ASSESSMENT

in Special *and* Inclusive Education

TWELFTH EDITION

John Salvia | *The Pennsylvania State University*

James E. Ysseldyke | *University of Minnesota*

Sara Bolt | *Michigan State University*

Australia • Brazil • Japan • Korea • Mexico • Singapore • Spain • United Kingdom • United States

***Assessment: In Special and Inclusive Education*, Twelfth Edition**
John Salvia, James E. Ysseldyke, and Sara Bolt

Senior Publisher: Linda Schreiber-Ganster
Executive Editor: Mark Kerr
Development Editor: Melissa Kelleher
Assistant Editor: Joshua Taylor
Editorial Assistant: Greta Lindquist
Media Editor: Elizabeth Momb
Marketing Manager: Kara Kindstrom
Marketing Coordinator: Klaira Markenzon
Senior Marketing Communications Manager: Heather Baxley
Content Project Manager: Samen Iqbal
Design Director: Rob Hugel
Art Director: Jennifer Wahi
Print Buyer: Becky Cross
Rights Acquisitions Specialist: Don Schlotman
Production Service: PreMediaGlobal
Text Designer: Patti Hudepohl
Photo Researcher: Wendy Granger
Text Researcher: Pablo D'Stair
Copy Editor: Cindy Bond
Cover Designer: Jeff Bane
Cover Image: Courtesy of Dreamstime
Compositor: PreMediaGlobal

Library of Congress Control Number: 2011936820

Student Edition:

ISBN-13: 978-1-111-83341-1

ISBN-10: 1-111-83341-9

Loose-leaf Edition:

ISBN-13: 978-1-133-30754-9

ISBN-10: 1-133-30754-X

Wadsworth
20 Davis Drive
Belmont, CA 94002-3098
USA

Printed in the United States of America
1 2 3 4 5 6 7 15 14 13 12 11

TABLE of CONTENTS

Part 4

PREFACE

As indicated by the title of the twelfth edition, *Assessment: In Special and Inclusive Education*, we continue to be concerned about assessing the performance and progress of students with disabilities, regardless of whether their education occurs in general or special education settings. Educational assessment has undergone substantial change since the first publication of *Assessment: In Special and Inclusive Education* in 1978. Improvement and expansion in assessment tools and strategies is certainly evident. New models and technologies for assessment in school settings have emerged in an attempt to more efficiently address the increasingly diverse needs of students today. Federal laws and regulations related to school assessment practices have been revised in attempts to promote improvements in student outcomes, and are in the midst of revision as we complete this most recent edition. As we developed the twelfth edition, a theme of continuous change emerged.

At the same time, we remain committed to assessment approaches that promote data-based decision making, and believe many concepts and ideas are still essential for our readers to understand and know how to apply. Philosophical differences continue to divide the assessment community. Disputes continue over the value of standardized and unstandardized test administration, objective and subjective scoring, generalizable and nongeneralizable measurement, interpersonal and intrapersonal comparisons, and so forth. In the midst of these differences, we believe students and society are best served by the objective, reliable, and valid assessment of student abilities and skills and by meaningful links between assessment results and intervention. Our position is based on several conclusions. First, the IDEA requires objective assessment, largely because it usually leads to better decision making. Second, we are encouraged by the substantial improvement in assessment devices and practices over the past 30-plus years. Third, although some alternatives are merely unproven, other innovative approaches to assessment—especially those that celebrate subjectivity—have severe shortcomings that have been understood since the early 1900s. Fortunately, much of the initial enthusiasm for those approaches has waned. Fourth, we believe it is unwise to abandon effective procedures without substantial evidence that the proposed alternatives really are better. Too often, we learned that an educational innovation was ineffective after it had failed far too many students.

Overall Changes to the Twelfth Edition

In order to ensure that our readers have access to assessment information that is comprehensive and up-to-date, and that can be tailored to their unique learning needs, we have made greater use of the Internet in the development of this edition.

- Throughout the paper version of the text, you will notice icons highlighting where you can expect to find more information on the Education CourseMate website for the book.
- You will find on the website a link to Wrightslaw so that you can find out about any changes in legislation.
- Greater use of the book website allows us to offer more in depth information about specific topics that may be of particular interest to only a subset of readers.We now include in the text summaries of five chapters that are available in their entirety on the book website, including Chapter 10, "How to Evaluate a Test," Chapter 18, "Using Measures of Adaptive Behavior," Chapter 19,

"Assessment of Infants, Toddlers, and Preschoolers," Chapter 20, "Assessment of Sensory Acuity," and Chapter 25, "Using Portfolios in Assessment."

- In each chapter, we provide web resources and activities that can be used to assist students in developing deeper and more current understanding of information presented in the book.

We know that many school systems are moving toward use of models involving multi-tiered systems of support (MTSS), and therefore considered it necessary to provide more background for readers on these models for assessment and intervention. In addition to integrating related ideas throughout the book, we have created a chapter entirely focused on MTSS and response to intervention (RTI), as well as a chapter devoted to curriculum-based approaches to assessment that are commonly used in conjunction with MTSS and RTI. We also know that many challenges in assessing students from culturally and linguistically diverse backgrounds exist and that the diversity of students present in individual classrooms is increasing. We have therefore devoted an entire chapter of the book to this topic and incorporated related challenges into many of the scenarios that are used to illustrate the concepts covered in each chapter.

Overall, we intend to provide readers with a comprehensive textbook and website that together provide easy access to the assessment concepts and ideas necessary to facilitate the academic and social–emotional competence of all students in schools today.

Audience for This Book

Assessment: In Special and Inclusive Education, Twelfth Edition, is intended for a first course in assessment taken by those whose careers require understanding and informed use of assessment data. The primary audience is made up of those who are or will be teachers in special education at the elementary or secondary level. The secondary audience is the large support system for special educators: school psychologists, child development specialists, counselors, educational administrators, nurses, preschool educators, reading specialists, social workers, speech and language specialists, and specialists in therapeutic recreation. Additionally, in today's reform climate, many classroom teachers enroll in the assessment course as part of their own professional development. In writing for those who are taking their first course in assessment, we have assumed no prior knowledge of measurement and statistical concepts.

Purpose

Students with disabilities have the right to an appropriate evaluation and to an appropriate education in the least restrictive educational environment. Those who assess have a tremendous responsibility; assessment results are used to make decisions that directly and significantly affect students' lives. Those who assess are responsible for knowing the devices and procedures they use and for understanding the limitations of those devices and procedures. Decisions about a student's eligibility for special education and related services must be based on valid information; decisions about how and where to educate students with disabilities must be based on valid data. Best practices in assessment can help support the learning and development of not just those with disabilities, but all students needing a variety of different levels of support, and so we intend for many of the concepts presented to facilitate best practices for all students, and not just those with disabilities.

The New Edition

COVERAGE

The twelfth edition continues to offer straightforward and clear coverage of basic assessment concepts, evenhanded evaluations of standardized tests in each domain, and illustrations of applications to the decision-making process. Most chapters have been updated, and several have been revised substantially. Five new chapters have also been developed. The organization of the twelfth edition has changed. We now have five parts: Overview and Basic Considerations, Assessment in Classrooms, Assessment Using Formal Measures, Special Considerations in Assessment, and Using Assessment to Make Educational Decisions.

NEW PEDAGOGICAL FEATURES

For each chapter, we have created web resources and web activities that link students to more in-depth information on related areas. The activities are designed to facilitate their integration of the concepts and information presented in the book with current issues in educational settings. In addition, many of the chapter scenarios have been revised to ensure that a variety of student issues and difficulties are represented across the different chapters. Several chapters also have video clips that can be used to facilitate more in-depth discussion of the given topic area.

Five chapters that include content that may be of great interest to a small proportion of our readership are now included as short summaries, with access to the complete versions available at the website for the book.

Special icons presented within several chapters highlight where students can find up-to-date information on the Education CourseMate website for the book.

In order to facilitate linkages from the book content to the professional training standards held by a variety of organizations, we have created tables that link various standards for special educators and other school professionals to chapters in this book. These tables are available on the inside covers of the book.

TESTS REVIEWED

We continue to reduce the number of tests reviewed within the actual book, and have placed more reviews on the book website.

There are several new and revised tests and measures in the book and corresponding website, including the Wechsler Individual Achievement Test, Third Edition (WIAT-III), Beery-Buktenica Developmental Test of Visual–Motor Integration (Beery VMI), DIBELS Next, and the Social Skills Improvement System (SSIS).

NEW CHAPTERS

The following are brand-new chapters to this edition:

- Chapter 1, "Assessment in Social and Educational Contexts"
- Chapter 2, "Assessment and Decision Making in Schools"
- Chapter 8, "Curriculum-Based Approaches to Measuring Student Progress"
- Chapter 22, "Cultural and Linguistic Considerations"
- Chapter 24, "Multi-Tiered Systems of Support (MTSS) and Response to Intervention (RTI)"

ORGANIZATION

Part 1, "Overview and Basic Considerations," places testing in the broader context of assessment: In Chapter 1, "Assessment in Social and Educational Contexts," we describe current models for supporting the diverse needs of students in schools today, and the basic methods used to collect assessment information. In Chapter 2, "Assessment and Decision Making in Schools," we describe the main types of decisions made in school settings for which assessment is necessary. In Chapter 3, "Laws, Ethical Codes, and Professional Standards That Impact Assessment," we discuss the ways assessment practices are regulated and mandated by legislation and litigation, and various ethical principles that may be used to guide assessment practices. In Chapter 4, "Test Scores and How to Use Them," we describe the commonly used ways to quantify test performance and provide interpretative data. In Chapter 5, "Technical Adequacy," we explain the basic measurement concepts of reliability and validity.

Part 2, "Assessment in Classrooms," provides readers with fundamental knowledge necessary to conduct assessments in the classrooms. Chapter 6, "Assessing Behavior Through Observation," explains the major concepts in conducting systematic observations of student behavior. Chapter 7, "Teacher-Made Tests of Achievement," provides a systematic overview of tests that teachers can create to measure students' learning and progress in the curriculum. Chapter 8, "Curriculum-Based Approaches to Monitoring Student Progress," describes concepts, ideas, and strategies that can be used to measure student progress; and Chapter 9, "Managing Classroom Assessment," is devoted to helping educators plan assessment programs that are efficient and effective in the use of both teacher and student time.

In Part 3, "Assessment Using Formal Measures," we provide information about the abilities and skills most commonly tested in the schools. Part 3 begins with Chapter 10, "How to Evaluate a Test." This chapter is a primer on what to look for when considering the use of a commercially produced test. The next nine chapters in Part 3 provide an overview of the domain and reviews of the most frequently used measures: Chapter 11, "Assessment of Academic Achievement with Multiple-Skill Devices"; Chapter 12, "Using Diagnostic Reading Measures"; Chapter 13, "Using Diagnostic Mathematics Measures"; Chapter 14, "Using Measures of Oral and Written Language"; Chapter 15, "Using Measures of Intelligence"; Chapter 16, "Using Measures of Perceptual and Perceptual–Motor Skills"; Chapter 17, "Using Measures of Social and Emotional Behavior"; Chapter 18, "Using Measures of Adaptive Behavior"; Chapter 19, "Using Measures of Infants, Toddlers, and Preschoolers"; and Chapter 20, "Assessment of Sensory Acuity."

Part 4 "Special Considerations" is devoted to offering more information on a variety of topics that are important, particularly given current issues and trends in schools. This section begins with Chapter 21, "Using Test Adaptations and Accommodations," in which we discuss circumstances that may require a change in test administration procedures to meet the unique needs of individual students, and strategies for making such changes. Chapter 22, "Cultural and Linguistic Considerations," discusses strategies and approaches for assessing students who do not share the dominant language and culture present in the United States. Chapter 23, "Using Technology to Help Make Assessment Decisions," describes computerized approaches to testing and systematic observation. In Chapter 24, "Multi-Tiered System of Supports (MTSS) and Response to Intervention (RTI)," we go into greater depth about how assessment is used within these newer models. This section concludes with Chapter 25, "Using Portfolios in Assessment," which discusses advantages and disadvantages to using this method of assessment.

In Part 5, "Using Assessment Results to Make Educational Decisions," we discuss the most important decisions educators make on behalf of students with disabilities. In Chapter 26, "Making Instructional Decisions," we discuss the decisions that are made prior to a student's referral for special education and those that are made in special education settings. In Chapter 27, "Making Special Education Eligibility Decisions," we discuss the role of multidisciplinary teams and the process for determining a student's eligibility for special education and related services. In Chapter 28, "Making Accountability Decisions," we explain the legal requirements for states and districts to meet the standards of *No Child Left Behind* and *IDEA*, achievement standards, and important considerations in making accountability decisions. In Chapter 29, "Collaborative Team Decision Making," we provide an overview of communicating with school teams and parents about assessment and decision making, and include information about the characteristics of effective school teams, strategies for effectively communicating assessment information to parents, and the rules concerning data collection and record keeping.

Instructor and Student Websites

These websites extend the textbook content and provide resources for further exploration into assessment practices. There are chapters and test reviews from previous editions, appendices, and additional resources helpful for students and instructors.

EDUCATION COURSEMATE

Students can visit CengageBrain.com to go to the Education CourseMate website for additional tests and resources. Education CourseMate brings course concepts to life with interactive learning, study, and exam preparation tools that support the printed textbook. CourseMate includes an integrated eBook, quizzes, flashcards, videos, and more, and EngagementTracker, a first-of-its-kind tool that monitors student engagement in the course.

For instructors, the accompanying instructor website offers access to password-protected resources.

Online Resources for Instructors

INSTRUCTOR'S MANUAL

An online Instructor's Manual accompanies this book. The instructor's manual contains information to assist the instructor in designing the course, including a sample syllabus, learning objectives, teaching and learning activities, and additional print and online resources.

TEST BANK

For assessment support, the updated test bank includes true/false, multiple-choice, matching, short answer and essay questions for each chapter.

PRESENTATION SLIDES

Preassembled Microsoft® PowerPoint® lecture slides for each chapter cover content from the book.

EXAMVIEW

Available for download from the instructor website, ExamView® testing software includes all the test items from the printed Test Bank in electronic format, enabling you to create customized tests in print or online.

WEBTUTOR

Jump-start your course with customizable, rich, text-specific content within your Course Management System. Whether you want to web-enable your class or put an entire course online, WebTutor™ delivers. WebTutor™ offers a wide array of resources including access to the eBook, quizzes, videos, web links, exercises, and more.

Up-to-Date Information

Throughout the paper version of the text, you will notice icons highlighting where you can expect to find more information on the Education CourseMate website for the book. You will also find on the website a link to Wrightslaw so that you can find out about any changes in legislation.

Test development and legislative changes are ongoing processes. It is our intent to review new tests and provide links to recent changes in legislation as they are developed and occur.

Acknowledgments

Over the years, many people have assisted in our efforts. In the preparation of this edition, we express our sincere appreciation to Melissa Kelleher for her assistance throughout its development. We also thank Ashley Cronin, media editor, and Mark Kerr, executive editor, for their dedication to this edition; and Samen Iqbal and Sumathy Kumaran for their help. We remain indebted to Lisa Mafrici, senior developmental editor, and Loretta Wolozin, who sponsored eight of the previous editions. We also appreciate the assistance of Shawna Peterson-Brown for her work on the Instructor's Resource Manual with Test Items, which accompanies this text.

Finally, specific thanks to the reviewers of this edition: Gail Ahearn, Rivier College; Alida Anderson, American University; Gena Barnhill, Lynchburg College; Manuel Barrera, Metropolitan State University; Abigail Baxter, University of South Alabama; Donna Bergman, Spring Arbor University; Mary Brady, Wayne State University; Sarah Jane DeHaas, Juniata College; Catharina de Wet, University of Alabama; Caroline DiPipi-Hoy, East Stroudsburg University; Mary Esposito, CSU Dominguez Hills; Rebecca Fogarty, Eastern Illinois University; Cathleen Geraghty, University of California, Riverside; and Jennifer Lindstrom, University of Georgia.

John Salvia • Jim Ysseldyke • Sara Bolt

ASSESSMENT

in SPECIAL *and* INCLUSIVE EDUCATION

Part 1

Overview and Basic Considerations

School personnel regularly use assessment information to make important decisions about students. Part 1 of this text looks at basic considerations in psychological and educational assessment of students, and introduces concepts and principles that constitute a foundation for informed and critical use of assessment information.

Chapter 1 provides a description of the multiple levels of support that students may require to achieve the educational standards required by state and federal regulations and the types of information provided by different kinds of assessment procedures. Assessment is of great importance to a variety of stakeholders who demand fair and accurate data to use in decision making. Chapter 2 describes the numerous instructional decisions that are made each day in the schools. Chapter 3 includes a description of the major laws that affect assessment in schools, and describes ethical considerations in best assessment practices.

Chapter 4 includes a description of the kinds of scores one obtains from tests and a set of considerations on how to use those scores. It is intended for the person with little or no background in descriptive statistics; it contains a discussion of the major concepts necessary for understanding most of the remaining chapters in this part and later parts of the book. Chapter 5 is focused on the technical adequacy of tests. The main focus is on reliability (the important concept that scores are fallible, and the amount of error associated with scores) and validity (the extent to which a test or other procedure leads to valid inferences about tested performance). Validity is the most important and inclusive aspect of a test's technical adequacy.

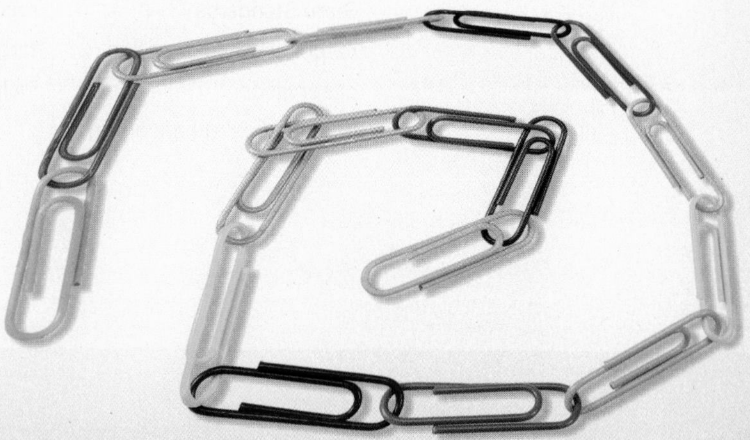

Assessment in Social and Educational Contexts

CHAPTER GOALS

1. Understand individual differences in skills, abilities, and behaviors and how these differences can require different levels of support to succeed in school.
2. Understand the concept of multi-tiered system of supports (MTSS) and how it applies to differentiated assessment and instruction.
3. Describe five methods of gathering assessment data (information).
4. Understand why assessment is important in school and society.
5. Understand what you will learn in this textbook.
6. Understand that significant improvements in assessment have happened and continue to happen.

KEY TERMS

assessment

testing

Common Core State Standards

response to intervention

observation

competence enhancement

capacity building

No Child Left Behind Act (NCLB)

recollections

targeted supports

inclusive education

multi-tiered system of supports (MTSS)

Individuals with Disabilities Education Improvement Act (IDEA)

professional judgment

Education is intended to provide *all* students with the skills and competencies they need to enhance their lives and the lives of their fellow citizens. School personnel are expected to provide all students with a predetermined set of competencies, usually those specified in national core content standards or in specific state education standards. This function would be extremely difficult even if all students entered school with the same abilities and competencies and even if all students learned in the same way and at the same rate. However, they do not. For example, it is the first day of school at Stevenson Elementary, and several students show up for kindergarten:

- Kim is dropped at the front door. He speaks no English and the school staff had no idea he was coming.
- Marshall comes knowing how to read, print, add, and subtract.
- Joyce is afraid to come to school and cries incessantly when her mother tries to leave.
- Kamryn and her mother arrive with a folder that includes all of her preschool records, her immunization and medical records, and reports from the two psychologists she has been seeing since age 2.
- Mike doesn't show up. The school has his name on a list, his completed registration records, and notes from a social worker indicating that he is eligible for free and reduced price lunch.

Not only do students not begin school with the same skills and abilities, they make progress through the curriculum at different rates and have different instructional needs. For example, midway through the first grade, Sally has picked up all she has been taught with no additional help. She just "gets it." Bill needs instruction specifically targeted to help him overcome his deficiencies in letter–sound correspondence; he sees a tutor twice a week. Joe needs so much help that he receives intensive special education services.

Students attending schools today are a much more diverse group than in the past. Today's classrooms are multicultural, multiethnic, and multilingual. Students demonstrate a significant range of academic skills; in some large urban environments, for example, 75 percent of sixth graders are reading more than 2 years below grade level, and there is as much as a 10-year range in skill level in math in a sixth-grade classroom. More than 6.5 million children and youth with disabilities (approximately 13 percent of the school-age population) receive special education and related services. Most of these children and youth are attending schools in their own neighborhoods in classes with their peers—this was not always the case in the past—and fewer students with disabilities receive special education services in separate buildings or separate classes. The focus of this book is on students in both special and inclusive education.

SCENARIO *in* ASSESSMENT

MRS. JOHNSON | The week before her fourth-grade class begins, Mrs. Johnson looks over her class roster. She has a heterogeneous group: 4 students who are receiving enrichment for 1 hour per week, 2 students who receive speech therapy for 30 minutes twice a week, 2 students with learning disabilities who receive itinerant (special education) services daily, 12 students who are functioning at grade level in all academic areas, and 6 students who are functioning below average in one or more academic areas. She also has two students whose educational records have yet to arrive from out-of-state.

Mrs. Johnson intends to spend the first week of school in a review of academic content and assessment of each student's prior knowledge so that she can differentiate her instruction. She will meet with the specialists who will be providing pull-out services to her students: with the itinerant special education teacher, to begin coordinating the instructional support her two students with learning disabilities receive; with the speech therapist, to schedule times when the two students needing therapy will be removed from her class; and with the enrichment teacher, to schedule times when the four gifted students will be seen for enrichment activities that will also be part of her curriculum. It looks like another busy year in her fourth-grade class.

What implications about your own professional role can you draw from this scenario? Go to the Education CourseMate website for this textbook for more reflection questions about this Scenario in Assessment.

1 Individual Students Need Different Levels of Support to Succeed

We as teachers and related services personnel are faced with providing education matched to the needs of students with few skills and those with highly developed skills in the same class. No matter what level of skills they bring with them and no matter how motivated students are to learn, it is our job to enhance their competence and to build the capacity of systems to meet student needs. In a larger social context, the assessor or a case coordinator must take into account these multiple influences as he or she assesses students and develops supports to meet individual student needs. For example, the tutoring Rosa is receiving at the local Hispanic community center could actually be interfering rather than helping. Or we may find that a really effective way to help Mohammed is to work with the local Somali neighborhood organization that provides students with homework help. As citizens and members of a variety of communities, we are also interested in the capacity of systems to support students in these ways, and we much enhance our effectiveness by taking into account these multiple perspectives and systems. To discuss all these influences is beyond the scope of this text.

Schools must provide multiple levels of support to enable each individual student to be successful in attaining the common core standards as required by state and federal regulations. School personnel must decide who gets what kinds of support and the level of instructional intensity needed by a student, how instruction will be delivered, and the extent to which instruction is working. **Assessment** is the process of collecting information (data) for the purpose of making these kinds of decisions about students.

2 The Concept of Multi-Tiered System of Supports and Differentiated Student Needs

We gather information about Kim, Bill, Sally, Kamryn, Rosa, Mohammed, and others by reviewing their records, interviewing their parents/caregivers and prior teachers, and watching them and/or testing them. We generate hypotheses about what will work best with them, that is, how to teach them, what materials to use, how fast to go, and whether they need special education services in order to succeed. Educators now typically talk about the provision of a multi-tiered system of supports (MTSS) to enable students to be successful. We find it helpful to view the system of supports as a funnel, with all students entering a school or specific classroom and then receiving varying intensity of supports to help them succeed. We illustrate this "funneling" concept in Figure 1.1. Notice that some supports are provided to all students, targeted supports are provided to those who need still extra help, and intensive supports are provided to the few students who experience the most difficulty. Students move up and down in the system of supports as school personnel decide they need more or less intensive support.

Some educators depict the multi-tiered system of supports as a triangle or pyramid, as shown in Figure 1.2. A multi-tiered system is illustrated in which students receive increasingly intensive levels of service and supports until interventions are identified that result in a positive response to intervention. Whether a pyramid, triangle, or funnel is used to illustrate the concept, what is communicated by these drawings is that (1) there are individual differences in the intensity of supports that students need to be successful, and (2) the numbers of students served decreases as more intensive supports are needed and provided. Assessment helps you figure out what skills and skill deficits students have, the intensity of supports that students need, whether good instruction is happening with students and the extent to which

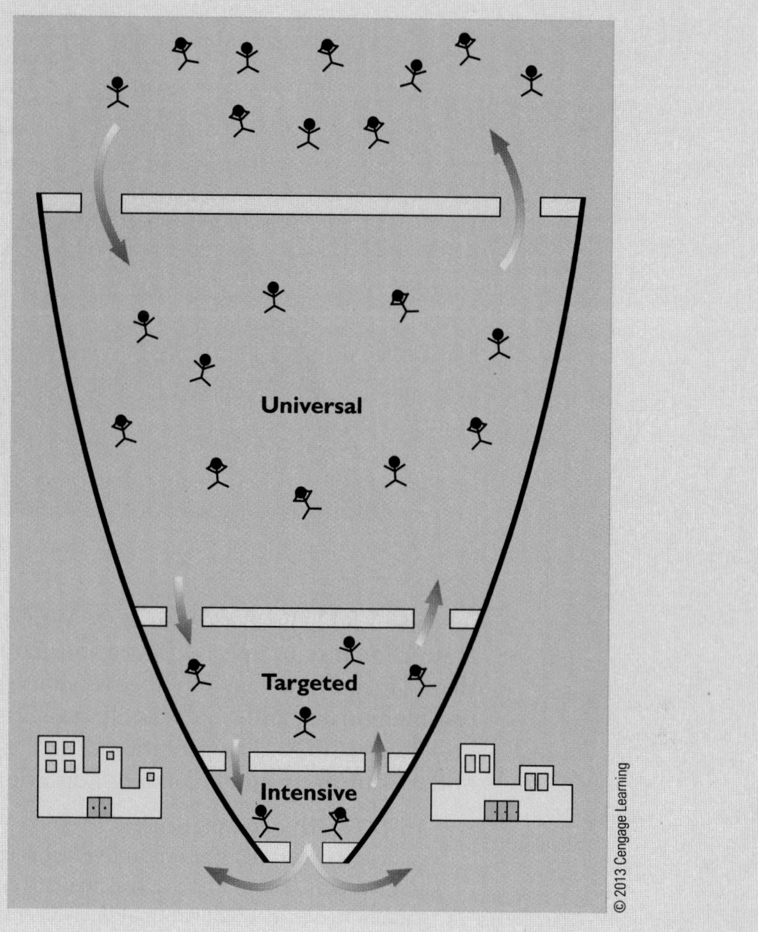

FIGURE 1.1
Students Receive Multiple Tiers of Support That Increase in Intensity if They Are Not Successful in School

they are profiting from it, and the extent to which teachers and schools are "effective." In this book you will learn about the specific kinds of information school personnel gather and how they use that information to enhance individual student competence and to build the capacity of systems to meet students' needs.

A multi-tiered system of supports (**MTSS**) is "a coherent continuum of evidence-based, system-wide practices to support a rapid response to academic and behavior needs with frequent data-based monitoring for instructional decision making to empower each student to high standards" www.kansasmtss.org/overview.htm.

The development of the concept of a multi-tiered system of supports came about in response to legal mandates or permissions. In the 2002 No Child Left Behind Act, Congress called for renewed and intensified focus on assessment and accountability. In the 2004 revision of the Individuals with Disabilities Education Improvement Act (IDEA), Congress added the assessment requirements of universal screening and progress monitoring. The law also indicated that decisions about eligibility for some kinds of special education services could be made based on the examination of student response to evidence-based effective instruction (RTI). Since the passage of IDEA, RTI has been a buzzword in federal, state, and school district discussions of assessment and in the professional literature. Yet, the basic conceptual framework for RTI has existed in the psychological and educational literature for many years; it has its foundation in the prevention sciences (Caplan, 1964), where physicians talked about primary, secondary, and tertiary prevention or treatment. In education and psychology, the concept likely originated in the early work of Lindsley (1964) on precision teaching and was first implemented as an assessment model by Beck (1979) in the Sacajawea Project in Great Falls, Montana. There are many

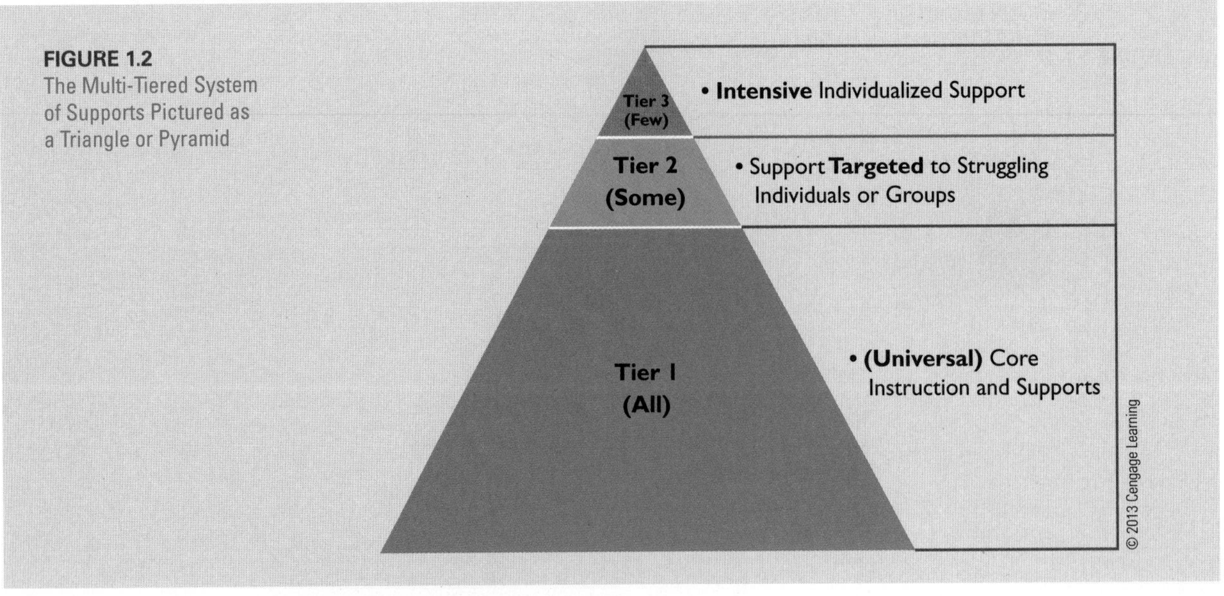

FIGURE 1.2 The Multi-Tiered System of Supports Pictured as a Triangle or Pyramid

models of RTI (Jimerson, Burns, & VanDerHeyden, 2007; National Association of State Directors of Special Education, 2005; Sugai & Horner, 2009), but they all share (1) multiple tiers of effective intervention service delivery, (2) ongoing progress monitoring, and (3) data collection/assessment to inform decisions at each tier (Ysseldyke, 2008). The definition of MTSS consistently used in the reauthorization of the Elementary and Secondary Education Act (ESEA) is as follows:

> An MTSS is a comprehensive system of differentiated supports that includes evidence-based instruction, universal screening, progress monitoring, formative assessments, summative assessments, research-based interventions matched to student needs, and educational decision-making using academic progress over time (Proposed ESEA Legislation, 2011).

MTSS has a variety of names at local, district, and state level: response to instruction/intervention (CA, CO, SC, VA), instructional support team (PA), problem solving/RTI (FL, IA, MI, MN), instructionally based assessment (OH), and three-tier RTI (AZ).

The MTSS framework is designed to address the academic and behavioral needs of all students, whether they are struggling or have advanced learning needs. The key assessment question is, "What supports do students need to be successful?" A "problem-solving" model is used throughout the provision of an MTSS. Problem solving is a data-based decision-making process that includes the steps illustrated in Figure 1.3: problem definition, problem analysis, deciding what action to take, intervening, monitoring student progress, and problem evaluation.

The foundation of an MTSS begins in general education programming that includes a focus on the provision of effective instruction and supports that assist in preventing academic and behavior problems. Throughout an MTSS, progress is closely monitored at each stage of instruction or intervention to verify that students are making appropriate progress on their instructional or behavioral goals. When progress is less than adequate, decisions are made about instructional content and methods as well as the intensity of the supports and services that the student needs. Within an MTSS, the collection of assessment information provides the following information about a student:

- An indication of the student's skill level relative to peers or a standard
- An indication of the success or lack of success of particular interventions
- A sense of the intensity of supports a student will need to perform at a proficient level

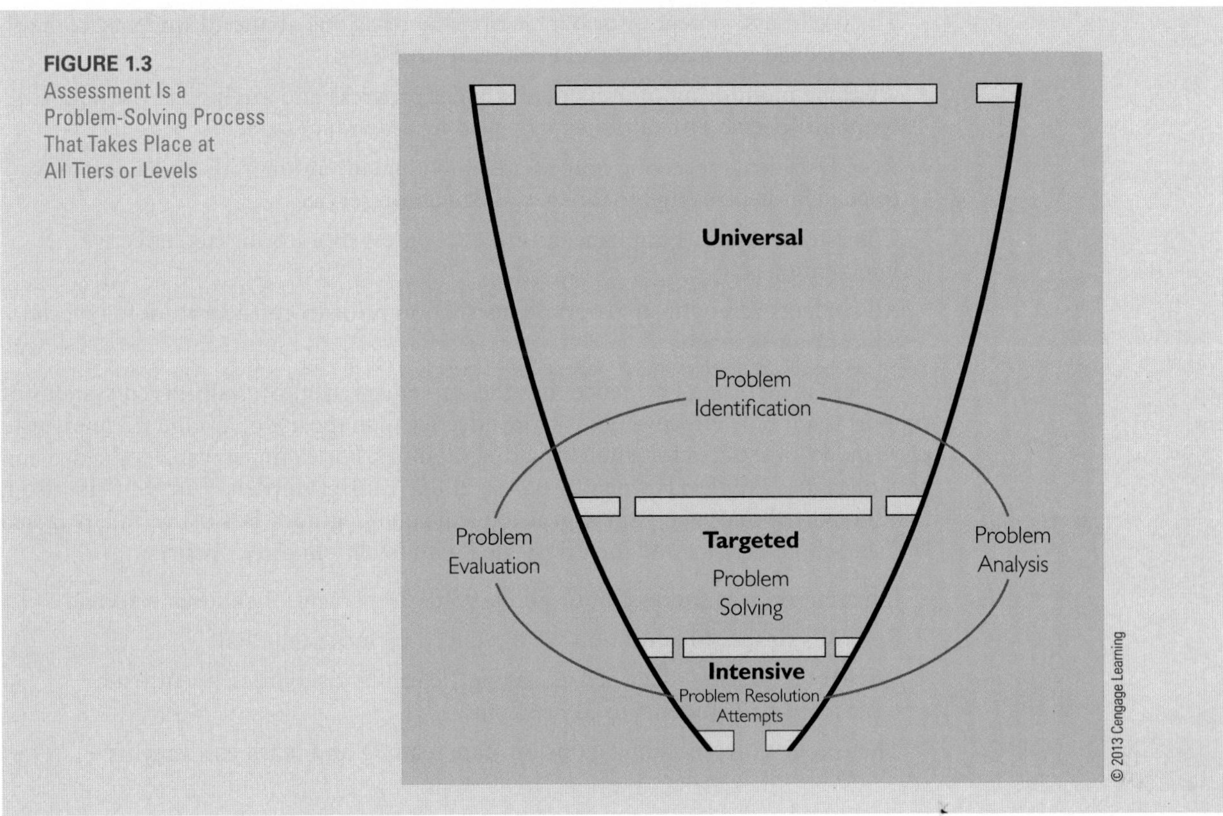

FIGURE 1.3
Assessment Is a Problem-Solving Process That Takes Place at All Tiers or Levels

Think of MTSS as a **series of tiers.** Tiers within the funnel or triangle describe the intensity of instruction, not specific places, programs or types of students, or staff. The **first tier** is instruction in the general classroom. Screening tests (e.g., formative assessments) given in the classroom show which students are at risk for reading, math, and other learning difficulties. Brief follow-up tests for those who are at risk may show that a student who has difficulty reading needs additional instruction in word fluency. In the **second tier,** the classroom teacher might provide corrective feedback and extra instruction. In other cases, another educator who has expertise in reading and fluency might instruct the student along with other students who are having the same difficulty. Or specific standard instructional programs like *Successful Reader, Read Naturally*, or *Read Well* may be implemented. Students who fail to respond to specific targeted interventions may then be considered for more specialized instruction in the **third tier,** where instruction may occur with increased intensity—that is, instructional sessions of longer duration and/or increased frequency. If difficulties persist, a team of educators may complete a comprehensive evaluation to determine eligibility for special education and related services. **The goal is to use student performance data to inform ways to provide the type of instruction and educational assistance that the student needs to be successful.** Typical assessments in tier 1 include universal screening and continuous or periodic (e.g., three times per year) progress monitoring to identify students at risk. At tier 2, typical assessments include diagnostic assessment in academic content areas to inform instruction and intervention as well as progress monitoring designed to help in making instructional decisions. At tier 3, assessment consists primarily of continuous or very frequent collection of information, consideration of referral to a multidisciplinary child study team, and assessment designed to determine eligibility for special education services. When correctly implemented, an MTSS results in:

- All students receiving high-quality instruction in the general education setting
- A reduction of referrals for special education eligibility consideration

- The use of assessment information to make decisions about all students as they are screened for academics and behavior problems
- Ongoing monitoring of individual student progress and analysis of the data to pinpoint specific difficulties experienced by individual students
- At-risk students receiving immediate individual attention without having to wait to be identified as eligible for special education services
- Consistent, rigorous implementation of progress monitoring and effective interventions
- All students receiving appropriate instruction prior to consideration for special education placement

There is increasing evidence that the implementation of multi-tiered systems of support is not only effective but is more effective than the use of a standard refer–test–serve model of services for students with disabilities. For example, VanDerHeyden and her colleagues (VanDerHeyden & Burns, 2005; VanDerHeyden, Witt, & Gilbertson, 2007) reported that when MTSS was implemented in grades 1–8 in the Vail, Arizona, Unified School District and then replicated with fidelity in three districts:

- Intervention was successful for about 95 to 98 percent of children screened
- Referrals to special education were reduced by more than half
- Percent of students identified as having "learning disabilities" went from 6 percent of all students to 3.5 percent
- There were corresponding gains on state reading and math assessments

3 How Are Assessment Data Collected?

When most people hear the term "assessment," they think of testing. Assessment is broader than testing. Testing consists of administering a particular set of questions to an individual or group of individuals to obtain a score. That score is the end product of testing. A test is only one of several assessment techniques or procedures for gathering information. During the process of assessment, data from observations, recollections, tests, professional judgments, and record reviews all come into play. To be most efficient, it can be helpful to first seek relevant information through a review of records, followed by interviews with those with special expertise and those who know the individuals(s) well, and then through observations. The use of testing can be reserved for the collection of more targeted information that can inform instructional changes, and for those decisions that require the use of very current and highly precise information about student skills and behavior.

RECORD REVIEW

Student cumulative records or medical records are yet another source of assessment data. In student records, school personnel retain demographic information, previous test scores, attendance data, and teacher comments about student behavior and performance. Assessors nearly always examine the prior records of the individual students with whom they work. Record reviews are useful in documenting when problems first appeared, their severity, and the interventions attempted. Similarly, record reviews are helpful when a student has not previously demonstrated difficulties.

PROFESSIONAL JUDGMENTS

The judgments and assessments made by others can play an important role in assessment. Diagnosticians occasionally seek out other professionals to complement their own skills and background. Thus, referring a student to various specialists (hearing specialists, vision specialists, reading teachers, and so on) is a common and desirable practice in assessment. Judgments by teachers, counselors, psychologists, and practically any other professional school employee may be useful in particular circumstances.

Expertise in making judgments is often a function of familiarity with the student being assessed. Teachers regularly express professional judgments; for example, teacher comments on a student's report card represent a teacher's judgment.

OBSERVATIONS

Observations can provide highly accurate, detailed, verifiable information not only about the person being assessed but also about the surrounding contexts. Observations can be categorized as either nonsystematic or systematic. In *nonsystematic,* or informal, observation, the observer simply watches an individual in his or her environment and notes the behaviors, characteristics, and personal interactions that seem significant. In *systematic observation*, the observer sets out to observe one or more precisely defined behaviors. The observer specifies observable events that define the behavior and then counts the frequency or measures the frequency, duration, amplitude, or latency of the behaviors.

RECOLLECTIONS

Recalled observations and interpretations of behavior and events are frequently used as an additional source of information. People who are familiar with the student can be very useful in providing information through interviews and rating scales. Interviews can range in structure from casual conversations to highly structured processes in which the interviewer has a predetermined set of questions that are asked in a specified sequence. Generally, the more structured the interview, the more accurate are the comparisons of the results of several different interviews. Rating scales can be considered the most formal type of interview. Rating scales allow questions to be asked in a standardized way and to be accompanied by the same stimulus materials, and they provide a standardized and limited set of response options.

TESTS

A *test* is a predetermined set of questions or tasks for which predetermined types of behavioral responses are sought. Tests are particularly useful because they permit tasks and questions to be presented in exactly the same way to each person tested. Because a tester elicits and scores behavior in a predetermined and consistent manner, the performances of several different test takers can be compared, no matter who does the testing. Hence, tests tend to make many contextual factors in assessment consistent for all those tested. The price of this consistency is that the predetermined questions, tasks, and responses may not be equally relevant to all students. Tests yield two types of information—quantitative and qualitative. *Quantitative data* are the actual scores achieved on the test. An example of quantitative data is Lee's score of 80 on her math test. *Qualitative data* consist of other observations made while a student is tested; they tell us how Lee achieved her score. For example, Lee may have solved all of the addition and subtraction problems with the exception of those that required regrouping. When tests are used, we usually want to know both the scores and how the student earned those scores.

4 The Importance of Assessment in Schools and Society

The end goal of assessment is improved educational outcomes for students. This is where teachers, school psychologists, speech and language pathologists, administrators, and other school personnel get their rewards: seeing students become more competent over time. School personnel tell us this is exciting work.

Assessment touches everyone's life. It especially affects the lives of people who work with children and youth, and who work in schools. Here are just a few examples of the ways in which assessment affects people's lives:

- You learn that as part of the state certification process, you must take tests that assess your knowledge of teaching practices, learning, and child development.
- Mr. and Mrs. Johnson receive a call from their daughter Morgan's third-grade teacher, who says he is concerned about her performance on a reading test. He would like to refer Morgan for further testing to determine whether she has a learning disability.
- Mr. and Mrs. Erffmeyer tell you that their son is not eligible for special education services because he scored "too high" on an intelligence test.
- In response to publication of test results showing that U.S. students rank low in comparison to students in other industrialized nations, the U.S. secretary of education issues a call for more rigorous educational standards for all students and increased federal aid.
- The superintendent of schools in a large urban district learns that only 40 percent of the students in her school district passed the state graduation test.
- Your local school district asks for volunteers to serve on a task force to design a measure of technological literacy to use as a test with students.

In the United States, almost everyone goes to school. And it seems like everyone has an opinion about testing. Test-based decision making can create "haves" and "have-nots." The "haves" tend to be happy with the decision, but the "have nots" are not happy. The procedures for gathering data and conducting assessments are matters that are rightfully of great concern to the general public—both individuals who are directly affected by the assessments (such as parents, students, and classroom teachers) and individuals who are indirectly affected (for example, taxpayers and elected officials). These matters are also of great concern to individuals and agencies that license or certify assessors to work in the schools. Finally, these matters are of great concern to the assessment community. For convenience, the concerns of these groups are discussed separately; however, the reader should recognize that many of the concerns overlap and are not the exclusive domain of one group or another.

CONCERNS OF STUDENTS, THEIR FAMILIES, AND TEACHERS

People react strongly when test scores are used to make interpersonal comparisons in which they or those they love look inferior. We expect parents to react strongly when test scores are used to make decisions about their children's life opportunities—for example, whether their child could enter college, pass a class, be promoted to the next grade, receive special education, or be placed in a program for gifted and talented students. Parents never want to hear that their children are not succeeding or that their children's prospects for adult life are limited. Students do not want to hear that they are different or not doing as well as their peers; they certainly do not want to be called handicapped or disabled. Poor student performance also affects teachers. Some teachers deny that student achievement really is inadequate; they opine that tests measure trivial knowledge (not the important things they teach), decontextualize knowledge, make it fragmented and artificial, and so on. Other teachers accept their students' failures as a fact of life (these teachers burn out). The good teachers work harder (for example, learn instructional techniques that actually work and individualize instruction).

Unwanted outcomes of assessment often lead to questions about the kinds of tests used, the skills or behaviors they measure, and their technical adequacy. Decisions about special and remedial education have consequences. Some consequences are desired, such as extra services for students who are entitled to special education.

Other consequences are unwanted, such as denial of special education services or diminished self-esteem resulting from a disability label.

CONCERNS OF THE GENERAL PUBLIC

Entire communities are keenly interested when test scores from their schools are reported and compared with scores from schools in other communities. Districts with "good" test scores are desirable, and real estate prices reflect the fact that parents want to live in those districts. This is especially true for parents of students who have disabilities. Good special education programs are a magnet for many such parents.

Often, test results are used to make high-stakes decisions that may have a direct and significant effect on the continued funding or even closing of schools and school systems, modifying state curricula, and salary negotiations. Finally, individuals who take tests outside of the schools are also affected. We take a test to earn the privilege of a driver's license. We usually have to take tests to gain admission to college. When test results restrict access to privileges, those denied access often view the tests as undemocratic, elitist, or simply unfair.

CONCERNS OF CERTIFICATION BOARDS

Certification and licensure boards establish standards to ensure that assessors are appropriately qualified to conduct assessments. Test administration, scoring, and interpretation require different degrees of training and expertise, depending on the kind of test being administered. All states certify teachers and psychologists who work in the schools; all states require formal training, and some require competency testing. Although most teachers can readily administer or learn to administer group intelligence and achievement tests as well as classroom assessments of achievement, a person must have considerable training to score and interpret most individual intelligence and personality tests. Therefore, when pupils are tested, we should be able to assume that the person doing the testing has adequate training to conduct the testing correctly (that is, establish rapport, administer the test correctly, score the test, and accurately interpret the test).

The joint committee of three professional associations that developed a set of standards for test construction and use has addressed the importance of testing:

> Educational and psychological testing are among the most important contributions of behavioral science to our society, providing fundamental and significant improvements over previous practices. Although not all tests are well developed nor are all testing practices wise and beneficial, there is extensive evidence documenting the effectiveness of well-constructed tests for uses supported by validity evidence.

SCENARIO *in* ASSESSMENT

MICHAEL | Sam has just been promoted and transferred to a different state. He and his wife, Virginia, and their three children are house-hunting. Their son Michael is autistic; one of the family's primary considerations in selecting a new home is the school district's programs for students with autism.

The area to which the family is moving is served by three school districts, one religious school, and one charter school. School district one has three autistic students (one who is about the same age as Michael), and those students are placed in classrooms for severely retarded students. School district two is more rural and buses all of its elementary students with autism to one classroom, where they are educated and included in activities with nondisabled peers. School district three is the largest and maintains classes for students with varying degrees of autism (i.e., both higher- and lower-functioning students) in several school buildings. The charter school has no students with disabilities. Students with disabilities in the religious school are fully included and may receive speech, occupational, and physical therapies through school district three. Sam and Virginia contact the local autism support group to see if it has a recommendation about the school systems. The group strongly recommends school district three. Besides having an excellent special education program, it is known to provide strong education for students without disabilities.

Even though houses cost several thousand dollars more in school district three, Sam and Virginia purchase their new home there.

What implications about your own professional role can you draw from this scenario? Go to the Education CourseMate website for this textbook for more reflection questions about this Scenario in Assessment.

> The proper use of tests can result in wiser decisions about individuals and programs than would be the case without their use and also can provide a route to broader and more equitable access to education and employment. The improper use of tests, however, can cause considerable harm to test takers and other parties affected by test-based decisions (American Educational Research Association, American Psychological Association, & National Council on Measurement in Education, 1999, p. 1).

5 What You Will Learn in This Book

NOT ALL TESTS ARE EQUAL

Test reviews are provided at the Education CourseMate website for this textbook.

Tests are samples of behavior. Different tests sample different behavior, and tests differ in their technical adequacy. (See Chapter 5 for more information on technical adequacy.) It is important when interpreting test results that users take into account the kinds of behaviors sampled by the tests and the tests' technical adequacy. If a test does not sample the kinds of behaviors in which you are interested, it is not worth giving the test. In addition, it is always critical to use technically adequate instruments. Thus, throughout the book, we describe the kinds of behaviors sampled by tests; we also include information on their technical adequacy. In Part 2, we provide you with the necessary standards and criteria to make good judgments about technical adequacy.

By reading this text, you will learn about the kinds of tests that are available for use in educational settings, the kinds of behaviors sampled by tests that are said to assess the same domain (for example, reading), and the technical adequacy of the tests. We focus on the extent to which students who are assessed are representative of those on whom and for whom a test was built. We also focus on the extent to which tests provide consistent results (are reliable) and actually measure what their authors say they measure (validity). When tests do not meet professional standards, we say so. Assessment is a process of collecting data for the purpose of making decisions about students. It is critical that testing be done correctly and that those who assess students do so with technical accuracy, fidelity, and integrity.

ASSESSMENT PRACTICES ARE DYNAMIC

Educational personnel regularly change their assessment practices. New federal or state laws, regulations, or guidelines specify and, in some cases, mandate, new assessment practices. New tests become available, and old ones go away. States change their special education eligibility criteria, and technological advances enable us to gather data in new and more efficient ways. The population of students attending schools also changes, bringing new challenges to the educational personnel who are working to enhance the academic and behavioral competence of all students. We address the dynamic nature of assessment by maintaining a website for this book. On that website we can inform you of changes that take place in laws, instruments, practices, or procedures.

WHY LEARN ABOUT ASSESSMENT IN SPECIAL AND INCLUSIVE EDUCATION?

Educational professionals must assess. Assessment is a critical practice that serves the purpose of matching instruction to the level of students' skills, monitoring student progress, modifying instruction, and working hard to enhance student competence. It is a critical component of teaching, and so it is necessary for teachers to have good skills in assessment and a good understanding of assessment information.

Although assessment can be a scary topic for practicing professionals as well as individuals training to become professionals, learning its different important facets helps people become less apprehensive. Educational assessments always have consequences that are important for students and their families. We can expect that good assessments lead to good decisions—decisions that facilitate a student's progress toward the desired goal (especially long term) of becoming a happy, well-adjusted, independent, productive member of society. Poor assessments can slow, stop, and sometimes reverse progress. The assessment process is also scary because there is so much to know; a student of assessment can easily get lost in the details of measurement theory, legal requirements, teaching implications, and national politics. Things were much simpler when the first edition of this book was published in 1978. The federal legislation and court cases that governed assessment were minimal. Some states had various legal protections for the assessment of students; others did not. There were many fewer tests used with students in special education, and many of them were technically inadequate (that is, they lacked validity for various reasons). Psychologists decided if a student was entitled to special education, and students did not have IEPs. Back then, the major problems we addressed were how to choose a technically adequate test, how to use it appropriately, and how to interpret test scores correctly. Although the quality of published tests has increased dramatically throughout the years, there are still poor tests being used.

Things are more complex today. Federal law regulates the assessment of children for and in special education. Educators and psychologists have many more tools at their disposal—some excellent, some not so good. Educators and psychologists must make more difficult decisions than ever before. For example, the law recognizes a greater number of disabilities, and educators need to be able to distinguish important differences among them.

Measurement theory and scoring remain difficult but integral parts of assessment. Failure to understand the basic requirements for valid measurement or the precise meaning of test scores inescapably leads to faulty decision making.

6 Good News: Significant Improvements in Assessment Have Happened and Continue to Happen

The good news is that there have been significant improvements in assessment since the first edition of *Assessment* in 1978. Assessment is evolving in a number of important ways.

- Methods of test construction have changed.
- Better statistical analyses have enabled test authors to do a better job of building their assessments.
- Skills and abilities that we assess have changed as theory and knowledge have evolved. We recognize attention deficit disorder and autism as separate disabilities; intelligence tests reflect theories of intelligence; measures of achievement are more closely aligned with the way in which students learn.
- The federal government has specified a comprehensive core set of standards in reading, math, and other subjects that they want students in all states to work toward. Each state once had separate standards, which resulted in confusing comparisons among states.
- Better assessment methods have worked their way into practice, including systematic observation, functional assessment, curriculum-based measurement, curriculum-based assessment, and technology-enhanced assessment and instructional management.
- The adoption by states and school districts of the concept of multi-tiered systems of support (MTSS) has led to assessment practices that are focused on instruction and instructional interventions designed to enhance student competence and build the capacity of systems to meet students' needs.

- Advancements in technology are making the collection, storage, and analysis of assessment data much more manageable and user-friendly.
- Federal laws prescribe the procedures that schools must follow in conducting assessments and hold schools more accountable for the assessments they conduct.

We have every reason to expect that assessment practices will continue to change for the better.

Chapter Comprehension Questions

Write your answers to each of the following questions and then compare your responses to the text.

1. What is meant by "individual differences"? Give two examples and indicate why it is important to take individual differences into account as we endeavor to help students succeed in school.
2. How do educational personnel decide what supports students need to succeed in school?
3. What are multi-tiered systems of support, and how do schools use them?
4. Name and describe four methods of gathering assessment data (information).
5. State reasons why assessment is important in school and society.
6. Describe what the authors said you will learn in this textbook.

Web Activities 

1. Use your Internet browser to identify three websites that address assessment practices in schools. What content is addressed on each of these sites? Share your list of websites with your fellow students and/or colleagues.
2. Go to the website for the National Association of School Psychologists and read its statement of best practices in assessment. Then interview a local teacher or school psychologist and ask if these practices are present in his or her school.
3. Go to the Cengage website for this book and read the reviews of two tests. What kind of information is provided about each of the tests?

Web Resources

Intervention Central
http://interventioncentral.org
This website includes free resources for teachers and related services personnel. It includes academic interventions, behavior resources, and assessment resources.

National Association of School Psychologists
http://nasponline.org
The website of the National Association of School Psychologists includes resources for assessment and intervention.

Council for Exceptional Children
www.CEC.sped.org
The Council for Exceptional Children (CEC) is the major professional organization for educators of students with disabilities. CEC works to improve the educational success of individuals with disabilities and/or gifts and talents.

Additional resources for this chapter can be found on the Education CourseMate website. Go to CengageBrain.com to access the site.

AP Photo/Denis Poroy

2 Assessment and Decision Making in Schools

CHAPTER GOALS

1 List and describe seven kinds of educational decisions made using assessment information.

2 Describe the sequence of activities and decisions that are made at each tier (universal, targeted, intensive) in the assessment process.

KEY TERMS

discrepancy

progress monitoring decision

resource allocation decision

program evaluation decision

Common Core State Standards

multidisciplinary team

universal screening

screening decision

instructional planning decision

eligibility decision

accountability decision

state-specific standards

individualized education plan

1 Types of Assessment Decisions Made by Educators

When you work in schools you will gather and use assessment information to make decisions for or about students. Educational assessment decisions address problems. Some of these assessment decisions involve problem identification (deciding whether there is a problem), whereas others address problem analysis and problem solving. Most educational problems begin as discrepancies between our expectations for students and their actual performance. Students may be discrepant academically (they are not learning to read as fast as they are expected), behaviorally (they are not acting as they are expected), or physically (they are not able to sense or respond as expected). At some point, a discrepancy is sufficiently large that it is seen as a problem rather than benign human variation. The crossover point between a discrepancy and a problem is a function of many factors: the importance of the discrepancy (for example, the inability to print a letter versus forgetting to dot the "i"), the intensiveness of the discrepancy (for example, a throat-clearing tic versus shouting obscenities in class), and so forth. Other assessment decisions address problem solving (how to solve problems and thereby improve students' education). Table 2.1 lists the kinds of decisions school personnel make using assessment information.

SCREENING DECISIONS: ARE THERE UNRECOGNIZED PROBLEMS?

Educators now know that it is very important to identify physical, academic, or behavior problems early in students' school careers. Early identification enables us to develop treatments or interventions that may alleviate or eliminate difficulties. Educators also understand that it is important to screen for specific conditions such as visual difficulties because prescription of corrective lenses enables students to be more successful in school. School personnel engage in universal screening (they test everyone) for some kinds of potential problems. All young children are screened for vision or hearing problems with the understanding that identification of sensory problems allows us to prescribe corrective measures (glasses, contacts, hearing aids, or amplification equipment) that will alleviate the problems. All students are required to have a physical examination, and most students are assessed for "school readiness" prior to entrance into school. Screening tests typically are given at tier 1 to all students in regular classes to identify students who are dis-

TABLE 2.1 Decisions Made Using Assessment Information

Screening	Are there unrecognized problems?
Progress monitoring	Is the student making adequate progress? Toward individual goals Toward state standards
Instructional planning and modification	What can we do to enhance competence and build capacity, and how can we do it?
Resource allocation	Are additional resources needed?
Eligibility for special education services	Is the student eligible for special education and related services?
Program evaluation	Are the instructional programs that are being used effective?
Accountability	Are we achieving desired outcomes?

crepant from an expected level of performance. Such screening is called universal screening.

PROGRESS MONITORING DECISIONS: IS THE STUDENT MAKING ADEQUATE PROGRESS?

School personnel assess students for the purpose of making two kinds of progress monitoring decisions: (1) Is the student making adequate progress toward individual goals? and (2) Is the student making adequate progress toward state standards?

Monitoring Progress Toward Individual Goals

School personnel regularly assess the specific skills that students do or do not have in specific academic content areas such as decoding words, comprehending what they read, performing math calculations, solving math problems, or writing. We want to know whether the student's rate of acquisition will allow the completion of all instructional goals within the time allotted (for example, by the end of the school year or by the completion of secondary education). The data are collected for the purpose of making decisions about what to teach and the level at which to teach. For example, students who have mastered single-digit addition need no further instruction (although they may still need practice) in single-digit addition. Students who do not demonstrate those skills need further instruction. The specific goals and objectives for students who receive special education services are listed in their individualized educational programs (IEPs).

The focus in assessment is helping students move toward the competencies we want them to attain so that we can modify instruction or interventions that are not meeting desired effects. Progress may be monitored continuously or periodically to ensure students have acquired the information and skills being taught, can maintain the newly acquired skills and information over time, and can appropriately generalize the newly acquired skills and information. The IEPs of students who receive special education services must contain statements about the methods that will be used to assess their progress toward attaining these goals. In any case, the information is used to make decisions about whether the instruction or intervention is working and whether there is a need to alter instruction.

Monitoring Progress Toward Common Core State Standards or Specific State Standards

School personnel set goals/standards/expectations for performance of schools, classes, and individual students. The U.S. Department of Education has developed a list of what are called Common Core State Standards, which all students are expected to meet. Some states use these standards as the basis for their state assessment and accountability systems. A website devoted entirely to the Common Core State Standards Initiative contains the latest information on that federal effort (http://www.corestandards.org/). All states have identified academic content and performance standards that specify what students are expected to learn in reading, mathematics, social studies, science, and so forth. Some students may have additional goals. Students with significant cognitive disabilities may be required to work toward a set of alternative achievement standards, or standards may be modified for students with disabilities that interfere with their movement toward state goals or standards (this is discussed in detail in Chapter 28). Moreover, states are required by law to have in place a system of assessments aligned with their goals/standards/expectations. The assessments that are used to identify the standing of groups are also used to ascertain if individuals have met or exceeded state standards/goals. The Common Core Standards Initiative likely will change significantly over time. Be sure to search the Internet for "Common Core Standards changes" and "NCLB changes" for the most recent information.

Find a link to the Common Core Standards Initiative on the Education CourseMate website for this textbook.

INSTRUCTIONAL PLANNING AND MODIFICATION DECISIONS: WHAT CAN WE DO TO ENHANCE COMPETENCE AND BUILD CAPACITY, AND HOW CAN WE DO IT?

Inclusive education teachers are able to take a standard curriculum and plan instruction based on it. Although curricula vary from district to district—largely as a function of the values of community and school—they are appropriate for most students at a given age or grade level. However, what should teachers do for those students who differ significantly from their peers or from district standards in their academic and behavioral competencies? These students need special help to benefit from classroom curriculum and instruction, and school personnel must gather data to plan special programs for these students.

Three kinds of decisions are made in instructional planning: (1) what to teach, (2) how to teach it, and (3) what expectations are realistic. Deciding what to teach is a content decision usually made on the basis of a systematic analysis of the skills that students do and do not have. Scores on tests and other information help teachers decide whether students have specific competencies. Test information may be used to determine placement in reading groups or assignment to specific compensatory or remedial programs. Teachers also use information gathered from observations and interviews in deciding what to teach. They obtain information about how to teach by trying different methods of teaching and monitoring students' progress toward instructional goals. Finally, decisions about realistic expectations are always inferences, based largely on observations of performance in school settings and performance on tests.

One of the provisions of the No Child Left Behind Act, the major federal law governing delivery of elementary and secondary education, states that schools are to use "evidence-based" instructional practices. There are a number of interventions with empirical evidence to support their use with students with special needs. A number of websites are devoted to evidence-based teaching, including the U.S. Department of Education (www.ed.gov), The Campbell Collaboration (www.campbellcollaboration.org), and the What Works Clearinghouse from the U.S. Department of Education (www.whatworks.ed.gov).

Find more information about websites devoted to evidence-based teaching on the Education CourseMate website for this textbook.

RESOURCE ALLOCATION DECISIONS: ARE ADDITIONAL RESOURCES NECESSARY?

Assessment results may indicate that individual students need special help or enrichment. These students may be referred to a teacher assistance team,[1] or they may be referred for evaluation to a multidisciplinary team that will decide whether these students are entitled to special education services.[2] School personnel gather data on student sensory difficulties or on academic skills for the purpose of deciding whether additional resources are necessary. They also use assessment information to make decisions about how to enlist parents, schools, teachers, or community agencies in enhancing student competence.

[1] Two kinds of teams typically operate in schools. The first, usually composed of teachers only, is designed as a first line of assistance to help classroom teachers solve problems with individual students in their class. These teams, often called teacher assistance teams, mainstream assistance teams, or schoolwide assistance teams, meet regularly to brainstorm possible solutions to problems that teachers confront. The second kind of team is the multidisciplinary team that is required by law for purposes of making special education eligibility decisions. These teams are usually made up of a principal; regular and special education teachers; and related services personnel, such as school psychologists, speech and language pathologists, occupational therapists, and nurses. These teams have different names in different places. Most often they are called child study teams, but in Minneapolis, for example, they are called special education referral committees or IEP teams.

[2] Students who are gifted and talented are considered exceptional. Yet, they are not entitled to special education services under IDEA. Some states have special provisions that entitle gifted and talented students to receive special services. Be sure to check your state department of education website to see whether and how gifted and talented students are entitled to special services.

When it is clear that many or all students require additional programs or support, system change and increased capacity may be indicated. Clear examples of building the capacity of schools to meet student needs include preschool education for all, federal funding to increase student competence in math and science, implementation of positive behavior support programs, and federal requirements for school personnel to develop individualized plans to guide the transition from high school to postschool employment.

ELIGIBILITY FOR SPECIAL EDUCATION SERVICES DECISIONS: IS THE STUDENT ELIGIBLE FOR SPECIAL EDUCATION AND RELATED SERVICES?

School personnel use assessment information to make decisions about whether students are eligible for special education and related services. Before a student may be declared eligible for special education services, he or she must be shown to be exceptional (have a disability or a gift or talent) *and* to have special learning needs. It is not enough to be disabled *or* to have special learning needs. Students can be disabled and not require special education services. Students can have special learning needs but not meet the state criteria for being declared disabled. For example, there is no federal mandate for provision of special education services to students with behavior disorders, and in many states students with behavior disorders are not eligible for special education services (students need to be identified as emotionally disturbed to receive special education services). Students who receive special education (1) have diagnosed disabilities and (2) need special education services to achieve educational outcomes.

In addition to the classification system employed by the federal government, every state has an education code that specifies the kinds of students who are considered disabled. States may have different names for the same disability. For example, in California, some students are called "deaf" or "hard of hearing"; in other states, such as Colorado, the same kinds of students are called "hearing impaired." States may expand special education services to provide for students with disabilities that are not listed in the Individuals with Disabilities Education Improvement Act (IDEA), but states may not exclude from services the disabilities listed in the IDEA. Finally, while a state may provide gifted students with special programs and protections, gifted students are not included in the IDEA and are not entitled to federal funding for special education.

PROGRAM EVALUATION: ARE INSTRUCTIONAL PROGRAMS EFFECTIVE?

Assessment data are collected to evaluate specific programs. Here the emphasis is on gauging the effectiveness of the curriculum in meeting the goals and objectives of the school. School personnel typically use this information for schoolwide curriculum planning. For example, schools can compare two approaches to teaching in a content area by (1) giving tests at the beginning of the year, (2) teaching comparable groups two different ways, and (3) giving tests at the end of the year. By comparing students' performances before and after, the schools are able to evaluate the effectiveness of the two competing approaches.

The process of assessing educational programs can be complex if numerous students are involved and if the criteria for making decisions are written in statistical terms. For example, an evaluation of two instructional programs might involve gathering data from hundreds of students and comparing their performances and applying many statistical tests. Program costs, teacher and student opinions, and the nature of each program's goals and objectives might be compared to determine which program is more effective. This kind of large-scale evaluation probably would be undertaken by a group of administrators working for a school district. Of course, program evaluations can be much less formal. For example, Mackenzie is a third-grade teacher. When Mackenzie wants to know the effectiveness of an instructional method she is using, she does her own evaluation. Recently, she wanted to know whether phonics instruction in reading is better than using flashcards to teach word

SCENARIO *in* ASSESSMENT

JOAN | Joan is an eighth-grader who was retained in first grade and identified as a student with a learning disability at the end of the third grade. She has progressed from grade to grade and remained in special education since that time. Currently, Joan receives resource services and in-class support for English, mathematics, science, and social studies taken in the general education classroom. In her resource room she receives instruction in writing (especially spelling) and in reading, where her lack of fluency hampers her comprehension.

Joan does have a number of strengths. She attends school regularly and, until recently, enthusiastically. She demonstrates excellent auditory comprehension and her attention to task is above average. She actively participates in class activities and discussions. She has good ideas and communicates them well orally. She asks for and accepts help from her teachers and is well accepted by her peers.

Recently, however, she has begun to exhibit signs of low self-esteem. Joan's parents are becoming concerned. Because Joan will be entering high school next year, her parents are concerned that time is running out and that Joan really needs to feel better about herself and how far she has come. So her parents ask for an IEP team meeting to address their concerns about Joan's reading, writing, and self-esteem. They wonder if Joan needs a more intensive special education program.

What implications about your own professional role can you draw from this scenario? Go to the Education CourseMate website for this textbook for more reflection questions about this Scenario in Assessment.

recognition. She used both approaches for 2 weeks and found that students learned to recognize words much more rapidly when she used a phonics approach.

ACCOUNTABILITY DECISIONS: DOES WHAT WE DO LEAD TO DESIRED OUTCOMES?

Under the provisions of the No Child Left Behind Act, schools, school districts, and state education agencies are now held accountable for individual student performance and progress. School districts must report annually to their state's department of education the performance of all students, including students with disabilities, on tests the state requires students to take. By law, states, districts, and individual schools must demonstrate that the students they teach are making adequate yearly progress (AYP). When it is judged by the state that a school is not making AYP, or when specified subgroups of students (disadvantaged students, students with disabilities, or specific racial/ethnic groups) are not making AYP, sanctions are applied. The school is said to be a school in need of improvement. When schools fail to make AYP for 2 years, parents of the children who attend those schools are permitted to transfer their children to other schools that are not considered in need of improvement. When the school fails to make AYP for 3 years, students are entitled to supplemental educational services (usually after-school tutoring). Failure to make AYP for longer periods of time results in increasing sanctions until finally the state can take over the school or district and reconstitute it.

2 The Assessment Process

The assessment and decision-making process differs for individual students, but there are commonalities in the sequence of activities that take place. Figure 2.1 shows the flow of activities from initial concern by a classroom teacher to the implementation of prereferral interventions in the general education classroom. Student progress is monitored and, depending on how students perform, they either receive more or less intensive services. Also illustrated is the fact that assessment information is collected for the purpose of deciding whether students are eligible for special education services and for the purpose of making accountability decisions. This simple chart is intended to illustrate the process in general. Recognize that for individual students, the process may include some extra steps, and certainly that it takes varying amounts of time for different individuals to proceed through the steps. Recognize also that many students with disabilities receive special education services before they enter school.

FIGURE 2.1
The Assessment Process

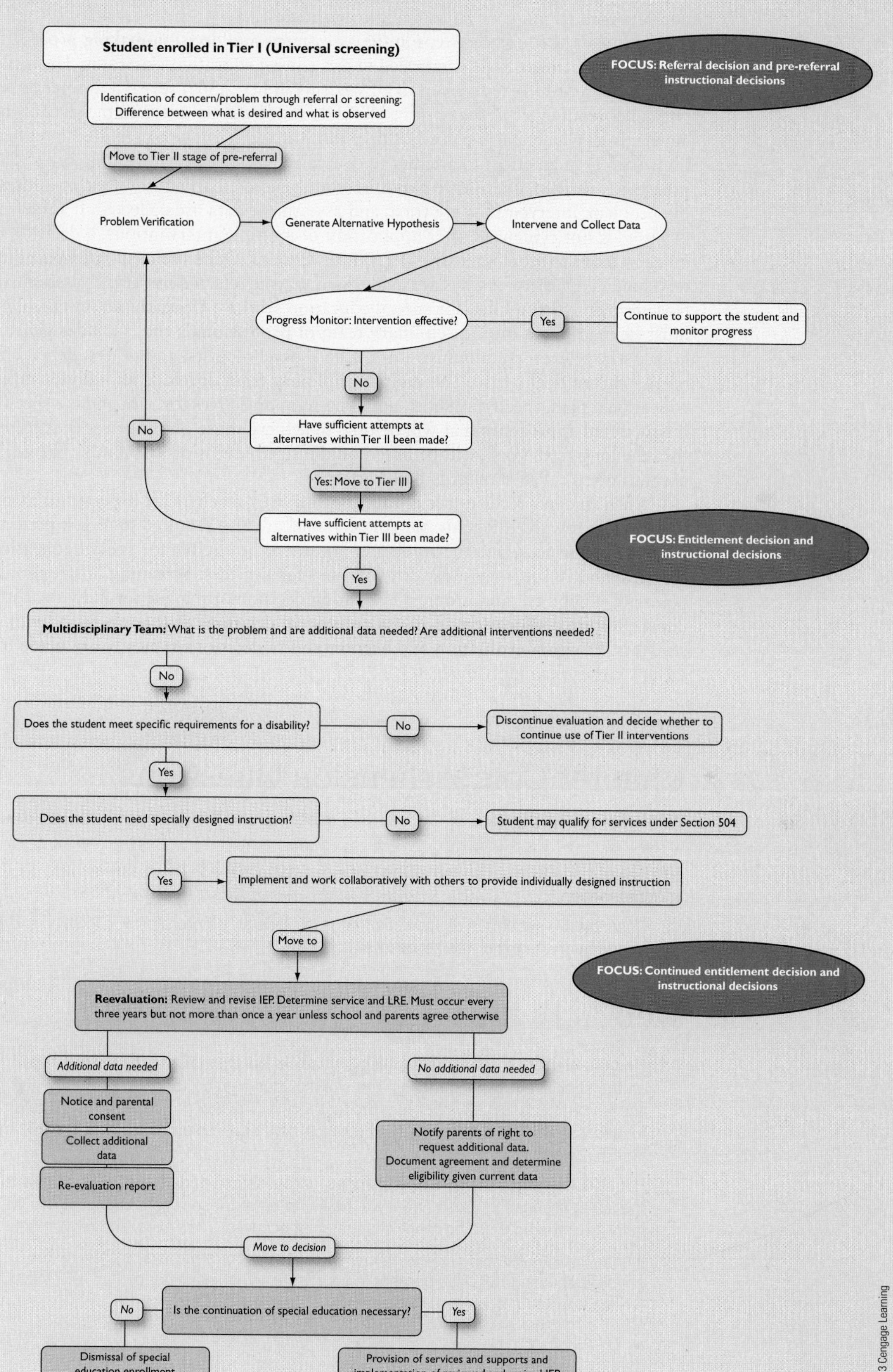

This is especially true for students who are blind, deaf, have medical conditions that interfere with learning, or have multiple disabilities.

Let's walk through the steps in the assessment and decision-making process. A student, let's call her Sara, is enrolled in the general education classroom. Universal screeening (screening tests given to all students in her grade) reveal a difference between her reading level (the observed level on the screening test) and the level of the materials in which she is placed. A decision is made to move to targeted interventions (tier 2) in an effort to attempt to overcome Sara's deficit in reading skills. The problem is verified, alternative hypotheses are generated about how best to address the problem, interventions are tried, and assessment data are collected. If sufficient progress is not evidenced after application of multiple interventions, a decision is made to move to more intensive (tier 3) interventions. Once sufficient attempts at intervening in a variety of ways are made, Sara may be referred for further assessment to determine her eligibility for special education services. Decisions about eligibility must be made by a multidisciplinary team of professionals that includes general and special educators, administrators, school psychologists, and others, depending on the nature of the case. The multidisiciplinary team develops an individualized educational plan, specifying short- and long-term objectives for Sara and the specific instructional approaches that will be used to achieve those objectives. It is expected that the long-term goals will be based on the state education standards. The goals are thus often called standards-based goals.

When students receive special education services, teachers are expected to monitor progress toward IEP goals. School personnel are also required to review periodically the extent to which the student continues to be eligible for special education services, and if not, they must discontinue such services. Screening, instructional planning, eligibility, and progress evaluation decisions are made for individual students. Resource allocation decisions are system decisions that apply to individual students. Program evaluation and accountability decisions typically are made for groups rather than individuals.

Chapter Comprehension Questions

Write your answers to each of the following questions and then compare your responses to the text.

1. List and briefly describe the seven kinds of decisions made using assessment information.
2. Describe the sequence of activities that take place at the prereferral, eligibility, and reevaluation stages of the assessment process.

Web Activities 

1. Find the website for the Los Angeles Unified School District and review the page on the special education process. The site includes a guide for parents on how the assessment and IEP development process works. Review the sections on (1) referral for assessment, (2) assessment, (3) development and implementation of the IEP, and (4) IEP review.
2. Put "IDEA changes" and "NCLB changes" into a search engine. You will get links to the latest changes in these two laws. Make notes of these recent changes. This will help you keep up with the many changes that occur to laws, rules, and regulations.
3. Find a website that details how the IEP process in your state works. Review the principles guiding IEP development in your state. What is included in an IEP? What are the important questions to be answered during the IEP meeting?

4. Search the Internet for "NCLB changes" and "IDEA changes" and note recent changes to NCLB and IDEA that may affect the special education assessment and decision-making process.

Web Resources

Fairtest: The National Center for Fair and Open Testing
http://fairtest.org
Fairtest is a nonprofit advocacy organization dedicated to preventing misuse of standardized tests.

Additional resources for this chapter can be found on the Education CourseMate website. Go to CengageBrain.com to access the site.

Chris Maddaloni/Roll Call/Getty Images

Laws, Ethical Codes, and Professional Standards that Impact Assessment

CHAPTER GOALS

1 Understand the major laws that affect assessment, along with the specific provisions (for example, individualized education program, least restrictive environment, and due process provisions) of the laws.

2 Understand the ethical standards for assessment that have been developed by professional associations and consider examples of ethical and unethical assessment practices.

KEY TERMS

Education for All Handicapped Children Act

Individuals with Disabilities Education Act

Elementary and Secondary Education Act

individualized education program

least restrictive environment

Americans with Disabilities Act (ADA)

Section 504 of the Rehabilitation Act of 1973

Race to the Top

ADAA

due process

Ethical Principles of Psychologists

Code of Conduct for Psychologists

beneficence

evidence-based instructional practice

National Association of School Psychologists' *Principles for Professional Ethics*

National Education Association's *Code of Ethics of the Education Profession*

No Child Left Behind Act (NCLB)

harassment

supplemental educaservices

protection in evaluation procedures (PEPs)

Public Law 94-142

Standards for Educational and Psychological Testing

Much of the practice of assessing students is the direct result of federal laws, court rulings, and professional standards and ethics. Federal laws mandate that students be assessed before they are entitled to special education services. Federal laws also mandate that there be an individualized education program for every student with a disability; that instructional objectives for each of these students be derived from a comprehensive individualized assessment; and that states provide an annual report to the U.S. Department of Education on the academic performance of all students, including students with disabilities. Professional associations (for example, the Council for Exceptional Children, the National Association of School Psychologists, and the American Psychological Association) specify standards for good professional practice and ethical principles to guide the behavior of those who assess students.

1 Evolving Nature of Rules, Regulations, and Guidelines

Laws, rules, and regulations change frequently. Therefore, as you read this chapter, we suggest that you enter "IDEA changes," "ESEA changes," or "NCLB changes" into a search engine and read the latest changes to the law.

2 Laws

It is very important that you understand the history of federal legislation on the education and assessment of individuals with disabilities.

Prior to 1975, there was no federal requirement that students with disabilities attend school, or that schools should make an effort to teach students with disabilities. Requirements were on a state-by-state basis, and they differed and were applied differently in the states. Since the mid-1970s, the delivery of services to students in special and inclusive education has been governed by federal laws. An important federal law, called Section 504 of the Rehabilitation Act of 1973, gave individuals with disabilities equal access to programs and services funded by federal monies. In 1975, Congress passed the Education for All Handicapped Children Act (Public Law 94-142), which included many instructional and assessment requirements. The law was reauthorized, amended, and updated in 1986, 1990, 1997, and 2004. In 1990, the law was given a new name: the Individuals with Disabilities Education Act (IDEA). To reflect contemporary practices, Congress replaced references to "handicapped children" with "children with disabilities." In the 2004 reauthorization, the law was again retitled the Individuals with Disabilities Education Improvement Act to highlight the fact that the major intent of the law is to improve educational services for students with disabilities.

Another federal law, the 2001 Elementary and Secondary Education Act (commonly referred to as the No Child Left Behind Act (NCLB)), is especially important to contemporary assessment practices because it requires that states must report to the U.S. Department of Education every year data on the performance and progress of all students. States get the information from districts, so this law requires that school districts report to state departments of education on the performance and progress of all students, including students with disabilities and English learners. Table 3.1 lists the federal laws that are especially important to assessment practices, and the major new provisions of each of the laws are highlighted.

TABLE 3.1 Major Federal Laws and Their Key Provisions Relevant to Assessment

Act	Provisions
Section 504 of the Rehabilitation Act of 1973 (Public Law 93-112)	It is illegal to deny participation in activities or benefits of programs, or to in any way discriminate against a person with a disability solely because of the disability. Individuals with disabilities must have equal access to programs and services. Auxiliary aids must be provided to individuals with impaired speaking, manual, or sensory skills.
Education for All Handicapped Children Act of 1975 (Public Law 94-142)	Students with disabilities have the right to a free, appropriate public education. Schools must have on file an individualized education program for each student determined to be eligible for services under the act. Parents have the right to inspect school records on their children. When changes are made in a student's educational placement or program, parents must be informed. Parents have the right to challenge what is in records or to challenge changes in placement. Students with disabilities have the right to be educated in the least restrictive educational environment. Students with disabilities must be assessed in ways that are considered fair and nondiscriminatory. They have specific protections.
1986 Amendments to the Education for All Handicapped Children Act (Public Law 99-457)	All rights of the Education for All Handicapped Children Act are extended to preschoolers with disabilities. Each school district must conduct a multidisciplinary assessment and develop an individualized family service plan for each preschool child with a disability.
Individuals with Disabilities Education Act of 1990 (Public Law 101-476)	This act reauthorizes the Education for All Handicapped Children Act. Two new disability categories (traumatic brain injury and autism) are added to the definition of students with disabilities. A comprehensive definition of transition services is added.
1990 Americans with Disabilities Act	Guarantees equal opportunity to individuals with disabilities in employment, public services, transportation, state and local government services, and telecommunications.
1997 Amendments to the Individuals with Disabilities Education Act (IDEA; Public Law 105-17)	These amendments add a number of significant provisions to IDEA and restructure the law. A number of changes in the individualized education program and participation of students with disabilities in state and district assessments are mandated. Significant provisions on mediation of disputes and discipline of students with disabilities are added.
2001 Elementary and Secondary Education Act (No Child Left Behind Act; Public Law 107-110)	Targeted resources are provided to help ensure that disadvantaged students have access to a quality public education (Funds Title 1). The act aims to maximize student learning, provide for teacher development, and enhance school system capacity. The act requires states and districts to report on annual yearly progress for all students, including students with disabilities. The act provides increased flexibility to districts in exchange for increased accountability. The act gives parents whose children attend schools on state "failing schools list" for 2 years the right to transfer their children to another school. Students in "failing schools" for 3 years are eligible for supplemental education services.
2004 Reauthorization of IDEA	New approaches are introduced to prevent overidentification by race or ethnicity. State must have measurable annual objectives for students with disabilities. Districts are not required to use severe discrepancy between ability and achievement in identifying learning disabled students.
2008 Americans with Disabilities Act Amendments	This act further defines and clarifies criteria necessary for determining whether a student has a disability under ADA and Section 504.

SECTION 504 OF THE REHABILITATION ACT OF 1973

Section 504 of the Rehabilitation Act of 1973 is civil rights legislation that prohibits discrimination against persons with disabilities. The act states:

> No otherwise qualified handicapped individual shall, solely by reason of his handicap, be excluded from the participation in, be denied the benefits of, or be subjected to discrimination in any program or activity receiving federal financial assistance.

Section 504 (1) prohibits schools from excluding students with disabilities from any activities solely because of their disability, (2) requires schools to take reasonable steps to prevent harassment based on disability, and (3) requires schools to make those accommodations necessary to enable students with disabilities to participate in all its activities and services (Jacob, Dekker, & Hartshorne, 2011). If the Office of Civil Rights (OCR) of the U.S. Department of Education finds that a state education agency (SEA) or local education agency (LEA) is not in compliance with Section 504, and that a state or district chooses not to act to correct the noncompliance, the OCR may withhold federal funds from that SEA or LEA.

Most of the provisions of Section 504 were incorporated into and expanded in the Education for All Handicapped Children Act of 1975 (Public Law 94-142) and are a part of the Individuals with Disabilities Education Improvement Act of 2004. Section 504 is broader than those other acts because its provisions are not restricted to a specific age group or to education.

Section 504 has been used to secure services for students with conditions not formally listed in the disabilities education legislation. The most frequent of these conditions are attention deficit disorder (ADD) and attention deficit disorder with hyperactivity (ADHD). Unlike IDEA, Section 504 does not provide any funds to schools. Yet, any school that receives federal funds for any purpose at all must comply with the provisions of Section 504 or they lose their funds. And, to make matters more complex, Section 504 and the Americans with Disabilities Act Amendments of 2008 require that schools must provide students with the necessary accommodations to participate in individual and standards-based assessments. It is illegal to refuse to let students use accommodations (like extra time, testing sessions broken into short intervals, or sign language) necessary to be successful in school and/or to participate in individual or standards-based assessment. Those who assess students are required to evaluate the extent to which they are eligible for accommodations in classrooms and/or those necessary to take tests. The accommodations must always be determined by a group of people (usually the child study or IEP team) and they must be based on individual student need rather than on disability type or category.

MAJOR ASSESSMENT PROVISIONS OF THE INDIVIDUALS WITH DISABILITIES EDUCATION IMPROVEMENT ACT

When Congress passed the Education for All Handicapped Children Act in 1975, it included four major requirements relative to assessment: (1) an individualized education program (IEP) for each student with a disability, (2) protection in evaluation procedures, (3) education in the least restrictive appropriate environment (LRE), and (4) due process rights. The provisions of federal law continued with the 2004 reauthorized Individuals with Disabilities Education Improvement Act.

The Individualized Education Program Provisions

Public Law 94-142 (the Education for All Handicapped Children Act of 1975) specified that all students with disabilities have the right to a free, appropriate public education and that schools must have an IEP for each student with a disability who is determined to need specially designed instruction. In the IEP, school personnel must specify the long- and short-term goals of the instructional program. IEPs must be based on a comprehensive assessment by a multidisciplinary team. We stress that assessment data are collected for the purpose of helping team members specify the components of the IEP. The team must specify not only goals and objectives but also

Go to the Education CourseMate website for this textbook to see an annotated IEP from the Pennsylvania Department of Education.

plans for implementing the instructional program. They must specify how and when progress toward accomplishment of objectives will be evaluated. Note that specific assessment activities that form the basis of the program are listed, as are specific instructional goals or objectives. IEPs are to be formulated by a multidisciplinary child study team that meets with the parents. Parents have the right to agree or disagree with the contents of the program.

In the 1997 amendments, Congress mandated a number of changes to the IEP. The core IEP team was expanded to include both a special education teacher and a general education teacher. The 1997 law also specified that students with disabilities are to be included in state- and districtwide assessments and that states must report annually on the performance and progress of all students, including students with disabilities. The IEP team must decide whether the student will take the assessments with or without accommodations or take an alternate or modified assessment.

Protection in Evaluation Procedures Provisions

Congress included a number of specific requirements in Public Law 94-142. These requirements were designed to protect students and help ensure that assessment procedures and activities would be fair, equitable, and nondiscriminatory. Specifically, Congress mandated eight provisions:

1. Tests are to be selected and administered so as to be racially and culturally nondiscriminatory.
2. To the extent feasible, students are to be assessed in their native language or primary mode of communication (such as American Sign Language or communication board).
3. Tests must have been validated for the specific purpose for which they are used.
4. Tests must be administered by trained personnel in conformance with the instructions provided by the test producer.

SCENARIO *in* ASSESSMENT

LEE | Lee is a young man with moderate mental retardation. He was diagnosed at birth with a genetic syndrome that is closely associated with mental retardation. Consequently, Lee's parents were concerned with his development and monitored it closely. Unfortunately, it soon became clear that he was lagging in passing developmental milestones such as recognizing faces, sitting up, making prespeech sounds, and so forth. At age 2, he was identified as eligible for early intervention services because of his delayed development. An Individual Family Service Plan (See Part C of IDEA) was developed. Not only did Lee receive special services, his family received various support services. Lee and his family continued to receive special education services when he enrolled in his neighborhood school, where he received a free, appropriate public education as described in an individualized educational plan (IEP) that his parents helped develop. In the primary grades, Lee also received speech therapy for articulation problems and occupational therapy for pencil and scissor use. Lee's parents received parent counseling to learn how to manage bedtime and toileting behavior. Lee made good progress throughout his elementary school program. He mastered self-help skills, some sight vocabulary, coin recognition, etc. In short, he met the annual goals in his IEP, seemed to enjoy school, and made friends, mostly in his special education classroom.

The year Lee entered high school he turned 14, and his education emphasized Lee's postsecondary training, employment, and community living. It stressed helping Lee become more independent in life after high school. Therefore, his educational goals addressed his employment options and preferences, recreation and leisure activities, personal management (e.g., using public transportation, doing laundry, money management, etc.), family and social relationships, and advocacy. Lee participated in a work-study program and had a job coach for his job at a local supermarket. Lee continued his public education until the year he turned 21.

Today, Lee lives in a subsidized apartment, works full time at the same supermarket, and has several friends. He plans on marrying his long-time girlfriend in the near future. He has an advocate who advises him on a number of topics.

Fifty years ago—before PL 94-142, IDEA, and PL 99-457 and before states and the federal government began guaranteeing educational rights for students with moderate or severe disabilities—Lee would have faced a much different life. There would not have been an early education or a public education. Lee would not have been prepared to live so independently—to work, to have his own home, etc.

What implications about your own professional role can you draw from this scenario? Go to the Education CourseMate website for this textbook for more reflection questions about this Scenario in Assessment.

5. Tests used with students must include those designed to provide information about specific educational needs, not just a general intelligence quotient.
6. Decisions about students are to be based on more than their performance on a single test.
7. Evaluations are to be made by a multidisciplinary team that includes at least one teacher or other specialist with knowledge in the area of suspected disability.
8. Children must be assessed in all areas related to a specific disability, including—where appropriate—health, vision, hearing, social and emotional status, general intelligence, academic performance, communicative skills, and motor skills.

In passing the 1997 amendments and the 2004 amendments, Congress reauthorized these provisions.

Least Restrictive Environment Provisions

In writing the 1975 Education for All Handicapped Children Act, Congress wanted to ensure that, to the greatest extent appropriate, students with disabilities would be placed in settings that would maximize their opportunities to interact with students without disabilities. Section 612(S)(B) states:

> To the maximum extent appropriate, handicapped children ... are educated with children who are not handicapped, and that special classes, separate schooling, or other removal of handicapped children from the regular educational environment occurs only when the nature or the severity of the handicap is such that education in regular classes with the use of supplementary aids and services cannot be achieved satisfactorily.

The LRE provisions arose out of court cases in which state and federal courts had ruled that when two equally appropriate placements were available for a student with a disability, the most normal (that is, least restrictive) placement was preferred. The LRE provisions were reauthorized in all revisions of the law.

Due Process Provisions

In Public Law 94-142, Congress specified the procedures that schools and school personnel would have to follow to ensure due process in decision making. Specifically, when a decision affecting identification, evaluation, or placement of a student with disabilities is to be made, the student's parents or guardians must be given both the opportunity to be heard and the right to have an impartial due process hearing to resolve conflicting opinions.

Schools must provide opportunities for parents to inspect the records that are kept on their children and to challenge material that they believe should not be included in those records. Parents have the right to have their child evaluated by an independent party and to have the results of that evaluation considered when psychoeducational decisions are made. In addition, parents must receive written notification before any education agency can begin an evaluation that might result in changes in the placement of a student.

In the 1997 amendments to IDEA, Congress specified that states must offer mediation as a voluntary option to parents and educators as an initial part of dispute resolution. If mediation is not successful, either party may request a due process hearing. The due process provisions were reauthorized in the 2004 IDEA.

THE NO CHILD LEFT BEHIND ACT OF 2001

The No Child Left Behind Act of 2001 is the reform of the federal Elementary and Secondary Education Act. Signed into law on January 8, 2002, the act has several major provisions that affect assessment and instruction of students with disabilities and disadvantaged students. The law requires stronger accountability for results by specifying that states must have challenging state educational standards, test children in grades 3–8 every year, and specify statewide progress objectives that ensure proficiency of every child by grade 12. The law also provides increased flexibility and local control, specifying that states can decide their standards and procedures but at the same time must be held accountable for results. Parents are given expanded educational options under this law, and students who are attending schools judged to be "failing schools" have the right to enroll in other public schools, including public charter schools. A major provision of this law is called "putting reading first," a set of provisions ensuring all-out effort to have every child reading by the end of third grade. These provisions provide funding to schools for intensive reading interventions for children in grades K–3. Finally, the law specifies that all students have the right to be taught using "evidence-based instructional methods"—that is, teaching methods proven to work. The provisions of this law require that states include all students, among them students with disabilities and English-language learners, in their statewide accountability systems.

2004 REAUTHORIZATION OF IDEA

The Individuals with Disabilities Education Act was reauthorized in 2004. Several of the new requirements of the law have special implications for assessment of students with disabilities.[1] After much debate, Congress removed the requirement that students must have a severe discrepancy between ability and achievement in order to be considered as having a learning disability. It replaced this provision with permission to states and districts to use data on student responsiveness to intervention in making service eligibility decisions. We provide an extensive discussion of assessing response to intervention in Chapter 24. Congress also specified that states must have measurable goals, standards, or objectives for all students with disabilities.

AMERICANS WITH DISABILITIES ACT OF 1990 (ADA)

ADA is the law most often cited in court cases involving either employment of people with disabilities or appropriate education in colleges and universities for students with disabilities. Simply put, any agency or organization that receives federal funds must provide access (like building ramps), transportation (like special buses or wheelchair lifts), or accommodations (like sign language interpreters at plays and musical events) necessary to enable students with disabilities to participate in its services and events.

AMERICANS WITH DISABILITIES ACT AMENDMENTS OF 2008 (ADAA)

In 2008, Congress reauthorized and revised the Americans with Disabilities Act, primarily for the purpose of clarifying the criteria for making decisions about eligibility for entitlements like special education services. The term 504/ADAA impairment is used to refer to those students who qualify as having a disability under Section 504/ADAA, but who are not eligible for special education and related services under IDEA. As long as they also meet the "need" criterion, they are entitled to special education services as a protection under Section 504/ADAA.

3 Ethical Considerations

Professionals who assess students have the responsibility to engage in ethical behavior. Most professional associations have put together sets of standards to guide the ethical practice of their members; many of these standards relate directly to assessment practices. Those most relevant to the concerns of education professionals are the ethical principles of the Council for Exceptional Children (http://www.cec.sped.org), National Education Association (http://www.nea.org/), American Federation of Teachers (http://www.aft.org/), National Association of School Psychologists

[1] The law was retitled the Individuals with Disabilities Education Improvement Act, but the acronym IDEA is still used to refer to the new law.

Find more information about websites devoted to evidence-based teaching on the Education CourseMate website for this textbook.

(http://www.nasponline.org/), and American Psychological Association (http://www.apa.org/). In our work with teachers and related services personnel, we consistently have found that the most helpful set of ethical principles and guidelines are those of the National Association of School Psychologists (these are based heavily on the ethical principles of the Canadian Psychological Association).

In publishing ethical and professional standards, the associations express serious commitment to promoting high technical standards for assessment instruments and high ethical standards for the behavior of individuals who work with assessments. Here, we cite a number of important ethical considerations, borrowing heavily from the National Association of School Psychologists' (2010) *Principles for Professional Ethics*, the American Psychological Association's (2002) *Ethical Principles of Psychologists and Code of Conduct*, and the National Education Association's *Code of Ethics of the Education Profession*. We have not cited the standards explicitly, but we have distilled from them a number of broad ethical principles that guide assessment practice and behavior.

The term *ethics* generally refers to a system of principles of conduct that guide the behavior of an individual. Codes of ethics serve to protect the public. However, ethical conduct is not synonymous with simple conformity to a set of rules outlined as principles and professional standards. NASP's Code of Ethics 2010 is organized around four broad ethical themes: Respecting the Dignity and Rights of All Persons; Professional Competence and Responsibility; Honesty and Integrity in Professional Relationships; and Responsibility to Schools, Families, Communities, the Profession, and Society" (Jacob, Decker, & Hartshorne, 2011, p. 9). We briefly describe these four broad ethical themes in the sections that follow.

FOUR BROAD ETHICAL PRINCIPLES

Respect for the Dignity of Persons

School personnel are committed to "promoting improvement in the quality of life for all students, their families and school communities" (Jacob et al., 2011). (For a fuller discussion of these principles see Jacobs et al., 2011). The discussion applies equally to all school personnel. In brief, this broad principle means that we always recognize that students and their families have the right to participate in decisions that affect student welfare, and that students have the right to decide for themselves whether they want to share their thoughts, feelings, and behaviors.

Those who assess students regularly obtain a considerable amount of very personal information about those students. Such information must be held in strict confidence. A general ethical principle held by most professional organizations is that confidentiality may be broken only when there is clear and imminent danger to an individual or to society. Results of pupil performance on tests must not be discussed informally with school staff members. Formal reports of pupil performance on tests must be released only with the permission of the persons tested or their parents or guardians.

Those who assess students are to make provisions for maintaining confidentiality in the storage and disposal of records. When working with minors or other persons who are unable to give voluntary informed consent, assessors are to take special care to protect these persons' best interests. Those who assess students are expected to maintain test security. It is expected that assessors will not reveal to others the content of specific tests or test items. At the same time, assessors must be willing and able to back up with test data decisions that may adversely affect individuals.

Professional Competence and Responsibility (Responsible Caring and Beneficence)

The ethical codes of all helping professions share a common theme referred to generally as the *beneficence* principle. Beneficence, or responsible caring, means educational professionals do things that are likely to maximize benefit to students, or at least do no harm. This means that educational professionals always act in the best interests of the students they serve. The assessment of students is a social act that has specific social and educational consequences. Those who assess students use assessment data to make decisions about the students, and these decisions can significantly affect an individual's life opportunities. Those who assess students must accept responsibility for the consequences of their work, and they must make every effort to be certain that their services are used appropriately. In short, they are committed to the application of professional expertise to promote improvement in the quality of life available to the student, family, school, and community. For the individual who assesses students, this ethical standard may mean refusing to engage in assessment activities that are desired by a school system but that are clearly inappropriate.

Honesty and Integrity in Professional Relationships

We must all recognize the boundaries of our professional competence. Those who are entrusted with the responsibility for assessing and making decisions about students have differing degrees of competence. Not only must professionals regularly engage in self-assessment to be aware of their own limitations but also they should recognize the limitations of the techniques they use. For individuals, this sometimes means refusing to engage in activities in areas in which they lack competence. It also means using techniques that meet recognized standards and engaging in the continuing education necessary to maintain high standards of competence. As a professional who will assess students, it is imperative that you accept responsibility for the consequences of your work and work to offset any negative consequences of your work.

As schools become increasingly diverse, professionals must demonstrate sensitivity in working with people from different cultural and linguistic backgrounds and with children who have different types of disabling conditions. Assessors should have experience working with students of diverse backgrounds and should demonstrate competence in doing so, or they should refrain from assessing and making decisions about such students.

Responsibility to Schools, Families, Communities, One's Profession, and Society

Those who are entrusted to educate students have responsibilities to the societies and communities in which they work. This means behaving professionally and not doing things that reflect badly on one's employer or profession. As professionals, we are responsible for promoting healthy school, family, and community environments, respecting and obeying laws, contributing to our profession by supervising, mentoring, and educating professional colleagues, and ensuring that *Or all* students can attend school, learn, and develop their personal identities in environments free from discrimination, harassment, violence, and abuse (Jacobs et al., 2011). Often the students with whom we work (especially students with disabilities) are among the most vulnerable members of society. We have a responsibility to protect their rights.

Those who assess students are responsible for selecting and administering tests in a fair and nonbiased manner. Assessment approaches must be selected that are valid and that provide an accurate representation of students' skills and abilities rather than of their disabilities. Tests are to be selected and administered so as to be racially and culturally nondiscriminatory, and students should be assessed in their native language or primary mode of communication (for example, Braille or communication boards).

4 Standards

Those who assess students adhere to professional standards on assessment.

A joint committee of the American Educational Research Association, the American Psychological Association, and the National Council on Measurement in Education (1999) published a document titled *Standards for Educational and Psychological Testing*. These standards specify a set of requirements for test development and use. It is imperative that those who develop tests behave in accordance with the standards, and that those who assess students use instruments and techniques that meet the standards.

In Parts 3 and 4 of this text and on the website that accompanies this text, we review commonly used tests and discuss the extent to which those tests meet the standards specified in *Standards for Educational and Psychological Testing*. We provide information to help test users make informed judgments about the technical adequacy of specific tests. There is no federal or state agency that acts to limit the publication or use of technically inadequate tests. Only by refusing to use technically inadequate tests will users force developers to improve them. After all, if you were a test developer, would you continue to publish a test that few people purchased and used? Would you invest your company's resources to make changes in a technically inadequate test that yielded a large annual profit to your firm if people continued to buy and use it the way it was?

Those who assess students are expected to maintain test security. It is expected that assessors will not reveal to others the content of specific tests or test items. At the same time, assessors must be willing and able to back up with test data decisions that may adversely affect individuals.

HOW DO YOU RESOLVE AN ETHICAL DILEMMA?

Using a Problem-Solving Model to Resolve Legal and Ethical Dilemmas

How do you decide what kinds of actions are legal and ethical?

Jacobs et al. provide an eight-step problem-solving model that walks us through the following steps:

1. Describe the parameters of the situation.
2. Define the potential ethical–legal issues involved.
3. Consult ethical and legal guidelines and district policies that might apply to resolution of each issue.
4. Evaluate the rights, responsibilities, and welfare of all affected persons (students, peers, teachers, other school staff, parents, siblings).
5. Generate a list of alternative things you could do in response to the situation.
6. List the consequences of taking each action.
7. Consider any evidence that the various consequences or benefits resulting from each decision will actually happen (conduct a risk–benefit analysis).
8. Make the decision.

What Do You Do When You Encounter Illegal or Unethical Behavior by Professionals in Schools?

In general, you go through a set of four steps.

1. Speak personally with the person who has committed the behavior about what you have observed. Let him or her know that the behavior might be considered illegal or unethical. Often people do not know or recognize that what they are doing is illegal, wrong, or harmful. (Of course, they often do).
2. If the behavior persists (e.g., repeated use of technically inadequate tests), take another professional with you and talk to the person about what the two of you have observed.
3. If the behavior persists, report the behavior to the person's supervisor and ask the supervisor to take action. If your school district has an attorney, include the attorney in this discussion.
4. If the behavior persists, either report the behavior to the relevant ethics board or committee or let the school attorney take action deemed necessary.

Adapted from Jacob, S., Decker, D., and Hartshorne, T. *Ethics and Law for School Psychologists, 6e*. Reprinted by permission of John Wiley and Sons, Inc.

Chapter Comprehension Questions

Write your answers to each of the following questions and then compare your responses to the text.

1. What three major laws affect assessment practices?
2. How do the major components of IDEA (individualized educational plan, least restrictive environment, protection in evaluation procedures, and due process) affect assessment practices?
3. Identify the ethical principles that you believe should guide the behavior of individuals in two of the following professions: plumber, stockbroker, grocery store manager, used car salesman, physician, bartender, and professor. Then write a brief paragraph on why you selected the principles and how they differ for different professions. Are there commonalities?
4. How do the broad ethical principles of beneficence, competence boundaries, respect for the dignity of persons, confidentiality, and fairness affect assessment practices?
5. Special education is, as we promised you, a field of acronyms. SWD are entitled to services under IDEA; others, who are labeled ADHD, are not eligible for services under IDEA but once received services under ADA and are now eligible under ADAA/504. Because of NCLD, Title I students are eligible for services. Students with disabilities are put on an IEP, but school personnel do not have to write one for SW/OD. Students with disabilities are entitled to a FAPE, PEP, and education in the LRE. Translate these sentence in a way that your mother or grandmother could understand.

Web Activities 

1. Go to the U.S. Department of Education website. Can you locate information about the most recent amendments to the Elementary and Secondary Education Act and to IDEA? Report what you find.
2. Go to the website for your state department of education. Download a copy of the rules, guidelines, and regulations regarding special education as well as any state laws specific to assessment. Make a list of relevant state laws. Discuss with classmates what state laws, rules, guidelines, and regulations say about assessment of students with disabilities.
3. Go to the Wrightslaw website, find the section on "Law School Exam," and then find the link to an oral argument on least restrictive environment. There is a video of a lawyer arguing a case on LRE and responding to questions. View the video and state what you learned.
4. Go to the website for the special education division for your state department of education. Look at the suggestions provided for writing IEPs for your state. Discuss with your instructor and classmates any questions you have about IEP content or format.

Web Resources

Wrightslaw
http://www.wrightslaw.org
This website provides many resources, including a glossary of legal terms; a glossary of assessment terms; recent laws; and changes to major federal laws, rules, regulations, and guidelines.

National Association of School Psychologists
http://nasponline.org
This website includes a complete copy of the NASP Principles for Professional Ethics 2010.

Additional resources for this chapter can be found on the Education CourseMate website. Go to CengageBrain.com to access the site.

Test Scores and How to Use Them

CHAPTER GOALS

1 Understand the basic quantitative concepts that deal with scales of measurement, characteristics of distributions, average scores, measures of dispersion, and correlation.

2 Understand how student performances are scored objectively using percent correct, accuracy, fluency, and retention.

3 Understand how test performances are made meaningful through criterion-referenced, achievement standards-referenced, and norm-referenced interpretations.

4 Understand that norms are constructed to be proportionally representative of the population in terms of important personal characteristics (for example, gender and age), contain a large number of people, be representative of today's population, and be relevant for the purposes of assessment.

KEY TERMS

ordinal scale
equal-interval scale
mean
variance
standard deviation
skew
kurtosis
mode
median
range
variance
correlation coefficient
objective scoring
subjective scoring
percent correct
accuracy
instructional level
frustration level
independent level
fluency
retention
age equivalent
grade equivalent
percentile ranks (percentiles)
standard scores
z scores
T scores
IQs
stanines
normal curve equivalents (NCEs)
norms
criterion-referenced
norm-referenced
achievement standards-referenced

More details are available at the Education CourseMate website for this text.

This chapter introduces some basic quantitative concepts needed to understand what various test scores mean and how they should be interpreted. You will find more detailed explanations, information about how various scores or statistics are calculated, and information about more advanced topics on the student website.

School personnel need to understand what test scores mean because they will be using them throughout their professional careers. Correct interpretations of scores can lead to good decision making, whereas incorrect interpretations cannot. To illustrate, suppose you are a teacher and learn that 65 percent of the students in your class earned scores of "proficient" in reading when they took the state test last spring; 22 percent of your students earned scores of "basic." You are told that Willis has an IQ of 87 and is considered a "slow learner," and that he scored at the 22nd percentile on a measure of vocabulary. Elaine is said to have a grade equivalent of 4.2 on a math test. You are also told that your class scored at the state median on a measure of writing. Obviously, this information is supposed to mean something to you and could affect how you will teach. What do these scores mean? How do they affect the instructional decisions you will make?

1 Basic Quantitative Concepts

The basic quantitative concepts for beginning students deal with scales of measurement, characteristics of sets of scores, average scores, measures of dispersion, and correlation.

SCALES OF MEASUREMENT

More information about *Scales of Measurement* is available at the Education CourseMate website for this text.

Assessment in the real world is a quantitative activity. The type of mathematical operations that can be properly done depends on the nature of the score. There are four types of scores: nominal, ordinal, ratio, and equal interval (Stevens, 1951). The four scales differ in the relationship between possible consecutive values on the measurement continuum, for example, the difference between 1 and 2 inches on a ruler. In education and psychology, ordinal and equal interval are by far the most commonly used scales; nominal and ratio scales are fairly rare.[1]

Ordinal scales order things from better to worse or from worse to better (for example, good, better, best, or novice, intermediate, and expert). On ordinal scales, the magnitude of the difference between adjacent values is unknown and unlikely to be equal. Thus, we cannot determine how much better an *intermediate* performance is than a *novice* performance or if the difference between *novice* and *intermediate* is the same as the difference between *intermediate* and *expert.* Because the differences between adjacent values are unknown and presumed unequal, ordinal scores cannot be added together or averaged.

Equal-interval scales also order things from better to worse. However, unlike ordinal scales, the magnitude of the difference between adjacent values is known and is equal. Examples of equal-interval scales in everyday life include the measurement of time, length, weight, and so forth. Because the differences between adjacent values are equal, equal-interval scores can be added, subtracted, multiplied, and divided.

[1] On *nominal scales*, adjacent values have no inherent relationship; they merely name values on the scale (for example, male and female or telephone numbers that name a specific telephone). Thus, it makes no sense to find the average value on a nominal scale; for example, there is no meaning for a number that is the average of the telephone numbers of all of one's friends. *Ratio scales* are equal-interval scales that have an absolute and logical zero, whereas equal-interval scales do not. For example, 0°C is not the absence of heat, nor is 0°F. Because equal-interval scales do not have a logical zero, ratios using equal-interval (or ordinal, of course) data make no sense; for example, 100°C is not twice as hot as 50°C. Ratio scales do have an absolute zero. Thus, if John weighs 300 pounds and Bob weighs 150 pounds, John weighs twice as much as Bob.

More information about *Distributions* is available at the Education CourseMate website for this text.

CHARACTERISTICS OF DISTRIBUTIONS

Sets of equal-interval scores (for example, student scores on a classroom test) can be described in terms of four characteristics: mean, variance, skew, and kurtosis. Each of these characteristics can be calculated, although there is no need for us to go into their calculations. The *mean* is the arithmetic average of the scores (for example, the mean height for U.S. women is their average height). The *variance* describes the distance between each score and every other score in the set. These characteristics are very important and are discussed repeatedly throughout this book.

Skew refers to the symmetry of a distribution of scores. In a symmetrical set of scores, the scores above the mean mirror the scores below the mean. When a test is easy and many students earn high scores, whereas only a few students earn low scores, the distribution of scores is not symmetrical; it is skewed. There are more scores above the mean and more extreme scores below the mean, as shown in Figure 4.1 (left). The opposite happens when a test is difficult; many students earn low scores, whereas a few students earn high scores. There are more scores below the mean and more extreme scores above the mean, as shown in Figure 4.1 (right).

Kurtosis describes the peakedness of a curve—that is, the rate at which a curve rises and falls. Relatively flat distributions spread out test takers and are called *platykurtic*. (The prefix *plat-* means flat, as in platypus or plateau.) Relatively fast-rising distributions do not spread out test takers and are called *leptokurtic*. Figure 4.2 illustrates a platykurtic and a leptokurtic curve.

More information about *Measures of Central Tendency* is available at the Education CourseMate website for this text.

AVERAGE SCORES

An average gives us a general description of how a group as a whole performed. There are three different averages: mode, median, and mean.

The *mode* is defined as the score most frequently obtained. A mode (if there is one) can be found for data on a nominal, ordinal, ratio, or equal-interval

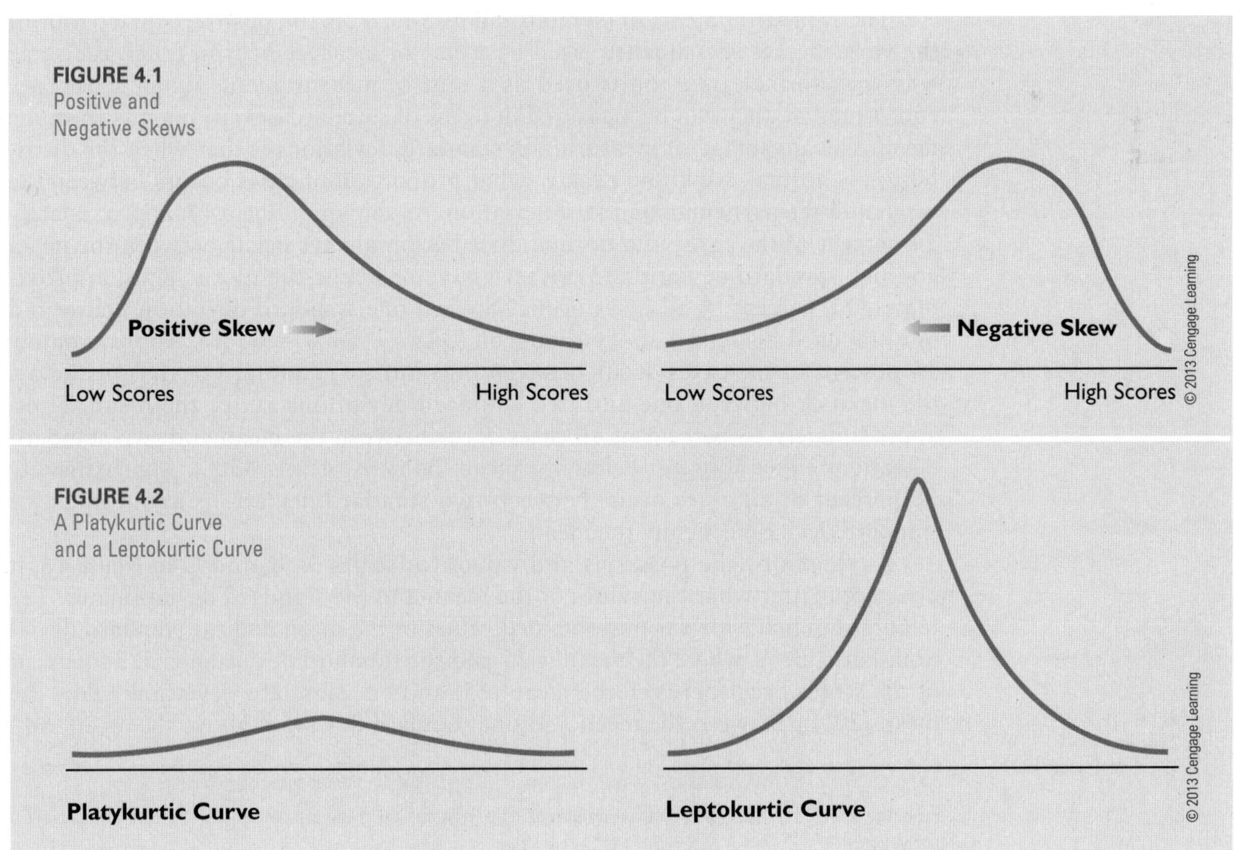

FIGURE 4.1 Positive and Negative Skews

FIGURE 4.2 A Platykurtic Curve and a Leptokurtic Curve

scale. Distributions may have two modes (if they do, they are called "bimodal distributions"), or they may have more than two.

The *median* is the point in a distribution above which are 50 percent of test takers (not test scores) and below which are 50 percent of test takers (not test scores). Medians can be found for data on ordinal, equal-interval, and ratio scales; they must not be used with nominal scales. The median score may or may not actually be earned by a student.

The *mean* is the arithmetic average of the scores in a distribution and is the most important average for use in assessment. It is the sum of the scores divided by the number of scores; its symbol *is* $\overline{X}$. The mean, like the median, may or may not be earned by any child in the distribution. Means should be computed only for data equal-interval (and ratio) scales.

MEASURES OF DISPERSION

More information about *Measures of Dispersion* is available at the Education CourseMate website for this text.

Dispersion tells us how scores are spread out above and below the average score. Three measures of dispersion are range, variance, and standard deviation. The *range* is the distance between the extremes of a distribution, including the extremes; it is the highest score less the lowest score plus 1. Range is a relatively crude measure of dispersion because it is based on only two pieces of information. Range can be calculated with ordinal data (for example, "ratings ranged from excellent to poor") and equal-interval data.

The variance and the standard deviation are the most important indexes of dispersion. The *variance* (symbolized as S^2 or σ^2) is a numerical index describing the dispersion of a set of scores around the mean of the distribution.[2] Because the variance is an average, the number of cases in the set or the distribution does not affect it. Large sets of scores may have large or small variances; small sets of scores may have large or small variances. In addition, because the variance is measured in terms of distance from the mean, it is not related to the actual value of the mean. Distributions with large means may have large or small variances; distributions with small means may have large or small variances.

The *standard deviation* (symbolized as S or σ) is the positive square root of the variance.[3] It is frequently used as a unit of measurement in much the same way that an inch or a ton is used as a unit of measurement. When scores are equal interval, they can be measured in terms of standard deviation units from the mean. The advantage of measuring in standard deviations is that when the distribution is normal, we know exactly what proportion of cases occurs between the mean and the particular standard deviation. As shown in Figure 4.3, approximately 34 percent of the cases in a normal distribution always occur between the mean and one standard deviation (S) either above or below the mean. Thus, approximately 68 percent of all cases occur between one standard deviation below and one standard deviation above the mean (34% + 34% = 68%). Approximately 14 percent of the cases occur between one and two standard deviations below the mean or between one and two standard deviations above the mean. Thus, approximately 48 percent of all cases occur between the mean and two standard deviations either above or below the mean (34% + 14% = 48%). Approximately 96 percent of all cases occur between two standard deviations above and two standard deviations below the mean.

As shown by the positions and values for scales A, B, and C in Figure 4.3, it does not matter what the values of the mean and the standard deviation are. The relationship holds for various obtained values of the mean and the standard deviation. For scale A, where the mean is 25 and the standard deviation is 5, 34 percent of the scores occur between the mean (25) and one standard deviation below the mean (20) or between the mean and one standard deviation above the mean (30).

[2] S^2 is the symbol for the variance of a sample, whereas σ^2 is the symbol for the variance of a population.

[3] S is the symbol for the standard deviation of a sample, whereas σ^2 is the symbol for the standard deviation of a population.

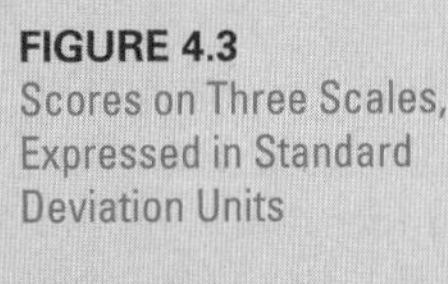

FIGURE 4.3
Scores on Three Scales, Expressed in Standard Deviation Units

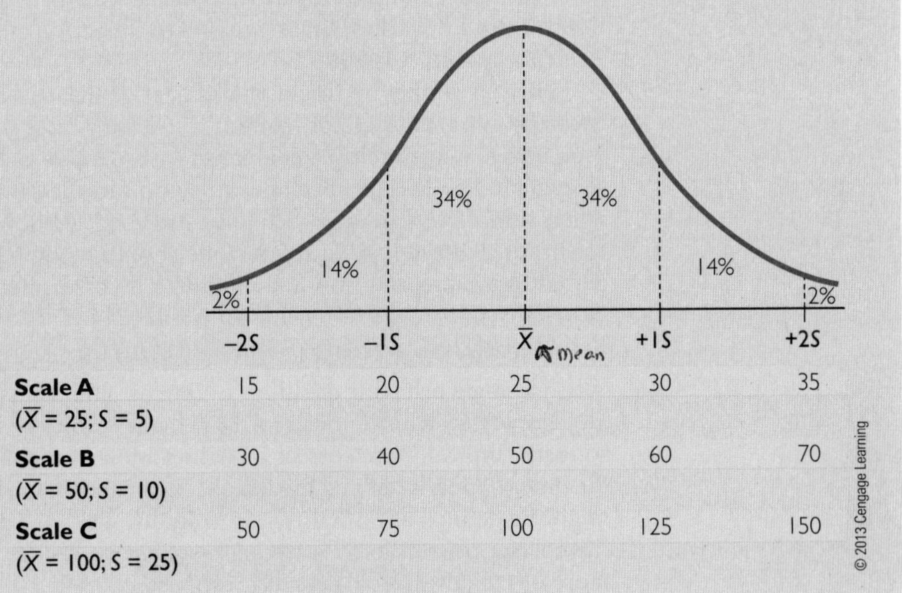

Similarly, for scale B, where the mean is 50 and the standard deviation is 10, 34 percent of the cases occur between the mean (50) and one standard deviation below the mean (40) or between the mean and one standard deviation above the mean (60).

CORRELATION

More information about *Correlation* is available at the Education CourseMate website for this text.

Correlation quantifies relationships between variables. *Correlation coefficients* are numerical indexes of these relationships. They tell us the extent to which any two variables go together—that is, the extent to which changes in one variable are reflected by changes in the second variable. These coefficients are used in measurement to estimate both the reliability and the validity of a test. Correlation coefficients can range in value from .00 to either +1.00 or −1.00. The sign (+ or −) indicates the direction of the relationship; the number indicates the magnitude of the relationship. A correlation coefficient of .00 between two variables means that there is no relationship between the variables. The variables are independent; changes in one variable are not related to changes in the second variable. A correlation coefficient of either +1.00 or −1.00 indicates a perfect relationship between two variables. Thus, if you know a person's score on one variable, you can predict that person's score on the second variable without error. Correlation coefficients between .00 and 1.00 (or −1.00) allow some prediction, and the greater the coefficient, the greater its predictive power.

2 Scoring Student Performance

Tests are structured situations in which predetermined materials are presented to an individual in a predetermined manner in order to evaluate that individual's responses. How a person's responses are scored and interpreted depends on the materials used, the intent of the test author, and the diagnostician's intention.

OBJECTIVE VERSUS SUBJECTIVE SCORING

There are two approaches to scoring a student's response: objective and subjective. By *objective scoring*, we mean scoring that is based on observable qualities and not influenced by emotion, guess, or personal bias. By *subjective scoring*, we mean scoring that is not based on observable qualities but relies on personal impressions and private criteria. The clear intent of the Individuals with Disabilities Education Act is to require objective measurement (*Federal Register* 71(156), August 14, 2006).

There is simply no doubt that objective measurement is less likely to be influenced by extraneous factors such as a student's race, gender, appearance, religion, or even name. When multiple examiners or observers use objective scoring procedures to evaluate student performance, they obtain the same scores. This is not the case when subjective scoring procedures are used. Although some educators advocate celebrating subjectivity in scoring, we should be skeptical of scores associated with global ratings, scoring rubrics, and portfolio assessments.

SUMMARIZING STUDENT PERFORMANCE

When a single behavior or skill is of interest and assessed only once, evaluators usually employ a dichotomous scoring scheme: right or wrong, present or absent, and so forth. Typically, the correct or right option of the dichotomy is defined precisely; the other option is defined by default. For example, a correct response to "1 + 2 = ?" might be defined as "3, written intelligibly, written after the = sign, and written in the correct orientation"; a wrong response would be one that fails to meet one or more of the criteria for a correct response.

A single response can also be awarded partial credit that can range along a continuum from completely correct to completely incorrect. For example, a teacher might objectively score a student response and give partial credit for a response because the student used the correct procedures to solve a mathematics problem even though the student made a computational error. Partial credit can be useful when trying to document slow progress toward a goal. For example, in a life-skills curriculum, a teacher might scale the item "drinking from a cup without assistance" as shown in Table 4.1. Of course, each point on the continuum requires a definition for the partial credit to be awarded.

When an evaluation is concerned with multiple items, a tester may simply report how a student performed on each and every item. More often, however, the tester summarizes the student's performance over all the test items to provide an index of total performance. The sum of correct responses is usually the first summary index computed.

Although the number correct provides a limited amount of information about student performance, it lacks important information that provides a context for understanding that performance. Five summary scores are commonly used to provide a more meaningful context for the total score: the percent correct, percent accuracy, and the rate of correct response, fluency, and retention.

Percent correct is widely used in a variety of assessment contexts. The percent correct is calculated by dividing the number correct by the number possible and multiplying that quotient by 100. This index is best used with *power tests*—tests for which students have sufficient time to answer all of the questions.

Accuracy is the number of correct responses divided by the number of attempted responses multiplied by 100. Accuracy is appropriately used when an assessment

TABLE 4.1 Drinking from a Cup

Level	Definition
Well	Drinks with little spilling or assistance
Acceptably	Dribbles a few drops
Learning	Requires substantial prompting or spills
Beginning	Requires manual guidance

procedure precludes a student from responding to all items.[4] For example, a teacher may ask a student to read orally for 2 minutes, but it may not be possible for that student (or any other student) to read the entire passage in the time allotted. Thus, Benny may attempt 175 words in a 350-word passage in 2 minutes; if he reads 150 words correctly, his percentage correct would be approximately 86 percent—that is, $100 \times (150/175)$.

Percentages are given verbal labels that are intended to facilitate instruction. The two most commonly used labels are "mastery" and "instructional level." *Mastery* divides the percentage continuum in two: Mastery is generally set at 90 or 95 percent correct, and nonmastery is less than the level of mastery. The criterion for mastery is arbitrary, and in real life we frequently set the level for mastery too low.

Instructional level divides the percentage range into three segments: frustration, instructional, and independent levels. When material is too difficult for a student, it is said to be at the *frustration level*; this level is usually defined as material for which a student knows less than 85 percent of it. An *instructional level* provides a degree of challenge where a student is likely to be successful, but success is not guaranteed; this level is usually defined by student responses between 85 and 95 percent correct. The *independent level* is defined as the point where a student can perform without assistance; this level is usually defined as student performance of more than 95 percent correct. For example, in reading, students who decode more than 95 percent of the words should be able to read a passage without assistance; students who decode between 85 and 95 percent of the words in a passage should be able to read and comprehend that passage with assistance; and students who cannot decode 85 percent of the words in a passage will probably have great difficulty decoding and comprehending the material, even with assistance.[5]

Fluency is the number of correct responses per minute. Teachers often want their students to have a supply of information at their fingertips so that they can respond fluently (or automatically) without thinking. For example, teachers may want their students to recognize sight words without having to sound them out, recall addition facts without having to think about them, or supply Spanish words for their English equivalents. Criterion rates for successful performance are usually determined empirically. For example, readers with satisfactory comprehension usually read connected prose at rates of 100 or more words per minute, depending on their grade level. (See, e.g., Read Naturally, Inc., 2010; National Assessment of Educational Progress, Oral Reading Rate, 2002; Mercer & Mercer, 1985.)

Retention refers to the percentage of learned information that is recalled. Retention may also be termed recall, maintenance, or memory of what has been learned. Regardless of the label, it is calculated in the same way: Divide the number recalled by the number originally learned, and multiply that ratio by 100. For example, if Helen learned 40 sight vocabulary words and recalled 30 of them 2 weeks later, her retention would be 75 percent—that is, $100 \times (30/40)$. Because forgetting becomes more likely as the interval between the learning and the retention assessment increases, retention is usually qualified by the period of time between attainment of mastery and assessment of recall. Thus, Helen's retention would be stated as 75 percent over a 2-week period.

3 Interpretation of Test Performance

There are three common ways to interpret an individual student's performance in special and inclusive education: criterion-referenced, standards-referenced, and norm-referenced.

[4] A situation in which there are more opportunities to respond than time to respond is termed a *free operant*. Free operant situations arise in assessments that are timed to allow the opportunity for unlimited increases in rate.

[5] Students should not be given homework (independent practice) until they are at the independent level.

CRITERION-REFERENCED INTERPRETATIONS

When we are interested in a student's knowledge about a single fact, we compare a student's performance against an objective and absolute standard (criterion) of performance. Thus, to be considered criterion-referenced, there must be a clear, objective criterion for each of the correct responses to each question or to each portion of the question if partial credit is to be awarded.

ACHIEVEMENT STANDARDS-REFERENCED INTERPRETATIONS

In large-scale assessments, school districts must ascertain the degree to which they are meeting state and national achievement standards. To do so, states specify the qualities and skills that competent learners need to demonstrate. These indices consist of four components.

- Levels of performance: The entire range of possible student performances (from very poor to excellent) is divided into a number of bands or ranges. Verbal labels that are attached to each of these ranges indicate increasing levels of accomplishment. For example, an *emerging* performance is less accomplished than an *advanced* performance, whereas an *advanced* performance is less accomplished than a *proficient* performance.
- Objective criteria: Each level of performance is defined by precise, objective descriptions of student accomplishment relative to the task. These descriptions can be quantified.
- Examples: Examples of student work at each level are provided. These examples illustrate the range of performance within each level.
- Cut scores: Cutoff scores are provided. These scores provide quantitative criteria that clearly delineate student performance level.

NORM-REFERENCED INTERPRETATIONS

Sometimes testers are interested in knowing how a student's performance compares to the performances of other students—usually students of similar demographic characteristics (age, gender, grade in school, and so forth). In order to make this type of comparison, a student's score is transformed into a *derived score*. There are two types of derived scores: developmental scores and scores of relative standing.

Developmental Scores

There are two types of developmental scores: developmental equivalents and developmental quotients. *Developmental equivalents* may be age equivalents or grade

SCENARIO *in* ASSESSMENT

MR. STANLEY | Mr. Stanley is a first-year special education teacher who teaches intermediate-level children with learning problems in a district elementary school. His school's principal asked him to participate in a multidisciplinary team meeting for a student who has been experiencing serious learning difficulties. Because Mr. Stanley had never participated in an initial evaluation before and was a bit nervous, he asked the school psychologist what would happen at the meeting. The psychologist told him that she (the psychologist) would go over the student's test results, specifically her scores on the Wechsler Intelligence Scale for Children (IV) and the Woodcock–Johnson Tests of Achievement (III). She also told him to expect that parents and the general education teacher would provide their input to the process.

To prepare for the meeting, Mr. Stanley looked up the Wechsler and Woodcock–Johnson tests in his college assessment text. Therein he reviewed what behaviors the tests sampled and the derived scores he could expect to see reported. At the meeting, the psychologist reported the percentiles and standard scores earned by the student, and Mr. Stanley knew exactly what each meant. With this knowledge, he was able to participate meaningfully in the team's discussion of the student's disability and possible need for special education.

What implications about your personal professional role can you draw from this scenario? Go to the Education CourseMate website for this textbook for more reflection questions about this Scenario in Assessment.

equivalents. Developmental scores are based on the average performance of individuals of a given age or grade. Suppose the average performance of 10-year-old children on a test was 27 correct. Furthermore, suppose that Horace answered 27 questions correctly. Horace answered as many questions correctly as the average of 10-year-old children. He would earn an age equivalent of 10 years. An *age equivalent* means that a child's raw score is the average (the median or mean) performance for that age group. Age equivalents are expressed in years and months; a hyphen is used in age scores (for example, 7-1 for 7 years, 1 month old). If the test measured mental ability, Horace's score would have a mental age; if the test measured language, it would be called a language age. A *grade equivalent* means that a child's raw score is the average (the median or mean) performance for a particular grade. Grade equivalents are expressed in grades and tenths of grades; a decimal point is used in grade scores (for example, 7.1). Age-equivalent and grade-equivalent scores are interpreted as a performance equal to the average of X-year-olds and the average of Xth graders' performance, respectively.

The interpretation of age and grade equivalents requires great care. Five problems occur in the use of developmental scores.

1. *Systematic misinterpretation:* Students who earn an age equivalent of 12-0 have merely answered as many questions correctly as the average for children 12 years of age. They have not necessarily performed as a 12-year-old child would; they may well have attacked the problems in a different way or demonstrated a different performance pattern from many 12-year-old students. For example, a second grader and a ninth grader might both earn grade equivalents of 4.0, but they probably have not performed identically. We have known for more than 30 years that younger children perform lower level work with greater accuracy (for instance, successfully answered 38 of the 45 problems attempted), whereas older children attempt more problems with less accuracy (for instance, successfully answered 38 of the 78 problems attempted) (Thorndike & Hagen, 1978).
2. *Need for interpolation and extrapolation:* Average age and grade scores are estimated for groups of children who are never tested. Interpolated scores are estimated for groups of students between groups actually tested. For example, students within 30 days of their eighth birthday may be tested, but age equivalents are estimated for students who are 8-1, 8-2, and so on. Extrapolated scores are estimated for students who are younger and older than the children tested. For example, a student may earn an age equivalent of 5-0 even though no child younger than 6 was tested.
3. *Promotion of typological thinking:* An average 12-0 pupil is a statistical abstraction. The average 12-year-old is in a family with 1.2 other children, 0.8 of a dog, and 2.3 automobiles; in other words, the average child does not exist. Average 12-0 children more accurately represent a range of performances, typically the middle 50 percent.
4. *Implication of a false standard of performance:* Educators expect a third grader to perform at a third-grade level and a 9-year-old to perform at a 9-year-old level. However, the way in which equivalent scores are constructed ensures that 50 percent of any age or grade group will perform below age or grade level because half of the test takers earn scores below the median.
5. *Tendency for scales to be ordinal, not equal interval:* The line relating the number correct to the various ages is typically curved, with a flattening of the curve at higher ages or grades. Figure 4.4 is a typical developmental curve. Because the scales are ordinal and not based on equal interval units, scores on these scales should not be added or multiplied in any computation.

To interpret a developmental score (for example, a mental age), it is usually helpful to know the age of the person whose score is being interpreted. Knowing developmental age as well as chronological age (CA) allows us to judge an individual's

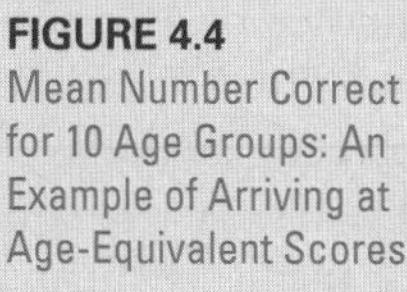

FIGURE 4.4
Mean Number Correct for 10 Age Groups: An Example of Arriving at Age-Equivalent Scores

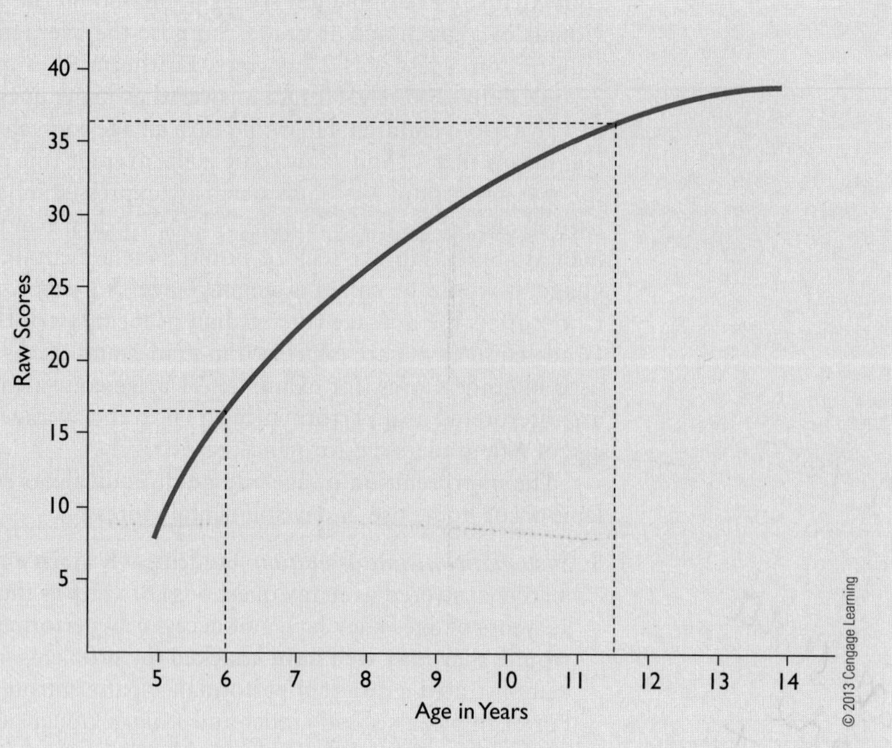

relative performance. Suppose that Ana earns a mental age (MA) of 120 months. If Ana is 8 years (96 months) old, her performance is above average. If she is 35 years old, however, it is below average. The relationship between developmental age and chronological age is often quantified as a developmental quotient. For example, a *ratio IQ* is

$$\mathbf{IQ = MA\ (in\ months) \times 100 \div CA\ (in\ months)}$$

All the problems that apply to developmental levels also apply to developmental quotients.

Percentile Family

More information about how *percentiles* are calculated is available at the Education CourseMate website for this text.

Percentile ranks (*percentiles*) are derived scores that indicate the percentage of people whose scores are at or below a given raw score. Although percentiles are easily calculated, test authors usually provide tables that convert raw scores on a test to percentiles for each age or grade of test takers. Interpretation of percentiles is straightforward. If Bill earns a percentile of 48 on a test, Bill's test score is equal to or better than those of 48 percent of the test takers. (It is also correct to say that 53 percent of the test takers earned scores equal to or better than that of Bill.) Theoretically, percentiles can range from 0.1 to 99.9—that is, a performance that is equal to or better than those of one-tenth of 1 percent of the test takers to a performance that is equal to or better than those of 99.9 percent of the test takers. The 50th percentile rank is the median.

Occasionally, a score is reported within a percentile band. The two most common are deciles and quartiles:

- *Deciles* are bands of percentiles that are 10 percentile ranks in width; each decile contains 10 percent of the norm group. The first decile is percentiles wide, from 0.1 to 9.9; the second ranges from 10 to 19.9; the tenth decile goes from 90 to 99.9.
- *Quartiles* are bands of percentiles that are 25 percentiles wide; each quartile contains 25 percent of the norm group. The first quartile contains percentile from 0.1 to 24.9; the fourth quartile contains the ranks 75 to 99.9.

Percentiles allow us to compare the performances of several students even when they differ in age or grade. For example, it is not particularly helpful to know that George is 70 inches tall, Bridget is 6 feet 3 inches tall, Bruce is 1.93 meters tall, and Alexandra is 177.8 centimeters tall. It is much simpler to compare their heights when the measurements are in the same units. Converting their heights to feet and inches, we see that George is 5 feet 10 inches, Bridget is 6 feet 3 inches, Bruce is 6 feet 4 inches, and Alexandra is 5 feet 10 inches. Percentiles put raw scores into comparable units. Similarly, it is not particularly helpful to know that George got 75 percent correct on the spelling portion of a group-administered test of achievement, 56 percent correct on the reading comprehension portion, and 63 percent on the mathematics portion. Without knowing how other students scored, such information offers little, if any, insight into George's achievement. However, converting the percents correct into percentiles allows direct and easy comparison: 54th percentile in spelling, 47th percentile in reading comprehension, and 61st percentile in mathematics. The major disadvantage of percentiles is that they are not equal-interval scores. Therefore, they cannot be added together or subtracted from one another. Thus, it would be incorrect to say that George is 7 percentiles better in reading comprehension than in spelling, although it is correct to say that George did relatively better in spelling than in reading comprehension.

Standard Score Family

More information about the calculation of various standard scores is available at the Education CourseMate website for this text.

Standard scores are derived scores with a predetermined mean and standard deviation. The most basic standard score is the *z* distribution. In the distribution of *z* scores, the mean is always equal to 0.[6] In the distribution of *z* scores, the standard deviation is always equal to 1.[7] Thus, regardless of the mean and standard deviation of the raw (obtained) scores, *z* scores transform those scores into a new distribution with a mean of 0 and a standard deviation of 1. Positive scores are above the mean; negative scores are below the mean. The larger the number, the more above or below the mean is the score. *z* scores are interpreted as being *X* number of standard deviations above or below the mean. When the distribution of scores is bell shaped or normal, we know the exact percentile that corresponds to a *z* score.

In assessment, it is customary to transform *z* scores into different standard scores with predetermined means and standard deviations. Four such scores are common in assessment: *T* scores, IQs,[8] normal curve equivalents, and stanines.

- A *T score* is a standard score with a mean of 50 and a standard deviation of 10. A person earning a *T* score of 40 scored one standard deviation below the mean, whereas a person earning a *T* score of 60 scored one standard deviation above the mean.
- *IQs* are standard scores with a mean of 100 and a standard deviation of 15.[9] A person earning an IQ of 85 scored one standard deviation below the mean, whereas a person earning an IQ of 115 scored one standard deviation above the mean.
- *Normal curve equivalents* (NCEs) are standard scores with a mean equal to 50 and a standard deviation equal to 21.06. Although the standard deviation may at first appear strange, this scale divides the normal curve into 100 equal intervals.

[6] This transformation is achieved by subtracting the mean of the obtained scores from each obtained score.

[7] This transformation is achieved by dividing the difference between the obtained score less the mean of the obtained scores by the obtained standard deviation.

[8] When it was first introduced, the IQ was defined as the ratio of mental age to chronological age, multiplied by 100. Statisticians soon found that MA has different variances and standard deviations at different chronological ages. Consequently, the same ratio IQ has different meanings at different ages—the same ratio IQ corresponds to different *z* scores and percentiles at different ages. To remedy this situation, scientists stopped using ratio IQs and began converting scores to standard scores.

[9] Some older tests have standard deviations that are 16 or another value.

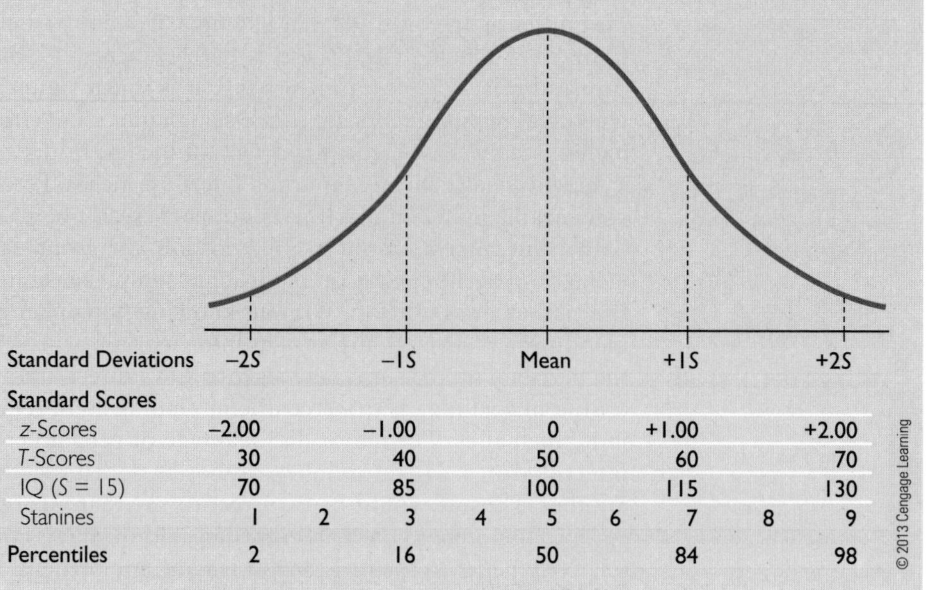

FIGURE 4.5 Relationship Among Selected Standard Scores, Percentiles, and the Normal Curve

- *Stanines* (short for standard nines) are standard-score bands that divide a distribution into nine parts. The first stanine includes all scores that are 1.75 standard deviations or more below the mean, and the ninth stanine includes all scores 1.75 or more standard deviations above the mean. The second through eighth stanines are each 0.5 standard deviation in width, with the fifth stanine ranging from 0.25 standard deviations below the mean to 0.25 standard deviations above the mean.

Standard scores are frequently more difficult to interpret than percentile scores because the concepts of means and standard deviations are not widely understood by people without some statistical knowledge. Thus, standard scores may be more difficult for students and their parents to understand. Aside from this disadvantage, standard scores offer all the advantages of percentiles plus an additional advantage: Because standard scores are equal-interval, they can be combined (for example, added or averaged).[10]

Concluding Comments on Derived Scores

Test authors provide tables to convert raw scores into derived scores. Thus, test users do not have to calculate derived scores. Standard scores can be transformed into other standard scores readily; they can be converted to percentiles without conversion tables only when the distribution of scores is normal. In normal distributions, the relationship between percentiles and standard scores is known. Figure 4.5 compares various standard scores and percentiles for normal distributions. When the distribution of scores is not normal, conversion tables are necessary in order to convert percentiles to standard scores (or vice versa). These conversion tables are test specific, so only a test author can provide them. Moreover, conversion tables are always required in order to convert developmental scores to scores of relative standing, even when the distribution of test scores is normal. If the only derived score

[10] Standard scores also solve another subtle problem. When scores are combined in a total or composite, the elements of that composite (for example, 18 scores from weekly spelling tests that are combined to obtain a semester average) do not count the same (that is, they do not carry the same weight) unless they have equal variances. Tests that have larger variances contribute more to the composite than tests with smaller variances. When each of the elements has been standardized into the same standard scores (for example, when each of the weekly spelling tests has been standardized as *z* scores), the elements (that is, the weekly scores) will carry exactly the same weight when they are combined. Moreover, the only way a teacher can weight tests differentially is to standardize all the tests and then multiply by the weight. For example, if a teacher wished to count the second test as three times the first test, the scores on both tests would have to be standardized, and the scores on the second test would then be multiplied by three before the scores were combined.

SCENARIO *in* ASSESSMENT

KATE | Kate returned from her first day of junior high school and told her parents about her classes. Everything seemed to be just what she had expected, except for her math class: None of her friends were in the class, and she already knew how to do all the math the teacher talked about teaching them that year. Her father called the school the next day and was able to meet with Kate's counselor that afternoon. The counselor explained that math class was tracked on the basis of the students' IQs, and since Kate's IQ was less than 100, she was put into the slowest math group.

Because all of Kate's previous intelligence tests were well above average, her dad asked to see the actual results of her test. The counselor produced the computer printout with all of his students' IQs, covered the names of all the students except for Kate's, and showed Kate's dad the printout. Sure enough, the number next to his daughter's name was 95. When her dad scanned up the column to the heading, he found the word "percentile." The counselor had read a percentile as a standard score, and his error made quite a difference. Kate's IQ was not 95; it was 124. She did not belong in the slowest math group; she belonged in pre-algebra.

Knowing the meaning of derived scores is essential when educational decisions are based on those scores.

What implications about your personal professional role can you draw from this scenario? Go to the Education CourseMate website for this textbook for more reflection questions about this Scenario in Assessment.

available for a test is an age equivalent, then there is no way for a test user to convert raw scores to percentiles. However, age or grade equivalents can be converted back to raw scores, which can be converted to standard scores if the raw score mean and standard deviation are provided.

The selection of the particular type of score to use and to report depends on the purpose of testing and the sophistication of the consumer. In our opinion, developmental scores should never be used. Both laypeople and professionals readily misinterpret these scores. In order to understand the precise meaning of developmental scores, the interpreter must generally know both the mean and the standard deviation and then convert the developmental score to a more meaningful score, a score of relative standing. Various professional organizations (for example, the International Reading Association, the American Psychological Association, the National Council on Measurement in Education, and the Council for Exceptional Children) also hold very negative official opinions about developmental scores and quotients.

Standard scores are convenient for test authors. Their use allows an author to give equal weight to various test components or subtests. Their utility for the consumer is twofold. First, if the score distribution is normal, the consumer can readily convert standard scores to percentile ranks. Second, because standard scores are equal-interval scores, they are useful in analyzing strengths and weaknesses of individual students and in research.

We favor the use of percentiles. These unpretentious scores require the fewest assumptions for accurate interpretation. The scale of measurement need only be ordinal, although it is very appropriate to compute percentiles on equal-interval or ratio data. The distribution of scores need not be normal; percentiles can be computed for any shape of distribution. Professionals, parents, and students readily understand them. Most important, however, is the fact that percentiles tell us nothing more than what any norm-referenced derived score can tell us—namely, an individual's relative standing in a group. Reporting scores in percentiles may remove some of the aura surrounding test scores, and it permits test results to be presented in terms users can understand.

4 Norms

Normative groups allow us to compare one person's performance to the performance of others. Whenever we make such a comparison, it is important to know who those other persons are. For example, suppose Kareem earned a percentile rank of 50 on an intelligence test. If the norm group comprised only students enrolled in programs for the mentally retarded, a score at the 50th percentile would indicate limited intellectual ability. However, if the norm group consisted of individuals enrolled in programs for the gifted, Kareem's score would indicate superior intellectual ability. If we wanted to know Kareem's general intellectual ability, it would make sense to compare his test performance to a representative sample of all children.

It is important that a person's performance is compared to that of an appropriate group. Normative comparisons can range from national to local. Local norms vary from entire states to individual classrooms. When statewide assessments are instituted to monitor student progress on state standards, the statewide norms are local norms. When school districts develop their own norms by administering an achievement test that matches their curricula to all their students, the resulting norms are local norms. When school districts institute response-to-intervention programs (see Chapter 8, Curriculum-Based Approaches to Monitoring Student Progress), their students' achievement scores are the local norms. When a teacher uses social comparison to evaluate a problem behavior, the norms are local. To illustrate social comparison, suppose a teacher (Ms. Lane) is concerned that Mike is not participating sufficiently in classroom discussions. She selects three students who are participating at appropriate levels—not the best participants, but satisfactory participants. During the next day or two, she counts the number of times Mike offers a contribution to a discussion and compares his participation with that of the three comparison students who become a normative group. If Mike's performance is comparable to the normative group (which is by her definition, satisfactory), Mike's performance is also satisfactory.

State and district norms allow two useful comparisons. First, the achievement of individual students can be compared to that of other students in the district in order to identify students in need of additional services, either remedial or enriching. Second, standard scores averaged by school allow school-by-school comparisons that can identify schools in which achievement is generally a problem. States do essentially the same thing to evaluate the educational attainment by individual school districts.

Unlike local norms where an entire population of students is tested, national norms always involve sampling, and it is essential that we know the characteristics and abilities of the people sampled. Obviously, the accuracy and meaningfulness of a derived score for one student is inextricably tied to the characteristics of the norm sample. Thus, "it is important that the reference populations be carefully and clearly described" (American Educational Research Association [AERA], American Psychological Association, & National Council on Measurement in Education, 1999, p. 51).[11] This description is absolutely essential for test users to judge if a test taker can be reasonably compared to the individuals within the norm sample. Representativeness hinges on two questions: (1) Does the norm sample contain individuals with relevant characteristics and experiences? and (2) Are the characteristics and experiences present in the sample in the same proportion as they are in the population of reference?[12]

IMPORTANT CHARACTERISTICS

What makes a characteristic relevant depends on the construct being measured. Some characteristics have a clear logical and empirical relationship to a person's development and are important for any psychoeducational construct.

Gender

Some differences between males and females may be relevant in understanding a student's test score. For example, girls tend to develop physically faster than boys during the first year or two, and many more boys have delayed maturation than do girls during the preschool and primary school years. After puberty, men tend to be

[11] In practice, it is also impossible to test the entire population because the membership of the population is constantly changing. Fortunately, the characteristics of a population can be accurately estimated from the characteristics of a representative sample.

[12] Characteristics expressed by less than 1 or 2 percent of the population may not be represented accurately.

bigger and stronger than women. In addition to physical differences, gender role expectations may differ and systematically limit the types of activities in which a child participates because of modeling, peer pressure, or the responses of significant adults.

Nevertheless, on most psychological and educational tests, gender differences are small, and the distributions of scores of males and females tend to overlap considerably. When gender differences are minor, norm groups clearly should contain the appropriate proportions of males (approximately 48 percent) and females (approximately 52 percent)—the proportion found in the general U.S. population. However, when gender differences are substantial, the correct course of action depends on the purpose of the normative comparison. If a test is intended to identify students with developmental lags and if gender differences are pronounced, it is better to have separate norms for males and females. For example, if 3-year-old Aaron earns a percentile of 45 on a developmental test that has both boys and girls in the norms, his score indicates that his development is slightly behind that of other children. However, he may actually be doing well for a boy at that age. On the other hand, if the purpose is to identify the students with the best background for advanced placement in a subject where there are gender differences, it is probably better to have a single norm sample composed of males and females.

Age

Chronological age is an important consideration for developmental skills and abilities. Norms for tests of ability compare the performances of individuals of essentially the same age. It would make no sense to compare the running performance of a 2-year-old to that of a 4-year-old.

We have known for more than 40 years that different psychological abilities develop at different rates.[13] When an ability or skill is developing rapidly (for example, locomotion in infants and toddlers), the age range of the norm group must be much less than 1 year. Thus, on scales used to assess infants and young children, we often see norms in 3-month ranges. For children of school age, differences of less than a few months are usually unimportant. Thus, we typically see norms in 6-month and 12-month ranges. After an ability has matured, there may be no meaningful differences over several years. As a result, we often see norms in 10-year ranges on adult scales. Therefore, although 1-year norms are most common, developmental theory and research can suggest norms of lesser or greater age ranges.

Grade in School

All achievement tests should measure learned facts and concepts that have been taught in school. The more grades completed by students (that is, the more schooling), the more they should have been taught. Thus, the most useful norm comparisons are usually made to students of the same grade, regardless of their ages.[14] It is also important to note that students of different ages are present in most grades; for example, some 7-year-old children may not be enrolled in school, some may be in kindergarten, some in first grade, some in second grade, and some even in third grade.

Acculturation of Parents

Acculturation is an imprecise concept that refers to an understanding of the language (including conventions and pragmatics), history, values, and social conventions of society at large. Nowhere are the complexities of acculturation more readily illustrated than in the area of language. Acculturation requires people to know more than standard American English; they must also know the appropriate contexts for various words and idioms, appropriate volume and distance between speaker and listener, appropriate posture to indicate respect, and so forth.

Because acculturation is a broad and somewhat diffuse construct, it is difficult to define or measure precisely. Typically, test authors use the socioeconomic status of the

[13] See, for example, Guilford (1967, pp. 417–426).

[14] In situations in which students are not grouped by grade, it may be necessary to use age comparisons.

parents (usually some combination of education, and occupation of the parents) as a general indication of the level of acculturation of the home. The socioeconomic status of a student's parents is strongly related to that student's scores on all sorts of tests, including intelligence, achievement, adaptive behavior, and social functioning. The children of middle- and upper-class parents have tended to score higher on such tests (see Gottesman, 1968; Herrnstein & Murray, 1994). Whatever the reasons for such differences in child development, norm samples certainly must include all segments of society (in the same proportion as in the general population) in order to be representative.

Race and Cultural Identity

Race and culture are particularly relevant to our discussion of norms for two reasons. First, the scientific and educational communities have often been insensitive and occasionally blatantly racist. Second, differences in *tested* achievement and ability persist among races and cultural groups, although these differences continue to narrow.[15] Inclusion of individuals of all racial, cultural, and socioeconomic groups is important for two reasons. First, to the extent that individuals of different groups undergo cultural experiences that differ even within a given social class and geographic region, norm samples that exclude (or underrepresent) one group are unrepresentative of the total population. Second, if individuals from various groups are excluded from field tests of test items, various statistics used in test development may be inaccurate,[16] and the test's scaling may be in error.

Geography

There are systematic differences in the attainment of individuals living in different geographic regions of the United States, and various psychoeducational tests reflect these regional differences. Most consistently, the average scores of individuals living in the southeastern United States (excluding Florida) are often lower than the average scores of individuals living in other regions of the country. Moreover, community size, population density (that is, urban, suburban, and rural communities), and gains or losses of population have also been related to academic and intellectual development.

There are several seemingly logical explanations for many of these relationships. For example, well-educated young adults tend to move away from communities with limited employment and cultural opportunities. When brighter and better educated individuals leave a community, the average intellectual ability and educational attainment in that community decline, and the average ability and attainment of the communities to which the brighter individuals move increase. Regardless of the reasons for geographical differences, test norms should include individuals from all geographic regions, as well as from urban, suburban, and rural communities.

Intelligence

A representative sample of individuals in terms of their level of intellectual functioning is essential for standardizing an intelligence test and most other kinds of tests, including tests of achievement, linguistic or psycholinguistic ability, perceptual skills, and perceptual–motor skills. In the development of norms, it is essential to test the full range of intellectual ability. Limiting the sample to students enrolled in and attending school (usually general education classes) restricts the norms. Failure to consider individuals with mental retardation in standardization procedures introduces systematic bias into test norms by underestimating the population mean and standard deviation.

PROPORTIONAL REPRESENTATION

Implicit in the preceding discussion of characteristics of people in a representative normative sample is the idea that various kinds of people should be included in the sample in the same proportion as they occur in the general population. No matter

[15] We also note that perhaps as much as 90 percent of observed racial and cultural differences can be attributed to socioeconomic differences.

[16] For example, item difficulty estimates (*p* values) and various item-total correlations.

how test norms are constructed, test authors should systematically compare the relevant characteristics of the population and their standardization samples. Although we frequently use the singular (that is, norm sample or group) when discussing norms, it is important to understand that tests have multiple normative samples. For example, an achievement test intended for use with students in kindergarten through twelfth grade has 13 norm groups (1 for each grade). If that achievement test has separate norms for males and females at each grade, then there are 26 norm groups. When we test a second-grade boy, we do not compare his performance with the performances of all students in the total norm sample. Rather, we compare the boy's performance with that of other second graders (or of other second-grade boys if there are separate norms for boys and girls). Thus, the preceding discussions of representatives and the number of subjects apply to each specific comparison group within the norms—not to the aggregated or combined samples. Representativeness should be demonstrated for each comparison group.

NUMBER OF SUBJECTS

The number of participants in a norm sample is important for several reasons. First, the number of subjects should be large enough to guarantee stability. If a sample is very small, another group of participants might have a different mean and standard deviation. Second, the number of participants should be large enough to represent infrequent characteristics. For example, if approximately 1 percent of the population is Native American, a sample of 25 or 50 people will be unlikely to contain even 1 Native American. Third, there should be enough subjects so that there can be a full range of derived scores. In practice, 100 participants in each age or grade is considered the minimum.

AGE OF NORMS

For a norm sample to be representative, it must represent the current population. Levels of skill and ability change over time. Skilled athletes of today run faster, jump higher, and are stronger than the best athletes of a generation ago. Some of the improvement can be attributed to better training, but some can also be attributed to better nutrition and societal changes. Similarly, intellectual and educational performances have increased from generation to generation, although these increases are neither steady nor linear.

For example, on norm-referenced achievement tests, considerably more than half the students score above the average after the test has been in use for 5 to 7 years.[17] In such cases, the test norms are clearly dated because only half the population can ever be above the median. Although some increase in tested achievement can be attributed to teacher familiarity with test content, there is little doubt that some of the changes represent real improvement in achievement.

The important point is that old norms tend to overestimate a student's relative standing in the population because the old norms are too easy. The point at which norms become outdated will depend in part on the ability or skill being assessed. With this caution, it seems to us that approximately 15 years is the maximum useful life for norm samples used in ability testing; 7 years appears to be the maximum for norm life for achievement tests. Although test publishers should ensure that up-to-date norms are readily available, test users ultimately are responsible for avoiding the inappropriate use of out-of-date norms (AERA et al., 1999, p. 59).

RELEVANCE OF NORMS

Norms must provide comparisons that are relevant to the purpose of assessment. National norms are the most appropriate if we are interested in knowing how a particular student is developing intellectually, perceptually, linguistically, or physically. Norms developed on a particular portion of the population may be meaningful in special circumstances. Local norms can be useful in ascertaining

[17] See, for example, Linn, Graue, and Sanders (1990).

the degree to which individual students have profited from their schooling in the local school district as well as in retrospective interpretations of a student's performance. Norms based on particular groups may be more relevant than those based on the population as a whole. For example, the American Association on Mental Retardation's Adaptive Behavior Scale was standardized on individuals who were mentally retarded; aptitude tests are often standardized on individuals in specific trades or professions. Whether national or local, "norms that are presented should refer to clearly described groups. These groups should be the ones with whom users of the test will ordinarily wish to compare the people who are tested" (AERA et al., 1997, p. 33).

Chapter Comprehension Questions

Write your answers to each of the following questions and then compare your responses to the text.

1. Compare and contrast the two scales of measurement most commonly used in educational and psychological measurement.
2. Explain the following terms: mean, median, mode, variance, skew, and correlation coefficient.
3. Explain the statistical meaning of the following scores: percentile, *z* score, IQ, NCE, age equivalent, and grade equivalent.
4. Why is the acculturation of the parents of students in normative samples important?

Web Activities

1. Go to Chapter 18 (Using Measures of Adaptive Behavior) on the CourseMate website for this textbook and read about the scores provided on the *Vineland Adaptive Behavior Scales, Second Edition.* What does an Adaptive Behavior Composite of 70 mean? What does a v-score of 13 mean?
2. Also in Chapter 18, read about the norms for that test. Why or why not do they appear generally representative?

Web Resources

Some Common Errors in Interpreting Test Scores
http://www.nctm.org/news/release.aspx?id=762
This short article provides a nontechnical explanation of three common errors of the interpretation of test scores.

Interpreting Your Child's Tests and Evaluations
http://www.cerebralpalsy.org/education/interpreting-test-and-evaluations/
Designed for parents, this website provides a brief discussion of how test scores are reported and defines composite scores, norm-referenced and criterion-referenced scores, and standard scores.

Additional resources for this chapter can be found on the Education CourseMate website. Go to CengageBrain.com to access the site.

Learning Module

Go to the Education CourseMate website to complete the learning module entitled, "**Descriptive Statistics.**"

What is the relationship between mean, median, and mode?

Aspen Photo/Shutterstock.com

5

Technical Adequacy

CHAPTER GOALS

1 Understand the basic concept of reliability, including error in measurement, reliability coefficients, standard error of measurement, estimated true scores, and confidence intervals.

2 Understand the general concept of validity, how tests are validated, factors affecting general reliability, and responsibility for valid assessment.

KEY TERMS

measurement error
reliability coefficient
item reliability
alternate form reliability
internal consistency
stability
interobserver agreement
simple agreement
point-to-point agreement
standard error of measurement
estimated true scores
confidence intervals
validity
content validity
concurrent criterion-related validity
predictive criterion-related validity
systematic bias

1 Reliability

None of us would consider having heart surgery on the basis of a diagnostic test known for its inaccuracy. Although educational decisions are not this dramatic, every day school personnel select, create, and use assessment procedures that lead to educational decisions. Accurate evaluation results lead to good decision making, whereas inaccurate results cannot. To illustrate, suppose you learn that other teachers would count as correct test responses that you have marked incorrect, that students earned good grades on their weekly spelling tests but made numerous errors in their written work, and that students who were earning As in reading were scoring at the 30th percentile on standardized reading tests. What do these things suggest about the accuracy of your assessments? What do they suggest about the decisions based on these assessments?

When we test students, we want to get accurate information that is unlikely to be misinterpreted. The very nature of schooling presumes students will generalize what they have learned to situations and contexts outside of the school and after graduation. Except for school-specific rules (for example, no running in the halls), nothing a student learns in school would have any value unless it generalized to life outside of school. When we test students or otherwise observe their performances, we always want to be able to generalize what we observe in a variety of ways. Moreover, we want those generalizations to be accurate—to be reliable. We also want to draw conclusions about their performances, and we want those conclusions to be correct.

ERROR IN MEASUREMENT

In educational and psychological measurement, there are two types of error. *Systematic* or *predictable error* (also called bias) is error that affects a person's (or group's) score in one direction. Bias inflates people's measured abilities above their true abilities. For example, suppose a teacher used only multiple-choice tests with a class of boys and girls. Since boys, as a group, tend to do better on this type of test, the boys' abilities may be somewhat overestimated due to the way their knowledge was measured. Bias can also deflate people's measured abilities above their true abilities. Girls' abilities may be somewhat underestimated due to the use of multiple-choice tests that tested their knowledge; they may well have scored higher on an essay examination. The other type of error is *random error*; its direction and magnitude cannot be known for an individual test taker. This type of error can just as easily raise as lower estimates of student's ability or knowledge. Reliability refers to the relative absence of random error present during measurement.

THE RELIABILITY COEFFICIENT

The reliability coefficient is a special use of a correlation coefficient. The symbol for a correlation coefficient (*r*) is used with two identical subscripts (for example, r_{xx} or r_{aa}) to indicate a reliability coefficient. The reliability coefficient indicates the proportion of variability in a set of scores that reflects true differences among individuals. If there is relatively little error, the ratio of true-score variance to obtained-score variance approaches a reliability index of 1.00 (perfect reliability); if there is a relatively large amount of error, the ratio of true-score variance to obtained-score variance approaches .00 (total unreliability). Thus, a test with a reliability coefficient of .90 has relatively less error of measurement and is more reliable than a test with a reliability coefficient of .50. Subtracting the proportion of true-score variance from 1 yields the proportion of error variance in the distribution of scores. Thus, if the reliability coefficient is .90, 10 percent of the variability in the distribution is attributable to error.

All other things being equal, we want to use the most reliable procedures and tests that are available. Since perfectly reliable devices are quite rare, the choice of test becomes a question of minimum reliability or the specific purpose of assessment. We recommend that the standards for reliability presented in Table 5.1 be used in applied settings.

TABLE 5.1 Standards for Reliability

1. If test scores are to be used for administrative purposes and are reported for groups of individuals, a reliability of .60 should be the minimum. This relatively low standard is acceptable because group means are not affected by a test's lack of reliability.
2. If weekly (or more frequent) testing is used to monitor pupil progress, a reliability of .70 should be the minimum. This relatively low standard is acceptable because random fluctuations can be taken into account when a behavior or skill is measured often.
3. If the decision being made is a screening decision (for example, a recommendation for further assessment), there is still a need for higher reliability. For screening devices, we recommend a standard of .80.
4. If a test score is to be used to make an important decision concerning an individual student (for example, tracking or special education placement), the minimum standard should be .90.

Three Types of Reliability

In educational and psychological assessment, we are concerned with three types of reliability or generalizations: generalization to other similar items, generalization to other times, and generalization to other observers. These three generalizations have different names (that is, item reliability, stability, and interobserver agreement) and are separately estimated by different procedures.

Item Reliability It is seldom possible or practical to administer all possible test items of interest. Instead, testers use a sample of items (that is, a subset of items) from all the possible items (that is, the domain of items). We would like to assume that students' performances on the sample of items are similar to their performances on all the items if it were possible or practical to administer all items. When our generalizations about student performance on a domain are correctly generalized from performance on the test, the test is said to be reliable. Sometimes our sample of test items leads us to overestimate a student's knowledge or ability; in such cases, the sample is unreliable. Sometimes our sample of test items leads us to underestimate a student's knowledge or ability; in such cases, the sample is unreliable.

There are two main approaches to estimating the extent to which we can generalize to different samples of items: alternate-form reliability and internal consistency.

Alternate-form reliability requires two or more forms of the same test. These forms (1) measure the same trait or skill to the same extent and (2) are standardized on the same population. Alternate forms offer essentially equivalent tests (but not identical items); sometimes, in fact, they are called equivalent forms. The means and variances for the alternate forms are assumed to be (or should be) the same. In the absence of error of measurement, any subject would be expected to earn the same score on both forms. To estimate the reliability of two alternate forms of a test (for example, form A and form B), a large sample of students is tested with both forms. Half the subjects receive form A and then form B; the other half receive form B and then form A. Scores from the two forms are correlated. The resulting correlation coefficient is a reliability coefficient.

SCENARIO *in* ASSESSMENT

GEORGE AND JULES | George and Jules were going to take a test on World War II in their history class. To study, George concentrated his efforts on the causes and consequences of the war. Jules reviewed his notes and then watched the movie *Patton.* The next day, the boys took the history test, which contained three short-answer questions and one major essay question, "Discuss Patton's role in the European theater of war." George got a C on his test; Jules got an A. George complained that his test score was not an accurate reflection of what he knew about the war and that it was unfair because it did not address the war's causes and consequences. On the other hand, Jules was very pleased with his score, even though it would have been considerably lower if the teacher had asked a different question. The test did not provide a reliable estimate of either's knowledge of World War II.

What implications about your own professional role can you draw from this scenario? Go to the Education CourseMate website for this textbook for more reflection questions about this Scenario in Assessment.

Internal consistency is the second approach to estimating the extent to which we can generalize to different test items. It does not require two or more test forms. Instead, after a test is given, it is split into two halves that are correlated to produce an estimate of reliability. For example, suppose we wanted to use this method to estimate the reliability of a 10-item test. The results of this hypothetical test are presented in Table 5.2. After administering the test to a group of students, we divide the test into two 5-item tests by summing the even-numbered items and the odd-numbered items for each student. This creates two alternate forms of the test, each containing one half of the total number of test items. We can then correlate the sums of the odd-numbered items with the sums of the even-numbered items to obtain an estimate of the reliability of each of the two halves. This procedure for estimating a test's reliability is called a *split-half reliability estimate.*

It should be apparent that there are many ways to divide a test into two equal-length tests. The aforementioned 10-item test can be divided into many different pairs of 5-item tests. If the 10 items in our full test are arranged in order of increasing difficulty, both halves should contain items from the beginning of the test (that is, easier items) and items from the end of the test (that is, more difficult items). There are many ways of dividing such a test (for example, grouping items 1, 4, 5, 8, and 9 and items 2, 3, 6, 7, and 10).

TABLE 5.2 Hypothetical Performance of 20 Children on a 10-Item Test

	Items										**Totals**		
Child	*1*	*2*	*3*	*4*	*5*	*6*	*7*	*8*	*9*	*10*	*Total Test*	*Evens Correct*	*Odds Correct*
1	+	+	+	−	+	−	−	−	+	−	5	1	4
2	+	+	+	+	−	+	+	+	−	+	8	5	3
3	+	+	−	+	+	+	+	−	+	+	8	4	4
4	+	+	+	+	+	+	+	+	−	+	9	5	4
5	+	+	+	+	+	+	+	+	+	−	9	4	5
6	+	+	−	+	−	+	+	+	+	+	8	5	3
7	+	+	+	+	+	−	+	−	+	+	8	3	5
8	+	+	+	−	+	+	+	+	+	+	9	4	5
9	+	+	+	+	+	+	−	+	+	+	9	5	4
10	+	+	+	+	+	−	+	+	+	+	9	4	5
11	+	+	+	+	+	−	+	−	−	−	6	2	4
12	+	+	−	+	+	+	+	+	+	+	9	5	4
13	+	+	+	−	−	+	−	+	−	−	5	3	2
14	+	+	+	+	+	+	+	−	+	+	9	4	5
15	+	+	−	+	+	−	−	−	−	−	4	2	2
16	+	+	+	+	+	+	+	+	+	+	10	5	5
17	+	−	+	−	−	−	−	−	−	−	2	0	2
18	+	−	+	+	+	+	+	+	+	+	9	4	5
19	+	+	+	+	−	+	+	+	+	+	9	5	4
20	+	−	−	−	−	+	−	+	−	−	3	2	1

The most common way to divide a test is by odd-numbered and even-numbered items (see the columns labeled "Evens Correct" and "Odds Correct" in Table 5.2).

A better method of estimating internal consistency was developed by Cronbach (1951) and is called coefficient alpha. *Coefficient alpha* is the average split-half correlation based on all possible divisions of a test into two parts. In practice, there is no need to compute all possible correlation coefficients; coefficient alpha can be computed from the variances of individual test items and the variance of the total test score.

Coefficient alpha can be used when test items are scored pass–fail or when more than 1 point is awarded for a correct response. An earlier, more restricted method of estimating a test's reliability, based on the average correlation between all possible split halves, was developed by Kuder and Richardson. This procedure, called *KR-20*, is coefficient alpha for dichotomously scored test items (that is, items that can be scored only right or wrong).

Stability When students have learned information and behavior, we want to be confident that students can access that information and demonstrate those behaviors at times other than when they are assessed. We would like to be able to generalize today's test results to other times in the future. Educators are interested in many human traits and characteristics that, theoretically, change very little over time. For example, children diagnosed as color blind at age 5 years are expected to be diagnosed as colorblind at any time in their lives. Color blindness is an inherited trait that cannot be corrected. Consequently, the trait should be perfectly stable. When an assessment identifies a student as colorblind on one occasion and not colorblind on a later occasion, the assessment is unreliable.

Other traits are developmental. For example, people's heights will increase from birth through adulthood. The increases are relatively slow and predictable. Consequently, we would not expect many changes in height over a 2-week period. Radical changes in people's heights (especially decreases) over short periods of time would cause us to question the reliability of the measurement device. Most educational and psychological characteristics are conceptualized much as height is conceptualized. For example, we expect reading achievement to increase with length of schooling but to be relatively stable over short periods of time, such as 2 weeks. Devices used to assess traits and characteristics must produce sufficiently consistent and stable results if those results are to have practical meaning for making educational decisions. When our generalizations about student performance on a domain are correctly generalized from one time to another, the test is said to be stable or have test–retest reliability. Obviously, the notion of stability excludes changes that occur as the result of systematic interventions to change the behavior. Thus, if a test indicates that a student does not know the long vowel sounds and we teach those sounds to the student, the change in the student's test performance would not be considered a lack of reliability.

The procedure for obtaining a stability coefficient is straightforward. A large number of students are tested and then retested after a short period of time (preferably 2 weeks later). The students' scores from the two administrations are then correlated, and the obtained correlation coefficient is the stability coefficient.

Interobserver Agreement We would like to assume that if any other comparably qualified examiner were to give the test, the results would be the same—we would like to be able to generalize to similar testers. Suppose Ms. Amig listened to her students say the letters of the alphabet. It would not be very useful if she assigned Barney a score of 70 percent correct, whereas another teacher (or education professional) who listened to Barney awarded a score of 50 percent correct or 90 percent correct for the same performance. When our scoring or other observations agree with those of comparably trained observers who observe the same phenomena at the same time, the observations are said to have interobserver reliability or agreement.[1] Ms. Amig would like to assume that any other education professional would score her students' responses in the same way.

[1] Agreement among observers has several different names. Observers can be referred to as testers, scorers, or raters; it depends on the nature of their actions. Agreement can also be called reliability.

There are two very different approaches to estimating the extent to which we can generalize to different scorers: a correlational approach and a percentage of agreement approach. The correlational approach is similar to estimating reliability with alternate forms, which was previously discussed. Two testers score a set of tests independently. Scores obtained by each tester for the set are then correlated. The resulting correlation coefficient is a reliability coefficient for scorers.

Percentage of agreement is more common in classrooms and applied behavioral analysis. Instead of the correlation between two scorers' ratings, a percentage of agreement between raters is computed. There are four ways of calculating percent agreement. The first two types of agreement we discuss are the most common, but the last two are more common in research publications.

Simple agreement is calculated by dividing the smaller number of occurrences by the larger number of occurrences and multiplying the quotient by 100. For example, suppose Ms. Amig and her teacher's aide, Ms. Carter, observe Sam on 20 occasions to determine how frequently he is on task during reading instruction. The results of their observations are shown in Table 5.3. Ms. Amig observes 12 occasions when

TABLE 5.3 Observations of Sam's On-Task Behavior During Reading, Where "–" Is Off Task and "+" Is On Task

Observation	Ms. Amig	Ms. Carter	Observers Agree
1	+	+	Yes
2	–	–	Yes
3	–	+	No
4	+	+	Yes
5	+	+	Yes
6	–	–	Yes
7	–	–	Yes
8	–	+	No
9	+	+	Yes
10	+	–	No
11	–	–	Yes
12	+	+	Yes
13	+	+	Yes
14	+	+	Yes
15	–	–	Yes
16	+	–	No
17	+	+	Yes
18	–	–	Yes
19	+	–	No
20	+	–	No
Total No. of occurrences	12	10	14

Sam is on task, whereas Ms. Carter observes 10 occasions. Simple agreement is 83 percent; that is, 100 × (10/12).

The second type of percent agreement, *point-to-point agreement*, is a more precise way of computing percentage of agreement because each data point is considered. Point-to-point agreement is calculated by dividing the number of observations for which both observers agree (occurrence and nonoccurrence) by the total number of observations and multiplying the quotient by 100. Using data shown in Table 5.3, there are 14 occasions when Ms. Amig's and Ms. Carter's observations agree. Point-to-point agreement is 70 percent; that is, 100 × (14/20).

The two other indices of percent agreement are agreement for occurrence and kappa.

Explanations of these indices and their calculation are available on the Education CourseMate website for this textbook.

Concluding Comments About the Reliability Coefficient

Generalization to other items, times, and observers are independent of each other. Therefore, each index of reliability provides information about only a part of the error associated with measurement.

In school settings, item reliability is not a problem when we test students on the entire domain (for example, naming all upper- and lowercase letters of the alphabet). Item reliability should be estimated when we test students on a sample of items from the domain (for example, a 20-item test on multiplication facts that is used to infer master on all facts). Interscorer reliability is usually not a problem when our assessments are objective and our criteria for a correct response clear (for example, a multiple-choice test). Interscorer reliability should be assessed whenever subjective or qualitative criteria are used to score student responses (for example, using a scoring rubric to assess the quality of written responses). When students are assessed frequently with interchangeable tests or probes, stability is usually assessed directly prior to intervention by administering tests on 3 or more days until the student's performance has stabilized.[2] If a test is given once, its stability should be estimated, although in practice teachers seldom estimate the stability of their tests.

STANDARD ERROR OF MEASUREMENT

The *standard error of measurement* (SEM) is another index of test error. The SEM is the average standard deviation of error distributed around a person's true score. Although we can compute standard errors of measurement for scorers, times, and item samples, SEMs for scorers are seldom calculated.

To illustrate, suppose we wanted to assess students' emerging skill in naming letters of the alphabet using a 10-letter test. There are many samples of 10-letter tests that could be developed. If we constructed 100 of these tests and tested just one kindergartner, we would probably find that the distribution of scores for that kindergartner was approximately normal. The mean of that distribution would be the student's true score. The distribution around the true score would be the result of imperfect samples of letters; some letter samples would overestimate the pupil's ability, and others would underestimate it. Thus, the variance around the mean would be the result of error. The standard deviation of that distribution is the standard deviation of errors attributable to sampling and is called the standard error of measurement.

When students are assessed with norm-referenced tests, they are typically tested only once. Therefore, we cannot generate a distribution similar to those shown in Figure 5.1. Consequently, we do not know the test taker's true score or the variance of the measurement error that forms the distribution around that person's true score. By using what we know about the test's standard deviation and its reliability for items, we can estimate what that error distribution would be. However, when estimating the error distribution for one student, test users should understand that the SEM is an average; some standard errors will be greater than that average, and some will be less.

[2] The period during which students are assessed prior to observation is generally called the baseline.

FIGURE 5.1
The Standard Error of Measurement: The Standard Deviation of the Error Distribution Around a True Score for One Subject

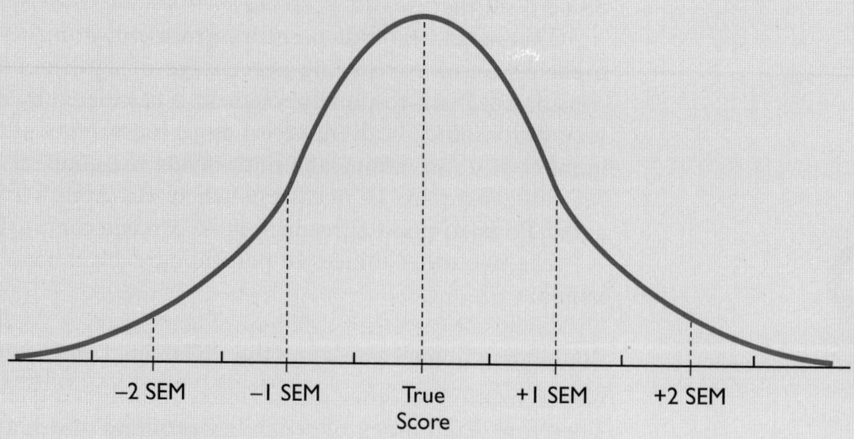

–2 SEM –I SEM True Score +I SEM +2 SEM

Equation 5.1 is the general formula for finding the SEM. The SEM equals the standard deviation of the obtained scores (*S*) multiplied by the square root of 1 minus the reliability coefficient. The type of unit (IQ, raw score, and so forth) in which the standard deviation is expressed is the unit in which the SEM is expressed. Thus, if the test scores have been converted to *T* scores, the standard deviation is in *T* score units and is 10; the SEM is also in *T* score units. From Equation 5.1, it is apparent that as the standard deviation increases, the SEM increases, and as the reliability coefficient decreases, the SEM increases.

$$\text{SEM} = S\sqrt{1 - r_{xx}} \tag{5.1}$$

The SEM provides information about the certainty or confidence with which a test score can be interpreted. When the SEM is relatively large, the uncertainty is large; we cannot be very sure of the individual's score. When the SEM is relatively small, the uncertainty is small; we can be more certain of the score.

ESTIMATED TRUE SCORES

More information about estimated true scores and their calculation is available at the Education CourseMate website for this text.

An obtained score on a test is not the best estimate of the true score because obtained scores and errors are correlated. Scores above the test mean have more "lucky" error (error that raises the obtained score above the true score), whereas scores below the mean have more "unlucky" error (error that lowers the obtained score below the true score). An easy way to understand this effect is to think of a test on which Mike guesses on several test items. If all Mike's guesses are correct, he has been very lucky and earns a score that is not representative of what he truly knows. However, if all his guesses are incorrect, Mike has been unlucky and earns a score that is lower than a score that represents what he truly knows.

CONFIDENCE INTERVALS

More information about confidence intervals and their calculation is available at the Education CourseMate website for this text.

Although we can never know a person's true score, we can estimate the likelihood that a person's true score will be found within a specified range of scores. This range is called a *confidence interval.* Confidence intervals have two components. The first component is the score range within which a true score is likely to be found. For example, a range of 80 to 90 indicates that a person's true score is likely to be contained within that range. The second component is the level of confidence, generally between 50 and 95 percent. The level of confidence tells us how certain we can be that the true score will be contained within the interval. Thus, if a 90 percent confidence interval for Jo's IQ is 106 to 112, we can be 90 percent sure that Jo's true IQ is between 106 and 112. It also means that there is a 5 percent chance her true IQ is higher than 112 and a 5 percent chance her true IQ is lower than 106. To have greater confidence would require a wider confidence interval.

Sometimes confidence intervals are implied. A score may be followed by a "±" and a number (for example, 109 ± 2). Unless otherwise noted, this notation implies a 68 percent confidence interval with the number following the ± being the SEM. Thus, the lower limit of the confidence interval equals the score less the SEM (that is, 109 − 2) and the upper limit equals the score plus the SEM (that is, 109 + 2). The interpretation of this confidence interval is that we can be 68 percent sure that the student's true score is between 107 and 111.

Another confidence interval is implied when a score is given with the probable error (PE) of measurement. For example, a score might be reported as 105 PE ± 1. A PE yields 50 percent confidence. Thus, 105 PE ± 1 means a 50 percent confidence interval that ranges from 104 to 106. The interpretation of this confidence interval is that we can be 50 percent sure that the student's true score is between 104 and 106; 25 percent of the time the true score will be less than 104, and 25 percent of the time the true score will be greater than 106.

2 Validity

Validity refers to "the degree to which evidence and theory support the interpretation of test scores entailed by proposed uses of tests" (American Educational Research Association [AERA], American Psychological Association, & National Council on Measurement in Education, 1999, p. 9). Validity is therefore the most fundamental consideration in developing and evaluating tests and other assessment procedures. Although much of the discussion that follows is necessarily general, it must always be remembered that all questions of validity are specific to the individual student being tested. The specific question that must always be asked is whether the testing process leads to correct inferences about a specific person in a specific situation for a specific purpose.

A test that leads to valid inferences in general or about most students may not yield valid inferences about a specific student. Two circumstances illustrate this. First, unless a student has been systematically acculturated in the values, behavior, and knowledge found in the public culture of the United States, a test that assumes such cultural information is unlikely to lead to appropriate inferences about that student. Consider, for example, the inappropriateness of administering a verbally loaded intelligence test to a recent U.S. immigrant. Correct inferences about this person's intellectual ability cannot be drawn from the testing because

SCENARIO *in* ASSESSMENT

ELMWOOD AREA SCHOOL DISTRICT

The Elmwood Area School District has adopted a child-centered, conceptual mathematics investigations curriculum that stresses problem solving as well as writing and thinking about mathematics. Students are expected to discover mathematical principles and explain them in writing. In the spring, the district administered the TerraNova achievement test for the purpose of determining whether students were learning what the district intended for them to learn. Much to its dismay, the mean scores on the mathematics subtests were substantially below average, and many students previously thought to be doing well in school were referred to determine if they had a specific learning disability in mathematics calculation. After the school psychologists completed their initial review of student records, the problem became clear. The TerraNova, although generally a good test, did not measure what was being taught in the Elmwood Area School District. Because mathematical calculations were not emphasized (or even systematically taught), Elmwood students had not had the same opportunities to learn as students in other districts. TerraNova was not a valid test within the school district, although it was appropriately used in many others. The validity of a test is validity for the specific child being assessed.

What implications about your personal professional role can you draw from this scenario? Go to the Education CourseMate website for this textbook for more reflection questions about this Scenario in Assessment.

the intelligence test requires not only proficiency in English but also proficiency in U.S. culture and mores.

Second, unless a student has been systematically instructed in the content of an achievement test, a test assuming such academic instruction is unlikely to lead to appropriate inferences about that student's ability to profit from instruction. It would be inappropriate to administer a standardized test of written language (which counts misspelled words as errors) to a student who has been encouraged to use inventive spelling and reinforced for doing so. It is unlikely that the test results would lead to correct inferences about that student's ability to profit from systematic instruction in spelling.

GENERAL VALIDITY

Because it is impossible to validate all inferences that might be drawn from a test performance, test authors typically validate just the most common inferences. Thus, test users should expect some information about the degree to which each commonly encouraged inference has (or lacks) validity. Although the validity of each inference is based on all the information that accumulates over time, test authors are expected to provide some evidence of a test's validity for specific inferences at the time the test is offered for use. In addition, test authors should validate the inferences for groups of students with whom the test will typically be used.

EVIDENCE THAT TEST INFERENCES ARE VALID

The process of gathering information about the appropriateness of inferences is called validation. Five general types of evidence are usually considered (AERA et al., 1999, pp. 11–17).

1. Evidence based on test content
2. Evidence based on internal structure
3. Evidence based on relations to other variables
4. Evidence based on the consequences of testing
5. Evidence based on response processes

These five types of evidence are not discrete. Rather, they are artificial categories that are merely intended to help organize a complex topic. Thus, one could as readily consider evidence based on internal structure to be part of a test's content as easily as a separate type of evidence.

1. Evidence Based on Test Content

By a test's content, we mean the specific information or tasks required by test items (e.g., the test questions) as well as the procedures for test administration and scoring. Specifically, we are concerned with the extent to which a test's items actually represent the domain or universe to be measured. It is a major source of evidence for the validation for any educational (especially tests of achievement) or psychological tests and many other forms of assessment (e.g., observations and ratings). Any analysis of a test's content necessarily begins with a clear definition of the domain or universe that the test's content is intended to represent. Ultimately a test's content validity is determined by the appropriateness of the items included, the importance of items not included, and the way in which the items assess the content.

Appropriateness of Included Items In examining the appropriateness of the items included in a test, we must ask: Is this an appropriate test question, and does this test item really measure the domain or construct? Consider the four test items from a hypothetical primary (kindergarten through grade 2) arithmetic achievement test presented in Figure 5.2. The first item requires the student to read and add two single-digit numbers, the sum of which is less than 10. This seems to be an appropriate item for an elementary arithmetic achievement test. The second item requires the student to complete a geometric progression. Although this item is

FIGURE 5.2
Sample Multiple-Choice Questions for a Primary Grade (K–2) Arithmetic Achievement Test

1. Three and six are ____________.
   a. 4
   b. 7
   c. 8
   d. 9

2. What number follows in this series?
   1, 2.5, 6.25, ____________
   a. 10
   b. 12.5
   c. 15.625
   d. 18.50

3. ¿Cuántos son tres y dos? ____________
   a. 3
   b. 4
   c. 5
   d. 6

4. Ille puer puellas ____________.
   a. amo
   b. amat
   c. amamus

mathematical, the skills and knowledge required to complete the question correctly are not taught in any elementary school curriculum by the second grade. Therefore, the question should be rejected as an invalid item for an arithmetic achievement test to be used with children from kindergarten through the second grade. The third item likewise requires the student to read and add two single-digit numbers, the sum of which is less than 10. However, the question is written in Spanish. Although the content of the question is suitable (this is an elementary addition problem), the method of presentation requires language skills that most U.S. students do not have. Failure to complete the item correctly could be attributed either to the fact that the child does not know Spanish or to the fact that the child does not know that $3 + 2 = 5$. Test givers should conclude that the item is not valid for an arithmetic test for children who do not read Spanish. The fourth item requires that the student select the correct form of the Latin verb *amare* ("to love"). Clearly, this is an inappropriate item for an arithmetic test and should be rejected as invalid.

Content Not Included Test content must also be examined to see if important content is not included. For example, the validity of any elementary arithmetic test would be questioned if it included only problems requiring the addition of single-digit numbers with a sum less than 10. Educators would reasonably expect an arithmetic test to include a far broader sample of tasks (for example, addition of two- and three-digit numbers, subtraction, understanding of the process of addition, and so forth). Incomplete test content results in an incomplete (and usually invalid) appraisal.

How Content Is Measured This aspect of validity is currently being hotly debated by those favoring constructed responses such as extended answers, performances, or demonstrations.[3] However, there is an emerging consensus that the methods used to assess student knowledge or ability should closely parallel those used in instruction. Unless we are testing an entire domain (e.g., all of the single-digit addition facts or all of the upper case letters of the alphabet), tests are samples of content. We usually expect that a test will contain a sufficiently large sample of content to allow meaningful inferences about a student's knowledge or skill were all of the content tested.

How we assess content directly influences the results of assessment. For example, when students are tested to see if they know the sum of two single-digit numbers, their knowledge can be evaluated in a variety of ways. Children might be required to recognize the correct answer in a multiple-choice array, supply the correct answer, demonstrate the addition process with manipulatives, apply the proper addition facts in a word problem, or write an explanation of the process they followed in solving the problem. However, there is an emerging consensus that the methods used to assess student knowledge should closely parallel those used in instruction.

[3] Current theory and research methods as they apply to trait or ability congruence under different methods of measurement are still emerging. Much of the current methodology grew out of Campbell and Fiske's (1959) early work on convergent and discriminant validity and is beyond the scope of this text.

2. Evidence Based on Internal Structure

Quite similar to evidence for a test's content is a test's internal structure. Internal structure refers the way(s) in which test items and subtests represent a test's components and/or total score. Most test domains have more than one dimension or component. For example, reading tests typically assess oral reading and comprehension; math tests typically assess computation and problem solving using whole numbers, fractions and decimals, etc.

One would rightly expect test authors to present evidence that their tests do have the structure hypothesized. When a test assesses a unidimensional skill or trait, we would expect to see evidence that the test items are homogeneous (e.g., coefficient alpha). When a test is multidimensional, we would expect to find the results of factor analytic studies that demonstrate the congruence between theoretical and obtained factor structure.

3. Evidence Based on Relations to Other Variables

See the Education CourseMate website for this text for statistical procedures that can be used by test authors to help validate the content validity of a test.

The relationship between a test's results and the results obtained from other sources is of key importance. The evidence falls into two broad categories: First, the test measures the desired skills and abilities, and second, the test does not measure unintended skills or abilities.

Measuring the Right Skills and Abilities The extent to which a person's performance on a criterion measure can be estimated from that person's performance on the assessment procedure being validated is an important indication that a new test is measuring what it is intended to measure. This relationship is usually expressed as a correlation between the new assessment procedure (for example, a test) and the criterion. The correlation coefficient is termed a *validity coefficient*. Two types of criterion-related validity are commonly described: concurrent validity and predictive validity. These terms denote the time at which a person's performance on the criterion measure is obtained. *Concurrent criterion-related validity* refers to how accurately a person's current performance (for example, test score) estimates that person's performance on the criterion measure at the same time. Basically, does a person's performance measured with a new or experimental test allow the accurate estimation of that person's performance on a criterion measure that has been widely accepted as valid? *Predictive criterion-related validity* refers to how accurately a person's current performance (for example, test score) estimates that person's performance on the criterion measure at a later time. Thus, concurrent and predictive criterion-related validity refer to the temporal sequence by which a person's performance on some criterion measure is estimated on the basis of that person's current assessment; concurrent and predictive validity differ in the time at which scores on the criterion measure are obtained.

Positive correlations between test scores and other variables can also provide evidence of a test's validity. For example many skills and abilities are developmental. Thus, we would expect a student's grade level or mental age would correlate positively with chronological age.[4]

Not Measuring the Wrong Skills and Abilities It is also important that a test not measure skills and abilities not intended by a test author or test user. Sometimes how one tests a skill or ability has more to do with the student's performance than the particular skill or ability is being assessed. A simple example is power versus speed tests. Power tests are untimed; speed tests are timed. Some students with learning disabilities or emotional problems may perform poorly on speed tests purely as a manifestation of their disability. In such a situation, student scores in math and reading based on fluency may be similar while power tests may reveal differences in reading and math achievement.

[4] Many test authors systematically ensure that their tests will be correlated with age by requiring that each item correlate positively with age or grade and passing. Also, in addition to intelligence, many other abilities correlate with chronological age—for example, achievement, perceptual abilities, and language skills.

4. Evidence Based on Response Processes

Response process refers to the way in which students go about answering test questions as well as how examiners go about scoring student responses. In some cases, we want to assess students' skill in using the correct process to solve problems. For example, did they follow the correct mathematical algorithm in solving a long division problem? If a test is intended to measure response processes, we would expect to find evidence that test takers actually are using the desired process. Evidence of this type would include interviews with test takers, having test takers "show their work" or having test takers write essays explaining how they arrived at their answers.

5. Evidence Based on the Consequences of Testing

As noted by AERA et al. (1999, p. 16):

> Tests are commonly administered in the expectation that some benefit will be realized from the intended use of the scores. A few of the many possible benefits are selection of efficacious treatments for therapy, placement of workers in suitable jobs, prevention of unqualified individuals from entering a profession, or improvement of classroom instructional practices. A fundamental purpose of validation is to indicate whether these specific benefits are likely to be realized. Thus, in the case of a test used in placement decisions, the validation would be informed by evidence that alternate placements, in fact, are differentially beneficial to the persons and the institution.

Although this type of evidence has been adopted by the joint committee of the American Educational Research Association, American Psychological Association, and the National Council on Measurement in Education, it does not seem to have been widely accepted in educational circles. Clearly, a test is but one of many factors that enter into the degree to which various decisions benefit a test taker. However, blaming a test for outcomes that may not be desired seems to us misplaced. For example, if a test correctly indicates a tenth-grade student cannot read second-grade materials, what a school does with that information has nothing to do with the accuracy of that information. If the school decides nothing is to be done, the test results are accurate; if the school decides to provide the student with ineffective instruction, the test results are still accurate; if the school provides effective remediation, the test results were still correct.

FACTORS AFFECTING GENERAL VALIDITY

Whenever an assessment procedure fails to measure what it purports to measure, validity is threatened. Consequently, any factor that results in measuring "something else" affects validity. Both unsystematic error (unreliability) and systematic error (bias) threaten validity.

Reliability

Reliability sets the upper limit of a test's validity, so reliability is a necessary but not a sufficient condition for valid measurement. Thus, all valid tests are reliable, unreliable tests are not valid, and reliable tests may or may not be valid. The validity of a particular procedure can never exceed the reliability of that procedure because unreliable procedures measure error; valid procedures measure the traits they are designed to measure.

Systematic Bias

Several systematic biases can limit a test's validity. The following are among the most common.

Enabling Behaviors Enabling behaviors and knowledge are skills and facts that a person must rely on to demonstrate a target behavior or knowledge. For example, to demonstrate knowledge of causes of the American Civil War on an essay examination, a student must be able to write. The student cannot produce the targeted behavior (the written answer) without the enabling behavior (writing). Similarly, knowledge of the language of assessment is crucial. Many of the abuses in assessment are directly attributable to examiners' failures in this area. For example, intelligence testing in English of non-English-speaking children at one time was sufficiently commonplace that a group of parents brought suit against a school district (*Diana v. State Board of Education*, 1970). Students who are deaf are routinely given the Performance subtests of the Wechsler Adult Intelligence Scales (Baumgardner, 1993) even though they cannot hear the directions. Children with communication disorders are often required to respond orally to test questions. Such obvious limitations in or absences of enabling behaviors are frequently overlooked in testing situations, even though they invalidate the test's inferences for these students.

Differential Item Effectiveness Test items should work the same way for various groups of students. Jensen (1980) discussed several empirical ways to assess item effectiveness for different groups of test takers. First, we should expect that the relative difficulty of items is maintained across different groups. For example, the most difficult item for males should also be the most difficult item for females, the easiest item for whites should be the easiest item for nonwhites, and so forth. We should also expect that reliabilities and validities will be the same for all groups of test takers.

The most likely explanation for items having differential effectiveness for different groups of people is differential exposure to test content. Test items may not work in the same ways for students who experience different acculturation or different academic instruction. For example, standardized achievement tests presume that the students who are taking the tests have been exposed to similar curricula. If teachers have not taught the content being tested, that content will be more difficult for their students (and inferences about the students' ability to profit from instruction will probably be incorrect).

Systematic Administration Errors

Unless a test is administered according to the standardized procedures, the inferences based on the test are invalid. Suppose Ms. Williams wishes to demonstrate how effective her teaching is by administering an intelligence test and an achievement test to her class. She allows the students 5 minutes less than the standardized time limits on the intelligence test and 5 minutes more on the standardized achievement test. The result is that the students earn higher achievement test scores (because they had too much time) and lower intelligence test scores (because they did not have enough time). The inference that less intelligent students have learned more than anticipated is not valid.

Norms

Scores based on the performance of unrepresentative norms lead to incorrect estimates of relative standing in the general population. To the extent that the normative sample is systematically unrepresentative of the general population in either central tendency or variability, the differences based on such scores are incorrect and invalid.

3 Responsibility for Valid Assessment

The valid use of assessment procedures is the responsibility of both the author and the user of the assessment procedure. Test authors are expected to present evidence for the major types of inferences for which the use of a test is recommended, and a rationale should be provided to support the particular mix of evidence presented for the intended uses (AERA et al., 1997, p. 13). Test users are expected to ensure that the test is appropriate for the specific students being assessed.

SCENARIO *in* ASSESSMENT

CRINA | Crina was born in Eastern Europe and spent most of the first 10 years of her life in an orphanage, where she looked after younger children. She was adopted shortly before her 11th birthday by an Ohio family. The only papers that accompanied Crina to the United States were her passport, baptismal certificate, and letter from the orphanage stating that Crina's parents were deceased.

Crina's adoptive parents learned some of Crina's language, and Crina tried to learn English in the months before she was enrolled in the local school system. When she was enrolled in the local public school, she was placed in an age-appropriate regular classroom and received additional support from an English as a second language (ESL) teacher.

Things did not go well. Crina did not adapt to the school routine, had virtually no understanding of any content area, and was viewed as essentially unteachable. She spent most of her school time trying to help the teacher by neatening up the room, passing out materials, and running errands. Within Crina's first week in school, her teacher sought additional help from the ESL teacher, the school principal, and the school psychologist. Although all offered suggestions, none of them seemed to work; the school was unable to find a native speaker of Crina's language. Within the first month of school, Crina was referred to a child study team that in turn referred her for psychological and educational assessment.

The school psychologist administered the current Wechsler Intelligence Scale for Children and the Wechsler Individual Achievement Test, although both tests are administered in English. Crina did much better on tests that did not require her to speak or understand English—for example, block designs. Her estimated IQ was in the 40s and her achievement was so low that no derived scores were available.

Given her age and the extent of her needs, the school team recommended that she be placed in a life skills class with other moderately retarded students. Crina's mother rejected that placement because Crina had already mastered most of the life skills she would be taught there; at the orphanage, she cleaned, cooked, bathed and tended younger children, and so forth. In addition, her mother believed more verbal students than the ones in the life skills class would be better language models for Crina. Basically, her mother wanted a program of basic academics that would be more appropriate—a program in which Crina could learn to read and write English, learn basic computational skills, make friends, and become acculturated.

For reasons that were never entirely clear, the school refused to compromise, and the dispute went to a due process hearing. The mother obtained an independent educational evaluation. Her psychologist assessed Crina's adaptive behavior; because the test had limited validity due to Crina's unique circumstances, the psychologist estimated that Crina was functioning within the average range for a person her age. Her psychologist also administered a nonverbal test of intelligence—one that neither required her to understand verbal directions nor to make verbal responses. With the same caveats, Crina was again estimated to be functioning in the average range for a person her age. To make a long story short, the school lost; Crina and her parents won.

The Moral. All validity is local. The district followed its policies for providing the teacher with support, for providing Crina with support, for convening a multidisciplinary team, etc. The tests administered by the school were generally reliable, valid, and well normed. However, they were not appropriate for Crina and her unique circumstances. Obviously, she lacked the language skills, cultural knowledge, and academic background to be assessed validly by the tests given by the school. Although the tests given by the parents' psychologist were better, they still had to be considered minimum estimates of her abilities due to the cultural considerations.

A Happy Ending. Crina learned enough English during the next several years to develop friendships, to read and write enough to be gainfully employed, and to leave school feeling positive about the experience and her accomplishments.

What implications about your personal professional role can you draw from this scenario? Go to the Education CourseMate website for this textbook for more reflection questions about this Scenario in Assessment.

Chapter Comprehension Questions

Write your answers to each of the following questions and then compare your responses to the text.

1. Explain the concept of measurement error.
2. What does a reliability coefficient of .75 tell you about true-score variability and error variability?
3. Compare and contrast item reliability, stability, and interobserver agreement.
4. What is the difference between simple agreement and point-to-point agreement, and when might you use each appropriately?
5. What is a standard error of measurement?
6. Explain evidence of validity based on relations to other measures.
7. Explain evidence of validity based on test content.
8. Explain three factors that can affect a test's validity.

Web Activities

1. Go to Chapter 18 (Using Measures of Adaptive Behavior) on the Education CourseMate website for this text and read about the reliability of the *Vineland Adaptive Behavior Scales, Second Edition.* What types of reliability evidence are offered? How do you judge the scale's reliability?
2. Also in Chapter 18, read about the evidence of the scale's validity. Why or why not does the scale appear to have adequate evidence of validity?

Web Resources

Test Validity and Reliability
http://allpsych.com/researchmethods/validityreliability.html
This short article provides a brief discussion of the kinds of validity and reliability.

Traditional and Modern Concepts of Validity
http://www.findarticles.com/p/articles/mi_pric/is_199912/ai_1959115104/
This paper, written by Amy Brualdi in 1999, compares more traditional concepts of validity (e.g., criterion-related, content-related, and construct-related validity) with new concepts (e.g., substantive, generalizability, consequental, etc.)

Additional resources for this chapter can be found on the Education CourseMate website. Go to CengageBrain.com to access the site.

Part 2

Assessment in Classrooms

Some educators still rely on norm-referenced achievement tests to plan and evaluate instruction; some rely on systematic observation; some rely on teacher-made tests and curriculum-based assessment; some rely on subjective and qualitative judgments to assess classroom learning; and some rely on a combination of approaches.

In Part 2 of this text, we discuss the approaches most likely to be used by classroom teachers. We do not consider these approaches to be informal or unstandardized. They are frequently formal: Students know that they are being assessed and that the assessments count for something. They are also frequently standardized: Students receive the same directions and tasks, and their responses are frequently scored using the same criteria. These approaches to assessment are used most frequently by classroom teachers, but we recognize that some specialists (such as school psychologists and speech and language therapists) may also use these approaches.

Part 2 begins with Chapter 6, on observation, which provides a general overview of basic considerations and good practice. Chapter 7 provides an overview of objective and performance measures constructed by teachers. Chapter 8 is an introduction to curriculum-based approaches to measurement, including the types of measurement tools and goal. Chapter 9 gives you a set of steps and procedures for preparing for and managing mandated tests, monitoring progress, and interpreting data.

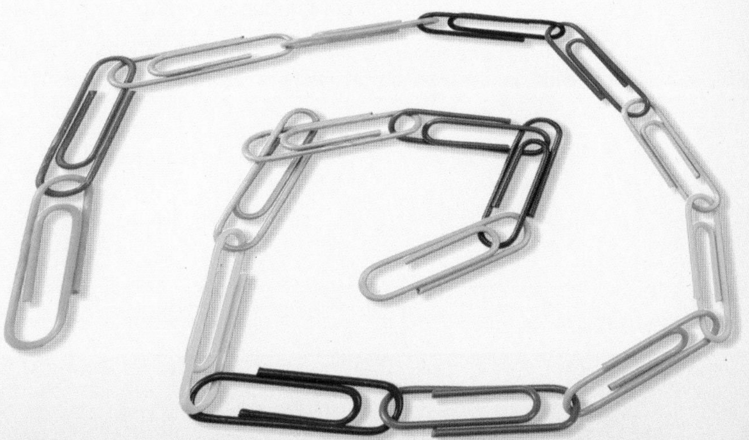

Assessing Behavior Through Observation

CHAPTER GOALS

1 Understand the general considerations in conducting the conditions of observation, defining behaviors to be observed, behavioral topographies and functions, and measurable characteristics of behavior.

2 Understand that observations require careful sampling of contexts, times, and behaviors.

3 Understand that conducting systematic observations requires careful preparation, precise data gathering, procedures for summarizing data, and criteria for evaluating the observed performances.

KEY TERMS

qualitative observation
quantitative observation
aided observation
obtrusive observations
amplitude
continuous recording
unobtrusive observations
contrived observations
naturalistic observations
topography of behavior
whole-interval sampling
partial-interval sampling
momentary time sampling
function of behavior
duration
latency
frequency
social comparison
social tolerance
aimline

1 General Considerations

Teachers are constantly monitoring themselves and their students. Sometimes they are just keeping an eye on things to make sure that their classrooms are safe and goal oriented, to anticipate disruptive or dangerous situations, or just to keep track of how things are going in a general sense. Often, teachers notice behavior or situations that seem important and require their attention: the fire alarm has sounded, Harvey has a knife, Betty is asleep, Jo is wandering around the classroom. In other situations, often as a result of their general monitoring, teachers look for very specific behavior to observe: social behavior that should be reinforced, attention to task, performance of particular skills, and so forth.

Systematic observations are also used to inform placement and instructional decisions. When assessment does not rely on permanent products (that is, written examinations and physical creations such as a table in shop or a dinner in home economics), observation is usually involved. Clearly, social behavior, learning behavior (for example, attention to task), and aberrant behavior (for example, hand flapping) are all suitable targets of systematic observation. Obviously, behavior can be an integral part of assessing physical and mental states, physical characteristics, and educational handicaps as well as monitoring student progress and attainment.

There are two basic approaches to observation: qualitative and quantitative. *Qualitative observations* can describe behavior as well as its contexts (that is, antecedents and consequences). These observations usually occur without predetermining the behaviors to be observed or the times and contexts in which to observe. Instead, an observer monitors the situation and memorializes the observations in a narrative, the most common form being anecdotal records. Good anecdotal records contain a complete description of the behavior and the context in which it occurred and can set the stage for more focused and precise *quantitative observations*.

We stress behavioral observation, a quantitative approach to observation. Measuring behavior through observation is distinguished by five steps that occur in advance of the actual observations: (1) The behavior is defined precisely and objectively, (2) the characteristics of the behavior (for example, frequency) are specified, (3) procedures for recording are developed, (4) the times and places for observation are selected and specified, and (5) procedures are developed to assess interobserver agreement. Beyond these defining characteristics, behavioral observations can vary on a number of dimensions.

LIVE OR AIDED OBSERVATION

Quantitative analysis of behavior can occur in real time or after the behavior has occurred by means of devices such as video or audio recorders that can replay, slow down, or speed up records of behavior. Observation can be enhanced with equipment (for example, a telescope), or it can occur with only the observer's unaided senses.

OBTRUSIVE VERSUS UNOBTRUSIVE OBSERVATION

Observations are called obtrusive when it is obvious to the person being observed that he or she is being observed. The presence of an observer makes observation obvious; for example, the presence of a practicum supervisor in the back of the classroom makes it obvious to student teachers that they are being observed. The presence of observation equipment makes it obvious; for example, a video camera with a red light on makes it obvious that observation is occurring. Something added to a situation can signal that someone is observing. For example, a dark, late-model, four-door sedan idling on the side of the road with a radar gun protruding from the driver's window makes it obvious to approaching motorists that they are being observed; a flickering light and noise coming from behind a mirror in a testing room indicate to test takers that there is someone or something watching from behind the mirror.

SCENARIO *in* ASSESSMENT

ZACK, PART 1 | Ms. Lawson notices that during sustained silent reading time, Zack is walking around the room a lot and disturbing students who are reading. When she tells him to return to his seat, he always does, but he does not seem to remain there for long. She decides to keep an eye on him and to document his behavior before developing a more systematic intervention.

She notes the context, antecedents, consequences, and specifics of Zack's behavior. Figure 6.1 contains the first 3 days of relevant notes.

What implications about your personal professional role can you draw from this scenario? Go to the Education CourseMate website for this textbook for more reflection questions about this Scenario in Assessment.

FIGURE 6.1
Observations of Zack's Behavior

Day:	Monday
Context:	Sustained Silent Reading—all students in their own seats. Zack was on task for activities other than independent seat work.
Antecedents:	I tell the class to take out their novels and begin reading where they had left off on Friday.
Behavior:	Zack takes out his novel, but does not open it. He fidgets a minute or two and then gets out of his seat, wanders around the room, talks to Cindy and Marie.
Consequences:	The girls initially ignore Zack, then tell him to go away. Zack giggles, and I scold him and tell him to return to his seat. Zack is falling behind in reading.
Day:	Tuesday
Context:	Science Activity Center—students working on time unit.
Antecedents:	I tell the class to write up their observations from their measurement experiments independently.
Behavior:	Zack requires help to find his lab book. After writing a few words, he gets up to sharpen his pencil but ends up strolling around the room. He talks to Cindy and Marie again.
Consequences:	The girls complain that Zack is bothering them again. Zack says he was just asking them about the project. I tell him to get back to work or he will get a time out. Zack is falling behind in science.
Note:	Zack was on task for activities other than independent seat work.
Day:	Wednesday
Context:	Sustained Silent Reading—all students in their own seats.
Antecedents:	I tell the class to take out their novels and begin reading where they had left off on Monday.
Behavior:	Zack puts his head down on the open pages of his novel. After about 5 minutes, he gets up and wanders around again.
Consequences:	Time out. Zack is far behind his peers in completing his novel.
Note:	Zack was again on task for activities other than independent seat work.

When observations are unobtrusive, the people being observed do not realize they are being watched. Observers may pretend that they are not observing or observe from hidden positions. They may use telescopes to watch from afar. They may use hidden cameras and microphones.

Unobtrusive observations are preferable for two reasons. First, people are reluctant to engage in certain types of behavior if another person is looking. Thus, when antisocial, offensive, or illegal behaviors are targeted for assessment, observation should be conducted surreptitiously. Behavior of these types tends not to occur if they are overtly monitored. For example, Billy is unlikely to steal Bob's lunch money when the teacher is looking; Rosie is unlikely to bully Sandy in front of teachers; and Rodney is unlikely to spray-paint gang graffiti on the front doors of the school when other students are present.

Likewise, if people are being observed, they are reluctant to engage in highly personal behaviors in which they must expose private body parts. In these instances, the observer should obtain the permission of the person or the person's guardian before conducting such observations. Moreover, a same-sex observer who does not know the person being observed (and whom the person being observed does not know) should conduct the observations.

The second reason that unobtrusive observations are preferable is that the presence of an observer alters the observation situation. Observation can change the behavior of those in the observation situation. For example, when a principal sits in the back of a probationary teacher's classroom to conduct an annual evaluation, both the teacher's and the students' behavior may be affected by the principal's presence. Students may be better behaved or respond more enthusiastically in the mistaken belief that the principal is there to watch them. The teacher may write on the chalkboard more frequently or give more positive reinforcement than usual in the belief that the principal values those techniques. Observation can also eliminate other types of behavior. For example, retail stores may mount circuit TV cameras and video monitors in obvious places to let potential thieves know that they are being watched constantly and to try to discourage shoplifting.

When the target behavior is not antisocial, offensive, highly personal, or undesirable, obtrusive observation may be used provided the persons being observed have been desensitized to the observers and/or equipment. It is fortunate that most people quickly become accustomed to observers in their daily environment—especially if observers make themselves part of the surroundings by avoiding eye contact, not engaging in social interactions, remaining quiet and not moving around, and so on. Observation and recording can become part of the everyday classroom routine. In any event, obtrusive observation should not begin until the persons to be observed are desensitized and are acting in their usual ways.

CONTRIVED VERSUS NATURALISTIC OBSERVATION

Contrived observations occur when a situation is set up before a student is introduced into it. For example, a playroom may be set up with toys that encourage aggressive play (such as guns or punching-bag dolls) or with items that promote other types of behavior. A child may be given a book and told to go into the room and read or may simply be told to wait in the room. Other adults or children in the situation may be confederates of the observer and may be instructed to behave in particular ways. For example, an older child may be told not to share toys with the child who is the target of the observation, or an adult may be told to initiate a conversation on a specific topic with the target child.

In contrast, naturalistic observations occur in settings that are not contrived. For example, specific toys are not added to or removed from a playroom; the furniture is arranged as it always is arranged.

DEFINING BEHAVIOR

Behavior is usually defined in terms of its topography, its function, and its characteristics. The function that a behavior serves in the environment is not directly observable, whereas the characteristics and topography of behavior can be measured directly.

Topography of Behavior

Behavioral topography refers to the way in which a behavior is performed. For example, suppose the behavior of interest is holding a pencil to write and we are interested in Patty's topography for that behavior. The topography is readily observable: Patty holds the pencil at a 45-degree angle to the paper, grasped between her thumb and index finger; she supports the pencil with her middle finger; and so forth. Paul's topography for holding a pencil is quite different. He holds the pencil between his great toe and second toe so that the point of the pencil is aimed toward the sole of his foot, and so forth.

Function of Behavior

The function of a behavior is the reason a person behaves as he or she does or the purpose the behavior serves. Obviously, the reason for a behavior cannot be observed; it can only be inferred. Sometimes, a person may offer an explanation of a behavior's function—for example, "I was screaming to make him stop." We can accept the explanation of the behavior's function if it is consistent with the circumstances, or we can reject the explanation of the function when it is not consistent with the circumstances or is unreasonable. Other times, we can infer a behavior's function from its consequences. For example, Johnny stands screaming at the rear door of his house until his mother opens the door and then runs into the backyard and stops screaming. We might infer that the function of Johnny's screaming is to have the door opened. Behavior typically serves one or more of five functions: (1) social attention/communication; (2) access to tangibles or preferred activities; (3) escape, delay, reduction, or avoidance of aversive tasks or activities; (4) escape or avoidance of other individuals; and (5) internal stimulation (Alberto & Troutman, 2006).

MEASURABLE CHARACTERISTICS OF BEHAVIOR

The measurement of behavior, whether individual behavior or a category of behavior, is based on four characteristics: duration, latency, frequency, and amplitude. These characteristics can be measured directly (Shapiro & Kratochwill, 2000).

Duration

Behaviors that have discrete beginnings and endings may be assessed in terms of their *duration*—that is, the length of time a behavior lasts. The duration of a behavior is usually standardized in two ways: average duration and total duration. For example, in computing average duration, suppose that Janice is out of her seat four times during a 30-minute activity, and the durations of the episodes are 1 minute, 3 minutes, 7 minutes, and 5 minutes. In this example, the average duration is 4 minutes—that is, (1 + 3 + 7 + 5)/4. To compute Janice's total duration, we add 1 + 3 + 7 + 5 to conclude that she was out of her seat a total of 16 minutes. Often, total duration is expressed as a rate by dividing the total occurrence by the length of an observation. This proportion of duration is often called the "prevalence of the behavior." In the preceding example, Janice's prevalence is .53 (that is, 16/30).

Latency

Latency refers to the length of time between a signal to perform and the beginning of the behavior. For example, a teacher might ask students to take out their books. Sam's latency for that task is the length of time between the teacher's request and Sam's placing his book on his desk. For latency to be assessed, the behavior must have a discrete beginning.

Frequency

For behaviors with discrete beginnings and endings, we often count *frequency*—that is, the number of times the behaviors occur. When behavior is counted during variable time periods, frequencies are usually converted to rates. Using rate of behavior allows observers to compare the occurrence of behavior across different time periods and settings. For example, three episodes of out-of-seat behavior in 15 minutes may be converted to a rate of 12 per hour.

Alberto and Troutman (2005) suggest that frequency should not be used under two conditions: (1) when the behavior occurs at such a high rate that it cannot be counted accurately (for example, many stereotypic behaviors, such as foot tapping, can occur almost constantly) and (2) when the behavior occurs over a prolonged period of time (for example, cooperative play during a game of Monopoly).

Amplitude

Amplitude refers to the intensity of the behavior. In many settings, amplitude can be measured precisely (for example, with noise meters). However, in the classroom, it is usually estimated with less precision. For example, amplitude can be estimated using a rating scale that calibrates the amplitude of the behavior (for example, crying might be scaled as "whimpering," "sobbing," "crying," and "screaming"). Amplitude may also be calibrated in terms of its objective or subjective impact on others. For example, the objective impact of hitting might be scaled as "without apparent physical damage," "resulting in bruising," and "causing bleeding." More subjective behavior ratings estimate the internal impact on others; for example, a student's humming could be scaled as "does not disturb others," "disturbs students seated nearby," or "disturbs students in the adjoining classroom."

Selecting the Characteristic to Measure

The behavioral characteristic to be assessed should make sense; we should assess the most relevant aspect of behavior in a particular situation. For example, if Burl is wandering around the classroom during the reading period, observing the duration of that behavior makes more sense than observing the frequency, latency, or amplitude of the behavior. If Camilla's teacher is concerned about her loud utterances, amplitude may be the most salient characteristic to observe. If Molly is always slow to follow directions, observing her latency makes more sense than assessing the frequency or amplitude of her behavior. For most behaviors, however, frequency and duration are the characteristics measured.

2 Sampling Behavior

As with any assessment procedure, we can assess the entire domain if it is finite and convenient. If it is not, we can sample from the domain. Important dimension for sampling behavior include the contexts in which the behaviors occur, the times at which the behaviors occur, and the behaviors themselves.

CONTEXTS

When specific behaviors become the targets of intervention, it is useful to measure the behavior in a variety of contexts. Usually, the sampling of contexts is purposeful rather than random. We might want to know, for example, how Jesse's behavior in the resource room differs from his behavior in the general education classroom. Consistent or inconsistent performance across settings and contexts can provide useful information about what events might set the occasion for the behavior. Differences between the settings in which a behavior does and does not occur can provide potentially useful hypotheses about *setting events* (that is, environmental events that set the occasion for the performance of an action) and *discriminative stimuli* (that is, stimuli that are consistently present when a behavior is reinforced and that come to bring out behavior even in the absence of the original reinforcer).[1] Bringing behavior under the control of a discriminative stimulus is often an effective way of modifying it. For example, students might be taught to talk quietly (to use their "inside voice") when they are in the classroom or hallway.

Similarly, consistent or inconsistent performance across settings and contexts can provide useful information about how the consequences of a behavior are affecting that behavior. Some consequences of a behavior maintain, increase, or decrease behavior. Thus, manipulating the consequences of a behavior can increase or decrease its occurrence. For example, assume that Joey's friends usually laugh

[1] Discriminative stimuli are not conditioned stimuli in the Pavlovian sense that they elicit reflexive behavior. Discriminative stimuli provide a signal to the individual to engage in a particular behavior because that behavior has been reinforced in the presence of that signal.

and congratulate him when he makes a sexist remark and that Joey is reinforced by his friends' behavior. If his friends could be made to stop laughing and congratulating him, Joey would probably make fewer sexist remarks.

TIMES

With the exception of some criminal acts, few behaviors are noteworthy unless they happen more than once. Behavioral recurrence over time is termed *stability* or *maintenance*. In a person's lifetime, there are almost an infinite number of times to exhibit a particular behavior. Moreover, it is probably impossible and certainly unnecessary to observe a person continuously during his or her entire life. Thus, temporal sampling is always performed, and any single observation is merely a sample from the person's behavioral domain.

Time sampling always requires the establishment of blocks of time, termed *observation sessions*, in which observations will be made. A session might consist of a continuous period of time (for example, one school day). More often, sessions are discontinuous blocks of time (for example, every Monday for a semester or during daily reading time).

Continuous Recording

Observers can record behavior continuously within sessions. They count each occurrence of a behavior in the observation session; they can time the duration or latency of each occurrence within the observation session.

When the observation session is long (for example, when it spans several days), continuous sampling can be very expensive and is often intrusive. Two options are commonly used to estimate behavior in very long observation sessions: the use of rating scales to make estimates and time sampling. In the first option, rating scales are used to estimate one (or more) of the four characteristics of behavior. Following are some examples of such ratings:

- *Frequency:* A parent might be asked to rate the frequency of a behavior. How often does Patsy usually pick up her toys—always, frequently, seldom, never?
- *Duration:* A parent might be asked to rate how long Bernie typically watches TV each night—more than 3 hours, 2 or 3 hours, 1 or 2 hours, or less than 1 hour?
- *Latency:* A parent might be asked to rate how quickly Marisa usually responds to requests—immediately, quickly, slowly, or not at all (ignores requests)?
- *Amplitude:* A parent might be asked to rate how much of a fuss Jessica usually makes at bedtime—screams, cries, begs to stay up, or goes to bed without fuss?

In the second observation option, duration and frequency are sampled systematically during prolonged observation intervals. Three different sampling plans have been advocated: whole-interval recording, partial-interval recording, and momentary time sampling.

Time Sampling

Continuous observation requires the expenditure of more resources than does discontinuous observation. Therefore, it is common to observe for a sample of times within an observation session.

In *interval sampling*, an observation session is subdivided into intervals during which behavior is observed. Usually, observation intervals of equal length are spaced equally through the session, although the recording and observation intervals need not be the same length. Three types of interval sampling and scoring are common.

1. In *whole-interval* sampling, a behavior is scored as having occurred only when it occurs throughout the entire interval. Thus, it is scored only if it is occurring when the interval begins and continues through the end of the interval.
2. *Partial-interval sampling* is quite similar to whole-interval recording. The difference between the two procedures is that in partial-interval recording, an

occurrence is scored if it occurs during any part of the interval. Thus, if a behavior begins before the interval begins and ends within the interval, an occurrence is scored; if a behavior starts after the beginning of the interval, an occurrence is scored; if two or more episodes of behavior begin and end within the interval, one occurrence is scored.

3. *Momentary time sampling* is the most efficient sampling procedure. An observation session is subdivided into intervals. If a behavior is occurring at the last moment of the interval, an occurrence is recorded; if the behavior is not occurring at the last moment of the interval, a nonoccurrence is recorded. For example, suppose we observe Robin during her 20-minute reading period. We first select the interval length (for example, 10 seconds). At the end of the first 10-second interval, we observe if the behavior is occurring; at the end of the second 10-second interval, we again observe. We continue observing until we have observed Robin at the end of the 60th 10-second interval.[2]

Salvia and Hughes (1990) have summarized a number of studies investigating the accuracy of these time-sampling procedures. Both whole-interval and partial-interval sampling procedures provide inaccurate estimates of duration and frequency.[3] Momentary time sampling provides an unbiased estimate of the proportion of time that is very accurate when small intervals are used (that is, 10- to 15-second intervals). Continuous recording with shorter observation sessions is the better method of estimating the frequency of a behavior.

BEHAVIORS

Teachers and psychologists may be interested in measurement of a particular behavior or a constellation of behaviors thought to represent a trait (for example, cooperation). When an observer views a target behavior as important in and of itself, only that specific behavior is observed. However, when a specific behavior is thought to be one element in a constellation of behaviors, other important behaviors within the constellation must also be observed in order to establish the content validity of the behavioral constellation. For example, if taking turns on a slide were viewed as one element of cooperation, we should also observe other behaviors indicative of cooperation (such as taking turns on other equipment, following the rules of games, and working with others to attain a common goal). Each of the behaviors in a behavioral constellation can be treated separately or aggregated for the purposes of observation and reporting.

Observations are usually conducted on two types of behavior. First, we regularly observe behavior that is desirable and that we are trying to increase. Behavior of this type includes all academic performances (for example, oral reading or science knowledge) and prosocial behavior (for example, cooperative behavior or polite language). Second, we regularly observe behavior that is undesirable or may indicate a disabling condition. These behaviors are harmful, stereotypic, inappropriately infrequent, or inappropriate at the times exhibited.

- *Harmful behavior:* Behavior that is self-injurious or physically dangerous to others is almost always targeted for intervention. Self-injurious behavior includes such actions as head banging, eye gouging, self-biting or self-hitting, smoking, and drug abuse. Potentially harmful behavior can include leaning back in a desk or being careless with reagents in a chemistry experiment. Behaviors harmful to others are those that directly inflict injury (for example, hitting or stabbing) or are likely to injure others (for example, pushing other

[2] Time sampling has been made easier by various digital devices such as personal digital assistants (PDAs) and observation programs such as the Behavioral Observation of Students in Schools (Shapiro, 2003). See Chapter 23 for further discussion of the use of technology in classrooms.

[3] Suen and Ary (1989) have provided procedures whereby the sampled frequencies can be adjusted to provide accurate frequency estimates, and the error associated with estimates of prevalence can be readily determined for each sampling plan.

students on stairs or subway platforms, bullying, or verbally instigating physical altercations). Unusually aggressive behavior may also be targeted for intervention. Although most students will display aggressive behavior, some children go far beyond what can be considered typical or acceptable. These students may be described as hot-tempered, quick-tempered, or volatile. Overly aggressive behavior may be physical or verbal. In addition to the possibility of causing physical harm, high rates of aggressive behavior may isolate the aggressor socially.

- *Stereotypic behavior:* Stereotypic behaviors, or stereotypies (for example, hand flapping, rocking, and certain verbalizations such as inappropriate shrieks), are outside the realm of culturally normative behavior. Such behavior calls attention to students and marks them as abnormal to trained psychologists or unusual to untrained observers. Stereotypic behaviors are often targeted for intervention.
- *Infrequent or absent desirable behavior:* Incompletely developed behavior, especially behavior related to physiological development (for example, walking), is often targeted for intervention. Intervention usually occurs when development of these behaviors will enable desirable functional skills or social acceptance. Shaping is usually used to develop absent behavior, whereas reinforcement is used to increase the frequency of behavior that is within a student's repertoire but exhibited at rates that are too low.
- *Normal behavior exhibited in inappropriate contexts:* Many behaviors are appropriate in very specific contexts but are considered inappropriate or even abnormal when exhibited in other contexts. Usually, the problems caused by behavior in inappropriate contexts are attributed to lack of stimulus control. Behavior that is commonly called "private" falls into this category; elimination and sexual activity are two examples. The goal of intervention should be not to get rid of these behaviors but to confine them to socially appropriate conditions. Behavior that is often called "disruptive" also falls into this category. For example, running and yelling are very acceptable and normal when exhibited on the playground; they are disruptive in a classroom.

A teacher may decide on the basis of logic and experience that a particular behavior should be modified. For example, harmful behavior should not be tolerated in a classroom or school, and behavior that is a prerequisite for learning academic material must be developed. In other cases, a teacher may seek the advice of a colleague, supervisor, or parent about the desirability of intervention. For example, a teacher might not know whether certain behavior is typical of a student's culture. In yet other cases, a teacher might rely on the judgments of students or adults as to whether a particular behavior is troublesome or distracting for them. For example, are others bothered when Bob reads problems aloud during arithmetic tests? To ascertain whether a particular behavior bothers others, teachers can ask students directly, have them rate disturbing or distracting behavior, or perhaps use sociometric techniques to learn whether a student is being rejected or isolated because of his or her behavior. The sociometric technique is a method for evaluating the social acceptance of individual pupils and the social structure of a group: Students complete a form indicating their choice of companions for seating, work, or play. Teachers look at the number of times an individual student is chosen by others. They also look at who chooses whom.

For infrequent prosocial behavior or frequent disturbing behavior, a teacher may wish to get a better idea of the magnitude and pervasiveness of the problem before initiating a comprehensive observational analysis. Casual observation can provide information about the frequency and amplitude of the behavior; carefully noting the antecedents, consequences, and contexts may provide useful information about possible interventions if an intervention is warranted. If casual observations are made, anecdotal records of these casual observations should be maintained.

3 Conducting Systematic Observations

PREPARATION

Careful preparation is essential to obtaining accurate and valid observational data that are useful in decision making. Five steps should guide the preparation for systematic observation:

1. *Define target behaviors.*
    - Use definitions that describe behavior in observable terms.
    - Avoid references to internal processes (for example, understanding or appreciating).
    - Anticipate potentially difficult discriminations and provide examples of instances and noninstances of the behavior. Include subtle instances of the target behavior, and use related behaviors and behavior with similar topographies as noninstances.
    - State the characteristic of the behavior that will be measured (for example, frequency or latency).
2. *Select contexts.* Observe the target behavior systematically in at least three contexts: the context in which the behavior was noted as troublesome (for example, in reading instruction), a similar context (for example, in math instruction), and a dissimilar context (for example, in physical education or recess).
3. *Select an observation schedule.*
    - Choose the session length. In schools, session length is usually related to instructional periods or blocks of time within an instructional period (for example, 15 minutes in the middle of small-group reading instruction).
    - Decide between continuous and discontinuous observation. The choice of continuous or discontinuous observation will depend on the resources available and the specific behaviors that are to be observed. When very low-frequency behavior or behavior that must be stopped (for example, physical assaults) is observed, continuous recording is convenient and efficient. For other behavior, discontinuous observation is usually preferred, and momentary time sampling is usually the easiest and most accurate for teachers and psychologists to use. When a discontinuous observation schedule is used, the observer requires some equipment to signal exactly when observation is to occur. The most common equipment is a portable audiocassette player and a tape with pure tones, recorded at the desired intervals. One student or several students in sequence may be observed. For example, three students can be observed in a series of 5-second intervals. An audiotape would signal every 5 seconds. On the first signal, Henry would be observed; on the second signal, Joyce would be observed; on the third signal, Bruce would be observed; on the fourth signal, Henry would be observed again; and so forth.
4. *Develop recording procedures.* The recording of observations must also be planned. When a few students are observed for the occurrence of relatively infrequent behaviors, simple procedures can be used. The behaviors can be observed continuously and counted using a tally sheet or a wrist counter. When time sampling is used, observations must be recorded for each time interval; thus, some type of recording form is required. In the simplest form, the recording sheet contains identifying information (for example, name of target student, name of observer, date and time of observation session, and observation-interval length) and two columns. The first column shows the time interval, and the second column contains space for the observer to indicate whether the behavior occurred during each interval. More complicated recording forms may be used for multiple behaviors and/or multiple students. When multiple behaviors are observed, they

are often given code numbers. For example, "out of seat" might be coded as 1, "in seat but off task" might be coded as 2, "in seat and on task" might be coded as 3, and "no opportunity to observe" might be coded as 4. Such codes should be included on the observation record form. Figure 6.2 shows a simple form on which to record multiple behaviors of students. The observer writes the code number(s) in the box corresponding to the interval. Complex observational systems tend to be less accurate than simple ones. Complexity increases as a function of the number of different behaviors that are assessed and the number of individuals who are observed. Moreover, both the proportion of target individuals to total individuals and the proportion of target behaviors observed to the number of target behaviors to be recorded also have an impact on accuracy. The surest way to reduce inaccuracies is to keep things relatively simple.

5. *Select the means of observation.* The choice of human observers or electronic recorders will depend on the availability of resources. If electronic recorders are available and can be used in the desired environments and contexts, they may be appropriate when continuous observation is warranted. If other personnel are available, they can be trained to observe and record the target behaviors accurately. Training should include didactic instruction in defining the target behavior, the use of time sampling (if it is to be used), and the way in which to record behavior, as well as practice in using the observation system. Training is always continued until the desired level of accuracy is reached. Observers' accuracy is evaluated by comparing each observer's responses with those of the others or with a criterion rating (usually a previously

FIGURE 6.2
A Simple Recording Form for Three Students and Two Behaviors

Observer: Mr. Kowalski

Date: 2/15/11

Times of observation: 10:15 to 11:00

Observation interval: 10 sec

Instructional activity: Oral reading

Students observed:

S1 = Henry J.
S2 = Bruce H.
S3 = Joyce W.

Codes:

1 = out of seat
2 = in seat but off task
3 = in seat, on task
4 = no opportunity to observe

	S1	S2	S3
1	___	___	___
2	___	___	___
3	___	___	___
4	___	___	___
5	___	___	___
.			
.			
.			
179	___	___	___
180	___	___	___

scored videotape). Generally, very high agreement is required before anyone can assume that observers are ready to conduct observations independently. Ultimately, the decision of how to collect the data should also be based on efficiency. For example, if it takes longer to desensitize students to an obtrusive video recorder than it takes to train observers, then human observers are preferred.

DATA GATHERING

Observers should prepare a checklist of equipment and materials that will be used during the observation and assemble everything that is needed, including an extra supply of recording forms, spare pens or pencils, and something to write on (for example, a clipboard or tabletop). When electronic recording (for example, personal digital assistants or PDAs) is used, equipment should be checked before every observation session to make sure it is in good working condition and fully charged, and the observer should bring needed extras (for example, batteries, signal tapes, and recording tapes). Also, before the observation session, the observer should check the setting to locate appropriate vantage points for equipment or furniture. During observation, care should be taken to conduct the observations as planned. Thus, the observer should make sure that he or she adheres to the definitions of behavior, the observation schedules, and recording protocols. Careful preparation can head off trouble.

As with any type of assessment information, two general sources of error can reduce the accuracy of observation. Random error can result in over- or underestimates of behavior. Systematic error can bias the data in a consistent direction—for example, behavior may be systematically overcounted or undercounted.

Random Error

Random errors in observation and recording usually affect observer agreement. Observers may change the criteria for the occurrence of a behavior, they may forget behavior codes, or they may use the recording forms incorrectly. Because changes in agreement can signal that something is wrong, the accuracy of observational data should be checked periodically. The usual procedure is to have two people observe and record on the same schedule in the same session. The two records are then compared, and an index of agreement (for example, point-to-point agreement) is computed. Poor agreement suggests the need for retraining or for revision of the observation procedures. To alleviate some of these problems, we can provide periodic retraining and allow observers to keep the definitions and codes for target behaviors with them. Finally, when observers know that their accuracy is being systematically checked, they are usually more accurate. Thus, observers should not be told when they are being observed but to expect their observations to be checked.

See the Education CourseMate website for this textbook for a discussion and examples of calculating indices of agreement.

One of the most vexing factors affecting the accuracy of observations is the incorrect recording of correctly observed behavior. Even when observers have applied the criterion for the occurrence of a behavior correctly, they may record their decision incorrectly. For example, if 1 is used to indicate occurrence and 0 is used to indicate nonoccurrence, the observer might accidentally record 0 for a behavior that has occurred. Inaccuracy can be attributed to three related factors.

1. *Lack of familiarity with the recording system:* Observers definitely need practice in using a recording system when several behaviors or several students are to be observed. They also need practice when the target behaviors are difficult to define or when they are difficult to observe.
2. *Insufficient time to record:* Sufficient time must be allowed to record the occurrence of behavior. Problems can arise when using momentary time sampling if the observation intervals are spaced too closely (for example, 1- or 5-second intervals). Observers who are counting several different high-frequency behaviors may record inaccurately. Generally, inadequate

opportunities for observers to record can be circumvented by electronic recording of the observation session; when observers can stop and replay segments of interest, they essentially have unlimited time to observe and record.

3. *Lack of concentration:* It may be difficult for observers to remain alert for long periods of time (for example, 1 hour), especially if the target behavior occurs infrequently and is difficult to detect. Observers can reduce the time that they must maintain vigilance by either taking turns with several observers or recording observation sessions for later evaluation. Similarly, when it is difficult to maintain vigilance because the observational context is noisy, busy, or otherwise distracting, electronic recording may be useful in focusing on target subjects and eliminating ambient noise.

Systematic Error

Systematic errors are difficult to detect. To minimize error, four steps can be taken.

1. *Guard against unintended changes in the observation process.*[4] When assessment is carried out over extended periods of time, observers may talk to each other about the definitions that they are using or about how they cope with difficult discriminations. Consequently, one observer's departure from standardized procedures may spread to other observers. When the observers change together, modifications of the standard procedures and definitions will not be detected by examining interobserver agreement. Techniques for reducing changes in observers over time include keeping the scoring criteria available to observers, meeting with the observers on a regular basis to discuss difficulties encountered during observation, and providing periodic retraining. Surprisingly, even recording equipment can change over time. Audio signal tapes (used to indicate the moment a student should be observed) may stretch after repeated uses; a 10-second interval may become an 11-second interval. Similarly, the batteries in playback units can lose power, and signal tapes may play more slowly. Therefore, equipment should be cleaned periodically, and signal tapes should be checked for accuracy.
2. *Desensitize students.* The introduction of equipment or new adults into a classroom, as well as changes in teacher routines, can signal to students that observations are going on. Overt measurement can alter the target behavior or the topography of the behavior. Usually, the pupil change is temporary. For example, when Janey knows that she is being observed, she may be more accurate, deliberate, or compliant. However, as observation becomes a part of the daily routine, students' behavior usually returns to what is typical for them. This return to typical patterns of behavior functionally defines desensitization. The data generated from systematic observation should not be used until the students who are observed are no longer affected by the observation procedures and equipment or personnel. However, sometimes the change in behavior is permanent. For example, if a teacher was watching for the extortion of lunch money, Robbie might wait until no observers were present or might demand the money in more subtle ways. In such cases, valid data would not be obtained through overt observation, and either different procedures would have to be developed or the observation would have to be abandoned.
3. *Minimize observer expectancies.* Sometimes, what an observer believes will happen affects what is seen and recorded. For example, if an observer expects an intervention to increase a behavior, that observer might unconsciously alter the criteria for evaluating that behavior or might evaluate approximations of the target behavior as having occurred. The more subtle or complex the target

[4] Technically, general changes in the observation process over time are called instrumentation problems.

behavior, the more susceptible it may be to expectation effects. The easiest way to avoid expectations during observations is for the observer to be blind to the purpose of the assessment. When video- or audiotapes are used to record behavior, the order in which they are evaluated can be randomized so that observers do not know what portion of an observation is being scored. When it is impossible or impractical to keep observers blind to the purpose, the importance of accurate observation should be stressed and such observation rewarded.

4. *Motivate observers.* Inaccurate observation is sometimes attributed to lack of motivation on the part of an observer. Motivation can be increased by providing rewards and feedback, stressing the importance of the observations, reducing the length of observation sessions, and not allowing observation sessions to become routine.

DATA SUMMARIZATION

Depending on the particular characteristic of behavior being measured, observational data may be summarized in different ways. When duration or frequency is the characteristic of interest, observations are usually summarized as rates (that is, the prevalence or the number of occurrences per minute or other time interval). Latency and amplitude should be summarized statistically by the mean and the standard deviation or by the median and the range. All counts and calculations should be checked for accuracy.

4 Criteria for Evaluating Observed Performances

Once accurate observational data have been collected and summarized, they must be interpreted. Behavior is interpreted in one of four ways.

1. A behavior's presence is an absolute criterion. Behaviors evaluated in this way include those that are unsafe, harmful, illegal, and taboo.
2. A behavior can be compared to the behavior of others. This comparison is generally called a normative comparison. Normative data may be available for some behaviors or, in some cases, data from behavior rating scales and tests. Social comparisons can be made using a peer whose behavior is considered appropriate. The peer's rate of behavior is then used as the standard against which to evaluate the target student's rate of behavior.
3. The social tolerance for a behavior can also be used as a criterion. For example, the degree to which different rates of out-of-seat behavior disturb a teacher or peers can be assessed. Teachers and peers could be asked to rate how disturbing the out-of-seat behavior of students who exhibit different rates of behavior is. In a somewhat different vein, the contagion of the behavior to others can be a crucial consideration in teacher judgments of unacceptable behavior. Thus, the effects of different rates of behavior can be assessed to determine whether there is a threshold above which other students initiate undesirable behavior.
4. Progress toward objectives or goals is frequently used as a standard with which to evaluate behavior. A common and useful procedure is graphing data against an aimline. As shown in Figure 6.3, an aimline connects a student's measured behavior at the start of an intervention with the point (called an aim) representing the terminal behavior and the date by which that behavior should be attained. When the goal is to accelerate a desirable behavior (Figure 6.3A), student performances above the aimline are evaluated as good progress. When the goal is to decelerate an undesirable behavior (Figure 6.3B), student performances below the aimline are evaluated as good progress. Good progress is progress that meets or exceeds the desired rate of behavior change.

FIGURE 6.3
Aimlines for Accelerating and Decelerating Behavior

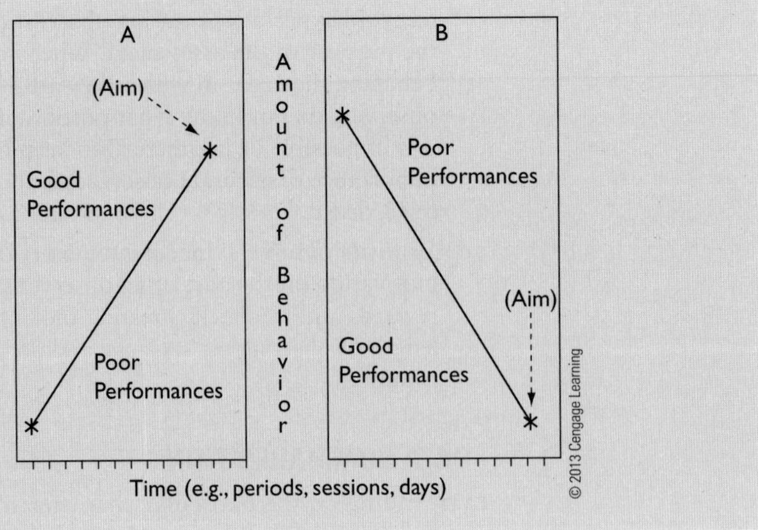

SCENARIO *in* ASSESSMENT

ZACK, PART 2 | Ms. Lawson has previously collected anecdotal information that suggests that Zack has a problem staying on task and in his seat when independent work is required, regardless of the subject matter or time of day. Before conducting systematic observations of Zack's *wanderings*, Ms. Lawson defines precisely what she means by wandering. She defines it as "walking around the classroom during seatwork assignments." She specifically excludes leaving his seat with her permission. She decides to count the frequency of both wandering and compliance during seatwork throughout the day for 4 days—Monday through Thursday. In addition, to have interpretive data, she decides to observe two other boys who she considers generally well behaved but not exceptionally so.

Ms. Lawson decides to record the behavior unobtrusively by using a wrist counter and transferring the frequencies to a chart after the students have left for the day. Fortunately, she has a student teacher who can make simultaneous observations in order to check reliability. However, she must first meet with the student teacher to discuss the definition of wandering and the procedures used to record behavior. Because the target behavior was so easy to observe and the procedures so simple, reliability was not thought to be a major issue. She would like to determine the function of Zack's wandering. The likely functions seemed to be avoidance from an unpleasant task or social attention, but more information would be needed to reach a conclusion.

Each day, Ms. Lawson and her student teacher transferred the frequencies of the number of times Zack and the two comparison boys wandered the room. She calculated simple agreement and transferred her frequencies to the graph shown in Figure 6.4.

The results were as expected. Simple agreement between Ms. Lawson and her student teacher was always 100 percent. The boys who were observed for social comparison seldom wandered, and Zack wandered approximately 20 percent of the time.

What implications about your own professional role can you draw from this scenario? Go to the Education CourseMate website for this textbook for more reflection questions about this Scenario in Assessment.

FIGURE 6.4
Comparison of Zack and Peer Wanderings

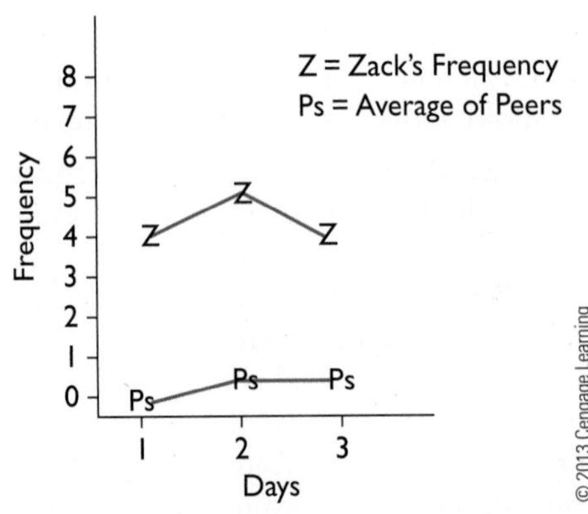

Chapter Comprehension Questions

Write your answers to each of the following questions and then compare your responses to the text.

1. What five steps should you follow in preparing to conduct systematic quantitative observations?
2. What is the difference between a behavior's topography and function?
3. What characteristics of behavior (for example, amplitude) can be observed?
4. Explain the three ways in which behavior can be sampled and identify which is the best way.
5. What can an observer do to minimize or prevent errors in observations?
6. Explain the four ways in which behavior can be interpreted.

Web Activities 

1. Search the Internet for a description of the Behavioral Observation of Students in Schools (**BOSS**) desktop application. How could you use BOSS in a general education classroom?
2. Search the Internet for "observation forms for teachers." Read about two in a curricular area in which you are interested.

Web Resources

North Central Regional Educational Laboratory
http://www.ncrel.org/sdrs/areas/issues/students/earlycld/ea5l141a.htm
This website provides a brief description of narratives, time sampling, and event sampling.

Observing Behavior Using A-B-C Data (Indiana Resource Center for Autism)
http://www.iidc.indiana.edu/?pageId=444
This website provides examples of and explanations for using antecedent-behavior-consequence observations.

Additional resources for this chapter can be found on the Education CourseMate website. Go to CengageBrain.com to access the site.

iStockphoto.com/sjlockesjlocke

Teacher-Made Tests of Achievement

CHAPTER GOALS

1 Understand that teacher-made tests can be used to ascertain skill development, monitor instruction, document instructional problems, and make summative judgments.

2 Understand that teacher-made tests vary on the dimensions of content specificity, testing frequency, and testing formats.

3 Know that considerations in preparing tests include selecting specific areas of the curriculum, writing relevant questions, organizing and sequencing items, developing formats for presentation and response modes, writing directions for administration, developing systematic procedures for scoring responses, and establishing criteria to interpret student performance.

4 Know that response formats use different types of questions and have special considerations for students with disabilities.

5 Understand that assessment in the core achievement areas of reading, mathematics, spelling, and writing differs for beginning and advanced students.

6 Understand the potential sources of difficulty in the use of teacher-made tests.

KEY TERMS

content specificity
frequency
testing formats
selection formats
supply formats
extended responses

Historically, teacher-made tests have not been held in high regard. Adjectives such as "informal" or "unstandardized" have been used to describe teacher-made tests. As a group, however, teacher-made tests cannot be considered informal because they are not given haphazardly or casually. They cannot be considered unstandardized because students usually receive the same materials and directions, and the same criteria are usually used in correcting student answers. Although there is a place for commercially available norm-referenced achievement tests, we think that their value has been overestimated. Indeed, teacher-made tests can be better suited to evaluation of student achievement than are commercially prepared, norm-referenced achievement tests.

Achievement refers to what has been directly taught and learned by a student. It is different from attainment (what has been learned anywhere). Teachers are in the best position to know what has been (or at least should be) taught in their classrooms. This simple fact stands in sharp contrast to commercially prepared tests that are not designed to assess achievement within specific curricula (see, for example, Crocker, Miller, & Franks, 1989) or to meet a specific state's standards. Rather, these tests are usually constructed to have general applicability so that they can be used with students in almost any curriculum or broad state standards. Moreover, it is clear that various curriculum series differ from one another in the particular educational objectives covered, the performance level expected of students, and the sequence of objectives; for example, DISTAR mathematics differs from Scott, Foresman mathematics (Shriner & Salvia, 1988). Even within the same curriculum series, teachers modify instruction to provide enrichment or remedial instruction. Thus, two teachers using the same curriculum series and trying to meet the same state standards may provide different instruction. Although teachers may not construct tests that match the curriculum and state standards, they are the only ones capable of knowing precisely what has been taught and what level of performance is expected from students. Consequently, they are the only ones who can match testing to instruction.

In addition, teacher-made tests are usually designed to assess what students are learning or have learned. Commercially prepared, norm-referenced tests are designed to assess which students know more and which students know less (that is, to discriminate among test takers on the basis of what they know). Thus, teachers include enough items on their tests to make valid estimates of what students have learned, whereas developers of norm-referenced tests try to include the minimum number of test items that allow reliable discrimination. This difference between teacher-made and commercially prepared tests has two important consequences. First, because teacher-made tests can include many more items (even all of the items of interest), they can be much more sensitive to small but important changes in student learning. For example, a teacher-made test that included all of the addition facts could show whether a student has learned single-digit addition facts with the number 9 in the past 2 days; norm-referenced tests usually assess all of the mathematical operations and necessarily have only a few addition problems so that this level of specificity is not possible to attain with them. Also, teacher-made tests can show what content requires additional instruction and student practice; norm-referenced tests cannot. Finally, teacher-made tests can indicate when students have mastered an instructional goal so instruction can be provided on new objectives; norm-referenced tests cannot.

In short, teachers need tests that reflect what they are teaching and are sensitive to changes in student achievement.[1] We strongly recommend that the assessments be objective—that is, based on observable phenomena and minimally affected by a variety of subjective factors. The use of objective methods is not merely a matter of personal preference. Federal regulations require that students with disabilities be

[1] Teachers assess frequently to detect changes in student achievement. However, frequent testing with exactly the same test usually produces a practice effect. Unless there are multiple forms for a test, student learning may be confused with practice effect.

evaluated using objective procedures.[2] This chapter provides a general overview of objective practices for teachers who develop their own tests for classroom assessment in the core areas of reading, mathematics, spelling, and written language.

1 Uses

Teachers regularly set aside time to assess their pupils for a variety of purposes. Most commonly, they make up tests to ascertain the extent to which their students have learned or are learning what has been taught or assigned. Student achievement is the basis on which teachers make decisions about student skill development, student progress and instructional problems, and grades. Often, an assessment can be used for more than one purpose. For example, assessments made to monitor instruction can be aggregated for use in making summative judgments.

A student's level of skill development is a fundamental consideration in planning instruction. We want to know what instructional objectives our students have met in order to decide what things we should be teaching our students. Obviously, if students have met an instructional objective, we should not waste their time by continuing to teach what they have already learned. Rather, we should build on their learning by extending their learning (for example, planning for generalization of learning) or moving on to the next objective in the instructional sequence. In addition, students who meet objectives so rapidly that they are being held back by slower peers can be grouped for enrichment activities or faster-paced instruction; slower students can be grouped so that they can learn necessary concepts to the point of mastery without impeding the progress of their faster-learning peers.

Another important use of classroom tests is to monitor instruction. Students are expected to progress through the curriculum at an acceptable pace. When students fail to learn or learn at an unacceptably slow rate, it is necessary to modify instruction. (See Chapter 24, Assessment in Multi-Tiered Systems of Support and Response to Intervention, for an extensive discussion of monitoring students' response to instruction.)

Finally, classroom assessments are used to make summary judgments about student attainment and teacher effectiveness. General student attainment is generally synonymous with the grade assigned to that student for a particular marking period. How grades are determined varies considerably from school district to school district. In some districts, there are districtwide policies that define each grade (for example, to earn an A, students must average 92 percent or more on all tests). Clearly, student grades should be based on what was taught and learned; the basis of a student's grade should be carefully explained at the beginning of the year (or marking period) so that all students know how they will be graded. We also recommend that grades be as objective as possible so that they avoid any hint of bias or favoritism.

Judgments about teaching effectiveness should be made on the basis of student achievement. When many students in a classroom fail to learn material, teachers should suspect that something is wrong with their instruction. Failure to modify instruction so that students succeed is unacceptable, and in the case of students with special needs, illegal.

2 Dimensions of Academic Assessment

Assessments differ along several dimensions: content specificity, frequency, and response quantification. Different purposes can require different degrees of specificity, different frequency, and different formats.

[2] Note that general educators are often trained in more subjective and holistic approaches, and the difference in approaches can cause many problems when general and special educators work together to provide an education for all students in an inclusive classroom.

CONTENT SPECIFICITY

By *content*, we mean simply the domain within which the testing will occur. When we think of teacher-made tests, we generally think of academic domains such as reading, arithmetic, spelling, and so forth. However, the domain to be tested can include supplementary curricula (for example, study skills).

By *specificity*, we mean the parts of the domain to be assessed. Any domain can be divided and subdivided into smaller and more precise chunks of content. For example, in reading we are unlikely to want to assess every possible thing within the domain of reading. Therefore, we would break down reading into the part or chunk in which we were interested in assessing: beginning reading, one-syllable words, one-syllable words with short vowel sounds, one-syllable words with short a, consonant-short a-consonant words, consonant-short a-specific consonants (–t, –n, and –r), and so forth.

The specificity of an assessment depends on the purpose of the assessment. Especially at the beginning of a school year or when a new student joins a class, educators want to know a student's level of skill development—what the student knows and does not know—in order to plan instruction. In this case, an appropriate assessment will begin with a broad sample of content to provide an estimate of student knowledge of the various topics that have been and will be covered. Areas in which a student lacks information or skills will be assessed with more precise procedures to identify the exact areas of deficiency so that appropriate remedial instruction can be provided.

When teachers assess to monitor instruction and document problems, their assessments are very specific. They should assess what they teach to ascertain if students have learned what was taught. If students are learning word families (for example, "bat," "cat," "fat," and "hat"), they should be tested on their proficiency with the word families they have been taught.

TESTING FREQUENCY

The time students have in school is finite, and time spent on testing is time not spent on other important activities. Therefore, the frequency of testing and the duration of tests must be balanced against the other demands on student and teacher time.

Most teacher-made tests are used to monitor instruction and assign grades. Although the frequency of assessment varies widely in practice, the research evidence is clear that more frequent assessments (two or more times a week) are associated with better learning than are less frequent assessments. When students are having difficulty learning or retaining content, teachers should measure performance and progress more frequently. Frequent measurement can provide immediate feedback about how students are doing and pinpoint the skills missing among students.[3] The more frequent the measurement, the quicker you can adapt instruction to ensure that students are making optimal progress. However, frequent measurement is only helpful when it can immediately direct teachers as to what to teach next or how to teach next. To the extent that teachers can use data efficiently, frequent assessment is valuable; if it consists simply of frequent measurement with no application, then it is not valuable. Student deficits in skill level and progress may dictate how frequently measurement should occur: Students with substantial deficits are monitored more frequently to ensure that instructional methods are effective. Those who want to know more about how expected rate is set or about the specific procedures used to monitor student progress are referred to Hintze, Christ, and Methe (2005), Hosp and Hosp (2003), or Shinn (1989).

[3] Many of the new measurement systems, such as those employing technology-enhanced assessments, call for continuous measurement of pupil performance and progress. They provide students with immediate feedback on how they are doing, give teachers daily status reports indicating the relative standing of all students in a class, and identify areas of skill deficits.

Broader assessments used for grading are given at the end of units or marking periods and cover considerable content. Thus, they must either be very general or be a limited sample of more specific content. In either case, the results of such assessments do not provide sufficiently detailed information about what a student knows and does not know for teachers to plan remediation.

TESTING FORMATS

When a teacher wants either to compare (1) the performance of several students on a skill or set of skills or (2) one pupil's performances on several occasions over time, the assessments must be the same. Standardization is the process of using the same materials, procedures (for example, directions and time allowed to complete a test), and scoring standards for each test taker each time the test is given. Without standardization, observed differences could be reasonably attributed to differences in testing procedures. Almost any test can be standardized if it results in observable behavior or a permanent product (for example, a student's written response).

The first step in creating a test is knowing what knowledge and skills students have been taught and how they have been taught. Thus, teachers will need to know the objectives, standards, or outcomes that they expect students to work toward mastering, and they will need to specify the level of performance that is acceptable.

Test formats can be classified along two dimensions: (1) the modality through which the item is presented—test items usually require a student to look at or to listen to the question, although other modalities may be substituted, depending on the particulars of a situation or on characteristics of students—and (2) the modality through which a student responds—test items usually require an oral or written response, although pointing responses are frequently used with students who are nonverbal. Teachers may use "see–write," "see–say," "hear–write," and "hear–say" to specify the testing modality dimensions.

In addition, "write" formats can be of two types. *Selection formats* require students to indicate their choice from an array of possible answers (usually termed response options). True–false, multiple-choice, and matching are the three common selection formats. However, they are not the only ones possible; for example, students may be required to circle incorrectly spelled words or words that should be capitalized in text. Formats requiring students to select the correct answer can be used to assess much more than the recognition of information, although they are certainly useful for that purpose. They can also be used to assess students' understanding, their ability to draw inferences, and their correct application of principles. Select questions are not usually well suited for assessing achievement at the levels of analysis, synthesis, and evaluation.

Supply formats require a student to produce a written or an oral response. This response can be as restricted as the answer to a computation problem or a one-word response to the question, "When did the potato famine begin in Ireland?" Often, the response to supply questions is more involved and can require a student to produce a sentence, a paragraph, or several pages.

As a general rule, supply questions can be prepared fairly quickly, but scoring them may be very time-consuming. Even when one-word responses or numbers are requested, teachers may have difficulty finding the response on a student's test paper, deciphering the handwriting, or correctly applying criteria for awarding points. In contrast, selection formats usually require a considerable amount of time to prepare, but once prepared, the tests can be scored quickly and by almost anyone.

The particular formats teachers choose are influenced by the purposes for testing and the characteristics of the test takers. Testing formats are essentially bottom up or top down. Bottom-up formats assess the mastery of specific objectives to allow generalizations about student competence in a particular domain. Top-down formats survey general competence in a domain and assess in greater depth those topics for which mastery is incomplete. For day-to-day monitoring of instruction and selecting short-term instructional objectives, we favor bottom-up assessment.

With this type of assessment, a teacher can be relatively sure that specific objectives have been mastered and that he or she is not spending needless instructional time teaching students what they already know. For determining starting places for instruction with new students and for assessing maintenance and generalization of previously learned material, we favor top-down assessment. Generally, this approach should be more efficient in terms of teachers' and students' time because broader survey tests can cover a lot of material in a short period of time.

For students who are able to read and write independently, see–write formats are generally more efficient for both individual students and groups. When testing individual students, teachers or teacher aides can give the testing materials to the students and can proceed with other activities while the students are completing the test. Moreover, when students write their responses, a teacher can defer correcting the examinations until a convenient time.

See–say formats are also useful. Teacher aides or other students can listen to the test takers' responses and can correct them on the spot or record them for later evaluation. Moreover, many teachers have access to electronic equipment that can greatly facilitate the use of see–say formats (for example, audio or video recorders).

The hear–write format is especially useful with selection formats for younger students and students who cannot read independently. This format can also be used for testing groups of students and is routinely used in the assessment of spelling when students are required to write words from dictation. With other content, teachers can give directions and read the test questions aloud, and students can mark their responses. The primary difficulty with a hear–write format with groups of students is the pacing of test items; teachers must allot sufficient time between items for slower-responding students to make their selections.

Hear–say formats are most suitable for assessing individual students who do not write independently or who write at such slow speeds that their written responses are unrepresentative of what they know. Even with this format, teachers need not preside over the assessment; other students or a teacher aide can administer, record, and perhaps evaluate the student's responses.

3 Considerations in Preparing Tests

Teachers need to build skills in developing tests that are fair, reliable, and valid. The following kinds of considerations are important in developing or preparing tests.

SELECTING SPECIFIC AREAS OF THE CURRICULUM

Tests are samples of behavior. When narrow skills are being assessed (for example, spelling words from dictation), either all the components of the domain should be tested (in this case, all the assigned spelling words) or a representative sample should be selected and assessed. The qualifier "representative" implies that an appropriate number of easy and difficult words—and of words from the beginning, middle, and end of the assignment—will be selected. When more complex domains are assessed, teachers should concentrate on the more important facts or relationships and avoid the trivial.

WRITING RELEVANT QUESTIONS

Teachers must select and use enough questions to allow valid inferences about students' mastery of short-term or long-term goals, and attainment of state standards. Nothing offends test takers quite as much as a test's failure to cover material they have studied and know, except perhaps their own failure to guess what content a teacher believes to be important enough to test. In addition, fairness demands that the way in which the question is asked be familiar and expected by the student. For example, if students were to take a test on the addition of single-digit integers, it would be a bad idea to test them using a missing-addend format (for example, "4 + ___ = 7") unless that format had been specifically taught and was expected by the students.

ORGANIZING AND SEQUENCING ITEMS

The organization of a test is a function of many factors. When a teacher wants a student to complete all the items and to indicate mastery of content (a power test), it is best to intersperse easy and difficult items. When the desire is to measure automaticity or the number of items that can be completed within a specific time period (a timed test), it is best to organize items from easy to difficult. Pages of test questions or problems to be solved should not be cluttered.

DEVELOPING FORMATS FOR PRESENTATION AND RESPONSE MODES

Different response formats can be used within the same test, although it is generally a good idea to group together questions with the same format. Regardless of the format used, the primary consideration is that the test questions be a fair sample of the material being assessed.

WRITING DIRECTIONS FOR ADMINISTRATION

Regardless of question format, the directions should indicate clearly what a student is to do—for example, "Circle the correct option," "Choose the best answer," and "Match each item in column b to one item in column a." Also, teachers should explain what, if any, materials may be used by students, any time limits, any unusual scoring procedures (for example, penalties for guessing), and point values when the students are mature enough to be given questions that have different point values.

DEVELOPING SYSTEMATIC PROCEDURES FOR SCORING RESPONSES

As discussed in the opening paragraphs of this chapter, teachers must have predetermined and systematic criteria for scoring responses. However, if a teacher discovers an error or omission in criteria, the criteria should be modified. Obviously, previously scored responses must be rescored with the revised criteria.

ESTABLISHING CRITERIA TO INTERPRET STUDENT PERFORMANCE

Teachers should specify in advance the criteria they will use for assigning grades or weighting assignments. For example, they may want to specify that students who earn a certain number of points on a test will earn a specific grade, or they may want to assign grades on the basis of the class distribution of performance. In either case, they must specify what it takes to earn certain grades or how assignments will be evaluated and weighted.

4 Response Formats

There are two basic types of test format. Selection formats require students to recognize a correct answer that is provided on the test. Supply formats require students to produce correct answers.

SELECTION FORMATS

Three types of selection formats are commonly used: multiple-choice, matching, and true–false. Of the three, multiple-choice questions are clearly the most useful.

Multiple-Choice Questions

Multiple-choice questions are the most difficult to prepare. These questions have two parts: (1) a *stem* that contains the question and (2) a response set that contains both the correct answer, termed the *keyed response*, and one or more incorrect options, termed *distractors*. In preparing multiple-choice questions, teachers should generally follow these guidelines:

- Keep the response options short and of approximately equal length. Students quickly learn that longer options tend to be correct.
- Keep material that is common to all options in the stem. For example, if the first word in each option is "the," it should be put into the stem and removed from the options.

  Improving a poorly worded question:
  A lasting contribution of the Eisenhower presidency was the creation of (the)

  a. ~~the~~ communication satellite system

  b. ~~the~~ interstate highway system

  c. ~~the~~ cable TV infrastructure

  d. ~~the~~ Eisenhower tank

- Avoid grammatical tip-offs. Students can discard grammatically incorrect options. For example, when the correct answer must be plural, alert students will disregard singular options; when the correct answer must be a noun, students will disregard options that are verbs.

  A poorly constructed question:
  An ___ test measures what a student has learned that has been taught in school.

  a. achievement

  b. intelligence

  c. social

  d. portfolio

  A better constructed question:
  ___ tests measure what a student has learned that has been taught in school.

  a. Achievement

  b. Intelligence

  c. Social

  d. Portfolio

- Avoid implausible options. In the best questions, distractors should be attractive to students who do not know the answer. Common errors and misconceptions are often good distractors.

  A poorly constructed question:
  Which of the following persons was NOT a candidate of the Republican Party for president of the United States in the 2008 primaries?

  a. Bart Simpson

  b. Mitt Romney

  c. Mike Huckabee

  d. Rudy Giuliani

  A better constructed question:
  Which of the following persons was NOT a candidate of the Republican Party for president of the United States in the 2008 primaries?

  a. John Edwards

  b. Mitt Romney

  c. Mike Huckabee

  d. Rudy Giuliani

- Make sure that one and only one option is correct. Students should not have to read their teacher's mind to guess which wrong answer is the least wrong or which right answer is the most correct.

A poorly constructed question:
Which of the following persons was NOT a candidate of the Republican Party for president of the United States in the 2008 primaries?

a. John Edwards
b. Mitt Romney
c. Mike Huckabee
d. Joseph Biden

A better constructed question:
Which of the following persons was NOT a candidate of the Republican Party for president of the United States in the 2008 primaries?

a. John Edwards
b. Mitt Romney
c. Mike Huckabee
d. Rudy Giuliani

- Avoid interdependent questions. Generally, it is bad practice to make the selection of the correct option dependent on getting a prior question correct.

An early question:
Which of the following persons was a candidate of the Democrat Party for president of the United States in the 2008 primaries?

a. Tom Tancredo
b. Mitt Romney
c. Mike Huckabee
d. Joseph Biden

A subsequent dependent question:
The candidate in the preceding question was or is a

a. governor
b. member of the U.S. House of Representatives
c. U.S. senator
d. U.S. ambassador to Russia

- Avoid options that indicate multiple correct options (for example, "all the above" or "both a and b are correct"). These options often simplify the question.

A poorly constructed question:
Which of the following persons was a candidate of the Democrat Party for president of the United States in the 2008 primaries?

a. John Edwards
b. Mitt Romney
c. Ron Paul
d. both b and c are correct

A better constructed question:
Which of the following persons was a candidate of the Democrat Party for president of the United States in the 2008 primaries?

a. John Edwards
b. Mitt Romney
c. Ron Paul
d. Rudy Giuliani

- Avoid similar incorrect options. Students who can eliminate one of the two similar options can readily dismiss the other one. For example, if citrus fruit is wrong, lemon must be wrong.

A poorly constructed question:
Eisenhower's inspiration for the interstate highway system was the

a. American turnpikes
b. modern German autobahns
c. Pennsylvania Turnpike
d. Alcan Highway

A better constructed question:
Eisenhower's inspiration for the interstate highway system was the

a. ancient Roman highways
b. modern German autobahns
c. Pennsylvania Turnpike
d. Alcan Highway

- Make sure that one question does not provide information that can be used to answer another question.

An early question:
A lasting contribution of the Eisenhower presidency was the creation of

a. the communication satellite system
b. the interstate highway system
c. the cable TV infrastructure
d. the Eisenhower tank

A later question that answers a prior question:
Eisenhower's inspiration for the interstate highway system was the

a. ancient Roman highways
b. modern German autobahns
c. Pennsylvania Turnpike
d. Alcan Highway

- Avoid using the same words and examples that were used in the students' texts or in class presentations.
- Vary the position of the correct response in the options. Students will recognize patterns of correct options (for example, when the correct answers to a sequence of questions are a, b, c, d, a, b, c, d) or a teacher's preference for a specific position (usually c).

When appropriate, teachers can make multiple-choice questions more challenging by asking students to recognize an instance of a rule or concept, by requiring students to recall and use material that is not present in the question, or by increasing the number of options. (For younger children, three options are generally difficult enough. Older students can be expected to answer questions with four or five options.) In no case should teachers deliberately mislead or trick students.

Matching Questions

Matching questions are a variant of multiple-choice questions in which a set of stems is simultaneously associated with a set of options. Generally, the content of matching questions is limited to simple factual associations (Gronlund, 2009). Teachers usually prepare matching questions so that there are as many options as stems, and an option can be associated only once with a stem in the set. Although we do not recommend their use, there are other possibilities: more options than stems, selection of all correct options for one stem, and multiple use of an option.[4] These additional possibilities increase the difficulty of the question set considerably.

[4] Scoring for these options is complicated. Generally, separate errors are counted for selecting an incorrect option and failing to select a correct option. Thus, the number of errors can be very large.

In general, we prefer multiple-choice questions to matching questions. Almost any matching question can be written as a series of multiple-choice questions in which the same or similar options are used. Of course, the correct response will change. However, teachers wishing to use matching questions should consider the following guidelines:

- Each set of matching items should have some dimension in common (for example, explorers and dates of discovery). This makes preparation easier for the teacher and provides the student with some insight into the relationship required to select the correct option.
- Keep the length of the stems approximately the same, and keep the length and grammar used in the options equivalent. At best, mixing grammatical forms will eliminate some options for some questions; at worst, it will provide the correct answer to several questions.
- Make sure that one and only one option is correct for each stem.
- Vary the sequence of correct responses when more than one matching question is asked.
- Avoid using the same words and examples that were used in the students' texts or in class presentations.

It is easier for a student when questions and options are presented in two columns. When there is a difference in the length of the items in each column, the longer item should be used as the stem. Stems should be placed on the left and options on the right, rather than stems above with options below them. Moreover, all the elements of the question should be kept on one page. Finally, teachers often allow students to draw lines to connect questions and options. Although this has the obvious advantage of helping students keep track of where their answers should be placed, erasures or scratch-outs can be a headache to the person who corrects the test. A commercially available product (Learning Wrap-Ups) has cards printed with stems and answers and a shoelace with which to "lace" stems to correct answers. The correct lacing pattern is printed on the back, so it is self-correcting. Teachers could make such cards fairly easily as an alternative to trying to correct tests with lots of erasures.

True–False Statements

In most cases, true–false statements should simply not be used. Their utility lies primarily in assessing knowledge of factual information, which can be better assessed with other formats. Effective true–false items are difficult to prepare. Because guessing the correct answer is likely—it happens 50 percent of the time—the reliability of true–false tests is generally low. As a result, they may well have limited validity. Nonetheless, if a teacher chooses to use this format, a few suggestions should be followed:

- Avoid specific determiners such as "all," "never," "always," and so on.
- Avoid sweeping generalizations. Such statements tend to be true, but students can often think of minor exceptions. Thus, there is a problem in the criterion for evaluating the truthfulness of the question. Attempts to avoid the problem by adding restrictive conditions (for example, "with minor exceptions") either render the question obviously true or leave a student trying to guess what the restrictive condition means.
- Avoid convoluted sentences. Tests should assess knowledge of content, not a student's ability to comprehend difficult prose.
- Keep true and false statements approximately the same length. As is the case with longer options on multiple-choice questions, longer true–false statements tend to be true.
- Balance the number of true and false statements. If a student recognizes that there is more of one type of statement than of the other, the odds of guessing the correct answer will exceed 50 percent.

SPECIAL CONSIDERATIONS FOR STUDENTS WITH DISABILITIES

In developing and using items that employ a selection format, teachers must pay attention to individual differences among students, particularly to disabilities that might interfere with performance. The individualized educational programs (IEPs) of students with disabilities often contain needed accommodations and adaptations. Prior to testing, it is always a good idea to double-check students' IEPs to make sure that any required accommodations and adaptations have been made. For example, students who have skill deficits in remembering things for short periods of time, or who do not attend well to verbally or visually presented information, may need multiple-choice tests with fewer distractors. Students who have difficulty with the organization of visually presented material may need to have matching questions rewritten as multiple-choice questions. Remember, it is important to assess the skills that students have, not the effects of disability conditions.

SCENARIO *in* ASSESSMENT

BARRY | Ms. Johnson is a special education teacher in a middle school. One of her students, Barry, has an IEP that requires adapted content area tests. Mr. Blumfield, the social studies teacher, sends Ms. Johnson a test that he will be giving in 8 days so that she can adapt it. The test contains both multiple-choice (five options) and true–false tests. Mr. Blumfield plans to allow students the entire period (37 minutes) to complete their tests.

Ms. Johnson has several concerns about the test. In her experience with Barry, she has found that he requires untimed and shorter tests, and that some questions must be read to him. In addition, when supply tests are used, he requires a couple of modifications. He cannot understand true–false questions, and he has unusual difficulty when there are more than three options on multiple-choice questions. Therefore, she schedules a meeting with Mr. Blumfield to discuss her adaptation of his test.

Mr. Blumfield has 127 students, and 8 of these students have IEPs. Ms. Johnson begins the meeting by reminding him that Barry's IEP provides for the adaptation of content area tests. She also tells Mr. Blumfield that she is willing to make the adaptations but will need some guidance from him. The first thing she wants to learn is what the important content is—the questions assessing the major ideas and important facts that Mr. Blumfield has stressed in his lessons. She also wants to learn which questions can be deleted.

Then Ms. Johnson explains how she will adapt the test:

- She will modify the content by deleting relatively unimportant ideas and concepts; she will retain all of the major ideas and important concepts.
- She will replace true–false questions that assess major ideas with multiple-choice questions that get at the same information.
- She will reduce the number of distractors in multiple-choice questions from five to three.
- She will reorder test items by grouping questions about related content together and ordering questions from easy to difficult whenever possible.

She also explains that she will read to Barry any part of the test that he requests, and that the test will not be timed, so he may not finish in one period. Finally, she offers to score the test for Mr. Blumfield.

Barry earns a B+ on the adapted teacher-made test.

What implications about your own professional role can you draw from this scenario? Go to the Education CourseMate website for this textbook for more reflection questions about this Scenario in Assessment.

SUPPLY FORMATS

It is useful to distinguish between items requiring a student to write one- or two-word responses (such as fill-in questions) and those requiring more extended responses (such as essay questions). Both types of items require careful delineation of what constitutes a correct response (that is, criteria for scoring). It is generally best for teachers to prepare criteria for a correct response at the time they prepare the question. In that way, they can ensure that the question is written in such a way as to elicit the correct types of answers—or at least not to mislead students—and perhaps save time when correcting exams. (If teachers change criteria for a correct response after they have scored a few questions, they should rescore all previously scored questions with the revised criteria.)

Fill-In Questions

Aside from mathematics problems that require students to calculate an answer and writing spelling words from dictation, fill-in questions require a student to complete a statement by adding a concept or fact—for example, "___ arrived in America in

1492." Fill-ins are useful in assessing knowledge and comprehension objectives; they are not useful in assessing application, analysis, synthesis, or evaluation objectives. Teachers preparing fill-in questions should follow these guidelines:

- Keep each sentence short. Generally, the less superfluous information in an item, the clearer the question will be to the student and the less likely it will be that one question will cue another.
- If a two-word answer is required, teachers should use two blanks to indicate this in the sentence.
- Avoid sentences with multiple blanks. For example, the item "In the year ___, ___ discovered ___" is so vague that practically any date, name, and event can be inserted correctly, even ones that are irrelevant to the content; for example, "In the year 2010, Henry discovered girls."
- Keep the size of all blanks consistent and large enough to accommodate readily the longest answer. The size of the blank should not provide a clue about the length of the correct word.

The most problematic aspect of fill-in questions is the necessity of developing an appropriate response bank of acceptable answers. Often, some student errors may consist of a partially correct response; teachers must decide which answers will receive partial credit, full credit, and no credit. For example, a question may anticipate "Columbus" as the correct response, but a student might write "that Italian dude who was looking for the shortcut to India for the Spanish king and queen." In deciding how far afield to go in crediting unanticipated responses, teachers should look over test questions carefully to determine whether the student's answer comes from information presented in another question (for example, "The Spanish monarch employed an Italian sailor to find a shorter route to").

Extended Responses

Essay questions are most useful in assessing comprehension, application, analysis, synthesis, and evaluation objectives. There are two major problems associated with extended response questions. First, teachers are generally able to sample only a limited amount of information because answers may take a long time for students to write. Second, extended-essay responses are the most difficult type of answer to score. To avoid subjectivity and inconsistency, teachers should use a scoring key that assigns specific point values for each element in the ideal or criterion answer. In most cases, spelling and grammatical errors should not be deducted from the point total. Moreover, bonus points should not be awarded for particularly detailed responses; many good students will provide a complete answer to one question and spend any extra time working on questions that are more difficult for them.

Finally, teachers should be prepared to deal with responses in which a student tries to bluff a correct answer. Rather than leave a question unanswered, some students may answer a related question that was not asked, or they may structure their response so that they can omit important information that they cannot remember or never knew. Sometimes, they will even write a poem or a treatise on why the question asked is unimportant or irrelevant. Therefore, teachers must be very specific about how they will award points, stick to their criteria unless they discover that something is wrong with them, and not give credit to creative bluffs.

Teachers should also be very precise in the directions that they give so that students will not have to guess what responses their teachers will credit. Following are a number of verbs (and their meanings) that are commonly used in essay questions. It is often worthwhile to explain these terms in the test directions to make sure that students know what kind of answer is desired.

- *Describe*, *define*, and *identify* mean to give the meaning, essential characteristics, or place within a taxonomy.
- *List* means to enumerate and implies that complete sentences and paragraphs are not required unless specifically requested.

- *Discuss* requires more than a description, definition, or identification; a student is expected to draw implications and elucidate relationships.
- *Explain* means to analyze and make clear or comprehensible a concept, event, principle, relationship, and so forth; thus, *explain* requires going beyond a definition to describe the hows or whys.
- *Compare* means to identify and explain similarities between two or among more things.
- *Contrast* means to identify and explain differences between two or among more things.
- *Evaluate* means to give the value of something and implies an enumeration and explanation of assets and liabilities, pros and cons.

Finally, unless students know the questions in advance, teachers should allow students sufficient time for planning and rereading answers. For example, if teachers believe that 10 minutes is necessary to write an extended essay to answer a question that requires original thinking, they might allow 20 minutes for the question. The less fluent the students are, the greater is the proportion of time that should be allotted.

5 Assessment in Core Achievement Areas

The assessment procedures used by teachers are a function of the content being taught, the criterion to which content is to be learned (such as 90 percent mastery), and the characteristics of the students. With primary-level curricula in core areas, teachers usually want more than knowledge from their students; they want the material learned so well that correct responses are automatic. For example, teachers do not want their students to think about forming the letter "a," sounding out the word "the," or using number lines to solve simple addition problems such as "3 + 5 = "; they want their students to respond immediately and correctly. Even for intermediate-level materials, teachers seek highly proficient responding from their students, whether that performance involves performing two-digit multiplication, reading short stories, writing short stories, or writing spelling words from dictation. However, teachers in all grades, but especially in secondary schools, are also interested in their students' understanding of vast amounts of information about their social, cultural, and physical worlds, as well as their acquisition and application of critical thinking skills. The assessment of skills taught to high degrees of proficiency is quite different from the assessment of understanding and critical thinking skills.

In the following sections, core achievement areas are discussed in terms of three important attributes: the skills and information to be learned within the major strands of most curricula, the assessment of skills to be learned to proficiency, and the assessment of understanding of information and concepts. Critical thinking skills are usually embedded within content areas and are assessed in the same ways as understanding of information is assessed—with written multiple-choice and extended-essay questions.

READING

Reading is usually divided into decoding skills and comprehension. The specific behaviors included in each of these subdomains will depend on the particular curriculum and its sequencing.

Beginning Skills

Beginning decoding relies on students' ability to analyze and manipulate sounds and syllables in words (Stanovich, 2000). Instruction in beginning reading can include letter recognition, letter–sound correspondences, sight vocabulary, phonics, and, in some curricula, morphology. Automaticity is the goal for the skills to be learned. See–say (for example, "What letter is this?") and hear–say (for example, "What sound does the letter make?") formats are regularly used for both instruction and assessment. During students' acquisition of specific skills, teachers should first stress the accuracy of student responses. Generally, this concern translates into allowing a moment or two for students to think about their responses. A generally accepted criterion for completion for early learning is 90 to 95 percent correct. As soon as accuracy has been attained (and sometimes before), teachers change their criteria from accurate responses to fast and accurate responses. For see–say formats, fluent students will need no thinking time for simple material; for example, they should be able to respond as rapidly as teachers can change stimuli to questions such as "What is this letter?" Once students accurately decode letters and letter combinations fluently, the emphasis shifts to fluency or the automatic retrieval of words. Fluency is a combination of speed and accuracy and is widely viewed as a fundamental prerequisite for reading comprehension (National Institute of Child Health and Human Development, 2000a, 2000b).

For beginners, reading comprehension is usually assessed in one of three ways: by assessing students' retelling, their responses to comprehension questions, or their rate of oral reading. The most direct method is to have students retell what they have read without access to the reading passage. Retold passages may be scored on the basis of the number of words recalled. Fuchs, Fuchs, and Maxwell (1988) have offered two relatively simple scoring procedures that appear to offer valid indications of comprehension. Retelling may be conducted orally or in writing. With students who have relatively undeveloped writing skills, retelling should be oral when it is used to assess comprehension, but it may be in writing as a practice or drill activity. Teachers can listen to students retell, or students can retell using tape recorders so that their efforts can be evaluated later.

A second common method of assessing comprehension is to ask students questions about what they have read. Questions should address main ideas, important relationships, and relevant details. Questions may be in supply or selection formats, and either hear–say or see–write formats can be used conveniently. As with retelling, teachers should concentrate their efforts on the gist of the passage.

A third convenient, although indirect, method of assessing reading comprehension is to assess the rate of oral reading. One of the earliest attempts to explain the relationship between rate of oral reading and comprehension was offered by LaBerge and Samuels (1974), who noted that poor decoding skills created a bottleneck that impeded the flow of information, thus impeding comprehension. The relationship makes theoretical sense: Slow readers must expend their energy decoding words (for example, attending to letters, remembering letter–sound associations, blending sounds, or searching for context cues) rather than concentrating on the meaning of what is written. Not only is the relationship between reading fluency and comprehension logical but also empirical research supports this relationship (Freeland, Skinner, Jackson, McDaniel, & Smith, 2000; National Institute of Child Health and Human Development, 2000a, 2000b; Sindelar, Monda, & O'Shea, 1990).

Therefore, teachers probably should concentrate on the rate of oral reading regularly with beginning readers. To assess reading rate, teachers should have students read for 2 minutes from appropriate materials. The reading passage should include familiar vocabulary, syntax, and content; the passage must be longer than the amount any student can read in the 2-minute period. Teachers have their own copy of the passage on which to note errors. The number of words read correctly and the number of errors made in 2 minutes are each divided by 2 to calculate the rate per minute. Mercer and Mercer (1985) suggest a rate of 80 words per minute (with two or fewer errors) as a desirable goal for reading words from lists and a rate of 100 words per minute (with two or fewer errors) for words in text. (See also, Read Naturally, Inc., 2010; National Assessment of Educational Progress, Oral Reading Rate, 2002). See Chapter 12 for a more complete discussion of errors in oral reading.

SCENARIO *in* ASSESSMENT

ROBERT | Robert has learned the basic alphabetic principles—letter sound associations, sound blending, and basic phonic rules. However, his reading fluency is very slow. This lack of fluency makes comprehension difficult and causes problems for him in completing his work in the times allotted. His IEP contains an annual goal of increasing his fluency to 100 words per minute with two or fewer errors in material written at his grade level. Mr. Williams, his special education teacher, has developed a program that relies on repeated readings. He recently read an article by Therrien (2004) that indicates the important aspects of repeated reading to follow in his program. He decides to check fluency daily using brief probes.

After Mr. Williams has determined the highest level reading materials that Robert can read with 95 percent accuracy, he prepares a series of 200-word passages at that level and one-third higher levels up to Robert's actual grade placement. Each passage forms a logical unit and begins with a new paragraph. The vocabulary is representative of Robert's reading level, and passage comprehension does not rely on preceding material that he has not read. He prepares two copies of each passage and places each in an acetate cover. (This allows him to indicate errors directly on the passage and then to wipe both copies clean after testing for reuse at another time.)

Mr. Williams then prepares instructions for Robert: "I want to see how fast you can read material the first time and a second or third time. I want you to read as fast as you can without making errors. If you don't know a word, just skip it. I'll tell you the word when you are done. Then I'll ask you to reread the passage. When I say start, you begin reading. After 1 minute, I'll say stop and you stop reading. Do you have any questions?"

Mr. Williams gives Robert two practice readings that he does not score. This gives Robert some experience with the process. He then begins giving Robert daily probes; he enters Robert's rate on the first reading and connects the data points for the same passage on different days. When Robert can read three consecutive probes at the target rate the first time, Mr. Williams increases the reading level of the material (for example, days 13, 14, and 15). The intervention will end when Robert is reading grade-level materials fluently—the third level above where the intervention has started.

As shown in Figure 7.1, Robert makes steady progress, both within reading levels and between reading levels. Mr. Williams is pleased with the intervention and will continue with it until it is no longer working or when Robert achieves the goal.

What implications about your own professional role can you draw from this scenario? Go to the Education CourseMate website for this textbook for more reflection questions about this Scenario in Assessment.

FIGURE 7.1
Robert's Progress in Reading

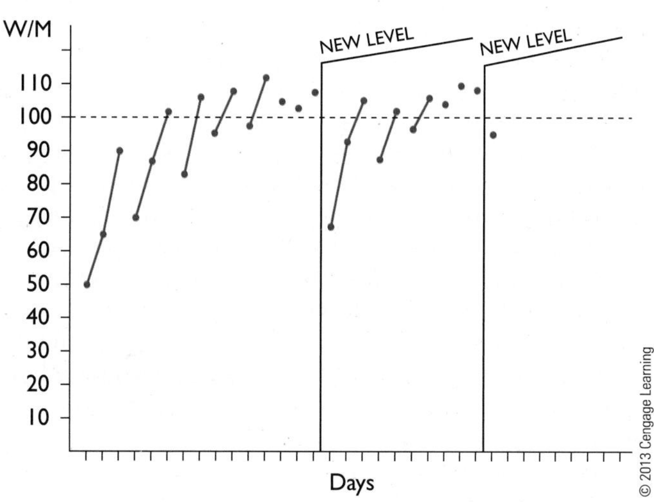

Advanced Skills

Students who have already mastered basic sight vocabulary and decoding skills generally read silently. Emphasis for these students shifts, and new demands are made. Decoding moves from oral reading to silent reading with subvocalization (that is, saying the words and phrases to themselves) to visual scanning without subvocalization; thus, the reading rates of some students may exceed 1,000 words per minute. Scanning for main ideas and information may also be taught systematically. The demands for reading comprehension may go well beyond the literal comprehension of a passage; summarizing, drawing inferences, recognizing and understanding symbolism, sarcasm, irony, and so forth may be systematically taught. For these advanced students, the gist of a passage is usually more important than the details. Teachers of more advanced students may wish to score retold passages on the basis of main ideas, important relationships, and details recalled correctly and the number of errors (that is, ideas, relationships, and details omitted plus the insertion of material not included in the passage). In such cases, the different types of information can be weighted differently, or the use of comprehension strategies (for example, summarization) can be encouraged. However, read–write assessment formats using multiple-choice and extended-essay questions are more commonly used.

INFORMAL READING INVENTORIES

When making decisions about referral or initial placement in a reading curriculum, teachers often develop *informal reading inventories* (IRIs), which assess decoding and reading comprehension over a wide range of skill levels within the specific reading curricula used in a classroom. Thus, they are top-down assessments that span several levels of difficulty.

IRIs are given to locate the reading levels at which a student reads independently, requires instruction, and is frustrated. Techniques for developing IRIs and the criteria used to define independent, instructional, and frustration reading levels vary. Teachers should use a series of graded reading passages that range from below a student's actual placement to a year or two above the actual placement. If a reading series prepared for several grade levels is used, passages can be selected from the beginning, middle, and end of each grade. Students begin reading the easiest material and continue reading until they can decode less than 85 percent of the words. Generally, an accuracy rate of 95 percent is recommended for independent reading and 85 to 95 percent accuracy is considered the level at which a student requires instruction.

MATHEMATICS

The National Council of Teachers of Mathematics has adopted standards for prekindergarten through secondary education. These standards deal with both content (that is, number, measurement, algebra, geometry, and data and statistics) and process (that is, reasoning, representation, problem solving, connections, and communication). Special education tends to share the goals of the National Mathematics Panel (2008), which has stressed computational proficiency and fluency in basic skills. In noninclusive special education settings, math content is generally stressed (that is, readiness skills, vocabulary and concepts, numeration, whole-number operations, fractions and decimals, ratios and percentages, measurement, and geometry). At any grade level, the specific skills and concepts included in each of these subdomains will depend on the state standards and the particular curriculum and its sequencing. Mathematics curricula usually contain both problem sets that require only computations and word problems that require selection and application of the correct algorithm as well as computation. The difficulty of application problems goes well beyond the difficulty of the computation involved and is related to three factors: (1) the number of steps involved in the solution (for example, a student might have to add and then multiply; Caldwell & Goldin, 1979), (2) the amount of extraneous information (Englert, Cullata, & Horn, 1987), and (3) whether the mathematical operation is directly implied by the vocabulary used in the problem (for example, words such as *and* or *more* imply addition, whereas words such as *each* may imply division; see Bachor, Stacy, & Freeze, 1986). Although reading level is popularly believed to affect the difficulty of word problems, its effect has not been clearly established (see Bachor, 1990; Paul, Nibbelink, & Hoover, 1986).

Beginning Skills

The whole-number operations of addition, subtraction, multiplication, and division are the core of the elementary mathematics curriculum. Readiness for beginning students includes such basics as classification, one-to-one correspondence, and counting. Vocabulary and concepts are generally restricted to quantitative words (for example, "same," "equal," and "larger") and spatial concepts (for example, "left," "above," and "next to"). Numeration deals with writing and identifying numerals, counting, ordering, and so forth.

See–write is probably the most frequently used assessment format for mathematical skills, although see–say formats are not uncommon. For content associated with readiness, vocabulary and concepts, numeration, and applications, matching formats are commonly used. Accuracy is stressed, and 90 to 95 percent correct is commonly used as the criterion. For computation, accuracy and fluency are stressed in beginning mathematics; teachers do not stop their instruction when students respond accurately, but they continue instruction to build automaticity. Consequently, a teacher may accept somewhat lower rates of accuracy (that is, 80 percent).

When working toward fluency, teachers usually use probes. Probes are small samples of behavior. For example, in assessment of skill in addition of single-digit numbers, a student might be given only five single-digit addition problems. Perhaps the most useful criterion for math probes assessing computation is the number of correct digits (in an answer) written per minute, not the number of correct answers per minute. The actual criterion rate will depend on the operation, the type of material (for example, addition facts versus addition of two-digit numbers with regrouping), and the characteristics of the particular students. Students with motor difficulties may be held to a lower criterion or assessed with see–say formats. For see–write formats, students may be expected to write answers to addition and subtraction problems at rates between 50 and 80 digits per minute and to write answers to simple multiplication and division problems at rates between 40 and 50 digits per minute.

Advanced Skills

The more advanced mathematical skills (that is, fractions, decimals, ratios, percentages, and geometry) build on whole-number operations. These skills are taught to levels of comprehension and application. Unlike those for beginning skills, assessment formats are almost exclusively see–write, and accuracy is stressed over fluency, except for a few facts such as "half equals 0.5 equals 50 percent." Teachers must take into account the extent to which specific student disabilities will interfere with performance of advanced skills. For example, difficulties in sequencing of information and in comprehension may interfere with students' performance on items that require problem solving and comprehension of mathematical concepts.

SPELLING

Although spelling is considered by many to be a component of written language, in elementary school it is generally taught as a separate subject. Therefore, we treat it separately in this chapter.

Spelling is the production of letters in the correct sequence to form a word. The specific words that are assigned as spelling words may come from several sources: spelling curricula, word lists, content areas, or a student's own written work. In high school and college, students are expected to use dictionaries and to spell correctly any word they use. Between that point and approximately fourth grade, spelling words are typically assigned, and students are left to their own devices to learn them. In the first three grades, spelling is usually taught systematically using phonics, morphology, rote memorization, or some combination of the three approaches.

Teachers may assess mastery of the prespelling rules associated with the particular approach they are teaching. For example, when a phonics approach is used, students may have to demonstrate mastery of writing the letters associated with specific vowels, consonants, consonant blends, diphthongs, and digraphs. Teachers assess mastery of spelling in at least four ways:

1. *Recognition response:* The teacher provides students with lists of alternative spellings of words (usually three or four alternatives) and reads a word to the student. The student must select the correct spelling of the dictated word from the alternatives. Emphasis is on accuracy.

2. *Spelling dictated single words:* Teachers dictate words, and students write them down. Although teachers often give a spelling word and then use it in a sentence, students find the task easier if just the spelling word is given (Horn, 1967). Moreover, the findings from research performed in 1988 suggest that a 7-second interval between words is sufficient (Shinn, Tindall, & Stein, 1988).
3. *Spelling words in context:* Students write paragraphs using words given by the teacher. This approach is as much a measure of written expression as of spelling. The teacher can also use this approach in instruction of written language by asking students to write paragraphs and counting the number of words spelled correctly.
4. *Students' self-monitoring of errors:* Some teachers teach students to monitor their own performance by finding and correcting spelling errors in the daily assignments they complete.

WRITTEN LANGUAGE

Written language is no doubt the most complex and difficult domain for teachers to assess. Assessment differs widely for beginners and advanced students. Once the preliminary skills of letter formation and rudimentary spelling have been mastered, written-language curricula usually stress both content and style (that is, grammar, mechanics, and diction).

Beginning Skills

The most basic instruction in written language is penmanship, in which the formation and spacing of uppercase (capital) and lowercase printed and cursive letters are taught. Early instruction stresses accuracy, and criteria are generally qualitative. After accuracy has been attained, teachers may provide extended practice to move students toward automaticity. If this is done, teachers will evaluate performance on the basis of students' rates of writing letters. Target rates are usually in the range of 80 to 100 letters per minute for students without motor handicaps.

Once students can fluently write letters and words, teachers focus on teaching students to write content. For beginners, content generation is often reduced to generation of words in meaningful sequence. Teachers may use story starters (that is, pictures or a few words that act as stimuli) to prompt student writing. When the allotted time for writing is over, teachers count the number of words or divide the number of words by the time to obtain a measure of rate. Although this sounds relatively easy, decisions as to what constitutes a word must be made. For example, one-letter words are seldom counted.

Teachers also use the percentage of correct words to assess content production. To be considered correct, the word must be spelled correctly, be capitalized if appropriate, be grammatically correct, and be followed by the correct punctuation (Isaacson, 1988). Criteria for an acceptable percentage of correct words are still the subject of discussion. For now, social comparison, by which one student's writing output is compared with the output of students whose writing is judged acceptable, can provide teachers with rough approximations. Teaching usually boils down to focusing on capitalization, simple punctuation, and basic grammar (for example, subject–verb agreement). Teachers may also use multiple-choice or fill-in tests to assess comprehension of grammatical conventions or rules.

Advanced Skills

Comprehension and application of advanced grammar and mechanics can be tested readily with multiple-choice or fill-in questions. Thus, this aspect of written language can be assessed systematically and objectively. The evaluation of content generation by advanced students is far more difficult than counting correct words. Teachers may consider the quality of ideas, the sequencing of ideas, the coherence of ideas, and consideration of the reading audience. In practice, teachers use holistic judgments of content (Cooper, 1977). In addition, they may point out errors in style or indicate topics that might benefit from greater elaboration or clarification.

SPECIAL CONSIDERATIONS FOR STUDENTS WITH DISABILITIES

In developing items that employ a supply format, teachers must pay attention to individual differences among learners, particularly to disabilities that may interfere with performance. For example, students who write very slowly can be expected to have difficulty with fill-in or essay questions. Students who have considerable difficulty expressing themselves in writing will probably have difficulty completing or performing well on essay examinations. Teachers should make sure that they have included the adaptations and accommodations required in student IEPs.

Objective scoring of any of these attributes is very difficult, and extended scoring keys and practice are necessary to obtain reliable judgments, if they are ever attained. More objective scoring systems for content require computer analysis and are currently beyond the resources of most classroom teachers.

6 Coping with Dilemmas in Current Practice

There are three pitfalls to be avoided: (1) relying on a single summative assessment, (2) using nonstandardized testing procedures, and (3) using technically inadequate assessment procedures. The first two are easily avoided; avoiding the third is more difficult.

First, teachers should not rely solely on a single summative assessment to evaluate student achievement after a course of instruction. Such assessments do not provide teachers with information they can use to plan and modify sequences of instruction. Moreover, minor technical inadequacies can be magnified when a single summative measure is used. Rather, teachers should test progress toward educational objectives at least two or three times a week. Frequent testing is most important when instruction is aimed at developing automatic or fluent responses in students. Although fluency is most commonly associated with primary curricula, it is not restricted to reading, writing, and arithmetic. For example, instruction in foreign languages, sports, and music is often aimed at automaticity.

Second, teachers should use standardized testing procedures. To conduct frequent assessments that are meaningful, the tests that are used to assess the same objectives must be equivalent. Therefore, the content must be equivalent from test to test; moreover, test directions, kinds of cues or hints, testing formats, criteria for correct responses, and type of score (for example, rates or percentage correct) must be the same.

Third, teachers should develop technically adequate assessment procedures. Two aspects of this adequacy are especially important: content validity and reliability. The tests must have content validity. There should seldom be problems with content validity when direct performances are used. For example, the materials used in determining a student's rate of oral reading should have content validity when they come from that student's reading materials; tests used to assess mastery of addition facts will have content validity because they assess the facts that have been taught. A problem with content validity is more likely when teachers use tests to assess achievement outside of the tool subjects (that is, other than reading, math, and language arts).

Although only teachers can develop tests that truly mirror instruction, teachers must not only know what has been taught but also prepare devices that test what has been taught. About the only way to guarantee that an assessment covers the content is to develop tables of specifications for the content of instruction and testing. However, test items geared to specific content may still be ineffective.

Careful preparation in and of itself cannot guarantee the validity of one question or set of questions. The only way a teacher can know that the questions are good is to field test the questions and make revisions based on the field test results. Realistically, teachers do not have time for field testing and revision prior to giving a test. Therefore, teachers must usually give a test and then delete or discount poor items. The poor items can be edited and the revised questions used the next time the examination is needed. In this way, the responses from one group of students become a field test for a subsequent group of students. When teachers use this approach, they should not return tests to students because students may pass questions down from year to year.

The tests must also be reliable. Interscorer agreement is a major concern for any test using a supply format but is especially important when extended responses are evaluated. Agreement can be increased by developing precise scoring guides for all questions of this type and by sticking with the criteria. Interscorer agreement should not be a problem for tests using select or restricted fill-in formats. For select and fill-in tests, internal consistency is of primary concern. Unfortunately, very few people can prepare a set of homogeneous test questions the first time. However, at the same time that they revise poor items, teachers can delete or revise items to increase a test's homogeneity (that is, delete or revise items that have correlations with the total score of .25 or less). Additional items can also be prepared for the next test.

Chapter Comprehension Questions

Write your answers to each of the following questions and then compare your responses to the text.

1. Explain three potential advantages of teacher-made tests.
2. How do skill attainment and progress monitoring differ?
3. Explain content specificity.
4. Explain why frequent testing is valuable.
5. Give examples of a see–write, see–say, hear–write, and see–write formats.
6. Explain six common errors to avoid in developing multiple-choice tests.
7. Explain three things a teacher can do to prepare better matching questions.
8. Explain three things a teacher can do to prepare better true–false questions.

Web Activities

1. Read about tables of specification in the technical adequacy chapter on the Education CourseMate website for this textbook. Prepare a table of specifications for a test that you (as the teacher) make to assess students on the election to the U.S. House of Representatives and Senate.
2. Explain how you would assess reading comprehension in a third grade classroom. Compare your answer to the reading section of the assessment in core achievement areas.

Web Resources

Tips for Teachers: Assessing for Instructional and Behavior Problems: Constructing Teacher-Made Tests
http://www.afcec.org/tipsforteachers/tips_a5.html
This site explains how to construct, administer, score, and interpret criterion-referenced tests.

Handbook on Test Development
http://testing.wisc.edu/Handbook%20on%20Test%20Construction.pdf
This paper by Allan S. Cohen and James A. Wollack from the Testing & Evaluation Services at the University of Wisconsin–Madison provides helpful tips for creating reliable and valid classroom tests.

Additional resources for this chapter can be found on the Education CourseMate website. Go to CengageBrain.com to access the site.

Curriculum-Based Approaches to Measuring Student Progress

CHAPTER GOALS

1 Know the defining characteristics of curriculum-based measurement (CBM).

2 Understand different types of CBM and the purposes for which they are used.

3 Describe two different ways in which to set goals using CBM.

4 Know some common tools and procedures for administering CBMs in reading, math, and writing.

5 Be familiar with self-generated and various off-the-shelf CBM packages.

6 Identify two diagnostic approaches that can be used with curriculum-based measures.

KEY TERMS

benchmark

curriculum-based assessment (CBA)

curriculum-based measurement (CBM)

curriculum-based evaluation (CBE)

general outcome measure (GOM)

skill-based measure (SBM)

subskill mastery measure (SMM)

In order to know whether a student is making progress according to grade-level standards so that appropriate instructional changes can be made as soon as possible, we need brief assessment tools that are technically adequate and sensitive to student progress within the curriculum. Some techniques that teachers can use to develop tests that measure student learning were discussed in Chapter 7. They all can be considered "curriculum-based," given that they are intended to measure student achievement according to the curriculum that is being taught. However, these tools vary substantially in the amount of time they take to develop and administer, and their technical adequacy is often questioned. Furthermore, if the tests don't directly measure important skills, students' scores may be unrepresentative of their achievement or influenced by chance (especially with multiple-choice tasks!), their performance may be influenced by other students (as in cheating, or using others to help in completing the given task), or the tests may measure certain subskills that don't necessarily represent students' ability to coordinate and maintain their knowledge to perform an important task.

1 Characteristics of Curriculum-Based Measurement

Over the past 30 years, a set of procedures called "curriculum-based measurement" (CBM) has grown in popularity; these procedures can provide teachers with very quick information on their students' progress in developing important basic skills. Developed by Dr. Stan Deno and others at the University of Minnesota Institute for Research on Learning Disabilities in the early 1980s (Deno, 1985), CBM is unique in that it involves a standardized set of procedures that allow one to directly measure important skills in a relatively short amount of time. Some have referred to CBMs as "academic thermometers"; they can allow us to know which students are "at-risk" in just a very short amount of time. Just like a thermometer, CBMs don't necessarily provide diagnostic information (a thermometer can't tell you what caused the fever!). But they do allow teachers to know early on who appears to be at-risk in their academic skill development so that follow-up assessment can be done that might help identify what intervention is needed to get the student back to an academically healthy state.

In addition to serving as brief screening tools, CBMs can also be used to track student progress toward important outcomes over an entire school year. Therefore, unlike other teacher-made procedures, we do not merely assess students on the material taught or reviewed; instead, we test students over the content of the entire year. Consequently, we do not expect students to know much of the material on early tests, but as students learn more material, we expect their scores to increase. In essence, we make sure there is room for students to show growth. This way, their progress can be effectively tracked over time as they respond to instruction.[1] Because CBMs can efficiently serve both screening and progress monitoring purposes, they fit very well into multi-tiered systems of support and response-to-intervention models and are increasingly used.

All CBMs share these characteristics:

- Direct measurement of student performance on basic skills. By direct, we mean that the student is asked to demonstrate the targeted basic skill. Indirect measurement would incorporate perceptions and judgments about the student's skills rather than asking the student to actually demonstrate the given skill.

[1] Because there are relatively few test items the students know in the beginning of the year and relatively few items they do not know at the end of the year, estimates of the tests internal consistency are lower than at times when students know about half of the material. Therefore, teachers should rely upon estimates of stability to assess their tests' reliability.

- Random selection from grade-level instructional materials of things that are intended to be taught for a predetermined period of time (i.e., usually one school year).
- Common standardized, timed administration procedures
- Common, pre-set objective scoring procedures

2 Types of Curriculum-Based Measurement Tools

Different types of measures are commonly referred to as CBMs. Hosp, Hosp, & Howell (2007) describe three types of CBMS that vary in terms of the complexity of skill assessed and the purposes for which they are commonly used, including general outcome measures, skill-based measures, and subskill mastery measures.

General Outcome Measures (GOMs)

These tools measure important outcomes that require maintenance and coordinated use of many skills. The most common general outcome measure is oral reading fluency, which requires students to read connected text that is selected to represent grade level instructional material. Students are asked to read aloud from a passage for between 1 and 3 minutes and are scored based on the number of words they read correctly per minute. Oral reading requires students to coordinate many different foundational skills (e.g., knowledge of letter sounds, skill and automaticity with blending sounds to produce words, skill in identifying and correctly reading words that don't fit common alphabetic rules, etc.) and represents students' ability to read connected text, a skill that is fundamental to academic achievement. Several different but equivalent reading passages (sometimes referred to as "probes") are developed to represent the reading level that the student would be expected to attain by the end of the school year, so that the student's performance level can be assessed repeatedly to measure progress. GOMs are typically used to measure progress toward long-term goals, for example, for a student to read at a certain rate by the end of the school year.

Skill-Based Measures (SBMs)

Although similar to GOMs in that they may be created to measure progress toward an end-of-year goal, skill-based measures allow for measurement of skills in a slightly more isolated manner. They often require students to demonstrate some coordination of multiple subskills, but not to the same extent as GOMs. One commonly used SBM is math computation. CBM math computation probes are created by randomly selecting various types of problems with operational components (e.g., those including carrying and borrowing etc.) that the student would be expected to learn and maintain by the end of the school year. The probes are created to be equivalent in difficulty level so that progress over time can be measured. Students are given a set period of time to complete the probe (this varies by grade level) and are scored in terms of the digits they write correctly in the given amount of time. An example of such a math computation probe is provided in the scenario provided with this chapter.

Subskill Mastery Measures (SMMs)

Subskill mastery measures (SMM) typically involve measurement of a subskill that is linked to SBMs or GOMs. For example, further analysis of results from an SBM may suggest that a student hasn't mastered single-digit subtraction. Several SSM probes could be developed that include just single-digit subtraction facts to measure student progress in learning that one subskill while the student receives additional instruction in single-digit subtraction. SMMs are typically used to measure progress toward short-term goals. An example of this kind of measure (a subtraction fact probe) is provided in the scenario included at the end of this chapter.

Although curriculum-based measurement tools can be used to measure a variety of important basic skills and to predict performance on other higher-level thinking tasks (i.e., reading comprehension, math problem solving), it is important to realize that they are not designed to accurately measure higher-level thinking skills. They can help us identify many students who are likely to struggle in developing these higher-level thinking skills without additional intervention; however, there are some important skills for which there are not currently CBMs available. For example, although CBM methods have been developed to monitor progress in the development of vocabulary terms associated with science, we are not aware of any common CBM methods for measuring student problem solving in science.

3 Goal-Setting with CBM

Because of the similar administration and scoring procedures of CBM, and its ability to track student progress in learning important skills over time, informed goal setting can occur. We describe two common approaches to CBM goal setting. However, it is important to note that newer goal-setting methodologies are available for use with technology enhanced measurement systems (Betebenner, 2008, 2009; Betts, 2010).

Benchmarks

Meaningful benchmarks for CBM can provide helpful information for goal setting. Benchmarks are performance levels that are associated with specific time-points that help to inform whether a student's academic development is on-track. Think of benchmarks as the clocks at mile-markers in a marathon. Let's say you are running a marathon (a 26.2-mile race), and your ultimate goal is to run it in under 4 hours. If the timer at the half-way point (13.1 miles in) says 2 hours 20 minutes, you know that you must increase your pace in order to meet your ultimate goal. The same thing is true when benchmarks are available for a CBM. If the long-term goal is reading fluently by the end of third grade (i.e., 140 words correct per minute on third-grade material), failing to meet the fall third-grade benchmark level for oral reading fluency means that the student is not on track to read at the proficient level by the end of third grade. Additional intervention support may be needed to ensure that the ultimate long-term goal is met.

Benchmarks are best when they are informed by research that has tracked the progress of many students over time. The Dynamic Indicators of Basic Early Literacy Skills (DIBELS) represent a set of tools with benchmarks available for goal setting. The *DIBELS Next* benchmark score for fall second-grade oral reading fluency is 52 words correct per minute. Therefore, if a student is substantially below that benchmark in the fall of second grade (e.g., scoring 40 words correct per minute), a goal might be set for the student to meet the spring of second-grade oral reading fluency benchmark of 87 words correct per minute. If additional intervention results in the student meeting this spring benchmark, we can be confident that the student is back on track in terms of his or her potential to meet the ultimate goal of reading by the end of third grade.

Norms

Another approach involves examining CBM performance and growth rates for students similar to the target student and using that information to guide goal setting. Some packages of CBM tools, such as AIMSweb, offer norms tables that can be used to determine approximately how students at a particular grade level should score during certain windows of time (e.g., a score at the 50th percentile for fall third-grade math computation = 22 digits correct per minute), as well as a typical rate of improvement for students at a particular grade level (e.g., a growth rate at the 50th percentile for third-grade math computation = 1.1 digits correct per minute per week). Using this information, a 10-week goal might be set for a third-grade student who scored at 22 digits correct per minute during the fall administration held on September 15 to score at 33 digits (22 digits correct per minute + (1.1 digits correct per minute per week × 10 weeks)) on November 26.

Betebenner (2008, 2009) points out the potential helpfulness of developing growth percentiles, which would allow one to have a reference point for growth.

Betts (2010) discusses the varying growth rates that are typically found among students at different levels of performance and offers a method for setting goals based on expected growth rates for a particular initial performance level. The Renaissance STAR Enterprise products (STAR Math, STAR Reading, and STAR Early Literacy) along with Accelerated Math Intervention (AMI) provide users with a "Goal Setting Wizard" that builds on Betts's research. This is a quick, button-clicking way to let the computer do all the calculations and to take both the level of current performance *and* the rate of typical progress by similar students into account.

The norms represented in tables put forth by various packages of CBM tools can be helpful; however, some schools and districts develop their own local norms by administering CBMs to all students across the course of a year. These norms help identify students with below-average performance who will need closer assessment and perhaps intervention. In general, when norms are used for goal setting, students performing at or below the 25th percentile are targeted for follow up.

OTHER CBM GOAL-SETTING CONCEPTS TO UNDERSTAND

Long- and Short-Term Goals

As noted above, GOMs can be helpful in setting long-term goals. For students who are not on track in developing their skills, it can be helpful to set short-term goals (e.g., weekly or monthly goals), and track their progress more closely over time to know whether any additional intervention that is provided is effective. In these cases, SMMs might be used to monitor progress in subskills that the student is lacking and for which instruction is provided. Within an MTSS model, progress toward both short- and long-term goals should be monitored frequently, and instructional changes made when students are not making appropriate progress.

High and Realistic Goals

Some people debate setting ambitious versus more reasonable goals using CBM.

Using the benchmark approach to set goals may result in goals that seem extremely high for those students who are currently low performing. Setting a goal that appears more reasonable can relieve educator's anxiety. However, we think it is important to have a very clear sense of where the student is at with regard to appropriate progress toward the finish line; the benchmark approach can help us keep the finish line in our mind so that we avoid having students fall farther and farther behind in the development of important skills.

At the same time, we know that continuous failure in meeting benchmark goals can be very frustrating for all involved (teachers, parents, students), and may contribute to an unfortunate neglect of the progress that the student may actually be making. It is extremely helpful to know if a student is making better progress than before—this can tell us that our intervention is having the intended effect. Furthermore, approaches that involve the use of growth norms (Betebenner, 2008, 2009; Betts, 2010) can allow teachers to set high and realistic goals that emphasize growth rather than focusing on whether a student meets a particular standard at a particular point in time.

In some (but ultimately very few) cases, after substantial intervention, it may be determined that the student will not be able to ultimately develop the target skill to an independent level of functioning. This is a decision that can only be made after substantial intervention and monitoring has occurred, and parents and teachers have come to a mutual agreement that a continued intensive focus on the given skill is unwarranted.

Decision-Making Pitfalls to Avoid

Although both benchmarks and norms can be helpful for goal setting, it is important to realize that as long as a student is meeting benchmarks, his or her individual growth rate is not necessarily that important. We have seen some teachers and parents get inappropriately worried about students who consistently meet benchmarks, but make no growth or actually decrease their scores between administrations. It is important to realize that increasing speed on certain tasks is really of no value; in fact, it may actually be detrimental to a student's learning. For example, once students can read approximately 140 words correct per minute, it is generally believed that their memory should be freed up to allow for comprehension. The use of effective comprehension strategies such as slowing down to better understand a complicated reading passage, or rereading for clarity, become more important once fluency has been attained. So if a student scores 150 words correct per minute in the fall, and then 140 words correct per minute in the spring, we should not worry. Increased speed at this level is not necessarily important; the student has reached sufficient fluency for comprehension.

In addition, it is important to recognize that even though studies have provided evidence for the technical adequacy of many CBM tools, they are not without error. In fact, recent studies have highlighted the importance of considering the standard error of measurement (SEM) within decision making using CBM (Ardoin & Christ, 2009). In other words, student performance may fluctuate considerably from passage to passage, and it is therefore important to use performance on multiple passages, or construct appropriate confidence intervals for scores in order to inform decision making. New advances using technology enhanced assessments make goal setting much more accurate and monitoring much more reliable. We discuss some of these advances in the chapter on using technology (Chapter 23).

One of the great advantages of CBM is that when goals are set and student progress is monitored, graphs can be created to effectively convey student progress. In Chapter 9 (Managing Classroom Assessment), we present further information on how to visually display students' progress toward goals in order to assist with effective communication and decision making.

4 Common CBMs for Reading, Math, and Written Expression

As noted earlier, CBM represents a set of tools with common administration and scoring frameworks. In Table 8.1 we provide some examples of several common CBM procedures. Many more are available than what we list in this table. However, it is

TABLE 8.1

Basic Skill	Specific Measures	Type*	Administration	Scoring
Early Reading	Letter Sound Fluency	SMM	Students are given a sheet with letters on it and asked to provide (in order, from left to right) as many of the sounds as they can in one minute.	Sounds correct per minute
	Phoneme Segmentation Fluency	SMM	The examiner reads a series of word to the student, and the student must provide the appropriate sound segmentation for the word (e.g., if examiner says "net," the student must say "nnnnn ... eh ... t").	Sounds correct per minute or words correct per minute

Basic Skill	Specific Measures	Type*	Administration	Scoring
	Nonsense Word Fluency	SBM	Students are given a sheet with three-letter words on it that are not real words (e.g., "SIF") and asked to read as many of the words/sounds that they can in 1 minute.	Sounds correct per minute or words correct per minute
Reading	Oral Reading Fluency	GOM	The student is given a grade-level reading passage and asked to read aloud for 1 minute.	Words correct per minute
	Retell	GOM	After reading aloud a passage for 1 minute, the student is asked to tell about what they read.	Number of words that the student provides in summary
	MAZE	SBM	The student is given a reading passage that includes complete first and last sentences, but for the remaining sentences, every fifth word is replaced with a blank that has three word choices written underneath. The student is typically given 3 minutes to circle one word that best fits each blank.	Number of correct words circled/percent of correct words circled
Math	Computation	SBM	The student is given a sheet with multiple grade-level appropriate math computation problems. The student is given a set time to complete as many of the items as possible.	Digits correct per minute
	Fact Probes (*addition, subtraction, multiplication, division, multiple fact probes*)	SMM	The student is given a sheet that lists certain math facts and is asked to complete as many of the items as possible within a set time.	Digits correct per minute
Writing	Story Starters	GOM	Students are given a story starter (e.g., "It was my birthday and I was going to . . .") and 1 minute to think about what they will write. After 1 minute, students are directed to write as much as they can about the topic.	Total words written per minute, total correct word sequences per minute, total words spelled correctly per minute
	Spelling	SBM	A student is given a piece of paper with numbered blanks. The examiner reads off 20 different words at a given rate that the students must spell on their paper.	Number of words spelled correctly, number of correct letter sequences

*NOTE: Some measures may be considered to fit multiple types.

important to remember that not all important skills can be measured using CBM. Failure to develop these basic skills puts students in danger of long-term poor achievement across many areas.

5 Developing or Selecting a CBM Measurement Package

When CBM was first developed, educators were encouraged to develop their own equivalent passages or probes based on material that students in a particular grade were expected to cover across the course of the year. Each probe or passage would include randomly selected material that would be covered during the entire year. Using such self-generated measures could ensure appropriate alignment between the actual instructional materials being used and the materials used for the purpose of assessment. Some school professionals may continue to take this approach; however, it is very time-consuming, and it is difficult to ensure that passages and probes generated in this way are of equivalent difficulty.

More recently, various off-the-shelf packages of CBM tools have been developed to help schools and teachers use CBM. Details about these different packages are provided in Table 8.2.

Some of these packages also provide data display and decision-making support. We discuss several of them in other chapters of this textbook. The National Center on Response to Intervention has been involved in conducting reviews of the technical adequacy of many of these measures.

Go to the Education CourseMate website for this textbook for a link to the National Center on Response to Intervention's reviews of many of these tools for different purposes.

One drawback of using a prepackaged set of CBM materials is that it may not necessarily represent the actual curriculum and instruction of the given school. When selecting a package, it is important to take into consideration whether the skills measured align with the curriculum and instructional materials used at your school.

Another option for developing CBMs is to use a program that helps generate probes that fit your particular classroom needs. One website that supports this approach to probe development is www.interventioncentral.org. Teachers can choose the types of skills they would like to measure, and the website creates probes that can allow for the measurement of progress in development of the selected skills.

6 Diagnostic Approaches

It is important to recognize that although curriculum-based measures can be used to screen and monitor progress, they are not necessarily designed to provide information about what intervention is needed. Just like a thermometer can't tell you how to cure a fever, a CBM score can't necessarily tell you how to solve a student's academic difficulty. Further analysis is necessary. Sometimes by analyzing the errors students make on a passage or probe, a teacher can make an educated guess about what kind of instruction is needed. However, additional curriculum-based frameworks for diagnosing student's difficulties in ways that can help in the design of effective interventions are available. Two approaches that offer assistance with the design of curriculum-based interventions include curriculum-based evaluation and curriculum-based assessment.

CBE. Curriculum-based evaluation (CBE) is a term coined by Howell and Morehead (1987) that represents a strategy for collecting and using data to make decisions about individual students or groups. Howell and Morehead offer a decision-making framework that can guide data collection and analysis within a particular content area. This process allows one to link assessment information to a potentially highly effective intervention. CBE is useful for determining what instructional sequences or skill deficits need to be taught.

TABLE 8.2 Existing Packages of Curriculum-Based Tools

Package	Measures	Grade-Level(s) Assessed*
AIMSweb (www.aimsweb.com)	Letter Naming Fluency Letter Sound Fluency Phoneme Segmentation Fluency Nonsense Word Fluency Oral Counting Number Identification Quantity Discrimination Missing Number Reading (*oral reading fluency*) MAZE Math Concepts and Applications Math Computation Addition Subtraction Addition/Subtraction Multiplication Division Multiplication/Division All Facts (*Several Spanish-language measures are also available*)	K–8
DIBELS Next (http://www.dibels.org/next.html)	First Sound Fluency Letter Naming Fluency Phoneme Segmentation Fluency Nonsense Word Fluency Oral Reading Fluency (*Retell can be incorporated within Oral Reading Fluency*) DAZE (*similar to MAZE*) (*Spanish-language measures are also available through DIBELS*)	K-6
Easy CBM (http://www.easycbm.com/)	Letter Names Letter Sounds Phonemic Segmenting Word Reading Fluency Passage Reading Fluency Vocabulary Multiple-Choice Reading Comprehension Math Numbers and Operations Math Geometry Math Number Operations and Algebra	K-8

*NOTE: Different tasks are available at different grade levels.

CBA. The term curriculum-based assessment (CBA) was first used by Gickling in 1977 in assessment practices for which the instructional needs of students were determined by measuring the ratio of known to unknown material in the curriculum. Over time, CBA referred to an assessment of accuracy and a system of monitoring student progress through the curriculum. Multiple models of CBA emerged, and eventually the term was replaced by "instructional assessment." CBA was used in the Pennsylvania instructional support team model to refer to an accuracy-based approach (Burns, MacQuarrie & Campbell (1999).

SCENARIO *in* ASSESSMENT

JENNIE | Jennie is a third-grade student at Sycamore Elementary, where teachers use CBM math computation to track student progress over time. Sycamore Elementary has developed its norms based on the third-grade students who have been instructed at the school over the past three years, with norms developed for three administrations across the course of the year (fall, winter, spring). The computation probes have been developed to include math problems that address double- and triple-digit addition problems with carrying, double- and triple-digit subtraction problems with borrowing, and double- and triple-digit multiplication, given that these skills are taught during the third-grade year. Each probe contains problems representing each of these skills. Jennie's performance on the administration of the fall probe is shown below.

12cd

Jennie's Performance on a 3rd grade Math Computation – Skill-Based Measure

1 48 + 24 72	53 × 10	478 − 23 434	676 − 94 692	11 345 + 489 834
1 934 + 248 1182	63 − 11 42	933 − 345	76 × 99	15 + 89
856 + 124	63 × 14	888 × 11	176 + 83	11 + 64
34 × 0	68 − 14	90 − 34	76 − 5	11 + 39
123 − 23	73 − 18	941 − 342	174 × 9	10 + 88
934 − 247	33 − 14	633 + 245	76 × 39	15 + 69

Her score of 12 digits correct per minute is below the 25th percentile (15 digits correct per minute) on the norms her school has developed. She has therefore been targeted for further analysis to determine if additional support is necessary. Further analysis indicates that Jennie has been attending Sycamore since kindergarten; interviews with her first- and second-grade teachers demonstrate that although they had taught some single- and double-digit addition and subtraction in those grades, they were not confident that Jennie had mastered those skills. An analysis of the errors Jennie made on the fall CBM probe suggests that although she has mastered her addition facts, she seems to have made a lot of mistakes on the subtraction facts. She also made many errors on the multiplication problems; however, that has not been taught yet, and so she is not expected to know those facts or how to compute using multiplication. To verify whether she knows her subtraction facts, a subskill mastery measurement is created to sample her subtraction fact fluency. Results indicate that she is not accurate with her subtraction facts (see her performance below)

7cd

Jennie's Performance on a Single Digit Subtraction Subskill Mastery Measure

9 − 2 4	5 − 1 3	4 − 2 2	12 − 2 11	10 − 4 5
8 − 5 3	13 − 2 10	8 − 2 5	17 − 9 16	10 − 3 13
9 − 6	8 − 1 7	9 − 3 5	15 − 4 1	6 − 4 2
4 − 2	5 − 3	7 − 2	17 − 2	10 − 6
8 − 1	5 − 5	4 − 2	13 − 2	13 − 9
4 − 4	2 − 1	4 − 2	19 − 9	10 − 4
6 − 2	11 − 1	4 − 2	12 − 4	14 − 7

she answered only 7 digits correct per minute on this task. As a result, a subtraction fact intervention is put in place for her. Additional mastery measurement subtraction fact probes are developed to measure progress on a weekly basis toward the short-term goal of her mastering subtraction facts. Her short-term goal is for her to score 27 digits correct per minute on a single-digit subtraction fact probe by November 1 (an expected growth rate of approximately 2 digits correct per minute per week). A long-term goal of having her make effective use of her subtraction knowledge on math computation CBMs is also set; this is for her to score at the 25th percentile compared to the third-grade level norms on the winter CBM math computation probe, which is a score of 35 digits correct per minute. Her progress toward this goal is monitored every two weeks. With the subtraction fact intervention, Jennie is able to steadily improve in her subtraction fact fluency. The results are seen to transfer to her math computation score such that she reaches the 25th percentile mark by the winter benchmark (see the graph of her progress below).

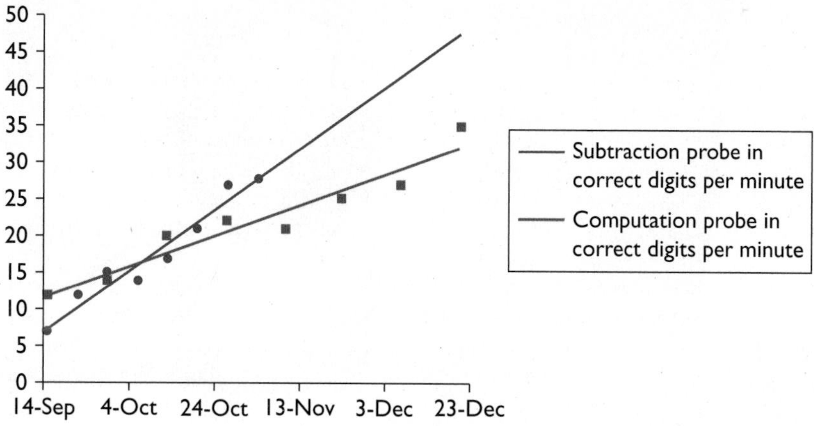

What implications for your own professional role can you draw from this scenario? Go to the Education CourseMate website for this textbook for more reflection questions about this Scenario in Assessment.

Chapter Comprehension Questions

Write your answers to each of the following questions and then compare your responses to the text.

1. What are the defining characteristics of curriculum-based measurement (CBM)?
2. Describe three different types of CBM. For what purposes are each used?
3. What are two ways to set goals using CBM? Provide an example of each.
4. Describe the administration procedures for three CBMs: one in math, one in reading, and one in writing.
5. Describe three different ways in which you could design or select a set of CBM tools. What are the advantages and drawbacks of each approach?
6. Describe two diagnostic approaches that can be used with curriculum-based measures.

Web Activities 

1. Search the Internet for reviews of progress monitoring tools provided at the National Center on Response to Intervention. Which tools are reported to have the greatest support for the purpose of screening? What about for the purpose of progress monitoring?
2. Search the Internet for training manuals on the AIMSweb website. Read one of the training manuals and practice scoring with the associated videos. Reflect on how difficult the various measures are to administer and score.
3. Search the Internet to compare and contrast the tools available through DIBELS Next and DIBELS, 6th edition. What changes were made in the revision process?

Web Resources

Create Your Own CBM Materials

http://www.interventioncentral.com/

http://www.easycbm.com/

You can create your own CBM measures at both of the sites listed here.

Additional resources for this chapter can be found on the Education CourseMate website. Go to CengageBrain.com to access the site.

Managing Classroom Assessment

CHAPTER GOALS

1. Know three characteristics of effective testing programs.
2. Be familiar with a process for putting a classroom assessment management program in place.
3. Understand various ways to make decisions using charts that display progress monitoring data.

KEY TERMS

progress monitoring	aimline	goal line
celeration charts	trendline	decision-making rules

Except for individual evaluations conducted by specialists such as psychologists and speech therapists, classroom teachers are responsible for most testing conducted in schools. When districts want group achievement tests on all their students (or those in particular grades), or when the state requires all students to complete standards-based assessments. teachers are the ones who administer these tests in their classrooms. Beyond these mandated assessments, teachers routinely test to monitor student progress and ascertain the degree of student achievement on instructional units. As schools move toward implementation of Multi-Tiered Systems of Support models, teachers become increasingly responsible for keeping track of data on student response to instruction and intervention, and this requires careful management and coordination of information.

Testing to monitor student progress during and after instruction is best when tests are carefully planned, thoughtfully managed, and fully incorporated into classroom routines. In short, testing should be an easy and natural part of classroom life. Teachers should plan their testing programs at the beginning of the year. Good testing programs have three characteristics: efficiency, ease, and integration.

- *Efficiency.* Time spent in testing (including administration, scoring, interpretation, and record keeping) is time not spent teaching and learning. Therefore, good assessment plans call for the least assessment necessary for decision making. This includes consideration of the amount of time both students and teachers must spend on assessment. Efficiency considerations are leading to greater emphasis on group testing, computer adaptive testing, and the use of technology systems to monitor and report frequently on student progress.
- *Ease.* Easy testing programs from the teacher's perspective are those that minimize teacher time and effort in all aspects of testing (that is, preparation, administration, scoring, and record keeping). The easiest testing programs are those that can be carried out by technology devices (computers, responders, smartphones, NEOs, iPads, etc.), paraprofessionals, or students. Easy testing programs from the student's perspective are those with which the student feels familiar and comfortable, and that he or she has confidence in. It is important to set expectations about how assessment works in the classroom early in the school year and reinforce these expectations periodically.
- *Integration.* Assessment activities can be integrated into the school day in two ways. First, teachers can monitor pupil performance during instructional activities. For example, basic skill drills can be structured to provide useful assessment information about accuracy and fluency, or computers can be used to manage instruction (See Chapter 23). Second, teachers can establish a regular schedule for brief assessments, such as daily 1-minute oral reading probes. Making assessments frequent and part of the regular classroom routine has the added benefit of reducing student anxiety associated with higher stakes testing.

1 Preparing for and Managing Mandated Tests

When districtwide and statewide assessments are conducted, they generally occur within classrooms. Teachers usually have advance notice about when various mandated tests will occur, how long they will take, and how they are to be administered. Teachers should become thoroughly familiar with expectations for their role in assessment, and they should be thoroughly prepared with backup supplies of pencils, timers, and answer sheets (if allowed). Teachers should also provide their students with advanced knowledge in such a way as to reduce anxiety about these tests without diminishing their importance. For example, it is a good idea to tell students that all students in the district or all students in their grade are taking the test, and that the tests are designed to help the district do a good job teaching all of the students.

In addition to these general considerations, teachers should check all of their students' individualized educational programs (IEPs) to verify the kinds of assessments that each student will take and what, if any, adaptations or accommodations must be provided. Teachers should check their students' IEPs to determine whether any student is to receive an alternate assessment and if individual students need any alternate assessment accommodations.

2 Preparing for and Managing Progress Monitoring

Even the most extensively researched curriculum and teaching techniques may not work with every student. Moreover, there is currently no way to discern the students for whom the curriculum or methods will be effective from those for whom the educational procedures will not work. The only way to know if educational procedures are effective is to determine if they were effective. That is, we can know if what we have done has worked, but we cannot know this before we do it. Thus, teachers are faced with a choice: They can either teach and hope that their instruction will work, or they can teach and measure the extent to which their instruction has worked. We advocate the latter approach.

Monitoring student achievement allows teachers the chance to reteach unlearned material, provide alternative content or methods for those students who have not learned, or get additional help for them. Moreover, student progress should be monitored frequently enough to allow early detection and error correction. Errors that are caught late in the learning process are much more difficult to correct because students have practiced the incorrect responses. Finally, the monitoring procedures must be sensitive to incremental changes in student achievement. Of all the ways in which teachers can monitor student learning, we prefer continuous (that is, daily or several times per week) and systematic monitoring rather than summative monitoring (that is, assessing student knowledge after instruction of large amounts of content or after several weeks of instruction).

Lack of time is the primary reason given by teachers for not measuring frequently or well. However, advanced planning and extra work in the beginning will save countless hours during the school year. Teachers can do five things to make assessment less time-consuming for themselves and their students:

1. Establish testing routines
2. Create assessment stations
3. Prepare and organize materials
4. Maintain assessment files
5. Involve other adults, students, and technology in the assessment process when possible

ESTABLISH ROUTINES

Establishing a consistent testing routine brings predictability for students. If students know that they will be taking a brief vocabulary test in Spanish class each Friday, or that a timer will be used for the 2-minute quiz at the start of math class every Tuesday and Thursday, they will require progressively fewer cues and less time to get ready to take the quizzes. For younger students, it helps to use the same cues that a quiz is coming. For example, "Okay students, it's time for a math probe. Clear your desks except for a pencil." Similarly, if the test-taking rules are the same every time, student compliance becomes easier to obtain and maintain. For example, when teaching an assessment course to college students, we do not allow them to wear baseball caps (some write notes inside the bill); we allow them to use calculators (but not those with alphanumeric displays because notes can be programmed into them); students must sit in every other seat so that there is no one to their immediate left or right; and we do not return the exams to students (to allow the reuse of questions without fear of students having a file of previous questions), although we do go over the exam with students individually if they wish. After the first exam or two, students know the rules and seldom need to be reminded.

To the extent feasible, the same directions and cues should be used. For example, a teacher might always announce a quiz in the same way: "Quiz time. Get ready." Directions for specific tests and quizzes may vary by content. For example, for an oral reading probe, the teacher may say, "When I say 'start,' begin reading at the top of the page. Try to read each word. If you don't know the word, you can skip it or I'll read it for you. At the end of a minute, I'll say 'stop.'" A teacher can use similar directions for a math probe: "Write your name at the top of the paper. When I say 'start,' begin writing your answers. Write neatly. If you don't know an answer, you can skip it. At the end of a minute, I'll say 'stop.'"

CREATE ASSESSMENT STATIONS

An assessment station is a place where individual testing can occur within a classroom. An assessment station should be large enough for an adult and student to work comfortably and be free of distractions. Stations are often placed in the back of the classroom, with chairs or desks facing the back wall and portable dividers walling off the left and right sides of the workspace.

Assessment stations allow classroom testing to occur concurrently with other classroom activities. They allow a teacher or an aide to test students or students to self-test. Student responses can be corrected during or after testing.

PREPARE ASSESSMENT MATERIALS

The first consideration in preparing assessment materials is that the assessment must match the instruction. Unless there is a good match between what is taught and what is tested, test results will lack validity. The best way for assessments to match curriculum is to use the actual content and formats that are used in instruction. For example, to assess mastery of addition facts that have been taught as number sentences, one would assess using number sentences as shown in Figure 9.1.[1]

If generic assessment devices are already available (see examples of such devices in Chapter 8, Curriculum-Based Approaches), there is no reason not to use them if they are appropriate. By appropriate, we mean that they represent measurement of the skills and knowledge that are part of the student's instruction. One advantage to using existing assessment devices is that many have been developed to ensure that the probes are of similar difficulty level across a year such that they can truly measure student progress over time. Now that Internet access is practically universal, teachers only need to go to their favorite search engine to find reading, writing, or math probes.

FIGURE 9.1
Matching Math Content to Assessment

How Addition Facts Are Taught

2 + 5 = ______ 6 + 3 = ______ 4 + 4 = ______

How Addition Facts Should Be Tested

6 + 3 = ______ 4 + 4 = ______ 2 + 5 = ______

How Addition Facts Should Not Be Tested

6 + ______ = 9 $\begin{array}{r} 4 \\ \underline{+4} \end{array}$ What are 2 and 5? ______

[1] Obviously, if testing is done to assess generalization or application of material, test content and perhaps formats will vary from those used during instruction.

There are numerous sites that generate a variety of probes (for example, Easy CBM and Intervention Central). Computer software can also be used to facilitate probe and quiz preparation (for example, Microsoft Word has a feature that provides summary data for print documents, including the number of words and the reading level). Any spreadsheet program allows the interchange of rows and columns so that a practically infinite number of parallel probes for word reading or math calculations can be created.

There is no need for teachers to create new assessment materials when they test the same content during subsequent semesters unless, of course, their instruction has changed enough to necessitate changing their tests. Tests, probes, projects, and other assessment devices take time to develop, and it is more efficient to use them again rather than start over. Like any other teaching material, tests may require revision. Sometimes a seemingly wonderful story starter used to measure writing skills does not work well with students. It is generally better to start the revision process while the problems or ideas are fresh—that is, immediately after a teacher has noticed that the tests are not working well. Sometimes all that is needed is a comment on the test that documents the problem. For example, "Students didn't like the story starter." Sometimes the course of action is obvious: "Words are too small—need bigger font and more space between words." If possible, teachers should make the revisions to the assessment materials as soon as they have a few moments of free time. Otherwise, the problems may be forgotten until the next time the teacher wants to use the test.

ORGANIZE MATERIALS

When assessment materials have been developed and perhaps revised, the major management problem is retrieval—both remembering that there are materials and where those materials are located. This problem is solved by organizing materials and maintaining a filing system.

One organizational strategy is to use codes. Teachers commonly color code tests and teaching materials. For example, instructional and assessment materials for oral reading might be located in folders with red tabs, whereas those for math may have blue tabs. Within content areas or units, codes may be based on instructional goals. For example, in reading, a teacher may have 10 folders with red tabs for regular C–V–C (consonant–short vowel–consonant) words. Student materials may be kept in different locations, such as a filing cabinet for reading probes with different drawers for different goals. Once the materials have been organized, teachers need only resupply their files at the beginning of each year (or semester in secondary schools).

INVOLVE OTHERS OR TECHNOLOGY

The process of assessment mainly requires professional judgment at two steps: (1) creating the assessment device and the procedures for its administration and (2) interpreting the results of the assessment. The other steps in the assessment process are routine and require only minimal training, not extensive professional expertise. Thus, although teachers must develop and interpret assessments, other adults or the students can be trained to conduct the assessments. Getting help with the actual administration of a test or probe frees teachers to perform other tasks that require professional judgment or skills while still providing the assessment data needed to guide instruction. And, as noted, technology devices now can be used to generate tests, monitor progress, provide teachers with assessment results, and serve as data warehouses.

3 Data Displays

After performances are scored, they must be recorded. Although tables and grade books are commonly used, they are not nearly as useful as charts and graphs. These displays greatly facilitate interpretation and decision making. There are two commonly used types of charts: equal interval and standard celeration charts. Both types of chart share common graphing conventions as shown in Figure 9.2.

SCENARIO *in* ASSESSMENT

PHIL SELF-ADMINISTERS A PROBE

After instruction and guided practice, Phil knows how to take his reading probes. He goes to the assessment center and follows the steps posted on the divider.

1. He checks his probe schedule and sees that he is supposed to take 2-minute oral reading probe No. 17.
2. He goes to the file, gets a copy of the probe, and lays it face up on the desk. He inserts a blank audio cassette into the tape recorder and rewinds to the beginning of the tape.
3. After locating the 3-minute timer on the desk, he starts recording.
4. He says the probe number and then sets the timer for 2 minutes.
5. He reads aloud into the tape recorder until the timer rings.
6. He stops the tape recorder, ejects it, and places it in the inbox on his teacher's desk.

Phil then returns to his seat and begins working. At a convenient time, his teacher or the aide gets a copy of the probe that Phil read, slides it into an acetate cover, notes errors on the cover, tallies the errors, calculates Phil's scores, and enters them on his chart. Then the teacher rewinds Phil's tape, wipes the acetate cover clean, and places the probe back into the file for reuse.

What implications about your own professional role can you draw from this scenario? Go to the Education CourseMate website for this textbook for more reflection questions about this Scenario in Assessment.

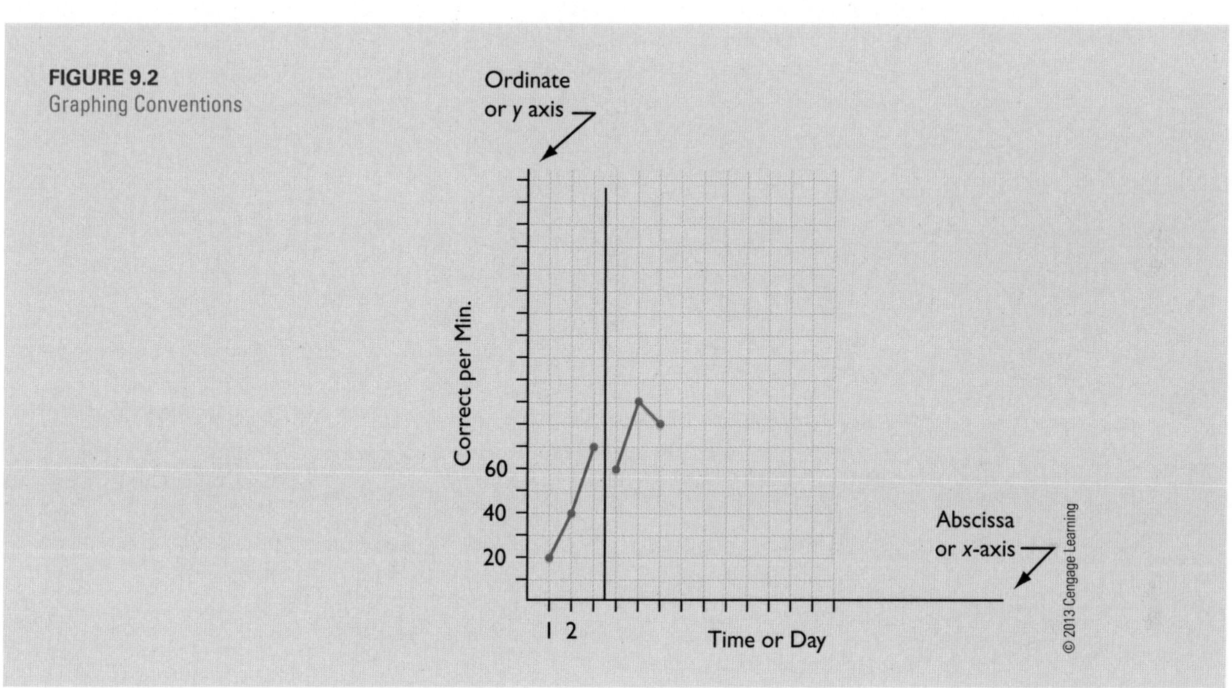

FIGURE 9.2
Graphing Conventions

- The vertical (y) axis indicates the amount of the variable (that is, its frequency, percent correct, rate of correct responses, and so forth). The axis is labeled (for example, correct responses per minute).
- The horizontal (x) axis indicates time, usually sessions or days. The axis is labeled (for example, school days).
- Dots represent performances on specific days; a dot's location on the chart is the intersection of the day or session in which the performance occurred and the amount (for example, rate) of performance.
- Dots on a single graph should represent only material that is of similar difficulty level; separate graphs are necessary to represent material of different difficulty levels (e.g., when a student switches from being monitored using 1st grade passages to being monitored using 2nd grade passages, a new graph should be created).
- Vertical lines separate different types of performances or different intervention conditions.
- Charts contain identifying data, such as the student's name and the objective being measured.

Two types of charts are used in special education: equal-interval charts and standard celeration charts. The difference between the two types of charts concerns the calibration of the vertical axis.

Equal-interval charts are most likely to be familiar to beginning educators. On these charts, the differences between adjacent points are additive and equal. The difference between one and two correct is the same as the difference between 50 and 51 correct. Figures 9.3, 9.4, and 9.5 are equal-interval graphs.

Standard celeration charts (also called standard behavior charts, semilogarithmic charts, or seven-cycle charts) are based on the principle that changes (increases or decreases) in the frequency of behavior within a specified time (for example,

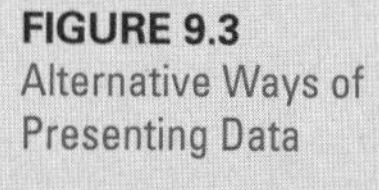

FIGURE 9.3
Alternative Ways of Presenting Data

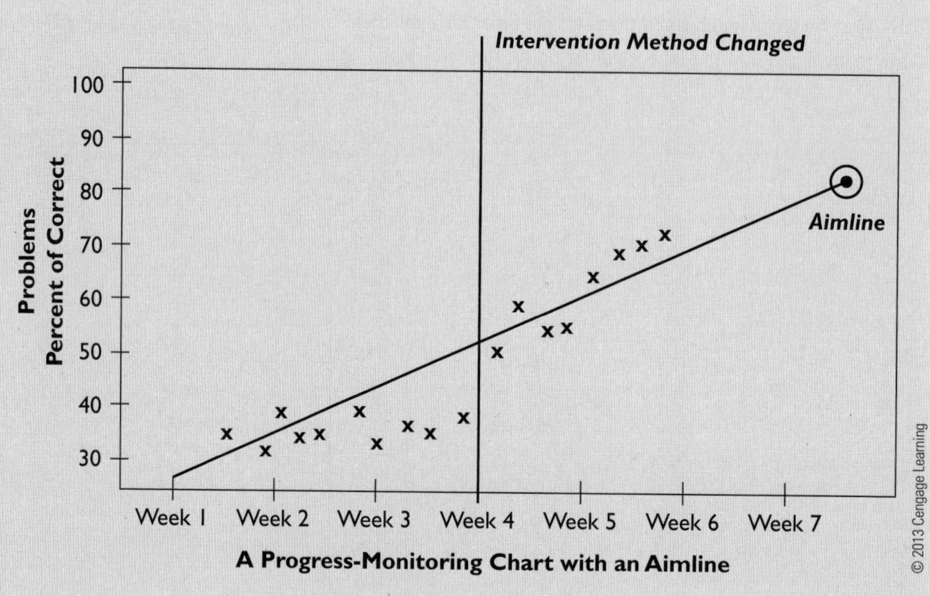

FIGURE 9.4
Alternative Ways of Presenting Data

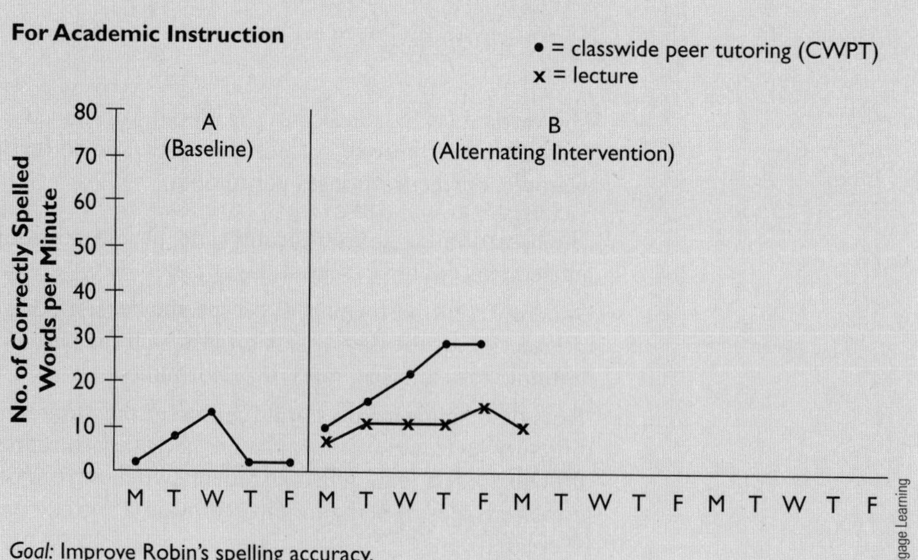

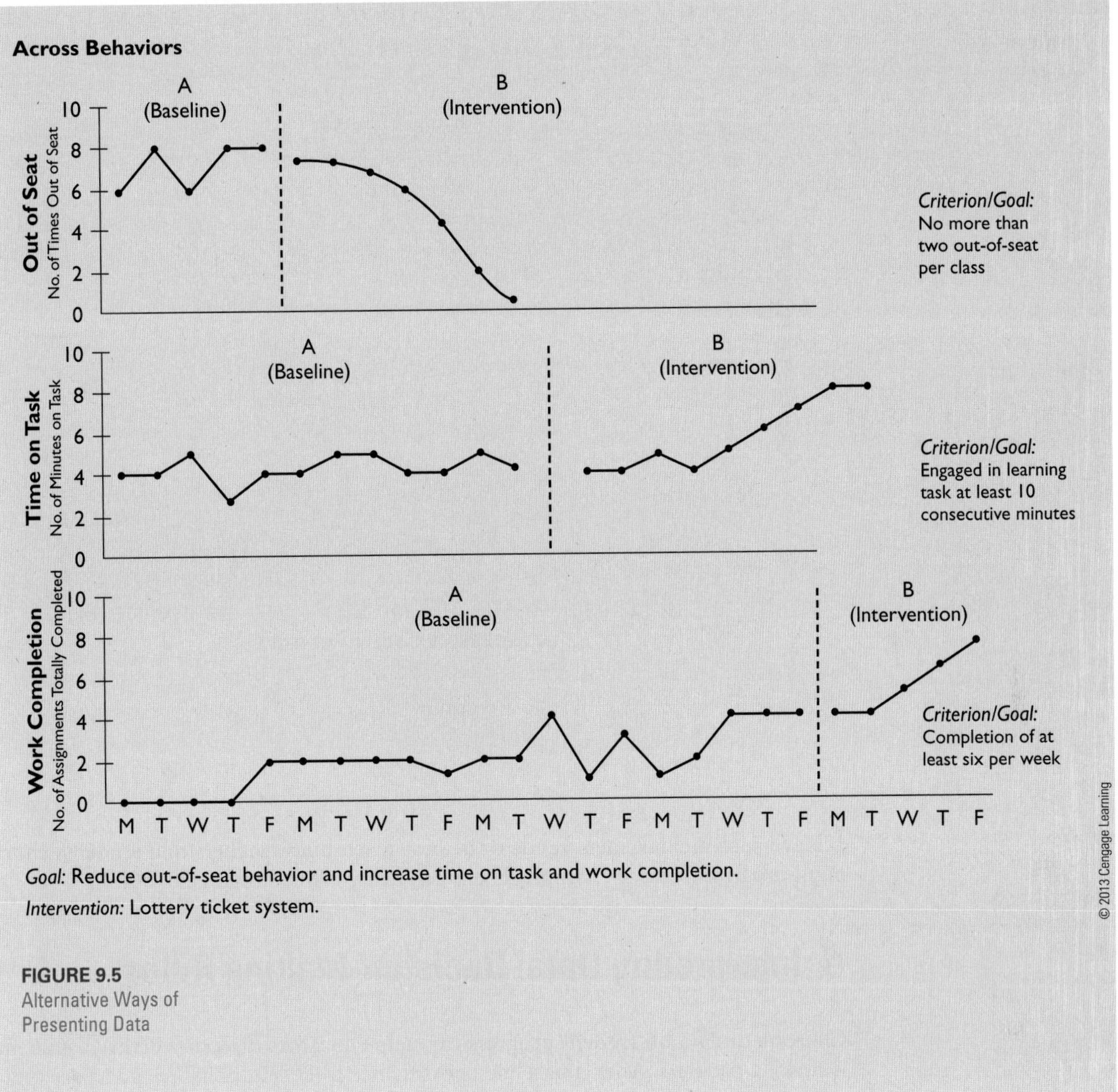

FIGURE 9.5
Alternative Ways of Presenting Data

number of correct responses per minute) are multiplicative, not additive. That is, the change from one correct to two correct is 100 percent and is the same as the change from 50 to 100. On daily celeration charts, the abscissa (x-axis) is divided into 140 days (that can be used as sessions). On the ordinate (y-axis), frequencies range from one per day to thousands per minute. A line from the bottom left corner of the chart to the top right corner indicates behavior that has doubled; any line parallel to that diagonal line similarly indicates behavior that has doubled. A line from the top left corner of the chart to the bottom right corner indicates that the behavior has reduced by half, and any diagonal line that is parallel to that line also indicates the behavior has halved. Figure 9.6 is a standard celeration day chart.

Although standard celeration charts allow one to see percentage change directly, it does not appear to matter which type of graph is used in terms of student achievement (Fuchs & Fuchs, 1987).

The benefits of charting student progress have been well documented since the 1960s. In general, students whose teachers chart pupil behavior have better achievement than students whose teachers do not chart. Students who chart their own performance have better achievement than students who do not chart their

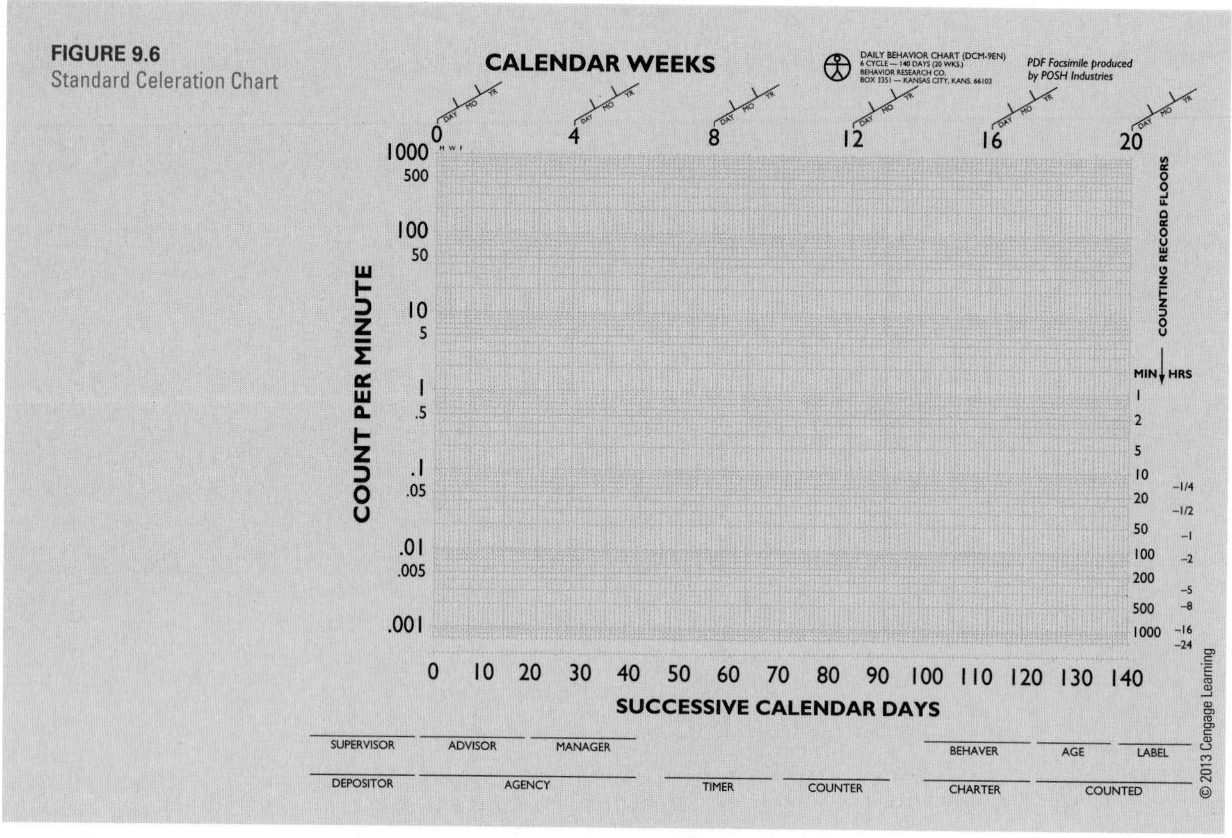

FIGURE 9.6
Standard Celeration Chart

achievement. Achievement tends to be best when both teachers and students chart pupil progress (see, for example, Fuchs & Fuchs, 1986; Santangelo, 2009).

4 Interpreting Data: Decision-Making Rules

Charting of data on student progress can help educators discern whether a student is making progress. After a baseline performance level is established, goals are typically set to assist with decision making. Goals may be set to ensure students reach the level of proficiency needed for them to be developmentally on track for a particular learning outcome (benchmark approach); they can be set using anticipated rates of growth established through prior research investigations, such as those described in Fuchs, Fuchs, Hamlett, Walz, and Germann (1993); or they can be set by using locally created norms for performance and growth.

It is said that we all "get sick of too much of a good thing." It is often the case that an intervention that "works" and is effective in moving a student toward an instructional goal will work for only a limited period of time. Students get satiated with specific instructional approaches or interventions. The construction of an aimline (see Chapter 6 for how to construct an aimline) and charting of student progress can help a teacher know when a change is needed. In Figure 9.3, after the third week of data collection, the teacher realized that the student was not on track to meet the goal, and so the intervention method was changed. Instructional decisions can also be informed by using charts to visually compare the effects of various instructional approaches that are used (as in Figure 9.4), and to see what effects the instructional approaches have on student different behaviors (as in Figure 9.5). In Chapter 23, we provide multiple examples of the kinds of charts that now can be generated by technology-enhanced assessment systems. Students and teachers no longer need to do their own charting.

Results from brief tests such as those frequently used to monitor progress can fluctuate, making it difficult to know whether the student is making progress toward meeting a goal. Sometimes fluctuations in performance are due to variations in the difficulty level of the test presented, sometimes they are due to student characteristics unrelated to what the test is intended to measure (for example, interest level and concentration level), and sometimes they are due to changes in student achievement, which are what you are intending to detect.

If a student is not improving in achievement at a rate needed to meet a predetermined goal, it is important that changes be made in instruction. However, given that there may be substantial fluctuation in the measures taken, how can we truly know whether the student is failing to make progress? Several decision-making strategies have been developed to help make appropriate decisions using progress monitoring data.

Four-point rule: Once a goal or aimline has been drawn, each data point collected after the determination of initial performance should be plotted soon after each probe is administered. If four consecutive data points fall below the goal line, a teaching change or intervention is considered warranted.

Parallel rule: Educators can draw an aimline as previously discussed. After several data points are collected, the trend in the student's performance can be compared to the aimline. If the instructional goal is the acquisition of a skill, the desired trendline is above the aimline and should be parallel or rise more steeply than the aimline. If the trendline does not meet the above criteria, instruction should be modified.

MODEL PROGRESS MONITORING PROJECTS

As people have recognized the benefits of frequent measurement of student learning, many educational systems have implemented systemwide changes that support progress monitoring efforts and have provided intervention as needed to those students who are not making adequate progress. The reauthorization of the Individuals with Disabilities Education Act in 2004 indicated that response to intervention (RTI) can be used to identify students in need of special education services, so many educational agencies are incorporating systematic procedures for managing progress monitoring data and using such data to make a variety of decisions.

See the website for more information and a summary table on projects that have supported such efforts.

Chapter Comprehension Questions

Write your answers to each of the following questions and then compare your responses to the text.

1. Name and describe three characteristics of effective testing programs.
2. What are three resources that you can use for setting up a plan for managing data collection and analysis in a classroom?
3. Provide two methods for making decisions using progress monitoring data.

Web Activities 

1. Go to the Cengage website and review the materials on five model progress-monitoring projects. Do a brief search on the web of two of these projects and provide a summary of what you find.
2. Search for and go to the websites for AIMSweb, DIBELS, Easy CBM, and Renaissance Learning and review the kinds of progress monitoring reports that can be generated by computers or web-based systems. Talk with others in your class about the relative merits of these reports.

Web Resources

"What the National Center on Student Progress Monitoring Can Do for You!"
http://www.studentprogress.org/library/Webinars.asp#webtour
Watch this webinar to see what resources at this center might be helpful to your work.

RTI Classroom Progress Monitoring Worksheet
http://www.interventioncentral.org/images/docs/blog/rti_tier_1_teacher_data_collection_form.pdf
You can review the RTI classroom progress monitoring worksheet and associated directions at this site.

Additional resources for this chapter can be found on the Education CourseMate website. Go to CengageBrain.com to access the site.

Part 3

Assessment Using Formal Measures

The chapters in Part 3 describe the most common domains in which assessment of processes (abilities) and products (skills) are conducted. With the exception of Chapter 10, each chapter in this part focuses on a different process or skill domain and opens with an explanation of why the domain is assessed. We next provide a general overview of the components of the domain (that is, the behaviors that are usually assessed) and then discuss the more commonly used tests within the domain. Each chapter concludes with some suggestions for coping with problems in assessing the domain.

The criteria we used in selecting and reviewing specific tests warrant some discussion. First, in selecting tests we could not, and did not, include all the available measures for each domain. Rather, we tried to select representative and commonly used devices in each area. Reviews of other tests are on the website for the book. Second, in evaluating the technical adequacy of each test, we restricted our evaluation to information in the test manuals. Each test review follows the same format: a description of the test's content, the derived scores, the standardization samples, evidence of reliability and validity and a summary.

Test users are ultimately responsible for test selection, administration, and interpretation. Thus, you may need to investigate the current research to support the validity of your assessment. Therefore, we urge our readers to go beyond our reviews.

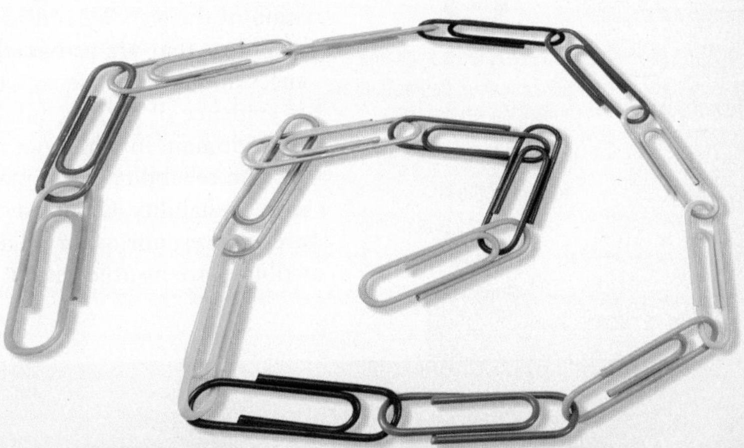

Web Chapter Preview

10

iStockphoto.com/sdominick

How to Evaluate a Test

CHAPTER GOALS

1. Understand the considerations in selecting a test to review.
2. Understand that reviewing a test requires an analysis of the test's purpose, content and assessment procedures, scores and norms, and reliability and validity in order to reach a summative evaluation.

KEY TERMS

pre-review
honing-in phase
"prove it" mind-set
test purposes

CHAPTER SUMMARY

The first step in evaluating a test is to choose a test to evaluate. Unless we know the specific test we want to evaluate, our first task is to find a test to use. Current publisher's catalogs or a reference work can generally help us find a test that we are qualified to administer and that can be used appropriately with students we want to test.

We usually begin by ascertaining the uses for the test recommended by the test's authors. Then we look for the authors' definition of the domain being tested and the procedures for testing that domain. Next we begin a more technical examination of the test. We consider the types of derived scores that are available and the norms that are provided. The scores and norms must lead to correct inferences about the students we are going to test. We want to make sure that there is evidence of good reliability (i.e., typically .90 or higher) for every score in each domain in which we are interested. Usually this will mean an indication of item reliability, but it may often also mean indications of stability and interscorer reliability. Obviously a test found generally lacking in its content, procedures, scores, norms, or reliability cannot yield valid inferences. However, these attributes are insufficient; all tests should present convincing evidence of general

The full chapter is available on the Education CourseMate website for this textbook.

Go to cengagebrain.com to access the site and download this chapter.

validity. General validity refers to evidence that a test leads to valid inferences for each recommended purpose of the test.

Finally, we reach an overall evaluation of a test. At this point, it is a good idea to remember that it is the test authors' responsibility to convince potential test users of the usefulness of their test. Having found that a test is generally useful, it is still necessary to determine if it is appropriately used with the specific students you intend to test. Of course, a test that is not generally useful will not be useful with a specific student. Remember, once you use a test, *you*—not the test author—become responsible for test-based inferences.

Chapter Comprehension Questions

Write your answers to each of the following questions and then compare your responses to the text.

1. What are five questions that you should ask when choosing a test for careful review?
2. What kinds of evidence should test authors provide to support the uses they recommend for their test?
3. What kinds of evidence should test authors provide to support the interpretations that they recommend for their test?
4. Justify a "prove it" approach to evaluating a test.
5. What reliability estimates should be reported in a test manual?

Web Activities 

1. Search the Internet for the PRO-ED website and Pearson's clinical assessment website for preK-16 education and special needs. Examine the multiple-skill achievement tests. Choose one or two tests that you would like more information about.
2. Search the Internet for the PRO-ED website for material about autism and Pearson's clinical assessment website for ADHD and autism (within the section on preK-16 education and special needs). Examine the assessment procedures for autism. Choose one or two devices that you would like more information about.

Web Resources

Questions to Ask When Evaluating Tests
http://pareonline.net/getvn.asp?v=4&n=2
Lawrence Rudner (ERIC Clearinghouse on Assessment and Evaluation) provides questions to ask about each aspect of test evaluation, including test coverage and use, appropriate samples for test validation and norming, reliability, different types of validity, test administration, test reporting, and test and item bias.

Technical Criteria for Evaluating Tests
http://www.rand.org/pubs/monograph_reports/MR1554/MR1554.ch3.pdf
Vi-Nhuan Le and Stephen Klein prepared this comprehensive 26-page chapter to explain the criteria to be used in test evaluations.

Assessment of Academic Achievement with Multiple-Skill Devices

CHAPTER GOALS

1. Know factors to consider in selecting an achievement test.
2. Know the categories of achievement tests: group versus individual, norm referenced versus standards referenced, multiple skill versus single skill, and diagnostic versus survey.
3. Know the reasons why we assess academic achievement.
4. Be able to describe and compare representative achievement tests.
5. Know how to get the most out of an achievement test.

KEY TERMS

achievement
attainment
norm referenced
standards referenced
diagnostic achievement test
instructional match
normative update

Achievement tests are the most frequently used tests in educational settings. Multiple-skill achievement tests evaluate knowledge and understanding in several curricular areas, such as reading, science, and math. These tests are intended to assess the extent to which students have profited from schooling and other life experiences, compared with other students of the same age or grade. Consequently, most achievement tests are norm referenced, although some are standards-referenced measures. Norm-referenced and standards-referenced achievement tests are designed in consultation with subject matter experts and are believed to reflect national curricula and national curricular trends in general. Achievement tests are used to tell teachers the skills students do and do not have so that they can make reasoned estimates about where to start in instruction.

Achievement tests can be classified along several dimensions; perhaps the most important one describes their specificity and density of content. *Diagnostic achievement* tests have dense content; they have many more items to assess specific skills and concepts and allow finer analyses to pinpoint specific strengths and weaknesses in academic development. Tests with fewer items per skill allow comparisons among test takers but do not have enough items to pinpoint students' strengths and weaknesses. These tests may still be useful for estimating a student's current general level of functioning in comparison with other students, and they estimate the extent to which an individual has acquired the skills and concepts that other students of the same age or grade have acquired.

Another important dimension is the number of students who can be tested at once. Achievement tests are designed to be given to groups of students or to individual students. Generally, group tests require students to read and either write or mark answers; individually administered tests may require an examiner to read questions to a student and may allow students to respond orally. The primary advantage of individually administered tests is that they afford examiners the opportunity to observe students working and solving problems. Therefore, examiners can glean valuable qualitative information in addition to the quantitative information that scores provide. Finally, a group test may be appropriately given to one student at a time, but individual tests should not be given to a group of students.

Table 11.1 shows the different categories of achievement tests. The Stanford Achievement Test (SAT), for example, is both a norm-referenced and a standards-referenced (objective-referenced) group-administered screening test that samples skill development in many content areas. The Stanford Diagnostic Reading Test (SDRT), detailed on the Education CourseMate website for this textbook in Chapter 12, is both a norm-referenced, group-administered test and a standards-referenced, individually administered diagnostic test that samples skill development strengths and weaknesses in the single skill of reading. The SDRT is intended to provide a classroom teacher with a more detailed analysis of students' strengths and weaknesses in reading, which may be of assistance in program planning and evaluation.

Group-administered multiple-skill achievement tests have limited use in planning instruction for individual students. Their primary use in schools today is for purposes of making accountability decisions. We do not review the many group-administered measures in this chapter, but do include selected reviews on the Education CourseMate website for this textbook.

1 Considerations for Selecting a Test

In selecting a multiple-skill achievement test, teachers must consider four factors: content validity, stimulus–response modes, the standards used in their state, and relevant norms. First, teachers must evaluate evidence for content validity, the most important kind of validity for achievement tests. Many multiple-skill tests have general content validity—the tests measure important concepts and skills that are generally part of most curricula. This validity makes their content suitable for

TABLE 11.1 Commonly Used Achievement Tests

Test	Author	Publisher	Year	Ages/ Grades	Administered	NRT/ CRT	Subtests
Metropolitan Achievement Tests (survey battery)		Pearson	2002	Grades 1–10 and 11/12	Group	NRT	Sounds and Print, Reading Vocabulary, Reading Comprehension, Open-Ended Reading, Mathematics, Mathematics Concepts and Problem Solving, Mathematics Computation, Open-Ended Mathematics, Language, Spelling, Open-Ended Writing, Science, Social Studies
Stanford Achievement Test Series		Pearson	2004	Grades K–12	Group	NRT and CRT	Sounds and Letters, Word Study Skills, Word Reading, Sentence Reading, Reading Vocabulary, Reading Comprehension, Mathematics, Mathematics Problem Solving, Mathematics Procedures, Language, Spelling, Listening to Words and Stories, Listening, Environment, Science, Social Science
TerraNova 3		CTB/ McGraw-Hill	2008	Grades K–12	Group	NRT	Reading, Language, Mathematics, Science, Social Studies
Kaufman Test of Educational Achievement-II	Kaufman & Kaufman	Pearson	1998	Grades 1–12	Individual	NRT	Reading, Decoding, Reading Comprehension, Mathematics Application, Mathematics Computation, Spelling
Peabody Individual Achievement Test-Revised-Normative update	Dunn & Markwardt	Pearson	1998	Grades K–12	Individual	NRT	Mathematics, Reading Recognition, Reading Comprehension, Spelling, General Information, Written Expression
Wide Range Achievement Test–4	Wilkinson & Robertson	Pro-Ed	2007	Ages 5–75	Individual	NRT	Word Reading, Sentence Comprehension, Spelling, Math Computation
Woodcock–Johnson Psychoeducational Battery III (reviewed in Chapter 15)	Woodcock, McGrew, Mather	Riverside	2001	Ages 2–90+	Individual	NRT	Story Recall, Picture Vocabulary, Understanding Directions, Oral Comprehension, Letter–Word Identification, Word Attack, Passage Comprehension, Reading Vocabulary, Calculation, Math Fluency, Applied Problems, Quantitative Concepts, Writing Samples, Writing Fluency

Test	Author	Publisher	Year	Ages/ Grades	Administered	NRT/ CRT	Subtests
Wechsler Individual Achievement Test–III	Wechsler	Pearson	2009	Grades pre-K–12	Individual	NRT	Word Reading, Reading Comprehension, Pseudoword Decoding, Numerical Operations, Math Reasoning, Spelling, Written Expression, Listening Comprehension, Oral Expression
Iowa Tests of Basic Skills		Riverside	2001	Grades K–8	Group	CRT	Vocabulary, Reading/Reading Comprehension, Listening, Language, Mathematics, Social Studies, Science, Sources of Information
Metropolitan Achievement Tests (instructional battery)		Pearson	2002	Grades K–12	Group	CRT	Sounds and Print, Reading Vocabulary, Reading Comprehension, Open-Ended Reading, Mathematics, Mathematics Concepts and Problem Solving, Mathematics Computation, Open-Ended Mathematics, Language, Spelling, Open-Ended Writing, Science, Social Studies
Stanford Achievement Test Series		Pearson	2004	Grades K–12	Group	CRT	Sounds and Letters, Word Study Skills, Word Reading, Sentence Reading, Reading Vocabulary, Reading Comprehension, Mathematics, Mathematics Problem Solving, Mathematics Procedures, Language, Spelling, Listening to Words and Stories, Listening, Environment, Science, Social Studies
Diagnostic Achievement Battery–3	Newcomer	Pro-Ed	2001	Ages 6–14	Individual	NRT	Story Comprehension, Capitalization, Characteristics, Punctuation, Synonyms, Spelling, Grammatic Completion, Contextual Language, Alphabet/Word Knowledge, Math Reasoning, Reading Comprehension, Math Calculation, Story Construction, Phonemic Analysis

assessing general attainment.[1] However, if a test is to be used to assess the extent to which students have profited from school instruction—that is, to measure student achievement—more than general content validity is required: the test must match the instruction provided. Tests that do not match instruction lack content validity, and decisions based on such tests should be restricted. When making decisions about

[1] Recall the previous discussion on the distinction between attainment and achievement. Achievement generally refers to content that has been learned as a product of schooling. Attainment is a broader term referring to what individuals have learned as a result of both schooling and other life experiences.

content validity for students with disabilities, educators must consider the extent to which the student has had an opportunity to learn the content of the test. Some students with disabilities are assigned to a curriculum (often a functional curriculum) that differs from the curriculum to which nondisabled students are exposed. These students are often assessed using the same test that others take, but they are provided adaptations or accommodations to compensate for their disability (see Chapter 21). Many students with severe cognitive impairments are given alternate assessments, and their performance is evaluated relative to modified achievement standards or alternate achievement standards. We discuss alternate assessment and modified assessment practices in Chapter 28.

Second, educators who use achievement tests for students with disabilities need to consider whether the stimulus–response modes of subtests may be exceptionally difficult for students with physical or motor problems. Tests that are timed may be inappropriately difficult for students whose reading or motor difficulties cause them to take more time on specific tasks. (Many of these issues are described in greater detail in Chapter 21.)

Third, educators must consider the common core standards and the state education standards for the state in which they work. In doing so, they should examine the extent to which the achievement test they select measures the content of their state standards.

Fourth, educational professionals must evaluate the adequacy of each test's norms by asking whether the normative group is composed of the kinds of individuals to whom they wish to compare their students. If a test is used to estimate general attainment, a representative sample of students from throughout the nation is preferred. However, if a test is used to estimate achievement in a school system, local norms are probably better. Finally, teachers should examine the extent to which a total test and its components have the reliability necessary for making decisions about what students have learned.

2 Categories of Achievement Tests

Table 11.1 provides a list of commonly used tests, indicates ages and grades for which the tests are appropriate, mode of administration, and specific subtests.

3 Why Do We Assess Academic Achievement?

Achievement tests are used most often as a broad assessment of academic skill development in making universal screening or accountability decisions. Their primary use is in making universal screening or accountability decisions. They also may be used to identify individual students for whom educational intervention is necessary, either in the form of remediation (for those who demonstrate relatively low-level skill development) or in the form of academic enrichment (for those who exhibit exceptionally high-level skill development). However, screening tests have limited behavior samples. Therefore, students who are identified with screening tests should be further assessed with diagnostic tests to verify their need for specific educational intervention.

Although multiple-skill, group-administered achievement tests are usually considered to be screening devices, scores earned on the tests occasionally are used in making eligibility decisions. In principle, such a use is generally inappropriate, although it may be justifiable and even desirable when the group tests (for example, the Stanford Achievement Test Series or the Metropolitan Achievement Tests) contain behavior samples that are more complete than those contained in some individually administered tests of achievement (such as the Wide Range Achievement Test 4 [WRAT4]). Use of an achievement test with a more comprehensive behavior sample is desirable if the tester goes beyond the scores earned to examine performance on specific test items.

Multiple-skill achievement tests may also be used for progress evaluation. Most school districts have routine testing programs at various grade levels to evaluate the extent to which pupils in their schools are progressing in comparison with state standards. Scores on achievement tests provide communities, school boards, and parents with an index of the quality of schooling. Schools and the teachers within those schools are often subject to question when pupils fail to demonstrate expected progress.

Finally, achievement tests are used to evaluate the relative effectiveness of alternative curricula. For instance, Brown School may choose to use the Read Well Reading Series in third grade, whereas Green School decides to use the Open Court Reading Program. If school personnel can assume that children were at relatively comparable reading levels when they entered the third grade, then achievement tests may be administered at the end of the year to ascertain the relative effectiveness of the Read Well and the Open Court programs. Educators must, of course, avoid many assumptions in such evaluations (for example, that the quality of individual teachers and the instructional environment are comparable in the two schools) and many research pitfalls if comparative evaluation is to have meaning.

SPECIFIC TESTS OF ACADEMIC ACHIEVEMENT

The remainder of this chapter addresses three individually administered multiple-skill devices (the Peabody Individual Achievement Test [PIAT-R/NU], Wide Range Achievement Test 4 [WRAT4] and the Wechsler Individual Achievement Test 3 [WIAT-III). Later chapters discuss both screening and diagnostic tests that are devoted to specific content areas, such as reading and mathematics. In Chapter 15, we review the Woodcock-Johnson III Normative Update (NU) Tests of Achievement (WJIII NU)

Peabody Individual Achievement Test–Revised/Normative Update

The most recent edition of the Peabody Individual Achievement Test (PIAT-R/NU; Markwardt, 1998) is not a new edition of the test but a normative update of the 1989 edition of the PIAT-R. The test is an individually administered, norm-referenced instrument designed to provide a wide-ranging screening measure of academic achievement in six content areas. It can be used with students in kindergarten through grade 12. PIAT-R/NU test materials are contained in four easel kits, one for each volume of the test. Easel kit volumes present stimulus materials to the student at eye level; the examiner's instructions are placed on the reverse side. The student can see one side of the response plate, whereas the examiner can see both sides. The test is recommended by the author for use in individual evaluation, guidance, admissions and transfers, grouping of students, progress evaluation, and personnel selection.

The original PIAT (Dunn & Markwardt, 1970) included five subtests. The PIAT-R added a written expression subtest. The 1989 edition updated the content of the test. The 1998 edition is identical to the 1989 edition. Behaviors sampled by the six subtests of the PIAT-R/NU follow.

Subtests

Mathematics This subtest contains 100 multiple-choice items, ranging from items that assess such early skills as matching, discriminating, and recognizing numerals to items that assess advanced concepts in geometry and trigonometry. The test is a measure of the student's knowledge and application of math concepts and facts.

Reading Recognition This subtest contains 100 items, ranging in difficulty from preschool level through high school level. Items assess skill development in matching letters, naming capital and lowercase letters, and recognizing words in isolation.

Reading Comprehension This subtest contains 81 multiple-choice items assessing skill development in understanding what is read. After reading a sentence, the student must indicate comprehension by choosing the correct picture out of a group of four.

Spelling This subtest consists of 100 items sampling behaviors from kindergarten level through high school level. Initial items assess the student's ability to distinguish a printed letter of the alphabet from pictured objects and to associate letter symbols with speech sounds. More difficult items assess the student's ability to identify, from a response bank of four words, the correct spelling of a word read aloud by the examiner.

General Information This subtest consists of 100 questions presented orally, which the student must answer orally. Items assess the extent to which the student has learned facts in social studies, science, sports, and the fine arts.

Written Expression This subtest assesses written-language skills at two levels. Level I, appropriate for students in kindergarten and first grade, is a measure of prewriting skills, such as skill in copying and writing letters, words, and sentences from dictation. At Level II, the student writes a story in response to a picture prompt.

Scores

All but one of the PIAT-R/NU subtests are scored in the same way: The student's response to each item is rated pass–fail. On these five subtests, raw scores are converted to grade and age equivalents, grade- and age-based standard scores, percentile ranks, normal-curve equivalents, and stanines. The Written Expression subtest is scored differently from the other subtests. The examiner uses a set of scoring criteria included in an appendix in the test manual. At Level I, the examiner scores the student's writing of his or her name and then scores 18 items pass–fail. For the more difficult items at Level I, the student must earn a specified number of subcredits to pass the item. Methods for assigning subcredits are specified clearly in the manual. At Level II, the student generates a free response, and the assessor examines the response for certain specified characteristics. For example, the student is given credit for each letter correctly capitalized, each correct punctuation, and the absence of inappropriate words. Scores earned on the Written Expression subtest include grade-based stanines and developmental scaled scores (with mean = 8 and standard deviation = 3).

Three composite scores are used to summarize student performance on the PIAT-R/NU: total reading, total test, and written language. Total reading is described as an overall measure of "reading ability" and is obtained by combining scores on Reading Recognition and Reading Comprehension. The total test score is obtained by combining performance on the General Information, Reading Recognition, Reading Comprehension, Mathematics, and Spelling subtests. A third composite score, the written-language composite score, is optional and is obtained by combining performance on the Spelling and Written Expression subtests.

Norms

The 1989 edition of the PIAT-R/NU was standardized on 1,563 students in kindergarten through grade 12. The 1998 normative update was completed in conjunction with normative updating of the Kaufman Test of Educational Achievement, the Key Math–Revised, and the Woodcock Reading Mastery Tests–Revised. The sample for the normative updates was 3,184 students in kindergarten through grade 12. A stratified multistage sampling procedure was used to ensure selection of a nationally representative group at each grade level. Students in the norm group did not all take each of the five tests. Rather, one-fifth of the students took each test, along with portions of each of the other tests. Thus, the norm groups for the brief and comprehensive forms consist of approximately 600 students. There are as few as 91 students at 3-year age ranges. Because multiple measures were given to each student, the authors could use linking and equating to increase the size of the norm sample.

Approximately 10 years separate the data-collection periods for the original PIAT norms and the updated norms. Changes during that time in curriculum and educational practice, in population demographics, and in the general cultural environment may have affected levels of academic achievement.

Reliability

All data on the reliability of the PIAT-R/NU are for the original PIAT-R. The performance of students on the two measures has changed, and so the authors should have conducted a few reliability studies on students in the late 1990s. Generalizations from the reliability of the original PIAT-R to reliability of the PIAT-R/NU are suspect.

Validity

All data on validity of the PIAT-R/NU are for the original PIAT-R. The performance of students on the two measures has changed, and so the authors should have conducted a few validity studies on students in the late 1990s. Generalizations from the validity of the original PIAT-R to validity of PIAT-R/NU are suspect. This is especially true for measures of validity based on relations with external measures where the measures (for example, the Wide Range Achievement Test or the Peabody Picture Vocabulary Test) have been revised.

Summary

The PIAT-R/NU is an individually administered achievement test that was renormed in 1998. Reliability and validity information is based on studies of the 1989 edition of the test. As with any achievement test, the most crucial concern is content validity. Users must be sensitive to the correspondence of the content of the PIAT-R/NU to a student's curriculum. The test is essentially a 1970 test that was revised and renormed in 1989 and then renormed again in

1998. Data on reliability and validity are based on the earlier version of the scale, which of course has gone unchanged. The practice of updating norms without gathering data on continued technical adequacy is dubious. This test now should be considered very dated and of questionable relevance to current curricula.

Wide Range Achievement Test 4

The Wide Range Achievement Test 4 (WRAT4; Wilkinson & Robertson, 2007) is an individually administered norm-referenced test designed to measure word recognition, spelling, and math computation skills in individuals 5 to 94 years of age. The test takes approximately 15 to 25 minutes to administer to students ages 5 to 7 years and approximately 35 to 45 minutes for older students. There are two alternate forms of the WRAT4. The test contains four subtests.

Subtests

Word Reading The student is required to name letters and read words.

Sentence Comprehension The student is shown sentences and is to indicate understanding of the sentences by filling in missing words.

Spelling The examiner dictates words and the student must write these down, earning credit for each word spelled correctly.

Math Computation The student is required to solve basic computation problems through counting, identifying numbers, solving simple oral problems, and calculating written math problems.

Scores

The raw scores that students earn on the WRAT4 can be converted to standard scores, confidence intervals (85, 90, and 95%), percentiles, grade equivalents, normal curve equivalents, and stanines. Separate scores are available for each subtest and for a reading composite (made up of Word Recognition and Sentence Comprehension).

Norms

The WRAT4 was standardized on a national sample of more than 3,000 individuals, ages 5 to 94 years. The sample was stratified on the basis of age, gender, ethnicity, geographic region, and parental education. Although tables in the manual report the relationship between the standardization sample and the composition of the U.S. population, cross-tabs (indicating, for example, the number of boys of each ethnicity from each geographic region) are not provided.

Reliability

Two kinds of reliability information are provided for the WRAT4: internal consistency and alternate-form reliability. Internal consistency coefficients range from .81 to .99, with median internal consistency coefficients ranging from .87 to .96. Alternate-form reliabilities range from .78 to .89 for an age-based sample and from .86 to .90 for a grade-based sample. The reliabilities of the Math Computation subtest are noticeably lower than those for other subtests. Test–retest reliabilities are sufficient, again with the exception of the Math Computation subtest. With the exception of the Math Computation subtest, the test is reliable enough for use in making screening decisions.

Validity

The WRAT4 is a screening test that covers a broad range of behaviors, so there are few items of each specific type. This results in a relatively limited behavior sample. The authors provide evidence of validity by demonstrating that test scores increase with age, that intercorrelations among the various subtests are as theoretically would be expected, and that correlations are high among performance on WRAT4 and previous versions of the test. Validity is also demonstrated by high correlations among subtests of the WRAT4 and comparable samples of behavior from the WIAT-II, Kaufman Test of Educational Achievement–II (KTEA-II), and the Woodcock–Johnson III Tests of Achievement (note: not the new normative update for this test).

Summary

The WRAT4 provides a very limited sample of behaviors in 4 content areas. Evidence for reliability is good, but evidence for validity is based on correlations to forms of other tests that since have been updated. Its use is limited to making screening decisions.

Wechsler Individual Achievement Test–Third Edition[2]

The Wechsler Individual Achievement Test–Third Edition (WIAT-III; Psychological Corporation, 2009) is a diagnostic, norm-referenced achievement test designed to assess reading, mathematics, written expression, listening, and speaking of individuals ages 4 years, 0 months to 19, years 11 months (or prekindergarten through grade 12). In this third edition, the authors contend that the WIAT-III better captures and aligns with recent federal legislation and state regulation changes in the identification of learning disabilities. They further argue that the WIAT-III, which includes 16 subtests (organized into seven domain composite scores and one total achievement composite; see Table 11.2), fully assesses each of the eight achievement areas in which specific learning

[2] Jill Fortain, Kristen S. Girard, Nathan von der Embse

TABLE 11.2 Description of the WIAT-III Composites and Subtests

Composite	Subtest	Description
Total Reading		
Basic Reading	Word Reading	Assess word recognition, word reading, and decoding skills ■ Fluently pronounce or read aloud individual words presented in isolation
	Pseudoword Decoding	Assess the ability to apply phonetic decoding skills ■ Read aloud non-sense, made-up words that conform to typical English language phonetic structures
Reading Comprehension and Fluency	Reading Comprehension	Assess skills in drawing meaning from text. ■ Reading passages (out loud or silently) and providing oral responses to content questions
	Oral Reading Fluency	Assess the ability to read text quickly, accurately, and with comprehension ■ Read a series of grade-level passages aloud ■ Answer a question pertaining to the passage's content
	Early Reading Skills*	Assess decoding and pre-reading skills ■ Identify letters by name and by sound ■ Identify words that begin/end with the same sound(s) ■ Word rhyming and letter blending activities ■ Match printed words to the appropriate picture
Mathematics	Math Problem Solving	Assess mathematical reasoning skills ■ Count ■ Identify shapes ■ Solve single- and multiple-step story problems ■ Interpret graphs and charts ■ Solve problems using geometry, statistics and probability
	Numerical Operations	Assess the ability to identify and write numbers; perform mathematical computations ■ Solve written computation problems ■ Solve basic equations involving addition, subtraction, multiplication, or division of whole numbers, decimals, and/or fractions
Math Fluency	Math Fluency—Addition	Evaluate computational fluency ■ Solve basic addition problems quickly and accurately
	Math Fluency—Subtraction	Evaluate computational fluency ■ Solve basic subtraction problems quickly and accurately
	Math Fluency—Multiplication	Evaluate computational fluency ■ Solve basic multiplication problems quickly and accurately
Written Expression	Alphabet Writing Fluency	Assess automatic letter writing skills ■ Write the letters of the alphabet in any order, in print or cursive, lower- or uppercase
	Spelling	Assess spelling skills ■ Write dictated letters, letter blends, and whole words

Composite	Subtest	Description
	Sentence Composition	Evaluate the ability to write well-formulated sentences ■ Combine multiple sentences into single sentences while preserving meaning and using correct spelling, capitalization, and punctuation ■ Build sentences using target words
	Essay Composition	■ Measure writing skills, including theme development text organization, and grammar and mechanics ■ Construct a narrative essay based on the given prompt
Oral Language	Listening Comprehension	Measure comprehension of single sentences and extended orally presented discourse ■ Pointing to objects upon request ■ Orally responding to questions about passages presented aloud
	Oral Expression	Measure expressive vocabulary and word retrieval skills ■ Providing words orally to match described constructs ■ Repeating orally presented sentences verbatim

*NOTE: Although the Early Reading Skills subtest does measure students' pre-reading skills, it is *not* included in the calculation of the Total Reading Composite score or any of the other two reading-related composites. It is *only* included in the calculation of students' Total Achievement Score.

disabilities can be identified under the Individuals with Disabilities Education Improvement Act of 2004 (IDEA, 2004; basic reading skills, reading fluency, reading comprehension, written expression, oral expression, listening comprehension, mathematics calculation, mathematics problem solving) in greater depth than previous versions of the test. New subtests on the WIAT-III that were not included on the WIAT-II include the oral reading fluency and mathematics fluency subtests. For children in pre-kindergarten or kindergarten, the length of administration is approximately 45 to 50 minutes; administration to students in grades 1 through 6 lasts approximately 1.5 hours and for grades 7 through 12 is approximately 1.5 to 2 hours.

Scores

Seven types of scores are available on the WIAT-III, including standard scores, percentile ranks, normal curve equivalents, stanines, and age and grade equivalents as well as growth scale value scores. In order to attain these scores, examiners must first obtain the students' raw subtest scores following the appropriate basal and ceiling rules or item-set guidelines for each subtest. Additionally, two subtests (Reading Comprehension and Oral Reading Fluency) require raw scores be converted to weighted raw scores prior to obtaining the corresponding standard scores.

Norms

The WIAT-III was standardized on a national sample of 2,775 students. A stratified sampling procedure was used to ensure that the normative samples for both grade and age were representative of students in grades pre-kindergarten through grade 12 on each of the following demographic variables (based on the U.S. Bureau of the Census data from October 2005): grade, age, race/ethnicity, sex, parent education level, and geographic region. The grade-based normative sample included 1,400 and 1,375 students (a fall and a spring sample, respectively), reflecting 14 grade-level groups. With the exception of a pre-kindergarten sample in the spring, which only had 75 participants, all grade groups had 100 participants at both fall and spring samples. The age-based normative sample included 1,826 students, which, like the grade-based groups, were divided into 14 groups based on age. The racial-ethnic makeups of each age and grade sample, as well as the geographic representation within each age and grade sample, were reported to reflect those of the U.S. population.

Reliability

Split-half reliability coefficients were calculated with the exception of timed subtests and those subtests that do not provide data at the individual item-level (i.e., Alphabet Writing Fluency, Math Fluency, Alphabet Writing Fluency, Sentence Composition, Essay Composition, Oral Expression, and Oral Reading Fluency). All eight composites across all school-ages and grades had split-half reliabilities higher than .90 except for the Oral Language and Written Expression composites, which were equal to or higher than .85 across all school ages and grades.

Test-Retest reliability was also calculated in order to demonstrate the stability of the WIAT-III using a sample of 131 students. The reported average test-retest interval for pre-kindergarten through fifth grades was 13 days, and 14 days for grades six through twelve. Correlations suggested generally adequate stability for both grade level groups. Specifically, the average correlation coefficients for the Reading Comprehension, Word Reading, Pseudoword Decoding, Oral Reading Fluency, Oral Reading Rate, and Spelling subtests were the highest, ranging from .90 to .94. Early Reading Skills, Math Problem Solving, Essay Composition, Essay Composition: Grammar and Mechanics, Numerical Operations, Oral Expression, Oral Reading Accuracy, and Math Fluency (Addition, Subtraction, and Multiplication subtests) also demonstrated strong levels of stability with average correlation coefficients ranging from .82 to .89. Two subtests, Listening Comprehension and Sentence Composition, demonstrated lower yet still acceptable levels of stability with average correlation coefficients of .75 and .79.

Finally, interrater agreement was calculated for subtests with objective and more subjective scoring criteria. For the objective subtests, agreement was reported to range from 98% to 99%. Intra-class correlation procedures were used to obtain interrater reliability coefficients for those subtests or subtest components in which scoring is more subjective (i.e., Reading Comprehension, Alphabet Writing Fluency, Sentence Composition, Essay Composition, Oral Expression). The authors report that the interrater reliability coefficients for these subtests ranged from .92 to .99. Thus, it appears that the more subjective subtests are still quite reliable despite the need for professional judgment in scoring.

Validity

Several methods were used to establish validity for the WIAT-III. In order to establish content validity, both the content of the previous test version and the suggested new subtests and specific items for the WIAT-III were subjected to exhaustive literature and expert reviews. Evidence for construct validity was established by examining the relationships among composites, subtests, and items scores (i.e., by examining the internal structure) of the WIAT-III. Student's response processes were also examined to demonstrate that the subtest items elicit the expected cognitive processes. Empirical and descriptive examinations of students' common errors and response patterns suggesting misunderstanding of questions, as well as comprehensive literature reviews and expert consultation are included in the technical manual to provide evidence for validity of the response processes required by subtest items.

Criterion-related validity was established by examining the relationships between the WIAT-III and several other measures (i.e., WIAT-II, WPPSI–III, WISC-IV, WAIS-IV, WNV, and DAS-II). For example, the corrected correlation coefficients between WIAT-III and WIAT-II composites ranged from .65 for Math Fluency—Math to .93 for Total Achievement—Total. In addition, the correlation coefficient for the WIAT-III Total Achievement and the WPPSI-III Full Scale IQ (FSIQ) was .78, and the correlation between the WIAT-III Total Achievement and the WISC-IV FSIQ was .82. The WISC-IV FSIQ and WIAT-III Composites correlation coefficients ranged from .53 to .75.

Finally, the authors of the WIAT-III also sought to determine the clinical utility of the WIAT-III by conducting special group studies with nonrandomly selected subsamples of students with disabilities (i.e., mild intellectual disability, reading disorder, mathematics disorder, disorder of written expression, and Individuals with expressive language disorder). In order to achieve this end, the average composite and subtest scores obtained by the special group and by a matched control group were compared. Participants were matched based on sex, race/ethnicity, parent education level, geographic region, grade, and semester. Students with mild intellectual impairment, on average, scored significantly lower on all WIAT-III composites and subtests than their matched counterparts (at the $p < .01$ level) with the mean standard score differences ranging from 22.08 on Alphabet Writing Fluency to 41.55 on Reading Comprehension.

Summary

The WIAT-III is an individually administered, norm-referenced diagnostic assessment tool. Made up of 16 subtests, it allows one to measure skills related to the eight learning disability categories defined by federal law. Overall, the WIAT-III demonstrates adequate evidence for being a reliable and valid tool for use with school-age populations.

4 Getting the Most Out of an Achievement Test

The achievement tests described in this chapter provide the teacher with global scores in areas such as word meaning and math computation skills. Although global scores can help in screening children, they generally lack the specificity to help in planning individualized instructional programs. The fact that Emily earned a standard score of 85 on the Mathematics Computation subtest of the ITBS does not tell us what math skills Emily has. In addition, a teacher cannot rely on test names as an indication of what is measured by a specific test. For example, a reading score of 115 on the WRAT4 tells a teacher nothing about reading comprehension or rate of oral reading. Teachers typically have other information, such as scores from cumulative records or their own observations of student performance, that they can use along with test scores to make judgments about the reasonable level at which to instruct students and the specific skills that need to be taught.

A teacher must look at any screening test (or any test, for that matter) in terms of the behaviors sampled by that test. Here is a case in point. Suppose Richard earned a standard score of 70 on a spelling subtest. What do we know about Richard? We know that Richard earned enough raw score points to place him two standard deviations below the mean of students in his grade. That is all we know without going beyond the score and examining the kinds of behaviors sampled by the test. The test title tells us only that the test measures skill development in spelling. However, we still do not know what Richard did to earn a score of 70.

First, we need to ask, "What is the nature of the behaviors sampled by the test?" Spelling tests can be of several kinds. Richard may have been asked to write a word read by his teacher, as is the case in the Spelling subtest of the WRAT4. Such a behavior sampling demands that he recall the correct spelling of a word and actually produce that correct spelling in writing. On the other hand, Richard's score of 70 may have been earned on a spelling test that asked him just to recognize the correct spelling of a word. For example, the Spelling subtest of the PIAT-R/NU presents the student with four alternative spellings of a word (for example, "empti," "empty," "impty," and "emity"), and the teacher asks a child to point to the word "empty." Such an item demands recognition and pointing, rather than recall and production. Thus, we need to look first at the nature of the behaviors sampled by the test.

Second, we must look at the specific items a student passes or fails. This requires going back to the original test protocol to analyze the specific nature of skill development in a given area. We need to ask, "What kinds of items did the child fail?" and then look for consistent patterns among the failures. In trying to identify the nature of spelling errors, we need to know, "Does the student consistently demonstrate errors in spelling words with long vowels? With silent *e*'s? With specific consonant blends?" and so on. The search is for specific patterns of errors, and we

Dilemmas *in* Current Practice

Unless the content assessed by an achievement test reflects the content of the curriculum, the results are meaningless. Students will not have had a formal opportunity to learn the material tested. When students are tested on material they have not been taught, or tested in ways other than those by which they are taught, the test results will not reflect their actual skills. Jenkins and Pany (1978) compared the contents of four reading achievement tests with the contents of five commercial reading series at grades 1 and 2. Their major concern was the extent to which students might earn different scores on different tests of reading achievement simply as a function of the degree of overlap in content between tests and curricula. Jenkins and Pany calculated the grade scores that would be earned by students who had mastered the words taught in the respective curricula and who had correctly read those words on the four tests. Grade scores are shown in Table 11.3. It is clear that different curricula result in different performances on different tests.

The data produced by Jenkins and Pany are now more than 30 years old. Yet the table is still the best visual illustration of test curriculum overlap. Shapiro and Derr (1987) showed that the degree of overlap between what is taught and what is tested varied considerably across tests and curricula. Also, Good and Salvia (1988) demonstrated significant differences in test performance for the same students on different reading tests. They indicate the significance of the test curriculum overlap issue, stating,

> Curriculum bias is undesirable because it severely limits the interpretation of a student's test score. For example, it is unclear whether a student's reading score of 78 reflects deficient reading skills or the selection of a test with poor content validity for the pupil's curriculum. (p. 56)

TABLE 11.3 Grade-Equivalent Scores Obtained by Matching Specific Reading Test Words to Standardized Reading Test Words

		MAT			
Curriculum	**PIAT**	**Word Knowledge**	**Word Analysis**	**SDRT**	**WRAT**
Bank Street Reading Series					
Grade 1	1.5	1.0	1.1	1.8	2.0
Grade 2	2.8	2.5	1.2	2.9	2.7
Keys to Reading					
Grade 1	2.0	1.4	1.2	2.2	2.2
Grade 2	3.3	1.9	1.0	3.0	3.0
Reading 360					
Grade 1	1.5	1.0	1.0	1.4	1.7
Grade 2	2.2	2.1	1.0	2.7	2.3
SRA Reading Program					
Grade 1	1.5	1.2	1.3	1.0	2.1
Grade 2	3.1	2.5	1.4	2.9	3.5
Sullivan Associates Programmed Reading					
Grade 1	1.8	1.4	1.2	1.1	2.0
Grade 2	2.2	2.4	1.1	2.5	2.5

SOURCE: From "Standardized Achievement Tests: How Useful for Special Education?" by J. Jenkins & D. Pany, *Exceptional Children*, 44 (1978), 450. Copyright 1978 by The Council for Exceptional Children. Reprinted with permission.

SCENARIO *in* ASSESSMENT

JOSH | In January, Josh, a sixth-grade student in the local middle school, was referred for a psychoeducational evaluation because of his deteriorating achievement in language arts and social studies. A multidisciplinary team met to formulate an assessment plan. Attending this meeting were Josh's mother; his language arts teacher, who represented the other teachers in his team (i.e., social studies, science, and math); the school principal, Josh's counselor, and the building's school psychologist.

Josh's teachers began the discussion by expressing their concern that Josh was not completing his homework and was earning poor scores on tests and quizzes in language arts and social studies; depending on his performance on the last tests in the marking period, he might pass those courses. In contrast, Josh was earning an A in science. In his mathematics class, Josh was a contradiction. He could do all of the calculations with speed and accuracy. He solved word problems accurately, but slowly. He was going to earn a C in math for the semester because he did not complete the homework and because his written explanations about how he solved the problems were incomplete. All of his teachers felt Josh was a bright student, but some worried that he was becoming discouraged.

Josh's mother reported that he is the youngest of three children. Josh's older brother and sister had not experienced any difficulties in school. The mother reported that Josh spent several hours every day working on his homework and studying for tests. Although he wanted to go to college to become an engineer and build bridges, he was doubting his ability to even pass sixth grade.

Josh's counselor summarized his elementary school records. Josh earned an IQ of 128 on the group intelligence test administered in the third grade. Yet his records indicated that he had had more difficulty than other students in reading. He was consistently evaluated as outstanding in math and science. Last year, his fifth-grade teacher had noted upon each report card that Josh was a slow reader.

The team felt that the school psychologist should complete a formal assessment of Josh's intelligence and achievement to see if he had a learning disability in reading that was affecting his school performance. The school psychologist administered the fourth edition of the Wechsler Intelligence Scale for Children (WISC-IV). The psychologist also administered the third edition of the Wechsler Individual Achievement Test (WIAT-III) because it corresponded nicely to the district's curriculum.

Josh earned the following standard scores (mean = 100; S = 15) on the WISC-IV.

Verbal Comprehension	125
Perceptual Reasoning	127

Working Memory	105
Processing Speed	115

He earned the following standard scores (mean = 100, S = 15) on the WIAT-III subtests, supplemental subtests, and composites.

Subtests	
Listening Comprehension	121
Reading Comprehension	102
Math Problem Solving	115
Sentence Composition	91
Word Reading	88
Essay Composition	97
Pseudoword Decoding	84
Numerical Operations	123
Oral Expression	119
Oral Reading Fluency	77
Spelling	100
Math Fluency–Addition	125
Math Fluency–Subtraction	123
Math Fluency–Multiplication	130
Supplemental Subtests	
Oral Reading Accuracy	91
Oral Reading Rate	79
Composites	
Oral Language	120
Reading	88
Written Expression	96
Mathematics	123

The psychologist also reported that Josh was quite forthcoming about how school was going and why he was having trouble in language arts and social studies. He said that the reading was really hard to understand and that he had to read the same passage a few times to get it. He also said that by the time he had finished his reading assignments, he was so tired that he just rushed through his written homework. He said that he did not like to write "that stuff in math class" and that it should be enough to get the right answer by doing the problem in the right way.

The team concluded that Josh clearly had difficulty with reading decoding. He was slow and inaccurate. Lack of reading fluency in and of itself reduces reading comprehension, and Josh was clearly below that threshold of reading fluency. His lack of fluency combined with his poor performances in word reading and pseudoword decoding strongly suggested that Josh was having a major problem in decoding. Given the nature of the school's curriculum in middle school, where reading is a primary way in which students acquire information, Josh's limited reading skills necessarily were causing achievement problems in language arts and social studies, where reading is stressed. His reading skills were also having an impact on science, but to a lesser degree. The team concluded that Josh was eligible for special education in the area of reading.

An IEP team was formed, and the team met and developed a plan whereby Josh received intensive instruction in phonics with emphases on both accuracy and fluency. By the end of the spring semester, Josh's reading accuracy and fluency had improved significantly. His grades had improved, although he still saw little relevance to the required writing in his mathematics class. Josh was again talking about becoming an engineer and building bridges.

What implications about your own professional role can you draw from this scenario? Go to the Education CourseMate website for this textbook for more reflection questions about this Scenario in Assessment.

try to ascertain the student's relative degree of consistency in making certain errors. Of course, fin-ding error patterns requires that the test content be sufficiently dense to allow a student to make the same error at least two times.

Similar procedures are followed with any screening device. Obviously, the information achieved is not nearly as specific as the information obtained from diagnostic tests. Administration of an achievement test that is a screening test gives the classroom teacher a general idea of where to start with any additional diagnostic assessment.

Chapter Comprehension Questions

Write your answers to each of the following questions and then compare your responses to the text.

1. Identify at least four important considerations in selecting a specific achievement test for use with the third graders in your local school system.
2. Describe the major advantages and disadvantages of using individually administered, multiple-skill achievement tests.
3. A new student is assessed in September using the WRAT4. Her achievement test scores (using the PIAT-R/NU) are forwarded from her previous school and place her in the 90th percentile overall. However, the latest assessment places her only in the 77th percentile. Give three possible explanations for this discrepancy.

Web Activities 

1. Go to the Education CourseMate website for this textbook and read the reviews of the Stanford Achievement Test and the TerraNova. Compare the tests on the following dimensions: (a) kinds of behaviors sampled, (b) reliability, and (c) validity.
2. Go to the website for Pearson publishers and identify two group-administered achievement tests.
3. Go to the website for your state department of education and identify the test or tests used statewide to assess academic achievement. Does your state use a commercially available test or does it have a test custom-made for use in the state?

Web Resources

Nationally Normed Elementary Achievement Testing in America's Schools: How All 50 States Are Above The National Average
http://onlinelibrary.wiley.com/doi/10.1111/j.1745-3992.1988.tb00424.x/abstract
The author addresses issues in explaining test results to the public.

Norm-Referenced Achievement Tests
http://fairtest.org/facts/nratests.htm
Includes a nice description of the kinds of achievement tests.

Additional resources for this chapter can be found on the Education CourseMate website. Go to CengageBrain.com to access the site.

Using Diagnostic Reading Measures

CHAPTER GOALS

1 Know why we assess reading.

2 Understand the ways in which reading is taught.

3 Know the areas assessed by diagnostic reading tests, including oral reading, comprehension, word-attack, reading recognition, and reading-related behaviors.

4 Be familiar with three reading tests.

5 Be familiar with some of the current dilemmas we face in using reading measures.

KEY TERMS

oral reading
word-attack skills
rate of reading
word recognition skills
oral reading errors
literal comprehension
inferential comprehension
critical comprehension
affective comprehension
lexical comprehension
text-to-speech software

1 Why Do We Assess Reading?

Reading is one of the most fundamental skills that students learn. For poor readers, life in school is likely to be difficult even with appropriate curricular and testing accommodations and adaptations, and life after school is likely to have constrained opportunities and less personal independence and satisfaction. Moreover, students who have not learned to read fluently by the end of third grade are unlikely ever to read fluently (Adams, 1990). For these reasons, students' development of reading skills is closely monitored in order to identify those with problems early enough to enable remediation.

Diagnostic tests are most often used at tiers 2 and 3 (targeted and intensive) levels in the multi-tiered systems of support model; they are used primarily to improve two educational decisions. First, they are administered to children who are experiencing difficulty in learning to read. In this case, tests identify a student's strengths and weaknesses so that educators can plan appropriate interventions. Second, they are given to ascertain a student's initial or continuing eligibility for special services. Tests given for this purpose are used to compare a student's achievement with the achievement of other students. Diagnostic reading tests may also be administered to evaluate the effects of instruction. However, this use of diagnostic reading tests is generally unwise. Lengthy individually administered tests are an inefficient way to evaluate instructional effectiveness for large groups of students; brief individually administered and group survey tests are generally more appropriate for this purpose. Diagnostic tests are generally too insensitive to identify small but important gains by individual students. Teachers should monitor students' daily or weekly progress with direct performance measures (such as having a student read aloud currently used materials to ascertain accuracy [percentage correct] and fluency [rate of correct words per minute]).

Because reading skills are fundamental to success in our society, their development should be closely monitored and informed instructional adjustments made as necessary. This way, all students will have an opportunity to learn to read, and to learn to do so quickly. However, there may be some students who, even with the most effective instruction, never manage to develop adequate reading skills. Fortunately, technologies such as text-to-speech converters and computer screen-readers are making it increasingly possible for such students to access printed information without the prerequisite reading skills. At the same time, this brings up a new dilemma: Under what conditions should we reduce reading intervention efforts in order to focus more on teaching a student to use reading accommodations (e.g., screen-readers, text-to-speech (TTS) software)? We unfortunately don't have a good answer to this right now. But we do know that some of these accommodations can actually facilitate reading development, and so we believe that their use should be encouraged, particularly for those students with the most severe reading difficulties. Overall, we can't predict who will and who will not learn to read, and so it is essential that we operate under the assumption that each student will learn to read when we assess and intervene appropriately.

2 The Ways in Which Reading Is Taught

For approximately 150 years, educators have been divided (sometimes acrimoniously) over the issue of teaching the language code (letters and sounds). Some educators favor a "look–say" (or whole-word) approach, in which students learn whole words and practice them by reading appropriate stories and other passages. Proponents of this approach stress the meaning of the words and usually believe that students learn the code incidentally (or with a little coaching). Finally, proponents of this approach offer the opinion (contradicted by empirical research) that drilling children in letters and sounds destroys their motivation to read. Other educators favor systematically teaching the language code: how letters represent sounds and how sounds and letters are combined to form words—both spoken and written. Proponents of this approach argue that specifically and systematically teaching phonics produces more skillful readers more easily; they also argue that reading failure destroys motivation to read.

For the first 100 years or so of the debate, observations of reading were too crude to indicate more than that the reader looked at print and said the printed words (or answered questions about the content conveyed by those printed words). Consequently, theoreticians speculated about the processes occurring inside the reader, and the speculations of advocates of whole-word instruction dominated the debate until the 1950s. Thereafter, phonics instruction (systematically teaching beginning readers the relationships among the alphabetic code, phonemes, and words) increasingly became part of prereading and reading instruction. Some of that increased emphasis on phonics may be attributable to *Why Johnny Can't Read* (Flesch, 1955), a book vigorously advocating phonics instruction; more importantly, the growing body of empirical evidence increasingly showed phonics instruction's effectiveness. By 1967, there was substantial evidence that systematic instruction in phonics produced better readers and that the effect of phonics instruction was greater for children of low ability or from disadvantaged backgrounds. With phonics instruction, beginning readers had better word recognition, better reading comprehension, and better reading vocabulary (Bond & Dykstra, 1967; Chall, 1967). Subsequent empirical evidence leads to the same conclusions (Rayner, Foorman, Perfetti, Pesetsky, & Seidenberg, 2001; National Institute of Child Health and Human Development, 2000a, 2000b; Adams, 1990; Foorman, Francis, Fletcher, Schatschneider, & Mehta, 1998; Pflaum, Walberg, Karegianes, & Rasher, 1980; Stanovich, 1986).

While some scholars were demonstrating the efficacy of phonics instruction, others began unraveling the ways in which beginners learn to read. Today, that process is much clearer than it was even in the 1970s. Armbruster and Osborn (2001) have provided an excellent summary of the processes involved in early reading. First, beginning readers must understand how words are made up of sounds before they need to read. This process, called "phonemic awareness," is the ability to recognize and manipulate phonemes, which are the spoken sounds that affect the meaning of a communication. Phonemic awareness can be taught if it has not already developed before reading instruction begins. Second, beginning readers must associate graphemes (alphabet letters) with phonemes. Beginning readers learn these associations best through explicit phonics instruction. Third, beginning readers must read fluently in order to comprehend what they are reading.

After students become fluent decoders, they read more difficult material. This material often contains advanced vocabulary that students must learn. It contains more complex sentence structure, more condensed and abstract ideas, and perhaps less literal and more inferential meaning. Finally, more difficult material frequently requires that readers read with the purpose of understanding what they are reading.

While learning more about how students begin to read, scholars also learned that some long-held beliefs were not valid. For example, it is incorrect to say that poor readers read letter by letter, but skilled readers read entire words and phrases as a unit. Actually, skilled readers read letter by letter and word by word, but they do it so quickly that they appear to be reading words and phrases (see, for example, Snow, Burns, & Griffin, 1998). It is also incorrect to say that good readers rely heavily on context cues to identify words (Share & Stanovich, 1995). Good readers do use context cues to verify their decoding accuracy. Poor readers rely on them heavily, however, probably because they lack skill in more appropriate word-attack skills (see, for example, Briggs & Underwood, 1984).

Today, despite clear evidence indicating the essential role of phonics in reading and strong indications of the superiority of reading programs with direct instruction in phonics (Foorman et al., 1998), some professionals continue to reject phonics

SCENARIO *in* ASSESSMENT

LLOYD | The Springfield School District uses a child-centered whole-language approach to teaching reading. Near the end of the school year, the district screened all first-grade students to identify students who would require supplementary services in reading the following year. Lloyd earned a score that was at the seventh percentile on the district's norms, and the district notified his parents that he would be receiving additional help the next year so that he could improve his skills. Lloyd's parents were upset by the news because until the notification, they thought that Lloyd was progressing well in all school subjects.

The parents requested a meeting with Lloyd's teacher, who also invited the reading specialist. At that meeting, the reading specialist told the parents that a fairly large percentage of first graders were in the same predicament as Lloyd, but not to worry, because many students matured into readers. She said that Lloyd only needed time. She urged the parents to let Lloyd enjoy his summer, and the district would retest him at the beginning of the second grade to determine if he still needed the extra help.

Lloyd's parents ignored the district's advice and enrolled him in a reading course at a local tutoring program. Lloyd was first tested to identify the exact nature of his problem. The test results indicated that he had excellent phonemic awareness, could print and name all upper- and lowercase letters, knew all the consonant sounds, knew the sounds of all long vowels, did not know any of the short vowel sounds, could not blend sounds, and had a sight vocabulary of approximately 50 words. Lloyd's tutor taught him the short vowel sounds rather quickly. However, he had trouble with sound blending until his tutor used his interest and skill in math to explain the principles. She wrote: c + a + t = cat, and then said each of the three sounds and "cat." As she explained to Lloyd's parents, it was like a light going on in his head. He got it. The tutor spent a few more sessions using phonics to help Lloyd increase his sight vocabulary.

In September, the district retested Lloyd as it had promised. The district sent home a form letter in which it explained that Lloyd was now at the 99th percentile in reading and no longer needed supplementary services. At the bottom was a handwritten note from the reading specialist: "Lloyd just needed a little time to become a reader. We're so glad you let him just enjoy his summer!"

Epigram Lloyd did enjoy his summer as well as the second grade. And he won an award as the best second-grade reader in the district.

What implications about your own professional role can you draw from this scenario? Go to the Education CourseMate website for this textbook for more reflection questions about this Scenario in Assessment.

What implications about your own professional role can you draw from this scenario? Go to the Education CourseMate website for this textbook for more reflection questions about this Scenario in Assessment.

instruction. Perhaps this may explain why most students who are referred for psychological assessment are referred because of reading problems, and why most of these students have problems changing the symbols (that is, alphabet letters) into sounds and words. The obvious connection between phonics instruction and beginning reading has not escaped the notice of many parents, however. They have become eager consumers of educational materials (such as "Hooked on Phonics" and "The Phonics Game") and private tutoring (for example, instruction at a Sylvan Learning Center).

Educators' views of how students learn to read and how students should be taught will determine their beliefs about reading assessment. Thus, diagnostic testing in reading is caught between the opposing camps. If the test includes an assessment of the skills needed to decode text, it is attacked by those who reject analytic approaches to reading. If the test does not include an assessment of decoding skills, it is attacked by those who know the importance of those skills in beginning reading.

3 Skills Assessed by Diagnostic Reading Tests

Reading is a complex process that changes as readers develop. Beginning readers rely heavily on a complex set of decoding skills that can be assessed holistically by having a student read orally and assessing his or her accuracy and fluency. Decoding skills may also be measured analytically by having students apply these skills in isolation (for example, using phonics to read nonsense words). Once fluency in decoding has been attained, readers are expected to go beyond the comprehension of simple language and simple ideas to the process of understanding and evaluating what is written. Advanced readers rely on different skills (that is, linguistic competence and abstract reasoning) and different facts (that is, vocabulary, prior knowledge and experience, and beliefs). Comprehension may be assessed by having a student read a passage that deals with an esoteric topic and is filled with abstract concepts and difficult vocabulary; moreover, the sentences in that passage may have complicated grammar with minimal redundancy.

ORAL READING

A number of tests and subtests are designed to assess the accuracy and/or fluency of a student's oral reading. Oral reading tests consist of a series of graded paragraphs that are read sequentially by a student. The examiner notes reading errors and behaviors that characterize the student's oral reading.

Rate of Reading

Good readers are fluent; they recognize words quickly (without having to rely on phonetic analysis) and are in a good position to construct meaning of sentences and paragraphs. Readers who are not fluent have problems comprehending what they read, and the problems become more severe as the complexity of the reading material increases. Indeed, reading fluency is an excellent general indicator of reading achievement. Consequently, increasingly more states are including reading fluency as part of their comprehensive reading assessment systems.

Nonetheless, many commercially available reading tests do not assess reading fluency. However, there are some exceptions. Two levels of the Stanford Diagnostic Reading Test have subtests to assess rate of reading. Tests such as the Gray Oral Reading Test–Fourth Edition (GORT-4) are timed. A pupil who reads a passage on the GORT-4 slowly but makes no errors in reading may earn a lower score than a rapid reader who makes one or two errors in reading.

Oral Reading Errors

Oral reading requires that students say the word that is printed on the page correctly. However, all errors made by a student are not equal. Some errors are relatively unimportant to the extent that they do not affect the student's comprehension of the material. Other errors are ignored. Examiners may note characteristics of a student's oral reading that are not counted as errors. Self-corrections are not counted as errors. Disregarded punctuation marks (for example, failing to pause for a comma or to inflect vocally to indicate a question mark) are not counted as errors. Repetitions and hesitations due to speech handicaps (for example, stuttering or stammering) are not counted as errors. Dialectic accents are not counted as mispronunciations.[1]

The following types of errors count against the student:

Teacher Pronunciation or Aid If a student either hesitates for a time without making an audible effort to pronounce a word or appears to be attempting for 3 seconds to pronounce the word, the examiner pronounces the word and records an error.

Hesitation The student hesitates for 3 or more seconds before pronouncing a word.

Gross Mispronunciation of a Word A gross mispronunciation is recorded when the pupil's pronunciation of a word bears so little resemblance to the proper pronunciation that the examiner must be looking at the word to recognize it. An example of gross mispronunciation is reading "encounter" as "actors."

Partial Mispronunciation of a Word A partial mispronunciation can be one of several different kinds of errors. The examiner may have to pronounce part of a word for the student (an aid); the student may phonetically mispronounce specific letters (for example, by reading "red" as "reed"); or the student may omit part of a word, insert elements of words, or make errors in syllabication, accent, or inversion.

Omission of a Word or Group of Words Omissions consist of skipping individual words or groups of words.

[1] Other characteristics of a student's oral reading are problematic (although not errors): poor posture, inappropriate head movement, finger pointing, loss of place, lack of expression (for example, word-by-word reading, lack of phrasing, or monotone voice), and strained voice.

Insertion of a Word or Group of Words Insertions consist of the student's putting one or more words into the sentence being read. The student may, for example, read "the dog" as "the mean dog." However, it is important to note that for some assessment instruments this counts against the student, but for others it does not.

Substitution of One Meaningful Word for Another Substitutions consist of the replacement of one or more words in the passage by one or more different meaningful words. The student might read "dense" as "depress." Students often replace entire sequences of words with others, as illustrated by the replacement of "he is his own mechanic" with "he sat on his own machine." Some oral reading tests require that examiners record the specific kind of substitution error. Substitutions are classified as meaning similarity (the words have similar meanings), function similarity (the two words have syntactically similar functions), graphic/phoneme similarity (the words look or sound alike), or a combination of the preceding.

Repetition Repetition occurs when students repeat words or groups of words while attempting to read sentences or paragraphs. In some cases, if a student repeats a group of words to correct an error, the original error is not recorded, but a repetition error is. In other cases, such behaviors are recorded simply as spontaneous self-corrections.

Inversion, or Changing of Word Order Errors of inversion are recorded when the child changes the order of words appearing in a sentence; for example, "house the" is an inversion.

ASSESSMENT OF READING COMPREHENSION

Diagnostic tests assess five different types of reading comprehension:

1. *Literal comprehension* entails understanding the information that is explicit in the reading material.
2. *Inferential comprehension* means interpreting, synthesizing, or extending the information that is explicit in the reading material.
3. *Critical comprehension* requires analyzing, evaluating, and making judgments about the material read.
4. *Affective comprehension* involves a reader's personal and emotional responses to the reading material.
5. *Lexical comprehension* means knowing the meaning of key vocabulary words.

In our opinion, the best way to assess reading comprehension is to give readers access to the material and have them restate or paraphrase what they have read.

Poor comprehension has many causes. The most common is poor decoding, which affects comprehension in two ways. First, if a student cannot convert the symbols to words, he or she cannot comprehend the message conveyed by those words. The second issue is more subtle. If a student expends all of his or her mental resources on sounding out the words, he or she will have no resources left to process their meaning. For that reason, increasing reading fluency frequently eliminates problems in comprehension.

Another problem is that students may not know how to read for comprehension (Taylor, Harris, Pearson, & Garcia, 1995). They may not actively focus on the meaning of what they read or know how to monitor their comprehension (for example, by asking themselves questions about what they have read or whether they understand what they have read). Students may not know how to foster comprehension (for example, by summarizing material, determining the main ideas and supporting facts, and integrating material with previous knowledge). Finally, individual characteristics can interact with the assessment of reading comprehension. For example, in an assessment of literal comprehension, a reader's memory capacity can affect comprehension scores unless the reader has access to the passage while answering questions about it or retelling its gist. Inferential comprehension depends on more than reading; it also depends on a reader's ability to see relationships (a defining element of intelligence) and on background information and experiences.

ASSESSMENT OF WORD-ATTACK SKILLS

Word-attack, or word analysis, skills are those used to derive the pronunciation or meaning of a word through phonic analysis, structural analysis, or context cues. Phonic analysis is the use of letter–sound correspondences and sound blending to identify words. Structural analysis is a process of breaking words into morphemes, or meaningful units. Words contain free morphemes (such as *farm*, *book*, and *land*) and bound morphemes (such as *-ed*, *-s*, and *-er*).

Because lack of word-attack skills is the principal reason why students have trouble reading, a variety of subtests of commonly used diagnostic reading tests specifically assess these skills. Subtests that assess word-attack skills range from such basic assessments as analysis of skill in associating letters with sounds to tests of syllabication and blending. Generally, for subtests that assess skill in associating letters with sounds, the examiner reads a word aloud and the student must identify the consonant–vowel–consonant cluster or digraph that has the same sound as the beginning, middle, or ending letters of the word. Syllabication subtests present polysyllabic words, and the student must either divide the word orally into syllables or circle specific syllables.

Blending subtests, on the other hand, are of three types. In the first method, the examiner may read syllables out loud (for example, "wa-ter-mel-on") and ask the student to pronounce the word. In the second type of subtest, the student may be asked to read word parts and to pronounce whole words. In the third method, the student may be presented with alternative beginning, middle, and ending sounds and asked to produce a word. Figure 12.1 illustrates the third method, used with the Stanford Diagnostic Reading Test, Fourth Edition (SDRT 4).

ASSESSMENT OF WORD RECOGNITION SKILLS

Subtests of diagnostic reading tests that assess a pupil's word recognition skills are designed to ascertain what many educators call "sight vocabulary." A student learns the correct pronunciation of letters and words through a variety of experiences. The more a student is exposed to specific words and the more familiar those words become to the student, the more readily he or she recognizes those words and is able to pronounce them correctly. Well-known words require very little reliance on word-attack skills. Most readers of this book immediately recognize the word *hemorrhage* and do not have to employ phonetic skills to pronounce it. On the other hand, a word such as *nephrocystanastomosis* is not a part of the sight vocabulary for most of us. Such words slow us down; we must use phonetics to analyze them.

Word recognition subtests form a major part of most diagnostic reading tests. Some tests use paper tachistoscopes to expose words for brief periods of time (usually one-half second). Students who recognize many words are said to have good sight vocabularies or good word recognition skills. Other subtests assess letter recognition, recognition of words in isolation, and recognition of words in context.

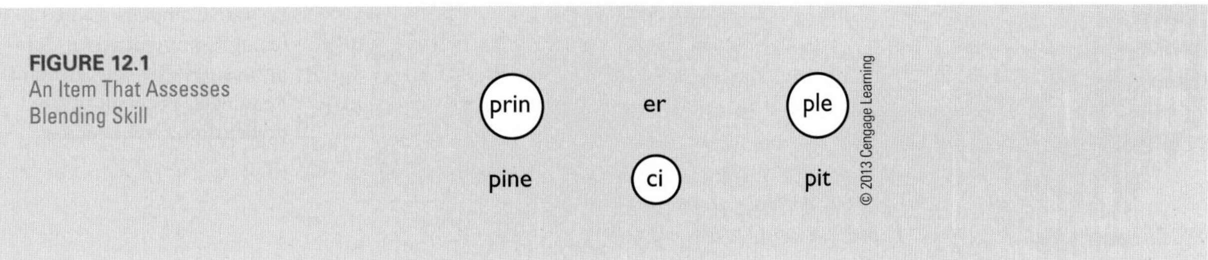

FIGURE 12.1
An Item That Assesses Blending Skill

SPECIFIC DIAGNOSTIC READING TESTS

In Table 12.1, we provide basic information about several commonly used diagnostic reading tests. Then we provide a detailed review of the Dynamic Indicators of Basic Early Literacy Skills Next (DIBELS Next); the Group Reading Assessment and Diagnostic Evaluation (GRADE); and the Test of Phonological Awareness–Second Edition: Plus.

TABLE 12.1 Commonly Used Diagnostic Reading Tests

Test	Author	Publisher	Year	Ages/Grades	Individual/ Group	NRT/SRT/ CRT	Subtests
Comprehensive Test of Phonological Processing	Wagner, Torgesen, & Rashotte	Pro-Ed	1999	Ages 5–25	Individual	NRT	Elision, Blending Words, Sound Matching, Blending Nonwords, Segmenting Nonwords, Memory for Digit, Nonword Repetition, Rapid Color Naming, Rapid Object Naming, Rapid Digit Naming, Rapid Letter Naming, Phoneme Reversal, Segmenting Words. Composites: Phonological Awareness, Phonological Memory, Rapid Naming
Dynamic Indicators of Basic Early Literacy Skills–6	Good & Kaminski	University of Oregon	No date	Grades K–6	Individual	NRT Norms are local	Subtests vary by grade: Initial Sound Fluency, Letter Naming Fluency, Phoneme Segmentation Fluency, Nonsense Word Fluency, Oral Reading Fluency, Retell Fluency
Dynamic Indicators of Basic Early Literacy Skills Next	Good & Kaminski	University of Oregon	2010	Grades K–6	Individual/ Group	NRT Norms are local	Subtests vary by grade: First Sound Fluency, Letter Naming Fluency, Phoneme Segmentation Fluency, Nonsense Word Fluency, Oral Reading Fluency, Daze
Gray Oral Reading Test–4 (GORT-4)	Wiederholt & Bryant	Pro-Ed	2001	Ages 6–0–18–11	Individual	NRT	Rate, Accuracy, Fluency, Comprehension
Group Reading Assessment and Diagnostic Evaluation	Williams	Pearson	2001	Ages 4–18 Grades pre-K–12	Individual or group	NRT	Picture Matching, Picture Differences, Verbal Concepts, Matching, Rhyming, Print Awareness, Letter Recognition, Same and Different Words, Phoneme–Grapheme Correspondence, Word Reading, Word Meaning, Vocabulary, Sentence Comprehension, Passage Comprehension, Listening Comprehension. Composites: Pre-Reading, Reading Readiness, Vocabulary, Comprehension, Oral Language

A student must choose which of four pictures represents what was read. Items require students to comprehend basic words, understand grammar structure, make inferences, understand idioms, and comprehend other nonliteral statements.

Scores

Subtest raw scores can be converted into stanines. Depending on the level administered, certain subtest raw scores can be added to produce composite scores. Similarly, each level has a different set of subtest raw scores that are added in computing the total test raw score. Composite and total test raw scores can be converted to unweighted standard scores (mean of 100 and standard deviation of 15), stanines, percentiles, normal-curve equivalents, grade equivalents, and growth scale values.[2] Conversion tables provide both fall and spring normative scores. For students who are very skilled or very unskilled readers in comparison to their same-grade peers, out-of-level tests may be administered. Appropriate normative tables are available for some out-of-level tests in the teacher's scoring and interpretative manuals. Other out-of-level normative scores are reported only in the scoring and reporting software.

Norms

The GRADE standardization sample included 16,408 students in the spring sample and 17,024 in the fall sample. Numbers of students tested in each grade ranged from 808 (seventh grade, spring) to 2,995 (kindergarten, spring). Gender characteristics of the sample were presented by grade level, and roughly equal numbers of males and females were represented in each grade and season level (fall and spring). Geographic region characteristics were presented without disaggregating results by grade and were compared to the population data as reported by the U.S. Census Bureau (1998). Southern states were slightly overrepresented, whereas Western states were slightly underrepresented in both the fall and the spring norm samples. Information on community type was also presented for the entire fall and spring norm samples; the samples are appropriately representative of urban, suburban, and rural communities. Information on students receiving free lunch was also provided. Information on race was also compared to the percentages reported by the U.S. Census Bureau (1998) and appeared to be representative of the population. It is important to note, again, that this information was not reported by grade level.

[2] Because growth scale values include all levels on the same scale, these scores make it possible to track a student's reading growth when the student has been given different GRADE levels throughout the years. It is important to note, however, that particular skills measured on the test vary from level to level, so growth scale values may not represent the same skills at different years.

Finally, the authors report that special education students were included in the sample but do not provide the number included.

Reliability

Total test coefficient alphas were calculated as measures of internal consistency for each form of the test, for each season of administration (fall and spring). These ranged from .89 to .98. Coefficient alphas were also computed for various subtests and subtest combinations (for example, Picture Matching and Picture Differences were combined into a Visual Skills category at the preschool and kindergarten levels). These were calculated for each GRADE level, form, and season of administration; several reliabilities were calculated for out-of-level tests (for example, separate alpha coefficients were computed for preschoolers and kindergartners taking the kindergarten-level test). These subtest–subtest combination coefficients ranged from .45 (Listening Comprehension, Form B, eleventh grade, spring administration) to .97 (Listening Comprehension, Form A, preschool, fall administration). Of the 350 coefficients calculated, 99 met or exceeded .90. The Comprehension Composite was found to be the most reliable composite score across levels. Listening Comprehension had consistently low coefficients from the first grade level to the highest level (Level A); thus, these are not included in calculating the total test raw scores for these levels. Alternate-forms reliability was determined across a sample of 696 students (students were included at each grade level). Average time between testing ranged from 8 to 32.2 days. Correlation coefficients ranged from .81 (eleventh grade) to .94 (preschool and third grade). Test–retest reliability was determined from a sample of 816 students. The average interval between testing ranged from 3.5 days (eighth-grade students taking Form A of Level M) to 42 days (fifth-grade students taking Form A of Level 5). Test–retest correlation coefficients ranged from .77 (fifth-grade students taking Form A of Level 5) to .98 (fourth-grade students taking Form A of Level 4). Reliability data were not provided on growth scale values.

Validity

The author presents three types of validity: content, criterion-related, and construct validity. A rationale is provided for why particular item formats and subtests were included at particular ages and what skills each subtest is intended to measure. Also, a comprehensive item tryout was conducted on a sample of children throughout the nation. Information from this tryout informed item revision procedures. Statistical tests and qualitative investigations of item bias were also conducted during the tryout. Finally, teachers were surveyed, and this information was used in modifying content and administration procedures (although specific information on this survey is not provided). Criterion-related validity provided by the author included correlations of the GRADE total test standard score with five other measures of reading achievement: the total reading standard score of the Iowa Test of Basic Skills, the California Achievement Test total reading score, the Gates–MacGinitie Reading Tests total score, the Peabody Individual Achievement Test–Revised (PIAT-R) scores (General Information, Reading Recognition, Reading Comprehension, and Total Reading subtests), and the TerraNova. Each of these correlation studies was conducted with somewhat limited samples of elementary and middle school students. Coefficients ranged from .61 (GRADE total test score correlated with PIAT-R General Information among 30 fifth-grade students) to .90 (GRADE total test score correlated with Gates total reading score for 177 first-, second-, and sixth-grade students). Finally, construct validity was addressed by showing that the GRADE scores were correlated with age. Also, scores for students with dyslexia ($N = 242$) and learning disabilities in reading ($N = 191$) were compared with scores for students included in the standardization sample that were matched on GRADE level, form taken, gender, and race/ethnicity but who were not receiving special education services. As a group, students with dyslexia performed significantly below the matched control group. Similarly, students with learning disabilities in reading performed significantly below the matched control group.

Summary

The GRADE is a standardized, norm-referenced test of reading achievement that can be group administered. It can be used with children of a variety of ages (4 to 18 years) and provides a "growth scale value" score that can be used to track growth in reading achievement over several years. Different subtests and skills are tested, depending on the grade level tested; 11 forms corresponding to 11 GRADE levels are included. Although the norm sample is large, certain demographic information on the students in the sample is not provided, and in some cases, groups of students are over- or underrepresented. Total test score reliability data are strong. However, other subtest–subtest composite reliability data do not support the use of these particular scores for decision-making purposes, although the validity data provided in the manual suggest that this test is a useful measure of reading skills.

Dynamic Indicators of Basic Early Literacy Skills Next (*DIBELS Next*)[3]

The Dynamic Indicators of Basic Early Literacy Skills, Next edition (Good & Kaminski, 2010) are measures used to assess reading and early literacy skills for students in kindergarten through sixth grade. DIBELS Next can be used to screen and monitor progress, to identify students who may be at risk for reading difficulties, to help educators detect students' specific skill deficits to target for intervention, and to examine the effectiveness of a school's literacy curriculum and instructional supports. DIBELS Next consists of six measures assessing phonemic awareness, alphabetic principle, advanced phonics, fluent reading, reading comprehension, and vocabulary. Both English (DIBELS Next) and Spanish (*Indicadores Dinámicos del Éxito en la Lectura, 7a Edición*; IDEL) versions of the DIBELS tools can be downloaded from the Internet, free of charge (http://www.dibels.org/). The DIBELS team is also currently working on producing DIBELS Next probes in Braille, and a French version of DIBELS, known as *Indicateurs dynamiques d'habiletés précoces en lecture* (IDAPEL), is currently in the experimental stages of development.

DIBELS Next authors report has undergone several significant changes from previous editions of DIBELS: First Sound Fluency replaced the Initial Sound Fluency measure, a new maze procedure comprehension measure called Daze was added for grades three through six, the Oral Reading Fluency passages were updated and reported to be empirically leveled, and revised Nonsense Word Fluency with new scoring rules and directions were also incorporated. In addition, there are checklists for common student response patterns, updated reliability and validity data, and revised directions and scoring rules.

The six subtests of DIBELS Next are *First Sound Fluency* (FSF)—the student says the first sound of each word stated by the assessor; *Letter Naming Fluency* (LNF)—the student is asked to name letters presented on a sheet; *Phoneme Segmentation Fluency* (PSF)—the student says the individual sounds of each word said by the assessor; *Nonsense Word Fluency* (NWF)—the student is asked to read a list of nonsense words; *DIBELS Oral Reading Fluency* (DORF)—the student is asked to read aloud a passage and then retell what he/she just read; and *Daze*—the student reads a passage where some words are replaced by a multiple choice box with the correct word and two distractors from which the student must select the word that makes the most sense in the sentence.

Phonemic awareness is assessed with the DIBELS Next indicators First Sound Fluency and Phoneme Segmentation Fluency. Alphabetic principle and basic phonics are assessed with Nonsense Word Fluency, specifically correct letter sounds and whole words read. Students' skills in reading connected text—both fluency and accuracy—are assessed by the DIBELS Oral Reading Fluency (DORF). Using DORF, the number of words a student reads correctly in one minute, as well as the number of errors a student

[3] Contributions to this review were provided by Nathan von der Embse, Jill Fortain, and Kristen Girard.

makes are used to indicate the student's level of accuracy and fluency. Reading comprehension is assessed by the number of words that were part of the retell provided by the student as part of the DORF administration, as well as by the number of correct words selected on the Daze. Vocabulary is assessed with Word Use Fluency-Revised (an experimental measure from http://www.dibels.org/).

Scores

Performance is converted into the number of correct responses per minute, except for Daze, which indicate the number of correct responses in three minutes minus half the number of incorrect words. Raw scores on the six subtests are converted by grade placement into one of three ranges: low risk (indicating a high likelihood of achieving future literacy goals), some risk (students likely in need of strategic, targeted intervention), and at risk (students likely in need of substantial, intensive intervention). According to DIBELS Next materials provided at the website, these ranges were determined based on predictive validity studies that compare scores with later performance on the Group Reading and Diagnostic Evaluation (GRADE).

Norms

DIBELS Next is designed to offer information on how individual students compare to various benchmark expectations in their development of early reading skills. These benchmark expectations represent levels that were determined based on prediction studies that involved the development of probabilities of students' later reading success. In addition, given that scores can be examined at individual student, classroom, school, and district levels, it is possible to examine how the student is performing relative to other students at the respective levels locally.

Reliability

Alternate form reliability studies were conducted with DIBELS Next. Alternate form reliability was determined using three passages or samples for each measure and was based on the Spearman-Brown prophecy formula. This approach resulted in reliability estimates by grade ranging from .65 for fifth grade Retell to .98 for first grade Oral Reading Fluency for Nonsense Word Fluency (whole words read). Oral Reading Fluency Retell test–retest reliability was not significant for second grade (.27) and ranged from .36 for fourth grade to .69 for third grade. Interrater reliability scores ranged from .85 (for third grade accuracy) to 1.00 (for third grade Daze).

Validity

Content from DIBELS Next is based on empirical reading research illustrating the importance of several basic early literacy skills: comprehension, vocabulary, reading fluency, phonics and word-attack skills, alphabetic principle, and phonemic awareness. Research has extensively documented the importance of fluency on each subtest as essential for future literacy success. Additionally, benchmarks, score ranges, and cut points are based on research reviews.

Concurrent validity was examined by comparing students' scores for DIBELS Next to their scores on the Group Reading Assessment and Diagnostic Evaluation (GRADE). Composite scores for DIBELS Next and GRADE were correlated, and results included correlations ranging from .40 (end-of-year kindergarten administration) to .80 (second grade middle-of-year administration and fourth grade all administrations). Evidence of predictive validity was provided by computing correlations for each subtest at each administration (fall, winter, spring) and the middle-of-year and end-of-year composite scores. These ranged from .25 (phoneme segmentation fluency at beginning of year for first grade) to .90 (oral reading fluency at the beginning of the year for fourth grade). Additional correlations with the Comprehensive Test of Phonological Processing (CTOPP) and GRADE are provided by subtest, with results providing more support for certain measures (i.e., oral reading fluency) than others (i.e., first sound fluency, phoneme segmentation fluency).

Summary

DIBELS Next consists of six individually administered subtests assessing phonemic awareness, alphabetic principle, advanced phonics, fluent reading, reading comprehension, and vocabulary. (Note: The Daze can be administered in group format as well as individually.) Single administrations are generally sufficient for screening purposes; however, three or four administrations must be administered for there to be sufficient reliability to make important educational decisions regarding individual students. Evidence for content and criterion-related validity is good.

The Test of Phonological Awareness, Second Edition: Plus (TOPA 2+)

The Test of Phonological Awareness, Second Edition: Plus (TOPA 2+; Torgesen & Bryant, 2004) is a norm-referenced device intended to identify students who need supplemental services in phonemic awareness and letter–sound correspondence. The TOPA 2+ can be administered individually or to groups of students between the ages of 5 and 8 years to assess phonological awareness and letter–sound correspondences.

Two forms are available: the Kindergarten form and the Early Elementary form for students in first or second grades. The Kindergarten form has two subtests. The first, Phonological Awareness, has two parts, each consisting of 10 items. In the first part, students must select from a three-choice array the word that begins with the same sound as the stimulus word read by the examiner. In the second part, students must select from a three-choice array the word that begins with a different sound. The second subtest, Letter Sounds, consists of 15 items requiring students to mark the letter in a letter array that corresponds to a specific phoneme. The Early Elementary form also has two subtests. The first, Phonological Awareness, also has two parts, each consisting of 10 items. In the first part, students must select from a three-choice array the word that ends with the same sound as the stimulus word read by the examiner. In the second part, students must select from a three-choice array the word that ends with a different sound. The second subtest, Letter Sounds, requires students to spell 18 nonsense words that vary in length from two to five phonemes.

Scores

The number correct on each subtest is summed, and sums can be converted to percentiles and a variety of standard scores.

Norms

Separate norms for the Kindergarten form are in four 6-month age intervals (that is, 5-0 through 5-5, 5-6 through 5-11, 6-0 through 6-5, and 6-6 through 6-11). Separate norms for the Early Elementary form are in 12-month age groups (that is, 6-0 through 6-11, 7-0 through 7-11, and 8-0 through 8-11).

The TOPA 2+ was standardized on a total of 2,085 students: 1,035 of whom were in the Kindergarten form and 1,050 of whom were in the Early Elementary form. Norms for each form at each age are representative of the U.S. population in 2001 in terms of geographic regions, gender, race, ethnicity, and family income. Parents without a college education are slightly underrepresented.

Reliability

Coefficient alpha was calculated for each subtest at each age. For the Kindergarten form, only Letter Sounds for 6-year-olds fell below .90; that subtest reliability was .88. For the Early Elementary form, all alphas were between .80 and .87. In addition, alphas were calculated separately for males and females, whites, blacks, Hispanics, and students with language or learning disabilities. These alphas ranged from .82 to .91.

Test–retest correlations were used to estimate stabilities. For the Kindergarten form, 51 students were retested within approximately a 2-week interval. Stability for Phonological Awareness was .87, and stability for Letter Sounds was .85. For the Early Elementary form, 88 students were retested within approximately a 2-week interval. Stability for Phonological Awareness was .81, and stability for Letter Sounds was .84.

Finally, interscorer agreement was evaluated by having two trained examiners each score 50 tests. On the Kindergarten form, interscorer agreement for Phonological Awareness was .98 and for Letter Sounds was .99. On the Early Elementary form, interscorer agreement for Phonological Awareness was .98 and for Letter Sounds was .98.

Overall, care should be taken when interpreting the results of the TOPA 2+. The internal consistency is sufficient for screening and in some cases for use in making important educational decisions for students.

Validity

Evidence for the general validity of the TOPA 2+ comes from several sources. First, the contents of scales were carefully developed to represent phonemic awareness and knowledge of letter–sound correspondence. For example, the words in the Phonological Awareness subscales come from the 2,500 most frequently used words in first graders' oral language, and all consonant phonemes had a median age of customary articulation no later than 3.5 years of age. Next, the TOPA 2+ correlates well with another scale measuring similar skills and abilities (Dynamic Indicators of Basic Early Literacy Skills) and with teacher judgments of students' reading abilities. Evidence for differentiated validity comes from the scales' ability to distinguish students with language and learning disabilities from those without such problems. Other indices of validity include the absence of bias against males or females, whites, African Americans, and Hispanics.

Summary

The TOPA 2+ assesses phonemic awareness using beginning and ending sounds and letter–sound correspondence at the kindergarten and early elementary levels. The norms appear representative and are well described. Coefficient alpha for phonemic awareness is generally good for kindergartners but only suitable for screening students in the early elementary grades and for letter–sound correspondence for all students. Stability was estimated in the .80s, but interscorer agreement was excellent. Overall, care should be taken when interpreting the results of the TOPA 2+. Evidence for validity is adequate.

Dilemmas *in* Current Practice

There are four major problems in the diagnostic assessment of reading strengths and weaknesses. The first is the problem of curriculum match. Students enrolled in different reading curricula have different opportunities to learn specific skills. Reading series differ in the skills that are taught, in the emphasis placed on different skills, in the sequence in which skills are taught, and in the time at which skills are taught. Tests differ in the skills they assess. Thus, it can be expected that pupils studying different curricula will perform differently on the same reading test. It can also be expected that pupils studying the same curriculum will perform differently on different reading tests. Diagnostic personnel must be very careful to examine the match between skills taught in the students' curriculum and skills tested. Most teachers' manuals for reading series include a listing of the skills taught at each level in the series. Many authors of diagnostic reading tests now include in test manuals a list of the objectives measured by the test. At the very least, assessors should carefully examine the extent to which the test measures what has been taught. Ideally, assessors would select specific parts of tests to measure exactly what has been taught. To the extent that there is a difference between what has been taught and what is tested, the test is not a valid measure.

The second problem is also a test–curriculum match problem. Most reading instruction now takes place in general education classrooms, using the content of typical reading textbooks. This is true for developmental reading instruction, remedial reading instruction, and the teaching of reading to students with disabilities. Most diagnostic reading tests measure student skill-development competence in isolation. Also, they do not include assessments of the comprehension strategies, such as the metacognitive strategies that are now part of reading instruction.

A third problem is the selection of tests that are appropriate for making different kinds of educational decisions. We noted that there are different types of diagnostic reading tests. In making classification decisions, educators must administer tests individually. They may either use an individually administered test or give a group test to one individual. For making instructional planning decisions, the most precise and helpful information will be obtained by giving individually administered criterion-referenced measures. Educators can, of course, systematically analyze pupil performance on a norm-referenced test, but the approach is difficult and time-consuming. It may also be futile because norm-referenced tests usually do not contain enough items on which to base a diagnosis. When evaluating individual pupil progress, assessors must consider carefully the kinds of comparisons they want to make. If they want to compare pupils with same-age peers, norm-referenced measures are useful. If, on the other hand, they want to know the extent to which individual pupils are mastering curriculum objectives, criterion-referenced measures are the tests of choice.

The fourth problem is one of generalization. Assessors are faced with the difficult task of describing or predicting pupil performance in reading. Yet reading itself is difficult to describe, being a complex behavior composed of numerous subskills. Those who engage in reading diagnosis will do well to describe pupil performance in terms of specific skills or subskills (such as recognition of words in isolation, listening comprehension, and specific word-attack skills). They should also limit their predictions to making statements about probable performance of specific reading behaviors, not probable performance in reading.

Chapter Comprehension Questions

Write your answers to each of the following questions and then compare your responses to the text.

1. Why is reading important to assess?
2. Explain the two approaches traditionally used to teach reading.
3. Explain what is assessed in oral reading, word attack, reading recognition, and reading comprehension.
4. Explain two potential problems in diagnostic testing of reading.

Web Activities 

1. Search the Internet for the website of the What Works Clearinghouse. At the website, select three of the interventions listed as having "evidence of positive or potentially positive effects." Describe the reading skills that are the focus of the intervention, and the reading skills for which positive effects were identified.
2. Examine the skills included in the *DIBELS* and *DIBELS Next* assessment batteries (you can find associated reviews of these in this chapter and on the CourseMate website for this textbook). How are they the same? How are they different? What areas are more closely assessed in *DIBELS Next*?

3. Search the Internet for the Reading Rockets website. Select two of the resources available at the Assessment and Evaluation Area that you consider to be particularly helpful, and explain why.

Web Resources

What Works Clearinghouse
http://ies.ed.gov/ncee/wwc/
This website from the U.S. Department of Education Institute of Education Sciences is a source of scientific evidence for what works in education.

Reading Rockets
http://www.readingrockets.org/atoz/assessment_evaluation
This website provides information and resources on how kids learn to read, why many kids struggle, and how adults can help kids learn to read.

Additional resources for this chapter can be found on the Education CourseMate website. Go to CengageBrain.com to access the site.

Using Diagnostic Mathematics Measures

CHAPTER GOALS

1. Know why we administer and use diagnostic math tests.
2. Understand the differing ways in which mathematics is taught and how that affects assessment.
3. Understand the content and processes sampled by diagnostic mathematics tests.
4. Understand the distinction between assessment of mathematics content and assessment of mathematics process.
5. Understand the kinds of behaviors sampled by two commonly used diagnostic mathematics tests: G•MADE and KeyMath-3 DA.
6. Understand three major dilemmas in diagnostic testing in mathematics: (a) curriculum match, (b) selecting the correct tests for making specific decisions, and (c) adequate and sufficient behavior sampling.

KEY TERMS

NCTM standards
content standards
process standards
focal points
curriculum match
G•MADE
KeyMath-3 DA
STAR Math

Diagnostic testing in mathematics is designed to identify specific strengths and weaknesses in skill development. We have seen that all major achievement tests designed to assess multiple skills include subtests that measure mathematics competence. These tests are necessarily global; they most often are used at tier 1 in the multi-tiered system of supports and attempt to assess a wide range of skills. However, in most cases these multiple skills tests include only a small number of items assessing specific math skills, and the sample of math behaviors is insufficient for diagnostic purposes. Diagnostic testing in mathematics is more specific, providing more depth and a detailed assessment of skill development within specific areas. It is typically used at tiers 2 and 3 (targeted and intensive) levels in the multi-tiered system of supports model (see the discussion of the model in Chapter 1).

There are fewer diagnostic math tests than diagnostic reading tests, but math assessment is more clear-cut. Because the successful performance of some mathematical operations clearly depends on the successful performance of other operations (for example, multiplication depends on addition), it is easier to sequence skill development and assessment in math than in reading. Diagnostic math tests generally sample similar behaviors. They sample various mathematical contents, concepts, and operations as well as applications of mathematical facts and principles. Some now also include assessment of students' attitudes toward math.

1 Why Do We Assess Mathematics?

There are several reasons to assess mathematics skills. First, diagnostic math tests are intended to provide sufficiently detailed information so that teachers and intervention-assistance teams can ascertain a student's mastery of specific math skills and plan individualized math instruction. Second, some diagnostic math tests provide teachers with specific information on the kinds of items students in their classes pass and fail. This gives them information about the extent to which the curriculum and instruction in their class are working, and it provides opportunities to modify curricula. Third, all public school programs teach math facts and concepts. Teachers need to know whether pupils have mastered those facts and concepts. Finally, diagnostic math tests are occasionally used to make exceptionality and eligibility decisions. Individually administered tests are usually required for eligibility and placement decisions. Therefore, diagnostic math tests are often used to establish special learning needs and eligibility for programs for children with learning disabilities in mathematics.

2 The Ways to Teach Mathematics

There are major differences in the ways in which math is taught, and these influence how we assess performance and progress. Traditionally, mathematics emphasized the mastery of basic facts and algorithms, deductive reasoning, and proofs; teachers explained, modeled, and gave corrective feedback. With the launch of Sputnik in 1957 and the Soviet lead in space exploration, some reacted by blaming the way in which science and mathematics were taught in American schools. The old way was thought to stifle creativity and understanding.

In the 1960s, *new math* became popular in teacher-education programs in colleges and universities. Set theory; number bases; and the commutative, associative, and distributive properties became part of the curriculum. However, it soon became clear that the new math curricula were not improving student performances. In the mid-1970s, *Why Johnny Can't Add* convincingly criticized the many shortcomings of new math and advocated a return to more traditional mathematics curricula.

New math was replaced by a child-centered, constructivist approach, usually referred to as *standards-based math*. This approach provided students with the freedom to select activities that fit their interests and prior experiences. Using concrete materials, students created their own subjective mathematical understandings using their own feelings, thoughts, and intuition. Teachers played a major role in structuring the situations in which their students constructed knowledge with little or no help from the teacher.

By the 1990s, advocates of the child-centered approached were pitted against parents and mathematicians who wanted a return to more traditional mathematics curriculum and ways of teaching. Both sides had their experts, and the debate was often rancorous. However, it was becoming clear that the child-centered, standards approach was not producing the improvements envisioned. The results of the *Third International Mathematics and Science Study* (1995) provided some early indications: U.S. twelfth graders outperformed only two countries in math.

Today the evidence is unequivocal. Explicit systematic instruction improves the performance of low-achieving students and those with learning disabilities in a variety of mathematical components: computation, word problems, and problem solving (National Mathematics Advisory Panel, 2008, p. 48). Thus, students learn better when their teachers demonstrate algorithms, highlight critical features, provide opportunities to ask and answer questions, and sequence content precisely. The panel also stresses that struggling students require some explicit instruction regularly to ensure that they acquire the foundational skills and conceptual knowledge necessary for understanding their grade-level material.

The National Mathematics Advisory Panel also observed that there is clear evidence that math achievement is enhanced significantly when teachers monitor student progress. They recommended that all mathematics instruction be accompanied by ongoing monitoring of student progress toward objectives.

SCENARIO *in* ASSESSMENT

ALFRED | Alfred is a fifth-grade student who is having particular difficulty solving mathematics problems. Alfred's school uses a spiral math curriculum, in which students must discover and explain the process they use to solve problems. Now near the end of the year, he is not fluent in any of the basic whole number processes (i.e., addition, subtraction, multiplication, and simple division). Fractions and decimals are a mystery to him. His teacher has provided Alfred with extra time and encouragement as well as peer models; she followed all of the suggestions for students who are having difficulty learning that were included in the teacher's edition of the curriculum. None of these additional interventions brought about noticeable improvement.

Alfred's parents met with the teacher to express their concern about his lack of progress and to find out what they can do at home to help their son. The teacher explained that Alfred needs to learn how to solve the problems on his own and that the parents should do no more than encourage him to try hard. Alfred's parents were not persuaded by the teacher, so they met with the school principal to request an evaluation to determine if Alfred had a learning disability in mathematics.

As a first step, the principal referred Alfred to the school's student assistance team for a tier 2 intervention. A review of Alfred's records (including previous report cards, teacher comments, and the results of the GRADE administered at the end of third grade) indicated that Alfred's problems in math were not new; math had been a problem for him since at least the third grade. The team decided first to conduct a systematic assessment of Alfred's knowledge of the basic facts in whole number operations. A learning specialist conducted the evaluation that required both oral and written responses. Alfred responded fluently to some of the addition facts (i.e., 1, 2, and 5); he could calculate the remaining addition facts accurately using his fingers. He knew all subtraction facts where the subtrahend was 1 and could calculate subtraction facts with minuends of 10 or less accurately. He did not know or did not correctly calculate other subtraction facts as well as multiplication and division facts.

The team decided to provide direct instruction (relying on the commutative property, for example, teaching 3 + 4 and 4 + 3 together) in the memorization of paired addition facts. Alfred would be seen by the learning specialist twice a day for 10 minutes per session. In addition, Alfred's parents reviewed the addition facts with him nightly. Alfred made good progress and was proud of himself. He mastered the basic addition facts in two weeks. The instructional goal was then changed to basic subtraction facts. (Periodic reviews were also made of the addition facts.) Alfred made progress, but even though his retention of previously learned addition and subtraction facts was excellent, his progress was not deemed sufficient. Alfred's classroom performance was not showing improvement.

At this point, the team was faced with a decision. Should Alfred continue in tier 2 intervention or move to more intensive intervention? The answer depended on the school district's policies. In some districts, Alfred would remain in tier 2; in others, he would progress to tier 3 interventions; in still others, he would be evaluated for special education.

What implications about your own professional role can you draw from this scenario? Go to the Education CourseMate website for this textbook for more reflection questions about this Scenario in Assessment.

3 Behaviors Sampled by Diagnostic Mathematics Tests

The National Council of Teachers of Mathematics (NCTM) has specified a set of standards for learning and teaching in mathematics. The most recent specification of those standards was in a document titled *Principles and Standards for School Mathematics,* issued in 2000.[1] The NCTM specified five content standards and five process standards. Diagnostic math tests now typically assess knowledge and skill in some subset of those 10 standards, or they specify how what they assess relates to the NCTM standards. The standards are listed in Table 13.1, and for each of the standards we list the kinds of behaviors or skills identified by NCTM as important.

See the CourseMate website for this textbook for a link to the NCTM website.

Some math tests include survey questions that ask students about their attitudes toward math. Students are asked the extent to which they enjoy math, the extent to which their friends like math more than they do, and so on.

TABLE 13.1 NCTM Standards for Learning and Teaching in Mathematics

Content Standards

Number and Operations Instructional programs from pre-kindergarten through grade 12 should enable all students to

- understand numbers, ways of representing numbers, relationships among numbers, and number systems;
- understand meanings of operations and how they relate to one another; and
- compute fluently and make reasonable estimates.

Algebra Instructional programs from pre-kindergarten through grade 12 should enable all students to

- understand patterns, relations, and functions;
- represent and analyze mathematical situations and structures using algebraic symbols;
- use mathematical models to represent and understand quantitative relationships; and
- analyze change in various contexts.

Geometry Instructional programs from pre-kindergarten through grade 12 should enable all students to

- analyze characteristics and properties of two- and three-dimensional geometric shapes and develop mathematical arguments about geometric relationships;
- specify locations and describe spatial relationships using coordinate geometry and other representational systems;
- apply transformations and use symmetry to analyze mathematical situations; and
- use visualization, spatial reasoning, and geometric modeling to solve problems.

Measurement Instructional programs from pre-kindergarten through grade 12 should enable all students to

- understand measurable attributes of objects and the units, systems, and processes of measurement; and
- apply appropriate techniques, tools, and formulas to determine measurements.

Data Analysis and Probability Instructional programs from pre-kindergarten through grade 12 should enable all students to

- formulate questions that can be addressed with data and collect, organize, and display relevant data to answer them;
- select and use appropriate statistical methods to analyze data;
- develop and evaluate inferences and predictions that are based on data; and
- understand and apply basic concepts of probability.

[1] In 2006, NCTM published *Curriculum Focal Points for Prekindergarten Through Grade 8 Mathematics.* Focal points are a small number of mathematical topics or areas that teachers should focus on at each grade level. Currently, state and district math standards are not reflective of the focal points, but they probably will be in the near future. Therefore, practitioners must consider alignment of diagnostic math tests to the current standards and the focal points. (Keep abreast of changes by visiting www.nctm.org/standards/default.aspx?id=58.)

Process Standards

Problem Solving Instructional programs from pre-kindergarten through grade 12 should enable all students to

- build new mathematical knowledge through problem solving;
- solve problems that arise in mathematics and in other contexts;
- apply and adapt a variety of appropriate strategies to solve problems; and
- monitor and reflect on the process of mathematical problem solving.

Reasoning and Proof Instructional programs from pre-kindergarten through grade 12 should enable all students to

- recognize reasoning and proof as fundamental aspects of mathematics;
- make and investigate mathematical conjectures;
- develop and evaluate mathematical arguments and proofs; and
- select and use various types of reasoning and methods of proof.

Communication Instructional programs from pre-kindergarten through grade 12 should enable all students to

- organize and consolidate their mathematical thinking through communication;
- communicate their mathematical thinking coherently and clearly to peers, teachers, and others;
- analyze and evaluate the mathematical thinking and strategies of others; and
- use the language of mathematics to express mathematical ideas precisely.

Connections Instructional programs from pre-kindergarten through grade 12 should enable all students to

- recognize and use connections among mathematical ideas;
- understand how mathematical ideas interconnect and build on one another to produce a coherent whole; and
- recognize and apply mathematics in contexts outside of mathematics.

Representation Instructional programs from pre-kindergarten through grade 12 should enable all students to

- create and use representations to organize, record, and communicate mathematical ideas;
- select, apply, and translate among mathematical representations to solve problems; and
- use representations to model and interpret physical, social, and mathematical phenomena.

SOURCE: Reprinted with permission from *Principles & Standards for School Mathematics.* copyright © 2000–2004 by the National Council of Teachers of Mathematics (NCTM). All rights reserved. Standards are listed with the permission of the NCTM. NCTM does not endorse the content or validity of these alignments.

SPECIFIC DIAGNOSTIC MATHEMATICS TESTS

SPECIFIC DIAGNOSTIC MATHEMATICS TESTS

Detailed reviews of the other tests are provided at the CourseMate website for this textbook.

Commonly used diagnostic mathematics tests are listed in Table 13.2. Two of the tests (Group Mathematics Assessment and Diagnostic Evaluation [G•MADE] and KeyMath-3 Diagnostic Assessment [KeyMath-3 DA]) are reviewed in detail in this chapter.

Group Mathematics Assessment and Diagnostic Evaluation (G•MADE)

The Group Mathematics Assessment and Diagnostic Evaluation (G•MADE; Williams, 2004) is a group-administered, norm-referenced, standards-based test for assessing the math skills of students in grades K–12. It is norm referenced in that it is standardized on a nationally representative group. It is standards based in that the content assessed is based on the standards of NCTM.

G•MADE is a diagnostic test designed to identify specific math skill development strengths and weaknesses, and the test is designed to lead to teaching strategies. The test provides information about math skills and error patterns of each student, using the efficiencies of group administration. Test materials include a CD that provides a cross-reference between specific math skills and math teaching resources. Teaching resources are also available in print.

There are nine levels, each with two parallel forms. Eight of the nine levels have three subtests (the lowest level has two). The three subtests are Concepts and Communication, Operations and

TABLE 13.2 Commonly Used Diagnostic Mathematics Tests

Test	Author	Publisher	Year	Ages/ Grades	Individual/ Group	NRT/ SRT/CRT	Subtests
KeyMath-3 DA	Connolly	Pearson	2007	Ages 4–6 to 21	Individual	NRT	Numeration, Algebra, Geometry, Measurement, Data Analysis and Probability, Mental Computation and Estimation, Addition and Subtraction, Multiplication and Division, Foundations of Problem Solving, Applied Problem Solving Composite scores: Basic Concepts (conceptual knowledge), Operations (computational skills), Applications (problem solving)
Comprehensive Mathematical Abilities Test (CMAT)	Hresko, Schlieve, Heron, Swain, & Sherbenou	Pro-Ed	2003	Ages 7–0 to 18–11	Individual	NRT	Core subtests: Addition; Subtraction; Multiplication; Division; Problem Solving; Charts, Tables, and Graphs Supplemental subtests: Algebra, Geometry, Rational Numbers, Time, Money, Measurement Core composites: General Mathematics, Basic Calculations, Mathematical Reasoning Supplemental composites: Advanced Calculations, Practical Applications Global Composite: Global Mathematical Ability
Group Mathematics Assessment and Diagnostic Evaluation (G•MADE)	Williams	Pearson	2004	Grades K–12	Group	NRT and SRT	Concepts and Communication, Operations and Computation, Process and Applications In each subtest, the following content is assessed: numeration, quantity, geometry, measurement, time/sequence, money, comparison, statistics, and algebra
Stanford Diagnostic Mathematics Test (SDMT4)	Harcourt Brace Educational Measurement	Pearson	1996	Grades 1.5–13	Group	NRT	Concepts and Applications, Computation
Test of Early Mathematics Abilities (reviewed on website under Chapter 19)	Ginsburg & Baroody	Pro-Ed	2003	Ages 3–0 to 8–11	Individual	NRT	Formal Mathematical Thinking, Informal Mathematical Thinking
STAR Math (reviewed in Chapter 23)	Renaissance Learning	Renaissance Learning	2011	Grades 3–12	Individual	CAT	No subtests for this computer adaptive test

Computation, and Process and Applications. The items in each subtest fit the content of the following categories: numeration, quantity, geometry, measurement, time/sequence, money, comparison, statistics, and algebra. Diagnosis of skill development strengths and needs is fairly broad. For example, teachers learn that an individual student has difficulty with concepts and communication in the area of geometry.

Subtests

Concepts and Communication. This subtest measures students' knowledge of the language, vocabulary, and representations of math. A symbol, word, or short phrase is presented with four choices (pictures, symbols, or numbers). It is permissible for teachers to read words to students, but they may not define or explain the words. Figure 13.1 is a representation of the kinds of items used to measure concepts and communication skills.

Operations and Computation. This subtest measures students' skills in using the basic operations of addition, subtraction, multiplication, and division. This subtest is not included at Level R (the readiness level and lowest level of the test). There are 24 items on this subtest at each level, and each consists of an incomplete equation with four answer choices. An example is shown in Figure 13.2.

Process and Applications. This subtest measures students' skill in taking the language and concepts of math and applying the appropriate operations and computations to solve a word problem. Each item consists of a short passage of one or more sentences and four response choices. An example is shown in Figure 13.3. At lower levels of the test, the problems are one-step problems, whereas at higher levels they require application of multiple steps.

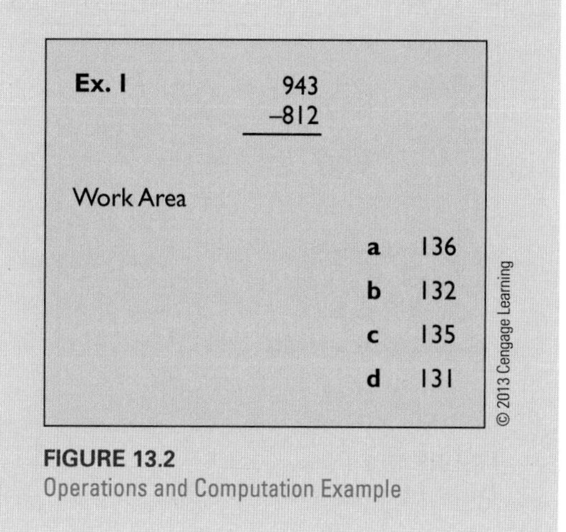

FIGURE 13.2
Operations and Computation Example

The G•MADE levels each contain items that are on grade level, items that are somewhat above level, and items that are below level. Each level can be administered on grade level or can be given out of level (matched to the ability level of the student). Teachers can choose to administer a lower or higher level of the test.

FIGURE 13.1
Concepts and Communication Example from Levels M and H

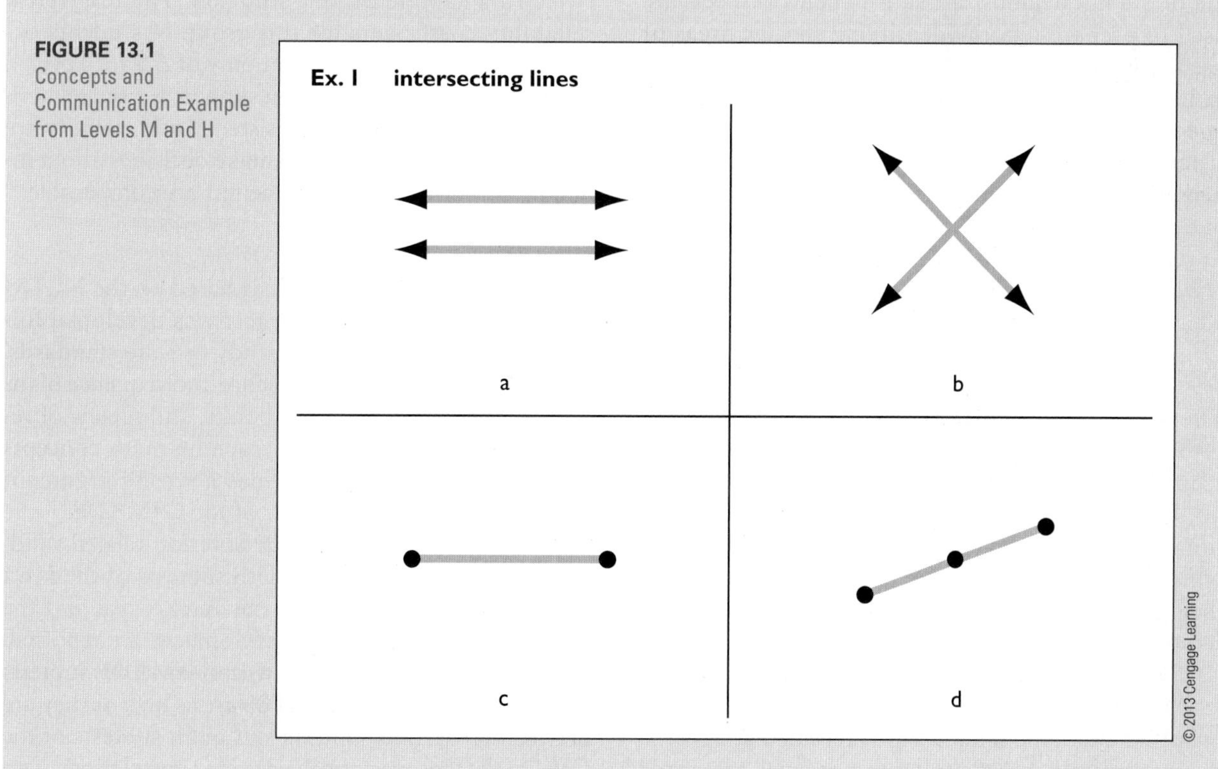

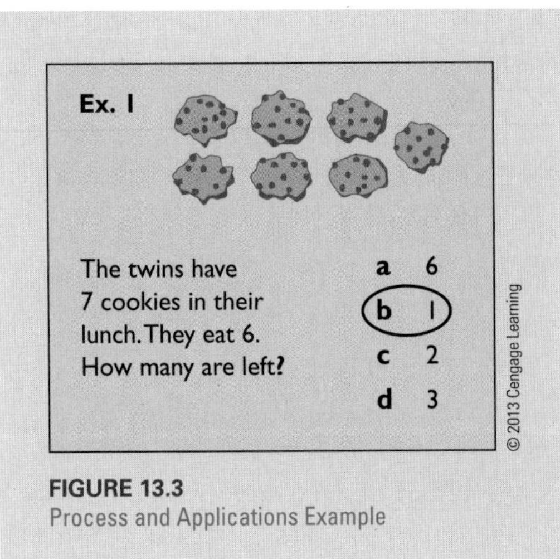

FIGURE 13.3
Process and Applications Example

Scores

Raw scores for the G•MADE can be converted to standard scores (with a mean of 100 and a standard deviation of 15) using fall or spring norms. Grade scores, stanines, percentiles, and normal curve equivalents are also available. Growth scale values are provided for the purpose of tracking growth in math skills for students who are given different levels of the test over the years. G•MADE can be used to track growth over the course of a year or from year to year.

The publisher provides diagnostic worksheets that consist of cross-tabulations of the subtests with the content areas. The worksheets are used to identify areas in which individual students or whole classes did or did not demonstrate skills. The worksheets are used to prepare reports identifying specific areas of need. For example, the objective assessed by item 28 in Level 1, Form B is skill in solving a one-step sequence problem that requires the ability to recognize a pattern. When reporting on performance on this item, the teacher might report that "Joe did not solve one-step sequence problems that require the ability to recognize a pattern." He might also indicate that "two-thirds of the class did not solve one-step problems that require the ability to recognize a pattern."

Norms

There were two phases to standardization of the G•MADE. First, a study of bias by gender, race/ethnicity, and region was conducted on more than 10,000 students during a national tryout. In addition, the test was reviewed by a panel of educators who represented minority perspectives, and items they identified as apparently biased were modified or removed.

During the fall of 2002, G•MADE was standardized on a nationwide sample of students at 72 sites. In spring 2003, the sampling was repeated at 71 sites. Approximately 1,000 students per level per grade participated in the standardization (a total of nearly 28,000 students). The sample was selected based on geographic region, community type (rural, and so on), and socioeconomic status (percentage of students on free and reduced-price lunch). Students with disabilities were included in the standardization if they attended regular education classes all or part of the day. Fall and spring grade-based and age-based norms are provided for each level of the G•MADE. Norms that allow for out-of-level testing are available in a G•MADE Out-of-Level Norms Supplement and through the scoring and reporting software. Templates are available for hand scoring, or the test can be scored and reported by computer.

Reliability

Data on internal consistency and stability over time are presented in the G•MADE manual. Internal consistency reliabilities were computed for each G•MADE subtest and the total test score for each level and form using the split-half method. All reliabilities exceed .74, with more than 90 percent exceeding .80. The only low reliabilities are at seventh grade for Concepts and Communications and for Process and Applications at all grades beyond grade 4. Thus, the only really questionable subtest is Process and Applications beyond grade 4. Internal consistency reliability coefficients are above .90 for the total score at all levels of the test.

Alternate-form reliability was established on a sample of 651 students, and all reliabilities exceeded .80. Stability of the test was established by giving it twice to a sample of 761 students. The test–retest reliability coefficients for this group of students exceeded .80, with the exception only of .78 for Level 4, Form A. Overall, there is good support for the reliability of the grade. Internal consistency and stability are sufficient for using the test to make decisions about individuals. The two forms of the test are comparable.

Validity

The content of the G•MADE is based on the NCTM Math Standards, though the test was developed following a year-long research study of state standards, curriculum benchmarks, the score and sequence plans of commonly used math textbooks, and review of research on best practices for teaching math concepts and skills. The author provides a strong argument for the validity of the content of the G•MADE.

Several studies support the criterion-related validity of the test. Correlations with subtests of the Iowa Tests of Basic Skills (ITBS), the TerraNova, and the Iowa Tests of Educational Development are reported. Surprisingly, correlations between G•MADE subtests and reading subtests of the ITBS are as high as they are between G•MADE subtests and math subtests of the G•MADE. This was not the case for correlations with the TerraNova, in which those with the math subtests exceeded by far correlations with the reading subtests. In a comparison of performance on KeyMath and the G•MADE, all correlations were in excess of .80. The two tests measure highly comparable skills.

Summary

The G•MADE is a group-administered, norm-referenced, standards-based, and diagnostic measure of student skill development in three separate areas. There is good evidence for the content validity of the test, and the test was appropriately and adequately standardized. Evidence for reliability and validity of the G•MADE is good. The lone exception to this is the finding that performance on the test is as highly correlated with the reading subtests of some other criterion measures as it is with the math subtests of those measures.

KeyMath-3 Diagnostic Assessment (KeyMath-3 DA)

KeyMath-3 Diagnostic Assessment (KeyMath-3 DA; Connolly, 2007) is the third revision of the test originally published in 1971. Over the three editions of the test, a number of "normative updates" have been published. KeyMath-3 DA is an untimed, individually administered, norm-referenced test designed to provide a comprehensive assessment of essential math concepts and skills in individuals aged 4 years, 6 months through 21 years. The test takes 30 to 40 minutes for students in the lower elementary grades and 75 to 90 minutes for older students. Four uses are suggested for the test: (1) assess math proficiency by providing comprehensive coverage of the concepts and skills taught in regular math instruction, (2) assess student progress in math, (3) support instructional planning, and (4) support educational placement decisions. The author designed this revision of the test to reflect the NCTM content and process standards described previously in this chapter.

KeyMath-3 DA includes a manual, two freestanding easels for either Form A or Form B, and 25 record forms with detachable Written Computation Examinee Booklets. Two ancillary products are available for KeyMath-3 DA: an ASSIST Scoring and Reporting Software program and a KeyMath-3 Essential Resources instructional program. There are two parallel forms (A and B) of the test, and each has 372 items divided into the following subtests: Numeration, Algebra, Geometry, Measurement, Data Analysis and Probability, Mental Computation and Estimation, Addition and Subtraction, Multiplication and Division, Foundations of Problem Solving, and Applied Problem Solving.

Scores

The test can be hand scored or scored by using the KeyMath-3 DA ASSIST Scoring and Reporting Software. Users can obtain three indices of relative standing (scale scores, standard scores, and percentile ranks) and three developmental scores (grade and age equivalents and growth scale values). Users also obtain three composite scores: Basic Concepts (conceptual knowledge), Operations (computational skills), and Application (problem solving). In addition, tools are available to help users analyze students' functional range in math, and they provide an analysis of students' performance specific to focus items and behavioral objectives. The scoring software can be used to create progress reports across multiple administrations of the test, produce a narrative summary report, export derived scores to Excel spreadsheets for statistical analysis, and generate reports for parents.

Norms

KeyMath-3 DA was standardized on 3,630 individuals, ages 4 years, 6 months to 21 years. The test was standardized by contacting examiners and having them get permission to assess students, sending the permissions to the publisher, and then randomly selecting students to participate in the norming. The sample closely approximates the distributions reported in the 2004 census, and cross-tabs (i.e., how many males were from the Northeast) are reported in the manual. In addition, the test was standardized on representative proportions of students with specific learning disability, speech/language impairment, intellectual disability, emotional/behavioral disturbance, and developmental delays. The test appears adequately standardized.

Reliability

The author reports data on internal consistency, alternate-form, and test–retest reliability. Internal consistency reliabilities for students in kindergarten and first grade are low. At other ages, internal consistency reliability coefficients generally exceed .80. Internal consistency coefficients for the composite scores exceed .90 except in grades K–2. Alternate-form reliabilities exceed .80 with the exception of the reliabilities for different forms of the Geometry and the Data Analysis and Probability subtests. Adjusted test–retest reliabilities based on the performance of 103 students (approximately half on each form) in grades K–12 generally exceed .80 with the exception of the Foundations of Problem Solving subtest (.70) and the Geometry subtest (.78). The reliability of all subtests and composites is adequate for screening purposes and good for diagnostic purposes.

Dilemmas *in* Current Practice

There are three major problems in the diagnostic assessment of math skills.

The first problem is the recurring issue of curriculum match. There is considerable variation in math curricula. This variation means that diagnostic math tests will not be equally representative of all curricula or even appropriate for some commonly used ones. As a result, great care must be exercised in using diagnostic math tests to make various educational decisions. Assessment personnel must be extremely careful to note the match between test content and school curriculum. This should involve far more than a quick inspection of test items by someone unfamiliar with the specific classroom curriculum. For example, a professional could inspect the teacher's manual to ensure that the teacher assesses only material that has been taught and that there is reasonable correspondence between the relative emphasis placed on teaching the material and testing the material. To do this, the professional might have to develop a table of specifications for the math curriculum and compare test items with that table. However, once a table of specifications has been developed for the curriculum, a better procedure would be to select items from a standards-referenced system to fit the cells in the table exactly.

The second problem is selecting an appropriate test for the type of decision to be made. School personnel are usually required to use individually administered norm-referenced devices in eligibility decisions. Decisions about a pupil's eligibility for special services, however, need not be based on detailed information about the pupil's strengths and weaknesses, as provided by diagnostic tests; diagnosticians are interested in a pupil's relative standing. In our opinion, the best mathematical achievement survey tests are subtests of group-administered tests. A practical solution is not to use a diagnostic math test for eligibility decisions but to administer individually a subtest from one of the better group-administered achievement tests.

The third problem is that most of the diagnostic tests in mathematics do not test a sufficiently detailed sample of facts and concepts. Consequently, assessors must generalize from a student's performance on the items tested to his or her performance on the items that are not tested. The reliabilities of the subtests of diagnostic math tests often are not high enough for educators to make such a generalization with any great degree of confidence. As a result, these tests are not very useful in assessing readiness or strengths and weaknesses in order to plan instructional programs. We believe that the preferred practice in diagnostic testing in mathematics is for teachers to develop curriculum-based achievement tests that exactly parallel the curriculum being taught.

Validity

The authors report extensive validity information in the manual. All validity data are for composite scores. KeyMath-3 DA composites correlate very highly with scores on the KeyMath-Revised normative update and math scores on the Kaufman Test of Educational Achievement (with the exception of the Applications and Mathematics Composite), ITBS, Measures of Academic Progress, and the G•MADE (with the exception of the operations composite [.63]). Evidence for content validity is good based on alignment with state and NCTM standards. The authors provide data on how representatives of special populations perform relative to the general population, and scores are within expected ranges.

Summary

KeyMath-3 DA is a norm-referenced, individually administered comprehensive assessment of skills and problem solving in math appropriate for use with students 4–6 to 21 years of age. The test is adequately standardized, and there is good evidence for reliability and validity. Comparative data are provided on the performance of students with disabilities.

Chapter Comprehension Questions

Write your answers to each of the following questions and then compare your responses to the text.

1. Why do we administer and use diagnostic math tests?
2. Provide two examples each of content and processes sampled by diagnostic mathematics tests.
3. What is the distinction between assessment of mathematics content and assessment of mathematics process?
4. Identify two differences in the kinds of behaviors sampled by two commonly used diagnostic mathematics tests: G•MADE and KeyMath-3 DA.
5. Briefly describe three major dilemmas in diagnostic testing in mathematics:
    a. Curriculum match
    b. Selecting the correct tests for making specific decisions
    c. Adequate and sufficient behavior sampling
6. How can educational professionals overcome the problem of curriculum match in the diagnostic assessment of mathematical competence?

Web Activities

1. Go to the CourseMate website for this textbook and read the review of the Stanford Diagnostic Math Test. How do the behaviors sampled for this test compare to those sampled by Key Math? How reliable and valid is the SDMT? When would you use it?
2. Search the Internet for the Intervention Central website and view the ways in which this site can be used to help with math assessment.
3. Search the Internet for the government website for the National Mathematics Advisory Panel. Read the panel recommendations regarding instructional practices (their recommendations 23–30). Note the recommendation regarding formative assessment (ongoing progress monitoring). Discuss with your classmates the implications of these recommendations for assessment practices.
4. Search the Internet for Easy CBM and read about how you can build curriculum-based tests in mathematics for use in classrooms and research projects.

Web Resources

National Council of Teachers of Mathematics (NCTM)
http://www.nctm.org
This website is designed for teachers of mathematics and contains information and resources related to the subject of math.

Easy CBM
http://www.easycbm.com/
Easy CBM was designed by researchers at the University of Oregon. The site can be used to generate CBMs in math for use as part of a multi-tiered system of supports model.

Additional resources for this chapter can be found on the Education CourseMate website. Go to CengageBrain.com to access the site.

Using Measures of Oral and Written Language

CHAPTER GOALS

1 Know why we assess oral and written language.
2 Understand various behaviors and skills associated with language.
3 Understand how cultural background may influence language assessment.
4 Know methods for eliciting oral language samples.
5 Be familiar with two language tests.
6 Be familiar with some of the current dilemmas we face in using language measures.

KEY TERMS

morphology	semantics	syntax
pragmatics	supralinguistic functioning	phonology

SCENARIO *in* ASSESSMENT

JILL | Jill's fifth-grade teacher and Jill's parents expressed concerns to the Teacher Assistance Team at Brownville Elementary School. According to her teacher and parents, Jill was demonstrating all the classic signs of a student with a central auditory processing disorder (CAPD). Her behavior in the classroom was characterized as often off task; she had difficulty attending to tasks and following oral directions, was easily distracted by noise, made frequent requests for repetition of information, daydreamed, often appeared not to be listening, and had poor memory skills. The teacher and parent completed checklists indicating concerns with central auditory processing. At the recommendation of the Teacher Assistance Team, Jill was taken to her family doctor to address concerns related to attention challenges and to rule these out as a possible reason for classroom performance issues. A trial of medication for attention deficit disorder was completed. Jill showed remarkable improvements in attention and focus, but continued to struggle with what appeared to be listening and comprehension components of classroom activities. The speech–language pathologist was brought in to assess Jill's language skills as well as make recommendations about audiological assessment for CAPD.

Jill completed the Clinical Evaluation of Language Fundamentals test. The results were surprising: Her receptive language standard score was 91, and her expressive language standard score was 76. This child did not have a CAPD but, rather, expressive language impairment. She could understand and process what was taking place and being asked of her, but she could not organize or formulate the response. The speech–language pathologist recommended extensive language therapy to address Jill's expressive language. The results have been amazing. Language testing is a vital component of assessing what disabilities are and are not present.

What implications about your own professional role can you draw from this scenario? Go to the Education CourseMate website for this textbook for more reflection questions about this Scenario in Assessment.

FIGURE 14.1
The Four Major Communication Processes

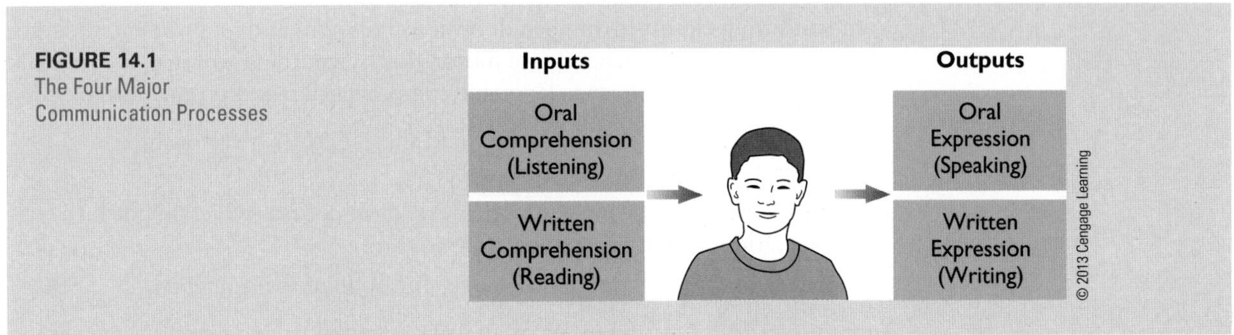

The assessment of language competence should include evaluation of a student's ability to process, both in comprehension and in expression, language in a spoken or written format. There are four major communication processes: oral comprehension (listening and comprehending speech), written comprehension (reading), oral expression (speaking), and written expression (writing). These are illustrated in Figure 14.1.

In assessing language skills, it is important to break language down into processes and measure each one because each process makes different demands on the person's ability to communicate. Performance in one area does not always predict performance in others. For example, a child who has normal comprehension does not necessarily have normal production skills. Also, a child with relatively normal expressive skills may have problems with receptive language. Therefore, a complete language assessment will include examination of both oral and written reception (comprehension) and expression (production).

1 Terminology

Educators, psychologists, linguists, and speech–language pathologists often have different perspectives on which skills make up language. These different views have resulted in the development of a plethora of language assessment tests, each with an apparently unique method of assessing language. The terminology used to describe the behaviors and skills assessed can be confusing as well. Terms such as *morphology*, *semantics*, *syntax*, and *supralinguistic functioning* are used, and sometimes different test authors use different terms to mean the same thing. One author's vocabulary subtest is another's measure of "lexical semantics."

We define *language* as a code for conveying ideas—a code that includes phonology, semantics, morphology, syntax, and pragmatics. These terms are defined as follows:

Phonology: the hearing and production of speech sounds. The term *articulation* is considered a synonym for phonology.

Semantics: the study of word meanings. In assessment, this term is generally used to refer to the derivation of meaning from single words. The term *vocabulary* is often used interchangeably with semantics.

Morphology: the use of affixes (prefixes and suffixes) to change the meaning of words used in sentences. Morphology also includes verb tense ("John *is* going" versus "John *was* going").

Syntax: the use of word order to convey meaning. Typically there are rules for arranging words into sentences. In language assessment, the word *grammar* is often used to refer to a combination of morphology and syntax.

Pragmatics: the social context in which a sentence occurs. Context influences both the way in which a message is expressed and the way in which it is interpreted. For example, the sentence, "Can you close the door?" can have different meanings to a student sitting closest to an open door in a classroom and to a student undergoing physical therapy to rehabilitate motor skills. According to Carrow-Woolfolk (1995), contexts that influence language comprehension and production include

- social variables, such as the setting and the age, roles, relationships, and number of participants in a discourse;
- linguistic variables produced by the type of discourse (which might be a conversation, narrative, lecture, or text); and
- the intention, motivation, knowledge, and style of the sender.

Supralinguistics: a second order of analysis required to understand the meaning of words or sentences. For example, much language must be interpreted in a nonliteral way (sarcasm, indirect requests, and figurative language). Dad may say that the lawn looks like a hay field, when he is actually implying that he wants his child to cut the grass. Mom may say that the weather is "great," when she really means that she is tired of all the cloudy and rainy weather.

Throughout this chapter, we use "comprehension" as a synonym for receptive language and "production" as a synonym for expressive language. Table 14.1 defines each of the basic language components for receptive and expressive modalities.

TABLE 14.1 Language Subskills for Each Channel of Communication

	Channel of Communication	
Language Component	**Reception (Comprehension)**	**Expression (Production)**
Phonology	Hearing and discriminating speech sounds	Articulating speech sounds
Morphology and syntax	Understanding the grammatical structure of language	Using the grammatical structure of language
Semantics	Understanding vocabulary, meaning, and concepts	Using vocabulary, meaning, and concepts
Pragmatics and supralinguistics	Understanding a speaker's or writer's intentions	Using awareness of social aspects of language
Ultimate language skill	Understanding spoken or written language	Speaking or writing

2 Why Assess Oral and Written Language?

There are two primary reasons for assessing language abilities. First, well-developed language abilities are desirable in and of themselves. The ability to converse and to express thoughts and feelings is a goal of most individuals. Those who have difficulties with various aspects of language are often eligible for special services from speech–language specialists or from special educators. Second, various language processes and skills are believed to underlie subsequent development. Students who experience language difficulties have also been shown to experience behavior disorders, learning disabilities, and reading disorders.

Written language and spelling are regularly taught in school, and these areas are singled out for assessment in the Individuals with Disabilities Education Act. Written and oral language tests are administered for purposes of screening, instructional planning and modification, eligibility, and progress monitoring.

CONSIDERATIONS IN ASSESSING ORAL LANGUAGE

Those who assess oral language must necessarily give consideration to cultural diversity and the developmental status of those they assess.

Cultural Diversity

Cultural background must be considered in assessing oral language competence. Although most children in the United States learn English, the form of English they learn depends on where they were born, who their parents are, and so on. For example, in central Pennsylvania, a child might say, "My hands need washed" instead of the standard "My hands need to be washed." In New York City, a child learning Black English might say "birfday" instead of "birthday," or "He be running" instead of "He is running." These and other culturally determined alternative constructions and pronunciations are not incorrect or inferior; they are just different. Indeed, they are appropriate within the child's surrounding community. Children should be viewed as having a language disorder only if they exhibit disordered production of their own primary language or dialect.

Cultural background is particularly important when the language assessment devices that are currently available are considered. Ideally, a child should be compared with others in the same language community. There should be separate norms for each language community, including Standard American English. Unfortunately, the norm samples of most language tests are heterogeneous, and scores on these tests may not be valid indicators of a child's language ability. Consider Plate 25 of the original Peabody Picture Vocabulary Test. This plate contained four pictures, and the examiner said, "Show me the wiener." There are many places in this country where the only word for that item is *hot dog* or *frankfurter.* Yet, because the test was standardized using *wiener*, the examiner was required to use that term. If a child had never heard "wiener," he or she was penalized and received a lower score, even though the error was cultural and not indicative of a semantic or intellectual deficiency. If there are a number of such items on a language test, the child's score can hardly be considered a valid indicator of language ability.

Developmental Considerations

Age is a major consideration in assessment of the child's language. Language acquisition is developmental; some sounds, linguistic structures, and even semantic elements are correctly produced at an earlier age than others. Thus, it is not unusual or indicative of language disorder for a 2-year-old child to say, "Kitty house" for "The cat is in the house," although the same phrase would be an indication of a disorder in a 3-year-old. It is important to be aware of developmental norms for language acquisition and to use those norms when making judgments about a child's language competence.

CONSIDERATIONS IN ASSESSING WRITTEN LANGUAGE

There are two major components of written language: content and form. The content of written expression is the product of considerable intellectual and linguistic activity: formulating, elaborating, sequencing, and then clarifying and revising ideas; choosing the precise word to convey meaning; and so forth. Moreover, much of what we consider to be content is the result of a creative endeavor. Our ability to use words to excite, to depict vividly, to imply, and to describe complex ideas is far more involved than simply putting symbols on paper.

The form of written language is far more mechanistic than its content. For writer and reader to communicate, three sets of conventions or rules are used: penmanship, spelling, and style rules. The most fundamental rules deal with *penmanship*, the formation of individual letters and letter sequences that make up words. Although letter formation tends to become more individualistic with age, there are a limited number of ways, for example, that the letter *A* can be written and still be recognized as an *A*. Moreover, there are conventions about the relative spacing of letters between and within words.

Spelling is also rule governed. Although American English is more irregular phonetically than other languages, it remains largely regular, and students should be able to spell most words by applying a few phonetic rules. For example, we have known since the mid-1960s that approximately 80 percent of all consonants have a single spelling (Hanna, Hanna, Hodges, & Rudoff, 1966). Short vowels are the major source of difficulty for most writers. The third set of conventions involves style. *Style* is a catchall term for rule-governed writing, which includes grammar (such as parts of speech, pronoun use, agreement, and verb voice and mood) and mechanics (such as punctuation, capitalization, abbreviations, and referencing).

The conventions of written language are tested on many standardized achievement tests. However, the spelling words that students are to learn vary considerably from curriculum to curriculum. For example, Ames (1965) examined seven spelling series and found that they introduced an average of 3,200 words between the second and eighth grades. However, only approximately 1,300 words were common to all the series; approximately 1,700 words were taught in only one series. Moreover, those words that were taught in several series varied considerably in their grade placement, sometimes by as many as five grades.

Capitalization and punctuation are also assessed on the current forms of several achievement batteries. Again, standardized tests are not well suited to measuring achievement in these areas because the grade level at which these skills are taught varies so much from one curriculum to another. To be valid, the measurement of achievement in these areas must be closely tied to the curriculum being taught. For example, pupils may learn in kindergarten, first grade, second grade, or later that a sentence always begins with a capital letter. They may learn in the sixth grade or several grades earlier that commercial brand names are capitalized. Students may be taught in the second or third grade that the apostrophe in "it's" makes the word a contraction of "it is" or may still be studying "it's" in high school. Finally, in assessing word usage, organization, and penmanship, we must take into account the emphasis that individual teachers place on these components of written language and when and how students are taught.

The more usual way to assess written language is to evaluate a student's written work and to develop vocabulary and spelling tests, as well as written expression rubrics, that parallel the curriculum. In this way, teachers can be sure that they are measuring precisely what has been taught. Most teacher's editions of language arts textbook series contain scope-and-sequence charts that specify fairly clearly the objectives that are taught in each unit. From these charts, teachers can develop appropriate criterion-referenced and curriculum-based assessments. There are also some rubrics available in the research literature that may be used by teachers to guide their instruction toward important components of writing content (Tindal & Hasbrouck, 1991).

SCENARIO *in* ASSESSMENT

JOSÉ | In the Fairfield School District, students are encouraged to use inventive spelling from kindergarten to second grade. In other words, they are encouraged to come up with their own spelling for words that they do not yet know how to spell. When completing independent writing assignments, Fairfield teachers simply encourage students to focus on getting their thoughts on paper. Although spelling is taught in Fairfield, it is not expected that students know how to correctly spell the words that they choose to use in their independent writing assignments. Students are provided feedback on the quality of description and organization evident in their writing. As long as the spelling makes sense, they are not corrected.

In the Lakewood School District, just to the north of Fairfield, the focus of writing instruction and feedback is on the form of writing (that is, handwriting, spelling, punctuation, and so on). Students are encouraged to use those words that have been taught as weekly spelling words in their weekly independent writing assignments. Teachers spend a substantial amount of time teaching letter formation, word spacing, capitalization, and spelling during writing instruction. Students' grades on their independent writing assignments are based on the percentage of words spelled correctly.

José is a first grader who just moved into the Lakewood School District after attending Fairfield for kindergarten and part of first grade. His new teacher is appalled when José turns in the following independent writing assignment:

Mi trip to flourda

I went to flourda on brake and it was rely wrm and i wint swemmin in a pul. I jummd of a dyving bord and mad a big splaz that mad evrywon wet. I wood like to go thare agin neckst yeer.

The teacher views this writing sample to be far below the quality of Meika's writing assignment, which is much shorter but includes correct spelling and capitalization. Meika's writing sample is as follows:

My Winter Break

I had fun with my sister. We played games. We watched T.V.

The teacher is very concerned that José will not be successful in her class and requests the assistance of the school psychologist to help determine whether he may have a writing disability and need additional services. Although José performs similarly to Meika on a standardized measure of written language in which scores are based on both spelling achievement and total words written, greater differences in their achievement are evident when applying the different writing standards associated with the two different districts. In Fairfield, where total words written in 3 minutes is the measure used, he scored at the 85th percentile. In Lakewood, where total words spelled correctly in 3 minutes is the measure used, he scored at the 9th percentile.

Instead of considering a full-blown special education evaluation, the school psychologist recommends that José be specifically instructed to use only the words he knows how to spell in his independent writing. As José receives more consistent feedback on his mechanics, he begins to increase his performance according to his new school district's standards and eventually is performing above average according to both total words written and words spelled correctly on the 3-minute writing task.

The message here is that measures of student achievement should be aligned with instruction. For students who have not had exposure to the associated instruction, it is important to be patient and provide opportunities to learn accordingly.

What implications about your own professional role can you draw from this scenario? Go to the Education CourseMate website for this textbook for more reflection questions about this Scenario in Assessment.

3 Observing Language Behavior

There has been some disagreement among language professionals about the most valid method of evaluating a child's language performance, especially in the expressive channel of communication. There are three procedures used to gather a sample of a child's language behavior: spontaneous, imitative, and elicited.

SPONTANEOUS LANGUAGE

One school of thought holds that the only valid measure of a child's language abilities is one that studies the language the child produces spontaneously (for example, see Miller, 1981). Using this approach, the examiner records 50 to 100 consecutive utterances produced as the child is talking to an adult or playing with toys. With older children, conversations or storytelling tasks are often used. The child's utterances are then analyzed in terms of phonology, semantics, morphology, syntax, and pragmatics in order to provide information about the child's conversational abilities. Because the construct of pragmatics has been developed only recently, there are few standard assessment instruments available to sample this domain. Therefore, spontaneous language-sampling procedures are widely used to evaluate pragmatic abilities (see Prutting & Kirshner, 1987). Although analysis of a child's spontaneous language production is not the purpose of any standard oral language assessment instruments, some interest has been shown in standard assessment of handwriting and spelling skills in an uncontrived, spontaneous situation (for example, the revised *Test of Written Language* by Hammill and Larsen, 2008).

IMITATION

Imitation tasks require a child to repeat directly the word, phrase, or sentence produced by the examiner. It might seem that such tasks bear little relation to spontaneous performance, but evidence suggests that such tasks are valid predictors of spontaneous production. In fact, many investigators have demonstrated that children's imitative language is essentially the same in content and structure as their spontaneous language (Blake, Austin, Cannon, Lisius, & Vaughn, 1994; Camarata & Nelson, 1994). Evidently, children translate adult sentences into their own language system and then repeat the sentences using their own language rules. A young child might imitate "The boy is running and jumping" as "Boy run and jump." Imitation thus seems to be a valuable tool for providing information about a child's language abilities. We note one caution, however: Features of a child's language systems can be obtained using imitation only if the stimulus sentences are long enough to tax the child's memory, because a child will imitate any sentence perfectly if the length of that sentence is within the child's memory capacity (Slobin & Welsh, 1973).

The use of imitation does not preclude the need for spontaneous sampling because the examiner also needs information derived from direct observation of conversational skills. Rather, imitation tasks should be used to augment the information obtained from the spontaneous sample because such tasks can be used to elicit forms that the child did not attempt in the conversations. Standardized imitation tasks are widely used in oral language assessment instruments (such as the Test of Language Development–P:4 and I:4). Assessment devices that use imitation usually contain a number of grammatically loaded words, phrases, or sentences that children are asked to imitate. The examiner records and transcribes the children's responses and then analyzes their phonology, morphology, and syntax. (Semantics and pragmatics are rarely assessed using an imitative mode.) Finally, imitation generally is used only in assessing expressive oral language.

ELICITED LANGUAGE

Using a picture stimulus to elicit language involves no imitation on the part of the child, but the procedure cannot be classified as totally spontaneous. In this type of task, the child is presented with a picture or pictures of objects or action scenes and is asked to do one of the following: (1) point to the correct object (a receptive vocabulary task), (2) point to the action picture that best describes a sentence (receptive language, including vocabulary), (3) name the picture (expressive vocabulary), or (4) describe the picture (expressive language, including vocabulary). Although only stimulus pictures are described in this section, some tests use concrete objects rather than pictures to elicit language responses.

ADVANTAGES AND DISADVANTAGES OF EACH PROCEDURE

There are advantages and disadvantages to all three methods of language observation (spontaneous, imitative, and elicited). The use of spontaneous language samples has two major advantages. First, a child's spontaneous language is undoubtedly the best and most natural indicator of everyday language performance. Second, the informality of the procedure often allows the examiner to assess children quite easily, without the difficulties sometimes associated with a formal testing atmosphere.

The disadvantages associated with this procedure relate to the nonstandardized nature of the data collection. Although some aspects of language sampling are stable across a variety of parameters, this procedure shows much wider variability than is seen with other standardized assessments. In addition, language sampling requires detailed analyses across language domains; such analyses are more time-consuming than administering a standardized instrument. Finally, because the examiner does not directly control the selection of target words and phrases, he or she may have difficulty understanding a young child, or there may be several different interpretations of what a child intended to say. Moreover, the child may have avoided, or may not have had an opportunity to attempt, a particular structure that is of interest to the examiner.

The use of imitation overcomes many of the disadvantages inherent in the spontaneous approach. An imitation task will often assess many different language elements and provide a representative view of a child's language system. Also, because of the structure of the test, the examiner knows at all times what elements of language are being assessed. Thus, even the language abilities of a child with a severe language disorder (especially a severe phonological disorder) can be quantified. Finally, imitation devices can be administered much more quickly than can spontaneous language samples.

Unfortunately, the advantages of the spontaneous approach become the disadvantages of the imitative method. First, a child's auditory memory may have some effect on the results. For example, an echolalic child may score well on an imitative test without demonstrating productive knowledge of the language structures being imitated. Second, a child may repeat part of a sentence exactly because the utterance is too simple or short to place a load on the child's memory. Therefore, accurate production is not necessarily evidence that the child uses the structure spontaneously. However, inaccurate productions often do reflect a child's lack of mastery of the structure. Thus, test givers should draw conclusions only about a child's errors from an imitative test. A third disadvantage of imitative tests is that they are often quite boring to the child. Not all children will sit still for the time required to repeat 50 to 100 sentences without any other stimulation, such as pictures or toys.

The use of pictures to elicit language production is an attempt to overcome the disadvantages of both imitation and spontaneous language. Pictures are easy to administer, are interesting to children, and require minimal administration time. They can be structured to test desired language elements and yet retain some of the impromptu nature of spontaneous language samples because children have to formulate the language on their own. Because there is no time limit, results do not depend on the child's word-retention skills. Despite these advantages, a major disadvantage limits the usefulness of picture stimuli in language assessment: It is difficult to create pictures guaranteed to elicit specific language elements. Although it is probably easiest to create pictures for object identification, difficulties arise even in this area. Thus, the disadvantage seen in spontaneous sampling is evident with picture stimuli as well—the child may not produce or attempt to produce the desired language structure.

In summary, all three methods of language observation have advantages and disadvantages. The examiner must decide which elements of language should be tested, which methods of observation are most appropriate for assessing those elements, and which assessment devices satisfy these needs. It should not be surprising that more than one test is often necessary to assess all components of language (phonology, semantics, morphology, syntax, and pragmatics), both receptively and expressively. As noted, standardized instruments should be supplemented with measures of conversational abilities within any oral language assessment. In addition, the different language domains are often best assessed by different procedures. For example, picture stimuli are particularly well suited for assessment of phonological abilities because the examiner should know the intended production. Similarly, imitation tasks are often employed to assess morphological abilities because the child having difficulty with this component will often delete suffixes and prefixes during imitation. Finally, because assessment of pragmatics involves determining the child's conversational use of language, this domain should be assessed with spontaneous production.

SPECIFIC ORAL AND WRITTEN LANGUAGE TESTS

Table 14.2 provides characteristics of several commonly administered tests of oral and written language. Reviews of four of these tests (that is, the Test of Written Language–Fourth Edition, the Test of Language Development: Primary–Fourth Edition, the Test of Language Development: Intermediate–Fourth Edition, and the Oral and Written Language Scales) are provided in the following section.

Test of Written Language–Fourth Edition (TOWL-4)

The Test of Written Language–4 (TOWL-4; Hammill & Larsen, 2008) is a norm-referenced device designed to assess the written language competence of students between the ages of 9-0 and 17-11. Although the TOWL-4 was designed to be individually administered, the authors provide a series of modifications to allow group administration, with follow-up testing of individual students to ensure valid testing. The recommended uses of the TOWL-4 include identifying students who have substantial difficulty in writing, determining strengths and weaknesses of individual students, documenting student progress, and conducting research. Two alternative forms (A and B) are available.

The TOWL-4 uses two writing formats (contrived and spontaneous) to evaluate written language. In a contrived format, students' linguistic options are purposely constrained to force the students to use specific words or conventions. The TOWL-4 uses these two formats to assess three components of written language (conventional, linguistic, and cognitive). The conventional component deals with using widely accepted rules in punctuation and spelling. The linguistic component deals with syntactic and semantic structures. The cognitive component deals with producing "logical, coherent, and contextual written material" (Hammill & Larsen, 2008, p. 25).

Subtests

The first five subtests, eliciting writing in contrived contexts, are briefly described here.

Vocabulary. This area is assessed by having a student write correct sentences containing stimulus words.

Spelling. The TOWL-4 assesses spelling by having a student write sentences from dictation.

Punctuation. Competence in this aspect of writing is assessed by evaluating the punctuation and capitalization in sentences written by a student from dictation.

Logical Sentences. Competence in this area is assessed by having a student rewrite illogical sentences so that they make sense.

Sentence Combining. The TOWL-4 requires a student to write one grammatically correct sentence based on the information in several short sentences.

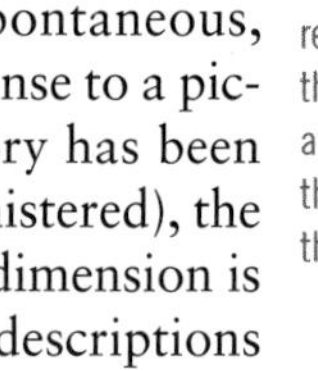

Reviews for the remaining test represented in the table are available on the website for this book.

The last two subtests elicit more spontaneous, contextual writing by the student in response to a picture used as a story starter. After the story has been written (and the other five subtests administered), the story is scored on two dimensions. Each dimension is treated as a subtest. Following are brief descriptions of these subtests:

Contextual Conventions. A student's ability to use appropriate grammatical rules and conventions of mechanics (such as punctuation and spelling) in context is assessed using the student's story.

Story Composition. As described by Hammill and Larsen (2008, p. 29), this subtest evaluates a student's story on the basis of the "quality of its composition (e.g., vocabulary, plot, prose, development of characters, and interest to the reader)."

Scores

Raw scores for each subtest can be converted to percentiles or standard scores. The standard scores have a mean of 10 and a standard deviation of 3. Various combinations of subtests result in three composites: contrived writing (Vocabulary, Spelling, Punctuation, Logical Sentences, and Sentence Combining), spontaneous writing (Contextual Conventions and Story Composition), and overall writing (all subtests). Subtest standard scores can be summed and converted to standard scores (that is, "index scores") and percentiles for each composite. The composite index scores have a mean of 100 and a standard deviation of 15. Both age and grade equivalents are available; however, the authors appropriately warn against reporting these scores.

Norms

Two different sampling techniques were used to establish norms for the TOWL-4. First, sites in each of the four geographic regions of the United States were selected, and 977 students were tested. Second, an additional 1,229 students were tested by volunteers who had previously purchased materials from the publisher. The total sample is distributed such that there are at least 200 students represented at each age level; however, at some age levels there are very few students represented in either the fall or the spring sample. The total sample varies no more than 5 percent from information provided by the U.S. Census Bureau for the 2005 school-age population on various demographic variables (that is, gender, geographic region, ethnicity,

TABLE 14.2 Commonly Used Diagnostic Language Tests

Test	Author	Publisher	Year	Ages/ Grades	Individual/ Group	NRT/ SRT/CRT	Subtests
Comprehensive Assessment of Spoken Language (CASL)	Carrow-Woolfolk	Pro-Ed	1999	Ages 3–21 years	Individual	NRT	Comprehension of Basic Concepts, Synonyms, Antonyms, Sentence Completion, Idiomatic Language, Syntax Construction, Paragraph Comprehension of Syntax, Grammatic Morphemes, Sentence Comprehension of Syntax, Grammaticality Judgment, Nonliteral Language Test, Meaning from Context, Inference Test, Ambiguous Sentences Test, Pragmatic Judgment
Comprehensive Receptive and Expressive Vocabulary Test–Second Edition (CREVT-2)	Wallace & Hammill	Pro-Ed	2002	Ages 4–0 to 89–11 years	Individual	NRT	Receptive Vocabulary, Expressive Vocabulary
Goldman–Fristoe Test of Articulation, Second Edition (GFTA-2)	Goldman & Fristoe	Pearson	2000	Ages 2–0 to 21–11 years	Individual	NRT	Sounds-in-Words, Sounds-in-Sentences, Stimulability
Illinois Test of Psycholinguistic Abilities–3 (ITPA-3)	Hammill, Mather, & Roberts	Pro-Ed	2001	Ages 5–0 to 12–11 years	Individual	NRT	Spoken Analogies, Spoken Vocabulary, Morphological Closure, Syntactic Sentences, Sound Deletion, Rhyming Sequences, Sentence Sequencing, Written Vocabulary, Sight Decoding, Sound Decoding, Sight Spelling, Sound Spelling
Oral and Written Language Scales	Carrow-Woolfolk	Pearson	1995	Ages 3–21 years	Individual	NRT	Listening Comprehension, Oral Expression, Written Expression

continued on the next page

TABLE 14.2 Commonly Used Diagnostic Language Tests, *continued*

Test	Author	Publisher	Year	Ages/Grades	Individual/Group	NRT/SRT/CRT	Subtests
Test for Auditory Comprehension of Language, Third Edition (TACL-3)	Carrow-Woolfolk	Pro-Ed	1999	Ages 3–0 to 9–11 years	Individual	NRT	Vocabulary, Grammatical Morphemes, Elaborated Phrases and Sentences
Test of Language Development: Intermediate–Fourth Edition (TOLD-I:4)	Hammill & Newcomer	Pro-Ed	2008	Ages 8–0 to 17–11 years	Individual	NRT	Sentence Combining, Picture Vocabulary, Word Ordering, Relational Vocabulary, Morphological Comprehension, Multiple Meanings
Test of Language Development: Primary–Fourth Edition (TOLD-P:4)	Newcomer & Hammill	Pro-Ed	2008	Ages 4–0 to 8–11 years	Individual	NRT	Picture Vocabulary, Relational Vocabulary, Oral Vocabulary, Syntactic Understanding, Sentence Imitation, Morphological Completion, Word Discrimination, Word Analysis, Word Articulation
Test of Written Language–Fourth Edition (TOWL-4)	Hammill & Larsen	Pro-Ed	2008	Ages 9–17 years	Individual, can be administered to a group	NRT	Vocabulary, Spelling, Punctuation, Logical Sentences, Sentence Combining, Contextual Conventions, Story Composition
Test of Written Spelling–Fourth Edition (TWS-4)	Larsen, Hammill, & Moats	Pro-Ed	1999	Ages 6–0 to 18–11 years	Individual, can be administered to a group	NRT	No separate subtests

family income, educational attainment of parents, and disability), with the exception that those with a very high household income are overrepresented (that is, 35 percent of the sample has a household income of more than $75,000, whereas just 27 percent of the population has this level of household income). The authors also present data for three age ranges (that is, 9 to 11, 12 to 14, and 15 to 17), showing that each age range also approximates information on the nationwide school-age population for 2005. However, the comparisons of interest (that is, the degree to which each normative group approximates the census) are absent.

Reliability

Three types of reliability are discussed in the TOWL-4 manual: internal consistencies (both coefficient alpha and alternate-form reliability), stability, and interscorer agreement.

Two procedures were used to estimate the internal consistency of the TOWL-4. First, a series of coefficient alphas was computed. Using the entire normative sample, coefficient alpha was used to estimate the internal consistency of each score (age and grade) and composite on each form at each age. Of the 238 alphas reported, 85 are in the .90s, 80 are in the .80s, 62 are in the .70s, 10 are in the .60s, and 1 is below .60. Alphas are consistently higher on the Vocabulary, Punctuation, and Spelling subtests and lowest on the Logical Sentences and Story Composition subtests. As is typical, coefficient alpha was substantially higher for the composites. For Contrived Writing and Overall Writing, all coefficients equaled or exceeded .95. For Spontaneous Writing, they were substantially lower, with all in the .70s and .80s. Thus, two of the composites are sufficiently reliable for making important educational decisions about students.

The authors are to be commended for also reporting subtest internal consistencies for several demographic subgroups (that is, males and females, Caucasian Americans, African Americans, Hispanic Americans, and Asian Americans), as well as students with disabilities (that is, learning disabled, speech impaired, and attention deficit hyperactive). The obtained coefficients for the various demographic subgroups are comparable to those for the entire normative sample.

Second, alternate-form reliability was also computed for each subtest and each composite at each age and grade, using the entire normative sample. These coefficients were distributed in approximately the same way as were the alphas.

The 2-week stability of each subtest and each composite on both forms was estimated with 84 students ranging in age from 9 to 17 years; results were examined according to two age and grade ranges. Of the 80 associated coefficients, 30 coefficients equaled or exceeded .90, 34 were in the .80s, 15 were in the .70s, and 1 was in the .60s. These followed the pattern of other reliability indices, with higher coefficients identified for the contrived writing and overall writing composites than for the spontaneous writing composite.

To estimate interscorer agreement, 41 TOWL-4 protocols were selected at random and scored. The correlations between scorers were remarkably consistent. Of the 40 coefficients associated with subtest and composite scoring agreement, 36 were in the .90s, 2 were in the .80s, and 2 were in the .70s. The scoring of written language samples is quite difficult, and unacceptably low levels of interscorer agreement appear to be the rule rather than the exception. It appears that the scoring criteria contained in the TOWL-4 manual are sufficiently precise and clear to allow for consistent scoring. The only subtest with interscorer reliability below .90 was Story Composition.

Validity

Support for content validity comes from the way in which the test was developed, the many dimensions of written language assessed, and the methods by which competence in written language is assessed. The evidence for criterion-related validity comes from a study in which three measures—the Written Language Observation Scale (Hammill & Larsen, 2009), the Reading Observation Scale (Hammill & Larsen, 2009), and the Test of Reading Comprehension–Fourth Edition (TORC-4; Brown, Wiederholt, & Hammill, 2009)—were correlated with each score on the TOWL-4. Correlations ranging from .34 (Story Composition correlated with the Written Language Observation Scale) to .80 (Spelling correlated with the TORC-4) provide somewhat limited support for the TOWL-4's validity; teacher ratings for reading correlated as well as or better than those for writing. The authors also conducted positive predictive analyses using these data on the three literacy measures. Based on the results, which indicate levels of sensitivity and specificity exist meeting the .70 threshold, the authors suggest that the TOWL-4 can be used to identify those students who have literacy difficulties.

Construct validity is considered at some length in the TOWL-4 manual. First, the authors present evidence to show that TOWL-4 scores increase with age and grade. The correlations with age are substantially stronger for students between the ages of 9 and 12 years than for students 13 to 17 years old, for whom correlations are small. Second, in examining the subtest intercorrelations and conducting a factor analysis, the TOWL-4 appears to assess a single factor for the sample as a whole. Thus, although individual subtests (or the contrived and spontaneous composites) may be of interest, they are not independent of the other skills measured on the test. Third, scores on the TOWL-4 for students with learning disabilities and speech/language impairments, who are anticipated to struggle in the area of written language, were generally lower than those for other subgroups. However, it is important to note that score differences for these exceptionality groups tended to be no more than one standard deviation below the average.

The authors were careful to examine the possibility of racial or ethnic bias in their assessment tool. They conducted reliability analyses separately by gender, race/ethnicity, and exceptionality grouping. They also conducted an analysis of differential item functioning in which they examined whether item characteristics varied by gender and ethnicity, which would suggest the possibility of item bias. Although two items were identified with differences in item characteristics across groups, these represented less than 5 percent of the test items.

Summary

The TOWL-4 is designed to assess written language competence of students aged 9-0 to 17-11. Contrived and spontaneous formats are used to evaluate the conventional, linguistic, and cognitive components of written language. The content and structure of the TOWL-4 appear appropriate.

Although the TOWL-4's norms appear representative in general, the fall and spring samples tend to be uneven by age group, with some of these seasonal samples including very few students at certain grade levels. Interscorer reliability is quite good for this type of test. The internal consistencies of one composite (that is, Contrived Writing) and the total composite are high enough for use in making individual decisions; the stabilities of subtests and the remaining composite (that is, Spontaneous Writing) are lower.

Although the test's content appears appropriate and well conceived, the validity of the inferences to be drawn from the scores is unclear. Specifically, group means are the only data to suggest that the TOWL-4 is useful in identifying students with disabilities or in determining strengths and weaknesses of individual students. Students with learning disabilities and speech/language disorders earn TOWL-4 subtest scores that are only 1 standard deviation (or less) below the mean; they earn composite scores that are no more than 1.2 standard deviations below the mean. However, because we do not know whether these students had disabilities in written language, their scores tell us little about the TOWL-4's ability to identify students with specific written language needs. Although positive predictive analyses were conducted to determine whether the TOWL-4 could identify students with literacy difficulties, these similarly do not provide evidence that the test is particularly helpful in identifying specific written language difficulties. Given that the TOWL-4 has only two forms and relatively low stability, its usefulness in evaluating pupil progress is also limited.

Test of Language Development: Primary–Fourth Edition

The Test of Language Development: Primary–Fourth Edition (TOLD-P:4; Newcomer & Hammill, 2008) is a norm-referenced, nontimed, individually administered test designed to (1) identify children who are significantly below their peers in oral language proficiency, (2) determine a child's specific strengths and weaknesses in oral language skills, (3) document progress in remedial programs, and (4) measure oral language in research studies (Newcomer & Hammill, 2008). The TOLD-P:4 is intended to be used with children ages 4-0 to 8-11 years. Although the test is not timed, the average student is able to complete the core subtests in 35 to 50 minutes and the supplemental tests in an additional 30 minutes.

Subtests

The TOLD-P:4 consists of nine subtests, each measuring different components of oral language. Six of the subtests are considered core subtests and their scores are combined to form composite scores. The composite scores cover the main areas of language: semantics and grammar; listening, organizing, and speaking; and overall language ability. The subtests measuring phonology are excluded from the composite scores in order to create a clear separation between speech competence and language competence, making it easier to determine specific disorders. Descriptions of the individual subtests are as follows:

Picture Vocabulary. This subtest assesses a child's ability to understand the meaning of spoken English words (semantics and listening).

Relational Vocabulary. This subtest assesses a child's understanding and ability to orally express the relationships between two words spoken by the examiner (semantics and organizing).

Oral Vocabulary This subtest assesses a child's ability to give oral directions to common English words that are spoken by the examiner (semantics and speaking).

Syntactic Understanding. This subtest assesses a child's ability to understand the meaning of sentences (grammar and listening).

Sentence Imitation. This subtest assesses a child's ability to imitate English sentences (grammar and organizing).

Morphological Completion. This subtest assesses a child's ability to recognize, understand, and use common English morphological forms (grammar and speaking).

Word Discrimination. This subtest assesses a child's ability to recognize the differences in speech sounds (phonology and listening).

Word Analysis. This subtest assesses a child's ability to segment words into smaller phonemic units (phonology and organizing)

Word Articulation. This subtest assesses a child's ability to produce various English speech sounds (phonology and speaking).

Scores

The TOLD-P:4 generates four types of normative scores: age equivalents, percentile ranks, scaled scores, and composite indexes. The subtests of the TOLD-P:4 are designed on a two-dimensional model of linguistic features and linguistic systems. The subtests can be combined into the following six composites:

1. Listening (Picture Vocabulary and Syntactic Understanding)
2. Organizing (Relational Vocabulary and Sentence Imitation)
3. Speaking (Oral Vocabulary and Morphological Completion)
4. Grammar (Syntactic Understanding, Sentence Imitation, and Morphological Completion)
5. Semantics (Picture Vocabulary, Relational Vocabulary, and Oral Vocabulary)
6. Spoken Language (Picture Vocabulary, Relational Vocabulary, Oral Vocabulary, Syntactic Understanding, Sentence Imitation, and Morphological Completion). This is a measure of the overall language ability.

Norms

The TOLD-P:4 was standardized in 2006 and 2007 on a demographic representative sample of 1,108 children from four regions of the United States. The norm sample was stratified on the basis of gender, age, race, geographic region, Hispanic status, exceptionality status (disability area), family income, and parental education level. The examiner's manual contains charts indicating the breakdown of the norm sample according to the 2007 census. Some cross-tabs (for example, the number of students in each specific racial/ethnic group from each region) are provided, and there is good correspondence between census and norm sample data.

Reliability

To determine test reliability, the TOLD-P:4 uses three types of correlation coefficients—coefficient alpha, test–retest, and scorer difference—to measure three types of error (content, time, and scorer). Coefficient alphas were calculated for each subtest and composite scores. The coefficients for the subtests exceeded .80, and seven of the nine subtest coefficients exceeded .90. The composite scores averaged coefficients greater than .90. Test–retest reliability was completed using two groups of students ages 4 to 6 years and ages 7 to 8 years; time between assessments was 1 or 2 weeks. With the exception of one subtest, the reliability coefficients for the subtests for both groups were greater than .80. The coefficients for the composites, with the exception of one, exceeded .90. Results indicate that TOLD-P:4 scores show little time sampling error. The scoring differences were calculated and all coefficients exceeded .90. The TOLD-P:4 appears to meet and often exceed the standards for reliability.

Validity

The examiner's manual includes extensive information on the validity of the TOLD-P:4, including various studies validating content—description validity, criterion prediction validity, and construct identification validity. The authors describe their theory of oral language development, indicate why they selected specific subtest measures, and provide a rationale for how each subtest matches their theory. The arguments are convincing. Evidence for criterion validity is based on correlations with scores on three other oral language measures: the Pragmatic Language Observation Scale, TOLD-I:4, and the WISC-IV Verbal Composite. Correlations were moderate, as would be expected, and comparable means and standard deviations were earned on the various measures.

Evidence for construct validity is based on testing hypotheses derived from theory, for example, "Because the TOLD-4:P subtests and composites are supposed to measure aspects of language, the test results should differentiate between groups of people known to be normal in language and those known to be poor in language" (Newcomer & Hammill, 2008, p. 60). Overall, there is good evidence for the validity of the TOLD-P:4.

Summary

The TOLD-P:4 is an individually administered, nontimed, norm-referenced test used to evaluate the spoken language abilities of children ages 4 years to 8 years, 11 months. The test contains nine subtests and yields subtest standard scores as well as composite scores. The TOLD-P:4 contains new normative data obtained from a demographic representation of the 2005 U.S. population, an expanded study on bias items, an increased number of validity studies, and an updated and easy to use examiner's manual. The TOLD-P:4 appears to meet and often exceed the standards for reliability. There is extensive information on content description validity, criterion prediction validity, and construct identification validity. The test seems appropriate to identify students' oral language strengths and weaknesses, identify those who are below their peers in oral language skills, and document progress in intervention programs.

Test of Language Development: Intermediate–Fourth Edition

The Test of Language Development: Intermediate–Fourth Edition (TOLD-I:4; Hammill & Newcomer, 2008) is a norm-referenced, nontimed, individually administered test designed to (1) identify students who are significantly below their peers in oral language proficiency, (2) determine students' specific strengths and weaknesses in oral language skills, (3) document their progress in remedial programs, and (4) measure oral language in research studies (Newcomer & Hammill, 2008). The TOLD-I:4 is intended to be used with students ages 8-0 to 17-11 years. Although the test is not timed, the average student is able to complete the entire test in 35 to 50 minutes.

Subtests

The TOLD-I:4 consists of six subtests, each measuring different components of semantics or grammar. The six scores students earn are converted to standard scores for each subtest, and the standard scores for subtests are combined to form composite scores. The composite scores cover the main areas of language: semantics and grammar; listening, organizing, and speaking; and overall language ability. Descriptions of the individual subtests are as follows:

Sentence Combining. The student is asked to create a compound sentence from two or more simple sentences presented verbally by the examiner (grammar and speaking).

Picture Vocabulary. Given a set of six pictures, the pupil is to identify, by pointing, the picture that represents the two-word stimulus.

Word Ordering. Given a randomly ordered word set, the student is to generate a complete, grammatically correct sentence (grammar and organizing).

Relational Vocabulary. Given three words from the examiner, the student must state how they are alike (semantics and organizing).

Morphological Comprehension. Given verbal sentences from the examiner, the student must identify grammatically correct and incorrect sentences (grammar and listening).

Multiple Meanings. Given a word from the examiner, the pupil is asked to generate as many different meanings for that word as he or she is able to (semantics and speaking).

Scores

The TOLD-I:4 yields four types of normative scores: age equivalents, percentile ranks, subtest standard (scaled) scores, and composite scores. The subtests of the TOLD-I:4 are designed on a two-dimensional model of linguistic features and linguistic systems. The subtests can be combined into the following six composite scores:

1. Listening (Picture Vocabulary and Morphological Comprehension)
2. Organizing (Word Ordering and Relational Vocabulary)
3. Speaking (Sentence Combining and Multiple Meanings)
4. Grammar (Sentence Combining, Word Ordering, and Morphological Comprehension)
5. Semantics (Picture Vocabulary, Relational Vocabulary, and Multiple Meanings)
6. Spoken Language (Sentence Combining, Picture Vocabulary, Word Ordering, Relational Vocabulary, Morphological Comprehension, and Multiple Meanings)

Norms

The TOLD-I:4 was standardized during 2006 and 2007 on a demographic representative sample of 1,097 students from four regions of the United States. The norm sample was gathered on the basis of gender, age, race, geographic region, Hispanic status, exceptionality status (disability area), family income, and parental education level. The manual contains charts indicating the breakdown of the norm sample according to the 2005 census. Some cross-tabs (number of males sampled from each geographic region) are provided and are further indicative of the representativeness of the sample.

Reliability

The TOLD-I:4 uses coefficient alpha, test–retest, and scorer differences to measure three different types of test error: content, time, and scorer. Coefficient alphas were calculated for each subtest at 10 age intervals; in all subtests, the average coefficient alphas exceed .90. The composite scores average a coefficient of .90 or greater. Test–retest reliability was completed using two groups of students, ages 8 to 12 years and ages 13 to 17 years; time between assessments was no more than 2 weeks. The reliability coefficients for all subtests were at or above .80 and for all composite scores were above .90. The coefficients for interscorer agreement all exceeded .90. The TOLD-I:4 appears to meet and often exceed the standards for reliability necessary for making screening and diagnostic decisions.

Validity

The examiner's manual included extensive information on the validity of the TOLD-I:4, including studies validating the content validity, criterion prediction validity, and construct validity. The authors provide an extensive rationale for selecting each of the subtests and for their method of measuring language skills. The arguments seem solid and are convincing. Criterion predictive validity was established by correlating performance on TOLD-I:4 subtests and composites with performance on eight other measures of spoken language, using a different sample of students for each comparison. There is good evidence for criterion predictive validity.

Evidence for construct validity is based on examination of the extent to which hypotheses based on theoretical analysis are supported; for example, "Because oral language ability is known to be related to literacy, the TOLD-4:I should correlate highly with tests of reading and writing." (Hammill & Newcomer, 2008, p. 56). There is good evidence for the construct validity of the test.

Summary

The TOLD-I:4 is an individually administered, nontimed, norm-referenced test used to evaluate the spoken language abilities of students ages 8 years, 0 months to 17 years, 11 months. The test contains six subtests and yields standard scores, composite scores, and an overall spoken language score. The TOLD-I:4 contains new normative data obtained from a demographic representation of the 2005 U.S. population, the floor effect has been eliminated, an expanded study of test bias is provided, and many validity studies have been completed and included in the manual. Also, it contains a new composite (Organizing) and a Multiple Meanings subtest. The General and Multiple Meanings subtests have been renamed to better represent what they assess; the new names are Relational Vocabulary and Morphological Comprehension. The age range has been extended to include students ages 13-0 to 17-11 years, and an updated, easy to use examiner's manual is included. The TOLD-I:4 appears to meet and often exceed reliability standards for making screening or diagnostic decisions. The manual contains extensive information on validity, and the evidence supports the validity of the scale. The test appears appropriate to identify students' oral language strengths and weaknesses, identify those who are below their peers in oral language functioning, and document progress in intervention programs.

Oral and Written Language Scales (OWLS)

The Oral and Written Language Scales (OWLS; Carrow-Woolfolk, 1995) are an individually administered assessment of receptive and expressive language for children and young adults ages 3 through 21 years. The test includes three scales: Listening Comprehension, Oral Expression, and Written Expression. Test results are used to determine broad levels of language skills and specific performance in listening, speaking, and writing. The scales are described here.

Subtests

Listening Comprehension. This scale is designed to measure understanding of spoken language. It consists of 111 items. The examiner reads aloud a verbal stimulus, and the student has to identify which of four pictures is the best response to the stimulus. The scale takes 5 to 15 minutes to administer.

Oral Expression. This scale is a measure of understanding and use of spoken language. It consists of 96 items. The examiner reads aloud a verbal stimulus and shows a picture. The student responds orally by answering a question, completing a sentence, or generating one or more sentences. The scale takes 10 to 25 minutes to administer.

Written Expression. This scale is an assessment of written language for students 5 to 21 years of age. It is designed to measure ability to use conventions (spelling, punctuation, and so on), use syntactical forms (modifiers, phrases, sentence structures, and so on), and communicate meaningfully (with appropriate content, coherence, organization, and so on). The student responds to direct writing prompts provided by the examiner.

The OWLS is designed to be used in identification of students with language difficulties and disorders, in intervention planning, and in monitoring student progress.

Norms

The OWLS standardization sample consisted of 1,985 students chosen to match the U.S. census data from the 1991 Current Population Survey. The sample was stratified within age group by gender, race, geographic region, and socioeconomic status. Tables in the manual show the comparison of the sample to the U.S. population. Cross-tabulations are shown only for age and not for other variables. The 14- to 21-year-old age group is overrepresented by students in the North Central region and underrepresented by students in the West.

Scores

The OWLS produces raw scores, which may be transformed to standard scores with a mean of 100 and a standard deviation of 15. In addition, test age equivalents, normal-curve equivalents, percentiles, and stanines can be obtained. Scores are obtained for each subtest, for an oral language composite, and for a written language composite.

Reliability

Internal consistency reliability was calculated using students in the standardization. Reliability coefficients range from .75 to .89 for Listening Comprehension, from .76 to .91 for Oral Expression, and from .87 to .94 for the oral composite. They range from .77 to .89 for Written Expression. Test–retest reliabilities were computed on a small sample of students who are not described. The coefficients range from .58 to

Dilemmas *in* Current Practice

Oral Language Issues

Three issues are particularly troublesome in the assessment of oral language: (1) ensuring that the elicited language assessment is a true reflection of the child's general spontaneous language capacity; (2) using the results of standardized tests to generate effective therapy; and (3) adapting assessment to individuals who do not match the characteristics of the standardization sample. All these dilemmas stem from the limited nature of the standardized tests and must be addressed in practice.

From a practical standpoint, the clinician must use standardized tests to identify a child with a language impairment. However, as noted previously in this chapter, such instruments may not directly measure a child's true language abilities. Thus, the clinician must supplement the standard tests with nonstandard spontaneous language sampling. In addition, if possible, the child should be observed in a number of settings outside the formal testing situation. After the spontaneous samples have been gathered, the results of these analyses should be compared with the performance on the standardized tests.

Selection of targets for intervention is one of the more difficult tasks facing the clinician. Many standardized tests that are useful for identifying language disorders in children may not lend themselves to determining efficient treatment. The clinician must evaluate the results of both the standard and the nonstandard assessment procedures and decide which language skills are most important to the child. Although it is tempting simply to train the child to perform better on a particular test (hence boosting performance on that instrument), the clinician must bear in mind that such tasks are often metalinguistic in nature and will not ultimately result in generalized language skills. Rather, the focus of treatment should be on those language behaviors and structures that are needed for improved language competence in the home and in the classroom.

In today's language assessment environment, with a plethora of multicultural and socioeconomic variation within caseloads, a clinician is bound to encounter many children who differ in one or more respects from the normative sample of a particular test. Indeed, clinicians are likely to see children who do not match the normative sample of any standardized test. When this occurs, the clinician must interpret the scores derived from these tests conservatively. Information from nonstandard assessment becomes even more important, and the clinician should obtain reports from parents, teachers, and peers regarding their impressions of the child's language competence. The clinician should also determine whether local norms have been developed for the standard and nonstandard assessment procedures. As previously noted, it is inappropriate to treat multicultural language differences as if they were language disorders. However, the clinician performing an assessment must judge whether the child's language is disordered within his or her language community and what impact such disorders may have on classroom performance and communication skills generally.

Written Language Issues

There are two serious problems in the assessment of written language.

Problem 1

The first problem involves assessing the content of written expression. The content of written language is usually scored holistically and subjectively. Holistic evaluations tend to be unreliable. When content on the same topic and of the same genre (such as narratives) is scored, interscorer agreement varies from the .50 to .65 range (as in Breland, 1983; Breland, Camp, Jones, Morris, & Rock, 1987) to the .75 to .90 range immediately following intensive training (such as Educational Testing Service, 1990). Consistent scoring is even more difficult when topics and genres vary. Interscorer agreement can decrease to a range of .35 to .45 when the writing tasks vary (as in Breland, 1983; Breland et al., 1987). Subjective scoring and decision making are susceptible to the biasing effects associated with racial, ethnic, social class, gender, and disability stereotypes.

We believe the best alternative to holistic and subjective scoring schemes is to use a measure of writing fluency as an indicator of content generation. Two options have received some support in the research literature: (1) the number of words written (Mather, Roberts, Hammill, & Allen, 2009; Shinn, Tindall, & Stein, 1988;) and (2) the percentage of correctly written words (Isaacson, 1988).

Problem 2

The second problem is in identifying a match between what is taught in the school curriculum and what is tested. The great variation in the time at which various skills and facts are taught renders a general test of achievement inappropriate. This dilemma also attends diagnostic assessment of written language. Commercially prepared tests have doubtful validity for planning individual programs and evaluating the progress of individual pupils.

We recommend that teachers and diagnosticians construct criterion-referenced achievement tests that closely parallel the curricula followed by the students being tested. In cases in which normative data are required, there are three choices. Diagnosticians can (1) select the devices that most closely parallel the curriculum, (2) develop local norms, or (3) select individual students for comparative purposes. Care should be exercised in selecting methods of assessing language skills. For example, it is probably better to test pupils in ways that are familiar to them. Thus, if the teacher's weekly spelling test is from dictation, then spelling tests using dictation are probably preferable to tests requiring the students to identify incorrectly spelled words.

.85 for the oral subtests and composite and from .66 to .83 for the Written Expression subtest. Reliabilities are sufficient to use this measure as a screening device. They are not sufficient to use it in making important decisions about individual students. This latter, of course, is the use the authors suggest for the test.

Validity

The authors report the results of a set of external validity studies, each consisting of a comparison of performance on the OWLS to performance on other measures. Sample sizes were small, but correlations were in the expected range. The Written Expression subtest was compared to the Kaufman Test of Educational Achievement, the Peabody Individual Achievement Test–Revised, the Woodcock Reading Mastery Test, and the Peabody Picture Vocabulary Test. Student performance on the Oral Expression and Listening Comprehension subtests was compared to performance on the Test for Auditory Comprehension of Language–Revised, the Peabody Picture Vocabulary Test, the Clinical Evaluation of Language Fundamentals–Revised, and the Kaufman Assessment Battery for Children.

Summary

The OWLS is a language test combining assessment of oral and written language. The test was standardized on the same population, so comparisons of student performance on oral and written measures are enhanced. The manual includes data showing that the standardization sample is generally representative of the U.S. population. Reliability coefficients are too low to permit use of this measure in making important decisions for individuals. Evidence for validity is good, although it is based on a set of studies with limited numbers of students.

Chapter Comprehension Questions

Write your answers to each of the following questions and then compare your responses to the text.

1. Describe five processes associated with communication.
2. Explain how cultural background may play a role in determining appropriate language expectations.
3. Identify and describe the three techniques for obtaining a sample of a child's language.
4. What are the two major components of written language, and how might they be assessed?
5. What are some of the dilemmas associated with assessment of oral and written language?

Web Activities 

1. Google the medical diagnosis of autism spectrum disorder vs. an educational diagnosis of autism spectrum disorder. How do they differ, and how are they the same? What potential issues do you see with parents who receive a medical diagnosis of ASD and school systems' responsibility to address educational implications and educational criteria?

Web Resources

Young children's oral language development
www.comeunity.com/disability/speech/young-children.html
A brief statement on when and how language is learned, oral language components, and nurturing language development

Additional resources for this chapter can be found on the Education CourseMate website. Go to CengageBrain.com to access the site.

Using Measures of Intelligence

CHAPTER GOALS

1 Understand how student characteristics, particularly acculturation, can affect student performance on intelligence tests.

2 Understand behaviors commonly sampled on intelligence tests.

3 Know the historical and theoretical foundation for the development of intelligence tests.

4 Know the factors that are commonly interpreted using intelligence tests.

5 Understand a recent advancement in intelligence testing—the assessment of processing deficits.

6 Know the various types of intelligence tests (that is, nonverbal and group administered).

7 Understand three commonly used measures of intelligence (WISC-IV, WJ-III NU, and PPVT-IV)

KEY TERMS

Thurstone

Cattell–Horn–Carroll theory

acculturation

processing deficits

nonverbal tests

intelligence factors

Wechsler Intelligence Scale for Children–IV (WISC-IV)

Woodcock–Johnson III Normative Update (WJ-III NU)

Peabody Picture Vocabulary Test–IV (PPVT-IV)

No other area of assessment has generated as much attention, controversy, and debate as the testing of what we call "intelligence." For centuries, philosophers, psychologists, educators, and laypeople have debated the meaning of intelligence. Numerous definitions of the term *intelligence* have been proposed, with each definition serving as a stimulus for counterdefinitions and counterproposals. Several theories have been advanced to describe and explain intelligence and its development. Some theorists argue that intelligence is a general ability that enables people to do many different things, whereas other theorists contend that there are multiple intelligences and that people are better at some things than others. Some argue that, for the most part, intelligence is genetically determined (hereditary), inborn, and something you get from your parents. Others contend that intelligence is, for the most part, learned—that it is acquired through experience. Most theorists today recognize the importance of both heredity and experience, including the impact of parental education, parental experience, maternal nutrition, maternal substance abuse, and many other factors. However, most theorists take positions on the relative importance of these factors.

Both the interpretation of group differences in performance on intelligence tests and the practice of testing the intelligence of schoolchildren have been topics of recurrent controversy and debate. In some instances, the courts have acted to curtail or halt intelligence testing in the public schools; in other cases, the courts have defined what composes intelligence testing. Debate and controversy have flourished about whether intelligence tests should be given, what they measure, and how different levels of performance attained by different populations are to be explained.

During the past 25 years, there has been a significant decline in the use of intelligence tests in schools as a result of several factors. Teachers and related services personnel have found that knowing the score a student earns on an intelligence test (IQ or mental age) has not been especially helpful in making decisions about specific instructional interventions or teaching approaches to use. It has only provided them with general information about how rapidly to pace instruction. Also, it is argued that scores on intelligence tests too often are used to set low expectations for students, resulting in diminished effort to teach students who earn low scores. This has been the case especially with students who were labeled mentally retarded on the basis of low scores on intelligence tests. In cases in which specific groups of students (such as African American or Hispanic students) have earned lower scores on tests and this has resulted in disproportionate placement of these groups of students in special education or in diminished expectations for performance, the courts have found intelligence tests discriminatory and mandated an end to their use.

No one has seen a specific thing called "intelligence." Rather, we observe differences in the ways people behave—either differences in everyday behavior in a variety of situations or differences in responses to standard stimuli or sets of stimuli; then we attribute those differences to something we describe as intelligence. In this sense, intelligence is an inferred entity—a term or construct we use to explain differences in present behavior and to predict differences in future behavior.

We have repeatedly stressed the fact that all tests, including intelligence tests, assess samples of behavior. Regardless of how an individual's performance on any given test is viewed and interpreted, intelligence tests—and the items on those tests—simply sample behaviors. A variety of different kinds of behavior samplings are used to assess intelligence; in most cases the kinds of behaviors sampled reflect a test author's conception of intelligence. The behavior samples are combined in different ways by different authors based on how they conceive of intelligence. In this chapter, we review the kinds of behaviors sampled by intelligence tests, with emphasis on the psychological demands of different item types, as a function of pupil characteristics. We also describe several ways in which intelligence theorists and test authors have conceptualized the structure of intelligence.

In evaluating the performance of individuals on intelligence tests, teachers, administrators, counselors, and diagnostic specialists must go beyond test names and scores to examine the kinds of behaviors sampled on the test. They must be willing to question the ways in which test stimuli are presented, to question the response requirements, and to evaluate the psychological demands placed on the individual.

1 The Effect of Pupil Characteristics on Assessment of Intelligence

Acculturation is the most important characteristic to consider in evaluating performance on intelligence tests. Acculturation refers to an individual's particular set of background experiences and opportunities to learn in both formal and informal educational settings. This, in turn, depends on the person's culture, the experiences available in the person's environment, and the length of time the person has had to assimilate those experiences. The culture in which an individual lives and the length of time the person has lived in that culture may influence the psychological demands presented by a test item. Simply knowing the kind of behavior sampled by a test is not enough because the same test item may create different psychological demands for people undergoing different experiences and acculturation.

Suppose, for example, that we assess intelligence by asking children to tell how hail and sleet are alike. Children may fail the item for very different reasons. Consider Juan (a student who recently moved to the United States from Mexico) and Marcie (a student from Michigan). Juan does not know what hail and sleet are, so he stands little chance of telling how hail and sleet are alike; he will fail the item simply because he does not know the meanings of the words. Marcie may know what hail is and what sleet is, but she fails the item because she is unable to integrate these two words into a conceptual category (precipitation). The psychological demand of the item changes as a function of the children's knowledge. For the child who has not learned the meanings of the words, the item assesses vocabulary. For the child who knows the meanings of the words, the item is a generalization task.

In considering how individuals perform on intelligence tests, we need to know how acculturation affects test performance. Items on intelligence tests range along a continuum from items that sample fundamental psychological behaviors that are relatively unaffected by the test taker's learning history to items that sample primarily learned behavior. To determine exactly what is being assessed, we need to know the essential background of the student. Consider the following item:

> Jeff went walking in the forest. He saw a porcupine that he tried to take home for a pet. It got away from him, but when he got home, his father took him to the doctor. Why?

For a student who knows what a porcupine is, that a porcupine has quills, and that quills are sharp, the item can assess comprehension, abstract reasoning, and problem-solving skill. The student who does not know any of this information may very well fail the item. In this case, failure is due not to an inability to comprehend or solve the problem but to a deficiency in background experience.

Similarly, we could ask a child to identify the seasons of the year. The experiences available in children's environments are reflected in the way they respond to this item. Children from central Illinois, who experience four discernibly different climatic conditions, may well respond "summer, fall, winter, and spring." Children from central Pennsylvania, who also experience four discernibly different climatic conditions but who live in an environment in which hunting is prevalent, might respond "buck season, doe season, small game, and fishing." Within specific cultures, both responses are logical and appropriate; only one is scored as correct.

Items on intelligence tests also sample different behaviors as a function of the age of the child assessed. Age and acculturation are positively related: Older children in general have had more opportunities to acquire the skills and cultural knowledge assessed by intelligence tests. The performances of 5-year-old children on an item requiring them to tell how a cardinal, a blue jay, and a swallow are alike are almost entirely a function of their knowledge of the word meanings. Most college students know the meanings of the three words; for them, the item assesses primarily their ability to identify similarities and to integrate words or objects into a conceptual category. As children get older, they have increasing opportunities to acquire the elements of the collective intelligence of a culture.

The interaction between acculturation and the behavior sampled determines the psychological demands of an intelligence test item. For this reason, it is impossible to define exactly what any one intelligence test would assess for any one student. Identical test items place different psychological demands on different children. Thirteen kinds of behaviors sampled by intelligence tests are described later in this chapter. These types of behavior will vary in their psychological demands based on the test taker's experience and acculturation. Given the great number of potential questions that could be asked for each type of question as well as the number of combinations of question types, the number of questions is practically infinite.

Used appropriately, intelligence tests can provide information that can lead to the enhancement of both individual opportunity and protection of the rights of students. Used inappropriately, they can restrict opportunity and rights.

SCENARIO *in* ASSESSMENT

INTELLIGENCE TESTING CAN HELP STUDENTS | Daraswan was born in Laos. Eventually, she and her family were brought to a suburb of Minneapolis by a church group. Daraswan and her sister were enrolled immediately in an elementary school. She was placed in the second grade with her younger sister although there was no indication that either child had ever attended school. The two girls were placed in an English language learner program option for part of the day and in classrooms with English-speaking teachers and students for nonacademic material. As the year went by, Daraswan's regular education teacher became increasingly concerned about her lack of progress in picking up appropriate English and school routines. In her English language learner program, Daraswan's progress was slow. Her younger sister was making more rapid progress: she could count, identify letters, and write her first name. Finally, the regular education teacher referred Daraswan for evaluation to determine if she was eligible for service as a mentally retarded student.

Several evaluations were conducted. The speech and language specialist declined to assess Daraswan for a language disorder because she had had so little exposure to the English language and the family continued to speak their native language at home. Reluctantly, the school psychologist agreed to attempt some assessments, in part because Daraswan's progress was notably slower than that of her sister. Due process procedures were followed. An interpreter discussed parental rights with Daraswan's mother and had her sign for permission to assess.

During the assessment process, the psychologist felt challenged in attempting to do a good assessment. She tried using an interpreter, but verbal items were outside of Daraswan's cultural experience. She tried using nonverbal subtests, but they still were not culturally appropriate. The psychologist administered the Nebraska Test of Learning Aptitude, a test that is given to deaf students and requires only pantomime directions. This test was used more to gain qualitative insight into Daraswan's performance; actual scores, while within the normal range, were not valid for Daraswan because the test is normed on deaf students. The psychologist also administered the Leiter International Performance Scale, a test requiring no verbal directions or response, and Daraswan earned a score that was somewhat above average. Adaptive behavior scales were administered to both Daraswan's teacher and mother. Although there were cultural factors that could bias the scores against Daraswan, the psychologist reported her somewhat-below-average scores.

A multidisciplinary individualized educational program (IEP) team met to consider the assessment data. The IEP conference complied with all state and federal guidelines and appropriate procedures were followed (that is, an interpreter was present, introductions were made, and assessment data were shared). The school psychologist was adamant that the testing data clearly ruled out the possibility that Daraswan was mentally retarded. Moreover, because of Daraswan's cultural and educational history, she would not agree to a diagnosis of learning disability. The team recommended that Daraswan receive more intensive instruction in English and remedial instruction in both reading and mathematics. Finally, a speech and language evaluation was conducted to ascertain if Daraswan might profit from individual therapy.

What implications about your own professional role can you draw from this scenario? Go to the Education CourseMate website for this textbook for more reflection questions about this Scenario in Assessment.

2 Behaviors Sampled by Intelligence Tests

Regardless of the interpretation of measured intelligence, it is a fact that intelligence tests simply sample behaviors. This section describes the kinds of behaviors sampled, including discrimination, generalization, motor behavior, general knowledge, vocabulary, induction, comprehension, sequencing, detail recognition, analogical reasoning, pattern completion, abstract reasoning, and memory.

DISCRIMINATION

Intelligence test items that sample skill in discrimination usually present a variety of stimuli and ask the student to find the one that differs from all the others. Figure 15.1 illustrates items assessing discrimination: Items a and b assess discrimination of figures, items c and d assess symbolic discrimination, and items e and f assess semantic discrimination. In each case, the student must identify the item that differs from the others.

GENERALIZATION

Items assessing generalization present a stimulus and ask the student to identify which of several response possibilities goes with the stimulus. Figure 15.2 illustrates several items assessing generalization. In each case, the student is given a stimulus element and is required to identify the one that is like it or that goes with it.

MOTOR BEHAVIOR

Many items on intelligence tests require a motor response. The intellectual level of very young children, for example, is often assessed by items requiring them to throw objects, walk, follow moving objects with their eyes, demonstrate a pincer grasp in picking up objects, build block towers, and place geometric forms in a recessed-form

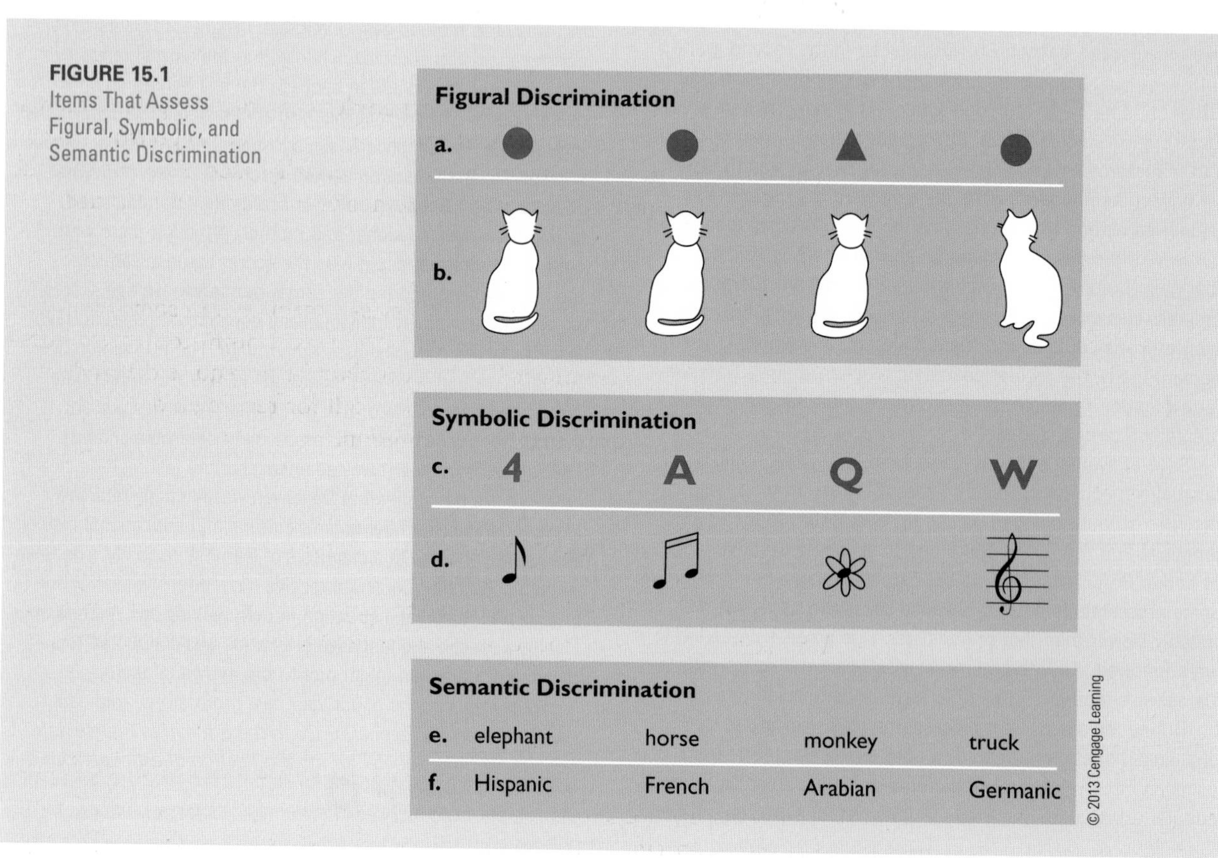

FIGURE 15.1
Items That Assess Figural, Symbolic, and Semantic Discrimination

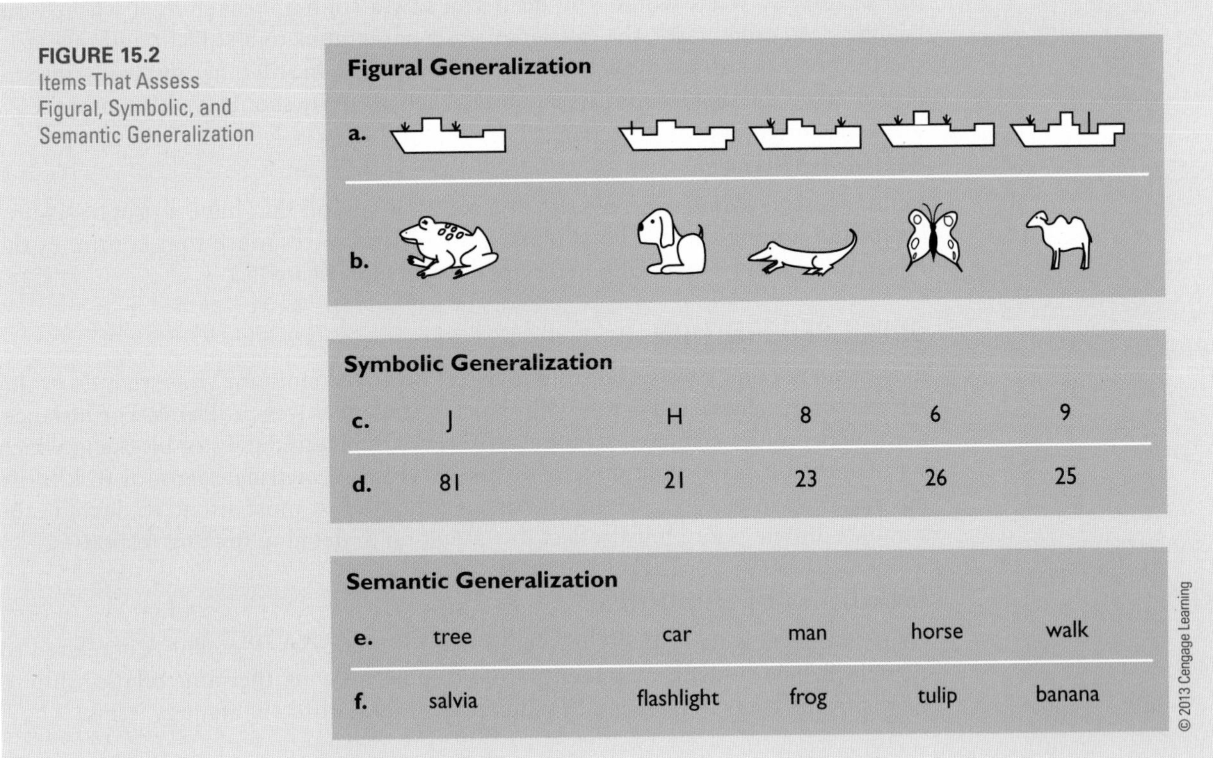

FIGURE 15.2 Items That Assess Figural, Symbolic, and Semantic Generalization

board. Most motor items at higher age levels are actually visual–motor items. The student may be required to copy geometric designs, trace paths through a maze, or reconstruct designs from memory.

GENERAL KNOWLEDGE

Items on intelligence tests sometimes require a student to answer specific factual questions, such as "In what direction would you travel if you were to go from Poland to Argentina?" and "What is the cube root of 8?" Essentially, such items are like the kinds of items in achievement tests; they assess primarily what has been learned.

VOCABULARY

Many different kinds of test items are used to assess vocabulary. In some cases, the student must name pictures, and in others he or she must point to objects in response to words read by the examiner. Some vocabulary items require the student to produce oral definitions of words, whereas others call for reading a definition and selecting one of several words to match the definition.

INDUCTION

Induction items present a series of examples and require the student to induce a governing principle. For example, the student is given a magnet and several different cloth, wooden, and metal objects and is asked to try to pick up the objects with the magnet. After several trials, the student is asked to state a rule or principle about the kinds of objects that magnets can pick up.

COMPREHENSION

There are three kinds of items used to assess comprehension: items related to directions, to printed material, and to societal customs and mores. In some instances, the examiner presents a specific situation and asks what actions the student would take (for example, "What would you do if you saw a train approaching a washed-out bridge?"). In other cases, the examiner reads paragraphs to a student and then asks specific questions about the content of the paragraphs. In still other instances, the student is asked questions about social mores, such as "Why should we keep promises?"

SEQUENCING

Items assessing sequencing consist of a series of stimuli that have a progressive relationship among them. The student must identify a response that continues the relationship. Four sequencing items are illustrated in Figure 15.3.

DETAIL RECOGNITION

In general, not many tests or test items assess detail recognition. Those that do evaluate the completeness and detail with which a student solves problems. For instance, items may require a student to count the blocks in pictured piles of blocks in which some of the blocks are not directly visible, to copy geometric designs, or to identify missing parts in pictures. To do so correctly, the student must attend to detail in the stimulus drawings and must reflect this attention to detail in making responses.

ANALOGICAL REASONING

"A is to B as C is to ___" is the usual form for analogies. Element A is related to element B. The student must identify the response having the same relationship to element C as B has to A. Figure 15.4 illustrates several different analogy items.

FIGURE 15.3
Items That Assess Sequencing Skill

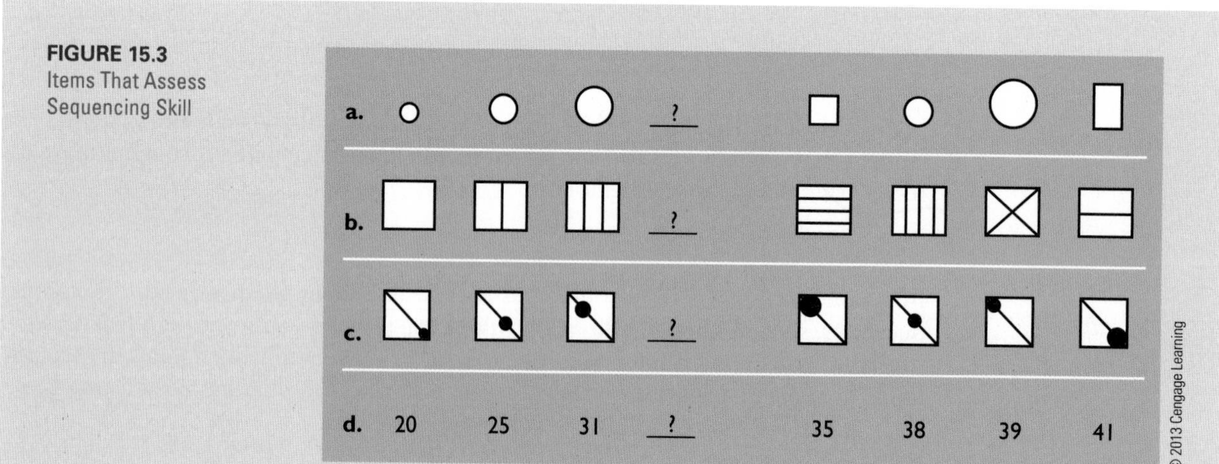

FIGURE 15.4
Analogy Items

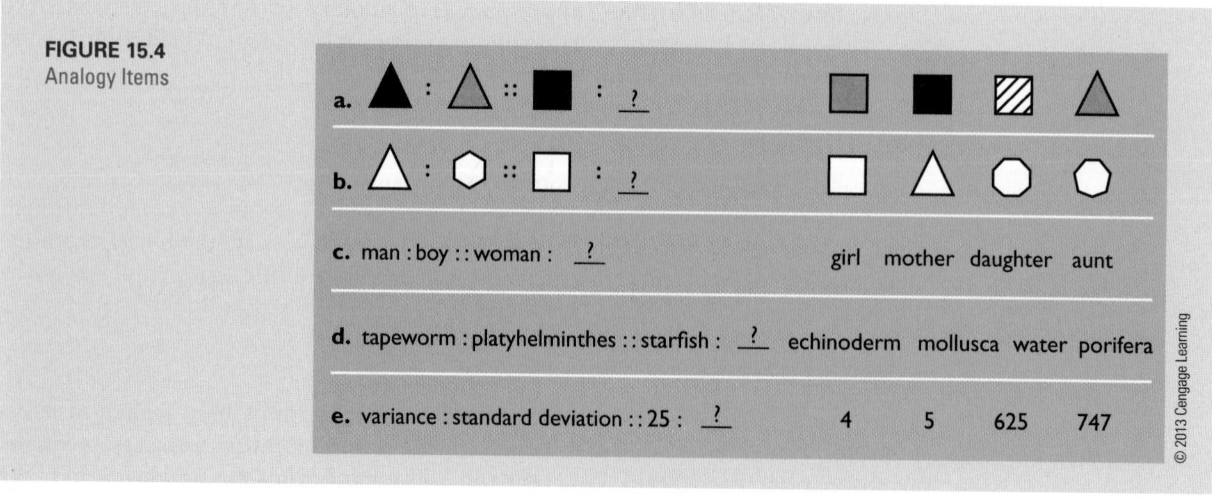

PATTERN COMPLETION

Some tests and test items require a student to select from several possibilities the missing part of a pattern or matrix. Figures 15.5 and 15.6 illustrate two different completion items. The item in Figure 15.5 requires identification of a missing part in a pattern. The item in Figure 15.6 calls for identification of the response that completes the matrix by continuing both the triangle, circle, rectangle sequence and the solid, striped, and clear sequence.

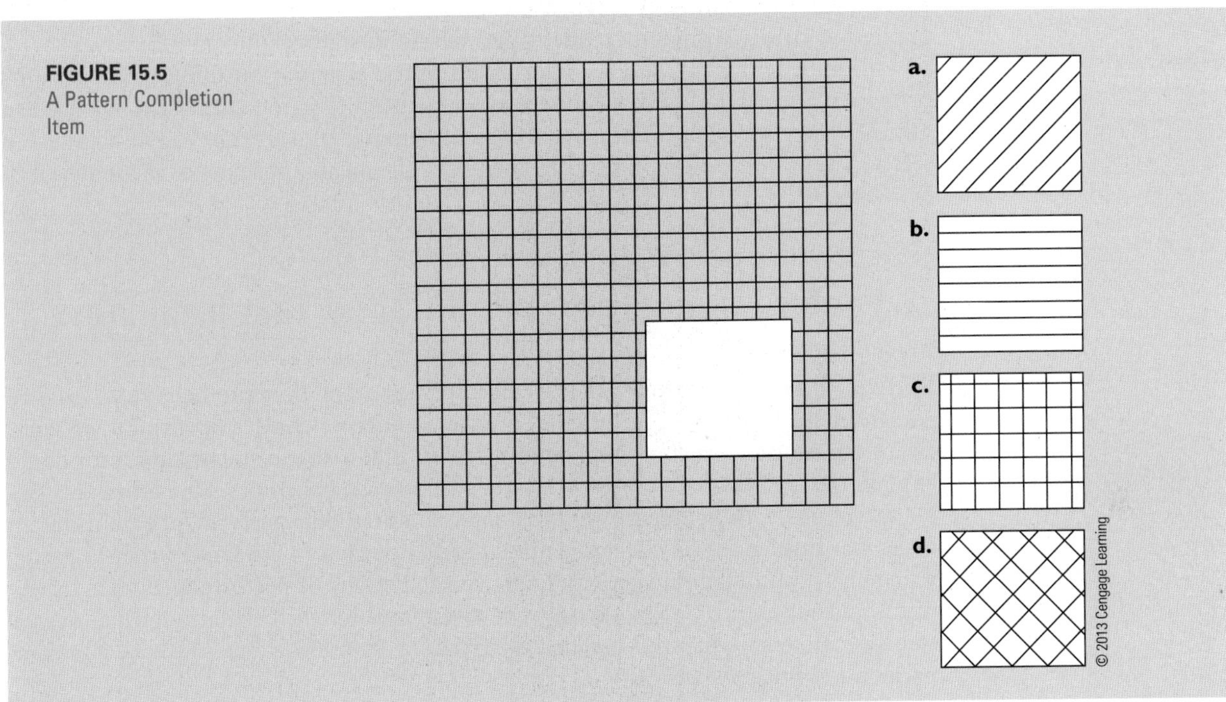

FIGURE 15.5
A Pattern Completion Item

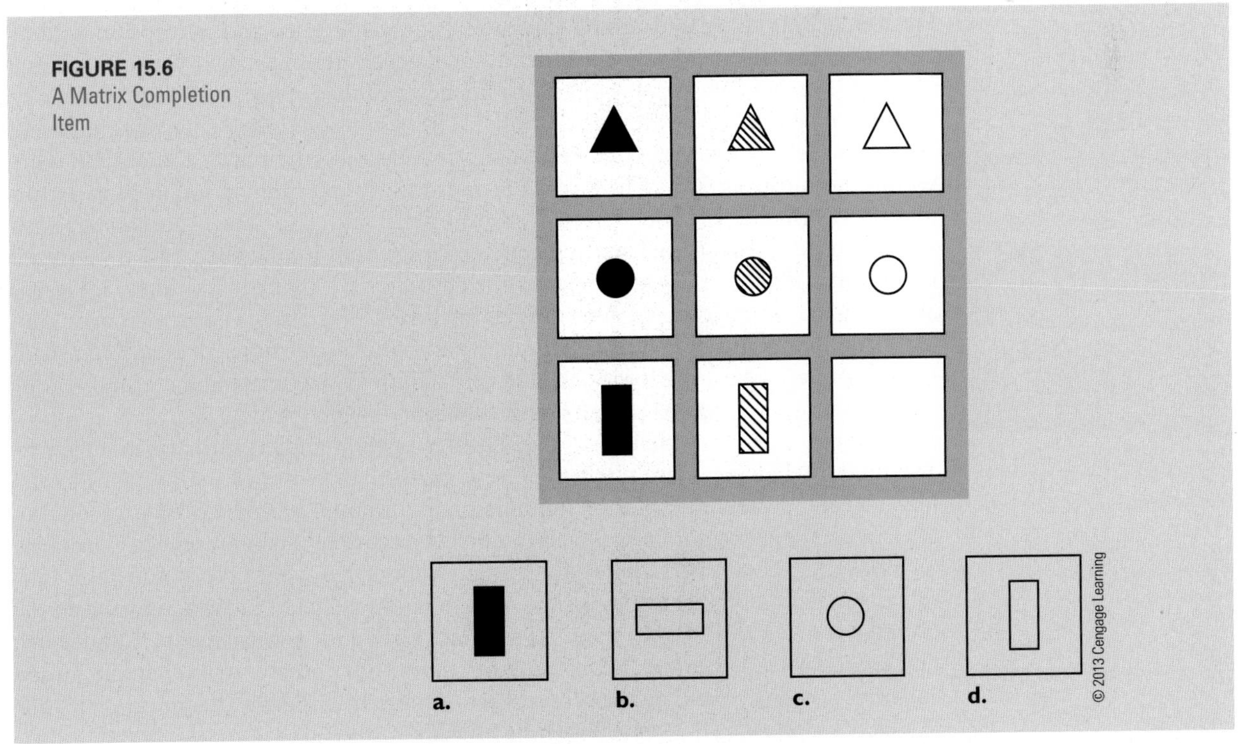

FIGURE 15.6
A Matrix Completion Item

ABSTRACT REASONING

A variety of items on intelligence tests sample abstract reasoning ability. The Stanford–Binet Intelligence Scale, for example, presents absurd verbal statements and pictures and asks the student to identify the absurdity. In the Stanford–Binet and other scales, arithmetic reasoning problems are often thought to assess abstract reasoning.

MEMORY

Several different kinds of tasks assess memory: repetition of sequences of digits presented orally, reproduction of geometric designs from memory, verbatim repetition of sentences, and reconstruction of the essential meaning of paragraphs or stories. Simply saying that an item assesses memory is too simplistic. We need to ask: Memory for what? The psychological demand of a memory task changes in relation to both the method of assessment and the meaningfulness of the material to be recalled.

3 Factors Underlying Intelligence Test Behaviors

Early in the study of intelligence, it became apparent that the behaviors used to assess intelligence were highly related to one another. Charles Spearman, an early twentieth-century psychologist, demonstrated that a single statistical factor could explain the high degree of intercorrelation among the behaviors. He named this single factor *general intelligence* (*g*). Although he noted that performance on different tasks was influenced by other specific intelligence factors, he argued that knowing a person's level of *g* could greatly improve predictions of performance on a variety of tasks. Today, nearly every intelligence test allows for the calculation of an overall test score that is frequently considered indicative of an individual's level of *g* in comparison to same-age peers.

Later, it became clear that different factor structures would emerge depending on the variables analyzed and the statistical procedures used. Thurstone (1941) proposed an alternative interpretation of the correlations among intelligence test behaviors. He conducted factor analyses of several tests of intelligence and perception, and he concluded that there exist seven different intelligences that he called "primary mental abilities": verbal comprehension, word fluency, number, space, associative memory, perceptual speed, and reasoning. Although Thurstone recognized that these different abilities were often positively correlated, he emphasized multiplicity rather than unity within the construct of intelligence. This approach to interpreting intellectual performance was further expanded by Raymond Cattell and associates. Cattell suggested the existence of two primary intelligence factors: fluid intelligence and crystallized intelligence. *Fluid intelligence* refers to the efficiency with which an individual learns and completes various tasks. This type of intelligence increases as a person ages until early adulthood and then decreases somewhat steadily over time. *Crystallized intelligence* represents the knowledge and skill one acquires over time and increases steadily throughout one's life. Several current tests of intelligence provide separate composite scores for behaviors that are representative of fluid and crystallized intelligence. The fluid intelligence score might represent performance on tasks such as memorizing and later recalling names of symbols or recalling unrelated words presented in a particular sequence. A crystallized intelligence score might represent performance on items that measure vocabulary or general knowledge. James Horn and John Carroll expanded on this theory to include additional intelligence factors, now called the Cattell–Horn–Carroll (CHC) theory. These factors include general memory and learning, broad visual perception, broad auditory perception, broad retrieval ability, broad cognitive speediness, and decision/reaction time/speed. This is the theory on which the Woodcock–Johnson III Tests of Cognitive Abilities is based.

4 Commonly Interpreted Factors on Intelligence Tests

Educational professionals will encounter many different terms that describe various intelligence test factors, clusters, indexes, and processes. We describe several common (and overlapping) terms in Table 15.1.

TABLE 15.1 Common Intelligence Test Terms, Associated Theorists and Tests, and Examples of Associated Behaviors Sampled

Term	Definition	Theorists[a]	Tests	Example of a Behavior Sampled	Source of Information Obtained
Attention	Alertness	Das, Naglieri	CAS, WJ-III	When given a target figure and many distracting stimuli, the individual must quickly select those that are identical to the target figure.	www.riverpub.com/products/cas/cas_pass.html
Auditory perception/processing	Ability to analyze, manipulate, and discriminate sounds	Cattell, Horn, Carroll	WJ-III	When given a set of pictures and listening to a recording in which a spoken word is presented along with noise distractions, the individual must select the picture that goes with the spoken word.	*WJ-III Examiner's Manual*
Cognitive efficiency/speediness	Ability to process information quickly and automatically	Carroll	WJ-III	When given several figures, the individual must quickly select the two that are most alike.	*WJ-III Examiner's Manual*
Cognitive fluency	Speed in completing cognitive tasks		WJ-III	When given a set of pictures, the individual must quickly say the names of the pictures.	*WJ-III Examiner's Manual*
Comprehension knowledge	Term used on the WJ-III to describe crystallized intelligence	Cattell, Horn, Carroll	WJ-III	When shown various pictures, the individual must provide the names for the pictures	*WJ-III Examiner's Manual*
Executive processing	Use of higher level thinking strategies to organize thought and behavior		WJ-III	When given a maze to complete, the individual must complete the maze correctly without mistakes on the first try.	*WJ-III Examiner's Manual*

continued on the next page

TABLE 15.1 Common Intelligence Test Terms, Associated Theorists and Tests, and Examples of Associated Behaviors Sampled, *continued*

Term	Definition	Theorists[a]	Tests	Example of a Behavior Sampled	Source of Information Obtained
Fluid reasoning/ intelligence	Efficiency with which an individual learns and completes various tasks	Cattell, Horn, Carroll	WJ-III	When given a set of simple relationships or rules among symbols, the individual must apply the rules to correctly identify missing links within increasingly complicated patterns.	*WJ-III Examiner's Manual*
Long-term retrieval/ delayed recall	Ability to store and easily recall information at a much later point in time	Cattell, Horn, Carroll	WJ-III	Two days after an individual was taught the words associated with certain symbols, the symbol is presented and the individual must recall the associated words.	*WJ-III Examiner's Manual*
Perceptual reasoning	Ability to identify and form patterns		WISC-IV	When given a pattern and various colored blocks, the individual must form the blocks in the shape of the given pattern.	*WISC-IV Technical and Interpretive Manual*
Planning	Ability to identify effective strategies to reach a particular goal	Das, Naglieri	CAS	When given multiple numbers, the individual must select the two that are the same.	http://www.riverpub.com/products/cas/cas_pass.html
Processing speed	Ability to quickly complete tasks that require limited complex thought	Cattell, Horn, Carroll	WJ-III, WISC-IV	The individual is presented with a key for converting numbers to symbols and must quickly write down the associated symbols for numbers that are presented.	*WISC-IV Technical and Interpretive Manual*
Quantitative knowledge	Mathematical knowledge and achievement	Cattell, Horn	WJ-III	The individual must answer math word problems correctly.	*WJ-III Examiner's Manual*
Short-term memory or working memory	Ability to quickly store and then immediately retrieve information within a short period of time	Cattell, Horn	WISC-IV, WJ-III	The examiner says several numbers, and the individual must repeat them accurately and in the same order.	*WISC-IV Technical and Interpretive Manual*
Simultaneous processing	Extent to which one can integrate pieces of information into a complete pattern	Das, Naglieri	CAS	When asked a question verbally and presented with figures, the individual must pick the figure that answers the question.	*WISC-IV Technical and Interpretive Manual*

Term	Definition	Theorists[a]	Tests	Example of a Behavior Sampled	Source of Information Obtained
Speed of lexical access	Fluency with which one can recall pronunciations of words, word parts, and letters	Carroll	WJ-III	When given many pictures, the individual must say the picture names as quickly as possible.	*WJ-III Examiner's Manual*
Successive processing	Extent to which one can recall things presented in a particular order	Das, Naglieri	Das, Naglieri	When given a set of words, the individual must repeat them back in the same order.	http://www.riverpub.com/products/cas/cas_pass.html
Thinking ability	Composite cluster within the WJ-III that is composed of performance on several less automatic cognitive tasks		WJ-III	This includes tasks associated with long-term retrieval, visual–spatial thinking, auditory processing, and fluid reasoning (see task examples for these terms in this table).	*WJ-III Technical Manual*
Verbal ability	Composite cluster within the WJ-III that is composed of language tasks		WJ-III	This includes tasks associated with comprehension/knowledge (see task example for this term above).	*WJ-III Technical Manual*
Verbal comprehension	"Verbal abilities utilizing reasoning, comprehension, and conceptualization" (p. 6)		WISC-IV	The individual must verbally express how two things are similar.	*WISC-IV Technical and Interpretive Manual*
Visual perception/ processing	Integrating and interpreting visual information	Cattell, Horn, Carroll	†	When presented only part of an image, the individual must identify what the entire image is.	*WJ-III Examiner's Manual*
Visual–spatial thinking	Ability to store and manipulate visual images in one's mind		WJ-III	A picture is briefly shown and removed; the individual must then select the originally shown picture from a set of additional pictures.	*WJ-III Technical Manual*

[a]There are often many theorists, researchers, and tests associated with a given intelligence term; we provide here just one or two individuals who were key in defining these terms and tests that involve measurement of behaviors associated with these terms.

†No test we reviewed specifically includes this as an index or factor, but it is a factor in CHC theory and is associated with many tasks included on intelligence tests.

CAS, Cognitive Assessment System; WISC-IV, Wechsler Intelligence Scale for Children–IV; WJ-III, Woodcock–Johnson III.

5 Assessment of Processing Deficits

People have become increasingly intrigued with the possibility of identifying specific cognitive processing deficits that contribute to a student's academic difficulties. Some current conceptualizations of learning disabilities include cognitive processing deficits as a defining characteristic. Test developers have begun to develop specific tests that are intended to measure particular weaknesses that students might have in processing information. For instance, there is now a supplemental instrument to the Wechsler Intelligence Scale for Children–IV (WISC-IV) called the WISC-IV Integrated. This supplemental material, which includes a variety of additional subtests that allow for the comparison of student performance across a variety of conditions, is intended to facilitate the identification of specific processing deficits. The Woodcock–Johnson III Tests of Cognitive Abilities includes a related vehicle for test score interpretation, whereby one can analyze student performance according to an information processing model.

6 Types of Intelligence Tests

Depending on what types of decisions are being made, as well as the specific characteristics of the student, different types of intelligence tests might be selected for administration. We describe three different types in the following sections.

INDIVIDUAL TESTS

Individually administered intelligence tests are most frequently used for making exceptionality, eligibility, and educational placement decisions. State special education eligibility guidelines and criteria typically specify that the collection of data about intellectual functioning must be included in the decision-making process for eligibility and placement decisions, and that these data must come from individual intellectual evaluation by a certified school psychologist.

GROUP TESTS

Group-administered intelligence tests are used for one of two purposes: as screening devices for individual students or as sources of descriptive information about groups of students. Most often, they are administered as screening devices to identify those students who differ enough from average to warrant further assessment. In these cases, the tests' merit is that teachers can administer them relatively quickly to large numbers of students. The tests suffer from the same limitations as any group test: They can be made to yield qualitative information only with difficulty, and they require students to sit still for approximately 20 minutes, to mark with a pencil, and, often, to read. During the past 25 years, it has become increasingly common for school districts to eliminate the practice of group intelligence testing. When administrators are asked why they are doing so, they cite (1) the limited relevance of knowing about students' capability, as opposed to knowing about the subject matter skills (such as for reading and math) that students do and do not have; (2) the difficulty teachers experience in trying to use the test results for instructional purposes; and (3) the cost of a schoolwide intellectual screening program.

NONVERBAL INTELLIGENCE TESTS

A number of nonverbal tests are among the most widely used tests for assessment of intelligence, particularly when there are questions about the intelligence of a child who is not proficient in English or who is deaf. Some nonverbal tests are designed to measure intelligence broadly; others are called "picture–vocabulary tests." The latter are not measures of intelligence per se; rather, they measure only one aspect of intelligence—receptive vocabulary. In picture–vocabulary tests, pictures are presented to the test taker, who is asked to identify those pictures that correspond to words read by the examiner. Some authors of picture–vocabulary measures state that the tests measure receptive vocabulary; others equate receptive vocabulary with intelligence and claim that their tests assess intelligence. Because the tests measure only one aspect of intelligence, they should not be used to make eligibility decisions.

ASSESSMENT OF INTELLIGENCE: COMMONLY USED TESTS

re extensive iews of ditional elligence ts are ilable at Education urseMate osite for this t.

In this section, we provide information on some of the most commonly used intelligence tests. Table 15.2 provides information on other intelligence tests that you may come across in educational settings; more extensive reviews of these tests are available on the website. We also provide more detailed reviews of several intelligence tests, with special reference to the kinds of behaviors they sample and to their technical adequacy. Although some individual intelligence tests may be appropriately administered by teachers, counselors, or other specialists, the intelligence tests on which school personnel rely most heavily must be given by psychologists.

Wechsler Intelligence Scale for Children–IV

The Wechsler Intelligence Scale for Children–IV (WISC-IV; Wechsler, 2003)[1] is the latest version of the WISC and is designed to assess the cognitive ability and problem-solving processes of individuals ranging in age from 6 years, 0 months to 16 years, 11 months.

Developed by David Wechsler in 1949, the WISC adapted the 11 subtests found in the original Wechsler Scale, the Wechsler–Bellevue Intelligence Scale (1939), for use with children, and added the Mazes subtest. In 1974, the Wechsler Intelligence Scale for Children–Revised (WISC-R) was developed. This revision retained the 12 subtests found in the original WISC but altered the age range from 5 to 15 years to 6 to 16 years. The Wechsler Intelligence Scale for Children–III (WISC-III) was developed in 1991. This scale retained the 12 subtests and added a new subtest, Symbol Search. Previous editions of the WISC provided verbal IQ, performance IQ, and full-scale IQ scores. The WISC-III maintained this tradition but introduced four new index scores: Verbal Comprehension Index (VCI), Perceptual Organization Index (POI), Freedom from Distractibility Index (FDI), and Processing Speed Index (PSI).

The WISC-IV provides a new scoring framework while maintaining the theory of intelligence underlying the previous scales. This theory was summarized by Wechsler when he stated that "intelligence is the overall capacity of an individual to understand and cope with the world around him" (Wechsler, 1974, p. 5). The definition is consistent with his original one, in which he stated that intelligence is "the capacity of the individual to act purposefully, to think rationally, and to deal effectively with his or her environment" (Wechsler, 1974, p. 3).

Based on the premise that intelligence is both global (characterizing an individual's behavior as a whole) and specific (composed of distinct elements) (Wechsler, 2004, p. 2), the WISC-IV measures overall global intelligence, as well as discrete domains of cognitive functioning.

The WISC-IV presents a new scoring framework. Unlike its predecessors, it does not provide verbal and performance IQ scores. However, it maintains both the full-scale IQ (FSIQ) as a measure of general intellectual functioning and the four index scores as measures of specific cognitive domains. The WISC-IV developed new terminology for the four index scores in order to more accurately reflect the cognitive abilities measured by the subtest composition of each index. The four indexes are the VCI, the Perceptual Reasoning Index (PRI), the Working Memory Index (WMI), and the PSI. A description of the subtests that comprise each index is provided next. Subtests can be categorized as either core or supplemental. Core subtests provide composite scores. Supplemental subtests (indicated by a "*") provide additional clinical information and can be used as substitutes for core subtests. Those familiar with the WISC-III will note that in the WISC-IV revisions, 3 subtests have been dropped, 10 subtests have been retained, and 5 subtests have been added (the supplemental subtests indicated with *).

Subtests

Verbal Comprehension Subtests

Similarities. This subtest requires identification of similarities or commonalities in superficially unrelated verbal stimuli.

Vocabulary. Items on this subtest assess ability to define words. Beginning items require individuals to name picture objects. Later items require individuals to verbally define words that are read aloud by the examiner.

Comprehension. This subtest assesses ability to comprehend verbal directions or to understand specific customs and mores. The examinee is asked questions such as "Why is it important to wear boots after a large snowfall?"

Information. This subtest assesses ability to answer specific factual questions. The content is learned; it consists of information that a person is expected to

[1] The WISC-IV is also available as the WISC-IV Integrated (Kaplan, Fein, Kramer, Morris, Delis, & Maerlender, 2004). The WISC-IV Integrated is composed of the core and supplemental subtests of the WISC-IV plus 16 additional process-oriented subtests. The WISC-IV Integrated is a clinical instrument that, in our opinion, has limited application to school settings. The process-oriented subtests of the WISC-IV Integrated do not have sufficient reliability to be used to make decisions in school settings. The 16 process-oriented subtests are in addition to the core and supplemental subtests, and they cannot be substituted for core or supplemental subtests.

TABLE 15.2 Commonly Used Intelligence Tests

Test	Author	Publisher	Year	Ages/ Grades	Individual/ Group	NRT/ SRT/ CRT	Subtests
Cognitive Abilities Test (CogAT)	Lohman & Hagan	Riverside	2001	Grades K–12	Group	NRT	Oral Vocabulary, Verbal Reasoning, Quantitative Concepts, Relational Concepts, Matrices, Figure Classification, Sentence Completion, Verbal Classification, Verbal Analogies, Quantitative Relations, Number Series, Equation Building, Figure Classification, Figure Analogies, Figure Analysis
Cognitive Assessment System	Das & Naglieri	Riverside	1997	Ages 5 to 17–11 years	Individual	NRT	Matching Numbers, Planned Codes, Planned Connections, Nonverbal Matrices, Verbal–Spatial Relations, Figure Memory, Expressive Attention, Number Detection, Receptive Attention, Word Series, Sentence Repetition, Speech Rate, Sentence Questions
Comprehensive Test of Nonverbal Intelligence (C-TONI)	Hammill, Pearson, & Wiederholt	Pro-Ed	1997	Ages 6 to 18–11 years	Individual	NRT	Pictorial Analogies, Geometric Analogies, Pictorial Categories, Geometric Categories, Pictorial Sequences, Geometric Sequences
Detroit Tests of Learning Aptitude, Fourth Edition (DTLA-4)	Hammill	Pro-Ed	1998	Ages 6 to 17–11 years	Individual	NRT	Word Opposites, Design Sequences, Sentence Imitation, Reversed Letters, Story Construction, Design Reproduction, Basic Information, Symbolic Relations, Word Sequences, Story Sequences
Kaufman Assessment Battery for Children, Second Edition (KABC-2)	Kaufman & Kaufman	Pearson	2004	Ages 3 to 18 years	Individual	NRT	Triangles, Face Recognition, Pattern Reasoning, Block Counting, Story Completion, Conceptual Thinking, Rover, Gestalt Closure, Word Order, Number Recall, Hand Movements, Atlantis, Atlantis-Delayed, Rebus, Rebus-Delayed, Riddles, Expressive Vocabulary, Verbal Knowledge

Test	Author	Publisher	Year	Ages/ Grades	Individual/ Group	NRT/ SRT/ CRT	Subtests
Leiter International Performance Scale–Revised	Roid & Miller	Stoelting	1997	Ages 2 to 20–11 years	Individual	NRT	Classification, Sequencing, Repeated Patterns, Design Analogies, Matching, Figure-Ground, Form Completion, Picture Context, Paper Folding, Figure Rotation, Immediate Recognition, Delayed Recognition, Associated Pairs, Delayed Pairs, Forward Memory, Reversed Memory, Spatial Memory, Visual Coding, Attention Sustained, Attention Divided
Otis–Lennon School Ability Test, Eighth Edition (OLSAT-8)	Harcourt Educational Measurement	Pearson	2003	Grades K–12	Group	NRT	Verbal Comprehension, Verbal Reasoning, Pictorial Reasoning, Figural Reasoning, Quantitative Reasoning
Peabody Picture Vocabulary Test–IV	Dunn & Dunn	Pearson	2007	Ages 2–6 to 90+ years	Individual	NRT	Not applicable
Test of Nonverbal Intelligence–3	Brown, Sherbenou, & Johnsen	Pro-Ed	2010	Ages 5 to 85–11 years	Individual	NRT	Matching, Analogies, Classification, Intersections, Progressions
Stanford–Binet Intelligence Scale, Fifth Edition	Roid	Riverside	2003	Ages 2 to 85+ years	Individual	NRT	Object Series/Matrices, Early Reasoning, Verbal Absurdities, Verbal Analogies, Procedural Knowledge, Picture Absurdities, Vocabulary, Quantitative Reasoning, Form Board, Form Patterns, Position and Direction, Delayed Response, Block Span, Memory for Sentences, Last Word
Universal Nonverbal Intelligence Test (UNIT)	Bracken & McCallem	Riverside	1996	Ages 5 to 17–11 years	Individual	NRT	Symbolic Memory, Object Memory, Analogic Reasoning, Spatial Memory, Cube Design, Mazes
Wechsler Intelligence Scale for Children–IV (WISC-IV)	Wechsler	Pearson	2003	Ages 6 to 16–11 years	Individual	NRT	Similarities, Vocabulary, Comprehension, Information, Word Reasoning, Block Design, Picture Concepts, Matrix Reasoning, Picture Completion, Digit Span, Letter–Number Sequencing, Arithmetic, Coding, Symbol Search, Cancellation

continued on the next page

TABLE 15.2 Commonly Used Intelligence Tests, *continued*

Test	Author	Publisher	Year	Ages/ Grades	Individual/ Group	NRT/ SRT/ CRT	Subtests
Wechsler Preschool and Primary Scale of Intelligence–III (WPPSI-III)	Wechsler	Pearson	2002	Ages 2–6 to 7–3 years	Individual	NRT	Information, Vocabulary, Word Reasoning, Receptive Vocabulary, Picture Naming, Comprehension, Similarities, Block Design, Object Assembly, Matrix Reasoning, Picture Concepts, Picture Completion, Coding, Symbol Search
Woodcock–Johnson III Tests of Cognitive Abilities (WJ-III)	Woodcock, McGrew, & Mather	Riverside	2001	Ages 2 to 90+ years	Individual	NRT	Verbal Comprehension, Visual–Auditory Learning, Visual–Auditory Learning–Delayed, Spatial Relations, Sound Blending, Incomplete Words, Concept Formation, Visual Matching, Numbers Reversed, Auditory Working Memory, General Information, Retrieval Fluency, Picture Recognition, Planning, Auditory Attention, Analysis-Synthesis, Planning, Decision Speed, Rapid Picture Naming, Pair Cancellation, Memory for Words

have acquired in both formal and informal educational settings. The examinee is asked questions such as "Which fast-food franchise is represented by the symbol of golden arches?"

Word Reasoning*. In this subtest, individuals are presented with a clue or a series of clues and must identify the common concept that each clue or group of clues describes. It is thought to measure comprehension, identification of analogies, generalization, and verbal abstraction. A sample item for this scale is "This has a long handle and is used with water to clean the floor" (mop). When partially correct responses are given, additional clues are provided.

Perceptual Reasoning Subtests

Block Design. In this subtest, individuals are given a specified amount of time to manipulate blocks in order to reproduce a stimulus design that is presented visually.

Picture Concepts*. In this subtest, an individual is shown two or three rows of pictures and must choose one picture from each row in order to form a group that shares a common characteristic. For example, an individual would choose the picture of the horse in row 1 and the picture of the mouse in row 2 because they are both animals. This is basically a picture classification task.

Matrix Reasoning*. In this subtest, children must select the missing portion of an incomplete matrix given five response options. Matrices range from 2 × 2 to 3 × 3. The last item differs from this general form, requiring individuals to identify the fifth square in a row of six.

Picture Completion. This subtest assesses the ability to identify missing parts in pictures within a specified time limit.

Working Memory Subtests

Digit Span. This subtest assesses immediate recall of orally presented digits. In Digit Span Forward, children repeat numbers in the same order that they were presented aloud by the examiner. In Digit Span Backward, children repeat numbers in the reverse of the order that they were presented by the examiner.

Letter–Number Sequencing*. This subtest assesses an individual's ability to recall and mentally manipulate a series of numbers and letters that are orally presented to them. After hearing a random sequence of numbers and letters, individuals must first repeat the numbers in ascending order and then repeat the letters in alphabetical order.

Arithmetic. This subtest assesses ability to solve problems requiring the application of arithmetic operations. In this subtest, children must mentally solve problems presented orally within a specified time limit.

Processing Speed Subtests

Coding. This subtest assesses the ability to associate symbols with either geometric shapes or numbers and to copy these symbols onto paper within a specified time limit.

Symbol Search. This subtest consists of a series of paired groups of symbols, with each pair including a target group and a search group. The child scans the two groups and indicates whether the target symbols appear in the search group within a specified time limit.

Cancellation*. In this subtest, individuals are presented with first a random and then a structured arrangement of pictures. For both arrangements, individuals must mark the target pictures within the specified time limit.

Scores

Subtest raw scores obtained on the WISC-IV are transformed to scaled scores with a mean of 10 and a standard deviation of 3. The scaled scores for 3 Verbal Comprehension subtests, 3 Perceptual Reasoning subtests, 2 Working Memory subtests, 2 Processing Speed subtests, and all 10 subtests are added and then transformed to obtain the composite VCI, PRI, WMI, PSI, and FSIQ scores, respectively. IQs for Wechsler scales are deviation IQs with a mean of 100 and a standard deviation of 15. Tables are provided for converting the subtest scaled scores and composite scores to percentile ranks and confidence intervals. Raw scores may also be transformed to test ages that represent the average performance on each of the subtests by individuals of specific ages. Seven process scores can also be derived. Process scores are "designed to provide more detailed information on the cognitive abilities that contribute to a child's subtest performance" (Wechsler, 2004, p. 107). The WISC-IV provides for subtest, index, and process score discrepancy comparisons. Tables provide the difference scores needed in order to be considered statistically significant at the .15 and .05 confidence level for each age group, and they also provide information on the percentage of children in the standardization sample who obtained the same or a greater discrepancy between scores.

The WISC-IV employs a differential scoring system for some of the subtests. Responses for the Digit Span, Picture Concepts, Letter–Number Sequencing, Matrix Reasoning, Picture Completion, Information, and Word Reasoning subtests are scored pass–fail. A weighted scoring system is used for the Similarities, Vocabulary, and Comprehension subtests. Incorrect responses receive a score of 0, lower level or lower quality responses are assigned a score of 1, and more abstract responses are assigned a score of 2. The remainder of the subtests are timed. Individuals who complete the tasks in shorter periods of time receive more credit. These differential weightings of responses must be given special consideration, especially when the timed tests are used with children who demonstrate motor impairments that interfere with the speed of response.

Norms

The WISC-IV was standardized on 2,200 children ages 6-0 to 16-11 years. This age range was divided into 11 whole-year groups (for example, 6-0 to 6-11). All groups had 200 participants. The standardization group was stratified on the basis of age, sex, race/ ethnicity (whites, African Americans, Hispanics, Asians, and others), parent education level (based on number of years and degree held), and geographic region (Northeast, South, Midwest, and West), according to 2000 U.S. census information. A representative sample of children from the special group studies (such as children with learning disorders, children identified as gifted, children with attention deficit hyperactivity disorder, and so on) conducted during the national tryout was included in the normative sample (approximately 5.7 percent) in order to accurately represent the population of children enrolled in school. Extensive tables in the manual are used to compare sample data with census data. These tables are stratified across the following characteristics: (1) age, race/ethnicity, and parent education level; (2) age, sex, and parent education level; (3) age, sex, and race/ethnicity; and (4) age, race/ethnicity, and geographic region. Overall, the samples appear representative of the U.S. population of children across the stratified variables.

Reliability

Because the Coding, Symbol Search, and Cancellation subtests are timed, reliability estimates for these subtests are based on test–retest coefficients. However, split-half reliability coefficient alphas corrected by the Spearman–Brown formula are reported for all the remaining subtest and composite scores. Moreover, standard errors of measurement (SEMs) are reported for all scores. Scores are reported for each age group and as an average across all age groups. As would be expected, subtest reliabilities (overall averages range from .79 to .90; age levels range from .72 to .94) are lower than index reliabilities (overall averages range from .88 to .94; age levels range from .81 to .95). Reliabilities for the full-scale IQ are excellent, with age-level coefficient alphas ranging from .96 to .97.

Test–retest stability data were collected on a sample of 243 children. These data were calculated for five age groups (6 to 7, 8 to 9, 10 to 11, 12 to 13, and 14 to 16) using Pearson's product–moment correlation. Scores for the overall sample were calculated using Fisher's z-transformation. Stability coefficients[2] are provided for each subtest, process, index, and IQ. Stability coefficients for the FSIQ among these five groups ranged from .91 to .96. Process stabilities ranged from .64 to .83. Index stabilities ranged from .84 (Working Memory, ages 8 to 9) to .95 (Verbal Comprehension, ages 14 to 16), and subtest stability correlations ranged from .71 (Picture Concepts, ages 6 to 7; Cancellation, ages 8 to 9) to .95 (Vocabulary, ages 14 to 16).

The full-scale IQ and index scores are reliable enough to be used to make important educational decisions. The subtests and process indicators are not sufficiently reliable to be used in making these important decisions.

Validity

The authors present evidence for validity based on four areas: test content, response processes, internal structure, and relationship to other variables. In terms of test content, they emphasize the extensive revision process, based on comprehensive literature and expert reviews, which was used to select items and subtests that would adequately sample the domains of intellectual functioning they sought to measure.

Evidence for appropriate response processes (child's cognitive process during subtest task) is based on (1) prior research that supports retained subtests and (2) literature reviews, expert opinion, and empirical examinations that support the new subtests. Furthermore, during development, the authors engaged in empirical (for instance, response frequencies conducted to identify incorrect answers that occurred frequently) and qualitative (for instance, directly questioned students regarding their use of problem-solving strategies) examination of response processes and made adjustments accordingly.

In terms of internal structure, evidence of convergent and discriminant validity is provided based on the correlations between subtests using Fisher's z-transformation. All subtests were found to significantly correlate with one another, as would be expected considering that they all presumably measure g (general intelligence). Moreover, subtests that contribute to the same index score (VC, PR, WM, or PS) were generally found to highly correlate with one another.

[2] Stability coefficients provided are based on corrected correlations.

Further evidence of internal structure is presented through both exploratory and confirmatory factor analysis. Exploratory factor analysis was conducted on two samples. Support for the four-factor structure and the stability of index scores across samples was found in cross-validation analysis. Moreover, confirmatory factor analysis using structural equation modeling and three goodness-of-fit measures confirmed that the four-factor model provided the best fit for the data.

In terms of relationships with other variables, evidence is provided based on correlations between WISC-IV and other Wechsler measures. The WISC-IV FSIQ score was correlated with the full-scale IQ or achievement measures from other Wechsler scales. The correlations are as follows: WISC-III, r =.89; WPPSI-III, r =.89; Wechsler Adult Intelligence Scale–III (WAIS-III), r =.89; Wechsler Abbreviated Scale of Intelligence (WASI), r =.83 (with FSIQ-4 measure) and r =.86 (with FSIQ-2 measure); and Wechsler Individual Achievement Test–II (WIAT-II), r=.87. Correlations were made with a set of specific intellectual measures, such as the Children's Memory Scale (CMS), Gifted Rating Scale–School Form (GRS-S), Bar On Emotional Quotient Inventory: Youth Edition (Bar On EQ), Adaptive Behavior Assessment System–II–Parent Form (ABAS-II-P), and Adaptive Behavior Assessment System–II–Teacher Form (ABAS-II-T). Correlations were very low (ranging from –.01 to .72). There is no evidence of the predictive validity of the WISC-IV.

The authors conclude by presenting special group studies that they conducted during standardization in order to examine the clinical utility of the WISC-IV. They note the following four limitations to these studies: (1) Random selection was not used, (2) diagnoses might have been based on different criteria due to the various clinical settings from which participants were selected, (3) small sample sizes that covered only a portion of the WISC-IV age range were used, and (4) only group performance is reported. The authors caution that these studies provide examples but are not fully representative of the diagnostic categories. The studies were conducted on children identified as intellectually gifted and children with mild to moderate mental retardation, learning disorders, and attention deficit hyperactivity disorder (ADHD) expressive language disorder, mixed receptive–expressive language disorder, traumatic brain injury, autistic disorder, Asperger's syndrome, and motor impairment.

Summary

The WISC-IV is a widely used individually administered intelligence test that assesses individuals ranging in age from 6 years, 0 months to 16 years, 11 months. Evidence for the reliability of the scales is good. Reliabilities are much lower for subtests, so subtest scores should not be used in making placement or instructional planning decisions. Evidence for validity, as presented in the manual, is based on four areas: test content, response processes, internal structure, and relationship to other variables. Evidence for validity is limited.

The WISC-IV is of limited usefulness in making educational decisions. The WISC-IV Integrated adds 16 process-oriented subtests to explain poor performance on WISC-IV subtests that have limited reliability. The process-oriented subtests are even less reliable than the WISC-IV core and supplemental subtests. Those who use the WISC-IV in educational settings would do well not to go beyond using the full-scale and four domain scores in making decisions about students.

Woodcock–Johnson III Normative Update: Tests of Cognitive Abilities and Tests of Achievement

The third edition of the Woodcock–Johnson Psychoeductional Battery (WJ-III) was developed in 2001 (Woodcock, McGrew, & Mather, 2001), and a normative update of the test (WJ-III NU) was conducted in 2007 (Woodcock, Schrank, McGrew, & Mather, 2007). The WJ-III is an individually administered, norm-referenced assessment system for the measurement of general intellectual ability, specific cognitive abilities, scholastic aptitudes, oral language, and achievement. The battery is intended for use from preschool to geriatric ages. The complete set of WJ-III test materials includes four easels for presenting the stimulus items: One for the standard battery cognitive tests, one for the extended battery cognitive tests, one for the standard achievement battery, and one for the extended achievement battery. Other materials include examiner's manuals for the cognitive and achievement tests, one technical manual, test records, and subject response booklets.

The WJ-III contains several modifications to the previous version of the battery (that is, WJ-R). The Tests of Cognitive Abilities (WJ-III-COG) were revised to reflect more current theory and research on intelligence, and several clusters have been added to the battery. New clusters were added to the Tests of Achievement (WJ-III-ACH) to assess several specific types of learning disabilities. Finally, a new procedure was added to ascertain intraindividual differences. The procedure allows professionals to compute discrepancies between cognitive and achievement scores within any specific domain. In 2007, normative calculation procedures were changed to more adequately represent the population according to updated 2005 census statistics, and associated materials were published as the WJ-III NU. These changes are described in the associated sections (that is, Norms, Reliability, and Validity) of this review.

WJ-III Tests of Cognitive Abilities

The 20 subtests of WJ-III-COG are based on the CHC theory of cognitive abilities. General Intellectual Ability is intended to represent the common ability underlying all intellectual performance. A Brief Intellectual Ability score is also available for screening purposes.

The primary interpretive scores on the WJ-III-COG are based on the broad cognitive clusters. Examiners are urged to note significant score differences among the tests comprising each broad ability to learn how the narrow abilities contribute. The broad and narrow abilities measured by the WJ-III-COG are presented in Table 15.3.

The standard WJ-III-COG subtests shown in Table 15.3 can be combined to create additional clusters: Verbal Ability, Thinking Ability, Cognitive Efficiency, Phonemic Awareness, and Working Memory. If the supplemental subtests are also administered, additional clusters can be created: Broad Attention, Cognitive Fluency, and Executive Processes.

Comprehension–Knowledge (Gc). Assesses a person's acquired knowledge, the ability to communicate one's knowledge (especially verbally), and the ability to reason using two subtests: *Verbal Comprehension* (measuring lexical knowledge and language development) and *General Information*.

Long-Term Retrieval (Glr). Assesses a person's ability to retrieve information from memory fluently. Two subtests are included: *Visual–Auditory Learning* (measuring associative memory) and *Retrieval Fluency* (measuring ideational fluency).

Visual–Spatial Thinking (Gv). Assesses a person's ability to think with visual patterns with two subtests: *Spatial Relations* (measuring visualization) and *Picture Recognition* (a visual memory task).

Auditory Processing (Ga). Assesses a person's ability to analyze, synthesize, and discriminate speech and other auditory stimuli with two subtests: *Sound Blending* and *Auditory Attention* (measuring one's understanding of distorted or masked speech).

Fluid Reasoning (Gf). Assesses a person's ability to reason and solve problems using unfamiliar information or novel procedures. The *Gf* cluster includes two subtests: *Concept Formation* (assessing induction) and *Analysis–Synthesis* (assessing sequential reasoning).

Processing Speed (Gs). Assesses a person's ability to perform automatic cognitive tasks. Two subtests are included: *Visual Matching* (a measure of perceptual

TABLE 15.3 Broad and Narrow Abilities Measured by the WJ-III Tests of Cognitive Abilities

Broad CHC Factor	WJ-III Tests of Cognitive Abilities: Standard Battery Test	Primary Narrow Abilities Measured	Extended Battery Test	Primary Narrow Abilities Measured
Comprehension–Knowledge (Gc)	Test 1:	Verbal Comprehension *Lexical knowledge Language development*	Test 11:	General Information *General (verbal) information*
Long-Term Retrieval (Glr)	Test 2:	Visual–Auditory Learning *Associative memory*	Test 12:	Retrieval Fluency *Ideational fluency*
	Test 10:	Visual–Auditory Learning–Delayed *Associative memory*		
Visual–Spatial Thinking (Gv)	Test 3:	Spatial Relations *Visualization Spatial relations*	Test 13:	Picture Recognition *Visual memory*
			Test 19:	Planning *Deductive reasoning* *Spatial scanning*
Auditory Processing (Ga)	Test 4:	Sound Blending *Phonetic coding: synthesis*	Test 14:	Auditory Attention *Speech–sound discrimination* *Resistance to auditory stimulus distortion*
	Test 8:	Incomplete Words *Phonetic coding: analysis*		
Fluid Reasoning (Gf)	Test 5:	Concept Formation *Induction*	Test 15:	Analysis–Synthesis *Sequential reasoning*
			Test 19:	Planning *Deductive reasoning* *Spatial scanning*
Processing Speed (Gs)	Test 6:	Visual Matching *Perceptual speed*	Test 16:	Decision Speed *Semantic processing speed*
			Test 18:	Rapid Picture Naming *Naming facility*
			Test 20:	Pair Cancellation *Attention and concentration*
Short-Term Memory (Gsm)	Test 7:	Numbers Reversed *Working memory*	Test 17:	Memory for Words *Memory span*
	Test 9:	Auditory Working Memory *Working memory*		

SOURCE: Copyright © 2007 by The Riverside Publishing Company. Table 2.2 "Broad and Narrow Abilities Measured by the WJ-III Tests of Cognitive Abilities" from the Woodcock-Johnson® III Normative Update (WJ III® NU) reproduced with permission of the publisher.

speed) and *Decision Speed* (a measure of semantic processing speed).

Short-Term Memory (Gsm). Is assessed by two subtests: *Numbers Reversed* and *Memory for Words.*

WJ-III Tests of Achievement

Several new subtests have been added to the WJ-III-ACH. As shown in Table 15.4, the WJ-III-ACH now contains 22 tests that can be combined to

TABLE 15.4 Broad and Narrow Abilities Measured by the WJ-III Tests of Achievement

	WJ-III Tests of Achievement			
Broad CHC Factor	**Standard Battery Test**		**Extended Battery Test**	
	Primary Narrow Abilities Measured		*Primary Narrow Abilities Measured*	
Reading–Writing (Grw)	Test 1:	Letter–Word Identification *Reading decoding*	Test 13:	Word Attack *Reading decoding* *Phonetic coding: analysis and synthesis*
	Test 2:	Reading Fluency *Reading speed*	Test 17:	Reading Vocabulary *Language development/ comprehension*
	Test 9:	Passage Comprehension *Reading comprehension* *Lexical knowledge*	Test 16	Editing *Language development* *English usage*
	Test 7:	Spelling *Spelling*	Test 22:	Punctuation and Capitalization *English usage*
	Test 8:	Writing Fluency *Writing ability*		
	Test 11:	Writing Samples *Writing ability*		
Mathematics (Gq)	Test 5:	Calculation *Mathematics achievement*	Test 18:	Quantitative Concepts *Knowledge of mathematics* *Quantitative reasoning*
	Test 6:	Math Fluency *Mathematics achievement* *Numerical facility*		
	Test 10:	Applied Problems *Quantitative reasoning* *Mathematics achievement* *Knowledge of mathematics*		
Comprehension Knowledge (Gc)	Test 3:	Story Recall *Language development* *Listening ability*	Test 14:	Picture Vocabulary *Language development* *Lexical knowledge*
	Test 4:	Understanding Directions *Listening ability Language development*	Test 15:	Oral Comprehension *Listening ability*
			Test 19:	Academic Knowledge *General information* *Science information* *Cultural information* *Geography achievement*
Auditory Processing (Ga)			Test 13:	Word Attack *Reading decoding* *Phonetic coding: analysis and synthesis*
			Test 20:	Spelling of Sounds *Spelling* *Phonetic coding: analysis*
			Test 21:	Sound Awareness *Phonetic coding: analysis Phonetic coding: synthesis*
Long-Term Retrieval (Glr)	Test 12:	Story Recall–Delayed *Meaningful memory*		

SOURCE: Copyright © 2007 by The Riverside Publishing Company. Table 2.2 "Broad and Narrow Abilities Measured by the WJ-III Tests of Cognitive Abilities" from the Woodcock-Johnson® III Normative Update (WJ III® NU) reproduced with permission of the publisher. All rights reserved.

form several clusters. The subtests and clusters from the standard battery can be combined to form scores for broad areas in reading, mathematics, and writing.

The Oral Expression. Cluster assesses linguistic competency and semantic expression with two subtests: *Story Recall* (measuring listening skills) and *Picture Vocabulary.*

The Listening Comprehension. Cluster assesses listening comprehension with two subtests: *Understanding Directions* and *Oral Comprehension.*

The Basic Reading Skills. Cluster assesses sight vocabulary and phonological awareness with two subtests: *Letter–Word Identification* and *Word Attack* (measuring one's skill in applying phonic and structural analysis skills to nonwords).

The Reading Comprehension. Cluster assesses reading comprehension and reasoning with two subtests: *Passage Comprehension* and *Reading Vocabulary.*

The Phoneme/Grapheme Knowledge. Cluster assesses knowledge of sound/symbol relationships.

The Math Calculation. Skills cluster assesses computational skills and automaticity with basic math facts using two subtests: *Calculation* and *Math Fluency.*

The Math Reasoning. Cluster assesses mathematical problem solving and vocabulary with two subtests: *Applied Problems* (measuring skill in solving word problems) and *Quantitative Concepts* (measuring mathematical knowledge and reasoning).

The Written Expression. Cluster assesses writing skills and fluency with two subtests: *Writing Samples* and *Writing Fluency.*

Scores

The WJ-III NU must be scored by a computer program—a change that eliminates complex hand-scoring procedures. Age norms (age 2 to 90+ years) and grade norms (from kindergarten to first-year graduate school) are included. Although WJ-III age and grade equivalents are not extrapolated, they still imply a false standard and promote typological thinking. (See Chapter 3 for a discussion of these issues.) A variety of other derived scores are also available: percentile ranks, standard scores, and Relative Proficiency Indexes. Scores can also be reported in 68 percent, 90 percent, or 95 percent confidence bands around the standard score. Discrepancy scores (predicted differences) are also available. Finally, each Test Record contains a seven-category Test Session Observation Checklist to rate a student's conversational proficiency, cooperation, activity, attention and concentration, self-confidence, care in responding, and response to difficult tasks.

Norms

WJ-III NU calculations are based on the performances of 8,782 individuals living in more than 100 geographically and economically diverse communities in the United States. Individuals were randomly selected within a stratified sampling design that controlled for 10 specific community and individual variables. The preschool sample includes 1,153 children from 2 to 5 years of age (not enrolled in kindergarten). The K–12 sample is composed of 4,740 students. The college/university sample is based on 1,162 students. The adult sample includes 2,889 individuals. An oversampling plan was employed to ensure that the resultant norms would match, as closely as possible, the statistics from the U.S. Department of Commerce, Bureau of the Census.

Reliability

The *WJ-III Normative Update Technical Manual* contains extensive information on the reliability of the WJ-III. The precision of each test and cluster score is reported in terms of the SEM. SEMs are provided for the *W* and standard scores at each age level. The precision with which relative standing in a group can be indicated (rather than the precision of the underlying scores) is reported for each test and cluster by the reliability coefficient. Odd–even correlations, corrected by the Spearman–Brown formulas, were used to estimate reliability for each untimed test.

Some human traits are more stable than others; consequently, some WJ-III tests that precisely measure important, but less stable, human traits show reliabilities in the .80s. However, in the WJ-III, individual tests are combined to provide clusters for educational decision making. Although cluster reliabilities for some age groups are less than .90, all median reliabilities (across age groups) for the standard broad cognitive and achievement clusters exceed .90.

Validity

Careful item selection is consistent with claims for the content validity of both the Tests of Cognitive Ability and the Tests of Achievement. All items retained had to fit the Rasch measurement model as well as other criteria, including bias and sensitivity.

The evidence for validity based on internal structure comes from studies using a broad age range of individuals.

Factor-analytic studies support the presence of seven CHC factors of cognitive ability and several domains of academic achievement. To augment evidence of validity based on internal structure, the authors examined the intercorrelations among tests within each battery. As expected, tests assessing the same broad cognitive ability or achievement area usually correlated more highly with each other than with tests assessing different cognitive abilities or areas of achievement.

For the Tests of Cognitive Ability, evidence of validity based on relations with other measures is provided. Scores were compared with performances on other intellectual measures appropriate for individuals at the ages tested. The criterion measures included the WISC-III, the Differential Ability Scale, the Universal Nonverbal Intelligence Test, and the Leiter International Performance Scale–Revised. The correlations between the WJ-III General Intellectual Ability score and the WISC-III Full-Scale IQ range from .69 to .73.

For the Tests of Achievement, scores were compared with other appropriate achievement measures (for example, the Wechsler Individual Achievement Tests, Kaufman Tests of Educational Achievement, and Wide Range Achievement Test–III). The pattern and magnitude of correlations suggest that the WJ-III-ACH is measuring skills similar to those measured by other achievement tests.

Summary

The WJ-III NU consists of two batteries—the WJ-III Tests of Cognitive Abilities and the WJ-III Tests of Achievement. These batteries provide a comprehensive system for measuring general intellectual ability, specific cognitive abilities, scholastic aptitude, oral language, and achievement over a broad age range. There are 20 cognitive tests and 22 achievement tests. A variety of scores are available for the tests and are combined to form clusters for interpretive purposes. A wide variety of derived scores are available. The WJ-III NU's norms, reliability, and validity appear adequate.

Peabody Picture Vocabulary Test–Fourth Edition (PPVT-4)

The Peabody Picture Vocabulary Test–4 (PPVT-4; Dunn & Dunn, 2007) is an individually administered, norm-referenced, nontimed test assessing the receptive (hearing) vocabulary of children and adults. The authors identify additional uses for the test results: "It is useful (perhaps as part of a broader assessment) when evaluating language competence, selecting the level and content of instruction, and measuring learning. In individuals whose primary language is English, vocabulary correlates highly with general verbal ability" (Dunn & Dunn, 2007, p. 1). The assessment of vocabulary can also be useful when evaluating the effects of injury or disease and is a key component of reading comprehension.

The PPVT-4 is a revised version of the PPVT, PPVT-R, and PPVT III, which were written and revised in 1959, 1981 and 1997, respectively. The new version contains many of the features of its predecessors, such as individual administration, efficient scoring, and the fact that it is untimed. The test continues to offer two parallel forms, broad samples of stimulus words, and it can be used to assess a wide range of examinees. The PPVT-4 has a streamlined administration and contains larger, full-color pictures; new stimulus words; expanded interpretive options to analyze items by parts of speech; a new growth scale value scale for measuring change; and a report to parents and letter to parents (available in Spanish and English). Other conveniences include a carrying tote and optional computerized scoring.

The PPVT-4 is administered using an easel. The examinee is shown a series of plates, each containing a set of four colored pictures. The examiner states a word and the examinee selects the picture that best represents the stimulus word. The PPVT-4 is an untimed power test, usually finished in 20 minutes or less. It consists of stimuli sets of 12 and examinees are tested at their ability or age level; therefore, test items that are either too difficult or too easy are not administered. The authors provide recommended starting points by age.

Scores

Examinees earn a raw score based on the number of pictures correctly identified between basal and ceiling items. A basal is defined as the lowest set administered that contains one or no errors. A ceiling is defined as the highest set administered that contains eight or more error responses. Once a ceiling is established, testing is discontinued. The raw score is determined by subtracting the total number of errors from the ceiling item. The PPVT-4 has two types of normative scores: deviation (standard scores, percentiles, normal curve equivalents, and stanines) and developmental (age equivalent and grade equivalent). The test also produces a nonnormative score called a growth scale value that measures change in PPVT-4 performance over time. It is a nonnormative score because it does not involve comparison with a norm group.

Norms

Two national tryouts were conducted in 2004 and 2005 to determine stimulus items for the test. Both classical and Rasch item analysis methods were applied to determine item difficulty, discrimination, bias, distracter performance, reliability, and the range of raw score by age. Some items from the previous versions of the PPVT were maintained in the development of the PPVT-4. The PPVT-4 contains two parallel forms with a total of 456 items, 340 of which were adapted from the third edition and 116 were created for this edition.

The PPVT-4 was standardized on a representative national sample of 3,540 people ages 2 years 6 months to 90 years or older (for age norms) and a subsample of 2,003 individuals from kindergarten through grade 12 (for grade norms). The goal was to have approximately 100 to 200 cases in each age group, with the exception of the oldest two age groups, for which the target was 60. Due to rapid vocabulary growth in young children, the samples were divided into 6-month age intervals at ages 2 years 6 months through 6 years. Whole-year intervals were used for ages 7 through 14 years. The adult age groups use multiyear age intervals. The manual includes a table showing the number of individuals at each age level included in the standardization.

The standardization sample for the PPVT-4 was composed of more than 450 examiners tested at 320 sites in four geographical areas of the United States. Background information, including birth date, sex, race/ethnicity, number of years of education completed, school enrollment status, special education status, and English language proficiency, was gathered either from the examinee (those older than 18 years) or from parents for children 17 years old or younger. All potential examinee information was entered, a stratified random sampling was made from the pool, and testing assignments for each site were determined. More cases were collected than planned, allowing the opportunity to choose final age and grade samples that closely matched the U.S. population characteristics. The test appears to adequately represent the population at each age and grade level.

Reliability

There are multiple kinds of reliability reported for the PPVT-4. The manual contains detailed information on reliability data. The PPVT-4 reports split-half reliability and coefficient alpha as indicators of internal consistency reliability; also included are alternate-form reliability and test–retest reliability. The split-half reliabilities average .94 or .95 for each form across the entire age and grade ranges. Coefficient alpha is also consistently high across all ages and grades, averaging .97 for Form A and .96 for Form B. During the standardization, a total of 508

Dilemmas *in* Current Practice

The practice of assessing children's intelligence is currently marked by controversy. Intelligence tests simply assess samples of behavior, and different intelligence tests sample different behaviors. For that reason, it is wrong to speak of a person's IQ. Instead, we can refer only to a person's IQ on a specific test. An IQ on the Stanford–Binet Intelligence Scale is not derived from the same samples of behavior as an IQ on any other intelligence test. Because the behavior samples are different for different tests, educators and others must always ask, "IQ on what test?"

This should also be considered when interpreting factor scores for different intelligence tests. Just as the measurement of overall intelligence varies across tests, factor structures and the behaviors that comprise factors differ across tests. Although authors of intelligence tests may include similar factor names, these factors may represent different behaviors across different tests. It is helpful to understand that, for the most part, the particular kinds of items and subtests found on an intelligence test are a matter of the way in which a test author defines intelligence and thinks about the kinds of behaviors that represent it.

When interpreting intelligence test scores, it is best to avoid making judgments that involve a high level of inference (judgments that suggest that the score represents much more than the specific behaviors sampled). Always remember that these factor, index, and cluster scores represent merely student performance on certain sampled behaviors and that the quality of measurement can be affected by a host of unique student characteristics that need to be taken into consideration.

Interpreting a student's performance on intelligence tests must be done with great caution. First, it is important to note that factor scores tend to be less reliable than total scores because they have fewer items. Second, the same test may make different psychological demands on various test takers, depending on their ages and acculturation. Test results mean different things for different students. It is imperative that we be especially aware of the relationship between a person's acculturation and the acculturation of the norm group with which that person is compared.

We think it is also important to note that many of the behaviors sampled on intelligence tests are more indicative of actual achievement than ability to achieve. For instance, quantitative reasoning (a factor commonly included in intelligence tests) typically involves measuring a student's math knowledge and skill. Students who have had more opportunities to learn and achieve are likely to perform better on intelligence tests than those who have had less exposure to information, even if they both have the same overall potential to learn. Intelligence tests, as they are currently available, are by no means a pure representation of a student's ability to learn.

examinees took both Form A and Form B (most during the same testing session, but some as many as 7 days apart). The alternate-form reliability is very high, falling between .87 and .93 with a mean of .89. The average test–retest correlation, reported on 349 examinees retested with the same form an average of 4 weeks after initial trial, is .93. The information on reliability indicates that the PPVT-4 scores are very precise and users can depend on consistent scores from the PPVT-4.

Validity

The manual discusses in detail validity information. Five studies were conducted comparing the PPVT-4 with the Expressive Vocabulary Test, second edition; the Comprehensive Assessment of Spoken Language; the Clinical Evaluation of Language Fundamentals, fourth edition; the PPVT-III; and the Group Reading Assessment and Diagnostic Evaluation. The PPVT-4 scores correlate highly with those of the previously mentioned assessments. Note that slightly lower correlations were found on assessments that measured broader areas of language than primarily vocabulary.

The authors provide data on how representatives of special populations (speech and language impairment, hearing impairment, specific learning disability, mental retardation, giftedness, emotional/behavioral disturbances, and ADHD) perform in relation to the general population. The results indicate the value of the PPVT-4 in assessing special populations.

Summary

The PPVT-4 is an individually administered, norm-referenced, nontimed test assessing the receptive vocabulary of children and adults. The test is adequately standardized, and there is good evidence for reliability and validity. Data are also included on the testing and performance of students with disabilities.

Chapter Comprehension Questions

Write your answers to each of the following questions and then compare your responses to the text.

1. Explain the possible impact of acculturation on intelligence test performance.
2. Describe four behaviors that are commonly sampled on intelligence tests.
3. Describe the theoretical contributions of three individuals to the development of intelligence tests.
4. Describe four commonly interpreted factors in intelligence testing.
5. What are processing deficits, and what tests are currently being used to assess them?
6. What are three types of intelligence testing, and for what purposes might you use each of them?
7. Compare and contrast three commonly used tests of intelligence.

Web Activities 

1. The Test of Non-Verbal Intelligence-4 (TONI 4) and the Comprehensive Test of Non-Verbal Intelligence (CTONI) are both published by Pro Ed, Inc. Go to the Education CourseMate website for this text and read the reviews of the two tests. Describe similarities and differences in behaviors sampled, reliability and validity of the two measures.
2. Go to the Education CourseMate website for this text and review the Leiter International Performance Scale. How might this device be used to assess the intelligence of students with disabilities? What kinds of students would it be useful for?
3. The following table of actual scores on intelligence tests is taken from a text by Kaufman (2009). It shows the scores pupils (pseudonyms used) earned on three different intelligence tests. What possible alternative explanations are there for the reported differences in scores?

Pupil	KABC II	WISC III	WJ III
Asher	90	95	111
Brianna	125	110	105
Colin	100	103	91
Danica	116	127	118
Elpha	93	105	93
Fritz	106	105	105
Georgi	95	100	90
Hector	112	113	103
Imelda	104	96	97
Jose	101	96	86
Keoku	81	78	75
Leo	116	124	102

Web Resources

Intelligent Intelligence Testing

www.apa.org/monitor/feb03/intelligent.aspx

A discussion of how psychologists are broadening the concept of intelligence and how to test it.

Additional resources for this chapter can be found on the Education CourseMate website. Go to CengageBrain.com to access the site.

Using Measures of Perceptual and Perceptual–Motor Skills

CHAPTER GOALS

1 Identify three reasons why educational personnel assess perceptual–motor skills.

2 Identify two technical difficulties in using perceptual–motor tests.

KEY TERMS

perception

perceptual–motor skills

visual discrimination

visual–motor integration

process deficits

BVMGT-2

Koppitz-2

Beery-Buktenica Developmental Test of Visual-Motor Integration (Beery VMI)

SCENARIO *in* ASSESSMENT

KENNETH | Kenneth is an 8-year-old second grader with noticeable motor impairments and considerable difficulty in acquiring basic reading skills. At age 6, his teacher referred him for a psychological evaluation, and the individualized educational program (IEP) team identified him as a student with development disabilities in visual–motor development and early reading skills. The IEP team thought that it would be better to work on development of skills that were believed to underlie reading difficulties before engaging in intensive reading instruction. The team recommended an adaptive physical education program and visual–motor services in a special education resource room. The resource teacher worked with Kenneth on tracing patterns, reproduction of designs, rhythm tapping, tracing paths through mazes, and figural discrimination and generalization skills (finding which of several shapes differed from the others and finding shapes that were alike). In adaptive physical education, the focus was on balance (balancing on his toes and walking on a balance beam) and locomotor skills such as jumping in place with both feet together, hopping, skipping, marching in place, and swinging his arms when walking. Kenneth also participated in "object control" activities, such as throwing a softball underhand, dribbling a basketball, and catching a softball.

For all of first grade, Kenneth participated in the perceptual and motor training. The IEP team met to draft an IEP for the second grade. The team noted Kenneth was better in directionality, rhythm, and throwing; his printing and fine motor skills had shown good improvement. He still had difficulty in balance and tasks requiring alternating left-to-right movements. He had made little progress in reading. Kenneth's special education teacher questioned if the time spent focusing on development of visual and motor skills might better have been spent teaching him to read.

What implications about your own professional role can you draw from this scenario? Go to the Education CourseMate website for this textbook for more reflection questions about this Scenario in Assessment.

Perception is the process of acquiring, interpreting, and organizing sensory information. Experience, learning, cognitive ability, and personality all influence how one interprets and organizes that sensory information. Perceptual–motor skills refer to the production of motor behavior that is dependent on sensory information.

Educators and psychologists recognize that adequate perception and perceptual–motor skills are important in and of themselves. Thus, perception and perceptual–motor tasks are regularly incorporated in tests of intelligence. For example, the Perceptual Organization portion of the Wechsler Intelligence Scale for Children–IV requires visual discrimination, attention to visual detail, sequencing, spatial and nonverbal problem solving, part-to-whole relationships, visual motor coordination, and concentration. Many perceptual and perceptual–motor skills (especially those involving vision, audition, and proprioception) are necessary for school success. For example, the ability to coordinate visual information with motor performance is essential in writing and drawing.

Psychologists have long been interested in perceptual distortions and perceptual–motor difficulties for at least two reasons. First, various groups of individuals with disabilities demonstrate distorted perceptions. Some individuals with diagnosed psychoses show distortions in visual, auditory, and olfactory perceptions. Many individuals known to have sustained brain damage have great difficulty writing and copying, regularly reverse letters and other symbols, have distortions in figure-ground perception, and show deficits in attention and focus. Moreover, some educators and psychologists believe that learning and behavior invariably build on and evolve out of early perceptual–motor integration, and any failures in early learning will adversely affect later learning. Thus, some professionals in the 1960s and 1980s sought to remediate learning disabilities by first remediating perceptual–motor problems (Barsch, 1966; Doman et al., 1967; Kephart, 1971), visual–perceptual problems (Frostig, 1968), psycholinguistic problems (Kirk & Kirk, 1971), or sensory integration (Johnson & Myklebust, 1967; Ayers, 1981). Although many of these approaches were recognized as lacking merit (see, for example, Ysseldyke & Salvia, 1974) and have subsequently been abandoned because of a lack of evidence of their efficacy, some (such as sensory integration) persist today. Recently, professional interest in process deficits and learning disabilities has increased and has resulted in much better assessment procedures.

1 Why Do We Assess Perceptual–Motor Skills?

Perceptual and perceptual–motor skills are assessed for four reasons. In the schools, these tests are used to screen students who may need instruction to remediate or ameliorate visual or auditory perceptual problems before they interfere with school learning. Second, they are used to assess perceptual and perceptual–motor problems in students who are already experiencing school learning problems. If such students also demonstrate poor perceptual–motor performance, they may also receive special instruction aimed at improving their perceptual abilities. Third, perceptual–motor tests are often used in assessments to determine a student's eligibility for special education. Students thought to be learning disabled are often given these tests to ascertain whether perceptual problems coexist with learning problems. Moreover, in some states, there is a specific category of "perceptually handicapped"; tests of perceptual–motor skills would likely be used in eligibility decisions for this category. Finally, perceptual–motor tests are often used by clinical psychologists as an adjunct in the diagnosis of brain injury or emotional disturbance.

SPECIFIC TESTS OF PERCEPTUAL AND PERCEPTUAL–MOTOR SKILLS

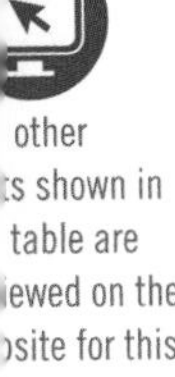
other ...s shown in ... table are ...ewed on the ...site for this ...

In Table 16.1, we provide a list of commonly used perceptual and perceptual–motor tests. In the sections that follow, we review the Bender Family of Tests with the Koppitz scoring system, and the Beery-Buktenica Developmental Test of Visual–Motor Integration (Beery VMI).

The Bender Visual–Motor Gestalt Test Family

Among the perceptual–motor tests used in schools are two tests that are derived from early work begun on assessment of visual–motor skills by Lauretta Bender in 1938. Bender built a test, the Bender Visual–Motor Gestalt Test (BVMGT), consisting of nine geometric designs (for example, a circle) that examinees were asked to copy. The examinees' reproductions of the designs were scored for accuracy. In 1963, Elizabeth Koppitz developed a 30-item method of scoring the BVMGT, scoring each design on as many as four criteria. The Koppitz developmental Bender scoring system was widely used in school and clinical settings between the mid-1960s and the early 2000s. In 2003, Brannigan and Decker revised the original BVMGT to produce the BVMGT-2, adding seven new designs and using a holistic scoring system (described in detail later) to score examinees' reproductions of the designs. In 2007, Reynolds obtained rights to the original Koppitz developmental scoring system, used the system to score the 16 designs that are a part of the BVMGT-2, and produced the Koppitz Developmental Scoring System for the Bender Gestalt Test, second edition (Koppitz-2). In the following sections, we review the BVMGT-2 and the Koppitz-2.

Bender Visual–Motor Gestalt Test, Second Edition

The second edition of the Bender Visual Motor Gestalt Test (BVMGT-2; Brannigan & Decker, 2003) is a norm-referenced, individually administered test intended to assess the visual–motor integration skills of individuals ages 4 years to 85 years. The BVMGT-2 consists of a copying test and three supplementary subtests. The copying test requires test takers to reproduce designs presented individually on stimulus cards that remain in view. There are two sets of designs, with 13 designs for children younger than 8 years of age and 12 designs for test takers 8 years of age or older. The two sets have eight designs that are common to both sets. The test is untimed. The three supplementary tests are a design recall subtest, a motor subtest, and a perception subtest.

Recalling Designs. After the designs and the stimulus materials have been copied and removed from sight, test takers are asked to draw as many of the designs as they can remember. The subtest is untimed.

Motor Test. This test consists of four test items, and each item contains three figures. Test takers are required to connect dots in each figure without lifting their pencil, erasing, or tilting their paper. Four minutes are allowed to complete the subtest.

Perception Test. This test consists of 10 items that require a test taker to match a design in a multiple-choice

TABLE 16.1 Common Perceptual and Perceptual–Motor Tests

Test	Author	Publisher	Year	Ages	Administration	NRT/SRT/CRT	Subtests
Developmental Test of Visual Perception, 2nd Edition	Hammill, Pearson, & Voress	Pearson	1993	4 to 10 years	Individual	NRT	Eye–Hand Coordination, Position in Space, Copying, Figure-Ground, Spatial Relations, Visual Closure, Visual–Motor Speed, Form Constancy
Bender Visual Motor Gestalt Test–2	Brannigan & Decker	Pearson	2003	4 to 85 years	Individual	NRT	Copying Designs, Recalling Designs, Motor Test, Perception Test
Koppitz-2 Scoring System	Reynolds	Pro-Ed	2007	4 to 85 years	Individual	NRT	
Developmental Test of Visual–Motor Integration (Beery VMI)	Beery, Buktenica, & Beery	Pro-Ed	2004	2 years to adult	Individual	NRT	

array to a stimulus design. Four minutes are allowed to complete the task.

Scores

Each copied and recalled design is scored holistically on a 5-point scale: 0 = no resemblance to the stimulus; 1 = slight or vague resemblance to the stimulus; 2 = some or moderate resemblance to the stimulus; 3 = strong or close resemblance to the stimulus; and 4 = nearly perfect. Examples of each score are presented for each design in the test manual. Each figure on the motor subtest and each item on the perception subtest are scored pass or fail. Raw scores from the copying and recall subtests can be converted to standard scores (mean = 100; standard deviation = 15) and percentiles; 90 percent and 95 percent confidence intervals are available for standard scores. Percentiles are available for the motor and perception subtests.

Norms

The normative sample consists of 4,000 individuals ages 4 years to 85 years. Individuals with limited English proficiency, severe sensory or communication deficits, traumatic brain injury, and severe behavioral or emotional disorders were excluded from the normative sample. Students placed in special education for more than 50 percent of the school day were also excluded from the normative sample. Approximately 5 percent of the school-age population was included in regular education classrooms. Thus, the normative sample systematically underrepresents the proportion of students with disabilities, the population with whom the BVMGT-2 is intended to be used. For students of preschool and school age, the norms appear generally representative in terms of race/ethnicity, educational level of parents, and geographical region for each age group.

Reliability

Corrected split-half correlations were used to estimate the internal consistency of the copying test. Of the 14 coefficients for students between 4 and 20 years of age, only 4 were less than .90, and they were in the .80s. Thus, the BVMGT-2 usually has sufficient reliability for use in making important education decisions.

Stability of the copying and recall tests was estimated by test–retest using the standard scores of 213 individuals in four age groups. There were 39 students in the 5- to 7-year-old group and 62 students in the 8- to 17-year-old group. The obtained correlation for the younger group was .77, and the correlation for the older group was .76. Thus, the BVMGT-2 is insufficiently stable to use in making important education decisions.

Interscorer agreement was assessed in two ways. Five experienced scorers scored 30 protocols independently. Correlations among scorers for copied designs ranged from .83 to .94; correlations for recalled designs were adequate, ranging from .94 to .97. The agreement between the scoring of 60 protocols by one experienced and one inexperienced scorer was also examined. The correlation for copied designs was .85, whereas the correlation for recalled designs was .92. Thus, the scoring of copied designs may not consistently have sufficient reliability for use in making important educational decisions on behalf of students.

No reliability data of any kind are presented for the motor or perception subtests.

Validity

Evidence for the internal validity of the copying test of the BVMGT-2 comes from three sources. First, the items were carefully developed to assess the ability to reproduce designs. Second, factor analysis of test items using the normative sample suggests that a single factor underlies copying test performance. Third, copying test performance varies with age in expected ways: It increases sharply at approximately age 7 years and continues to increase, although less rapidly, until approximately age 15 years, when it plateaus until approximately age 40 years, after which it begins to decline. No evidence of content validity is presented for the recall, motor, or perception subtests.

Criterion-related validity was examined by studying the relationship between the BVMGT-2 and the Beery-Buktenica Developmental Test of Visual–Motor Integration (DTVMI) with 75 individuals between the ages of 4 and 17 years. The obtained correlation between the copying score on the BVMGT-2 and the DTVMI was .55, whereas the obtained correlation between the recall score and the DTVMI was .32.

Other studies examined the relationship between copying and recall on the BVMGT-2 and academic achievement. Obtained correlations with the Woodcock–Johnson Psychoeducational Battery, Achievement Battery–III for the copying test ranged from .22 (with Basic Reading) to .43 (with Math Reasoning), and obtained correlations for the recall subtest ranged from .21 (with Basic Reading) to .38 (with Broad Math). Obtained correlations with the Wechsler Individual Achievement Test–II for the copying test ranged from .18 (with Oral Language) to .42 (with Written Language), and the obtained correlations for the recall subtest ranged from .18 (with Written Language) to .32 (with Math). The relationship between performance on this test and academic achievement is very low.

The relationship between BVMGT-2 scores and IQs was also examined. In one study, the Stanford–Binet Intelligence Scale, Fifth Edition, was used as the criterion measure. Obtained correlations for the copying test ranged from .47 with verbal IQ to .51 with nonverbal IQ; obtained correlations for the recall subtest ranged from .44 with verbal IQ to .47 with nonverbal IQ. In another study, copying and recall scores were correlated with IQs from the Wechsler Intelligence Scale for Children–III. Obtained correlations for the copying test ranged from .31 with verbal IQ to .62 with performance IQ; obtained correlations for the recall subtest ranged from .16 with VIQ to .32 with PIQ. A third study with the Wechsler Adult Intelligence Scale–III had similar findings.

Finally, evidence is presented for differential performance by groups of individuals with disabilities. The means of individuals with mental retardation, learning disabilities in reading, learning disabilities in math, learning disabilities in written language, autism, and attention deficit hyperactivity disorder are all significantly lower than those of nondisabled individuals on both the copying and the recall tests. Gifted students earn significantly higher scores on the copying and recall tests.

No evidence of validity is presented for motor or perception subtests.

Summary

The BVMGT-2 is a norm-referenced, individually administered test intended to assess an individual's ability to copy and recall geometric designs as well as to connect dots and perform match-to-sample tasks with such designs. The norms for school-age people appear generally representative, although they exclude some of the very individuals with whom the test is intended to be used. No reliability data of any kind are presented for the motor or perception subtests. The copying test appears generally to have adequate internal consistency, but there is no information about the internal consistency of the recall subtest. The copying and recall tests have poor stability and may have inadequate interscorer agreement. Evidence for the content validity of the copying test is adequate, but the correlations to establish criterion-related validity are too low to be compelling. Although the copying and recall tests of the BVMGT-2 can discriminate groups of individuals known to have disabilities, no evidence is presented regarding these tests' accuracy in categorizing undiagnosed individuals. Reliability and validity evidence for the motor and perception subtests is absent; these subtests should not be used in educational decision making and are of unknown value in clinical situations.

Koppitz-2 Scoring System for the BVMGT-2

The Koppitz developmental scoring system for the BVMGT, developed in 1963, received widespread application in school and clinic settings. Once the BVMGT was revised as the BVMGT-2 and PRO-ED received the rights to the original Koppitz scoring system, it was only a matter of time until the author (Reynolds, 2007) developed the Koppitz-2 as a scoring system for the BVMGT-2.

The Koppitz scoring system is applied to the same 16 cards given for the BVMGT-2. The cards can be obtained as part of the Koppitz-2, or the Koppitz materials may be ordered separately by those who already have the BVMGT-2 stimulus cards. Additional materials included with the Koppitz-2 are two record forms (one for ages 5 to 7 years and the other for individuals older than 8 years), a supplemental emotional indicators record form, a scoring template, and an examiner's manual that includes detailed instructions for scoring.

The Koppitz-2 developmental scoring system has 45 items as opposed to the 30 items that were part of the original Koppitz system. Examinees copy the BVMGT-2 designs and then a standardized set of rules is applied to score their performance. There are as many as five items for each design. The author states that the Koppitz-2 scoring system is designed to document the presence and degree of visual–motor difficulties, identify candidates for referral, assess effectiveness of intervention programs, research, and assist in differential diagnosis of various neuropsychological and psychological conditions.

Scores

Raw scores earned using the Koppitz-2 scoring system are converted to scaled scores with a mean of 100 and a standard deviation of 15. Descriptive ratings of performance (for example, average and below average) are assigned. Scaled scores can be converted to *T* scores, *Z* scores, normal curve equivalents, stanines, and age equivalents. Time to complete the drawings is also recorded. The author states that a short completion time may reflect impulsive responding and problems with impulse control and planning ability.

Norms

The standardization sample for the Koppitz-2 scoring system is identical to that for the BVMGT-2.

Reliability

Data on internal consistency are reported in the manual separately for each age range. Coefficients range from .77 to .91, with all but one coefficient greater than .80. Reliabilities are also shown for subgroups such as racial/ethnic groups and disability groups. Test–retest reliabilities are reported on 202 individuals ages 5 to 85 years, and they range from .75 to .84. The test is reliable for screening purposes but not for diagnostic purposes. Interscorer reliabilities average .91 for ages 5 to 7 years and .93 for those older than 8 years.

Validity

The author presents theory-based, logic-based, and empirically based evidence for the validity of the Koppitz-2 scoring system. The theory-based argument is relatively weak, consisting primarily of the contention that the test is valid because scores increase with age. As empirical evidence for validity of the Koppitz-2 scoring system, the test is compared to measures of intelligence, academic achievement, other visual–motor tests, and clinical and academic status. It is argued that the fact that the application of the scoring system to the BVMGT-2 shows that correlations with verbal measures (average .34) are half what they are with nonverbal measures (.63) is evidence for validity of the scoring system. In describing the relationship of scores earned on the Koppitz-2 system with other perceptual–motor measures, the author reports moderate correlations with an old version of the Beery VMI with only 45 examinees. The author states that demonstration of validity is a work in progress.

Summary

The Koppitz-2 is a revision of a 1963 Koppitz system of scoring, the BVMGT. The Koppitz-2 scoring system is applied to the BVMGT-2 as an alternative way to score that test. There is no comparison of results obtained when the two systems are compared, reliability is adequate for screening purposes, and evidence for validity is very limited.

Beery-Buktenica Developmental Test of Visual–Motor Integration (Beery VMI)

The Beery-Buktenica Developmental Test of Visual–Motor Integration (Beery VMI; Beery, Buktenica, & Beery, 2010) is a set of geometric forms to be copied on paper using a pencil. The authors contend that the set of forms is arranged in a developmental sequence from easy to more difficult. The Beery VMI is designed to assess the extent to which individuals can integrate their visual and motor abilities. The authors state that the primary purpose of the Beery VMI is to "help identify, through early screening, significant difficulties that some children have integrating, or coordinating their visual–perceptual and motor (finger and hand movement) abilities" (p. 9). The authors define visual–motor integration as the degree to which visual perception and finger–hand movements are well coordinated (p. 12). They indicate that if a child performs poorly on the Beery VMI, it could be because he or she has adequate visual–perceptual and motor coordination abilities but has not yet learned to integrate, or coordinate, these two domains. Two supplemental tests, the Beery VMI Visual Perception Test and the Beery VMI Motor Coordination Test, are provided to enable users to attempt to sort out the relative contribution of visual and motor difficulties to poor performance on measures of visual–motor integration.

There are two versions of the Beery VMI. The full Beery VMI is intended for use with individuals from age 2-18 years.. It contains all 30 VMI forms, including the initial 3 that are both imitated and copied directly. The short Beery VMI contains 21 items and is intended for use with children ages 2 to 7 years. Items for the supplemental tests are identical to items for the full VMI. The VMI may be administered individually or to groups. The test can be administered and scored by a classroom teacher and usually takes approximately 15 minutes. Scoring is relatively easy because the designs are scored pass–fail, and individual protocols can be scored in a few minutes.

Scores

The manual for the Beery VMI includes two pages of scoring information for each of the 30 designs. The child's reproduction of each design is scored pass–fail, and criteria for successful performance are clearly articulated. A raw score for the total test is obtained by adding the number of reproductions copied correctly before the test taker has three consecutive failures. Normative tables provided in the manual allow the examiner to convert the total raw score to a developmental age equivalent, grade equivalent, standard score, scaled score, stanine, or percentile.

Norms

The 2010 edition of the Beery VMI is a normative update only. The test has been standardized in the United States five times since its initial development in 1967. The test was originally standardized on 1,030 children in rural, urban, and suburban Illinois. In 1981, the test was cross-validated with samples of children "from various ethnic and income groups in California" (Beery, 1982, p. 10). In 1988, the test was again cross-validated with an unspecified group of students "from several Eastern, Northern and Southern states" (Beery, 1989, p. 10). The 1988 norm sample is not representative of the U.S. population with respect to ethnicity and residence of the students. A normative update of the Beery VMI and its supplemental tests was conducted in 2003 by contacting school psychologists and learning disabilities specialists chosen at random from membership lists of major professional organizations. Those who indicated a willingness to participate tested the subjects. The 2010 normative update was again completed by contacting school psychologists, asking them to participate, and then asking them to provide information about their school composition. School psychologists who agreed to participate provided data on the performance of 1,737 children ages 2 to 18. A table is provided in the manual showing norms distribution based on gender, ethnicity, parent educational level, residence, region, and age. Although the norms collectively were representative of the U.S. population, cross-tabulations are shown only for age by gender, ethnicity, socioeconomic status, and geographic region. Thus, we do not know whether, for example, all the African American students were from middle-socioeconomic status families, from the East, and so on.

Reliability

Nearly all data on reliability of the Beery VMI are on previous editions of the test. The authors indicate that reliability studies conducted previously have produced consistent stable results, so they added only two small new studies. A 14-day test–retest study was completed on an unspecified group of 142 children between 5 and 12 years of age and a reliability coefficient of .88 was obtained. They conducted an interscorer reliability study in which two individuals scored 100 tests. The resultant correlation was .93. The Beery VMI has adequate reliability for screening purposes.

Validity

The authors contend that the Beery VMI has good content validity because of the way in which the items were selected. For the 2010 normative update they provide an IRT analysis and very limited updates regarding content of the test.

They provide evidence for validity based on internal structure by (1) generating a set of hypotheses about what performance on the test would look like if it were measuring what is intended and (2) providing answers to the hypotheses. They show that the abilities measured by the Beery VMI are developmental and that they are related to one another.

Summary

The Beery VMI is designed to assess the integration of visual and motor skills by asking a child to copy geometric designs. As is the case with other such tests, the behavior sampling is limited, although the 30 items on the VMI certainly provide a larger sample of behavior than is provided by the 9 items on the BVMGT. The VMI has relatively high reliability and validity in comparison with other measures of perceptual–motor skills.

Dilemmas *in* Current Practice

The assessment of perceptual–motor skills or visual–motor integration is a difficult undertaking. Without an adequate definition of perceptual and perceptual–motor skills and with few technically adequate tests to rely on, the assessor is in a bind. Usually, the best way to cope with these problems is not to test. If assessments cannot be done properly or are not educationally necessary, they should not be conducted. Assessment of perceptual and perceptual–motor skills usually falls into this category. We encourage those who are concerned about development of these skills to engage in direct systematic observation in the natural environment in which these skills actually occur. After all, when students cannot print legibly, we do not need to know that they have difficulty copying geometric designs.

It is important to realize that when test authors write about perceptual–motor skills, they are talking only about a very small subset of those skills—visual perception and fine hand movements. These tests do not address auditory or proprioceptive perception, and they do not address gross motor skills or fine motor skills other than manual ones. It is also important to recognize that much of the theoretical importance of perceptual–motor assessment is not well founded. First, the specific mechanisms by which perceptual–motor development affects reading are seldom specified and never validated. Thus, theorists may opine that perceptual–motor skills are necessary for reading, but they do not specify what those skills are and how they affect reading. Other than focusing on print material and turning pages, the motor component of reading is unclear. Second, it is based on an incorrect interpretation of the correlation between achievement and perceptual–motor skills. For example, it is well established that poor readers also tend to have poorly developed perceptual–motor skills. However, it is not poor perceptual–motor skills that cause poor reading. Rather, it is poor reading that causes poor perceptual–motor skills. Perceptual–motor skills improve with practice, and learning academics provides that practice. Thus, good readers of material written in English typically develop good left-to-right tracking because they practice tracking from left to right as they read.

The practice of perceptual–motor assessment is linked directly to perceptual–motor training or remediation. There is an appalling lack of empirical evidence to support the claim that specific perceptual–motor training facilitates the acquisition of academic skills or improves the chances of academic success. In fact, major professional associations and insurance companies have taken strong stands against the practice of perceptual–motor assessment and training. Perceptual–motor training will improve perceptual–motor functioning. When the purpose of perceptual–motor assessment is to identify specific important perceptual and motor behaviors that children have not yet mastered, some of the devices reviewed in this chapter may provide useful information; performance on individual items will indicate the extent to which specific skills (for example, walking along a straight line) have been mastered. There is no support for the use of perceptual–motor tests in planning programs designed to facilitate academic learning or to remediate academic difficulties.

See the CourseMate education website for t text for mate published on the Cigna Insurance Company website.

Chapter Comprehension Questions

Write your answers to each of the following questions and then compare your responses to the text.

1. Identify three reasons why educational personnel administer perceptual–motor tests.
2. Identify two technical difficulties in using perceptual–motor tests.
3. Assume that you have to assess a student's perceptual–motor skills. How would you go about doing this in a way that would be appropriate?
4. Homer, age 6-3, takes two visual–perceptual–motor tests, the BVMGT-2 and the DTVMI. On the BVMGT-2, he earns a developmental age of 5-6, and on the DTVMI he earns a developmental age of 7-4. Give two different explanations for the discrepancy between the scores.
5. Performance on the BVMGT–2 is used as a criterion in the differential identification of children as brain injured, perceptually handicapped, or emotionally disturbed. Why must the examiner use caution in interpreting and using test results for these purposes?

Web Activities 

1. Enter "Cigna Statement on Visual–Perceptual Training" in a search engine. Read Cigna's statement on visual perceptual training. What do major medical and psychological professional organizations say about the validity of perceptual motor assessment and training? What are the implications for your practice?

2. Go to the CourseMate website for this book, read the review of the Developmental Test of Visual Perception, and make a table listing the behaviors sampled by that test. Complete the table by listing behaviors sampled by the BVMGT 2 and the Beery VMI. How do the behavior samples differ?
3. Go to the website for your state department of education and then the section on special education. Read the criteria for identifying students as learning disabled. Does your state require demonstration of process disorders? Compare your state's criteria to those at the Minnesota Department of Education website. Why would states require identification of visual perceptual or perceptual motor deficits?

Web Resources

Cigna Statement on Visual–Perceptual Training
http://www.cigna.com/customer_care/healthcare_professional/coverage_positions/medical/mm_0410_coveragepositioncriteria_visual_perceptual_training.pdf
This section of the Cigna Medical Coverage Policy discusses visual perceptual training and explains why visual perceptual training is not covered under Cigna's medical policy.

Additional resources for this chapter can be found on the Education CourseMate website. Go to CengageBrain.com to access the site.

Using Measures of Social and Emotional Behavior

CHAPTER GOALS

1 Know several methods for assessing social–emotional functioning.

2 Know two reasons for assessing social–emotional functioning.

3 Understand the components of a functional behavioral assessment.

4 Be familiar with some commonly used scales for assessing social–emotional functioning.

KEY TERMS

internalizing problems
externalizing problems
acquisition deficit
performance deficit
direct behavior ratings
multiple gating
peer-acceptance nomination scales
sociometric ranking
Systematic Screening for Behavior Disorders
functional behavioral assessment
Behavior Assessment System for Children, Second Edition (BASC-2)

Social and emotional functioning often plays an important role in the development of student academic skills. When students either lack or fail to demonstrate a certain repertoire of expected behavioral, coping, and social skills, their academic learning can be hindered. The reverse is also true: School experiences can impact student social–emotional well-being and related behaviors. To be successful in school, students frequently need to engage in certain positive social behaviors, such as turn taking and responding appropriately to criticism. Other behaviors, such as name calling and uttering self-deprecating remarks, may cause concern and can denote underlying social and emotional problems. In Chapter 6, we noted that teachers, psychologists, and other diagnosticians systematically observe a variety of student behaviors. In this chapter, we discuss additional methods and considerations for the assessment of behaviors variously called social, emotional, and problem behaviors.

The appropriateness of social and emotional behavior is somewhat dependent on societal expectations, which may vary according to the age of a child, the setting in which the behavior occurs, the frequency or duration of the behavior, and the intensity of the behavior. For example, it is not uncommon for preschool students to cry in front of other children when their parents send them off on the first day of school. However, the same behavior would be considered atypical if exhibited by an eleventh grader. It would be even more problematic if the eleventh grader cried every day in front of her peers at school. Some behaviors are of concern even when they occur infrequently, if they are very intense. For example, setting fire to an animal is significant even if it occurs rarely—only every year or so.

Although some social and emotional problems that students experience are clearly apparent, others may be much less easily observed, even though they have a similar negative impact on overall student functioning. Externalizing problems, particularly those that contribute to disruption in classroom routines, are typically quite easily detected. Excessive shouting, hitting or pushing of classmates, and talking back to the teacher are behaviors that are not easily overlooked. Internalizing problems, such as anxiety and depression, are often less readily identified. These problems might be manifested in the form of social isolation, excessive fatigue, or self-destructive behavior. In assessing both externalizing and internalizing problems, it can be helpful to identify both behavioral excesses (for instance, out-of-seat behavior or interrupting) and deficits (such as sharing, positive self-talk, and other coping skills) that can then become targets for intervention.

Sometimes students fail to behave in expected ways because they do not have the requisite coping or social skills; in other cases, students may actually have the necessary skills but fail to demonstrate them under certain conditions. Bandura (1969) points to the importance of distinguishing between such acquisition and performance deficits in the assessment of social behavior. If students never demonstrate certain expected social behaviors, they may need to be instructed how to do so, or it may be necessary for someone to more frequently model the expected behavior for them. If the behavior is expected to be demonstrated across all contexts and is restricted to one or few contexts, there may be discriminative stimuli unique to the few environments that occasion the behavior, or there may be specific contingencies in those environments that increase or at least maintain the behavior. An analysis of associated environmental variables can help determine how best to intervene. When problematic behavior is generalized across a variety of settings, it can be particularly difficult to modify and may have multiple determinants, including biological underpinnings.

1 Ways of Assessing Problem Behavior

Four methods are commonly used, singly or in combination, to gather information about social and emotional functioning: observational procedures, interview techniques, situational measures, and rating scales. Direct observation of social and emotional behavior is often preferred, given that the results using this method are generally quite accurate. However, obtaining useful observational data across multiple settings can be time-consuming, particularly when the behavior is very limited in frequency or duration. Furthermore, internalizing problems can go undetected unless specific questions are posited, given that the associated behaviors may be less readily detected. The use of rating scales and interviews can often allow for more efficient collection of data across multiple settings and informants, which is particularly important in the assessment of social and emotional behavior. Observational procedures were discussed in Chapter 6; the remaining methods are described in the following sections.

INTERVIEW TECHNIQUES

Interviews are most often used by experienced professionals to gain information about the perspectives of various knowledgeable individuals, as well as to gain further insight into a student's overall patterns of thinking and behaving. Martin (1988) maintains that self-reports of "aspirations, anxieties, feelings of self-worth, attributions about the causes of behavior, and attitudes about school are [important] regardless of the theoretical orientation of the psychologist" (p. 230). There are many variations on the interview method—most distinctions are made along a continuum from structured to unstructured or from formal to informal. Regardless of the format, Merrell (1994) suggests that most interviews probe for information in one or more of the following areas of functioning and development: medical/developmental history, social–emotional functioning, educational progress, and community involvement. Increasingly, the family as a unit (or individual family members) is the focus of interviews that seek to identify salient home environment factors that may be having an impact on the student (Broderick, 1993).

SITUATIONAL MEASURES

Situational measures of social–emotional behavior can include nearly any reasonable activity (D. K. Walker, 1973), but two well-known methods are peer-acceptance nomination scales and sociometric ranking techniques. Both types of measures provide an indication of an individual's social status and may help describe the attitude of a particular group (such as the class) toward the target student. Peer nomination techniques require that students identify other students whom they prefer on some set of criteria (such as students they would like to have as study partners). From these measurements, sociograms, pictorial representations of the results, can be created. Overall, sociometric techniques provide a contemporary point of reference for comparisons of a student's status among members of a specified group.

RATING SCALES

There are several types of rating scales; generally a parent, teacher, peer, or "significant other" in a student's environment must rate the extent to which that student demonstrates certain desirable or undesirable behaviors. Raters are often asked to determine the presence or absence of a particular behavior and may be asked to quantify the amount, intensity, or frequency of the behavior. Rating scales are popular because they are easy to administer and useful in providing basic information about a student's level of functioning. They bring structure to an assessment or evaluation and can be used in almost any environment to gather data from almost any source. The important concept to remember is that rating scales provide an index of someone's perception of a student's behavior. Different raters will probably have different perceptions of the same student's behavior and are likely to provide different ratings of the student; each is likely to have different views of acceptable and unacceptable expectations or standards. Chafouleus et al. (2010) suggest that training for raters should occur if results from multiple raters are going to be used for decision making. Self-report is also often a part of rating scale systems. Gresham and Elliott (1990) point out that rating scales are inexact and should be supplemented by other data collection methods.

Just as is the case for academic skills (e.g., reading, math, etc.), assessment of social–emotional behavior occurs at each tier within an educational system, with increasing comprehensiveness and frequency of assessment occurring at higher tiers. One procedure that has been developed to incorporate multiple methods in the assessment of social and emotional behavior, and that resembles a multi-tiered approach to assessment, is multiple gating (Walker & Severson, 1992). This procedure is evident in the Systematic Screening for Behavior Disorders, which involves the systematic screening of all students using brief rating scales. The screening is followed by the use of more extensive rating scales, interviews, and observations for those students who are identified as likely to have social–emotional problems. Multiple gating may help limit the number of undetected problems, as well as target time-consuming assessment methods toward the most severe problems.

2 Why Do We Assess Problem Behavior?

There are two major reasons for assessing problem behavior: (1) identification and classification and (2) intervention. First, some disabilities are defined, in part, by inappropriate behavior. For example, the regulations for implementing the Individuals with Disabilities Education Act (IDEA) describe in general terms the types of inappropriate behavior that are indicative of emotional disturbance and autism. Thus, to classify a pupil as having a disability and in need of special education, educators need to assess social and emotional behavior.

Second, assessment of problem behavior may lead to appropriate intervention. For students whose disabilities are defined by behavior problems, the need for intervention is obvious. However, the development and demonstration of social and coping skills, and the reduction of problem behavior, are worthwhile goals for any student. Both during and after intervention, behaviors are monitored and assessed to learn whether the treatment has been successful and the desired behavior has generalized.

See the CourseMate website for this textbook for a link to the Direct Behavior Ratings website.

Direct behavior rating (DBR) is a method that has become more widely recognized and used for both assessment and intervention in the area of problem behavior. It is also used to facilitate communication about a student's behavioral progress. Chafouleas, Riley-Tillman, and Christ (in press) describe their potential for use within a multi-tiered problem-solving model. The appeal of DBRs is in their simplicity and in their malleability. The overall procedure is as follows: a target behavior and observational time period is selected, an individual (typically the teacher) rates the student or groups of students on the target behavior, and the rating is communicated to someone else (typically the targeted students and parents). Target behavior(s), numbers of students to be rated, frequency of ratings, communication methods, and any associated reinforcement for behavioral improvements are determined in advance, but can be manipulated to address situational needs. For example, a teacher might decide to target an individual student's respectful behavior during transition times (e.g., gym class to class time, recess to class time). At each identified transition time, the student would be given a rating on a scale of 0 to 100 percent for the percent of time the student was showing respectful behavior during the given transition. This information could be communicated to the student as well as sent home to the parents each day.

3 Functional Behavioral Assessment and Analysis

Another assessment strategy that has become more commonly used to address problem behavior is functional behavioral assessment (FBA). An FBA represents a set of assessment procedures used to identify the function of a student's problematic behavior, as well as the various conditions under which it tends to occur. Those who conduct FBAs may use a variety of different assessment methods and tools (for example, interviews, observations, and rating scales), depending on the nature of the student's behavioral difficulties. Once an FBA has been conducted, a behavior intervention plan can be developed that has a high likelihood of reducing the problem behavior. According to IDEA 2004, an FBA must be conducted for any student undergoing special education eligibility evaluation in which problem behavior is of concern. An FBA must also be conducted (or reviewed) following a manifestation determination review[1] in which the associated suspensions from school were determined to be due to the child's disability. FBAs are to be conducted by those who have been appropriately trained.

STEPS FOR COMPLETING A FUNCTIONAL BEHAVIOR ASSESSMENT

Although a variety of different tools and measures might be used to conduct an FBA, certain steps are essential to the process. These include the following:

Defining the behavior. Although a student may display a variety of problematic behaviors, for the purpose of conducting a functional behavioral assessment, it is important to narrow in on just one or two of the most problematic behaviors. For example, although Annie may exhibit a variety of problematic behaviors, including excessive crying, self-mutilation (that is, repeatedly banging her head against her desk until she develops bruises), and noncompliance with teacher directions, a support team may decide to focus on her self-mutilation behavior, given that it is particularly intense and harmful to her body. It is important to define the behavior such that it is observable, measurable, and specific (see Chapter 6 for ways in which behaviors can be measured). A review of records, interviews with teachers and caregivers, and direct observations may help in defining the behavior of concern.

Identifying the conditions under which behavior is manifested. Once the behavior has been carefully defined, it is necessary to identify any patterns associated with occurrences of the behavior. In doing so, it is important to identify the following:

- Antecedents: These represent events that occur immediately before the problem behavior. They may include such things as being asked to complete a particular task, having a particularly disliked person enter the room, or receiving a bad grade.
- Setting events: These represent events that make it such that the student is particularly sensitive to the antecedents and consequences associated with the problem behavior. For example, a setting event might include not having gotten enough sleep the night before school, such that the student is particularly sensitive to a teacher's request for her to finish work quickly and subsequently acts out in response to the teacher's request.
- Consequences: These represent what happens as a result of the behavior. For example, the consequence for a student tearing up a paper that he or she does not want to work on may be that the student does not have to complete the difficult task presented on the paper. Or, if a student hits another student in the arm, the consequence may be that he is sent to the office and his parents are called to pick him up and take him home.

Developing a hypothesis about the function of the behavior. Using information that is collected about antecedents, setting events, and consequences through record review, interview, and observation, one can begin to develop hypotheses about the function of the behavior. In Chapter 6, we described several different functions of behavior, including (1) social attention/communication; (2) access to tangibles or preferred activities; (3) escape, delay, reduction, or avoidance of aversive tasks or activities; (4) escape or avoidance of other individuals; and (5) internal stimulation (Carr, 1994).

[1] A manifestation determination review must be conducted when a student receiving special education services has been the recipient of disciplinary action that constitutes a change of placement for more than 10 days within a school year.

Testing the hypothesized function of the behavior. Although this step is typically considered part of a functional behavioral *analysis* (as opposed to a functional behavioral *assessment*), it is important to verify that your hypothesis about the function of the behavior is correct. Otherwise, the associated intervention plan may not work. By manipulating the antecedents and consequences, one can determine whether the function is correct. For example, if it is assumed that escape from difficult tasks is a function of the student's problematic behavior of tearing up assignments, one could provide tasks that the student finds easy, and enjoys, and examine whether he or she tears up the paper. If not, this would provide evidence that the function of the behavior may be to escape from a difficult task.

Developing a behavioral intervention plan. Although this comes after the actual FBA, it is important to know how to use the assessment data that are collected to

SCENARIO *in* ASSESSMENT

JOSEPH | Joseph was a kindergarten student who, within the first 3 weeks of school, had been sent to the office more than 15 times for his inappropriate behavior, which included hitting and shouting at his peers. Joseph's teacher used a time-out procedure to discipline students in her classroom. Joseph frequently received multiple time-outs in a single morning. The teacher would then decide that he needed to receive a more substantial consequence. This typically included being sent to the principal's office.

After a very brief consultation with one of the school's special education teachers and another kindergarten teacher, Joseph's teacher decided to keep track of the antecedents and consequences associated with his behavior for a few days, using the following recording device. This is what Joseph's teacher recorded:

Antecedents	Behavior	Consequence
Morning large group time, students sitting on the floor while the teacher was pointing to the calendar	Hit the peer sitting next to him in the arm	Reprimanded, sent to the time-out corner
Morning group time, while the teacher was reading a story	Kicked the peer sitting next to him	Reprimanded, sent to the time-out corner
Afternoon group time, while watching a video	Shouted "I hate this; I hate this video!"	Peers laugh, Joseph is reprimanded and sent to the office
Morning group time, when a student was describing the weather	Kicked the peer sitting next to him	Reprimanded, sent to the time-out corner
Morning group time, when the teacher was asking questions about the story that was just read	Hit the peer sitting next to him	Reprimanded, sent to the office

Joseph's teacher brought this information to the other two teachers and sought their guidance. Based on the information, they thought that Joseph's behavior served an attention function. Joseph seemed to get quite a bit of negative attention from his teacher and peers following his behavior; he also likely got some attention from the principal when he was sent to her office. They suggested that Joseph be provided with more attention when he was behaving appropriately; they also suggested developing a very brief signal (rather than using words) to send him to the time-out area when he behaved inappropriately. This way the teacher would not have to verbally reprimand and call attention to his inappropriate behavior.

Unfortunately, this did not seem to help decrease Joseph's behavior. The other teachers suggested that they bring this to the attention of the district behavior consultant. After analyzing the data that had been collected and asking a few questions, the consultant decided to observe Joseph in the classroom environment. She made a couple of interesting observations that were pertinent to the situation: (1) The area where the teacher held group time was very crowded, (2) Joseph tended to engage in the problem behavior toward the end of group times, and (3) he had a very difficult time sitting still during group time. This led her to believe that the function of the behavior was to escape from having to do something he had not yet developed the skill to do (that is, sit and listen for long periods of time). If this was the case, the teacher's consequence of time-out would only serve to reinforce the problem behavior. The consultant suggested developing an intervention that involved initially reducing the length of time spent in group activity and reinforcing Joseph for his good behavior. Once Joseph's good behavior had been established, the teacher told the students that the group activity would be increased by 3 additional minutes. Joseph's good behavior continued to be reinforced. The teacher continued to increase the length of time in group activity each as Joseph's behavior allowed. Using this intervention plan, Joseph's behavioral problems decreased dramatically.

Conclusion: Make sure you appropriately identify the function of a problem behavior; without this, the intervention is not likely to work.

What implications about your own professional role can you draw from this scenario? Go to the Education CourseMate website for this textbook for more reflection questions about this Scenario in Assessment.

inform the development of an intervention plan. Ideally, a behavior intervention plan will involve the following:

- Identifying, teaching, and reinforcing a replacement behavior. As part of the behavior intervention plan, the support team needs to identify a behavior that the student can use to address the identified function in an appropriate manner. For example, if the function of a problematic behavior (such as tearing up work) is escape from a difficult task, the student might be taught how to request a break from the difficult task, such that the same function (escape) would be met when the student engaged in a more appropriate behavior. Although some might initially think that teaching replacement behaviors (that is, to ask for a break and have it granted) results in a lowering of standards, it is important to highlight that having the student ask for a break is certainly more socially appropriate behavior than tearing up an assignment, and it is a step in the right direction. In order to ensure that the student makes use of newly taught replacement behaviors, the intervention plan might include a reward for when the student initially makes appropriate use of the replacement behavior.
- Appropriately addressing setting events, antecedents, and consequences. Behavior intervention plans may include an alteration of the conditions surrounding antecedents and/or a change in consequences. For example, if escape from difficult items presented on a worksheet is the function of a behavior, and the antecedent is presentation of those difficult items, the teacher might set up a task to begin with a few very easy tasks, followed by a medium task, some more easy tasks, and perhaps one difficult task toward the end. If peer attention is the function of a behavior, the teacher might train the entire class how to ignore the target student's problematic behavior.

Once a behavior intervention plan is developed, it is important to also create a method for measuring implementation integrity as well as a monitoring strategy to determine whether the behavioral intervention plan is appropriately addressing the student's problem behavior.

SPECIFIC RATING SCALES OF SOCIAL–EMOTIONAL BEHAVIOR

In Table 17.1, we provide information on several commonly used scales of social–emotional behavior. In the following section, we provide a full review of the Behavior Assessment System for Children, Second Edition.

Full reviews for each of t[he] scales listed [in] the table are provided on [the] website.

TABLE 17.1 Commonly Used Scales for Measuring Social–Emotional Functioning and Problem Behavior

Test	Author	Publisher	Year	Ages/Grades	Individual/ Group	Norm vs. Criterion	Sections or Subscales
		Achenbach System of Empirically Based Assessment (ASEBA)					
Caregiver–Teacher Report Form (C-TRF)/1.5–5	Achenbach & Rescorla	Research Center for Children, Youth, & Families, University of Vermont	2000	Ages 1.5 to 5 years	Individual	Norm	Internalizing (Emotionally Reactive, Anxious/Depressed, Somatic Complaints, Withdrawn), Externalizing (Attention Problems, Aggressive Behavior)
Child Behavior Checklist (CBCL)/1.5–5	Achenbach & Rescorla	Research Center for Children, Youth, & Families, University of Vermont	2000	Ages 1.5 to 5 years	Individual	Norm	Internalizing (Emotionally Reactive, Anxious/Depressed, Somatic Complaints, Withdrawn), Externalizing (Attention Problems, Aggressive Behavior, Sleep Problems)

Test	Author	Publisher	Year	Ages/Grades	Individual/ Group	Norm vs. Criterion	Sections or Subscales
Child Behavior Checklist (CBCL)/6–18	Achenbach & Rescorla	Research Center for Children, Youth, & Families, University of Vermont	2001	Ages 6 to 18 years	Individual	Norm	Activities, Social, School, Internalizing (Anxious/ Depressed, Withdrawn/ Depressed, Somatic Complaints), Externalizing (Rule-Breaking Behavior, Aggressive Behavior, Social Problems, Thought Problems, Attention Problems)
Direct Observation Form (DOF)	Achenbach	Research Center for Children, Youth, & Families, University of Vermont	1986	None specified	Individual	Norm	On Task, Internalizing (Withdrawn/Inattentive, Nervous/Obsessive, Depressed), Externalizing (Hyperactive, Attention Demanding, Aggressive)
Teacher's Report Form (TRF)	Achenbach & Rescorla	Research Center for Children, Youth, & Families, University of Vermont	2001	Ages 6 to 18 years	Individual	Norm	Academic Performance, Working Hard, Behaving Appropriately, Learning, Happy, Internalizing (Anxious/Depressed, Withdrawn/Depressed, Somatic Complaints), Externalizing (Rule-Breaking Behavior, Aggressive Behavior, Social Problems, Thought Problems, Attention Problems)
Youth Self Report (YSF)	Achenbach & Rescorla	Research Center for Children, Youth, & Families, University of Vermont	2001	Ages 11 to 18 years	Individual	Norm	Activities, Social, Internalizing, (Anxious/Depressed, Withdrawn/Depressed, Somatic Complaints), Externalizing (Rule-Breaking Behavior, Aggressive Behavior, Social Problems, Thought Problems, Attention Problems)
				Other Measures			
Asperger Syndrome Diagnostic Scale (ASDS)	Myles, Bock, & Simpson	Pro-Ed	2001	Ages 5 to 18 years	Individual	Norm	Language, Social Skills, Maladaptive Behavior, Cognition, Sensorimotor Development
Behavioral and Emotional Rating Scale, 2nd Edition (BERS-2)	Epstein	Pro-Ed	2004	Ages 5 to 18 years	Individual	Norm	Interpersonal Strength, Family Involvement, Intrapersonal Strength, School Functioning, Affective Strength, Career Strength

continued on the next page

TABLE 17.1 Commonly Used Scales for Measuring Social–Emotional Functioning and Problem Behavior (*Continued*)

Test	Author	Publisher	Year	Ages/Grades	Individual/ Group	Norm vs. Criterion	Sections or Subscales
Behavior Assessment System for Children, Second Edition (BASC-2)	Reynolds & Kamphaus	Pearson	2004	Ages 2 to 25 years	Individual	Norm	Teacher Rating Scale: Externalizing Problems, Internalizing Problems, School Problems Parent Rating Scale: Externalizing Problems, Internalizing Problems, Activities of Daily Living Self-Report of Personality: Inattention/Hyperactivity, Internalizing Problems, Personal Adjustment, School Problems
Behavior Rating Profile, Second Edition	L. Brown & Hammill	Pro-Ed	1990	Ages 6-5 to 18-5 years	Individual	Norm	Includes three student rating scales (peers, home, school), a parent rating scale, a teacher rating scale, and a sociogram
Early Childhood Behavior Scale (reviewed on website under Chapter 19)	S. B. McCarney	Hawthorne	1992	Ages 36–72 months	Individual	Norm	Academic Progress, Social Relationships, Personal Adjustment
Gilliam Asperger's Disorder Scale (GADS)	Gilliam	Pro-Ed	2001	Ages 3 to 22 years	Individual	Norm	Social Interaction, Restricted Patterns of Behavior, Cognitive Patterns, Pragmatic Skills
Gilliam Autism Rating Scale–2nd edition	Gilliam	Pro-Ed	2006	Ages 3 to 22 years	Individual	Norm	Stereotyped Behaviors, Communication Behaviors, Social Interaction Behaviors
Social Skills Improvement System Rating Scales (SSIS)	Gresham & Elliott	Pearson	2010	Ages 3 to 18 years	Individual	Norm	Social Skills (Communication, Cooperation, Assertion, Responsibility, Empathy, Engagement, Self-Control), Problem Behaviors, (Externalizing, Bullying, Hyperactivity/ Inattention, Internalizing, Autism Spectrum), Academic Competence (Reading Achievement, Math Achievement, Motivation to Learn)
Systematic Screening for Behavior Disorders	H. M. Walker & Severson	Sopris–West	1992	Grades 1–6	Individual	Norm	Adaptive Behavior, Maladaptive Behavior, Academic Engaged Time, Peer Social Behavior
Temperament and Atypical Behavior Scale (TABS)	Neisworth, Bagnato, Salvia, & Hunt	Brookes	1999	Ages 11 to 71 months	Individual	Norm	Detached, Hypersensitive/ Active, Underactive, Dysregulated
Walker–McConnell Scale of Social Competence and School Adjustment, Elementary Version	H. M. Walker & McConnell	Wadsworth	1988	Grades K–6	Individual	Norm	Teacher Preferred Behavior, Peer Preferred Behavior, School Adjustment Behavior

Behavior Assessment System for Children, Second Edition (BASC-2)

The Behavior Assessment System for Children, Second Edition (BASC-2; Reynolds & Kamphaus, 2004) is a "multimethod, multidimensional system used to evaluate the behavior and self-perceptions of children and young adults aged 2 through 25 years" (p. 1). This comprehensive assessment system is designed to assess numerous aspects of an individual's adaptive and maladaptive behavior. The BASC-2 is composed of five main measures of behavior: (1) Teacher Rating Scale (TRS), (2) Parent Rating Scale (PRS), (3) Self-Report of Personality (SRP), (4) Structured Developmental History (SDH), and (5) Student Observation System (SOS). The test authors indicate that the BASC-2 can be used for clinical diagnosis, educational classification, and program evaluation. They indicate that it can facilitate treatment planning and describe how it may be used in forensic evaluation and research, as well as in making manifestation determination decisions.

Behaviors Sampled

The Teacher Rating Scale (TRS) is a comprehensive measure of both adaptive and problem behaviors that children exhibit in school and caregiving settings. Three different forms are available—preschool (2 to 5 years), child (6 to 11 years), and adolescent (12 to 21 years)—with the behavior items specifically tailored for each age range. Teachers, school personnel, or caregivers rate children on a list of behavioral descriptions using a 4-point scale of frequency ("never," "sometimes," "often," or "almost always"). Estimated time to complete the TRS is 10 to 15 minutes. The TRS for preschool is composed of 100 items; the TRS for children, 139 items; and the TRS for adolescents, 139 items. Items consist of ratings of behaviors similar to the following: "Has the flu," "Displays fear in new settings," "Speeds through assignments without careful thought," and "Works well with others."

The Parent Rating Scale (PRS) is a comprehensive measure of a child's adaptive and problem behavior exhibited in community and home settings. The PRS uses the same 4-point rating scale as the TRS. In addition, three forms are provided by age groups, as defined previously. Estimated time to complete this measure is 10 to 20 minutes.

The Self-Report of Personality (SRP) contains short statements that a student is expected to mark as either true or false or to provide a rating ranging from "never" to "almost always." Three forms are available by age/schooling level: child (8 to 11 years), adolescent (12 to 21 years), and young adult/college (for 18- to 25-year-old students in a postsecondary educational setting). Estimated administration time is 20 to 30 minutes. Spanish translations of the PRS and SRP are available.

The Structured Developmental History (SDH) is a broad-based developmental history instrument developed to obtain information on the following areas: social, psychological, developmental, educational, and medical history. The SDH may be used either as an interview format or as a questionnaire. The organization of the SDH may help in conducting interviews and obtaining important historical information that may be beneficial in the diagnostic process.

The Student Observation System (SOS) is an observation tool developed to facilitate diagnosis and monitoring of intervention programs. Both adaptive and maladaptive behaviors are coded during a 15-minute classroom observation. An electronic version of the SOS is available for use on a laptop computer or personal digital assistant.

The SOS is divided into three parts. The first section, the Behavior Key and Checklist, is a list of 65 specific behaviors organized into 13 categories (four categories of positive behavior and nine categories of problem behavior). Following the 15-minute observation, the coder rates the child on the 65 items according to a 3-point frequency gradation ("never observed," "sometimes observed," and "frequently observed"). The rater can separately indicate whether the behavior is disruptive.

The second part, Time Sampling of Behavior, requires the informant to decide whether a behavior is present during a 3-second period following each 30-second interval of the 15-minute observation. Observers place a check mark in separate time columns next to any of the 13 categories of behavior that occur during any one interval. The third section, Teacher's Interaction, is completed following the 15-minute observation. The observer scores the teacher's interactions with the students on three aspects of classroom interactions: (1) teacher position during the observation, (2) teacher techniques to change student behavior, and (3) additional observations that are relevant to the assessment process.

Scores

The BASC-2 can be either hand or computer scored. A hand-scored response form can be used for the first three instruments (TRS, PRS, and SRP). The hand-scored protocols are constructed in a unique format, using pressure-sensitive paper that provides the examiner with an immediate translation of ratings to scores. After administration of the different rating forms, the administrator removes the outer page to reveal a scoring key. Scale and composite scores are totaled easily, and a behavior profile is available to represent the data graphically. Validity scores are tabulated to evaluate the quality of completed forms and to guard against response patterns that may skew the data profiles positively or negatively. Detailed scoring procedures that use a 10-step procedure for each of these scales are described in the administration manual.

Raw scores for each scale are transferred to a summary table for each individual measure. *T*-scores (mean = 50, standard deviation = 10), 90 percent confidence intervals, and percentile ranks are obtained after selecting appropriate norm tables for comparisons. In addition, a high/low column is provided to give the assessor a quick and efficient method for evaluating whether differences among composite scores for the individual are statistically significant.

The TRS produces three composite scores of clinical problems: Externalizing Problems, Internalizing Problems, and School Problems. Externalizing problems include aggression, hyperactivity, and conduct problems. Internalizing problems include anxiety, depression, and somatization. School problems are broken down into attention and learning problems. A broad composite score of overall problem behaviors is provided on the Behavioral Symptoms Index, which includes several of the subscales listed previously in addition to Atypicality and Withdrawal. In addition, positive behaviors are included in an adaptive skills composite; these include the Leadership, Social Skills, Study Skills, Adaptability, and Functional Communication subscales. An optional content scale can also be used, which provides information according to the following subscales: Anger Control, Bullying, Developmental Social Disorders, Emotional Self-Control, Executive Functioning, Negative Emotionality, and Resiliency. The PRS provides the same scoring categories and subscales, with the exception that the School Problems composite scores, composed of subscales for learning problems and study skills, are omitted, and Activities of Daily Living is added.

The SRP produces four composite scores—Inattention/Hyperactivity, Internalizing Problems, Personal Adjustment, and School Problems—and an overall composite score referred to as an Emotion Symptoms Index (ESI). The composite ESI score includes both negative and adaptive scales. Inattention/Hyperactivity includes the Attention Problems and Hyperactivity subscales. The Internalizing Problems composite includes atypicality, locus of control, social stress, anxiety, depression, and sense of inadequacy. Personal Adjustment groupings include relations with parents, interpersonal relations, self-esteem, and self-reliance. The School Problems composite includes attitude to school and attitude to teachers. Additional subscales, including Sensation Seeking, Alcohol Abuse, School Adjustment, and Somatization, are included in the ESI. An optional content scale is also available that includes the following subscales: Anger Control, Ego Strength, Mania, and Test Anxiety.

Three validity scores are provided. To detect either consistently negative bias or consistently positive bias in the responses provided by the student, there is an F index ("fakes bad") and an L index ("fakes good"). The V index incorporates nonsensical items (similar to "Spiderman is a real person"), such that a child who consistently marks these items "true" may be exhibiting poor reading skills, may be uncooperative, or may have poor contact with reality.

The SDH and SOS are not norm-referenced measures and do not provide individual scores of comparison. Rather, these instruments provide additional information about a child, which may be used to describe his or her strengths and weaknesses.

Norms

Standardization and norm development for the general and clinical norms on the TRS, PRS, and SRP took place between August 2002 and May 2004. Data were collected from more than 375 sites. The number of children who received or provided behavioral ratings across the different measures were, for the TRS, N = 4,650; for the PRS, N = 4,800; and for the SRP, N = 3,400. Efforts were made to ensure that the standardization sample was representative of the U.S. population of children ages 2 to 18 years, including exceptional children. The standardization sample was compared with census data for gender, geographic region, socioeconomic status (SES; as measured by mother's education level), placement in special education and gifted/talented programs, and race/ethnicity. Several cross-tabulations are provided (for instance, geographic region by gender by age, race by gender by age, and so forth). Data collected through Spanish versions of the PRS and SRP are included in the standardization sample. The authors present data to support mostly balanced norms; however, the 2- to 3-year-old sample tends to vary somewhat from the characteristics of the population. For instance, 2- to 3-year-old students of low SES (mother's education level) tend to be underrepresented, whereas 2- to 3-year-old students of high SES tend to be overrepresented. The authors claim that children with behavioral–emotional disturbances are represented appropriately at each grade level of each instrument, and the data provided in the manual support this claim.

A separate norm sample was collected for the college level of the SRP. This sample consisted of 706 students ages 18 to 25 years who were attending various postsecondary educational institutions. Information on the degrees sought by participants is presented, along with information on the frequency by age and gender of participants in this standardization sample. No comparisons to the U.S. population are presented. Females appear to be overrepresented in this sample.

Clinical population sample norms consist of data collected on children receiving school or clinical services for emotional, behavioral, or physical problems. Sample sizes were, for the TRS, N = 1,779; for the PRS, N = 1,975; and for the SRP, N = 1,527. The authors state that the clinical sample was not controlled demographically because this subgroup is not a random set of children. For example, significantly more males were included than females.

Reliability

The manual has a chapter devoted to the technical information supporting reliability and validity for each normed scale (TRS, PRS, and SRP). Three types of reliability are provided within the technical manual: internal consistency, test–retest, and interrater agreement.

Internal Consistency. Coefficient alpha reliabilities are provided for the TRS and PRS by gender according to the following six age levels: ages 2 to 3, ages 4 to 5, ages 6 to 7, ages 8 to 11, ages 12 to 14, and ages 15 to 18 years. Median reliabilities for the TRS subscales for these age/gender groups range from .84 to .89. Lower reliabilities are evident for subscales associated with the Internalizing Problems scale (including Anxiety, Depression, and Somatization) than for those associated with the Externalizing Problems scale. Median reliabilities for the PRS subscales range from .80 to .87 across these age/gender groups; reliabilities tend to be lower at the preschool-and-below ages. SRP coefficient alpha reliabilities are provided according to the following age levels: ages 8 to 11, ages 12 to 14, ages 15 to 18, and ages 18 to 25 years. Median subscale reliabilities for the SRP range from .79 to .83. The Sensation Seeking, Somatization, and Self-Reliance subscales tended to be particularly low (<.70) at certain age levels. Internal consistency reliabilities for the composite scales exceeded .80 across all three scales for each age/gender group. Coefficient alphas are also provided for certain disability groups within the clinical sample by gender (such as learning disabilities, ADHD, and all clinical) and for those taking the Spanish version of the SRP and the PRS. Coefficient alpha reliabilities for the clinical groups are similar to those provided for the general norm sample; those for the Spanish version are slightly lower.

Test-Retest Reliability. TRS test–retest reliability was computed by having teachers rate the same child twice, with 8 to 65 days intervening between rating periods; this was done for a total of 240 students. Results are presented by age level (preschool, child, and adolescent) for each subscale and composite. Adjusted reliabilities ranged from .81 to .93 for composites and from .64 to .90 for the subscales. PRS test–retest reliability was determined based on parent ratings of 252 students, with an intervening time period of 9 to 70 days. Adjusted reliabilities for the PRS composites ranged from .78 to .92; those for the subscales ranged from .72 to .88. Test–retest reliabilities for the SRP were based on ratings provided by 279 students, for which there was an intervening time period of 13 to 66 days. Adjusted composite reliabilities ranged from .74 to .93; adjusted subscale reliabilities ranged from .61 to .99.

Interrater Reliability. A total of 170 students were rated according to the TRS by two teachers to determine interrater reliability of the TRS. Adjusted reliabilities ranged from .48 to .81 for the composite scales and from .19 to .82 for the subscales. Parents and caregivers completed the PRS for 134 students, such that two rating scales were completed for each student by different individuals. Adjusted reliabilities for the PRS composite scales ranged from .65 to .86; associated reliabilities for the PRS subscales ranged from .53 to .88. No interrater reliability study was conducted for the SRP, given that the scale is a self-report instrument.

Correlations were calculated across the PRS and the TRS by age level (preschool, child, and adolescent) for students in the standardization samples that had both forms completed (N = 2,324). Correlations for the related composites ranged from .17 to .52 for the preschool forms, from .22 to .50 for the child forms, and from .36 to .51 for the adolescent forms. The internalization composite scale tended to have the lowest correlations across forms. Correlations between the SRP and both the PRS and the TRS are also provided; however, the composites are substantially different for the SRP, making the presence of lower correlations among composites difficult to interpret.

Validity

The authors describe the procedures used to develop and select items for inclusion in the BASC-2. Many of the items included on the BASC-2 are taken directly from the original BASC. In the development of the original items, alternate behavior rating scales and related instruments were examined, and clinicians provided consultation in the selection of items to measure both problem and adaptive behaviors. Students and teachers were also involved in item development. The items went through several cycles of testing via expert and statistical review for inclusion in the original BASC. Several new items were developed for the BASC-2 to replace those with poor technical characteristics. More extensive revisions were conducted for the SRP, in which the item response format was altered from the previous edition, based on results of research studies examining internal consistency and factor loadings across the two formats. Confirmatory factor analysis was used to examine item characteristics to assist with decision making about inclusion in the final instrument. Items that correlated substantially with alternate composite scales that were not intended to be measured with the item, as well as those items that had low factor loadings on the intended composite scale, were eliminated. Analyses of partial correlations and differential item-functioning analyses were conducted to examine whether items were measuring appropriately across various student demographic groups (for instance, females versus males, African Americans versus non-Hispanics, and Hispanics versus non-Hispanics). A total of five items were eliminated based on bias reviews. Both exploratory and confirmatory factor analytic procedures were used to examine the appropriateness of the composite scale structure for the TRS, PRS, and SRP. These analyses supported the three-factor and four-factor child and adolescent composite scores.

Criterion-Related Validity. The TRS was compared with several related behavior rating scales, including various portions of the Achenbach System of Empirically Based Assessment (ASEBA; Achenbach & Rescorla, 2001), the Conners Teacher Rating Scale–Revised (Conners, 1997), and the original BASC TRS. Ratings from the preschool form of the TRS were compared to an associated form of the ASEBA among 46 children ages 2 to 5 years. Fifty-seven children ages 6 to 11 years and 39 adolescents ages 12 to 18 years similarly had corresponding rating forms from the BASC and the ASEBA compared. Correlations for related subscales were primarily in the .60 to .90 range, with the exception of Somatization subscales, which tended to be very weakly correlated across rating scales. Correlations across composite scales were higher; however, Internalizing Problems composites tended to be lower than the other composite scale correlations.

Correlations with the Conners Teacher Rating Scale–Revised were based on teacher ratings for 59 children ages 6 to 11 years and 45 adolescents ages 12 to 18 years. Associated subscale adjusted correlations ranged from .26 (Anxiety scales for adolescents) to .94 (Aggression/Oppositional scales for adolescents). Composite behavior scale correlations (Conners Global Index and the BASC Behavioral Symptoms Index) were .84 at the child level and .69 at the adolescent level. Information is presented on the correlations with ratings from the original BASC for the standardization samples. As expected, the results for the BASC and the BASC-2 were very similar, with correlations exceeding .90 for the majority of composite and subscales.

The PRS was also compared to a variety of similar rating scales, including the following: related forms of the ASEBA, Conners Parent Rating Scale–Revised, the Behavior Rating Inventory of Executive Functioning (Gioia, Isquith, Guy, & Kenworthy, 2000), and the original BASC PRS. The associated parent rating forms for the ASEBA and the BASC-2 were completed for 53 young children, 65 school-age children, and 67 adolescents. Adjusted correlations for associated subscales ranged from .34 to .77; adjusted correlations for associated composites ranged from .67 to .84. Internalizing Problems composites tend to have weaker correlations than Externalizing Problems composites.

Correlations with the Conners Parent Rating Scale were determined based on 60 children ages 6 to 11 years and 55 adolescents ages 12 to 18 years. The Conners Global Index and the BASC-2 Behavioral Symptoms Index correlated .79 at the child level and .65 at the adolescent level. Subscale adjusted correlations ranged from .41 to .84 at the child level and .35 to .64 at the adolescent level. The BASC-2 and the Behavior Rating Inventory of Executive Functioning (Gioia et al., 2000) were administered to 51 children ages 6 to 11 years and 40 adolescents ages 12 to 18 years. Broad composite scores correlated .67 at the child level and .80 at the adolescent level. Finally, correlations with the original BASC PRS were primarily in the .80 to .95 range, as expected.

Criterion-related validity of the SRP was evidenced through correlations with the associated forms of the ASEBA, the Conners–Wells Adolescent Self-Report Scale (Conners, 1997), the Children's Depression Inventory (Kovacs, 1992), and the Revised Children's Manifest Anxiety Scale (Reynolds & Richmond, 2000). The associated scale of the ASEBA was administered concurrently with the SRP among 51 adolescents. Associated composite adjusted correlations were in the .75 to .80 range. All associated subscales of the Conners–Wells Adolescent Self-Report correlated positively (.52 to .67) with the BASC-2 scales among 54 adolescents, with an exception being the negative correlations showing up as expected for the relationship between "family problems" and "relations with parents" across these scales. Finally, the associated scales of the Children's Depression Inventory and the Children's Manifest Anxiety Scale correlated positively with the Depression and Anxiety scales on the BASC-2 SRP. Correlations for a group ($N = 86$) of students in postsecondary settings who took the college level of the SRP and the ASEBA self-report ranged from .38 to .61 for associated composite and subscales.

Evidence for criterion-related validity of the college level of the BASC-2 SRP is also presented using the Brief Symptom Inventory (Derogatis, 1993) and the Minnesota Multiphasic Personality Inventory–2 (Butcher, Graham, BenPorath, Tellegen, Dahlstrom, & Kaemmer, 2001). Correlations of the BASC-2 SRP with the original BASC SRP were lower than corresponding correlations for the TRS and PRS, but they were still positive.

Although there appears to be evidence of validity for using the BASC-2 in making diagnostic decisions, no evidence of validity for the purposes of program evaluation and treatment planning is provided.

Summary

The BASC-2 is a comprehensive instrument that may be used to evaluate the behavior and self-perception of children ages 2 to 25 years. The integrated system comprises five separate measures of behavior: (1) Teacher Rating Scale, (2) Parent Rating Scale, (3) Self-Report of Personality, (4) Structured Developmental History Inventory, and (5) Student Observation Scale. Although the multimethod and multidimensional approach should be commended, the TRS, PRS, and SRP are the only scales for which normative data are provided on which any classification statements can be made. Norms for the BASC are more than adequate, with general and clinical norm data provided. Reliability of the composite scales is good, although the internalizing composites tend to have lower reliability coefficients, along with lower reliability coefficients evident for very young children. The BASC-2, like the ASEBA, provides one of the most comprehensive assessment tools on the market today. Good evidence of reliability and validity is presented via analysis of standardization sample data and correlations with additional behavior rating scales; however, validity evidence is not present for all of the possible uses described by the authors.

Chapter Comprehension Questions

Write your answers to each of the following questions and then compare your responses to the text.

1. What are four methods for assessing social–emotional functioning?
2. Describe two reasons for assessing social–emotional functioning.
3. Describe the steps that you would follow in conducting a functional behavioral assessment.
4. Name and describe one commonly used measure of social–emotional functioning. What evidence of reliability and validity is available for this measure?

Web Activities 

1. Search the Internet for information about how Direct Behavior Rating (DBR) is used to monitor student behavior. Identify one advantage and one disadvantage of this approach when compared to the systematic observational methods discussed in Chapter 6.
2. The Gilliam Asperger's Disorder Scale (GADS) and the Gilliam Autism Rating Scale, 2nd edition (GARS-2) are both commonly used in the diagnosis of students with autism spectrum disorder (ASD). Using the corresponding reviews provided on the textbook website, compare these two scales. What are the similarities and differences with respect to behaviors sampled? What are the similarities and differences with respect to technical adequacy?
3. Search the Internet for the module on Functional Behavioral Assessment (FBA) provided by the IRIS center at Vanderbilt University. Walk through the module and describe what additional things you learned from this module.
4. Considering the test reviews provided at the textbook website, and the assessment tools discussed in this and prior chapters, identify assessment tools that would be used for each of the following purposes, and explain why:

   (a) Monitoring behavioral progress
   (b) Analyzing problem behavior to inform the development of an intervention plan
   (c) Determining if a student has an internalizing disorder

Web Resources

Direct Behavior Ratings
http://www.directbehaviorratings.com/
This website contains training modules and associated materials to assist with the use of direct behavior ratings.

OSEP Technical Assistance Center on Positive Behavioral Interventions and Supports
http://www.pbis.org/
This website provides background information and tools to assist with implementing positive behavior supports, including a training manual on functional behavioral assessment.

Additional resources for this chapter can be found on the Education CourseMate website. Go to CengageBrain.com to access the site.

Web Chapter Preview

18

MIXA next/Jupiterimages Corporation

Using Measures of Adaptive Behavior

CHAPTER GOALS

1 Understand the concept of adaptive behavior, including the role of physical environment, social and cultural expectations, and age in the definition of adaptation.

2 Understand the concept of maladaptive behavior, including the role of the context in which behavior occurs and its frequency and amplitude.

3 Know how we assess adaptive behavior.

4 Be familiar with the second edition of the Vineland Adaptive Behavior Scales.

5 Be familiar with some of the current dilemmas we face in using adaptive behavior measures.

KEY TERMS

adaptive behavior
maladaption
respondent
daily living skills
interrespondent reliability
social skills and relationships
interinterviewer reliability

CHAPTER SUMMARY

The full chapter is available on the Education CourseMate website for this textbook.

Go to cengagebrain.com to access the site and download this chapter.

In the assessment of adaptive behavior, we are interested in what an individual regularly does, not what the individual is capable of doing. Ultimately, the behaviors of interest in adults are those that allow individuals to manage their affairs sufficiently well that they do not require societal intervention to protect them or others. The behaviors that are believed to be important vary from time to time and from theory to theory as a function of the demands of the physical environment as well as social, cultural, and age expectations. In general, in the United States, adults are expected to take reasonable care of themselves (by managing their own health, dressing, eating, and so on), to work, and to engage in socially acceptable recreational or leisure activities. In children and adolescents, the behaviors of interest are of two kinds. We assess behaviors that demonstrate age-appropriate independence and responsibility. We assess those behaviors that are believed to enable the development or acquisition of desired adult behaviors.

The assessment of adaptive behavior usually takes the form of a structured interview with a person (for example, a parent or teacher) who is very familiar with the person being assessed (the subject of the interview). The assessment of adaptive behavior has been plagued by inadequate instruments—scales that lack reliability and are poorly normed. Assessors must select scales (or parts of scales) with great care. We review the Vineland Adaptive Behavior Scales, Second Edition (VABS II).

The reasons we usually assess adaptive behavior (determining the eligibility of students as students with intellectual disability and planning educational programs) are discussed. This is followed by a discussion of the dilemmas in current practice.

Chapter Comprehension Questions

Write your answers to each of the following questions and then compare your responses to the text.

1. How do the physical environment, age, and social and cultural expectations affect the definition of adaptation?
2. How do the context in which behavior occurs and its frequency and amplitude affect the definition of maladaption?
3. Why do we assess adaptive behavior?
4. Explain two potential problems in the assessment of adaptive behavior.

Web Activities 

1. Visit the website for your state's department of education. Find the part of the site that deals with special education. Read the definition of mental retardation or mentally retarded student and adaptive behavior, if there is one. Does your state specify how adaptive behavior is to be assessed? Does your state specify the degree of impairment in adaptive behavior necessary for a student to be identified as mentally retarded?
2. Search the Internet for the definition of intellectual disability at the American Association on Intellectual and Developmental Disabilities (AAIDD) web site. What role does adaptive behavior play in the definition of intellectual disability?

Web Resources

Best Practices in the Assessment of Adaptive Behavior
http://faculty.unlv.edu/sloe/Courses/EPY%20715/Best%20Practices%20in%20Adaptive%20Beh%20Assessment.pdf
This article provides a framework for data-based decision making regarding an individual's functional limitations and service needs.

Adaptive and Maladaptive Behavior Scales
http://www.assessmentpsychology.com/adaptivebehavior.htm
This webpage compares four commonly used measures of adaptive behavior in terms of behaviors sampled, purpose of assessment, standardization, and norming.

Additional resources for this chapter can be found on the Education CourseMate website. Go to CengageBrain.com to access the site.

Web Chapter Preview

19

Using Measures of Infants, Toddlers, and Preschoolers

CHAPTER GOALS

1 Know why we assess infants, toddlers, and preschoolers.

2 Understand the unique challenges associated with measuring development among young children.

3 Understand methods that are commonly used for assessing young children.

4 Be familiar with several commonly used infant, toddler, and preschool measures.

KEY TERMS

developmental milestones

Head Start/Early Head Start

Individual Growth and Developmental Indicators (IGDIs)

Bayley Scales of Infant and Toddler Development, Third Edition (Bayley-III)

Developmental Indicators for the Assessment of Learning–Third Edition (DIAL-3)

CHAPTER SUMMARY

The assessment of young children is quite different from the assessment of older individuals. Infant assessment frequently involves neurobiological appraisal in four areas: neurological integrity (for example, reflexes and postural responses), behavioral organization (for example, attention and response to social stimuli), temperament (for example, consolability and responsivity) and state of consciousness (for example, sleep patterns and attention). Assessment of toddlers and preschoolers frequently involves appraisal of communication, cognition, personal–social behavior, and motor behavior.

The full chapter is available on the Education CourseMate website for this textbook.

Go to cengagebrain.com to access the site and download this chapter.

The evaluation of toddlers and preschoolers generally relies on their attainment of developmental milestones (significant developmental accomplishments), such as using words and walking. Although children's development is quite variable, children usually are considered to be at risk for later problems when their attainment of developmental milestones is delayed. Those who assess young children need a thorough understanding of normal development. We review the Bayley Scales of Infant and Toddler Development, Third Edition (Bayley-III) and the Developmental Indicators for the Assessment of Learning–Third Edition (DIAL-3). We conclude with a discussion of dilemmas in current practice.

Chapter Comprehension Questions

Write your answers to each of the following questions and then compare your responses to the text.

1. Describe four reasons why you might assess infants, toddlers, and preschoolers.
2. What characteristics of young children can make it particularly challenging to assess their skill development?
3. Describe a measure you might use to monitor the progress of a toddler.
4. Describe one commonly used measure for the assessment of infant development. Include information on the reliability and validity of the measure.

Web Activities 

1. Go to the Education CourseMate website and read the review of the DIAL-3. What evidence is there for its validity?
2. Search the Internet to find the LENA Pro Link Go at the website for the Language Environment Assessment. View the demo on LENA Pro. What is a LENA digital language processor, and how is it used? How might this new technology be used in a preschool setting to analyze children's language environments?
3. Find and read about Assessment of Preschool Children on the ERIC website.

Web Resources

Preschool Assessment: A Guide to Developing a Balanced Approach
http://nieer.org/resources/policybriefs/7.pdf
This article, at the National Institute for Early Education Research's website, discusses how to develop a balanced approach for preschool assessment.

Additional resources for this chapter can be found on the Education CourseMate website. Go to CengageBrain.com to access the site.

Web Chapter Preview

20

Lars Christensen/Shutterstock.com

Assessment of Sensory Acuity

CHAPTER GOALS

1 Learn the kinds of visual difficulties that affect students' performance in school.
2 Learn several kinds of visual screening and assessment techniques.
3 Learn the signs that students are experiencing hearing difficulties.
4 Know the various types of auditory screening tests.

KEY TERMS

sensory
visual acuity
functional vision
clinical low vision
Braille Assessment Inventory
sensorineural hearing loss
tympanometry
audiogram
conductive hearing loss
central auditory hearing loss
audiometer
Snellen Wall Chart

CHAPTER SUMMARY

The first thing to check when a child is having academic or social difficulties is whether he or she is adequately and properly receiving environmental information. Vision and hearing difficulties interfere with the educational progress of a significant number of schoolchildren. The teacher's role in the assessment of sensory acuity is twofold. First, the teacher must be aware of behaviors that may indicate sensory difficulties, and thus must have at least cursory knowledge of the kinds of sensory difficulties that children experience. Second, the teacher must know the instructional implications of sensory difficulties. Communication with vision specialists (teachers of students with visual impairments, ophthalmologists, optometrists, and orientation and mobility specialists) and hearing specialists (speech and language pathologists, teachers of students with hearing impairments, audiologists, and otolaryngologists) is the most effective way to gain such information. The teacher must have basic knowledge about the procedures used for

The full chapter is available on the Education CourseMate website for this textbook.

Go to cengagebrain.com to access the site and download this chapter.

assessing sensory acuity in order to comprehend and use data from specialists. This chapter provides basic knowledge about the kinds of vision and hearing difficulties that students experience, as well as an overview of procedures and devices used to assess sensory acuity.

We review basic vision and hearing screening measures in the chapter, differentiating between measures of visual acuity, clinical measures of low vision, functional vision assessment, learning-media assessment, and the Braille Assessment Inventory. In the hearing section of the chapter, we describe signs of hearing loss and types of screening and assessment, including hearing screening, hearing-threshold testing, and tympanometry screening. We differentiate between conductive hearing loss, sensorimeural hearing loss, mixed hearing loss, and central auditory hearing loss.

Chapter Comprehension Questions

Write your answers to each of the following questions and then compare your responses to the text.

1. Identify several characteristics (behaviors) a student might demonstrate that would make you question whether that student is seeing adequately.
2. Identify several characteristics (behaviors) a student might demonstrate that would make you question whether that student is hearing adequately.
3. After a complete visual examination, the doctor reported that "Peter demonstrates 20/20 corrected vision, and his visual field subtends and angular distance of 15 degrees." Glasses were prescribed. Translate the report into nontechnical terms. Will Peter's vsion have any implications for instructional procedures?
4. Theia's hearing test, administered in November, showed a 35 db loss on a pure-tone audiometric sweep in the speech range. In December, she was assessed using the Wechsler Intelligence Scale for Children-III and the Test of Adolescent Language and scored very poorly on subtests requiring auditory reception. In April, the audiologist reported a 10 db loss in the speech range. In July (and following several months of intensive remediation), Theia was reevaluated in the school and performed substantially better on both intelligence measures and tests of oral language. What conclusions can be drawn about Theia's performance?

Web Activities 

1. Contact your local school district and find out what provisions are made for educating students with sensory disorders. What factors determine when the child will be sent to a special school for the blind or deaf?
2. Find "[PPT] No Slide Title—American Printing House for the Blind" on the website for the American Printing House for the Blind. What do they recommend about the use of color in presentations for individuals with visual impairments?
3. Search the Internet for information about colorblindness. Do boys or girls have a higher incidence of colorblindness? Why? What are the instructional implications of a child being colorblind?
4. Search the Internet for the Gallaudet Research Institute. Read the data that researchers gather and analyze about the demographic and academic characteristics of deaf and hard of hearing populations.

Web Resources

Vischeck
http://www.vischeck.com/
Find out what a person with colorblindness sees when looking at colorful materials.

Part 4 contains four chapters that cut across the entire assessment process. Chapter 21 describes the important considerations in adapting tests to accommodate the specific needs of students with disabilities, and considers when and how to make accommodation decisions. Chapter 22 includes a description of important considerations in assessing students from different cultural backgrounds and those who are English language learners. Chapter 23 discusses how computers are playing increasingly important roles in the testing process. Computer programs are now able to generate individual tests, score the tests, evaluate a student's test performance, and even recommend specific instruction. Chapter 24 describes how student performance in response to specific interventions or instruction is used to make decisions about the nature and intensity of subsequent interventions. Chapter 25 discusses the unresolved problems in assembling the content of portfolios, scoring them, and their instructional utility. A number of suggestions are offered for improving the use of portfolios in educational decision making.

Part 4

Special Considerations in Assessment

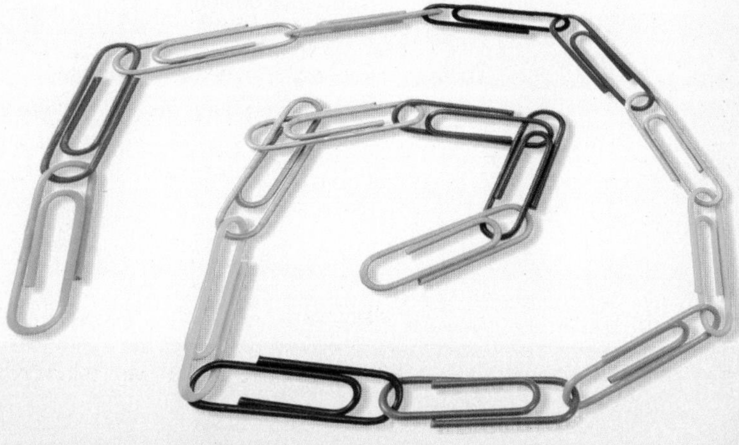

Using Test Adaptations and Accommodations

CHAPTER GOALS

1 Understand four reasons why you should be concerned with test adaptations and accommodations.

2 Know factors to consider when deciding whether test changes are necessary and, if so, which test changes might be appropriate.

3 Know two categorization schemes for accommodations, including one associated with accommodation type and one associated with accommodation validity.

4 Know accommodation guidelines you can use in making accommodation decisions for eligibility testing.

5 Know accommodation guidelines you can use in making accommodation decisions for accountability testing.

KEY TERMS

504 plan

accommodation

universal design for assessment

presentation accommodations

response accommodations

setting accommodations

scheduling accommodations

Although the use of well-designed standardized tests can enhance assessment decision making, it does not result in optimal measurement for every student. In fact, for some students, the way in which a test is administered under standardized conditions may actually prohibit their demonstration of true knowledge and skill. For example, some tests require that students print their answers in a test booklet; this can make it difficult for some students with motor impairments to demonstrate their knowledge. Some tests require that students remain focused for long periods of time at a desk; this can make it difficult for some students with hyperactivity problems to demonstrate their knowledge. Clearly, changes in test conditions may be needed. However, some changes can have a negative impact on the validity of test scores. Educators must attend to the kinds of adaptations that can be made without compromising the technical adequacy of tests. In this chapter, we consider issues associated with adapting tests and providing accommodations for students with disabilities.

1 Why Be Concerned About Testing Adaptations?

There are many reasons why it is important to understand appropriate ways in which to adapt tests. The reasons we discuss in this chapter include the increased diversity in today's schools and legal requirements for all students to be appropriately measured toward the same standards.

INCREASED DIVERSITY

Student diversity has increased substantially in the last decade. As we discuss in Chapter 22, schools are more culturally diverse, both in terms of the numbers of students who are culturally different and in terms of the cultures they represent. However, in addition to racial, ethnic, and cultural differences, students within these groups enter school these days with a very diverse set of academic background experiences and opportunities. Within the same classroom, students often vary considerably in their academic skill development. Educators face two clear challenges: (1) designing instruction that will be effective with this vast range in skills and abilities and (2) using assessments that will evaluate validly the large range in student skills.

Since the mid-1970s, considerable attention has been focused on including all students in neighborhood schools and general education settings. Much attention has been focused on including students who are considered developmentally, physically, or emotionally impaired. As federal and state officials create educational policies, they are now compelled to make them for all children and youth, including those with severe disabilities. Also, as policymakers attempt to develop practices that will result in improved educational results, they rely on data from district- and state-administered tests. However, relying on assessment data presents challenges associated with deciding whom to include in the multiple kinds of assessments and the kinds of changes that can be made to include them.

Although meaningful assessment of the skills of such a diverse student population is challenging, it is clear that all students need to be included in large-scale assessment programs. If students are excluded from large-scale assessments, then the data on which policy decisions are made represent only part of the school population. If students are excluded from accountability systems, they may also be denied access to the general education curriculum. If data are going to be gathered on all students, then major decisions must be made regarding the kinds of data to be collected and how tests are to be modified or adapted to include students with special needs. Historically, there has been widespread exclusion of students with disabilities from state and national testing (Thompson & Thurlow, 2001; McGrew, Thurlow, Shriner, & Spiegel, 1992). Participation in large-scale assessments is now recognized by many educators and parents as a critical element of equal opportunity and access to education. Thurlow and Thompson (2004) report that all states now require participation of all students. Furthermore, all states now have accommodation policies that indicate how students can participate in large-scale assessment programs with accommodations. However, many questions remain about which participation and accommodation strategies are the best for particular students. It is up to school teams to determine which accommodations are appropriate for individual students.

CHANGES IN EDUCATIONAL STANDARDS

Part of major efforts to reform or restructure schools has been a push to specify high standards for student achievement and an accompanying push to measure the extent to which students meet those high standards. It is expected that schools will include students with disabilities and ELLs in assessments, especially those completed for accountability purposes.

State education agencies in nearly every state are engaging in critical analyses of the standards, objectives, outcomes, results, skills, or behaviors that they want students to demonstrate upon completion of school. Additionally, nationwide efforts are underway to develop a set of common core standards. In all of these efforts, decisions must be made about the extent to which standards should be the same for students with and without disabilities. In Chapter 28 (Making Accountability Decisions), you will learn about current state efforts to develop alternate achievement standards for students with disabilities. Development of standards is not enough. Groups that develop standards must develop ways of assessing the extent to which students are meeting the standards.

THE NEED FOR ACCURATE MEASUREMENT

It is critical that the assessment practices used for gathering information on individual students provide accurate information. Without accommodations, testing runs the risk of being unfair for certain students. Some test formats make it more difficult for students with disabilities to understand what they are supposed to do or what the response requirements are. Because of their disabilities, some students find it impossible to respond in a way that can be evaluated accurately.

IT IS REQUIRED BY LAW

By law, students with disabilities have a right to be included in assessments used for accountability purposes, and accommodations in testing should be made to enable them to participate. This legal argument is derived largely from the Fourteenth Amendment to the U.S. Constitution (which guarantees the right to equal protection and to due process of law). The Individuals with Disabilities Education Act (IDEA) guarantees the right to education and to due process. Also, Section 504 of the Rehabilitation Act of 1973 indicates that it is illegal to exclude people from participation solely because of a disability. If a student is receiving special education services due to an educational disability, that student's instructional and testing accommodations are to be documented on an individualized education plan (IEP). If a student with a disability does not necessarily need special education services but instead simply needs accommodations to allow appropriate participation in the general curriculum, then the student's accommodation needs are documented on what is commonly referred to as a 504 plan.

The Americans with Disabilities Act of 1992 mandates that all individuals must have access to exams used to provide credentials or licenses. Agencies administering tests must provide either auxiliary aids or modifications to enable individuals with disabilities to participate in assessment, and these agencies may not charge the individual for costs incurred in making special provisions. Adaptations that may be provided include an architecturally accessible testing site, a distraction-free space, or an alternative location; a test schedule variation or extended time; the use of a scribe, sign language interpreter, reader, or adaptive equipment; and modifications of the test presentation or response format.

SCENARIO *in* ASSESSMENT

AMY | Amy has a visual impairment that does not quite meet the definition of legal blindness. Her teacher provides her with accommodations during instruction. For example, Amy's seat is positioned in class directly under the large fluorescent light fixture, the spot considered by the teacher to have the brightest light. On several occasions when Amy has expressed difficulty seeing, the teacher has given her a special desk lamp that brightens her work surface. The teacher tries to arrange the daily schedule so that work that requires lots of vision (for example, reading) occurs early in the day. In doing so, her teacher hopes that Amy experiences less eye strain. Similar accommodations are made in classroom testing, and on the day of the state test, the following testing accommodations are provided for Amy:

- She is tested in an individual setting, where extra bright light shines directly on her test materials.
- The test is administered on three separate mornings rather than over an entire day. This helps minimize her eye strain.
- The test is administered with frequent breaks because of fatigue to eyes created by extra bright light and intense strain at deciphering text.
- The teacher uses a copy machine to enlarge the print on pages requiring reading.
- A scribe records Amy's responses to avoid her spending extra time and experiencing eye strain trying to find the appropriate location for a response and to give the response.

What implications about your own professional role can you draw from this scenario? Go to the Education CourseMate website for this textbook for more reflection questions about this Scenario in Assessment.

The 1997 and 2004 IDEA mandate that states include students with disabilities in their statewide assessment systems. The necessary accommodations are to be provided to enable students to participate. By July 2000, states were to have available alternate assessments. These are to be used by students who are unable to participate in the regular assessment even with accommodations. Alternate assessments are substitute ways of gathering data, often by means of portfolios or performance measures. The No Child Left Behind Act of 2001 requires states to report annually on the performance and progress of all students, and this principle was reiterated in the 2004 reauthorization of IDEA. Furthermore, states are expected to report on the numbers of students using accommodations for state and district assessment programs.

In this chapter, we first describe factors that may contribute to a student's need for accommodations, and then discuss accommodations that may address those needs. Finally, we offer recommendations for making accommodation decisions.

As you read this chapter, remember that the major objective of assessment is to benefit students. Assessment can do so either by enabling us to develop intervention and accommodation plans that help a child achieve the objectives of schooling or by informing local, state, and national policy decisions that benefit all students, including those with diverse needs.

2 The Importance of Promoting Test Accessibility

More information about the concept of universal design is available at the Education CourseMate website for this textbook.

The extent to which test adaptations and accommodations are needed depends in part on the way in which an assessment program is designed. When test development involves careful consideration of the unique needs of all students who may eventually participate, less "after-the-fact" changes in test conditions will be needed. Application of the principles of universal design to assessment can improve accessibility, such that appropriate testing for all students is promoted.

ABILITY TO UNDERSTAND ASSESSMENT STIMULI

Six factors can impede getting an accurate picture of students' abilities and skills during assessment: (1) the students' ability to understand assessment stimuli, (2) the students' ability to respond to assessment stimuli, (3) the nature of the norm group, (4) the appropriateness of the level of the items (sufficient basal and ceiling items), (5) the students' exposure to the curriculum being tested (opportunity to learn), and

(6) the nature of the testing environment. Assessments are considered unfair if the test stimuli are in a format that, because of a disability, the student does not understand. For example, tests only available in print are considered unfair for students with severe visual impairments. Tests with oral directions are considered unfair for students with certain hearing impairments. In fact, because the law requires that students be assessed in their primary language and because the primary language of many deaf students is not English, written assessments in English are considered unfair and invalid for many deaf students. When students cannot understand test stimuli because of a sensory or mental limitation that is unrelated to what the test is targeted to measure, accurate measurement of the targeted skills is hindered by the sensory or mental limitation. Such a test is invalid, and failure to provide an accommodation is illegal.

ABILITY TO RESPOND TO ASSESSMENT STIMULI

Tests typically require students to produce a response. For example, intelligence tests require verbal, motor (pointing or arranging), or written (including multiple-choice) responses. To the extent that physical or sensory limitations inhibit accurate responding, these test results are invalid. For example, some students with cerebral palsy may lack sufficient motor ability to arrange blocks. Others may have sufficient motor ability but have such slowed responses that timed tests are inappropriate estimates of their abilities. Yet others may be able to respond quickly but expend so much energy that they cannot sustain their efforts throughout the test. Not only are test results invalid in such instances, but also the use of such test results is proscribed by federal law.

NORMATIVE COMPARISONS

Norm-referenced tests are standardized on groups of individuals, and the performance of the person assessed is compared with the performance of the norm group. To the extent that the test was administered to the student differently than the way it was administered to the norm group, you must be very careful in interpreting the results. Adaptations of measures require changing either stimulus presentation or response requirements. The adaptation may make the test items easier or more difficult, and it may change the construct being measured. Although qualitative or criterion-referenced interpretations of such test performances are often acceptable, norm-referenced comparisons can be flawed. *Standards for Educational and Psychological Testing* (American Educational Research Association, American Psychological Association, & National Council on Measurement in Education, 1999) specifies that when tests are adapted, it is important that there is validity evidence for the change that is made. Otherwise, it is important to describe the change when reporting the score and to use caution in score interpretation.

APPROPRIATENESS OF THE LEVEL OF THE ITEMS

Tests are often developed for students who are in specific age ranges or who have a particular range of skills. They can sometimes seem inappropriate for students who are either very high or very low functioning compared to their age-mates. Assessors are tempted to give out-of-level tests when an age-appropriate test contains either an insufficient number of easy items or not enough easy items for the student being assessed. Of course, when out-of-level tests are given and norm-referenced interpretations are made, the students are compared with a group of students who differ from them. We have no idea how same-age or same-grade students would perform on the given test. Out-of-level testing may be appropriate to identify a student's current level of educational performance or to evaluate the effectiveness of instruction with a student who is instructed out of grade level. It is inappropriate for accountability purposes.

EXPOSURE TO THE CURRICULUM BEING TESTED (OPPORTUNITY TO LEARN)

One of the issues of fairness raised by the general public is the administration of tests that contain material that students have not had an opportunity to learn. This same issue applies to the making of accommodation decisions. Students with sensory impairments have not had an opportunity to learn the content of test items that use verbal or auditory stimuli. Students receiving special education services who have not had adequate access to the general education curriculum have not had the same opportunity to master the general education curriculum.

To the extent that students have not had an opportunity to learn the content of the test (that is, they were absent when the content was taught, the content is not taught in the schools in which they were present, or the content was taught in ways that were not effective for the students), they probably will not perform well on the test. Their performance will reflect more a lack of opportunity to learn than limited skill and ability.

ENVIRONMENTAL CONSIDERATIONS

Students should be tested in settings in which they can demonstrate maximal performance. If students cannot easily gain access to a testing setting, this may diminish their performance. Tests should always be given in settings that students with disabilities can access with ease. The settings should also be quiet enough to minimize distractibility. Also, because fatigue is an issue, tests should be given in multiple short sessions (broken up with breaks) so students do not become overly tired.

3 Categories of Testing Accommodations

An accommodation is any change in testing materials or procedures that enables students to participate in assessments so that their abilities with respect to what is intended to be measured can be more accurately assessed. There are four general types of accommodations:

- Presentation (for example, repeat directions, read aloud)
- Response (for example, mark answers in book, point to answers)
- Setting (for example, study carrel, separate room, special lighting)
- Timing/schedule (for example, extended time, frequent breaks, multiple days)

Concern about accommodation applies to individually administered and large-scale testing. The concerns are legal (Is an individual sufficiently disabled to require taking an accommodated test?), technical (To what extent can we adapt measures and still have technically adequate tests?), and political (Is it fair to give accommodations to some students, yet deny them to others?).

It is important to recognize that the appropriateness of an accommodation will depend on the skills targeted for measurement, as well as the types of decisions that are intended to be made. In addition, the specific needs, preferences, and experiences of the student may affect which accommodations are most appropriate. Although it may initially appear to you that it is easy to determine exactly which accommodations allow for better measurement of targeted skills and fair and appropriate assessment, people actually tend to disagree on which accommodations maintain the validity of tests, making it a more complicated issue. Based on input from a variety of stakeholders (that is, teachers, state assessment directors, and researchers), one test publisher has created a framework for accommodations and classified common accommodations into one of three categories: accommodations that have no impact on test validity, accommodations that may affect validity, and accommodations that are known to affect validity (CTB/McGraw-Hill, 2004). Extended descriptions of these categories, as well as accommodations that are considered to fit within these categories, are provided in Figure 21.1.

FIGURE 21.1
Categories of Testing Accommodations

Category 1 The accommodations listed in category 1 are not expected to influence student performance in a way that alters the interpretation of either criterion- or norm-referenced test scores. Individual student scores obtained using category 1 accommodations should be interpreted in the same way as the scores of other students who take the test under default conditions. These students' scores may be included in summaries of results without notation of accommodation(s).

Presentation

- Use visual magnifying equipment
- Use a large-print edition of the test
- Use audio amplification equipment
- Use markers to maintain place
- Have directions read aloud
- Use a tape recording of directions
- Have directions presented through sign language
- Use directions that have been marked with highlighting

Response

- Mark responses in test booklet
- Mark responses on large-print answer document
- For selected-response items, indicate responses to a scribe
- Record responses on audio tape (except for constructed-response writing tests)
- For selected-response items, use sign language to indicate response
- Use a computer, typewriter, Braille writer, or other machine (for example, communication board) to respond
- Use template to maintain place for responding
- Indicate response with other communication devices (for example, speech synthesizer)
- Use a spelling checker except with a test for which spelling will be scored

Setting

- Take the test alone or in a study carrel
- Take the test with a small group or different class
- Take the test at home or in a care facility (for example, hospital), with supervision
- Use adaptive furniture
- Use special lighting and/or acoustics

Timing/scheduling

- Take more breaks that do not result in extra time or opportunity to study information in a test already begun
- Have flexible scheduling (for example, time of day and days between sessions) that does not result in extra time or opportunity to study information in a test already begun

Category 2 Category 2 accommodations may have an effect on student performance that should be considered when interpreting individual criterion- and norm-referenced test scores. In the absence of research demonstrating otherwise, scores and any consequences or decisions associated with them should be interpreted in light of the accommodation(s) used.

Presentation

- Have stimulus material, questions, and/or answer choices read aloud, except for a reading test
- Use a tape recorder for stimulus material, questions, and/or answer choices, except for a reading test

- Have stimulus material, questions, and/or answer choices presented through sign language, except for a reading test
- Communication devices (for example, text talk converter), except for a reading test
- Use a calculator or arithmetic tables, except for a mathematics computation test

Response

- Use graph paper to align work
- For constructed-response items, indicate responses to a scribe, except for a writing test

Timing/scheduling

- Use extra time for any timed test
- Take more breaks that result in extra time for any timed test
- Extend the timed section of a test over more than one day, even if extra time does not result
- Have flexible scheduling that results in extra time

Category 3 Category 3 accommodations change what is being measured and are likely to have an effect that alters the interpretation of individual criterion- and norm-referenced scores. This occurs when the accommodation is strongly related to the knowledge, skill, or ability being measured (for example, having a reading comprehension test read aloud). In the absence of research demonstrating otherwise, criterion- and norm-referenced test scores and any consequences or decisions associated with them should be interpreted not only in light of the accommodation(s) used but also in light of how the accommodation(s) may alter what is measured.

Presentation

- Use Braille or other tactile form of print
- On a reading (decoding) test, have stimulus material, questions, and/or answer choices presented through sign language
- On a reading (decoding) test, use a text-talk converter, where the reader is required to construct meaning and decode words from text
- On a reading (decoding) test, use a tape recording of stimulus material, questions, and/or answer choices
- Have directions, stimulus material, questions, and/or answer choices paraphrased
- For a mathematics computation test, use of a calculator or arithmetic tables
- Use a dictionary, where language conventions are assessed

Response

- For a constructed-response writing test, indicate responses to a scribe
- Spelling aids, such as spelling dictionaries (without definitions) and spell/grammar checkers, provided for a test for which spelling and grammar conventions will be scored
- Use a dictionary to look up words on a writing test

Over the past 20 years, much research on the validity of accommodated test scores has been conducted. Research continues to be conducted on accommodations to refine and provide justification for how these accommodations are assigned to the various validity categories. We emphasize throughout this book the importance of considering test purpose and the decisions that assessment is intended to inform when deciding what assessment tools to use. Deciding whether a particular accommodation is appropriate for testing is no different. When deciding on accommodation appropriateness, careful attention must be paid to what the test is intended to measure and what decisions are intended to be made with the results.

Progress is rapid in designing and validating test accommodations. You are advised to visit the website for the National Center on Educational Outcomes at the University of Minnesota to read the latest research and publications on state and national practice in testing accommodations.

4 Recommendations for Making Accommodation Decisions for Individual Students

There are major debates about the kinds of accommodations that should be permitted during testing for accountability purposes. There are also major arguments about the extent to which accommodations in testing destroy the technical adequacy of tests used for determining instructional needs and eligibility for special education. We think there are some reasonable guidelines for best practice in making decisions about individuals, and we offer associated guidelines here. We first provide recommendations for making accommodation decisions on tests that are commonly used to make decisions about individuals (for example, eligibility and instructional planning for exceptional children). Then, we provide recommendations for making accommodation decisions on tests that are typically administered at the group level and used for accountability purposes.

RECOMMENDATIONS FOR MAKING ACCOMMODATION DECISIONS DURING INSTRUCTIONAL PLANNING AND ELIGIBILITY DECISIONS FOR EXCEPTIONAL STUDENTS

When making decisions about what to teach, it is important to collect information about the student's current skills in a way that the student can adequately demonstrate his or her knowledge. For example, if you want to know whether students have specific math problem-solving skills, it may be necessary to present the questions in an oral format rather than a written format to students who cannot yet accurately read. Otherwise, students may fail to answer correctly because they cannot read the item, even though they have the given math problem-solving skills. The result would unfortunately be that you continue to plan your instruction around the given math problem-solving skill even when the student already has mastered the given skill.

However, if you are using data from tests with specific standardized administration procedures and intending to compare to a normative sample, it is important to follow the rules set forth in the administration manual. Published tests are increasingly providing specific rules for testing with accommodations in administration manuals. Such rules should be carefully consulted when using these tests for determining students instruction needs and making eligibility decisions.

Some related recommendations that we suggest are provided below:

- Conduct all assessments in the student's primary language or mode of communication. The mode of communication is that normally used by the person during instruction (such as sign language, Braille, or oral communication); however, note that there are additional considerations that should be made in assessing students who are English language learners (see Chapter 22, Cultural and Linguistic Considerations). Loeding and Crittenden (1993, p. 19) note that for students who are deaf, the primary communication mode is either a visual–spatial, natural sign language used by members of the American Deaf Community called American Sign Language (ASL), or a manually coded form of English, such as Signed English, Pidgin Sign English, Seeing Essential English, Signing Exact English, or Sign-Supported Speech/English. Therefore, they argue, "traditional paper-and-pencil tests are inaccessible, invalid, and inappropriate to the deaf student because the tests are written in English only."

- Make accommodations in format when the purpose of testing is not substantially impaired. For example, a student might be allowed to provide an oral response instead of a written response if the purpose is not to measure writing skills. Or a student might be given more frequent breaks when completing a task if the purpose is not to measure his or her ability to attend for long periods of time. It should be demonstrated that the accommodations assist the individual in responding but do not provide content assistance (for example, a scribe should record the response of the person being tested—not interpret what the person says, include his or her additional knowledge, and then record a response). Personal assistants who are provided during testing, such as readers, scribes, and interpreters, should be trained in how to provide associated accommodations to ensure proper administration.
- Make normative comparisons only with groups whose membership includes students with background sets of experiences and opportunities like those of the students being tested. For example, if you provide a signed interpretation of a norm-referenced test, you should only compare the student's results with those of a group of students who also had the test signed using the same language.

RECOMMENDATIONS FOR MAKING ACCOMMODATION DECISIONS DURING ACCOUNTABILITY TESTING

Many other accommodation recommendations can be implemented when collecting assessment data to make decisions about groups of students, specifically for the purpose of making accountability decisions. Decisions about which accommodations to provide should be made separately for each individual student determined to need them; however, decisions are often guided by state accommodation policies. Thurlow, Elliott, and Ysseldyke (2003) suggest the following recommendations about accommodation decision making for the purpose of accountability:

- States and districts should have written guidelines for the use of accommodations in large-scale assessments used for accountability purposes.
- Decisions about accommodations should be made by one or more persons who know the student, including the student's strengths and weaknesses.
- Decision makers should consider the student's learning characteristics and the accommodations currently used during classroom instruction and classroom testing.
- The student's category of disability or program setting should not influence the decision.
- The goal is to ensure that accommodations have been used by the student prior to their use in an assessment—generally, in the classroom during instruction and in classroom testing situations. New accommodations should not be introduced for the district- or statewide assessment.
- The decision is made systematically, using a form that lists questions to answer or variables to consider in making the accommodation decision. Ideally, classroom data on the effects of accommodations are part of the information entered into decisions. Decisions and the reasons for them should be noted on the form.
- Decisions about accommodations should be documented on the student's individualized educational program.
- Parents should be involved in the decision by either participating in the decision-making process or being given the analysis of the need for accommodations and by signing the form that indicates accommodations that are to be used.[1]
- Accommodation decisions made to address individual student needs should be reconsidered at least once a year, given that student needs are likely to change over time.

[1] Adapted from Thurlow, Elliott, and Ysseldyke (2003), pp. 46–47, with permission.

Chapter Comprehension Questions

Write your answers to each of the following questions and then compare your responses to the text.

1. What are four reasons why you should be concerned with test adaptations and accommodations?
2. Describe at least four factors to be considered when deciding whether test changes are necessary and what test changes may be appropriate.
3. Describe two schemes for categorizing accommodations, and provide examples of accommodations that might fit each category within those categorization schemes.
4. What are some guidelines to use in making decisions about which accommodations to provide when making eligibility decisions?
5. What are some accommodation guidelines to use in making decisions about which accommodations to provide when making accountability decisions?

Web Activities

1. Search the Internet to find and read your state's accommodation policy. To what extent does your state's policy reflect the recommendations presented in this chapter for making accommodation decisions for accountability decisions?
2. Search on the website for the National Center on Educational Outcomes at the University of Minnesota for the Accommodations Manual that was developed for the Council of Chief State School Officers (CCSSO). Examine the tools that can be used to make accommodation decisions for individual students.
3. Look on the website for the National Center on Educational Outcomes at the University of Minnesota for a report on access assistants for state assessments. What types of guidelines for readers, scribes, and interpreters are described? What guidelines does your state have for these assistants? Why are such guidelines necessary?
4. Select and locate a manual for one of the published standardized tests in math that is reviewed on the textbook website. What information does the manual provide about the use of accommodations?

Web Resources

The NCEO Accommodations Bibliography
http://apps.cehd.umn.edu/nceo/accommodations/
This tool allows you to search for research studies on various accommodations. Summaries of each study related to your search word are provided.

NECO's Accommodations for Students with Disabilities
http://www.cehd.umn.edu/NCEO/TopicAreas/Accommodations/Accomtopic.htm
This website provides links to state accommodation policies, answers to frequently asked questions, and other helpful manuals to assist with accommodation decision making for students with disabilities.

Additional resources for this chapter can be found on the Education CourseMate website. Go to CengageBrain.com to access the site.

Cultural and Linguistic Considerations

CHAPTER GOALS

1 Begin to understand the magnitude of cultural and linguistic diversity present in U.S. public schools.

2 Understand various legal protections and testing requirements for students who are English language learners (ELLs).

3 Be familiar with several questions that should be used to guide the assessment process for students from culturally and linguistically diverse backgrounds.

4 Know several approaches to testing students who are English language learners (ELLs), along with their merits and drawbacks.

KEY TERMS

acculturation pattern

basic interpersonal communication skills

cognitive academic language proficiency

English language learner (ELL)

limited English proficiency (LEP)

nonverbal test

test translations

The assessment of students with unique cultural and linguistic backgrounds is a particularly difficult task for educators and psychologists. The overwhelming majority of classroom and commercially prepared tests are administered in English. Students who do not speak or read English cannot access the content and respond verbally to these tests. For example, suppose Lupe does not understand English but is given an intelligence test. She might be asked, "What is a sled?" or "What is an orange?" She would not understand the questions, although she might be able to define these words. Similarly, she might respond, "*¿Que?*" The examiner might not understand that she was asking, "What?" Obviously, this test is not valid for Lupe; her lack of English language proficiency creates a barrier to effective testing such that her score may not reflect her true abilities with respect to what is intended to be measured.

Challenges in assessing students with cultural and language differences go beyond not knowing the language used for testing. They relate to a host of issues associated with acculturation and linguistic development. Students who are English language learners (sometimes called students with limited English proficiency or LEP) may speak some English. However, knowing enough English for social conversation is not the same as knowing enough English for instruction or for the nuances of highly abstract concepts. Moreover, many English language learners may come from a culture that is very different from the public culture of the United States. As a result, whenever a test item relies on a student's cultural knowledge to test some other area of achievement or aptitude, the test will necessarily be invalid because it will also test the student's knowledge of American culture. In this chapter, we discuss social, political, and demographic issues that complicate the assessment process, as well as how to assess students who are English language learners.

1 The Diversity of English Language Learners

According to information from the U.S. Census Bureau, large numbers of individuals who live in the United States do not speak English. Table 22.1 shows the languages most frequently spoken by these individuals, the number of speakers of each of these languages, and how numbers have changed over time. Spanish, Chinese, and French are among the most common languages other than English spoken in homes in the United States.

The number of different languages and the distribution of speakers of those languages cause problems for test makers and testers. First, because there are many languages with relatively few LEP speakers, it would be unprofitable for test publishers to develop and norm test versions in these languages. Second, even if the tests were available it is unlikely that there would be many bilingual psychologists and teachers able to use foreign-language versions of those tests. Finally, students within the same language group will not be culturally homogeneous. For example, there are French speakers from Montreal and French speakers from Port-au-Prince; there are Russian speakers from Kazakhstan and Russian speakers from Belarus. Students speaking the same language do not necessarily share a culture and a history.

Although the number of Spanish-speaking English language learners is large enough to make it profitable for test publishers to develop Spanish-language versions of their tests, Spanish-speaking students are not a homogeneous group, either. In the United States, about 64 percent of Spanish speakers are of Mexican descent, about 13 percent are of Central or South American descent, about 9 percent are of Puerto Rican descent, and about 3 percent are of Cuban descent (U.S. Census Bureau, 2006). Moreover, Spanish-speaking students of Mexican descent include those born in East Los Angeles and those who emigrated from Mexico; Spanish-speaking students of Puerto Rican descent include those born in New York City

TABLE 22.1 Languages Spoken at Home: 1980, 1990, 2000, and 2007.

(For information on confidentiality protection, sampling error, nonsampling error, and definitions, see *www.census.gov/acs/www/*)

Characteristic	1980	1990	2000	2007	Percentage change 1980–2007
Population 5 years and older	**210,247,455**	**230,445,777**	**262,375,152**	**280,950,438**	33.6
Spoke only English at home	187,187,416	198,600,798	215,423,557	225,505,953	20.5
Spoke a language other than English at home[1]	23,060,040	31,844,979	46,951,595	55,444.485	140.4
Spoke a language other than English at home[2]	**23,060,040**	**31,844,979**	**46,951,595**	**55,444,405**	**140.4**
Spanish or Spanish Creole	11,116,194	17,345,064	28,101,052	34,547,077	210.8
French (incl. Patois, Cajun, Creole)	1,550,751	1,930,404	2,097,206	1,984,824	28.0
Italian	1,618,344	1,308,648	1,008,370	798,801	–50.6
Portuguese or Portuguese Creole	351,875	430,610	564,630	687,126	95.3
German	1,586,593	1,547,987	1,383,442	1,104,354	–30.4
Yiddish	315,953	213,064	178,945	158,991	–49.7
Greek	401,443	388,260	365,436	329,825	–17.8
Russian	173,226	241,798	706,242	851,174	391.4
Polish	820,647	723,483	667,414	638,059	–22.2
Serbo-Croatian	150,255	70,964	233,865	276,550	84.1
Armenian	100,634	149,694	202,708	221,865	120.5
Persian	106,992	201,865	312,085	349,686	226.8
Chinese	630,806	1,319,482	2,022,143	2,464,572	290.7
Japanese	336,318	427,657	477,997	458,717	36.4
Korean	266,280	626,478	894,063	1,062,337	299.0
Vietnamese	197,588	507,069	1,009,627	1,207,004	510.9
Tagalog	474,150	843,251	1,224,241	1,480,429	212.2

[1] The languages highlighted in this table are the languages for which data were available for the four time periods: 1980, 1990, 2000, and 2007.

[2] The total does not match the sum of the 17 languages listed in this table because the total includes all the other languages that are not highlighted here.

Note: Margins of error for all estimates can be found in Appendix Table 2 at <http://www.census.gov/hhes/socdemo/language/data/acs/appendix.html>. For more information on the ACS, see <http://www.census.gov/acs/www/>.

Source: U.S. Census Bureau, 1980 and 1990 Census, Census 2000, and 2007 American Community Survey.

and those from San Juan. Spanish speakers from Central or South America may speak a Native American language (for example, Quechua) in addition to Spanish. Thus because students speak Spanish does not mean that they share a culture and a history with everyone else in the United States for whom Spanish is the first and primary language.

Finally, there are political and social differences among students who are ELLs, and these differences affect their learning of English and their understanding of the culture of the United States. Regardless of the language they speak, how the students and their parents came to the United States has social and political implications. Some students are immigrants or the children of immigrants who intend to make the United States their new home. Some immigrants are simply seeking a better life in the United States; others are fleeing repressive governments. Some have arrived at JFK or LAX by jet; others have negotiated the Straits of Florida on a raft to arrive in Miami. Some come with or join extended families; others come alone or with one parent. Some immigrants prefer to maintain their own culture and remain separate from the United States and U.S. schools' cultures. All of these things may affect their acculturation pattern, the way they find to either merge with or stay separate from U.S. culture.

Some parents of ELL students embrace the culture and ideals of the United States, and English is likely to eventually become their primary language educationally and socially. Other parents are short-term visitors to the country. For example, they may be the children of graduate students attending U.S. colleges and universities, of business people working for foreign corporations, of diplomats, of individuals seeking political asylum—all of whom intend to return permanently to their homeland in the future. For these students, the U.S. culture is more likely to be seen as something to understand rather than something to be embraced, and assimilation into the U.S. culture may actually be disadvantageous. English is likely to be their temporary instructional language, whereas their first language is stressed in their home.

Finally, some students are the descendants of people who were neither immigrants nor visitors, but who were living on lands captured or purchased by the U.S. government—for example, many Native Americans, Pacific Islanders, and Mexican Americans. These students and their parents can have attitudes toward English and U.S. culture that run the gamut from wanting to assimilate, to having multiple national or ethnic identities, to continuing resistance to the U.S. government by rejecting English and American culture.

U.S. policy toward students who are ELLs has evolved over the last 35 years. Prior to the mid-1960s, a number of practices were accepted that today would be considered illegal and repugnant. Voter registration in some states required potential voters to pass a literacy test, and these tests were sometimes used to disfranchise minority voters. Native American students were punished for speaking their first language during recess. One particularly offensive punishment was washing their mouths out with soap—as if their language consisted of dirty words. More pertinent to this text, ELLs were routinely tested in English to ascertain whether they had mental retardation. When they could not pass the intelligence test in English, they were placed in segregated special education classes.

Today the United States officially celebrates the diversity of its citizenry, and we are a collage of ethnic music, dance, art, and food. Formally, the United States welcomes visitors and immigrants, but unofficially acceptance is neither all encompassing nor embraced by all citizens. For example, most Americans reject cultural practices that limit opportunities for women or that sexually mutilate girls.

In addition, although the state and federal governments champion diversity, it is the local communities that must pay for the services needed to make diversity workable. The federal government controls immigration, but local school districts must bear the added costs of educating ELLs.

In many ways, the debate about how to deal with ELLs is a debate about the very nature of who we are as a country. This debate lurks at the edges of discussions about assessing students who are ELLs. Although we acknowledge this debate, in this chapter we shall try, to the extent possible, to avoid the political and social issues surrounding the assessment of students who are ELLs. Instead, we first focus on legal considerations in testing students who are ELLs. Then we identify questions that should be considered when assessing students from culturally and linguistically diverse backgrounds. Finally, we discuss specific strategies that might be used in the assessment of such students.

2 Legal Considerations

Both IDEA and NCLB include specific information related to assessment of students who are ELLs. IDEA specifies certain protections for both students and parents who are involved in assessment for the purpose of determining eligibility for special education services. NCLB discusses how students with LEP are to be included in assessments for the purpose of accountability.

IDEA PROTECTIONS

Protections for Students Being Assessed

The fundamental principle when assessing students who are ELLs is to assure that the assessment materials and procedures used actually assess students' target knowledge, skill, or ability, not their inability (or limited ability) to understand and use English. For example, suppose that Antonio cannot answer a word problem involving two 2-digit addends and one extraneous fact (also a 2-digit number). To what does the tester attribute Antonio's failure—a lack of skill in adding numbers or an inability to read English? Antonio must have sufficient knowledge of English in order for the tester to rule out his failure as a lack of proficiency in English.

Clearly, the intent of the Individuals with Disabilities Education Act (IDEA) and all other pertinent court decisions is to assess students' achievement and abilities unbiased by their limited proficiency in English. The principal rationale for protecting students who are ELLs during the assessment process can be found in the IDEA. As §300.532(a)(2) states, "Materials and procedures used to assess a child with limited English proficiency [must be] selected and administered to ensure that they measure the extent to which the child has a disability and needs special education, rather than measuring the child's English language skills." To accomplish this goal, tests must be selected and administered in such a way that they are not racially or culturally discriminatory. Indeed, to the extent feasible, tests and evaluation materials must be administered in the student's native language or other mode of communication. This principle is echoed in §300.534(b) of the IDEA, which forbids a student to be identified as in need of special educational services if the determining factor is limited proficiency in English.

However, it is important to note that, if the goal of assessment is to ascertain a student's current level of functioning in English, then it is appropriate to test the student in English. If the student cannot decode the words in a passage written in English, then the student cannot decode the passage written in English. If a student cannot comprehend the meaning of the individual words in a passage written in English, then the student cannot comprehend the meaning of that passage. The assessment has provided an indication of the student's current ability to use English.

Protections for Parents in the Assessment Process

Parents are the principal advocates for their children within the educational system, and the IDEA contains a number of protections for them as well, especially in terms of notice, participation, and consent. For example, §300.503(b) requires that parents receive prior notice if the school intends to initiate or change their child's identification as a student with a disability. That notice must "be provided in the native language of the parent or other mode of communication used by the parent, unless it is clearly not feasible to do so." Although notice is usually in written form, the IDEA also provides that interpreters be used if the native language or mode of communication of the parent is not written language. Parents must be given notice of their procedural safeguards. This notice must be in the parents' native language or other mode of communication if they do not understand English (§300.504[c]). Schools must take steps to make sure that the parents of a student with a disability have the opportunity to participate in team meetings. To that end, §300.345(e) requires the use of interpreters or other appropriate measures "for parents with deafness or whose native language is other than English." In those instances when parental consent is required (for example, to conduct an initial assessment of a student), that consent must be given in the parents' native language or mode of communication (§300.500[b][1]).

NCLB REQUIREMENTS

In Chapter 28 ("Making Accountability Decisions"), we discuss the No Child Left Behind requirements for school accountability. According to NCLB, students, including students with LEP, must participate in assessments used for the purpose of holding schools accountable. In fact, when sufficient numbers of students who are ELLs exist for results to be reliable, it is expected that scores for students who are ELLs will be both aggregated in school reports of student proficiency and disaggregated so that people can know specifically how students who are ELLs are doing. When sufficient numbers of students who are ELLs exist, the progress of these students is specifically taken into account when determining whether a school or district meets adequate yearly progress. Although they can be excluded from participation in the English/language arts tests used to hold schools accountable during their first year of public school instruction in the United States, it is expected that they will participate in all other sections of the test during their first year, and every section of the test (including English/language arts) in the years that follow. They are expected to take an additional English language proficiency test as part of NCLB. They may be provided a variety of different accommodations to assist with removing language barriers from testing in certain areas; each state provides a list of approved accommodations for students who are ELLs.

3 Important Questions to Consider in Assessing Students from Culturally and Linguistically Diverse Backgrounds

To assess students in a way that reduces language and cultural barriers to effective measurement of targeted skills, knowledge, and abilities among students, we provide several important questions that should be taken into consideration.

WHAT BACKGROUND EXPERIENCES DOES THE STUDENT HAVE IN ENGLISH AND IN THEIR NATIVE LANGUAGE?

Students who are ELLs vary considerably in the rate at which they learn a new language. Many different factors can affect this rate, such as the age at which they were first exposed to the new language and the extent to which they are exposed to the new language in their home, school, and community environments. They also vary in terms of the languages in which they have received instruction, with some having received considerable instruction in both their native language and English and others receiving only instruction in English. These factors should be taken into consideration during assessment, and are further described below.

English as a Second Language

It is critical to distinguish between social/interpersonal uses of language and cognitive/academic uses. Students learning English as a second language usually need at least 2 years to develop social and interpersonal communication skills, sometimes referred to as basic interpersonal communication skills (BICS). However, they require 5 to 6 years to develop language sufficient for cognitive academic language proficiency (CALP; Cummins, 1984). Thus, after even 3 or 4 years of schooling, students who demonstrate few problems with English usage in social situations still probably lack sufficient language competence to be tested in English.

At least three factors can affect the time required for students to attain cognitive and academic sufficiency in English. Related questions that should be considered when deciding how to assess students who are ELLs are provided below.

1. *At what age did the student first begin to learn English?* Young children are programmed to learn language. As children get older, learning another language becomes more difficult (Johnson & Newport, 1989). Thus, all things being equal, one should expect younger students to acquire English faster than older students.
2. *In what contexts has the student been exposed to English?* The more contexts in which English is used, the faster will be its acquisition. Thus a student's learning of English as a second language will depend in part on the language the parents speak at home. If the native language is spoken at home, progress in English will be slower. This creates a dilemma for parents who want their children to learn (or remember) their first language and also learn English.
3. *To what extent is the student's native language similar to English?* Languages can vary along several dimensions. The phonology may be different. The 44 speech sounds of English may be the same or different from the speech sounds of other languages. For example, Xhosa (an African language) has three different click sounds; English has none. English lacks the sound equivalent of the Spanish *ñ*, the Portuguese-*nh*, and the Italian-*gn*. The orthography may be different. English uses the Latin alphabet. Other languages may use different alphabets (for example, Cyrillic) or no alphabet (Mandarin). English does not use diacritical marks; other languages do. The letter–sound correspondences may be different. The letter *h* is silent in Spanish but pronounced as an English *r* in one Brazilian dialect. The grammar may be different. Whereas English tends to be noun dominated, other languages tend to be verb dominated. Word order varies. Adjectives precede nouns in English, but they follow nouns in Spanish. The more language features the second language has in common with the first language, the easier it is to learn the second language.

Bilingual Students

"Bilingual" implies equal proficiency in two languages. Nevertheless, young children must learn which language to use with specific people. For example, they may be able to switch between English and Spanish with their siblings; speak only Spanish with their grandparents; and use only English with their older sister's husband, who still has not learned Spanish. Although children can switch between languages, sometimes in mid-sentence, they are seldom truly bilingual.

When students grow up in a home where two languages are spoken, they are seldom equally competent or comfortable in using both languages, regardless of the context or situation. These students tend to prefer one language or the other for specific situations or contexts. For example, Spanish may be spoken at home and in the neighborhood, whereas English is spoken at school. Moreover, when two languages are spoken in the home, the family may develop a hybrid language borrowing a little from each. For example, in Spanish, *caro* means "expensive"; in English, *car* means "automobile." In some bilingual homes (and communities), *caro* comes to mean "automobile." These speakers may not be speaking "proper" Spanish or English, although they have no problem communicating.

These factors enormously complicate the testing of bilingual students. Some bilingual students may understand academic questions better in English, but the language in which they answer can vary. If the content was learned in English, they may be better able to answer in English. However, if the answer calls for a logical explanation or an integration of information, they may be better able to answer in their other language. Finally, it cannot be emphasized strongly enough that language dominance is not the same as language competence for testing purposes. Because a student knows more Spanish than English does not mean that the student knows enough Spanish to be tested in that language.

WHAT UNIQUE CULTURAL CHARACTERISTICS OF THE STUDENT MAY AFFECT TESTING?

Cultural factors can complicate the testing of students. In some cultures, children are expected to speak minimally to adults or authority figures; elaboration or extensive verbal output may be seen as disrespectful. In some cultures, answering questions may be seen as self-aggrandizing, competitive, and immodest. These cultural values work against students in most testing situations.

Male–female relations are subject to cultural differences. Female students may be hesitant to speak to male teachers; male students (and their fathers) may not see female teachers as authority figures.

Children may be hesitant to speak to adults from other cultures, and testers may be reluctant to encourage or say no to children whose culture is unfamiliar. It is also important to remember that many French-speaking children with limited English proficiency may have fled the strife in Haiti or that many Spanish-speaking children with limited English proficiency may have fled repression in Cuba or civil strife in Peru, Nicaragua, El Salvador, or Colombia. These children may have been traumatized by the civil strife and therefore be wary of or frightened by strangers.

It may be difficult for an examiner to establish rapport with a student who is an ELL. Some evidence suggests that children do better with examiners of the same race and cultural background (Fuchs & Fuchs, 1989).

Immigrant students and their families may have little experience with the types of testing done in U.S. schools. Consequently, these students may lack test-taking skills. Finally, doing well on tests may not be as valued within the first cultures of immigrant students.

4 Alternative Ways to Test Students Who Are ELLs

Circumstances exist in which students who are ELLs need to be tested. As noted earlier, they need to be included in testing for the purpose of school accountability. In addition, in some situations, it may be deemed necessary to administer a test to help make a decision about whether a student with LEP is eligible to receive special education services. In the following sections, we provide information about strategies that are sometimes used with regard to testing students who are ELLs.

ENGAGE IN DENIAL

A common procedure is to pretend that a student has sufficient proficiency to be tested in English. Denial is frequently accompanied by self-delusion or coercion. Self-delusion manifests itself when the tester talks with the student and believes that the student's adequate social language indicates sufficient academic language to be tested in English. Coercion is present when the tester's supervisor insists that the student be tested. Sometimes denial is only denial; in this case, the tester admits that the student's language may have somewhat limited his or her ability to take the test.

USE NONVERBAL TESTS

Several nonverbal tests are available for testing intelligence. This type of test is believed to reduce the effects of language and culture on the assessment of intellectual abilities. (Nonverbal tests do not, however, completely eliminate the effects of language and culture.) Some tests (see Chapter 15, "Using Measures of Intelligence") do not require a student to speak—for example, the performance subscale of the third edition of the Wechsler Intelligence Scale for Children. However, these tests frequently have directions in English. Some tests (for example, the Comprehensive Test of Nonverbal Intelligence) allow testers to use either oral or pantomime directions. A few tests are exclusively nonverbal (for example, the Leiter International Performance Scale) and do not require language for directions or responses.

Because students' skills in language comprehension usually precede their skills in language production, performance tests with oral directions might be useful with some students. However, the testers should have objective evidence that a student sufficiently comprehends academic language for the test to be valid, and such evidence is generally not available. Tests that do not rely on oral directions or responses are more useful because they do not make any assumptions about students' language competence. However, other validity issues cloud the use of performance tests in the schools. For example, the nature of the tasks on nonverbal intelligence tests is usually less related to success in school than are the tasks on verbal intelligence tests.

Moreover, some cultural considerations are beyond the scope of directions and responses. For example, the very nature of testing may be more familiar in U.S. culture than in the cultures of other countries. When students are familiar with the testing process, they are likely to perform better. As another example, students from other cultures may respond differently to adults in authority, and these differences may alter estimates of their ability derived from tests. Thus, although performance and nonverbal tests may be a better option than verbal tests administered in English, they are not without problems.

TEST IN THE STUDENT'S NATIVE LANGUAGE

There are several ways to test students using directions and materials in their native language. Commercial tests may have been developed in the student's native language. If such tests are not available, testers may locate a foreign-language version of the test. If foreign-language versions are not available, testers may be able to translate a test from English to the student's native language.

Use Commercially Translated Tests

Several tests are currently available in language versions other than English—most frequently, Spanish. These tests run the gamut from those that are translated, to those that are renormed, to those that are reformatted for another language and culture. The difference among these approaches is significant.

When tests are only translated, we can assume that the child understands the directions and the questions. However, the questions may be of different difficulty in U.S. culture and the English language for two reasons. First, the difficulty of the vocabulary can vary from language to language. For example, reading *cat* in English is different from reading *gato* in Spanish. *Cat* is a three-letter, one-syllable word containing two of the first three letters of the English alphabet; *gato* is a four-letter, two-syllable word with the first, seventh, fifteenth, and twentieth letters of the alphabet. The frequency of *cat* in each language is likely different, as is the popularity of cats as house pets.

The second reason that translated questions may be of different difficulty is that the difficulty of the content can vary from culture to culture because children from different cultures have not had the same opportunity to learn the information. For example, suppose we asked Spanish-speaking students from Venezuela, Cuba, and California who attended school in the United States to identify Simón Bolívar, Ernesto "Che" Guevara, and César Chávez. We could speculate that the three groups of students would probably identify the three men with different degrees of accuracy. The students from California would be most likely to recognize Chávez as an American labor organizer but less frequently recognize Bolívar and Guevara. Students from Venezuela would likely recognize Bolívar as a liberator of South America more often than would students from Cuba and the United States. Students from Cuba would be more likely to recognize Guevara as a revolutionary than would students from the other two countries. Thus the difficulty of test content is embedded in culture.

Also, when tests are translated, we cannot assume that the psychological demands made by test items remain the same. For example, an intelligence test might ask a child to define *peach*. A child from equatorial South America may never have eaten, seen, or heard of a peach, whereas U.S. students are quite likely to have seen and eaten peaches. For U.S. students, the psychological demand of identifying a peach is to recall the biological class and essential characteristics of something they have experienced. For South American children, the item measures their knowledge of an exotic fruit. For American children, the test would measure intelligence; for South American children, the test would measure achievement.

Some of the problems associated with a simple translation of a test can be circumvented if the test is renormed on the target population and items reordered in terms of their translated difficulties. For example, to use the Wechsler Intelligence Scale for Children, third edition, effectively with Spanish-speaking Puerto Ricans, the test could be normed on a representative sample of Spanish-speaking Puerto Rican students. Based on the performance of the new normative sample, the items could be reordered as necessary. However, renorming and reordering do not reproduce the psychological demands made by test items in English.

Develop and Validate a Version of the Test for Each Cultural/Linguistic Group

Given the problems associated with translations, tests developed in the student's language and culture are clearly preferable to those that are not. For example, suppose one wished to develop a version of the Wechsler Intelligence Scale for Children *para los Niños de Cuba*.Test items could be developed within the Cuban American culture according to the general framework of the Wechsler scale. Specific items might or might not be the same. The new test would then need to be validated. For example, factor–analytic studies could be undertaken to ascertain whether the same four factors underlie the new test (that is, verbal comprehension, perceptual organization, freedom from distractibility, and processing speed).

Although they may be preferable, culture-and language-specific tests are not economically justifiable for test publishers except in the case of the very largest-minorities—for example, Spanish-speaking students with quite a bit of U.S. acculturation. The cost of standardizing a test is sizable, and the market for intelligence tests in, for example, Hmong, Ilocano, or Gujarathi is far too small to offset the development costs. For Spanish-speaking students, many publishers offer both English and Spanish versions. Some of these are translations, others are adaptations, and still others are independent tests. Test users must be careful to assess the appropriateness of the Spanish version to make sure that it is culturally appropriate for the test taker.

Use an Interpreter

If the tester is fluent in the student's native language or if a qualified interpreter is available, it is possible (although undesirable) to administer tests that are interpreted for a student who is an ELL. Interpretations can occur on an as-needed basis. For example, the tester can translate or interpret directions or test content and answer questions in the student's native language. Although interpretation is an appealing, simple approach, it presents numerous problems. In addition to the problems associated with the commercial availability of translations, the accuracy of the interpretation is unknown.

OTHER ACCOMMODATIONS

Testing in a student's native language is sometimes considered an "accommodation" (accommodations are discussed in Chapter 21). Other accommodations are sometimes used when assessing ELLs, particularly during the administration of tests used for making accountability decisions. For example, a side-by-side English/native language version of the test might be provided. Test directions and items might use simplified English language. ELLs might be allowed to use specialized English dictionaries containing the definitions for difficult words on the test. They might be allowed access to certain accommodations that other students have (e.g., extended time, small group setting, dictated response to a scribe). Many state accommodation policies indicate which accommodations ELLs can receive on the statewide test used for accountability purposes. However, it is important to recognize that certain native language and English language accommodations would not be appropriate if the test is intended to measure English proficiency.

TEST FIRST TO SEE IF THE STUDENT IS PROFICIENT ENOUGH IN ENGLISH TO TAKE THE ENGLISH VERSION

Increasingly, especially pertaining to accountability measures and national tests like the national Assessment of Educational Progress, the common practice is to give students an English proficiency test and to require a certain level of proficiency before having them take the test in English. Remember the fundamental ethical principle you learned in Chapter 3: it is our responsibility to do no harm. Administration of two tests takes valuable time away from activities in which students might otherwise engage. It also singles them out as "different" and puts the burden of the decision on the student. Furthermore, there are very few reliable measures of English proficiency, especially for selected areas like science and social studies that have their own vocabulary.

DO NOT TEST

Not all educational decisions and not all assessments require testing. For students who are ELLs from a variety of cultures, testing is usually a bad idea. Most states include language in their laws or regulations specifying that students must be in school a minimum amount of time before they can participate in the state testing program.

5 Making Entitlement Decisions Without Testing

Lack of progress in learning English is the most common reason students who are ELLs are referred to ascertain eligibility for special education (Figueroa, 1990). It seems that most teachers do not understand that it usually takes several years to acquire sufficient fluency to be fully functional academically and cognitively in English. However, the school cannot overlook the possibility that students who are ELLs are really handicapped beyond their English abilities.

Determination of disability can be made without psychological or educational testing. The determination of sensory or physical disability can be readily made with the use of interpreters. Students or their parents need little proficiency in English for professionals to determine if a student has a traumatic brain injury, other health impairments, or orthopedic, visual, or auditory disabilities. Disabilities based on impaired social function (such as emotional disturbance and autism) can be identified through direct observation of a student or interviews with family members (using interpreters if necessary), teachers, and so forth.

The appraisal of intellectual ability is required to identify students with mental retardation. When students have moderate to severe forms of mental retardation, it may be possible to determine that they have limited intellectual ability without ever testing. For example, direct observation may reveal that a student has not acquired language (either English or the native language), communicates only by pointing and making grunting noises, is not toilet trained, and engages in inappropriate play whether judged by standards of the primary culture or by U.S. culture. The student's parents may recognize that the student is much slower than their other children and would be judged to have mental retardation in their native culture. In this case, parents may want special educational services for their child. In such a situation, identification would not be impeded by the student's (or parents') lack of

SCENARIO *in* ASSESSMENT

DMETRI | Dmetri is a 12-year-old student with two elementary-age younger brothers. The family emigrated to the United States from Astana (the capital of Kazakhstan) 3 years ago. In Kazakhstan, Dmetri and his brothers (Yuri and Vasili) attended a Russian-language school. Dmetri's family speaks Russian at home; Dmetri's parents also both speak Kazakh. The father and children are learning English.

When the family arrived in the United States, Dmetri entered school immediately and was placed in an ESL program. His progress was slow the first year. In the spring semester, Dmitri's parents came to the parent-teacher conference accompanied by an interpreter. The parents were concerned about Dmetri's poor grades and dislike of school. They reported that Yuri and Vasili both enjoyed school and seemed to be learning English more rapidly. Dmetri's ESL teacher also expressed frustration with Dmetri's progress. He completed the minimum amount of work quickly and carelessly.

Dmetri's second year in school was academically similar to the first—poor grades, little effort, little progress. Dmetri had acquired some social English; his oral language was grammatically simple (e.g., present, future, and past tenses). His lexicon remained limited, and his main strategy for finding an appropriate word was the "that thing" strategy. For example, he would say, "that thing on wall you get water" when he didn't know "drinking fountain" or "that thing on arm [pointing to wrist] for time" when he didn't know "wristwatch." Unfortunately, Dmetri added some inappropriate behavior to his repertoire—bullying and extorting younger students. At the end of the second year, his ESL teacher suggested that the parents refer Dmetri for a psychoeductional evaluation to ascertain if he had a learning disability.

Dmetri was evaluated by both the speech and language specialist and the school psychologist. The speech and language specialist administered the Peabody Picture Vocabulary Test (IV) to assess Dmetri's vocabulary. He earned a standard score of 65, which is significantly below average. The specialist also engaged Dmetri in conversation and noted many speech problems associated with the differences between spoken Russian and English. He had difficulty with the r-controlled short vowel sound (as in fir, her, murmur); the *th* sound; and words beginning with *w*, which he pronounced as beginning with *v*. His speech gave the impression of being hurried and indistinct because he usually stressed only one syllable even when the word had more than one stressed syllable or weakly stressed syllables. Grammatically, Dmetri had not mastered the use of articles and used gender pronouns to refer to nouns (the ship she goes fast). Finally, spelling was particularly difficult for Demetri. The speech and language specialist believed that Dmetri's language problems were most likely the result of the short period of time he had been in this country and the differences between the English and Russian languages. She did not believe Dmetri had a speech or language disability, although she agreed that he was not learning English as rapidly as most students.

The school psychologist administered the Test of Nonverbal Intelligence–3, the Leiter International Performance Scale–Revised, and the Peabody Individual Achievement Test–Revised/Normative Update.[1] On the Test of Nonverbal Intelligence–3, Dmetri earned an IQ of 94. On the Leiter, Dmetri earned scaled scores (mean = 100; S = 15) ranging from 92 (Reasoning) to 103 (Attention); Visualization and Memory were 94 and 93 respectively. His IQ was 95. The psychologist chose the PIAT/NU to minimize the demands of expressive language on estimates of Dmetri's achievement. Dmetri earned the following standard scores: Mathematics 95, Reading Recognition 75, Reading Comprehension 70, Spelling 70, General Information 83, and Written Expression 74. In her written report, the psychologist stated that she believed the intelligence scores to be minimum estimates of Dmetri's ability and the achievement scores to be invalid due to his limited proficiency in English, differences in schooling between Kazakhstan and the United States, and lack of cultural knowledge.

At the multidisciplinary meeting to review the assessment results and determine if Dmetri was eligible for special education and related services, the team was initially divided. The ESL teacher and the general education teacher believed Dmetri may have a learning disability; the speech and language specialist and the school psychologist stated that he could not be considered learning disabled due to cultural and language differences. The parents did not believe Dmetri was disabled, and the principal did not initially express an opinion. After some discussion, the team found Dmetri not to be eligible for special education or 504 services. However, all of the members agreed that Dmetri needed more intensive ESL services and English language instruction. Unfortunately, those services were not available in the district.

What implications about your own professional role can you draw from this scenario? Go to the Education CourseMate website for this textbook for more reflection questions about this Scenario in Assessment.

[1] See Chapter 15 for information about the intelligence tests and Chapter 11 for information about the achievement test.

English. However, students with mild mental retardation do not demonstrate such pronounced developmental delays; rather, their disability is relative and not easily separated from their limited proficiency in English.

The identification of students with specific learning disabilities seems very difficult. The IDEA (§300.304-§300.309) requires that failure to achieve adequately in "oral expression, listening comprehension, written expression, basic reading skills, reading fluency, reading comprehension, math calculation or math problem-solving" be considered indicative of a specific learning disability only if the student has been "provided with learning experiences and instruction appropriate for the child's age or State-approved grade level standards" and has either failed to respond to a scientific, research-based intervention or demonstrates a certain pattern of strengths and weaknesses. In order to find a student eligible under this category, the associated results cannot be due to cultural disadvantage or limited English proficiency. Clearly, these conditions cannot be met for students who are ELLs, especially when the students are also culturally diverse. Furthermore, limited research has been done specifically on interventions to address the needs of ELLs, and so it may be difficult to identify and implement an appropriate intervention that both meets the legal requirements and addresses the unique characteristics of students who are ELLs.

Finally, limited English proficiency should not be considered a speech or language impairment. Although it is quite possible for a student with limited English to have a speech or language impairment, that impairment would also be present in the student's native language. Speakers of the student's native language, such as the student's parents, could verify the presence of stuttering, impaired articulation, or voice impairments; the identification of a language disorder would require a fluent speaker of the child's native language.

When it is not possible to determine whether a student has a disability, students who are ELLs who are experiencing academic difficulties still need to have services besides special education available. Districts should have programs in English as a second language (ESL) that could continue to help students after they have acquired social communication skills.

Chapter Comprehension Questions

Write your answers to each of the following questions and then compare your responses to the text.

1. Describe language and acculturation differences that are present among students in U.S. public schools.
2. Describe the legal protections and requirements for students who are ELLs included in IDEA and NCLB.
3. What are four questions that should be used to guide the assessment process for students from culturally and linguistically diverse backgrounds?
4. Describe the merits and drawbacks of three approaches to testing students who are ELLs.

Web Activities 

1. Search the Internet for the Center for Equity and Excellence in Education at George Washington University to find information on the ELL accommodations allowed for the statewide test in your state.
2. Search the Internet for the IRIS center at Vanderbilt University. At the site, under Resources, click on "Diversity" and then on "Information Briefs." Read the documents entitled "Disproportionality and Overidentification" and "Disproportionate Representation of Culturally and Linguistically Diverse Students in Special Education: Measuring the Problem." Summarize what you have learned.
3. Go to the University of Oregon's website and look for the Spanish version of DIBELS (i.e., the Indicadores Dinámicos del Éxito en la Lectura (®IDEL). Review the IDEL measures. Given the content provided in Chapter 22, under what circumstances would you consider using ®IDEL?
4. Go to the materials on Universal Design for Learning that are provided in Chapter 21 at the Education CourseMate website for this text. How might the concepts of Universal Design for Learning assist with instruction and assessment for students who are ELLs?
5. Search the Internet for English Proficiency Tests and read the latest information about efforts to assess students and ascertain their proficiency in English.

Web Resources

Center for Equity and Excellence in Education ELL Accommodations Online Toolkit and Database
http://ells.ceee.gwu.edu/tools.aspx
This website provides a searchable database of ELL accommodation research studies and related information about a variety of common ELL accommodations.

Teaching Diverse Learners from the Education Alliance at Brown University
http://www.alliance.brown.edu/tdl/index.shtml
This website provides research summaries and suggestions for teachers who work with students from culturally and linguistically diverse backgrounds.

Additional resources for this chapter can be found on the Education CourseMate website. Go to CengageBrain.com.com to access the site.

Using Technology to Help Make Assessment Decisions

CHAPTER GOALS

1. Understand the distinction between continuous and periodic progress monitoring.
2. Know the advantages of technology-enhanced progress monitoring and instructional management systems.
3. Understand representative technology-enhanced continuous progress monitoring measures.
4. Understand representative technology-enhanced periodic progress monitoring measures.
5. Know the advantages and limitations of computerized scoring and report-writing programs.

KEY TERMS

computer adaptive test
TOPS report
continuous progress monitoring measures
Status of the Class Report
periodic progress monitoring measures
diagnostic report
computerized scoring
computer-generated reports

Many regard educational technology as something new. However, it wasn't new in 1988, when the Technology-Related Assistance for Individuals with Disabilities Act was passed, or in 1990, when The Carl D. Perkins Vocational and Applied Technology Act was passed. It wasn't new when the IDEA included assistive technology as a related service. Special educators have long been familiar with FM voice amplification systems and electronic conversion of print to Braille. What is new is the almost universal access to technology that performs complex tasks, makes decisions, and connects us to the world. Today websites provide parents and students access to current and future assignments; e-mail allows fast parent-teacher communication and exchange of documents; the Internet provides access to information from around the world.

This chapter focuses on two uses of technology in assessment. First, we describe how computers are being used to facilitate instructional decision making. Second, we describe how computers are used to score and make sophisticated test interpretations.

1 Computers and Instructional Decision Making

For individual students, computer programs are now capable of determining where instruction should begin within a student's specific curriculum, assessing the presence or absence of prerequisite skills, identifying the specific skills a student is or is not mastering during instruction, and determining if a student is making adequate progress toward achieving instructional goals, attaining proficiency on state tests, and mastering common core state standards. For classrooms, computer programs can aggregate data on each student to make decisions about instructional grouping, curriculum sequence (e.g., do most students lack prerequisite knowledge?), the class' progress toward various outcomes, and the need for additional educational resources. All of the preceding decisions are derived from two types of information: What a student knows and the rate at which the student is learning.

WHAT A STUDENT KNOWS

Whether by traditional testing where students answer the same questions (or parallel forms of the same questions) or by "adaptive testing,"[1] a computer program examines the test questions passed and failed to ascertain what a student knows and what a student does not know. The computer provides teachers with printouts of that information and the teacher is able to use it to make data-driven instructional decisions, such as the following:

- What skills has the student mastered? In the aggregate, what skills have the students in the class mastered?
- Where should instruction begin? Teachers should instruct their students in what has not yet been learned and avoid repeating instruction on material the student already knows.
- Does the student have a group? Students who are learning the same content can be grouped for instruction.

Information about the starting points of instruction can also provide a snapshot of which students are behind and how far they are behind. Some computer programs can generate screening reports showing the proficiency levels of each of the students in their class (see Figure 23.1). Reports like these can help school personnel to

[1] In adaptive testing, the difficulty of each item in the item pool is calculated using Item-Response Theory (IRT). (See Coursemate website for this text for an explanation of IRT.) An item of middle difficulty is administered. Dependent on whether or not the student passes that item the computer administers an easier or a harder item. This process continues until the student's level of proficiency or level of skill development is identified, often after only a few test items have been administered. Thus, adaptive testing is more efficient that traditional testing procedures (McBride & Martin, 1983).

FIGURE 23.1
Screening Report

The Screening Report is available for STAR Early Literacy, STAR Reading, and STAR Math.

Screening Report
for <State>
Printed Friday, September 10, 2010 5:11:12 PM

Page 1 of the screening report shows a graphical representation of all students in the grade.

School: Oakwood Elementary School

Reporting Period: 9/1/2010–9/7/2010
(Fall Screening)

Report Options
Reporting Parameter Group: All Demographics [Default]

Report may be run for your state, school or district benchmarks.

Grade: 4

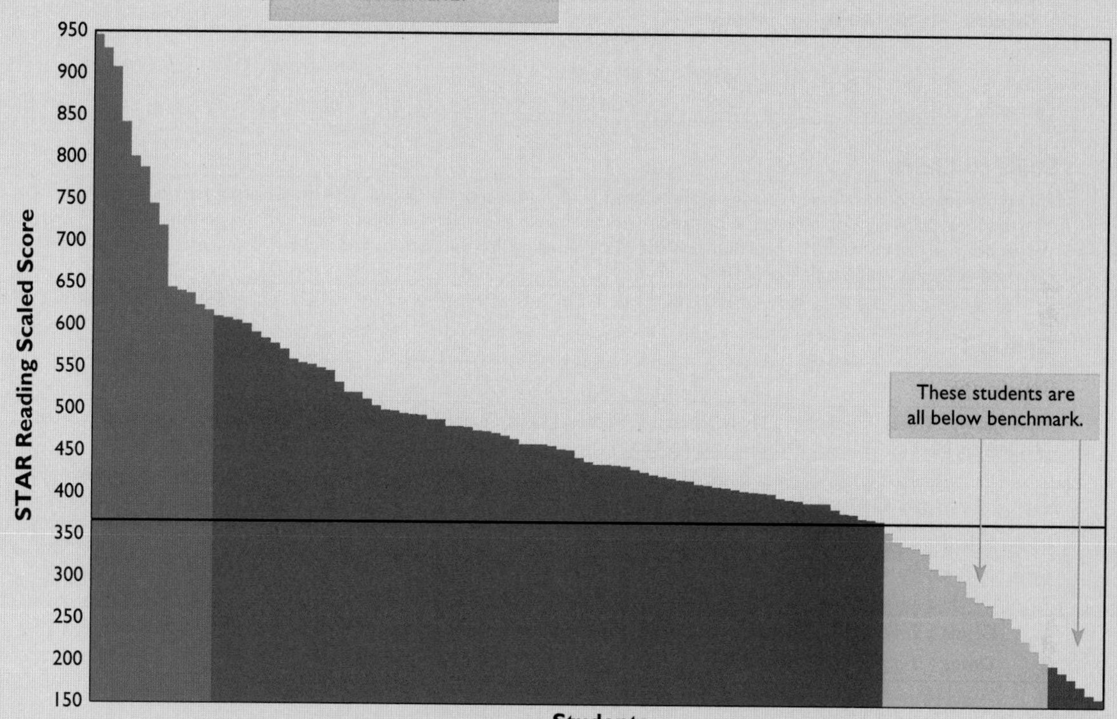

Categories/Levels	Current Benchmark[d]	Number	Percent	Benchmark At Time of State Test
Proficient				
Advanced	At/Above 618 SS	12	11%	At/Above 670 SS
Proficient	At/Above 367 SS	74	67%	At/Above 443 SS
Category Total		86	78%	
Less Than Proficient				
Basic	Below 367 SS	18	16%	Below 443 SS
Below Basic	Below 200 SS	6	5%	Below 283 SS
Category Total		24	22%	
Students Tested		110		

Key questions to ask based on this and other information: Are you satisfied with the number of students at the highest level of performance? Next, consider the level or score that indicates proficiency. Which students just above proficiency are you "worried about" and what support within or beyond core instruction is warranted? What support is needed for students just below? Do all students represented by your lowest level need urgent intervention?

Use these key questions to help determine next steps.

Screening is the first step in Response to Intervention (RTI). Use this report for grade-level planning and identifying students who need the most help.

[d]Benchmark adjusted for time of year using student growth norms.

Exclusively Available for STAR Reading™ Enterprise Customers R43439

FIGURE 23.2
Class Instructional Planning Report

The Class Instructional Planning Report is available for STAR Reading and STAR Math.

This report provides a list of skill recommendations for each group identified on the Instructional Report Groupings page.

Class Instructional Planning Report

Printed Monday, September 13, 2010 9:16:32 AM

School: Oakwood Elementary School

Reporting Period: 09/01/2010–09/13/2010

Group: Grade 4 Math

Instructional Groups	Number of Students	Scaled Score (0–1400)	
		Median	Range
Group 1	10	659	602–874
Group 2	4	569	537–588
Group 3	4	468	403–519

Skills to Learn

Skill recommendations are based on the median score for each Instructional Group. These skills are a starting point for instructional planning. Combine this information with your own knowledge of the student and use your professional judgment when designing an instructional program. Use the Math Learning Progressions to find additional information for each skill, worked examples, and example problems.

Students are listed in rank order.

Group 1

Students

Unger, Jerry; Thiess, Kimberly; O'Neil, Sarah; Gonzales, Maria; Richmond, Angela; Bell, Timothy; Rodriguez, Carlos; Anderson, Marcus; Chang, Michelle; Stone, Lisa

Recommended skills are based on the median Scaled Score for each Group.

Numbers and Operations

1. o Estimate a product of whole numbers using any method
2. o WP: Estimate a product of two whole numbers using any method
3. Divide a multi-digit whole number by 10 or 100 with no remainder
4. Divide a 2-digit whole number by a 1-digit whole number with no remainder in the quotient
5. Divide a 3-digit whole number by a 1-digit whole number with no remainder in the quotient

Algebra

1. o Determine a rule that relates to two variables
2. Extend a number pattern in a table of related pairs
3. Use a variable expression with one operation to represent a verbal expression
4. Use a verbal expression to represent a variable expression with one operation
5. WP: Use a variable expression with

Find more information on any skill listed using the Math Learning Progressions.

Geometry and Measurement

1. o Calculate elapsed time exceeding an hour with regrouping
2. WP: Calculate elapsed time exceeding an hour without regrouping hours
3. o WP: Calculate elapsed time exceeding an hour with regrouping hours
4. WP: Determine the end time given the start time and the elapsed time exceeding an hour
5. WP: Determine the start time given the end time and the elapsed time exceeding an hour

Data Analysis, Probability, and Statistics

1. Answer a question using information from a table
2. List possible outcomes of a simple event
3. Answer a question using information from a line graph that does not start at zero or has a broken vertical scale
4. WP: Extend a line graph to solve a problem
5. Read a double- or stacked-bar graph

Page 1 of a multipage report. Remaining groups are shown on following pages.

o Designates a core skill. Core skills identify the most critical skills to learn at each grade level.

Exclusively Available for STAR Math™ Enterprise Customers R45644 identify individual students who need intensified supports. Additional reports can identify students who can be grouped for instructional purposes (see Figure 23.2). These reports enable teachers to identify students who are at about the same instructional level and who could be taught in groups.

RATE OF LEARNING

A number of computer programs evaluate a student's rate of learning by combining information about what a student currently knows, what a student should learn, and the number of days that should be required for the student to learn the material. Assuming that students learn incrementally, one would expect student knowledge to increase with instruction. Schooling is finite; there are only so many hours in a school year and school career. Students are expected to master quite a lot of skills and acquire quite a bit of information in school. If students fail to progress expeditiously, they will not learn all that is expected and needed. Thus, information about the rate of student learning is essential in making decisions about the adequacy of progress in meeting both individual and state goals.

Several computer programs are currently available that are used to monitor student progress toward individual goals, passing the state proficiency examination, meeting the state content standards, or responding to interventions. AIMSweb (NCS Pearson, 2010) and Yearly Progress Pro (undated, CTB-McGraw-Hill) are two such web-based CBM data management systems. Other programs do more, such as develop and score tests as well as writing reports. For example, STAR Enterprise Assessments (Renaissance Learning, 2011) are web-based computer tests that can be used to help plot a student's progress toward a previously set goal (see Figure 23.3). The figure shows the progress Susan Halden will need to make in order to meet his goal, and the progress he currently is making. Similar reports can be generated to show progress toward state standards. Figure 23.4 is such a report and is labeled a pathway toward proficiency. The figure illustrates for Lydia Hansen that her current rate of progress predicts that she will demonstrate proficiency on the state test. The advantage of reports like this is that the computer does all the necessary calculations in the background and the teacher receives easy-to-use information that helps make decisions about whether the student is making sufficient progress or if interventions need to be changed.

FIGURE 23.3
Student Progress Monitoring Report

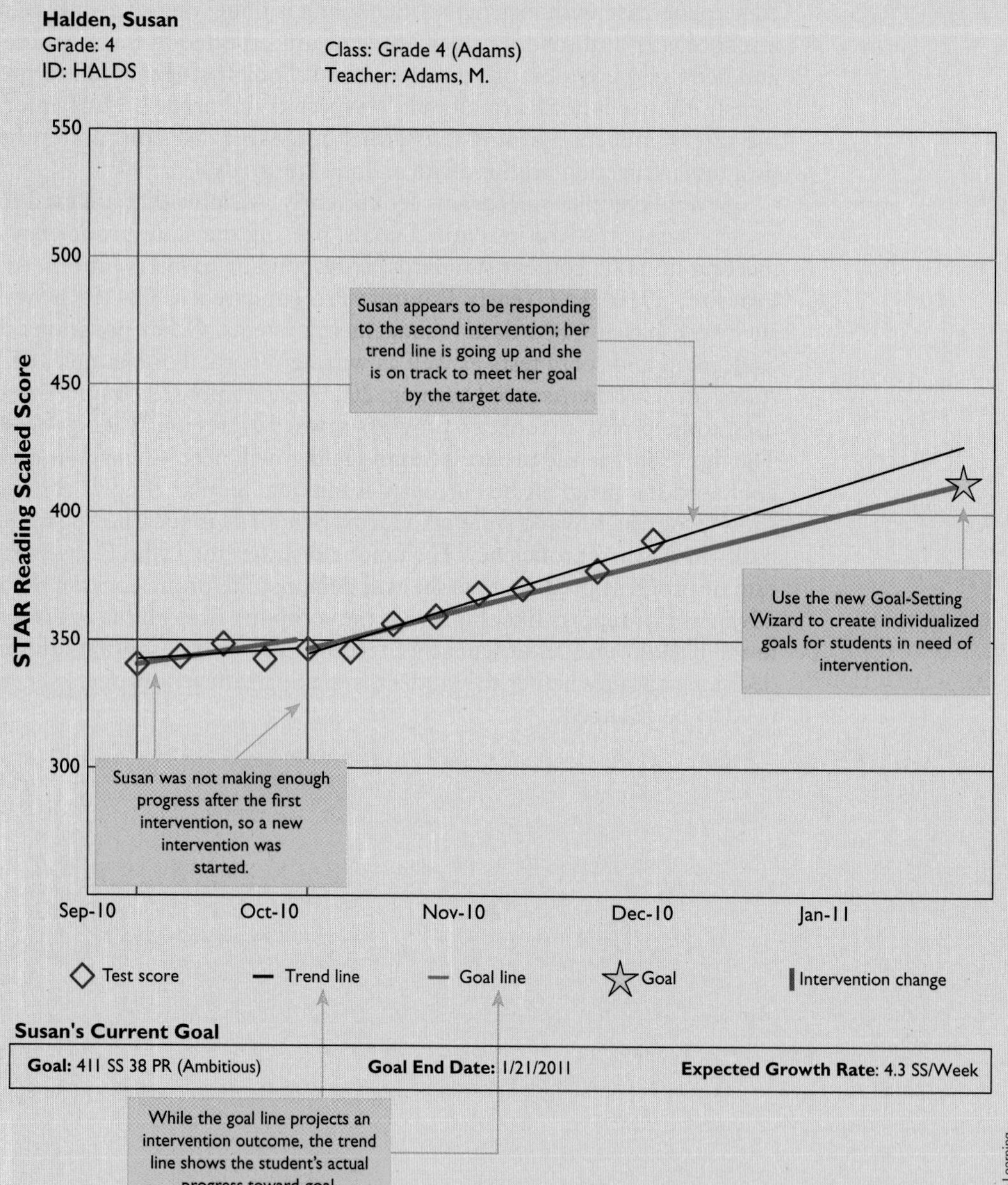

FIGURE 23.4
Student Performance Report: State Assessment

The Student Performance Report is available for STAR Reading and STAR Math.

Student Performance Report

State Assessment

Printed Thursday, February 10, 2011 3:45:12 PM

Predict performance on the state test in time to make adjustments to math instruction and math practice.

School: Oakwood Elementary School

Reporting Period: 9/1/2010–6/10/2011 (School Year)

Hansen, Lydia
Grade: 4
ID: H4329

Teacher: Carter, M.
Class: Math 4C (Carter)

Pathway to Proficiency

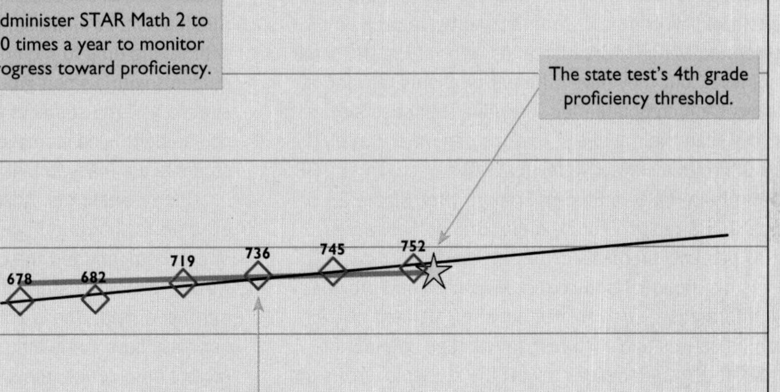

STAR Math and the State Mathematics Assessment

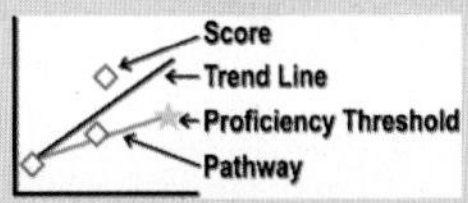

Research has shown that STAR Math scores are related to student performance on the State Mathematics Assessment. In the graph above, blue diamonds show the student's STAR Math test scores. The gold star notes the STAR Math scaled score that is approximately equivalent to the threshold for proficiency (Proficient) at the time of the state test. For grade 4, this score is approximately 610.

The green line represents the typical pathway to proficiency for students who are just at this threshold. A STAR Math score below the green line indicates that the student will need to improve at a higher than typical rate in order to achieve proficiency by the time of the state test. A STAR Math score above the green line indicates that the student was "on the pathway" to proficiency at the time that STAR test was taken. If the student has taken three or more tests, a black trend line displays the statistical tendency of the scores. If the trend line is higher than the gold star at the state test date, the student can be considered to be on the pathway toward proficiency.

The key and explanation are useful for teachers who want to share the report with parents and students.

State Mathematics Assessment information was updated on 7/29/2010 and is subject to change.

Exclusively Available for Renaissance Place™ Real Time Customers R43718

SCENARIO *in* ASSESSMENT

MARCIE ADAMS'S FOURTH-GRADE CLASS

The Oakwood Elementary School has used Star Math for 2 years. In the fall, Marcie Adams takes her fourth-grade class to the media center, where each student takes an individualized 15- or 20-minute math test on a computer. The computer selects items of different levels of difficulty based on a student's performance on previous tests. Students who pass an item get a more difficult follow-up item; students who do not pass an item get an easier follow-up item. Testing continues until the student's level of skill development in math is determined. When the testing is completed, Ms. Adams receives (1) a record of the math level of each student in her class, (2) the range of student performance, and (3) the numbers of students who are working at various levels.

Brandon and Carlos are students in Ms. Adams's class. Once she knows their instructional levels, she assigns them to a specific level of a computerized math software program called Accelerated Math™. Brandon and Carlos are at the same instructional level, but they have different problems to work on. When the boys each complete their individualized sheets of math problems, they scan their answers, and the computer scores their responses and prints a corrective feedback sheet known as TOPS (The Opportunity to Praise a Student) report. (See Figure 23.5 for Brandon's TOPS report.) For example, Brandon answered 16 of 20 (80 percent) problems correctly. The TOPS report also indicates his incorrect and correct responses and provides cumulative information, such as mastery of 62 percent of the fourth-grade objectives and a 75 percent average on practice exercises to date. Ms. Adams can review the students' errors and provide individualized instruction before the computer generates a new sheet of math problems at the same instructional level.

Students continue working on sheets of math practice items at their instructional level until they consistently achieve 75 percent accuracy on practice exercises for four objectives. The computer then signals Ms. Adams when students are ready to take a computer-generated test on the objective. Students take the test, scan it, and receive corrective feedback. When students reach 85 percent mastery, they are moved to the next objective. The practice–practice–practice–test process is repeated.

Each morning, Ms. Adams prints a report summarizing the progress of her class (i.e., Status of the Class Report). See Figure 23.6.[2] This report identifies students who need assignments and students who need help with two or more practice objectives. This morning, the Status of Class Report indicates that Brandon needs help with practice items for two objectives that he is currently working on, and that he is not yet ready to test on any objectives. At the bottom of the sheet, Ms. Adams sees the specific objectives for which Brandon needs help: multiplying money expressions by whole numbers, and word problems that require him to figure change. She is also able to see that Carlos is currently working but that she needs to print a test for him to take. Test printing is always under the control of the teacher.

The Status of Class Report also alerts Ms. Adams to specific objectives that are causing difficulty for three or more students. She learns that Michelle, Lisa, and Lawrence are having difficulty with telling time to the hour and minute; she provides those students with a small-group tutorial. The report also gives her a summary of the status of the students in her class. She learns that one student needs to have a specific objective assigned, three students are ready to test, and two students need intervention.

Once a week, Ms. Adams prints a diagnostic report (an example is shown in Figure 23.7). The report gives her a snapshot of every student and the class as a whole. She reviews the report weekly to monitor student performance and look for students who may need help. She is able to see that on average, students in her class have completed 380 problems, are getting 83 percent correct on practice items, and are averaging 86 percent correct on regular tests. Note that she is also able to see that Brandon is performing below expectation (only achieving 64 percent correct on practice exercise and 67 percent correct on regular tests). Brandon is identified as a student at risk and in need of intervention. When students are persistently at risk, teachers can use this information to make informed decisions to refer students for additional assistance or psychoeducational evaluation.

What implications about your own professional role can you draw from this scenario? Go to the Education CourseMate website for this textbook for more reflection questions about this Scenario in Assessment.

[2] Note that we have reduced the class size to 12 for simplicity.

FIGURE 23.5
Accelerated Math™ Practice TOPS Report for Brandon Bollig

Practice TOPS Report for Brandon Bollig

Printed Friday, March 11, 2011 10:45:20 AM

The Accelerated Math TOPS Report prints after each assignment is scored, giving immediate feedback to students.

School: Oakwood Elementary School
Class: Math 4A

Number Correct: 16 / 20 (80%)

Brandon is having problems with these objectives. Brandon will make corrections and share with his teacher before he continues.

Incorrect Responses (4)

Objective	Problem	Your Answer	Correct Answer
90. Generate a table of paired numbers based on a rule	7	A	D
90. Generate a table of paired numbers based on a rule	12	D	A
91. Determine a rule that relates two variables	15	B	C
91. Determine a rule that relates two variables	18	A	B

Objectives on this Practice (5)

Objective	Results		Overall	
89. Identify a missing figure in a repeating pictorial or nonnumeric pattern	6/6	100%	9/12	75%
90. Generate a table of paired numbers based on a rule	4/6	67%	9/18	50%
91. Determine a rule that relates two variables	4/6	67%	9/18	50%
39.[c] WP: Divide a 3-digit whole number by a 1-digit whole number with no remainder in the quotient	1/1	100%	4/4	100%
40.[c] WP: Divide a 2-digit whole number by a 1-digit whole number with a remainder in the quotient	1/1	100%	4/4	100%

Overall Progress

Average Percent Correct	Marking Period (79% Complete)	School Year (70% Complete)
Practice %:	67[a]	75[a]
Test %:	70[b]	83[b]
Review %:	73	79

Objective Summary

Ready to Test: 1
Goal for Marking Period: 32
Total Mastered this Marking Period: 21 (66% of Goal)
Total Mastered this Year: 93

The goal for Review is 80%. Brandon's score suggests he may be having trouble retaining concepts.

Teacher Comments:

The goal for Practice is 75%. Brandon is not meeting this goal; he may be having trouble with new concepts.

Parent

[a]Includes Exercise Results
[b]Includes Diagnostic Test Results
[c]Review Objectives

FIGURE 23.6
Accelerated Math™ Status of the Class Report

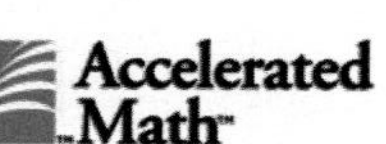

Status of the Class Report

Printed Monday, March 14, 2011 3:50:44 PM

Page 1 of the Status of the Class Report

School: Oakwood Elementary School

Class: Math 4A
Teacher: Adams, Marcie

Group Name: Class

Accelerated Math provides the data to differentiate practice to strengthen your core curriculum.

To aid with instructional planning, the report helps identify which math objectives are causing the most difficulty for students.

Assignment Status

Student	Action Needed	Objectives Ready to Test	Last Assignment Completed		Outstanding Assignments		
			Type	Date	Practice	Exercise	Test
Anderson, Marcus		2	Practice	03/11/11	03/11/11		
Bell, Timothy		1	Regular Test	03/14/11		03/14/11	
Bollig, Brandon	I Intervene (2)	1	Practice	03/11/11	03/14/11	03/11/11	
Chang, Michelle		0	Practice	03/11/11	03/11/11		
Gonzales, Maria		3	Practice	03/14/11	03/14/11		
Halden, Susan	I Intervene (2)	1	Regular Test	03/11/11		03/14/11	
O'Neil, Sarah	Assign Objs	0	Practice	03/14/11			03/11/11[a]
Richmond, Angela		0	Practice	03/14/11	03/14/11		
Rodrigues, Carlos		4	Practice	03/14/11	03/14/11		
Stone, Lisa		0	Practice	03/11/11	03/11/11		
Tyler, Lawrence	Print Assignment	3	Practice	03/11/11			
White, Jacob		0	Practice	03/14/11	03/14/11		

I Intervention Needed

Provide targeted instruction to help students having problems with specific objectives.

Student	Assignment Type	Objectives	Library Objective Code	Overall Results
Bollig, Brandon	Practice	90. Generate a table of paired numbers based on a rule	DMG4-090	11/18 (61%)
	Practice	91. Determine a rule that relates two variables	DMG4-091	12/18 (67%)
Halden, Susan	Regular Test	96. Convert between customary units of weight using whole numbers	DMG4-096	6/10 (60%)
	Regular Test	97. Convert between metric units of capacity using whole numbers	DMG4-097	5/10 (50%)

[a]Diagnostic Test

continued on the next page

FIGURE 23.6
(*Continued*)

Accelerated Math™

Status of the Class Report

Printed Monday, March 14, 2011 3:50:44 PM

Page 2 of the Status of the Class Report

School: Oakwood Elementary School

Class: Math 4A

Teacher: Adams, Marcie

Group Name: Class

Objectives Causing Difficulties

Minimum Students: 3

Use this information to determine how to group students to work on concepts.

Objectives	Assignment Type	Student	Library Objective Code	Overall Results
112. WP: Determine the perimeter of a square or rectangle	Practice	Chang, Michelle	DMG4-112	8/12 (67%)
	Practice	Stone, Lisa	DMG4-112	7/12 (58%)
	Practice	Tyler, Lawrence	DMG4-112	5/10 (50%)
114. Determine the area of a polygon on a grid	Practice	Richmond, Angela	DMG4-114	6/10 (60%)
	Practice	Rodrigues, Carlos	DMG4-114	6/10 (60%)
	Practice	White, Jacob	DMG4-114	5/12 (42%)

Outstanding Assignments

Student	School Days Since Last Work Printed	Practice			Exercise			Test		
		From	Problems	Date Printed	From	Problems	Date Printed	From	Problems	Date Printed
Anderson, Marcus	1	2431	1–18	03/11/11						
Bell, Timothy	Today				2487	1–8	03/14/11			
Bollig, Brandon	Today	2541	21–40	03/14/11	2453	1–16	03/11/11			
Chang, Michelle	1	2441	21–40	03/11/11						
Gonzales, Maria	Today	2509	1–20	03/14/11						
Halden, Susan	Today				2493	17–32	03/14/11			
O'Neil, Sarah	Today							2466[a]	1–20	03/14/11
Richmond, Angela	Today	2501	61–80	03/14/11						
Rodrigues, Carlos	Today	2476	21–48	03/14/11						
Stone, Lisa	1	2448	1–20	03/11/11						
Tyler, Lawrence										
White, Jacob	Today	2460	1–18	03/14/11						

[a]Diagnostic Test

The teacher needs to print an assignment for Lawrence.

continued on the next page

FIGURE 23.6
(Continued)

Accelerated Math™

Status of the Class Report

Printed Monday, March 14, 2011 3:50:44 PM

Page 3 of the Status of the Class Report

School: Oakwood Elementary School

Class: Math 4A
Teacher: Adams, Marcie

Group Name: Class

Group Summary

Action Summary	Total
Students Need Assignments Printed	1
Students Need Objs Assigned	1
Students Need Tests Printed	0
Students Need Intervention	2
Objectives with three or more students experiencing difficulty	2

Outstanding Assignments	Total
Practices	8
Exercises	3
Regular Tests	0
Diagnostic Tests	1

FIGURE 23.7
Accelerated Math™
Diagnostic Report

Accelerated Math

Diagnostic Report

Printed Wednesday, March 16, 2011 3:30:12 PM

This report helps to carefully monitor students' progress toward mastery of math objectives.

Reporting Period: 1/24/2011 – 3/16/2011
(3rd Quarter)

School: Oakwood Elementary School

Report Options

Reporting Parameter Group: All Demographics [Default]
Group By: Class

Class: Math 4A

Teacher: Adams, Marcie

Group Name: Class

Key indicators of successful math practice are Average Percent Correct on Practice, Average Percent Correct on Review, and Average Number of Objectives Mastered Per Week.

This indicates whether students are on pace and are mastering an average of four objectives per week.

Student	Diagnostic Codes	Average Percent Correct						Engaged Time[a]	Objectives Mastered				
		Practice	Exercise	Regular Test	Diagnostic Test	Total Tests	Review		Average Number Per Week	Regular Test	Diagnostic Test	Total Tests	Average Objective Level
Anderson, Marcus		92	94	93	94	94	95	40	4.0	27	5	32	4.5
Bell, Timothy		80	77	85	82	84	83	29	2.9	15	8	23	4.4
Bollig, Brandon	I, P, T, R	64 ◄	69	67 ◄	72	70	73 ◄	28	2.8	12	10	22	4.0
Chang, Michelle		85	87	88	87	88	90	33	3.3	19	7	26	4.3
Gonzales, Maria		91	88	91	89	90	91	38	3.8	23	7	30	4.4
Halden, Susan	I, P, T, R	70 ◄	67	74 ◄	75	75	77 ◄	28	2.8	11	11	22	4.1
O'Neil, Sarah		95	96	95	96	96	97	44	4.4	31	4	35	4.8
Richmond, Angela		83	86	86	84	85	84	30	3.0	15	9	24	4.4
Rodrigues, Carlos		84	81	87	85	86	88	34	3.4	17	10	27	4.6
Stone, Lisa		89	87	88	86	87	90	35	3.5	18	10	28	4.5
Tyler, Lawrence		81	76	85	84	85	80	31	3.1	19	6	25	4.3
White, Jacob		86	89	90	88	89	88	30	3.0	16	8	24	4.5
Average		83	83	86	85	86	86	33	3.3	19	8	27	4.4

Susan seems to be struggling with new concepts. Goal is 75%.

Brandon may be having problems retaining previously learned concepts. Goal is 80%.

Diagnostic Code Summary

Number of Students	% of Students	Diagnostic Code	Description
2	17	I	Teacher intervention needed (see Status of the Class Report)
2	17	P	Practice percentage lower than 75%
2	17	T	Regular Test percentage lower than 85%
2	17	R	Review percentage lower than 80%
0	0	M	Less than 1/2 of the median objectives mastered (1/2 the median = 13)

Students At Risk: 2 of 12 (17%)

Group Summary

Objectives Mastered	Total
Regular Tests	223
Diagnostic Tests	95
All Tests	318
Students	
Total	12
Number who did not take any Regular Tests	0

◄ Trouble value

[a]Engaged Time per Day: An estimate based on number of objectives mastered and an anticipated 40 minutes per day of math practice.

TECHNOLOGY ENHANCED PROGRESS MONITORING MEASURES

There are two types of progress monitoring measures: periodic and continuous. Periodic measures are given either by hand (e.g., AIMSweb) or by computer (STAR Enterprise measures in reading and math), and are administered "periodically" (typically every 3 to 5 weeks). Continuous progress monitoring measures typically are used daily to monitor overall progress and keep a "running record" of student performance.

Periodic Progress Monitoring Measures

Representative periodic progress monitoring measures are listed in Table 23.1. Computer adaptive tests can be used for periodic monitoring of student progress. In the remainder of this section, we review AIMSweb (PsychCorp/Pearson) and the STAR Enterprise System (Renaissance Learning, 2011), a system that consists of three computer adaptive measures that can be used to determine individual student skill level or measure individual and class growth toward accomplishing specific goals or objectives. These include STAR Reading™ and STAR Math™.

See the Education CourseMate website for the textbook for a review of STAR Early Literacy

AIMSweb[3]

AIMSweb (Pearson, 2001) is a web-based tool designed to help with collection and management of periodic progress monitoring data. Users can either download, administer, and enter results using curriculum-based

[3] Sarah Stebbe Rowe, Kristen S. Girard

TABLE 23.1 Software Packages for Periodic Progress Monitoring

Provider	Product	URL
AIMSweb	Basic, Pro, RTI	www.aimsweb.com
Compass Learning	Explorer, Odyssey Math	www.compasslearning.com
EasyCBM	EasyCBM Reading EasyCBM Math	www.easycbm.com
EduCare	KewUp!	www.educarelearning.com
McGraw-Hill Digital Learning	Yearly Progress Pro	www.mhdigitallearning.com
Northwest Evaluation Association	Measure of Academic Progress	www.nwea.org
Pearson Education	Pearson Prosper	www.scantron.com
Pearson School Systems	Pearson Benchmark	www.personschoolsystems.com
PLATO Learning	eduTest	www.edutest.com
PRO-ED	Monitoring Basic Skills Progress	www.proedinc.com
Renaissance Learning	STAR Math, STAR Reading, STAR Early Literacy	www.renlearn.com
Riverside Publishing	Assess2Know, Edusoft Assessment Management System	www.riverpub.com www.riverpub.com/products/edusoft/
Scantron	Achievement Series	www.scantron.com
Taylor Associates	ReadingPlus	www.readingplus.com
ThinkLink Learning	Predictive Assessment Series	www.thinklinklearning.com
Vantage Learning	Learning Access!	www.vantagelearning.com
Wireless Generation	mCLASS DIBELS	www.wirelessgeneration.com

measurement (CBM) probes provided on the AIMSweb website or they can enter results of student performance on the Dynamic Indicators of Basic Early Literacy Skills (DIBELS; see Chapter 8). CBM measures into the AIMSweb system. The web-based system allows users to enter data and create graphs and reports for distribution.

An important distinction between AIMSweb and STAR Enterprise measures is that AIMSweb requires that teachers select, administer, and (sometimes) score the CBM measures, while the STAR Assessments (STAR Early Literacy, STAR Math, STAR Reading) do that work for the teacher. The CBM measures available for AIMSweb are like those available for Easy CBM and DIBELS and are designed to monitor progress at specific grade levels. CBM probes are available for math concepts and applications, oral reading fluency (English and Spanish), reading comprehension, early literacy skills (English and Spanish), early numeracy skills, mathematics (computation and facts), spelling, and written expression. The newest edition to the AIMSweb system is a behavior module that allows users to screen students for behavior/emotional issues and social skills. Used together, the AIMSweb components create a comprehensive progress monitoring system that provides assessments in a wider array of academic content and behavior areas than measures like Yearly Progress Pro or STAR assessments. The AIMSweb probes can be used for universal screening, monitoring at-risk students, or writing individualized goals within a progress monitoring or problem solving framework. Training workbooks and technical manuals provided for each AIMSweb CBM area outline administration and scoring rules and describe the creation and technical features of the tools. AIMSweb provides norm tables that include growth rates for CBMs based on an aggregate national sample. Schools can also develop local norms.

There is good evidence for the technical adequacy of AIMSweb provided in the test manual. Reliability coefficients consistently exceed .90 and the measures have good content validity. But, as we noted in Chapter 8, recent research findings are casting significant doubt on the comparability and equivalence of CBM measures, noting specifically their lack of reliability in measuring growth (Ardoin & Christ, 2009; Bettebenner & Linn, 2010; Betts, 2010; Christ & Ardoin, 2009).

STAR Reading

STAR Reading (Renaissance Learning, 2009) is a computer adaptive test that is incorporated as a part of STAR Enterprise (Renaissance Learning, 2010) and is designed to provide teachers with quick and accurate estimates of students' instructional reading levels and estimates of their reading comprehension levels relative to national norms. The test is also used as a periodic measure of student progress toward individual goals and/or state or common core standards. The test is administered using computer software, so the specific test items each student receives are determined by his or her responses to previous test items. Using computer-adaptive procedures, a branching formula matches test items to student ability and performance level. Two item formats are used: short comprehension items and extended comprehension items. The test uses a vocabulary-in-context format in which students must identify the best choice for a missing word in a single-context sentence. Correct answers fit both the semantics and the syntax of the sentence. All incorrect answers either fit the syntax of the sentence or relate to the meaning of something in the sentence.

Scores

Users of STAR Reading may obtain grade equivalents, percentile ranks, normal-curve equivalents, and scaled scores. In addition, they may obtain information about the zone of proximal development, an index of the low and high ends of the range at which students can read. The software used to administer the test provides the information, and scores are obtained immediately. A Goal Setting Wizard can be used to set individual goals and the test can be used to monitor progress toward those goals.

Norms

Items for STAR Reading 2 were developed using 27,807 students from 247 schools. The development sample was stratified on the basis of gender, grade, geographic region, district socioeconomic status, school type, and district enrollment. The primary unit of selection was school rather than students. Tables in the manual contrast sample characteristics with national population characteristics. Sample characteristics approximate population characteristics.

STAR Reading initially was standardized in 1999 on 30,000 students from 269 schools in 47 states. In 2008 STAR Reading was renormed on 69,738 students who took STAR Reading as part of their in-school routine experience. The standardization sample was stratified on the basis of geographic region, school system and per-grade district enrollment, and socioeconomic status. Sample characteristics very closely approximate population characteristics. Students from all geographic regions, socioeconomic levels, and school sizes were selected in proportion to their presence in the population. Normative tables in the manual describe the close approximation of the sample to the U.S. population.

Reliability

STAR Reading is a computer-adaptive test that offers a virtually unlimited number of test forms, so traditional methods of conducting reliability analyses do not apply. The authors instead conducted reliability analyses using a test–retest methodology with alternative forms. Reliability was tested using both scaled scores and instructional reading levels. A total of 34,446 students were tested twice with STAR Reading, each taking the second test an average of 5 days after the first. Test–retest reliabilities ranged from .85 to .95 for scaled scores and averaged .91 for instructional reading level.

Validity

Performance on STAR Reading was correlated with performance on a number of different standardized measures of reading skills administered to those in the standardization group. An extensive table in the manual reports these results. Comparison tests included the California Achievement Test, Comprehensive Test of Basic Skills, Degrees of Reading Power, Gates–MacGinitie, Iowa Test of Basic Skills, Metropolitan Achievement Test, Stanford Achievement Test, and several state custom-built tests (Connecticut, Texas, Indiana, Tennessee, Kentucky, North Carolina, and New York). Performance on STAR Reading is closely related to performance on the other measures of reading.

Summary

STAR Reading is a norm-referenced, computer-adaptive reading test that provides teachers with information about students' instructional levels as well as their level of performance relative to a national sample. The test enables users to sample a wide range of reading behaviors in a relatively limited period of time. The test was standardized on a large and representative group of students. Evidence for reliability and validity is satisfactory. The test should be very useful to those who want immediate scoring and information about appropriate student instructional level.

STAR Math

STAR Math (Renaissance Learning, 2009) is part of a larger web-based tool called STAR Enterprise (Renaissance Learning, 2010). It is a computer adaptive test designed to provide teachers with quick and accurate estimates of students' math achievement levels relative to national norms and both individual and class progress toward individual goals, state standards, and common core standards. It is appropriate for use with students in grades 1 through 12. Using computer-adaptive procedures, a branching formula matches test items to students' ability and performance level. In other words, the specific test items that students receive depend on how well they perform on previous items. Thus, each test is unique, tailored to the individual student, and students can be given the test as many as 5 times in 1 year without being exposed to the same item more than once. The test is timed. Students have up to 3 minutes to solve each item and are given a warning when 30 seconds remain.

Items on STAR Math consist of some of the major strands of math content: numeration concepts, computation, word problems, estimation, statistics, charts, graphs, geometry, measurement, and algebra. Responses are four-item multiple-choice responses. The test consists of two parts: Concepts of numeration and computation are addressed in the first part, whereas the other content areas are addressed in the second part.

Scores

Users of STAR Math can obtain grade equivalents, percentile ranks, normal-curve equivalents, and scaled scores. The software provided with the test is used to score the test automatically and give users immediate feedback on student performance.

Norms

STAR Math was standardized on 29,185 students from 312 schools. These schools represented 48 states across the United States. Standardization was completed in spring 2002 using a sample that was stratified on the basis of geographic region, school location (urban, rural, and suburban), gender, and ethnicity. The sample is representative of the U.S. population, as are the proportions of the various kinds of students in the sample.

Reliability

Reliability was calculated using a test–retest method with 1,541 students, who took alternative forms of the test because of its computer-adaptive nature. Reliabilities at grades 3 through 6 are in the high .70s, whereas at higher grades they are in the .80s. The test has sufficient reliability for use as a screening test and a progress monitoring tool, but not for making eligibility decisions.

Validity

Performance on STAR Math was correlated with performance on a number of standardized math tests administered during standardization of the test. An extensive table in the manual reports these results. Comparison tests included the California Achievement Test, Comprehensive Test of Basic Skills, Iowa Tests of Basic Skills, and Metropolitan Achievement Test. Scores were moderately high and approximately as would be expected.

Summary

STAR Math is a norm-referenced, computer-adaptive math test that gives teachers information about students' instructional levels as well as their level of performance relative to a national sample. The test was standardized on a large representative sample. It provides teachers with immediate diagnostic profiles on student performance and is especially useful as a periodic progress monitoring measure. Evidence for reliability is limited, but evidence for validity is good.

Continuous Progress Monitoring Measures

Representative continuous progress monitoring measures are listed in Table 23.2. In this section, we review one measure (Accelerated Math).

Accelerated Math™ (AM)

Accelerated Math™ (AM) (Renaissance Learning, 1998) is a technology-enhanced system designed to monitor student progress toward instructional goals and manage student practice of relevant instructional tasks. We illustrated the system in the scenario about students in Marcie Adams's class. Students are placed at an instructional level dependent on their level of skill development in math as determined by an assessment such as STAR Math. They are taught at that level, and then they complete practice exercises that enable them to apply what they have learned. The computer is used to monitor accuracy and task completion, and students move at their own pace. The AM program is used to provide teachers with daily information on the progress of individual students, on the status of all students in the class, and to alert teachers when individual students are having difficulty. The program can be used by administrators to track the progress of all students in classes, schools, or districts. Steps in the program are like those used by students in Marcie Adams's class. Students take STAR Math as a locator test; it identifies the appropriate library of instructional objectives toward which students should work. The computer generates worksheets of problems that students use to practice math skills. Students score their practice exercises using the computer, and once they achieve sufficient proficiency (typically 85 percent correct) the computer signals the teacher that they are ready for a test. When students pass tests, they proceed to the next objective. Teachers are able to get the kinds of reports shown previously for students in Marcie Adams's class. Administrators have available to them an Accelerated Math Dashboard, which is a web-based system that allows them to monitor the performance of all students in their school(s).

Computer Scoring Systems

In addition to providing efficient ways to monitor progress and manage targeted practice opportunities, advances in technology have also made scoring of several other measures, including those commonly used for diagnostic and eligibility decisions, much more efficient. In the past, test users spent countless hours adding, subtracting, and converting test scores. Today, computerized scoring programs are available to ease this burden so that test users can spend more time interpreting scores and identifying appropriate instructional interventions.

Computerized scoring programs offer several advantages to traditional paper-and-pencil scoring. Most notably, they reduce the time needed to compute and convert test scores. In addition, they may reduce error associated with calculating scores and misreading conversion tables. They can also assist with calculating scores associated with more sophisticated statistical and measurement techniques, such as the W-scores that are used in the Woodcock–Johnson

TABLE 23.2 Software Packages for Continuous Progress Monitoring

Provider	Product	Website
Hosts Learning	LearnerLink	www.hosts.com
Leapfrog SchoolHouse	LeapTrack	www.leaptrack.com
Renaissance Learning	Accelerated Math™, Accelerated Reader	www.renlearn.com
Riverdeep	Destination Success, Skill Detective, Skill Navigator	www.riverdeep.net/teacheruniverse
Scantron	Skills Connection, Classroom Wizard	www.scantron.com
Wireless Generation (and Harcourt Achieve)	e*assessment	www.wirelessgeneration.com

TABLE 23.3 Assessment Tools with Computerized Scoring and Reporting Programs

Tool	Name of Associated Product(s)	Hand Scoring	Computer Scoring	Report Writing
Wechsler Scales	WISC-IV Writer and Scoring Assistant	X	X	X
Kaufman Scales	Assist	X	X	X
Stanford–Binet	SB5 ScoringPro	X	X	X
BASC-2	BASC-2 Assist and Assist Plus	X	X	X
Achenbach	Assessment Data Manager	X	X	X
Woodcock–Johnson Scales	WJ III Compuscore and Profiles Program Report-Writer for the WJ III	No	X	X
Vineland Adaptive Behavior Scales	Vineland-II Survey Forms Assist	X	X	X

Scales; calculating these scores by hand could be tedious. (See Table 23.3.)

Computer scoring programs (which are developed and used by humans, of course) are certainly not perfect, and they need to be carefully developed and applied by test users. On more than one occasion, even after test developers have conducted numerous demonstration trials and the product has gone to market, glitches in computer scoring have been identified. Unfortunately, in some cases, this has led to misinformed decision making such that students have been denied services that they otherwise should have received. Also, even though computers may help eliminate computation and table-reading errors, it is essential that the user enters scores and other information (for example, date of birth, grade, form, and norms to be used) accurately for correct scoring. It is recommended that users carefully check results even when using a computer and always use multiple sources of data when making important decisions. Storing electronic copies of scoring records can also pose challenges. It is important to ensure that only those individuals with a need to know the given test score results have access to such data. This may require the development of special electronic passwords known only to those who administer the test.

When first learning a new test that has both a hand and a computer scoring option, it may be beneficial to learn how to hand score the test in order to understand how the scores are derived. This can allow you to better understand the nature of the scores that you interpret. However, once you have a good understanding of how the test scores are calculated, use of a computer scoring program can help you score more quickly and accurately.

With advances in technology, computer programs are becoming more widely available to not only assist with calculating and converting scores but also discriminate correct and incorrect responses. Whereas it may be relatively simple to design a computer program to score selected response items, it is more difficult to design programs that can accurately score constructed response items and essay responses. Yet such programs are being created. Although such software may help reduce problems associated with poor interrater reliability, it may be difficult for such programs to accurately score unique and creative responses.

In addition to offering automated scoring, some test packages that are used to make special education eligibility decisions offer computer-generated psychoeducational reports. These kinds of reports make use of predetermined language and table formats that are intended to facilitate communication of score results to parents and educators. Although it may be appropriate to incorporate some of the language and tables from a computer-generated report program, it is important to recognize how such reports, when used in their entirety and without editing, may lead users away from incorporating multiple assessment methods and measures in their overall evaluation. Because a report-writing program is often specific to a given test, it will focus on presenting scores obtained through the given test alone, and it may not easily allow a user to incorporate additional data collected from multiple sources. Furthermore, standard language presented through a computer-generated report may not optimally convey the information to certain audiences; users should edit such information in order to communicate most effectively with the individuals with whom they are working. We discourage the use of computer-generated reports and instead encourage assessors to write reports that are tailored specifically to the students they test.

Chapter Comprehension Questions

Write your answers to each of the following questions and then compare your responses to the text.

1. What is the distinction between continuous and periodic progress monitoring?
2. What are the advantages of using technology-enhanced assessment systems?
3. How does a technology-enhanced continuous progress monitoring system work?
4. Identify representative technology-enhanced periodic progress monitoring measures.

Web Activities 

1. Go to the websites for any two of the periodic progress monitoring measures in Table 23.1. List the kinds of behaviors sampled by the measures and any evidence for technical adequacy.
2. Put AIMSweb in your search engine and go to the AIMSweb site. Download the brochure showing the kinds of reports available for AIMsweb. Then go to the website for Renaissance Learning and view the Renaissance reports. Which reports require teachers to enter the data on individual students; which do so automatically for the teacher? What are the relative merits and limitations of each set of reports?
3. Go to the website for the National Center on RTI and check out the list of progress monitoring measures. Examine the tables comparing the many progress monitoring measures available for use in schools.

Web Resources

See Table 23.1, Software Packages for Continuous Progress Monitoring, and Table 23.2, Software Packages for Periodic Progress Monitoring, for a variety of web resources.

Additional resources for this chapter can be found on the Education CourseMate website. Go to CengageBrain.com to access the site.

ABC News Video

Go to the Education CourseMate website to watch the video entitled, "Technology Is Making Teaching and Learning More Fun."

1 Note how classroom responders are used to collect student data in a different way than the traditional paper-and-pencil "pop-quiz." What are the potential benefits of this technology-enhanced approach in terms of managing classroom assessment?

2 Also note the discussion of the "digital divide," and how some students may not have as much experience in working with computers. How might you need to adapt to ensure these technology-enhanced methods are helpful and fair for all students?

Multi-Tiered System of Supports (MTSS) and Response to Intervention (RTI)

CHAPTER GOALS

1. Define and describe MTSS and RTI concepts that underlie school assessment practices.
2. Describe the steps school personnel go through in assessing student needs for differing levels of support.
3. Describe the fundamental assumptions in assessing response to instruction or response to intervention.
4. Describe dimensions of assessment (specificity and frequency) in MTSS and RTI models.
5. Discuss important considerations in MTSS and RTI.

KEY TERMS

multi-tiered system of supports
response to instruction
response to intervention
progress monitoring
specificity
intervention integrity

A major purpose of assessment has been to monitor pupil progress; this means assessing and documenting a student's achievement—that is, responses to or responsiveness to instruction. We have learned that standardized tests often are not satisfactory instruments for monitoring response to instruction. They are time-consuming, insensitive to small but important changes, expensive, not suitable for repeated administrations, and fail to match a student's curriculum and instruction. Over time, demands to develop new ways in which to monitor student progress and response to instruction have increased. These have gone under the titles multi-tiered system of supports (MTSS), response to intervention (RTI), response to instruction, and problem solving. In this chapter, we describe in more detail the assessment approaches and methods that typically take place when one engages in these methodologies for monitoring student progress.

As you begin reading and studying this chapter, recall what you already have learned. The primary purpose of schooling is to enhance competence and build the capacity of systems to meet student needs. Students need different levels of support to succeed in school, a fact that we illustrated earlier with Figure 1.1 (see Chapter 1). A major purpose of assessment is to monitor progress toward competence, usually expressed in the form of state educational standards or individual student goals. You learned earlier that the foundation of an MTSS begins in general education that involves focusing on provision of effective instruction and supports that help prevent learning and behavior problems. Three levels of supports are illustrated in the funnel: universal (for all), targeted (for some), and intensive (for a few). The overall goal in MTSS, or in RTI, as it is sometimes called, is to use student performance data to inform ways to provide the type of instruction and educational assistance a student needs to be successful.

Go to the Education CourseMate website for this textbook for a link to the National Center on Response to Intervention.

In Chapter 8, we elaborated on curriculum-based assessment (CBM)—one approach to progress monitoring—and in Chapter 23, we described recent developments in using technology-enhanced assessment systems in special and inclusive education. In subsequent chapters in Part 5 we describe applications of MTSS and RTI to making instructional, eligibility, and accountability decisions. We reported in Chapter 1 that there is considerable research support for use of these approaches, and that the effectiveness of measures to do so are documented by the National Center on Response to Intervention.

1 MTSS and RTI Conceptualizations

A multi-tiered system of supports (**MTSS**) is "a coherent continuum of evidence-based, system-wide practices to support a rapid response to academic and behavior needs with frequent data-based monitoring for instructional decision making to empower each student to high standards" (retrieved from the Kansas Department of Education website, 2011).

The acronym *RTI* currently is used to refer to *response to instruction* or *response to intervention*. We believe it is important to differentiate between these two terms, and we do so in this chapter. We use the terminology *response to instruction* to refer to response to core instruction or universal programming (the everyday instruction that occurs for students). Assessment of response to core instruction occurs for all students. Sometimes the assessment is continuous, sometimes it is periodic (occurring 3 to 10 times per month), and sometimes it is a one-time assessment occurring once per year.

We use the term *response to intervention* to refer to a student's response when substantial changes are made in regular programming (for the large group, the small group, or individual students. Over time, students who experience academic or behavioral difficulties in school receive increasingly intensive instruction. Those who demonstrate at-risk performance receive enhanced instruction, and those who do not respond to enhanced instruction are given intensive instruction.

Measurement is done similarly for the two RTIs, but one (response to intervention) involves a substantive change to instruction, and the other does not. In this chapter, the use of the term *response to intervention* is reserved for situations in which an instructional change is implemented and the corresponding effects on student achievement are measured. Assessing response to intervention goes slightly beyond assessing response to instruction and involves comparing the rate of learning during an intervention to the rate of learning during general instruction to determine whether the given change was helpful.

Response to instruction and response to intervention are measured in both general and special education. Response to instruction (RTI) is a concept with multiple meanings but without definition as yet in state or federal laws or regulations. Sometimes it is defined simply as collecting data on student performance and progress toward some goal; invariably it has to do with progress monitoring. The general notion is to monitor student progress (continuously, periodically, annually, or with some other degree of frequency) in order to spot deviance, ascertain skill development, or check the efficacy of academic or behavioral interventions being used with the student. Some would say it is all about catching children early so that they do not get left behind. Reports of assessments of response to instruction could consist of report cards every 6 weeks, simple statements that a student's overall progress is satisfactory, or more formal, highly specific statements such as "In 2 weeks, she has increased her single-digit addition accuracy from 4 out of 10 problems correct to 8 out of 10 problems correct." Obviously, these different kinds of reports have different meanings and differ in their usefulness for instructional decision making.

Assessment of response to instruction and progress monitoring are now encountered by educators in many different ways. The No Child Left Behind Act requires that schools implement "evidence-based instruction." Most often, this is interpreted to mean that someone has monitored the extent to which an instructional program "works" in general; that is, the extent to which students who receive the instruction make progress toward grade-level standards. And the ramifications of RTI assessment are seen when state departments of education punish schools where students are failing to make adequate yearly progress.

The extent to which any given program or intervention will be effective within a given educational context cannot be known until it is applied. Generally effective instruction may not work because of unique characteristics of the children or their teachers. Teachers need to know how to choose interventions that address individual students' needs. Yet, even when that happens, differences exist across school settings that may influence the efficacy of a given intervention. For instance, instructional materials vary across schools in terms of the extent to which they cover certain skills. A supplemental program with strong support in the research literature may not necessarily address the skills with which students at a particular school are struggling. It is therefore important to consider contextual factors when selecting a program that is supported in the research literature. Furthermore, it is important to monitor student progress over time to know whether a program or intervention, when applied, has the intended positive impact on student learning.

The federal government has funded a National Center on Response to Intervention (RTI4success.org), a center charged with evaluating progress-monitoring practices, reporting on effective practices, and providing the necessary technical assistance to states to enable them to implement effective progress-monitoring methodologies. On its website, the NCRTI periodically posts assessment devices that are shown to be scientifically validated and answers questions about RTI and progress monitoring.

2 Steps in Provision of Support

Douglas Fuchs and colleagues (2003) describe RTI in terms of the steps that educational professionals go through. They list these as follows. (We have modified steps 5 and 6 for purposes of this text.)

1. Students are provided with "generally effective" instruction by their classroom teachers.
2. Their progress is monitored.
3. Those who do not respond get something else, or something more, from their teacher or someone else. The "something else" should be an intervention for which there is evidence of a high probability of success.
4. Again, their progress is monitored.
5. Decisions about resource allocation and entitlement for supplemental programs (e.g., Title I, special education) are made.
6. Steps 1 through 4 are repeated until the teacher uses instruction that enables the student to reach desired levels of performance.

SCENARIO *in* ASSESSMENT

CHARLES | Charles, a second grader, is the oldest of three children who moved from the city into the suburban West Morgan School District over the summer. Several requests for Charles's records from the city district were never answered. By mid-September, it was clear that Charles was struggling in oral reading. Mrs. Buchanon, his teacher, noted that Charles was very inaccurate. After listening to Charles read aloud twice, she decided to tally the number of correct and incorrect words he read. The next time Charles read aloud, he read 56 percent of the words correctly and was unable to retell what he had read. Clearly, the beginning second-grade material was too difficult for Charles. Mrs. Buchanon tried material at the mid-first-grade level, but it too was too difficult. In beginning first-grade material, Charles could read with 85 percent accuracy, but his reading was very slow and he was able only to retell about 60 percent of what he had read.

Mrs. Buchanon decided to use a generally effective instructional strategy to improve Charles's reading. She paired him with Michelle, one of the better readers in the class. Charles would read beginning first-grade material aloud for 5 minutes, and Michelle would correct his errors. Mrs. Buchanon monitored the intervention twice a week. Although Charles seemed to enjoy working with Michelle, his reading accuracy showed no improvement after 4 weeks of intervention.

Mrs. Buchanon then developed a targeted intervention. She assessed Charles's knowledge of letter names and letter sounds. He could name all of the letters, all of the long vowel sounds, none of the short vowel sounds, and all of the common consonant sounds. She drilled him for 2 minutes daily on short vowel sounds and sent worksheets home for Charles to practice with his mother. Charles continued to read with Michelle for 5 minutes every day. However, instead of supplying a correct word for an incorrect one, La Donna provided the correct initial sound of the word before supplying the correct word. After a month, Charles had learned short o and improved his fluency from 35 correct sounds per minute to 45 correct sounds per minute. Increased accuracy in letter sounds was not accompanied by increases in oral reading.

At this point, it was clear that Charles was not making the kind of gains he needed to make; he was falling farther behind his classmates. Mrs. Buchanon consulted with the school building's Student Assistance Team. The team recommended an intensive intervention of explicit instruction targeting phonemic awareness, letter–sound associations, and fluency. The team did not specifically target reading comprehension because of the likelihood that Charles's poor comprehension was the result of his lack of reading fluency. Charles received 12 minutes each day of individual instruction from the reading specialist. Data were collected weekly on Charles's reading accuracy and fluency.

Charles progressed consistently in the intensive program. The number of correct words read per minute increased steadily in progressively more difficult reading materials. By the end of the first semester, Charles was reading beginning second-grade material independently. By the end of the second grade, he had caught up to his peers; he was reading end-second-grade material independently. The Student Assistance Team ended instructional intervention; however, it did continue to monitor Charles in the third grade to make sure he maintained his gains. Charles continued to progress at the rate of his peers.

What implications about your own professional role can you draw from this scenario? Go to the Education CourseMate website for this textbook for more reflection questions about this Scenario in Assessment.

3 Fundamental Assumptions in Assessing Response to Instruction

There are seven assumptions that underlie the practice of assessing RTI.

1. *Instruction occurs.* When we assess response to instruction, we assume that instruction actually occurs. However, some philosophies of education explicitly eschew direct or systematic instruction and value a student's discovering content, skills, and behavior.[1] Thus it is likely that some students could spend their time in instruction-free environments and would stand no chance of being instructed.
2. *Instruction occurs as intended.* It is assumed that instruction is implemented in the way in which it is intended to be implemented and that students are actively engaged in the instruction. Over the past decade, researchers have become increasingly interested in intervention integrity (also sometimes called treatment integrity or fidelity of treatment). For example, when we assess the extent to which a student responds to phonics instruction, we are assuming that the phonics instruction is implemented as the teacher intended and that the student is actively engaged in responding to the instruction.
3. *The instruction that is assessed is known to be generally effective.* There needs to be empirical evidence that the instruction that is implemented works for students in general and, more specifically, for students who are the same age and grade as the pupil being assessed.
4. *The measurement system is adequate to detect changes in student learning as a result of instruction.* There are four subcomponents to this assumption.
   a. The measurement system reflects the curriculum or assesses the effect of instruction in that curriculum. It is axiomatic that response to instruction must reflect the content being instructed.
   b. The measurement system can be used frequently. Frequent measurement is important to avoid wasting a student's and a teacher's time when instruction in not working. It is also important to prevent a student from practicing (and mastering) errors and making them more difficult to correct.
   c. The measurement system is sensitive to small changes in student performance. If measurement is conducted frequently, it is unlikely that there will be large changes in student learning. Thus, to be effective, the measurement system must be capable of detecting small, but meaningful, changes in student learning or performance.
   d. The measurement system actually assesses pupil performance, not simply what the teacher does. Clearly, what a teacher does is important because it goes directly to treatment fidelity. However, we are interested in whether the student is learning.
5. *There are links between the assessment data and modifications in instruction.* This is the concept of data-driven decision making and reiterates our earlier point that data collected and not used to make decisions are useless. It is assumed that the data are both useful and usable for purposes of instructional planning. Student failure to respond appropriately to instruction, as determined by the formative measures used, should trigger a change in instruction. Additional data may need to be collected to determine what change has the highest probability of leading to student success; nevertheless, a change would be needed in the type of instruction, amount of instruction, or instructional delivery method.
6. *There are consequences that sustain (a) improved student outcomes and (b) continued implementation of the measurement system.* It is assumed not

[1] Most parents would prefer that this procedure not be used to teach their children to swim.

only that the system is good, but that it is worth keeping in place. In our experience we have learned that the collection of direct frequent data on student performance is considered both time-consuming and arduous by some teachers. At the same time, teachers tell us that they and their students are "better off" when data are collected. Although many teachers are motivated by their students' progress, it is sometimes necessary to provide rewards to others for data collection if we want them to engage in direct and frequent measurement. These teachers have told us that, if it does not matter to someone that they monitor student progress, they will stop doing so.

7. *Assessment of RTI is not setting specific.* It is assumed that response to instruction can be assessed in both general and special education settings.

4 Examples of MTSS and RTI systems

On the website that accompanies this book we have included descriptions of some early RTI models used in the Minneapolis schools, Heartland Education Agency, and by the Pennsylvania and Ohio Departments of Education. Note that the models are referred to variously as problem solving, instructional support team, and intervention assistance team models. The reader also is referred to Jimerson, Burns, and VanDerHeyden's (2007) *Handbook of Response to Intervention* for detailed descriptions of the foundations of problem-solving and RTI strategies, assessment and measurement considerations, evidence-based practices, and lessons learned in implementing problem solving and RTI.

5 Dimensions of Assessment in MTSS and RTI Models

Assessments of student response to educational interventions vary along two dimensions: specificity and frequency. Technically adequate measures of RTI are those that are highly specific and very frequently administered. This concept is illustrated in Figure 24.1. Along the vertical axis, measures vary in their specificity from those

FIGURE 24.1
Frequency of Assessment

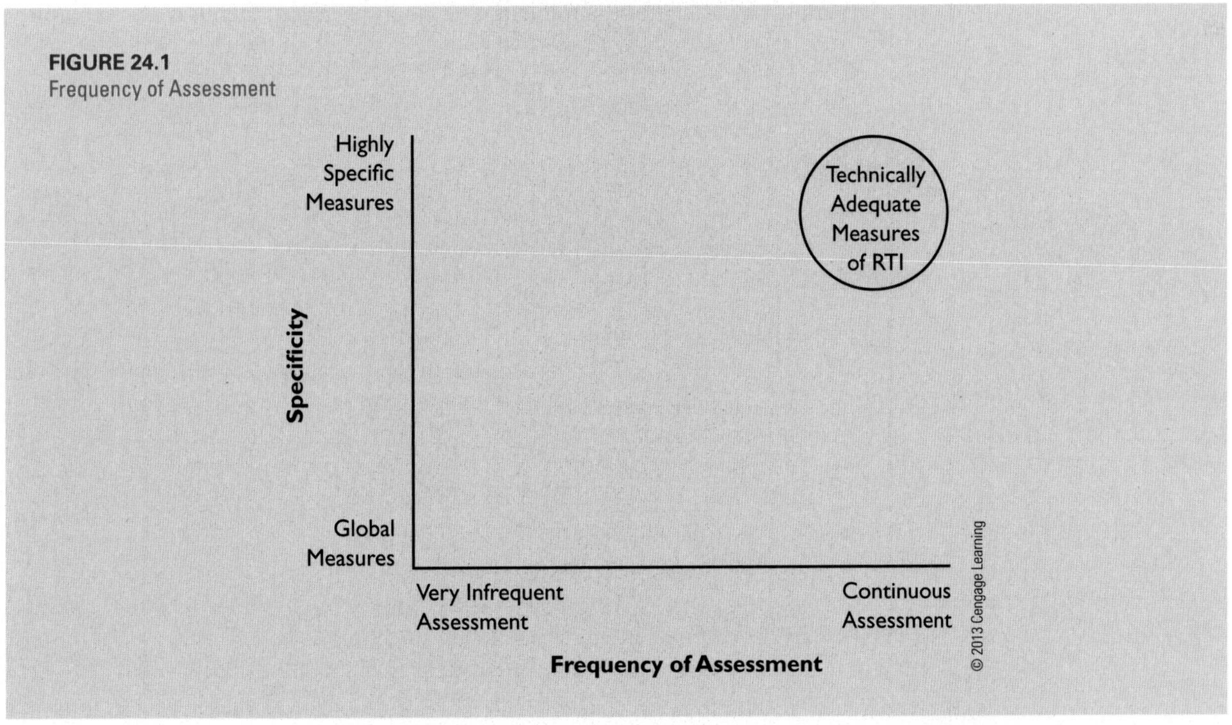

that are global to those that are highly specific. Along the horizontal axis measures vary in their frequency of assessment from those that are given very infrequently to those that are administered daily, hourly, or even continuously. The "best" measures, those that are most technically adequate for decision making, are in the upper right-hand quadrant (highly sensitive or specific and frequently administered).

SPECIFICITY

Assessments differ along a continuum of specificity. This is illustrated in Figure 24.2. The more specific the assessment and the more specific the information collected by or reported to the teacher, the more precise the teacher can be in planning instructional interventions. Think about where you would begin teaching a student who is "doing fine in reading."

FREQUENCY

Assessments also vary along a continuum of frequency. As illustrated in Figure 24.2, assessments range from annual assessments to daily assessments. In school settings, many measures (such as large-scale achievement tests) are given annually. These are broad assessments that must cover considerable content (material learned over an entire school year). Thus they must either be very general or be a limited sample of more specific content. In either case, the results of such assessments do not provide sufficiently detailed information about what a student knows and does not know to plan specific lessons. The results of unit tests or report cards are provided more frequently than standardized tests, but they are still inadequate to learn what a student specifically knows and does not know.

Increasingly, educators are measuring performance and progress very frequently. Many of the new measurement systems, such as those employing technology-enhanced assessments, call for continuous measurement of pupil performance and progress. They provide students with immediate feedback on how they are doing, give teachers daily status reports indicating the relative standing of all students in a class, and pinpoint the skills missing among students who are experiencing difficulty. The more frequent the measurement, the quicker you can adapt instruction to ensure that students are making optimal progress. However, frequent measurement is only helpful when it can immediately direct teachers as to what to teach or how to teach next. To the extent that teachers can use data efficiently, frequent assessment is valuable; if it consists simply of frequent measurement with no application, then it is not valuable.

FIGURE 24.2
Continuum of Specificity

- Given 10 consonant-vowel-consonant words with the short e sound, Bill says 8 correctly.
- Bill has mastered short vowel sounds.
- Bill is at the 70th percentile in decoding skills.
- Bill passed the unit test.
- Bill earned a B in reading.
- Bill is doing fine in reading.

6 Important Considerations in MTSS and RTI

INTERVENTION INTEGRITY

As school personnel assess response to intervention, it will be critical to demonstrate that intervention is occurring and that it is occurring in ways that it was intended. Imagine assessing student response to treatment, concluding that the student did not respond to the treatment, and then learning later that the treatment either was never put in place or was poorly implemented. Or imagine that a student starts to make substantial progress, but you are not sure what made the difference and thus are not sure what to maintain or change in a student's program. More than for other forms of assessment, RTI assessment models are dependent on effective instruction's being implemented with good integrity.

There are likely a number of ways to make sure that interventions are put in place with good integrity. First, teachers need to learn the nuances of implementing an intervention. If, for example, teachers are to implement the Success for All program with their classes, it would be important that they know the specifics of doing so. They might attend specific training in Success for All, read extensively about implementation of the program, or work for a time alongside another teacher in a setting where Success for All is being implemented. Similarly, if teachers are to work with individual students on phonemic awareness, it is important that they know how to do so and that they do so with implementation integrity.

Assessors can examine the extent to which interventions are implemented with integrity by listing the specific steps in the intervention. Then they can directly observe the extent to which the teacher implements the steps. Upah and Tilley (2002) identify a 12-component quality indicator model that can be used to indicate best practices in designing, implementing, and evaluating quality interventions. These quality indices are as follows

Problem Identification. The problem is defined as the difference between what is expected and the actual student behavior or performance.

- *Behavioral definition.* The behavior must be defined in observable and measurable terms.
- *Baseline data.* Current level of performance must be measured.
- *Problem validation.* The student's behavior must be shown to deviate from peers' behavior or classroom expectations.

Problem analysis. The team or teacher examines why the problem is occurring.

- *Problem analysis steps.* The team identifies relevant known and unknown information, generates a hypothesis, validates the hypothesis, and links the assessment information to the intervention design.

Plan implementation. The plan is put into place.

- *Goal setting.* Goals are stated clearly in a measurable way and indicate what the student's performance will look like if the intervention is successful.
- *Intervention plan development.* An intervention plan is developed.
- *Measurement strategy.* A way to gather progress data is identified.
- *Decision-making plan.* The team specifies how data will be used to drive improved instruction.

Program evaluation. The team analyzes the extent to which the program worked.

- *Progress monitoring.* The team decides whether to use CBM procedures, observations, frequency counts, checklists, portfolios, or rating scales.
- *Formative evaluation.* An assessment of the extent to which the intervention plan is working.

- *Treatment integrity*. An assessment of the extent to which the plan is being implemented as intended and as desired.
- *Summative evaluation*. An assessment of the extent to which the plan worked.

INTERVENTION EFFICACY

When examining response to intervention for individual students, there should be good evidence that the treatment itself is generally effective with students who are at the same age and grade as the student being assessed. This is especially true in models that require normative peer comparisons (examinations of pupil progress relative to that of classmates). Under the requirements of NCLB, school personnel are expected to be putting in place evidence-based treatments. Information about the extent to which treatments are generally effective is found by reviewing the research evidence in support of the treatments.

The What Works Clearinghouse can provide direction as to what treatments might be particularly effective. You can go to the WWC website, look up interventions for middle school math, and find a topic report listing the kinds of interventions that the clearinghouse reviewed on middle school math. Information on the extent to which there is good empirical support for a particular intervention can be obtained from the website.

However, always remember that efficacy is local. It is highly recommended that you consider the characteristics of the student and teachers when selecting an intervention rather than relying solely on what has been shown to be most effective in the research literature. If an intervention is not targeted appropriately to an individual child's or school's needs, it may not be effective. What works in general might not work for Billy. That is why we monitor Billy's performance to see if the treatment is efficacious for him, too.

RESPONSE STABILITY

In assessing response to intervention, it is important to document the extent to which the student's response varies over content and over time. We expect that in nearly all instances it will. Few students respond to the content of different subject matter in the same way, and their responses are seldom consistent over time. We are interested in the usual response to instruction, not response to instruction on a bad day.

It is said that we all "get sick of too much of a good thing." It is often the case that an intervention that "works" and is effective in moving a student toward an instructional goal will work for only a limited period of time. Students get satiated with specific instructional approaches or interventions. Indeed, one of the evidence-based principles of effective instruction is that variety in instructional presentation and in response demand enhances instructional outcomes. This presents significant challenges for those who teach students with learning and behavior problems. They must not only identify instructional approaches that work, they must also identify multiple competing instructional approaches that work. You may need to work to identify several different approaches to achieve the same instructional goals.

CRITERIA USED TO DETERMINE A STUDENT'S RESPONSIVENESS TO INTERVENTION

Determination of whether students are responding to interventions requires specification of decision rules based on the student's level and rate of progress. School personnel should establish these rules *before* interventions are implemented. Both level of performance (e.g., third-grade level) and rate of progress (e.g., objectives mastered, periodic measures or quizzes answered with 80 percent accuracy) should be specified. Stakeholder groups in states, districts, or individual schools often work on specification of criteria.

FREQUENCY OF PROGRESS MONITORING

As noted earlier, school personnel decide how often to monitor progress, and typically do so either periodically (e.g., twice a week or three times a month) or continuously. Periodic progress monitoring approaches are the most commonly used. Continuous progress monitoring approaches are the most effective (Ysseldyke & Bolt, 1997; Bolt, Ysseldyke, & Patterson, 2010).

CAN'T DO IT VERSUS WON'T DO IT

When we assess student response to intervention, we learn one of two things: The student demonstrates the skill (she or he does it) or does not demonstrate the skill (she or he does not do it). It is always critical that assessment personnel consider carefully whether failure to respond correctly is indicative of a skill deficit or a performance deficit. Some students have skills that they simply chose not to demonstrate. This distinction has important implications for how interventions should be designed to improve student functioning. If you think a student does not have the skill, but he or she actually does, and you spend time teaching the skill, this will be a serious waste of time and energy. Likewise, if you implement an intervention that merely rewards skill demonstration, the intervention will have no effect for a student who does not actually have the skill to begin with.

WHAT WOULD RTI LOOK LIKE IF IT WERE IMPLEMENTED WELL?

If RTI is being implemented well, one would see teachers engaged in evidence-based instruction, monitoring student progress toward intended goals, and adjusting instruction based on student response to instruction. Teachers would meet regularly in study groups to review and discuss students' progress and there would be clear criteria specified ahead of time indicating desired levels of performance and rates of progress. There would be lots of communication with parents whose children may be at risk, and the use of short, efficient assessments to monitor progress.

Chapter Comprehension Questions

Write your answers to each of the following questions and then compare your responses to the text.

1. State the difference between response to instruction and response to intervention, including MTSS in your answer. Then indicate why an educational professional would be concerned about each.
2. What are the major steps school personnel go through in implementing an MTSS model?
3. What are the fundamental assumptions in implementing an MTSS?

Web Activities

1. Type "response to intervention" into a search engine. This will yield several school district websites that describe the district's RTI practices. Select two school districts and compare their approaches.
2. Type "Intervention Central" into a search engine. Describe RTI resources available at that site.
3. Obtain a copy of the *Handbook of Response to Intervention*. Make a list of five things people say they learned in their efforts to implement MTSS/RTI models.
4. Type the name of a test company (e.g., CTB McGraw-Hill, Pearson, or Renaissance Learning) into a search engine. What web resources for MTSS or RTI do you find there?
5. Go to the website for the Kansas Department of Education. Kansas was the first state to implement an MTSS model, and coined the term. Describe what you learn about MTSS from reading information at this website.

6. Go to the website for the National Center on Response to Intervention and review the list of assessments that the center has approved. Click on the "Resources" and "Tools" sections. What useful material do you find there?
7. Go to the Education CourseMate website for this textbook. Read the descriptions of the various school system models. State similarities and differences between the approaches used in two of the settings.

Web Resources

Renaissance Learning
www.renlearn.com
This website includes tools for implementing MTSS and RTI.

Intervention Central
http://www.interventioncentral.org/
This website includes tools for implementing MTSS and RTI.

Kansas State Department of Education
http://www.ksde.org/
This website includes tools for implementing MTSS and RTI.

Additional resources for this chapter can be found on the Education CourseMate website. Go to CengageBrain.com to access the site.

Web Chapter Preview

Photo by John Salvia

Using Portfolios in Assessment

CHAPTER GOALS

1 Understand the criticisms by advocates of portfolio assessment of objective tests.

2 Understand the strengths cited by advocates of portfolio assessment.

3 Understand the unresolved issues in portfolio assessment.

4 Understand the ways in which portfolio assessment can be improved.

KEY TERMS

subjective evaluation
holistic evaluation
showcase portfolio
teacher–student portfolio
assessment portfolio

CHAPTER SUMMARY

Interest in portfolio assessment stems from a general concern about the validity and utility of norm-referenced achievement tests, the potential negative effects that standardized tests may have on learning, dissatisfaction in some circles with objective appraisal, and the belief that reform in the area of assessment can drive or support broader efforts in educational reform. Six elements define portfolio assessment: targeting valued outcomes for assessment, using tasks that mirror the work in the real world, encouraging cooperation among learners and between teacher and student, using multiple dimensions to evaluate student work, encouraging student reflection, and integrating assessment and instruction.

Depending on its purpose, the contents of a portfolio can vary considerably. Despite an initial surge of interest in the use of portfolios, several concerns and limitations have not been systematically addressed: selecting the criteria for including work in a student's portfolio, determining the nature of student participation in content selection, ensuring sufficient content generated by a student to reach valid decisions, and finding a way to make portfolio assessment more reliable, with consistency of scoring and breadth of sampling of student

The full chapter is available on the Education CourseMate website for this textbook.

Go to cengagebrain.com to access the site and download this chapter.

performances. In addition, there are concerns about biased scoring, instructional utility, and efficiency. Portfolio assessment will remain difficult and expensive for schools, and educators who wish to pursue this alternative should give serious attention to how portfolios are assembled and evaluated. Objectivity, less complexity, and comparability are the keys to better practice.

Chapter Comprehension Questions

Write your answers to each of the following questions and then compare your responses to the text.

1. Select and evaluate three criticisms of objective tests made by portfolio advocates.
2. Select and evaluate three claims of portfolio strengths made by portfolio advocates.
3. What measurement issues have yet to be resolved in the use of portfolios?
4. How can a teacher use portfolios more effectively?

Web Activities 

1. Look online for one study that provides a quantitative evaluation of the reliability of student assessment using portfolios.
2. Find two rubrics for evaluating written language. Do these rubrics provide data about the interscorer reliability of the evaluations? About the stability of student performance using the rubrics?

Web Resources

The Reliability of Scores from the 1992 Vermont Portfolio Assessment Program, Interim Report
http://www.eric.ed.gov/
This article by Daniel Koretz (1992) is available as ED355284 on the ERIC website.

A Report on the Reliability of a Large-Scale Portfolio Assessment for Language Arts, Mathematics, and Science
http://www.eric.ed.gov/
This article by Edward Wolfe (1996) is available as ED399285 on the ERIC website.

Additional resources for this chapter can be found on the Education CourseMate website. Go to CengageBrain.com to access the site.

TeachSource Video Case

Go to the Education CourseMate website to Watch the video entitled, *Portfolio Assessment: Elementary Classroom.*

1. Would you reach the same instructional decisions as the teacher?
2. What is the basis for your response to the previous question?

Part 5

Using Assessment Results to Make Educational Decisions

Assessment is the process of collecting data for the purpose of making decisions about students. The first four parts of this book set the stage for that. Part 1 discussed the context for assessment in schools, legal and ethical considerations in assessment, the test meaning of scores, and an overview of technical adequacy. Part 2 described assessment in classrooms: observation, teacher-made tests, curriculum-based approaches to monitoring student progress, and the management of classroom assessments. Part 3 described how to evaluate a test, the major domains assessed in school and a few representative tests. Part 4 discussed topics that cut across the entire assessment process: testing adaptations and accommodations, cultural and linguistic considerations in assessment, response-to-intervention and multi-tiered systems of support, and the use of portfolios in classroom assessment.

Part 5 discusses the use of assessment results in the decision-making process. Chapter 26 discusses various instructional decisions and the assessment information used to make those decisions. We differentiate those classroom instructional decisions that are made prior to referral and those that are made for students who receive special education. Chapter 27 discusses decisions related to special education eligibility and how they are made. Specifically, we discuss how to determine whether a student has a disability and whether a student with a disability needs special education. Chapter 28 describes current legal requirements and practices in developing and using standards-based large-scale accountability measures. Chapter 29 discusses collaborative decision-making, including characteristics of effective school teams, types of school teams, communicating information to parents, and the collection, maintenance, and dissemination of pupil information.

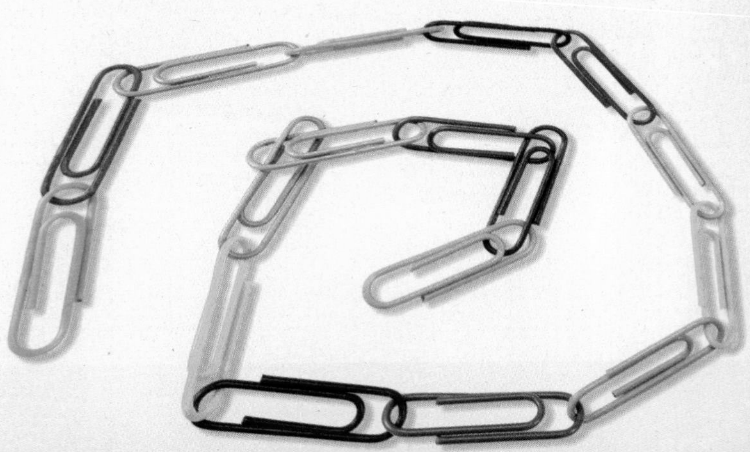

Making Instructional Decisions

CHAPTER GOALS

1 Understand first-, second-, and third-tier decisions that are made prior to a student becoming eligible for special education (for example, recognizing problems, intervention planning, and inadequate academic and behavioral progress).

2 Understand the decisions that are made in special education (for example, individualized educational program content, placement in the least restrictive (and appropriate) environment, and program effectiveness).

KEY TERMS

child find

audiologist

ophthalmologist

graphomotor skills

prereferral assessment

prereferral intervention

Each regular and special education teacher makes literally hundreds of professional decisions every day. In this chapter, we are primarily concerned with the decisions that teachers make about the effectiveness of instruction for students who are at risk, and students who have disabilities.

Both general and special educators share responsibility for students who are disabled. General educators are largely responsible for identifying general education students who are experiencing sensory, learning, or behavior problems. They are also responsible for addressing those problems with or without the assistance of other educators. Both general and special educators share responsibility for the education of students with disabilities who are instructed in general education classrooms. Special educators are additionally responsible for students whose disabilities are so severe that they cannot be educated in general education settings even with a full complement of related services and classroom adaptations and accommodations.

1 Decisions About Students Who Are Not Thought to Be Disabled

Children with moderate or severe disabilities usually are identified before the age of 3 or 4 years and enroll in school as students with disabilities. Approximately 40 percent of all students will experience difficulty during their school career. Most of these problems will be successfully addressed in general education by regular educators. When students' problems are not addressed successfully by regular educators, those students are often referred to multidisciplinary teams to ascertain if they are disabled and in need of special education (that is, eligible for special education). In this part of the chapter, we deal with those decisions that precede entitlement to special education.

DOES A STUDENT HAVE A HIDDEN DISABILITY?

The overwhelming majority of children enter school under the presumption that they do not have disabilities. However, educators know that some of these students have less severe disabilities that may not be apparent to parents or that other students will develop disabilities during their educations. Because disabilities are likely to be less severe if special services are provided early, federal regulations (§300.125) require states to have policies and procedures to ensure all children with disabilities who need special education and related services are located, evaluated, and identified. This requirement, generally referred to as *child find,* means that local school districts and other agencies must inform parents of available services through strategically placed flyers, notices in local newspapers, and so forth.

Universal screening by school districts may uncover additional disabilities. Some children may have undiagnosed sensory difficulties that are not apparent to parents, physicians, or teachers. Therefore, schools routinely screen all children to identify undetected hearing and vision problems and to provide services for those who need them. Sensory screening is usually conducted by a school nurse with the intention of finding children who require diagnosis by a health care professional—a hearing specialist such as an audiologist or a vision specialist such as an optometrist or ophthalmologist. The critical point is that screening, by itself, cannot be used to identify a student as disabled. There must be follow-up.

IS A STUDENT HAVING ACADEMIC DIFFICULTIES?

Some of the students in general education will not make adequate progress toward individual, classroom, or state goals. The threshold of recognition varies from teacher to teacher and may be a function of several factors: teacher skill and experience, class size, availability of alternative materials and curriculum, ability and behavior of other students in the class, and the teacher's tolerance for atypical progress or behavior. Generally, when a student is performing academically at a rate that is between 20 and 50 percent of the rate of other students, a teacher has reason to be concerned. Teachers will likely be concerned when a student

- asks questions that indicate that he or she does not understand new material.
- does not know material that was previously taught and presumed to be mastered.
- makes numerous errors and few correct responses.
- does not keep up with peers, in general or in his or her instructional groups.
- is so far behind that of peers that he or she cannot be maintained in the lowest instructional group in a class—that is, the student becomes instructionally isolated.
- changes from doing good or acceptable work to doing poor or unacceptable work.
- performs adequately in most academic areas but has extreme difficulty in one or more important core skill areas.

Why a student is having academic difficulty is seldom clear at this point in the decision-making process. There are multiple reasons for school failure, and these reasons may often interact with one another. The reasons for these differences generally fall into two broad categories: ineffective instruction or individual differences.

Ineffective Instruction

Some students make progress under almost any instructional conditions. When students with emerging skills and a wealth of information enter a learning situation, such students merely need the opportunity to continue learning and developing skills. These students often learn despite ineffective instructional methodology. However, some students enter a learning situation with poorly developed skills and require much more effective instruction. Without good instruction,

SCENARIO *in* ASSESSMENT

ALEX AND JENNA | **Example 1.** Alex is a third grader whose teacher is worried that he is falling behind his peers. Assessment information is of two types. First, his teacher notices that he has not kept up with the slowest students in the class nor acquired reading skills as quickly as those students. Second, his teacher assesses Alex and some of his peers and finds that the students in the lowest reading group are reading preprimer materials orally at a rate of 50 words per minute or more, with no more than two errors per minute. Alex reads the same materials at a rate of 20 words per minute with four errors per minute. The reading materials used by the lowest group are too difficult for Alex; easier reading materials are needed for effective instruction.

Example 2. Jenna is a fourth grader whose teacher is concerned about her writing skills. Assessment information is of two types. First, her teacher notes that Jenna has been placed in the classroom's highest instructional group for arithmetic, reading, social science, and music, where her performance is among the best in the class. However, her teacher notices that she struggles in her written work. Her writing is messy and often indecipherable. Her written work is like that of the least able students in the class. Second, her teacher assesses Jenna and some of her peers using timed writings with story starters. Jenna's writings contain relatively few words (7 words per minute), whereas peers judged to be progressing satisfactorily write almost twice as many (13) words per minute. Jenna has frequent misspellings (approximately 30 percent of her words), whereas peers progressing satisfactorily misspell approximately 10 percent of their words. Although not quantified, Jenna's writing demonstrates poor graphomotor skills (for example, letter formation, spacing within and between words, and text lines that move up and down as they go across the page), whereas her peers' writing is much neater and more legible.

What implications about your own professional role can you draw from this scenario? Go to the Education CourseMate website for this textbook for more reflection questions about this Scenario in Assessment.

these students are in danger of becoming casualties of the educational system. This situation can occur in at least five ways.

1. *Students' lack of prerequisite knowledge or skill.* Some students may lack the prerequisites for learning specific content. In such cases, the content to be learned may be too difficult because the student must learn the prerequisites and the new content simultaneously. For example, Mr. Santos may give Alex a reader in which he knows only 70 percent of the words. Alex will be forced to learn sight vocabulary that he lacks while trying to comprehend what he is reading. The chances are that he will not comprehend the material because he must read too many unknown words.
2. *Insufficient instructional time.* The school curriculum may be so cluttered with special events and extras that sufficient time cannot be devoted to core content areas. Students who need more extensive and intensive instruction in order to learn may suffer from the discrepancy between the amounts of instruction (or time) they need and the time allocated to teaching them.
3. *Teachers' lack of subject matter knowledge.* The teacher may lack the skills to teach specific subject matter. For example, in some rural areas, it may not be possible to attract physics teachers, so the biology teacher may have to teach the physics course and try to stay one or two lectures ahead of the students.
4. *Teachers' lack of pedagogical knowledge.* A teacher may lack sufficient pedagogical knowledge to teach students who are not independent learners. Although educators have known for a very long time about teaching methods that promote student learning (see Stevens & Rosenshine, 1981), this information is not as widely known to teachers and supervisors as one would hope. Thus, some educators may not know how to present new material, structure learning opportunities, provide opportunities for guided and independent practice, or give effective feedback. Also, given the number of families in which all adults work, there is less opportunity for parents to provide supplementary instruction at home to overcome ineffective instruction at school.
5. *Teachers' commitment to ineffective methods.* A teacher may be committed to ineffective instructional methods. A considerable amount of effort has gone into the empirical evaluation of various instructional approaches. Yet much of this research fails to find its way into the classroom. For example, a number of school districts have rejected systematic instruction in phonics. However, the empirical research has been clear for a long time that early and systematic phonics instruction leads to better reading (Adams, 1990; Foorman, Francis, Fletcher, Shatschneider, & Mehta, 1998; Pflaum, Walberg, Karegianes, & Rasher, 1980).

Individual Differences

A few students make little progress despite systematic application of sound instructional principles that have been shown to be generally effective. There are at least three reasons for this.

1. Student abilities affect learning. Obviously, instruction that relies heavily on visual or auditory presentation will be less effective with students who have severe visual or auditory impairments.[1] Just as obviously, slow learners require more practice to acquire various skills and knowledge.
2. Some students may find a particular subject inherently interesting and be motivated to learn, whereas other students may find the content to be boring and require additional incentives to learn.

[1] The instructional importance of other abilities has been asserted; however, there is scant evidence to support such assertions. There is limited and dated support for the notion that intelligence interacts with teaching methods in mathematics. Maynard and Strickland (1969) found that students with high IQs tended to learn mathematics somewhat better when discovery methods were used, although more direct methods were equally effective with students with lower IQs.

SCENARIO *in* ASSESSMENT

NICK | **Example 3.** Nick is a fifth grader who is earning unsatisfactory grades in all instructional areas. His teacher notices that Nick frequently does not understand new material and seldom turns in homework. His teacher also notices that Nick frequently stares into space or watches the tropical fish in the class aquarium at inappropriate times. He occasionally seems startled when his teacher calls on him. Although he usually begins seatwork, unlike the other students in class, he usually fails to complete his assignments. He seldom brings his homework to school even when his mother says that he has done it.

Nick's teacher systematically observes Nick and two of his peers who are progressing satisfactorily for their attention to task. Specifically, once each minute during language arts and arithmetic seatwork, the teacher notes if the boys are on task (that is, looking at their work, writing, or appear to be reading). After a week of observation, the teacher summarizes the data and finds that Nick is off task in both language arts and arithmetic approximately 60 percent of the time. His peers are off task less than 5 percent of the time. It is not surprising, given Nick's lack of attention, that he is doing poorly in school.

What implications about your own professional role can you draw from this scenario? Go to the Education CourseMate website for this textbook for more reflection questions about this Scenario in Assessment.

3. Cultural differences can affect academic learning and behavior. For example, reading is an interactive process in which an author's writing is interpreted on the basis of a reader's experience and knowledge. To the extent that students from different cultures have different experiences, their comprehension of some written materials may differ. Thus, students from different cultural groups may have different understandings of, for example, "all men are created equal." Similarly, cultural norms for instructional dialogues between teacher and student may also vary, especially when the teacher and student are of different genders. Boys and girls may be raised differently, with different expectations, in some cultures. Thus, it may be culturally appropriate for women and girls to be reticent in their responses to male teachers. Similarly, teachers may feel ill equipped to teach students from different cultures. For example, teachers may be hesitant to discipline students from another culture, or they may not have culturally relevant examples to illustrate concepts and ideas.

IS A STUDENT HAVING BEHAVIORAL DIFFICULTIES?

Some students may fail to meet behavioral expectations. As discussed in Chapter 6, any behavior that falls outside the range typically expected—for example, too much or too little compliance, too much or too little assertiveness—can be problematic in and of itself. In other cases, a behavior may be problematic because it interferes with learning, either of the students themselves or their peers. Finally, behavior that is dangerous to the student or the student's classmates cannot be ignored.

As is true with academic learning problems, why a student is having behavioral difficulty may be unclear. The problem may lie in the teacher's inability to manage classroom behavior, the individual student's distinctive behavior, or a combination of both.

A teacher may lack sufficient knowledge, skill, or willingness to structure and manage a classroom effectively. Many students come to school with well-developed interpersonal and intrapersonal skills, and such students are well behaved and easily directed or coached in almost any setting. Other students enter the classroom with far less developed skills. For these students, a teacher needs much better management skills. In a classroom in which the teacher lacks these skills, the behavior of such students may interfere with their own learning and the learning of their peers. Thus, a teacher must know how to manage classroom behavior and be willing to do so. Classroom management is one of the more emotional topics in education, and often teachers' personal values and beliefs affect their willingness to control their classrooms. Although for some time there has been extensive empirical research supporting the effectiveness of various management techniques (see Alberto & Troutman, 2005; Sulzer-Azaroff & Mayer, 1986), these techniques may be rejected by some teachers on philosophical grounds. Occasionally, teachers may know how to manage behavior and be willing to do so generally but be unwilling to deal with

SCENARIO *in* ASSESSMENT

NICK | **Example 4.** Because Nick has trouble paying attention, his teacher moves him to the front of class and away from the class aquarium. When his attention seems to wander, she taps his desk unobtrusively with her index finger; this usually brings him back to task. The teacher also has a conference with Nick's mother, and they agree that the teacher will send the parents each homework assignment via e-mail. The mother agrees to check Nick's book bag each morning to make sure that his completed homework is taken to school. It is important that the teacher monitors the effect of these interventions on Nick's attention and learning—that is, determine if the intervention improves Nick's behavior. The assessment data used by the teacher consist of the frequency of homework turned in before and after the homework intervention is introduced. The teacher also notes the duration of Nick's redirected attention.

What implications about your own professional role can you draw from this scenario? Go to the Education CourseMate website for this textbook for more reflection questions about this Scenario in Assessment.

specific students for some reason. For example, some European American teachers may be hesitant to discipline minority students.

Even when teachers use generally effective management strategies, they may be unable to control some students effectively. For example, some students may be difficult to manage because they have never had to control their behavior before, because they reject women as authority figures, or because they seek any kind of attention—positive or negative. Other students may not get enough sleep or nutritious food to be alert and ready to participate and learn in school. Thus, generally effective management strategies may be ill suited to a particular student. Because there is seldom a perfect relationship between undesirable behavior and its cause, it is impossible to know *a priori* whether a student's difficulties are the result of different values, lack of learning, or flawed management techniques without modifying some of the management strategies and observing the effect of the modifications. If a student begins to behave better with the modifications, the reasons for the initial difficulties are not particularly important (and no one should assume that the teacher has found the cause of the difficulty).

CAN WE INCREASE TEACHER COMPETENCE AND SCHOOL CAPACITY?

Many academic and behavioral problems can be remediated or eliminated when classroom teachers intervene quickly and effectively. When teachers recognize that students are experiencing difficulties, they usually provide those students with a little extra help.

However, when teachers are unable to remediate or eliminate the problem, they need help. Help can come in two basic forms: (1) increasing teachers' competence so that they can handle the problem themselves or (2) bring additional resources to bear on the problem. The former may take the form of informal consultation with other teachers or building specialists. The latter may take the form of Title I services or tier 2 and tier 3 services.

SCENARIO *in* ASSESSMENT

NICK | **Example 5.** The data on the effectiveness of the interventions on Nick's on-task behavior showed mixed results. Nick's rate of homework completion immediately jumped to 100 percent. Thus, Nick's completion problem was solved by providing the parents with each homework assignment and having them make sure that Nick actually brought his homework to school. Moving Nick to the front of the class, nearer to the teacher, stopped him from staring at the aquarium but had little effect on his staring into space in general. The tapping cue to redirect Nick's attention worked 100 percent of the time, but the duration of his redirected attention was short, averaging approximately 30 seconds. Moreover, the teacher found that increasingly harder tapping was required, and that this intervention had become intrusive and distracting to the students seated next to Nick. Because the teacher's classroom interventions had met with little success and because Nick's lack of attention was still affecting his learning, the teacher decided to consult with the school building's child study team to find out if they had other suggestions.

What implications about your own professional role can you draw from this scenario? Go to the Education CourseMate website for this textbook for more reflection questions about this Scenario in Assessment.

CAN AN INTERVENTION ASSISTANCE TEAM HELP?

A team can provide more intensive interventions; short-term consultation; continuous support; or information, resources, or training for teachers who request its help. By providing problem-specific support and assistance to teachers, those teachers become more skillful in their work with students. Although the team's makeup and job titles vary by state, team members should be skilled in areas of learning, assessment, behavior management, curriculum modification, and interpersonal communication.

Intervention assistance teams provide tiers of intervention between what was available in a regular classroom teacher and what is provided in special education. Obviously, students do not need, and should not receive, special education when better teaching or behavioral management would allow them to make satisfactory progress in regular education. Thus, when a teacher seeks more intensive help for students, the first form of help offered should be providing additional strategies and materials. The goals of intervention assistance are (1) to remediate, if possible, student difficulties before they become disabling; (2) to provide remediation in the least restrictive environment; and (3) to verify that if the problems cannot be resolved effectively, they are not caused by the school (that is, to establish that the problems reside within the child or the family). Typically, there are four (Bergen & Kratchowill, 1990) or five (Graden, Casey, & Bonstrom, 1983) stages of prereferral activities, depending how making a formal request for service is counted: (1) making a formal request for services, (2) clarifying the problem, (3) designing the interventions, (4) implementing the interventions, and (5) evaluating the interventions' effects.

Making the Request

Because prereferral intervention is a formalized process, a formal request for services may be required and might be made on a form similar to that shown in Figure 26.1. When a prereferral[2] form is used, it should contain identifying information (such as teacher and student names), the specific problems for which the teacher is seeking consultation, the interventions that have already been attempted in the classroom, the effectiveness of those interventions, and current academic instructional levels. This information allows those responsible for providing consultation to decide whether the problem warrants their further attention.

Clarifying the Problem

In the initial consultation, the team works with the classroom teacher to specify the nature of a problem or the specific areas of difficulty. These difficulties should be stated in terms of observable behavior, not hypothesized causes of the problem. For example, the teacher may specify a problem by saying that "Jenna does not write legibly" or that "Nick does not complete homework assignments as regularly as other students in his class." The focus is on the discrepancy between actual and desired performance.

The team may seek additional information. For example, the referring teacher may be asked to describe in detail the contexts in which problems occur, the student's curriculum, the way in which the teacher interacts with or responds to the student, the student's interactions with the teacher and with classmates, the student's instructional groupings and seating arrangements, and antecedents and consequences of the student's behaviors. The referring teacher may also be asked to specify the ways in which the student's behavior affects the teacher or other students and the extent to which the behavior is incongruent with the teacher's expectations. When multiple problems are identified, they may be ranked in order of importance for action.

[2] Early on, special educators adopted the term *referral* to designate a request that a student be evaluated for special education eligibility and entitlement. Subsequently, an additional step was inserted into the process. Because referral had already gained widespread acceptance, the new step was called "prereferral," although this step clearly involves referral, too. We use the term *prereferral* to describe assessment and intervention activities that occur prior to formal referral to determine eligibility for special education.

FIGURE 26.1
Request for Prereferral Consultation

Request for Prereferral Consultation

Student ______________________ Gender ________ Date of Birth ________

Referring Teacher ______________ Grade ________ School ____________

Specific Educational/Behavioral Problems:

Current Level or Materials in Deficit Areas:

Specific Interventions to Improve Performance in Deficit Areas and Their Effectiveness:

What Special Services Does the Student Receive (e.g., Title I Reading, Speech Therapy)?

Most Convenient Days and Times for Consultation:

Finally, as part of the consultation, a member of the staff support team may observe the pupil in the classroom to verify the nature and extent of the problem. In relevant school settings, a designated member of the team observes the student, notes the frequency and duration of behaviors of concern, and ascertains the extent to which the student's behavior differs from that of classmates. At this point (or later in the process), the perceptions of the student and the student's parents may also be sought.

Designing the Interventions

Next, the team and the referring teacher design interventions to remediate the most pressing problems. The team may need to coach the referring teacher on how to implement the interventions. Initially, the interventions should be based on empirically validated procedures that are known to be generally effective. In addition, parents, other school personnel, and the student may be involved in the intervention.

A major factor determining whether an intervention will be tried or implemented by teachers is feasibility. Those who conduct assessments and make recommendations about teaching must consider the extent to which the interventions they recommend are doable. (Unfortunately, too often feasibility is determined on the basis of how much of a hassle the intervention planning will be or how much work it will take to implement a given program.) Phillips (1990) identifies eight major considerations in making decisions about feasibility, which we suggest that assessors address.

1. *Degree of disruption.* How much will the intervention the teacher recommends disrupt school procedures or teacher routines?
2. *Side effects.* To what extent are there undesirable side effects for the student (for example, social ostracism), peers, home and family, and faculty?
3. *Support services required.* How readily available are the support services required, and are the costs reasonable?
4. *Prerequisite competencies.* Does the teacher have the necessary knowledge, motivation, and experience to be able to implement the intervention? Does the teacher have a philosophical bias against the recommended intervention?
5. *Control.* Does the teacher have control of the necessary variables to ensure the success of the intervention?
6. *Immediacy of results.* Will the student's behavioral change be quick enough for the teacher to be reinforced for implementing the intervention?
7. *Consequences of nonintervention.* What are the short- and long-term prognoses for the student if the behaviors are left uncorrected?
8. *Potential for transition.* Is it reasonable to expect that the intervention will lead to student self-regulation and generalize to other settings, curriculum areas, or even to other students who are experiencing similar difficulties?

The intervention plan should include a clear delineation of the skills to be developed or the behavior to be changed, the methods to be used to effect the change, the duration of the intervention, the location of the intervention, and the names of the individuals responsible for each aspect of the intervention. Moreover, the criteria for a successful intervention should be clear. At a minimum, the intervention should bring a student's performance to an acceptable or tolerable level. For academic difficulties, this usually means accelerating the rate of acquisition. For an instructional isolate, achievement must improve sufficiently to allow placement in an instructional group. For example, if Bernie currently cannot read the material used in the lowest reading group, the team would need to know the level of the materials used by the lowest instructional group. In addition, the team would need to know the probable level of materials that the group will be using when Bernie's intervention has been completed. For students with more variable patterns of achievement, intervention is directed toward improving performance in areas of weakness to a level that approximates performance in areas of strength.

Setting the criterion for a behavioral intervention involves much the same process as setting targets for academic problems. When the goal is to change behavior, the teacher should select two or three students who are behaving appropriately. These students should not be the best behaved students but, rather, those in the middle of the range of acceptable behavior. The frequency, duration, latency, or amplitude of their behavior should be used as the criterion. Usually, the behavior of the appropriate students is stable, so the team does not have to predict where they will be at the end of the intervention.

Implicit in this discussion is the idea that the interventions will reach the criterion for success within the time allotted. Thus, the team not only desires progress toward the criterion but also wants that progress to occur at a specific rate—or faster. Finally, it is generally a good idea to maintain a written record of these details. This record might be as informal as a set of notes from the team meeting, or it might be a formal document such as the Prereferral Intervention Plan shown in Figure 26.2.

FIGURE 26.2
Prereferral Intervention Plan

Prereferral Intervention Plan

Complete one form for each targeted problem.

Student ________________ Gender ______ Date of Birth ______

Referring Teacher ________________ Grade ______ School ______

Intervention Objectives

Behavior to be changed:

Criterion for success/termination of intervention:

Duration of intervention:

Location of intervention:

Person responsible for implementing the intervention:

Strategies

Instructional methods:

Instructional materials:

Special equipment:

Signatures

________________ ________
(Referring Teacher) (Date)

________________ ________
(Member, Teacher Assistance Team) (Date)

Implementing the Interventions

The interventions should then be conducted as planned. To ensure that the intervention is being carried out faithfully, a member of the team may observe the teacher using the planned strategy or special materials, or careful records may be kept and reviewed in order to document that the intervention occurred as planned.

Evaluating the Effects of the Interventions

The effects of the interventions should be evaluated frequently enough to allow fine-tuning of the teaching methods and materials. Frequently, student performance is graphed to make pictures of progress. Effective programs designed to increase desired behavior produce results like those shown in Figure 26.3: The student usually shows an increase in the desired behavior (correct responses) and a decrease in the number of errors (incorrect responses). It is also possible for successful programs to produce only increasingly correct responses or only a decrease in errors. Ineffective programs show no increase in the desired correct responses, no decrease in the unwanted errors, or both.

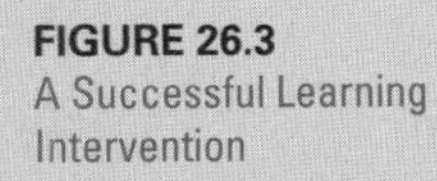

FIGURE 26.3
A Successful Learning Intervention

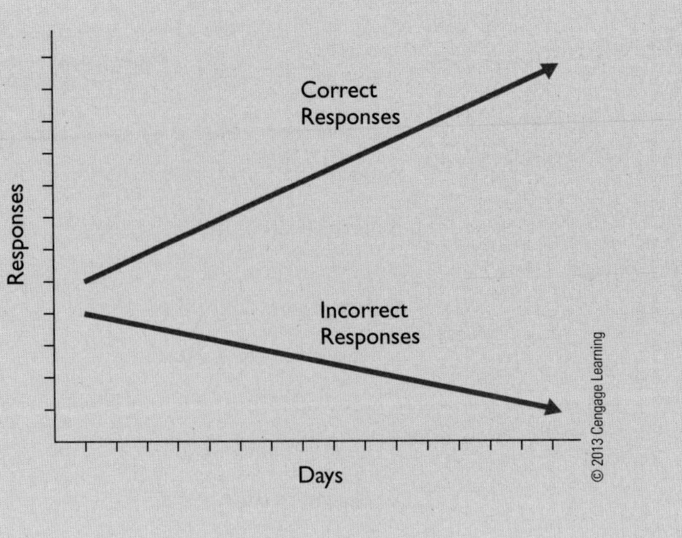

To assess a student's rate of behavior change, we graph the acceleration of a desired behavior (or the deceleration of an undesired behavior) with an aimline (See Chapter 6), as shown in Figure 26.4. The aimline connects the student's current level of performance with the point that represents both the desired level of behavior and the time at which the behavior is to be attained. When behavior is targeted for increase, we expect the student's progress to be at or above the aimline (as shown in Figure 26.4); when behavior is targeted for decrease, we expect the student's progress to be at or below the aimline (not shown). Thus, a teacher, the intervention assistance team, and the student can look at the graph and make a decision about the adequacy of progress.

When adequate progress is being made, the intervention should obviously be continued until the criterion is reached. When better than anticipated progress is being made, the teacher or team can decide to set a more ambitious goal (that is, raise the level of desired performance) without changing the aim date, or they can set an earlier target for achieving the criterion without changing the level of performance. When inadequate progress is being made, teachers can take several steps to fine-tune the student's program.

FIGURE 26.4
Student Progress with an Aimline

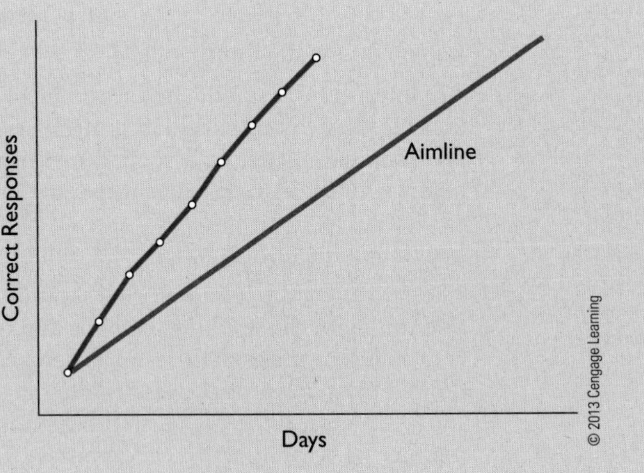

SHOULD THE STUDENT BE REFERRED FOR MULTIDISCIPLINARY EVALUATION?

When several attempted interventions at each level of a multi-tiered system of supports (MTSS) have not led to sufficient success, the student is likely to be referred for psychoeducational evaluation to ascertain eligibility for special education.

2 Decisions Made in Special Education

Approximately 10 to 12 percent of all students who enter school will experience sufficient difficulty to be identified as having a disability at some time during their school career. Most of these students will receive special education services because they need special instruction. Some students with disabilities (such as students with certain chronic health impairments) will not need special education but will require special related services that must be provided under Section 504 of the Rehabilitation Act of 1973.

After students have been determined to be eligible for special education, special education decisions revolve around design and implementation of their individualized education plans (IEPs). An IEP is a blueprint for instruction and specifies the goals, procedures, and related services for an individual eligible student. Assessment data are important for such planning. Numerous books and hundreds of articles in professional and scientific journals discuss the importance of using assessment data to plan instructional programs for students. The Individuals with Disabilities Education Act (IDEA) requires a thorough assessment that results in an IEP. Pupils are treated differentially on the basis of their IEPs. Moreover, most educators would agree that it is desirable to individualize programs for students in special and remedial education because the general education programs have not proved beneficial to them.

WHAT SHOULD BE INCLUDED IN A STUDENT'S IEP?

The Individuals with Disabilities Education Act of 1997 and subsequent revisions to the Act and its regulations set forth the requirements for IEPs. Instructionally, an IEP is a road map of a student's 1-year trip from point A to point B. This road map is prepared collaboratively by an IEP team composed of the parents and student

SCENARIO *in* ASSESSMENT

ALEX | **Example 6.** Alex's teacher finds an easier reader for him and reads individually with him for 5 minutes each day. During this time, the teacher corrects his errors and shows him how to sound out words. Although Alex can read the lower level materials more fluently, he is unable to advance to more grade-appropriate reading materials (that is, his fluency and error rate are below an instructional level). The building assistance team recommends that the teacher assess Alex's knowledge of letter–sound associations. Alex is found to know all long vowel sounds, the short *a* sound, and hard consonant sounds. Consequently, the team develops a program that targets the sounds of the consonants and vowels that he has not yet mastered. One of the district's reading specialists administers the intervention daily and evaluates his progress every other day. Assessment data to ascertain the effectiveness of the intervention consists of Alex's progress in learning letter–sound associations and his oral reading fluency. The reading specialist administers a letter–sound probe after each day's instruction. After 4 weeks of intervention, Alex has learned half of the unknown soft consonant sounds as well as the short *e* and *i* sounds. A retest of his oral reading fluency indicates that he has become fluent in the next higher reading level. At the rate he is improving, he will fall at least another half-year behind his peers at the end of the current school year. Because the intervention selected has support in the research literature but has not proved sufficiently effective with Alex, he is referred for multidisciplinary evaluation to ascertain if there are nonschool factors that could be impeding his learning (for example, a disability). Determination of eligibility requires further assessment by specialists, such as school psychologists, who use commercially prepared instruments.

What implications about your own professional role can you draw from this scenario? Go to the Education CourseMate website for this textbook for more reflection questions about this Scenario in Assessment.

(when appropriate), at least one general education teacher, at least one of the student's special education teachers, a representative of the school administration, an individual who can interpret the instructional implications of evaluation results, and other individuals who have knowledge or special expertise regarding the student.

The IEP begins with a description of the student's current educational levels—the starting point of the metaphoric trip. Next, the IEP specifies measurable, annual, academic, and functional goals (the student's destination). The IEP must include a description of how progress toward meeting annual goals will be measured and when progress reports will be provided to parents. The IEP must identify the special education and related services that are based on peer-reviewed research (to the extent practicable) needed by the student in order to reach the goals (the method of transportation and provisions that make the trip possible). Finally, the IEP requires measurement, evaluation, and reporting of the student's progress toward the annual goals (periodic checks to make sure the student is on the correct road and traveling fast enough).[3]

Current Levels

A student's current level of performance is not specifically defined in the regulations. However, because current levels are the starting points for instruction, a current level must be instructionally relevant and expressed quantitatively. Although legally permissible, scores from standardized achievement are not particularly useful. Even if there is adequate correspondence between test and curricular content, the fact that a student is reading less well than 90 percent of students in the grade is not useful information about where the teacher should begin instruction. If a student is physically aggressive in the third-grade classroom, that alone is too vague to allow a teacher, parents, and the student to tell whether progress toward acceptable behavior is being made. Although not defined in the IDEA, we think a current educational level in an academic area should be the level at which a student is appropriately instructed. For example, knowing that Sam is at an *instructional* reading level in third-grade materials (i.e., reads that material with between 90 and 95 percent accuracy) is directly related to where his instruction should begin.

SCENARIO *in* ASSESSMENT

ALEX AND NICK | **Example 7.** Alex is found eligible for special education services as a student with a learning disability in reading. To ascertain Alex's current level of performance in oral reading, he is again assessed by having him read from the materials actually used in his school. Two passages of 300 to 400 words that are representative of the beginning, middle, and end of each grade-level reading text are selected. Because Alex is already known to be reading only slightly above the preprimer level, he is asked to start reading at that level. He reads passages of increasing difficulty until he is no longer reading at an instructional level (that is, reading with 85 to 95 percent accuracy).[4] Alex reads beginning first-grade material with 95 percent accuracy, but he reads middle second-grade material with only 87 percent accuracy. Thus, his current instructional level in oral reading is determined to be middle second grade.

Current educational level in behavioral areas should also be quantified. Frequency, duration, latency, and amplitude can be quantified, and the results can be compared to those of a peer who is performing satisfactorily on the target skill or behavior.

Example 8. Nick has also been found eligible for special education services as a student with other health impairments (attention deficit disorder without hyperactivity). To ascertain the duration of Nick's attention to task during academic instruction, the school counselor systematically observes Nick and another student who is not reported to be having attention problems. Observations occurred between 10:00 and 10:45 for a week during reading and arithmetic instruction. Nick's teacher does not use the tapping cue during this time period. The counselor sits behind and to Nick's side and uses an audio signal tape with beeps at a fixed interval of 30 seconds. The counselor calculates that Nick is on task 35 percent of the time, whereas his peer is on task 93 percent of the time. Nick's current level of attention to academic tasks is 35 percent.

What implications about your own professional role can you draw from this scenario? Go to the Education CourseMate website for this textbook for more reflection questions about this Scenario in Assessment.

[3] See, for example, the website for the Los Angeles Unified School District (http://sped.lausd.net/sepg2s/pg2_gettingstarted.htm).

[4] To calculate accuracy, first find the number of words with two or more letters. Then count the number of errors; for example, words a reader cannot decode correctly and words a reader incorrectly adds to the text. See Chapter 12 for a discussion of errors in oral reading.

Annual Goals

IEPs must contain a statement of measurable annual goals, which meet each educational need arising from the student's disability and ensure the student's access to the general education curriculum (or appropriate activities, if a preschooler). Thus, for each area of need, parents and schools must agree on what should be a student's level of achievement after 1 year of instruction.

In part, the selection of long-term goals is based on the aspirations and prognosis for a student's postschool outcomes. Although these are not formally required by federal law until a special education student reaches 16 years of age, the expected or desired postschool outcomes shape the special education a student receives. For students with pervasive and severe cognitive disabilities, the prognosis may be assisted living with supported employment. With this prognosis, educational goals are likely to center on daily living, social skills, and leisure rather than academic areas. For students with moderate disabilities, the prognosis may be independent living and unskilled or semiskilled employment. With this prognosis, educational goals are likely to be basic academics and vocational skills. For students with mild disabilities, the prognosis may be professional or skilled employment. For these students, educational goals can prepare students for college or technical schools.

In part, the selection of long-term goals is based on the degree to which the educational deficit caused by the disability is remediable. All students receiving special education will lag significantly behind their nondisabled peers.[5] Except when students have severe and pervasive disabilities, special educators and parents generally try to remediate the educational deficits first. The benefit of this approach is that it allows the student the fullest access to later school and postschool opportunities. When remediation repeatedly fails, parents and teachers usually turn to compensatory mechanisms so that the student can attain the more generally desired educational outcomes. For example, if Cliff just cannot learn math facts, he may be allowed to use a calculator. The advantage of this option is that it allows Cliff to move to higher curricular goals; the disadvantage is that the deficits will always be with Cliff, and he will always behave to compensate for them. When a student cannot master the curriculum with compensatory mechanisms, parents and teachers may adapt the curriculum by reducing the complexity of some components. For example, in social studies all students might be required to learn about taxes, but LeShaun might not have to learn about the constitutional issues surrounding the creation of the federal income tax. If reducing the complexity is not appropriate, areas of the curriculum may be eliminated for individual students with disabilities. Obviously, this option is the last resort, but it may be appropriate when a child's disabilities are profound. For example, we would not expect all deaf students to be fluent oral communicators, although we would expect them to attain other generally prescribed educational outcomes; we would not expect quadriplegics to pass a swimming test, although we might well expect them to meet other educational outcomes.

Annual goals are derived directly from a student's curriculum and a student's current instructional levels. When continued academic integration is the desired educational outcome, a student's goals are mastery of the same content at the same rate as nondisabled peers. Thus, after 1 year, the student would be expected to be instructional in the same materials as his or her peers. When reintegration is the desired educational outcome, a student's goal depends on where the regular class peers will be in 1 year. For students pursuing alternative programming, the IEP team makes an educated guess about where the student should be after 1 year of instruction.

Specially Designed Instruction

IDEA defines special education, in part, as specially designed instruction that is provided in classrooms, the home, or other settings (see 34 CFR §300.26). It includes the adaptation of instructional content, methods, or delivery to meet the needs of a student with disabilities.

[5] Some gifted students have learning disabilities. Thus, these gifted students will also have significant deficits.

Currently, the best way to teach handicapped learners appears to rely on generally effective procedures.[6] Teachers can do several things to make it easier for their pupils to learn facts and concepts, skills, or behavior. They can model the desired behavior. They can break down the terminal goal into its component parts and teach each of the steps and their integration. They can teach the objective in a variety of contexts with a variety of materials to facilitate generalization. They can provide time for practice, and they can choose the schedule on which practice is done (in other words, they can offer distributed or massed practice). Several techniques that are under the direct control of the teacher can be employed to instruct any learner effectively. To help pupils recall information that has been taught, teachers may organize the material that a pupil is to learn, provide rehearsal strategies, or employ overlearning or distributed practice. There are also a number of things that teachers can do to elicit responses that have already been acquired: Various reinforcers and punishers have been shown to be effective in the control of behavior.

Assessment personnel can help teachers identify specific areas in which instructional difficulties exist, and they can help teachers plan interventions in light of information gained from assessments. Procedures such as the Functional Assessment of Academic Behavior (Ysseldyke & Christenson, 2002) may be used both to pinpoint the extent to which a student's academic or behavioral problems are a function of factors in the instructional environment and to identify likely starting points for designing appropriate interventions for individual students. Yet there is no way to know for certain ahead of time how best to teach a specific student.

There should be good evidence that the instructional interventions are generally effective with students who are at the same age and grade as the student being assessed. Under the requirements of No Child Left Behind, school personnel are expected to be putting in place evidence-based treatments. Information about the extent to which treatments are generally effective is found by reviewing the research evidence in support of the treatments. The What Works Clearinghouse (WWC) can provide direction as to what treatments might be particularly effective. At the WWC website, you can look up interventions for middle school math and find a topic report listing the kinds of interventions that WWC reviewed on middle school math.

Find the WWC address at the Education CourseMate website for this textbook.

SCENARIO *in* ASSESSMENT

ALEX | **Example 9.** Alex is finishing third grade, so his annual goal specifies his desired performance near the end of fourth grade. If he were to be completely caught up with his peers, Alex would read independently in his fourth-grade materials. (If his teacher or school uses different levels of reading materials for different tracks of students, he would need to read independently the materials used by the lowest track in regular education.) For the sake of this example, let us assume that the lowest group will use reading materials written at the middle third-grade level at the end of fourth grade. Thus, for Alex to be "caught up" with his peers, he would need to complete approximately 3.3 years in 1 year. Because this much growth in reading could not likely be attained without omitting instruction in other key curricular areas (such as science and written language), the IEP team decides to take 2 years to try to catch Alex up to his age peers. Thus, his annual goal becomes "At the end of 1 year of instruction in oral reading Alex will read material written at the end of second-grade difficulty level with 95 percent accuracy."

What implications about your own professional role can you draw from this scenario? Go to the Education CourseMate website for this textbook for more reflection questions about this Scenario in Assessment.

[6] Historically, some psychologists and educators have believed that students learn better when instruction is matched to test-identified abilities. This approach led to the development of instructional procedures that capitalized on areas of strength or avoided weaker abilities. For example, test scores from the first edition of the Developmental Test of Visual Perception (Frostig, Maslow, Lefever, & Whittlesey, 1964), the Illinois Test of Psycholinguistic Abilities (Kirk, McCarthy, & Kirk, 1968), and the Purdue Perceptual–Motor Survey (Roach & Kephart, 1966) were at one time believed to be instructionally useful. In part because test-identified abilities were frequently unreliable and in part because special instructional methods did not result in better learning, this approach to instruction gradually lost favor, although some educators today still cling to a belief in it. In the 1980s, attempts to match instruction to specific student attributes resurfaced. However, hypothetical cognitive structures and learning processes replaced the hypothetical abilities of the 1960s (for example, see Resnick, 1987). This approach is interesting but has yet to be validated.

Information on the extent to which there is good empirical support for a particular intervention can be obtained from that website.

However, always remember that efficacy is local. We recommend that teachers first rely on general principles that are known and demonstrated to be effective in facilitating learning for students with disabilities. However, even when we find studies that demonstrate that a particular application of a learning principle worked for a research sample, we still cannot be certain that it will work for specific students in a specific classroom. The odds are that it will, but we cannot be sure. Consequently, we must treat our translation of these principles, known to be effective, as tentative. In a real sense, we hypothesize that our treatment will work, but we need to verify that it has worked. The point was made years ago by Deno and Mirkin (1977) and remains true today:

> At the present time we are unable to prescribe specific and effective changes in instruction for individual pupils with certainty. Therefore, changes in instructional programs that are arranged for an individual child can be treated only as hypotheses that must be empirically tested before a decision can be made about whether they are effective for that child. (p. 11)

Teaching is often experimental in nature. When there is no database to guide our selection of specific tasks or materials, decisions must be tentative. The decision maker makes some good guesses about what will work and then implements an instructional program. We do not know whether a decision is correct until we gather data on the extent to which the instructional program actually works. We never know if the program will work until it has worked.

Tests do provide some very limited information about how to teach. Tests of intelligence, for example, yield information that gives a teacher some hints about teaching. Generally, the lower a pupil's intelligence, the more practice the student will require for mastery. A score of 55 on the Wechsler Intelligence Scale for Children–IV does not tell the teacher whether a pupil needs 25 percent or 250 percent more practice, but it does alert the teacher to the likelihood that the pupil will need more practice than the average student will need. Other tenuous hints can be derived, but we believe that it is better to rely on direct observation of how a student learns in order to make adjustments in the learning program. Thus, to determine whether we had provided enough practice, we would observe Sally's recall of information rather than looking at Sally's IQ. We cannot do anything about Sally's IQ, but we can do something about the amount of practice she gets.

Related Services

In addition to special instruction, eligible students are entitled to developmental, corrective, and other supportive services if such services are needed in order for the students to benefit from special education; federal legislation uses the term *related services*, which has been widely adopted by states and school districts. Related services include both those not typically provided by schools and those typically provided (34 CFR §300.24).

Schools must provide to students with disabilities a variety of services to which nondisabled students are seldom entitled. Services described in 34 CFR §300.24 include, but are not limited to, the following types:

1. *Audiology.* Allowable services include evaluation of hearing, habilitation (for example, programs in auditory training, speech reading, and speech conservation), amplification (including the fitting of hearing aids), and hearing conservation programs.
2. *Psychological services.* Psychological services allowed include testing, observation, and consultation.
3. *Physical and occupational therapy.* These therapies can be used to (a) improve, develop, or restore functional impairments caused by illness, injury, or deprivation; and (b) improve independent functioning. These therapies may also be used with preschool populations to prevent impairment or further loss of function.

SCENARIO *in* ASSESSMENT

NICK AND ALEX | **Example 10.** The assessment data pointed to areas where Nick needs specially designed instruction. Although Nick's physician prescribes Ritalin, Nick also needs systematic behavioral intervention to minimize the effects of his attention deficit disorder on school functioning.[7] The team develops a program of specially designed instruction that includes systematic reinforcement for appropriate attention and systematic instruction in self-monitoring his attention. The district behavior management specialist will be responsible for training Nick to self-monitor accurately, and Nick's teacher will be trained to implement the plan developed by the district specialist.

[7] Assume that Nick's psychoeducational evaluation does not reveal other intellectual, physical, or cognitive problems beyond his lack of attention.

Example 11. The assessment data also indicated that Alex needs specially designed instruction in reading. Although he has now mastered all of the sounds of consonants and vowels, he is slow and inaccurate in reading grade-appropriate materials. To improve Alex's accuracy, the IEP team decides that Alex should be taught the basic sight vocabulary needed to read the words in his language arts text as well as content-area curricula. To improve Alex's reading fluency, the IEP team decides to use the strategy of rereading.

What implications about your own professional role can you draw from this scenario? Go to the Education CourseMate website for this textbook for more reflection questions about this Scenario in Assessment.

4. *Recreation.* Allowable programs include those located in the schools and community agencies that provide general recreation programs, therapeutic recreation, and assessment of leisure functioning.
5. *Counseling services.* Either group or individual counseling may be provided for students and their parents. Student counseling includes rehabilitation counseling that focuses on career development, employment preparation, achievement of independence, and integration in the workplace and community; it also includes psychological counseling. Parental counseling includes therapies addressing problems in the student's living situation (that is, home, school, and community) that affect the student's schooling. Parental counseling also includes assistance to help parents understand their child's special needs, as well as information about child development.
6. *Medical services.* Diagnostic and evaluative services required to determine medically related disabilities are allowed.

The schools must also provide to students with disabilities the services they typically provide to all children. Thus, schools must provide to students with disabilities, as needed, speech and language services, school health and school social work services, and transportation. School-provided transportation includes whatever is needed to get students to and from school, as well as between schools or among school buildings, including any required special equipment such as ramps. Although these related services are mandatory for students who need them to profit from their special education, there is nothing to prohibit a school from offering other services. Thus, schools may offer additional services free of charge to eligible students.

Although federal law is very clear about the need to provide related services to students with disabilities, how that need should be established remains unclear. In practice, most schools or parents seek an evaluation by a specialist. The specialist notes a problem and expresses a belief that a specific therapy could be successful and benefit the student. Thus, need is frequently based on professional opinion. We must also note that related services can be very costly, and some school districts try to avoid providing them. We have heard of districts maintaining that they do not offer a particular service even though federal law mandates that service should be provided to students who need it.

WHAT IS THE LEAST RESTRICTIVE APPROPRIATE ENVIRONMENT?

Federal law expresses a clear preference for educating students with disabilities as close as possible to their home and with their nondisabled peers to the maximum extent appropriate. Education in "special classes, separate schooling or other removal of children with disabilities from the regular educational environment occurs only if the nature or severity of the disability is such that education in regular classes with the use of supplementary aids and services cannot be achieved satisfactorily" (34 CFR §300.550).

Placement Options

A hierarchy of placements ranges from the least restrictive (educating students with disabilities in a general education classroom with a general education teacher who receives consultative services from a special education teacher) to the most restrictive (educating students with disabilities in segregated residential facilities that provide services only to students with disabilities). Between these two extremes are at least five other options:

1. *Instructional support from a special education teacher in the general education classroom.* In this arrangement, eligible students remain in the general education classroom in their neighborhood schools, and the special education teacher comes to the student to provide whatever specialized instruction is necessary.
2. *Instructional support from a special education teacher in a resource room.* In this arrangement, eligible students remain in a general education classroom for most of the day. When they need specialized instruction, they go to a special education resource room to receive services from a special education teacher. Because districts may not have enough students with disabilities in each school to warrant establishing a resource room program at each school, a student may be assigned to a general education classroom that is not in the student's neighborhood school.
3. *Part-time instruction in a special education classroom.* In this arrangement, eligible students have some classes or subject matter taught by the special education teacher and the rest taught in the general education classroom. As is the case with resource rooms, the general education classroom may not be in the student's neighborhood school.
4. *Full-time instruction in a special education classroom, with limited integration.* In this arrangement, eligible students receive all academic instruction from a special education teacher in a special classroom. Eligible students may be integrated with nondisabled peers for special events or activities (such as lunch, recess, and assemblies) and nonacademic classes (such as art and music).
5. *Full-time instruction in a special education classroom, without integration.* In this arrangement, eligible students have no interaction with their nondisabled peers, and their classrooms may be in a special day school that serves only students with disabilities.

FACTORS AFFECTING THE PLACEMENT CHOICE

The selection of a particular option should be based on the intensity of education needed by the eligible student: The less intensive the intervention needed by the student, the less restrictive the environment; the more intensive the intervention needed by the student, the more restrictive the environment. The procedure for determining the intensity of an intervention is less than scientific. Frequently, there is some correspondence between the severity of disability and the intensity of service needed, but that correspondence is not perfect. Therefore, special education teachers and parents should consider the frequency and duration of the needed interventions. The more frequent an intervention is (for instance, every morning versus one morning per week) and the longer its duration (for example, 30 minutes versus 15 minutes per morning), the more likely it is that the intervention will be provided in more, rather than less, restrictive settings. When frequent and long interventions are needed, the student will have less opportunity to participate with nondisabled peers, no matter what the student's placement. Obviously, if students require round-the-clock intervention, they cannot get what they need from a resource room program.

In addition to the nature of needed interventions, parents and teachers may also reasonably consider the following factors when deciding on the type of placement:

1. *Disruption.* Bringing a special education teacher into or pulling a student out of a general education classroom may be disruptive. For example, some students with disabilities cannot handle transitions: They get lost between classrooms, or they forget to go to their resource rooms. When eligible students have a lot of difficulty changing schedules or making transitions between events, less restrictive options may not be appropriate.
2. *Well-being of nondisabled individuals.* Eligible students will seldom be integrated when they present a clear danger to the welfare of nondisabled peers or teachers. For example, assaultive and disruptive students are likely to be placed in more restrictive environments.
3. *Well-being of the student who has a disability.* Many students with disabilities require some degree of protection—in some cases, from nondisabled peers who may tease or physically abuse a student who is different; in other cases, from other students with disabilities. For example, the parents of a seriously withdrawn student may decide not to place their child in a classroom for students with emotional disabilities when those students are assaultive.
4. *Labeling.* Many parents, especially those of students with milder handicaps, reject disability labels. They desire special education services, but they want these services without having their child labeled. Such parents often prefer consultative or itinerant services for their children.
5. *Inclusion.* Some parents are willing to forgo the instructional benefits of special education for the potential social benefits of having their children educated exclusively with nondisabled peers. For such parents, full inclusion is the only option.

There are also pragmatic considerations in selecting the educational setting. One very real consideration is that a school district may, for economic reasons, not be able to provide a full range of options. In such districts, parents are offered a choice among existing options unless they are willing to go through a due process hearing or a court trial. A second consideration is instructional efficiency. When several students require the same intervention, the special education teacher can often form an instructional group. Thus, it will probably cost less to provide the special education services. A third consideration is the specific teachers. Some teachers are

SCENARIO *in* ASSESSMENT

NICK AND ALEX | **Example 12.** Although Nick's behavior is not disruptive or detrimental to the learning of his peers, the interventions that his regular class teacher has used are distracting to the other students. However, the team believes that the specially designed instruction (systematic reinforcement for appropriate attention and self-monitoring) that has been approved by the team will be much less intrusive. Therefore, the team believes that the impact of the intervention on Nick's peers will not be a consideration.

The classroom teacher, once properly trained by the behavior management specialist, can administer the positive reinforcement correctly. Although the behavior management specialist will remove Nick from class when teaching him to self-monitor, the special education teacher and the behavior specialist will evaluate Nick's use of the self-monitoring system in his classroom. Thus, Nick's needs can readily be met in the regular classroom; he will not be instructed in a special education setting.

Example 13. Because the reading interventions designed by the IEP team are not being used in Alex's classroom and because Alex requires more instruction in reading than can be provided in his regular classroom, the IEP team recommends placement in a special education resource room for 1 hour per day. The team decides that Alex will go to the resource room when the rest of his class is being instructed in social studies and art.

What implications about your own professional role can you draw from this scenario? Go to the Education CourseMate website for this textbook for more reflection questions about this Scenario in Assessment.

better than others, and parents may well opt for a more restrictive setting because the teacher there is highly regarded.

Parents and special education teachers must realize that selecting a placement option is an imprecise endeavor. Thus, although federal regulations are clear in their preference for less restrictive placements, the criteria that guide the selection of one option over another are unclear. Choices among placement options should be regarded as best guesses.

3 Is the Instructional Program Effective?

IEPs are supposed to result in effective instruction for students with disabilities. IDEA requires that each student's IEP contain a statement detailing the way in which progress toward annual goals will be measured and how parents will be informed of their child's progress (34 CFR §300.347). In addition, IDEA requires IEP teams to review each student's IEP "periodically, but not less than annually, to determine whether the annual goals for the child are being achieved" (34 CFR §300.343). If adequate progress is not being made, IEP teams are required to revise the IEPs of students who are not making expected progress toward their annual goals. An exception to this rule is that according to IDEA 2004, some states may put in place comprehensive multiyear IEPs for those students who have milder disabilities and for whom parents agree a multiyear IEP is sufficient.

Throughout this book, we have discussed procedures that are useful in collecting information about students' achievement and behavior. We have also discussed how that information can be systematized using graphs and charts. We have offered guidelines about how to reach decisions about a student's progress. All of these discussions are relevant to the decision about the effectiveness of each component of a student's instructional program. Judgments about the simultaneous effectiveness of all of the components of an instructional program are geometrically more complicated. Based on our personal experience, a program is effective if the most important goals are achieved. What makes a goal important varies by student. For an aggressive, acting-out student, self-control may be more important than quadratic equations. For a bright student with a learning disability, learning to read may be more important than improvement in spelling.

Chapter Comprehension Questions

Write your answers to each of the following questions and then compare your responses to the text.

1. List and explain three instructional decisions that are made prior to a student being found eligible for special education.
2. List and explain three instructional decisions that are made after a student has been found eligible for special education.

Web Activities 

1 Go to Chapter 25 (Using Portfolios in Assessment) at the website for this textbook. How can a teacher use portfolios to establish a student's current level of academic performance?

2. Review Chapter 18 (Using Measures of Adaptive Behavior) at the website for this textbook. Explain how you could establish current levels of adaptive behavior for a preschool child with moderate retardation.

Web Resources

Standards-Based Individualized Educational Program Examples
http://www.nasdse.org/Portals/0/Standards-BasedIEPExamples.pdf
Marla Holbrook prepared this 2007 12-page report that provides a seven-step process for developing standards-based IEPs. Two extended examples illustrate each step.

Related Services – A Closer Look
http://www.wrightslaw.com/info/relsvcs.indepth.htm
This web page is based on information from the National Information Center for Children and Youth with Disabilities. It provides a brief explanation of numerous related services: artistic/cultural programs, assistive technology, audiology, counseling services, medical services, occupational therapy, orientation and mobility services, parent counseling and training, physical therapy, psychological services, recreation, rehabilitation counseling services, school health services, social work services, speech-language services, and transportation services.

Additional resources for this chapter can be found on the Education CourseMate website. Go to CengageBrain.com to access the site.

Making Special Education Eligibility Decisions

CHAPTER GOALS

1 Understand the disabilities recognized by the Individuals with Disabilities Education Improvement Act.

2 Understand how the need for special education is established.

3 Understand multidisciplinary teams (their composition and responsibilities).

4 Understand the process for determining eligibility (including procedural safeguards, the requirements for valid assessment, and the team process).

5 Understand common problems in determining eligibility.

KEY TERMS

autism
mental retardation
specific learning disability
severe discrepancy
response to intervention
emotional disturbance
traumatic brain injury
speech or language impairment
deafness and hearing impairment
visual impairment
orthopedic impairments
other health impairments
deaf–blindness
multiple disabilities
developmental delay
need for special education
multidisciplinary team
procedural safeguards

The issue of eligibility for special education hinges on two questions: (1) Does the student have a disability? and (2) If so, does the student need special education? Both questions must be answered in the affirmative to be eligible for special education and related services. Students who have disabilities but do not need special education are not eligible (although they may well be eligible for services under Section 504 of the Rehabilitation Act of 1973). Students who do not have disabilities but need (or would benefit from) special education services are not eligible. Once students have been determined to be eligible for special education, they are automatically entitled to procedural safeguards, special services, altered outcome expectations, and special fiscal arrangements, as discussed in Chapter 3.

1 Official Student Disabilities

Students are classified as having a disability under several laws; three are particularly important: The Americans with Disabilities Act (Public Law 101-336), Section 504 of the Rehabilitation Act of 1973, and the Individuals with Disabilities Education Improvement Act (IDEA; 34 CFR §300.7). In the schools and other educational settings, the following disabilities, enumerated in regulations of the IDEA (34 CFR §300.7), are the most frequently used: autism, mental retardation, specific learning disability, emotional disturbance, traumatic brain injury, speech or language impairment, visual impairment, deafness and hearing impairment, orthopedic impairments, other health impairments, deaf–blindness, multiple disabilities, and developmental delay.[1] Identification under §300.306 of the IDEA requires that

- a team (i.e., group of qualified professionals and the parent(s) of the student) determine whether the student has a disability and the student's educational needs.
- a student cannot be determined to have a disability if that determination is based on (1) a lack of appropriate instruction in reading or math, (2) limited English proficiency, or (3) if the child does not otherwise meet the eligibility criteria.
- the team draw upon information from a variety of sources, including aptitude and achievement tests, input from parents, and teachers, as well as information about the child's physical condition, social or cultural background, and adaptive behavior; and
- the team ensure that information obtained from all of these sources is documented and carefully considered.

§300.8 of the IDEA regulations define the specific disabilities. These definitions are given below.

AUTISM

Autistic students are those who demonstrate "developmental disability significantly affecting verbal and nonverbal communication and social interaction, generally evident before age 3, that adversely affects a child's educational performance. Other characteristics often associated with autism are engagement in repetitive activities and stereotyped movements, resistance to environmental change or change in daily routines, and unusual responses to sensory experiences. Autism does not apply if a child's educational performance is adversely affected primarily because the child has an emotional disturbance."

Students with suspected autism are usually evaluated by speech and language specialists and psychologists after it has been determined that some aspects of their educational performance fall outside the normal range and various attempts to

[1]The definitions in IDEA (excluding the need for special education) are generally used for entitlements under Section 504.

remedy the educational problems have failed. Frequently, a speech and language specialist would look for impaired verbal and nonverbal communication. A large proportion of autistic children are mute, an impairment that is readily apparent. Autism in students with speech and language might manifest itself as overly concrete thinking. For example, an autistic student might react to a statement such as "don't cry over spilled milk" quite literally ("I didn't spill any milk"). Another manifestation would be a lack of conversational reciprocity (usually long, often tedious, orations about a favorite subject) and failure to recognize a listener's waning interest. Moreover, this impaired social communication would be a consistent feature of the student's behavior rather than an occasional overexuberance. A psychologist looks for behavior that defines the condition: repetitive activities (for example, self-stimulating behavior, spinning objects, aligning objects, and smelling objects), stereotyped movements (for example, hand flapping, rocking, and head banging), resistance to change (for example, eating only certain foods or tantruming when activities are ended). A psychologist may also administer a behavior rating scale (for example, the Gilliam Autism Rating Scale) as an aid to diagnosis. Finally, a psychologist rules out emotional disturbance as a cause of the student's behavior and impairments.

MENTAL RETARDATION

Students with mental retardation are those who demonstrate "significantly subaverage general intellectual functioning, existing concurrently with deficits in adaptive behavior and manifested during the developmental period, that adversely affects a child's educational performance." Students who are eventually labeled "mentally retarded" are often referred because of generalized slowness: They lag behind their age mates in most areas of academic achievement, social and emotional development, language ability, and, perhaps, physical development.

Usually, a psychologist will administer a test of intelligence that is appropriate in terms of the student's age, acculturation, and physical and sensory capabilities. In most states, students must have an IQ that is two standard deviations or more below the mean (usually 70 or less) on a validly administered test. However, a test of intelligence is not enough. The pupil must also demonstrate impairments in adaptive behavior. There is no federal requirement that a test or rating scale be used to assess adaptive behavior psychometrically. In practice, most school psychologists will administer an adaptive behavior scale (for example, the Vineland Adaptive Behavior Scales, second edition). However, when it is not possible to do so appropriately, a psychologist will interview parents or guardians and make a clinical judgment about a student's adaptive behavior.

SPECIFIC LEARNING DISABILITY

A student with a learning disability is one who "does not achieve adequately for the child's age or . . . meet state-approved grade-level standards in one or more of the following areas, when provided with learning experiences and instruction appropriate for the child's age or state-approved grade–level standards: oral expression, listening comprehension, written expression, basic reading skills, reading fluency skills, reading comprehension, mathematics calculation, [or] mathematics problem solving" (34 CFR 300.306). In addition, the student's failure to meet age or state standards cannot be due to: a visual, hearing, or motor disability; mental retardation; emotional disturbance; cultural factors; environmental or economic disadvantage; or limited English proficiency.

To ensure that the lack of progress is not due to lack of appropriate instruction in reading or math, there must be data to demonstrate that the student received appropriate instruction in regular education settings from qualified personnel, that there were repeated assessments of student progress at reasonable intervals, and that assessments of progress were provided to the child's parents (Office of Special Education, undated).

Therefore, initial evaluations to ascertain if a student has a learning disability have four components: rule outs, verification of achievement difficulties, documentation of unsuccessful attempts to remediate the achievement difficulties, and evidence of a disorder in a basic psychological process.

1. Rule Outs

Those responsible for making the actual determination that a student has a learning disability must rule out various potential causes for poor achievement. IDEA specifically forbids that the student's achievement problem be the result of a visual, hearing, or motor impairment; mental retardation; emotional disturbance; or environmental, cultural, or economic disadvantage. The presence of various medical conditions may also be used to rule out a diagnosis of learning disability.

2. Verification of Achievement Difficulties

It is expected that all students will meet age or grade and local and state achievement standards; however, students with high IQs may fail to meet expectations when their performance is only average. Only students who fail to meet expected grade level academic standards can be considered for a diagnosis of learning disability. Academic difficulties must be verified by direct observation during classroom instruction. In addition, school personnel will likely perform a records review to ascertain the intensity and duration of the problems. Previous grades, teacher comments, and the results of standardized achievement tests (e.g., from tier 1 screening) are useful. Finally, individual achievement tests may be administered by a school psychologist or learning specialist. The student may also be evaluated by a speech and language specialist who would look for manifestations of a disorder in producing or understanding language. This specialist may conduct an assessment of a student's spontaneous or elicited language during an interview or play situation; the specialist may administer a formal test.[2] There are no quantitative guidelines in the regulations to indicate a language disorder, but a child with a disability in language would be expected to earn scores that are substantially below average.

3. Unsuccessful Attempts at Remediation

Before it can be assumed that a student is unable to learn, educators must demonstrate that the student has had the opportunity to learn—that the teacher has used effective and appropriate teaching methods and curricula. Normally, this means that there have been numerous, documented attempts to remediate the educational problems using at least tier 2 (targeted) interventions and that these attempts have failed.

4. Evidence of a Learning Disability

Either of two approaches can be used to infer that a student has a disorder in a basic psychological process—response to intervention or severe discrepancy. Either approach can be used singly or in combination with the other approach.

Response to intervention[3] In this approach, students received targeted (i.e., tier 2) interventions. The academic problem is verified, alternative hypotheses about how to remediate the problem are generated, interventions are developed and applied, and assessment data are collected and interpreted. If a student fails to progress or if a student makes insufficient progress after several interventions, there is *prima facie* evidence of a learning disability. However, the rule outs still apply. The student cannot have mental retardation, and so forth. Thus, in this approach, students are thought to have a learning disability when they fail to progress sufficiently after

[2] For example, the Test for Auditory Comprehension of Language–Third Edition or the Test of Language Development–Primary, Fourth Edition.

[3] Chapter 24 [Multi-Tiered System of Supports (MTSS) and Response to Intervention (RTI)] deals extensively with response to intervention.

receiving intensive instruction using methods of proven effectiveness (that is, validated by objective, empirical research).

Severe discrepancy In this approach, students must exhibit a pattern of strengths and weaknesses in performance, achievement, or both, relative to age, state-approved grade level standards or intellectual development [34 CFR 300.309(a)(2)]. In this approach, a psychologist typically looks for large differences between a student's measured intelligence (i.e., scores on a test of intelligence)[4] and measured achievement (i.e., scores on a standardized test of achievement). A significant difference between ability and achievement is taken as a demonstration of a learning disability when the previously enumerated criteria are present. Schools may also consider a pattern of strengths and weaknesses within a student's achievement (for example, large differences between reading and mathematics scores on a standardized achievement). An analysis of strengths and weaknesses is based on differences between scores. Such differences are almost always less reliable than the individual scores on which the differences are based. For example, the difference between reading and math achievement will almost always be less reliable than either the reading or the math achievement score. Difference scores are discussed in detail on the student website.[5]

Finally, psychologists may also administer tests to assess specific psychological processes such as visual perception (for example, the Developmental Test of Visual Perception). Low scores may also be used to support a diagnosis of a learning disability.

EMOTIONAL DISTURBANCE

Emotional disturbance means "a condition exhibiting one or more of the following characteristics over a long period of time and to a marked degree that adversely affects a child's educational performance: (1) an inability to learn that cannot be explained by intellectual, sensory, or health factors; (2) an inability to build or maintain satisfactory interpersonal relationships with peers and teachers; (3) inappropriate types of behavior or feelings under normal circumstances; (4) a general pervasive mood of unhappiness or depression; (5) a tendency to develop physical symptoms or fears associated with personal or school problems" [§300.8(c)(4)]. This disability includes schizophrenia but excludes "children who are socially maladjusted, unless it is determined that they have an emotional disturbance." Students who are eventually labeled as having an emotional disorder are often referred for problems in interpersonal relations (for example, fighting or extreme noncompliance) or unusual behavior (for example, unexplained episodes of crying or extreme mood swings).

Students suspected of being emotionally disturbed are evaluated by a psychologist after it has been determined that some of their school performance falls outside the normal range and various attempts to remedy the school problems have failed. Requirements for establishing a pupil's eligibility as a student with emotional disturbance vary among the states. However, multidisciplinary teams usually obtain a developmental and health history from a student's parent or guardian to rule out sensory and health factors as causes of a student's inability to learn. A parent or guardian is usually interviewed about the student's relationships with peers, feelings (for example, anger, alienation, depression, and fears), and physical symptoms (for example, headaches or nausea). Parents or guardians may also be asked to complete a behavior rating scale such as Achenbach's Child Behavior Checklist to obtain normative data on the student's behavior. Teachers will likely be interviewed about their relationships with the student and the student's relationships with peers at

[4] Scores from an intelligence test can also be used to rule out mental retardation.

[5] Some psychologists will define a severe discrepancy as a difference greater than chance fluctuation. Psychologists who use this approach may use the reliability of an obtained difference or the reliability of the predicted difference to reach their decision. Some psychologists will use the rarity of a difference, which is often provided by test authors when they have normed both the intelligence and the achievement tests on the same sample.

school. They may also be asked to complete a rating scale (for example, the Walker–McConnell Scale of Social Competence and School Adjustment) to obtain normative data for in-school behavior. In addition, a psychologist might be asked to administer a norm-referenced achievement battery to verify that the student's educational performance has been negatively affected by the student's emotional problems.

TRAUMATIC BRAIN INJURY

Students with traumatic brain injury have "an acquired injury to the brain caused by an external physical force, resulting in total or partial functional disability or psychosocial impairment, or both, that adversely affects a child's educational performance. Traumatic brain injury applies to open or closed head injuries resulting in impairments in one or more areas, such as cognition; language; memory; attention; reasoning; abstract thinking; judgment; problem solving; sensory, perceptual, and motor abilities; psychosocial behavior; physical functions; information processing; and speech. Traumatic brain injury does not apply to brain injuries that are congenital or degenerative, or to brain injuries induced by birth trauma" [§300.8(c)(12)]. Students with traumatic brain injury have normal development until they sustain a severe head injury. As a result of this injury, they have a disability. Most head injuries are the result of an accident (frequently an automobile accident), but they may also occur as a result of physical abuse or intentional harm (for example, being shot).

Traumatic brain injury will be diagnosed by a physician, who is usually a specialist (a neurologist). The need of a student with brain injury for special education will be based first on a determination that the student's school performance falls outside the normal range and various attempts to remedy the educational problems have failed. Next, a school psychologist will likely administer a standardized achievement battery to verify that the student's achievement has been adversely affected.

SPEECH OR LANGUAGE IMPAIRMENT

A student with a speech or language impairment has "a communication disorder, such as stuttering, impaired articulation, a language impairment, or a voice impairment, that adversely affects a child's educational performance." [§300.8(c)(11)] Many children will experience some developmental problems in their speech and language. For example, children frequently have difficulty with the *r* sound and say "wabbit" instead of "rabbit." Similarly, many children will use incorrect grammar, especially with internal plurals; for example, children may say, "My dog has four foots." Such difficulties are so common as to be considered a part of normal speech development. However, when such speech and language errors continue to occur beyond the age when most children have developed correct speech or language, there is cause for concern. Not all students who require intervention for speech or language problems are eligible for special education. A student may be eligible for speech or language services but not have a problem that adversely affects his or her school performance. Thus, for a student to be eligible for special education as a person with a speech or language impairment, that student must not only have a speech/language impairment but also need special education.

The identification of students with speech and language impairments proceeds along two separate paths. School personnel identify the educational disability in the same way that other educational disabilities are identified. When extra help from a teacher does not solve the problem, the student is referred to a child study team for prereferral intervention. If those interventions fail to remedy the achievement problem, the student is referred for multidisciplinary evaluation. A psychologist or educational diagnostician will likely administer a norm-referenced achievement test to verify the achievement problem. At the same time, speech and language specialists will use a variety of assessment procedures (norm-referenced tests, systematic observation, and criterion-referenced tests) to identify the speech and language disability. If the student has both need and disability, the student will be eligible for special education and related services.

VISUAL IMPAIRMENT

A student with a visual impairment has "an impairment in vision that, even with correction, adversely affects a child's educational performance. The term includes both partial sight and blindness" [§300.8(c)(13)]. Students with severe visual impairments are usually identified by an ophthalmologist before they enter school. Many students who are partially sighted will be identified by routine vision screening that usually takes place in the primary grades; others will be identified when visual demands increase (for example, when font size is reduced from the larger print used in beginning reading materials). Severe visual impairment is always presumed to adversely affect their educational development, and students with this disability are presumed to require special education services and curricular adaptations (for example, mobility training, instruction in Braille, and talking books). A vision specialist usually assesses functional vision through systematic observation of a student's responses to various types of paper, print sizes, lighting conditions, and so forth.

For more information about vision screening, see the material on sensory screening on the Education CourseMate website for this textbook.

DEAFNESS AND HEARING IMPAIRMENT

Deafness is an impairment in hearing "that is so severe that the child is impaired in processing linguistic information through hearing, with or without amplification, and that adversely affects a child's educational performance" [§300.8(c)(3)]. A student with a hearing impairment has a permanent or fluctuating impairment "that adversely affects educational performance but that is not included under the definition of deafness."

Most students classified as deaf will be identified as such before they enter school. Deafness will be presumed to adversely affect a student's educational development, and students with this disability are presumed to require special education services and curricular adaptations. However, even severe hearing impairments may be difficult to identify in the first years of life, and students with milder hearing impairments may not be identified until school age. Referrals for undiagnosed hearing-impaired students may indicate expressive and receptive language problems, variable hearing performance, problems in attending to aural tasks, and perhaps problems in peer relationships. Diagnosis of hearing impairment is usually made by audiologists, who identify the auditory disability, in conjunction with school personnel, who identify the educational disability.

ORTHOPEDIC IMPAIRMENTS

An orthopedic impairment is "a severe impairment that adversely affects a child's educational performance. The term includes impairments caused by a congenital anomaly, impairments caused by disease (such as poliomyelitis and bone tuberculosis), and impairments from other causes (such as cerebral palsy, amputations, and fractures or burns that cause contractures)" [§300.8(c)(8)].

Physical disabilities are generally identified prior to entering school. However, accidents and disease may impair a student who previously did not have a disability. Medical diagnosis establishes the presence of the condition. The severity of the condition may be established in part by medical opinion and in part by systematic observation of the particular student. For many students with physical disabilities, the ability to learn is not affected. These students may not require special education classes, but they will need accommodations and modifications to the curriculum—and perhaps the school building—that can be managed through a 504 plan. For example, a student may require a personal care aide to help with positioning, braces, and catheterization; educational technology (for example, a voice-activated computer); and transportation to and from school that can accommodate a wheelchair. When such adaptations and accommodations are insufficient to allow adequate school progress, special education is indicated. The specially designed instruction can include alternate assignments, alternative curricula, alternative testing procedures, and special instruction.

OTHER HEALTH IMPAIRMENTS

Other health impairment "means having limited strength, vitality, or alertness, including a heightened alertness to environmental stimuli, that results in limited alertness with respect to the educational environment that (i) is due to chronic or acute health problems such as asthma, attention deficit disorder or attention deficit hyperactivity disorder, diabetes, epilepsy, a heart condition, hemophilia, lead poisoning, leukemia, nephritis, rheumatic fever, sickle cell anemia, and Tourette syndrome; and (ii) adversely affects a child's educational performance" [§300.8(c)(9)]. Diagnosis of health impairments is usually made by physicians, who identify the health problems, and school personnel, who identify the educational disability. For some students with other health impairments, the ability to learn is not affected. These students may not require special education classes, but they will need accommodations and modifications to the curriculum that can be managed through a 504 plan. For example, a student may require nursing services to administer medication, times and places to rest during the day, and provisions for instruction in the home. When health impairments adversely affect educational progress even with the curricular adaptations and modifications, special education is indicated.

DEAF–BLINDNESS

Deaf–blindness means "concomitant hearing and visual impairments, the combination of which causes such severe communication and other developmental and educational needs that they cannot be accommodated in special education programs solely for children with deafness or children with blindness" [§300.8(c)(2)].

Only a small number of students are deaf–blind, and their assessment is typically complex. Tests that compensate for loss of vision usually rely on auditory processes; tests that compensate for loss of hearing usually rely on visual processes. Psychological and educational evaluations of students who are both deaf and blind rely on observations as well as interviews of and ratings by individuals sufficiently familiar with the student to provide useful information.

MULTIPLE DISABILITIES

Multiple disabilities "means concomitant impairments (such as mental retardation–blindness or mental retardation–orthopedic impairment), the combination of which causes such severe educational needs that they cannot be accommodated in special education programs solely for one of the impairments. The term does not include deaf–blindness" [§300.8(c)(7)].

DEVELOPMENTAL DELAY

Although not mandated by IDEA, states may use the category of developmental delay for children between the ages of 3 and 9 years who are "(1) experiencing developmental delays, as defined by the state and as measured by appropriate diagnostic instruments and procedures, in one or more of the following areas: physical development, cognitive development, communication development, social or emotional development, or adaptive development; and (2) … need special education and related services" [§300.8(b)]. Diagnosis of developmental delay is usually made by school personnel, who identify the educational disability, and other professionals (such as speech and language specialists, physicians, and psychologists), who identify the delays in the developmental domains.

2 Establishing Educational Need for Special Education

In addition to having one (or more) of the disabilities specified in IDEA, a student must experience a lack of academic success. This criterion is either implicit or explicit in the IDEA definitions of disabilities. Autism, hearing impairment, mental retardation, and six other disabling conditions are defined as "adversely affecting a child's educational performance." Multiple disabilities (such as deaf–blindness) cause "severe educational needs." Learning disability results in an "imperfect ability" to learn basic academic skills.

Most students without obvious sensory or motor disabilities are presumed to not have disabilities when they enter school. However, during their education, it becomes clear to school personnel that these students have significant problems. They fail to behave appropriately or to meet state-approved grade-level standards in one or more core achievement areas when provided with appropriate instruction. In short, they demonstrate marked discrepancies from mainstream expectations or from the achievement and behavior of typical peers. The magnitude of the discrepancy necessary to consider a student for special education is not codified, and there are many opinions on this issue.

The presence of a discrepancy alone does not establish need, because there are many causes for a discrepancy. Thus, school personnel usually should engage in a number of remedial and compensatory activities designed to reduce or eliminate the discrepancy. As discussed in Chapter 26, interventions initially may be designed and implemented by the classroom teacher. When the teacher's interventions are unsuccessful, the student is referred to a teacher assistance team that designs and may help implement further interventions. Need for special educational services for students is established when one of two conditions is met. First, if a student fails to respond to validated and carefully implemented interventions, need for special education is indicated (see Chapter 8). Second, successful interventions may be too intensive or extensive for use in regular education. That is, the interventions needed to remediate the student's academic or behavioral deficits are so intrusive, labor-intensive, or specialized that a general education classroom teacher cannot implement them without the assistance of a special education teacher or without seriously detracting from the education of other students in the classroom.

We address the specifics of decision making at greater length in the response-to-intervention materials on the Education CourseMate website for this textbook.

Some students have such obvious sensory or motor problems that they are identified as having a disability before they enter school. From accumulated research and professional experience, educators know that students with certain disabilities (for example, blindness, deafness, and severe mental retardation) will not succeed in school without special education. Thus, educators (and relevant regulations) assume that the presence of a severe disability is sufficient to demonstrate the need for special educational services.

3 The Multidisciplinary Team

The determination that a student has a disability is made by a team of professionals called a multidisciplinary team (MDT). The team conducts a multidisciplinary evaluation (MDE) by collecting, assembling, and evaluating information to determine whether a student meets the conditions that define a handicap as set forth in IDEA and state law.[6]

COMPOSITION OF THE MDT

IDEA requires that the team have members with the same qualifications as those who must serve on IEP teams and "other qualified professionals, as appropriate" (34 CFR §300.533). Thus, the team must include the student's parents (and the student, if appropriate), a general education teacher, a special education teacher, a representative of the school administration, and an individual who can interpret the instructional implications of evaluation results. If the student is suspected of having

[6] Note that there are two types of teams required under special education law, and the same people may or may not serve on the two types of teams: evaluation teams (usually called MDTs) and individualized educational program (IEP) teams (always called IEP teams). In addition, many schools have teacher teams (often called child study teams) that deal with student difficulties before a student is referred for evaluation.

a learning disability, the team must also include "at least one person qualified to conduct individual diagnostic examinations of children, such as a school psychologist, speech–language pathologist, or remedial reading teacher" (34 CFR §300.540). In practice, school psychologists are usually members of most MDTs.

RESPONSIBILITIES OF THE MDT

The team is responsible for gathering information and determining if a student has a disability. In theory, the decision-making process is straightforward. The MDT assesses the student to determine whether he or she meets the criteria for a specific disability. Thus, the MDT must collect, at a minimum, information required by the definition of the disability being considered. Moreover, federal regulations (34 CFR §300.532) require that a student be "assessed in all areas related to the suspected disability, including, if appropriate, health, vision, hearing, social and emotional status, general intelligence, academic performance, communicative status, and motor abilities."

In reaching its decision about eligibility, the team must do two things. First, it must draw upon information from a variety of sources, including aptitude and achievement tests, parent input, and teacher recommendations, as well as information about the child's physical condition, social or cultural background, and adaptive behavior. Second, it must ensure that information obtained from all of these sources is documented and carefully considered [§300.306(c)].

4 The Process of Determining Eligibility

IDEA has established rules that MDTs must follow in determining whether a student is eligible for special education and related services. The first set of rules provides a variety of procedural safeguards intended to provide students and their parents the right to full and meaningful participation in the evaluation process.

PROCEDURAL SAFEGUARDS

As specified in §300.504, school districts and other public agencies must give parents a copy of the procedural safeguards relating to

- independent educational evaluation;
- prior written notice in the native language of the parent or other mode of communication used by the parent;
- parental consent;
- access to educational records;
- opportunity to present complaints to initiate due process hearings;
- the child's placement during pendency of due process proceedings;
- procedures for students who are subject to placement in an interim alternative educational setting;
- requirements for unilateral placement by parents of children in private schools at public expense;
- mediation;
- due process hearings, including requirements for disclosure of evaluation results and recommendations;
- state-level appeals (if applicable in that state);
- civil actions;
- attorneys' fees; and
- the state complaint procedures.

VALID ASSESSMENTS

The next set of rules requires valid and meaningful assessments. School districts and other public agencies must ensure that students are assessed in all areas related to their suspected disabilities, including, if appropriate, health, vision, hearing, social and emotional status, general intelligence, academic performance, communicative status, and motor abilities. The evaluations must be sufficiently comprehensive to identify all of the child's special education and related services needs, whether or not they are commonly linked to the disability category in which the child has been classified.

School districts and other public agencies must ensure that the assessment includes a variety of techniques, including information provided by the parent, that provide relevant information about

- whether the student is a student with a disability; and
- the student's involvement and progress in the general curriculum.

The assessments must be conducted by trained and knowledgeable personnel in accordance with any instructions provided by the producer of the tests (and if an assessment is not conducted under standard conditions, a description of the extent to which it varied from standard conditions must be provided in the evaluation report). As specified in §300.304(c), only tests or other evaluation materials may be used that are

- "not racially or culturally discriminatory";
- "administered in the child's native language or other mode of communication" (in addition, for students with limited English proficiency, districts and other public agencies must select and use materials and procedures that measure the extent to which the child has a disability and needs special education, rather than measuring the child's English language skills);
- "selected and administered so as best to ensure that if a test is administered to a child with impaired sensory, manual, or speaking skills, the test results accurately reflect the child's aptitude or achievement level or whatever other factors the test purports to measure, rather than reflecting the child's impaired sensory, manual, or speaking skills (unless those skills are the factors that the test purports to measure)";
- technically sound instruments that may assess the relative contribution of cognitive and behavioral factors, in addition to physical or developmental factors;
- "tailored to assess specific areas of educational need and not merely designed to provide a single general intelligence quotient"; and
- relevant in assisting persons determining the educational needs of the student.

TEAM PROCESS

The final set of requirements sets forth the process for determining a student's eligibility for special education and related services. The MDT team follows four basic steps as specified in §§300.305/306:

1. The team reviews existing evaluation data to determine if additional data are needed.
2. The team gathers any additional data that are needed, ensuring that information obtained from all sources is documented.
3. The team determines if the student is a child with a disability by considering information from a variety of sources (that is, aptitude and achievement tests, parent input, teacher recommendations (including response to intervention), physical condition, social or cultural background, and adaptive behavior) and comparing this information to the state and federal standards for the suspected disability.
4. The team prepares an evaluation report.

In practice, deciding whether a student is entitled to special education can be complex. Sometimes, the problems a student is experiencing can suggest a specific disability to team members. For example, having problems maintaining attention, being fidgety, and being disorganized may suggest the possibility of attention deficit disorder; persistent and major difficulties learning letter–sound correspondences despite many interventions may suggest a learning disability. MDTs should do more than simply confirm a disability. MDTs should adopt a point of view that is, in part, disconfirmatory—a point of view that seeks to disprove the working hypothesis.

Many behaviors are indicative of specific disabilities. For example, stereotypies hand flapping is associated with autism, severe retardation, and some emotional disturbances. Assessors must be open to alternative explanations for the behavior and, when appropriate, collect information that will allow them to reject a working hypothesis of a particular disability. For example, if Tom was referred for inconsistent performance in expressive language, even though his other skills—especially math and science—were average, an MDT might suspect that he could have a learning disability. What would it take to reject the hypothesis that he has such a disability? He would not be considered to have a learning disability if it could be shown that his problem was caused by a sensorineural hearing loss, if his problem arose because his primary language is a dialect of English, if he suffered from recurrent bouts of otitis media (middle ear infections), and so forth. Therefore, the MDT would have to consider other possible causes of his behavior. Moreover, when there is evidence that something other than the hypothesized disability is the cause of the educational problems, the MDT would need to collect additional data that would allow it to evaluate these other explanations. Thus, MDT evaluations frequently (and correctly) go beyond the information required by the entitlement criteria to rule out other possible disabling conditions or to arrive at a different diagnosis.

Finally, in attempting to establish that a student should be classified with a disability, we often must choose among competing procedures and tests. However, as indicated in Chapter 15, individual tests of intelligence are not interchangeable. They differ significantly in the behaviors they sample and in the adequacy of their norms and reliability and slightly in their standard deviations. A dull, but normal, person may earn an IQ of less than 70 on one or two tests of intelligence but earn scores greater than 70 on two others. Thus, if we had to assess such a student, we could be caught in a dilemma of conflicting information.

The routes around and through the eligibility process are easier to state than to accomplish. First, we should choose (and put the most faith in) objective, technically adequate (reliable and well normed) procedures that have demonstrated validity for the particular purpose of classification. Second, we must consider the specific validity. For example, we must consider the culture in which the student grew up and how that culture interacts with the content of the test. A test's technical manuals may contain information about the wisdom of using the test with individuals of various cultures, or the research literature may have information for the particular cultural group to which a student belongs. Often, theory can guide us in the absence of research. Sometimes it is just not possible to test validly, and we must also recognize that fact.

SCENARIO *in* ASSESSMENT

CHERYL | Cheryl was the youngest of Jack and Melinda Stenman's three children. She was a full-term baby but weighed only 1,800 grams (4 pounds) at birth. In addition to her significantly low birth weight, she was placed in the neonatal intensive care unit for almost 3 days and was not released from the hospital until she was 10 days old. Although her health during her early years was unremarkable, she was slower to attain the common developmental milestones (walking and talking) than her older siblings.

Cheryl entered a local daycare center at age 3. Little information is available from the center except the general perception that Cheryl did not engage in developmentally appropriate play activities. The daycare center provided no interventions because its philosophy was that each child developed uniquely and there was plenty of time for intervention.

Mrs. Stenman enrolled Cheryl in the local school district's half-day kindergarten the September when she was 5 years and 8 months of age. Cheryl was slow compared to her peers. She still had toileting accidents, had immature speech and language, and did not engage in cooperative play, preferring parallel play instead. At the end of the first semester of kindergarten, she had not learned her colors, whereas her peers had mastered the primary and additive colors (that is, red, green, blue, yellow, violet, blue-green, brown, black, and white); she recognized only five capital letters (A, B C, D, and S), whereas most of her peers recognized and could write all upper- and lowercase letters. Her teacher characterized her as following other children around but not joining in the various activities.

The teacher implemented several interventions known to be effective in teaching students to recognize and write letters, and several social interaction interventions. She monitored Cheryl's progress and showed that there was a consistent lack of progress. In January, Cheryl's teacher sought the help of the school's student assistance team. The teacher met with Mr. and Mrs. Stenman and agreed that some interventions would be appropriate to try to accelerate her academic progress. They agreed that Cheryl should attend all-day kindergarten and developed a program in which the teachers or the reading specialist provided individual direct instruction in the recognition and writing of all letters of the alphabet; they also developed a behavior plan that reinforced Cheryl for successive approximations of cooperative play. From the very beginning, the classroom interventions did not work. Cheryl seemed to learn one or two new letters but forget them the next day. The team met with the teacher several times and modified the instructional program, but Cheryl's progress was slow. She did not master more than two letters per week, and that rate of progress was simply not enough to get her ready for first grade. The results of the behavioral interventions were similarly unsuccessful. At the end of the year, all kindergartners received a district screening test. Cheryl scored at or below the first percentile in all academic areas.

The teacher and the student assistance team (which included the parents) weighed various options for Cheryl's next year: retention, promotion with help from the student assistance team, and referral for an MDE to determine if Cheryl had a disability that required special education and related services. After some discussion, the team was unanimous in its recommendation that Cheryl should be evaluated for eligibility for special education.

An MDT was appointed and consisted of Cheryl's kindergarten teacher, a special education teacher who worked with children of Cheryl's age, the school principal (who chaired the meetings), and the school psychologist assigned to Cheryl's school. At the first team meeting, the principal gave the parents a copy of a document listing the procedural safeguards guaranteed by IDEA and the state. The principal also explained each element carefully and answered all of the parents' questions to their satisfaction. Next, the team reviewed all relevant documents: attendance records, data from the interventions developed by the student assistance team, the results of the district's routine hearing and vision screening (which indicated Cheryl was normal), and the results from the district's first-grade readiness assessment. After reviewing the data and discussing Cheryl's strengths and weaknesses, the MDT decided that additional data would be necessary to determine if Cheryl was eligible for special education and related services. The team discussed the possibility of special language or cultural considerations and concluded there were none. The team then decided that it needed (1) the results of a valid, individually administered test of intelligence; (2) the results of a valid, individually administered test of achievement; (3) ratings from a validly administered scale of social and emotional development; and (4) the ratings from a valid evaluation of adaptive behavior. The principal would be responsible for distributing and collecting the results from the social–emotional rating scale; the school psychologist would be responsible for administering and scoring the test of intelligence and the adaptive behavior scale and also for scoring and interpreting the social–emotional ratings provided by the teachers.

The testing went smoothly. Teachers completed the Behavior Assessment System for Children, Second Edition; the parents completed the Vineland Adaptive Behavior Scales, Second Edition; and the school psychologist administered the Wechsler Intelligence Scale for Children–Fourth Edition and the Stanford–Binet Intelligence Scale, Fifth Edition. The school psychologist drafted an evaluation report and distributed copies to each team member. The MDT then met to consider the results of their evaluation and to decide if additional data might be needed to make sure that their evaluation examined all areas of potential disability. If the evaluation results were complete and sufficient, the team would decide if Cheryl was a student with a disability under IDEA and state law. The school psychologist affirmed that all of the instruments were administered under standard conditions and that she believed the results to be valid. She next interpreted the evaluation results and answered all of the questions posed by the parents and educators. The results indicated that Cheryl's level of general intellectual functioning was 59 ± 4 points. Her achievement in Reading, Mathematics, and Written Language was at the second percentile. Her parent's ratings of adaptive behavior resulted in a composite (total) score of 64, with Daily Living her area of highest functioning and Communication her lowest area. Although the evaluation results suggested that Cheryl was a student with mental retardation, the parents believed that Cheryl was too young to be diagnosed with such a stigmatizing diagnosis. After some discussion, the team unanimously agreed that a diagnosis of developmental delay would be appropriate at that time. Cheryl met the criteria for that disability, and she would not be 9 years of age for almost 3 years.

The MDT next turned to the question of need for special education. The team relied heavily on Cheryl's lack of progress when she was given the maximum amount of intervention services within the regular education curriculum. Clearly, she needed more services. The MDT added recommendations for special education and related services to the evaluation report. The team noted that Cheryl needed direct instruction in the core academic areas of reading, writing, and mathematics. The team recommended that Cheryl's social interactions be monitored for possible intervention later in the first semester. The MDT also recommended that Cheryl be evaluated by a speech and language therapist to determine if the teacher should have ongoing consultations with the therapist about curriculum or methods and/or if Cheryl would benefit from direct speech and language services. The team also recommended that Cheryl should be included in all nonacademic activities with her same-age peers. Finally, it recommended that Cheryl receive her special education services from an itinerant special education teacher in the general education classroom who would also consult with the regular education teacher, who would also be implementing portions of Cheryl's educational program.

What implications about your own professional role can you draw from this scenario? Go to the Education CourseMate website for this textbook for more reflection questions about this Scenario in Assessment.

5 Problems in Determining Special Education Eligibility

Four problems with the criteria used to determine eligibility for special services are especially noteworthy. First, we find the prevalent (but mistaken) belief that special educational services are for students who could benefit from them. Thus, in many circles, educational need is believed to be sufficient for entitlement. Clearly, this belief is contradicted by pertinent law, regulations, and litigation. Students must need the services *and* meet the criteria for a specific disability. Nonetheless, some educators have such strong humanitarian beliefs that when they see students with problems, they want to get those students the services that they believe are needed. Too often, the regulations may be bent so that students fit entitlement criteria.

Second, the definitions that appear in state and federal regulations are frequently very imprecise. The imprecision of federal regulations creates variability in standards among states, and the imprecision of state regulations creates variability in standards among districts within states. Thus, students who are eligible in one state or district may not be eligible in other states or districts. For example, some states and school districts may define a learning disability as a severe discrepancy between measured intellectual ability and actual school achievement. However, there is no consensus about the meaning of "severe discrepancy"; certainly, there is no widely accepted mathematical formula to ascertain severe discrepancy. To some extent, discrepancies between achievement and intelligence are determined by the specific tests used. Thus, one test battery might produce a significant discrepancy, whereas another battery would not produce such a discrepancy for the same student. Other states and school districts may define a learning disability by an inadequate response to intervention. Yet, what constitutes an inadequate response is ambiguous.

Third, the definitions treat disabilities as though they were discrete categories. However, most diagnosticians are hard-pressed to distinguish between primary and secondary mental retardation or between primary and secondary emotional disturbance. Also, for example, distinctions between individuals with autism and individuals with severe mental retardation and autistic-like behaviors are practically impossible to make with any certainty.

Fourth, parents may often prefer the label associated with one disability (for example, autism or learning disability) over the label associated with another (for example, mental retardation). Because of the procedural safeguards afforded students with special needs and their parents, school districts may become embroiled in lengthy and unnecessarily adversarial hearings in which each side has an expert testifying that a particular label is correct even though those labels are contradictory and sometimes mutually exclusive. School personnel find themselves in a no-win situation because the definitions and their operationalizations are so imprecise. As a result, school districts frequently give parents the label they want rather than what educators, in their best professional judgments, believe to be correct. Districts may be reluctant to risk litigation because parents can frequently find an expert to contradict the district staff members. In some states, special educational services are noncategorical. In these states, a label qualifies a student for special education but does not determine the nature of the special education; that is determined by the individual student's needs, not label.

Chapter Comprehension Questions

Write your answers to each of the following questions and then compare your responses to the text.

1. List and define each disability recognized by IDEA.
2. How is the need for special education established?

3. What are the responsibilities of the MDT?
4. What procedural safeguards are guaranteed by IDEA?
5. State two important considerations in assessment for purposes of making accountability decisions.

Web Activities

1. Locate your state's Department of Education web site that deals with special education. See if it has forms for multidisciplinary evaluations, with guidance for their completion. For example, Pennsylvania posts the required "Evaluation Report" form online.
2. Locate your state's Department of Education web site that deals with eligibility for special education services. Are students with Asperger's Syndrome or social maladjustment eligible for special education in your state?

Web Resources

Eligibility: Determining Whether a Child Is Eligible for Special Education Services (Learning Disabilities Association of America)
http://www.ldanatl.org/aboutld/parents/special_ed/eligibility.asp
This site provides a general description of the process through which students become eligible for special education. The discussion on children with development delay is particularly useful.

Tips for Parents: Multidisciplinary Team (MDT) Evaluation (Nebraska Advocacy Services, Center for Disability Rights, Law, and Advocacy)
https://secure.digital-community.com/english/nebraskaadvocacyservices.org/includes/downloads/0107tipsforparentsmdt.pdf?PHPSESSID=a84fa57626e6196a3d93f7a11ed8030b
This website explains for parents what the MDT evaluation is, what the MDT considers, what must be in the MDT evaluation, what must be done if a child does not qualify for special education, and how are MDT evaluations requested.

Additional resources for this chapter can be found on the Education CourseMate website. Go to CengageBrain.com to access the site.

Making Accountability Decisions

CHAPTER GOALS

1 Know the legal requirements for state and school district assessment and accountability systems specified in the No Child Left Behind Act and the Individuals with Disabilities Education Improvement Act.

2 Be able to define the important terms associated with assessment for the purpose of making accountability decisions.

3 Understand past and current trends related to standards-based educational reform.

4 Know the important considerations for making decisions about how students participate in accountability systems

KEY TERMS

accountability system
adequate yearly progress
content standards
achievement standards
alternate achievement standards
alignment
alternate assessment
cut scores
out-of-level testing
student accountability
system accountability

Are our schools producing the results we want? To what extent are individual students meeting the goals, standards, or outcomes that their schools have set for them? What goals or standards should we expect students and schools to meet? How should we assess progress toward meeting standards? During the past 20 years, there has been an increased focus on the results of education for all students, including students with disabilities. In this chapter, we examine the collection and use of assessment information for the purpose of making accountability decisions.

A powerful idea dominates policy discussions about schools: the notion that "students should be held to high, common standards for academic performance and that schools and the people who work in them should be held accountable for ensuring that students—all students—are able to meet those standards" (Elmore, 2002, p. 3). It has not always been that way. Until the early to mid-1990s, school personnel focused on the *process* of providing services to students. They provided evidence that they were teaching students, and often evidence that they were teaching specific types of students (for example, Title 1, mentally retarded, deaf, or disadvantaged students). When administrators were asked about special education students or services, typically they described the numbers and kinds of students who were tested or taught, the settings in which they were taught, or the numbers of special education teachers who tested and taught them (for example, "We have 2,321 students with disabilities in our district; 1,620 are educated in general education classes with special education supports, and the remainder are in resource rooms, self-contained classes and out-of-school settings; the students are served by 118 special education teachers and 19 related services personnel"). Few administrators could provide evidence for the results or outcomes of the services being provided. Since the early 1990s, there has been a dramatic shift in focus from serving students with disabilities to measuring the results of the services provided. This shift has paralleled the total quality management (TQM; Deming, 1994, 2000), results-based management, and management by objectives (Olson, 1964) movements in business and, more recently, in federal and state government.

Much of the impetus for this shift to a focus on results was the publication of *A Nation at Risk: The Imperative for Educational Reform* (National Commission of Excellence in Education, 1983). In this document, the then secretary of education revealed the low status of U.S. schoolchildren relative to their counterparts in other nations and reported that "the educational foundations of our society are presently being eroded by a rising tide of mediocrity that threatens our very future as a nation and a people" (p. 5). In this report, the secretary argued that the nation was at risk because mediocrity, not excellence, was the norm in education. Recommendations included more time for learning; better textbooks and other materials; more homework; higher expectations; stricter attendance policies; and improved standards, salaries, rewards, and incentives for teachers. The entire nation began to focus on raising educational standards, measuring performance, and achieving results. Policymakers and bureaucrats, who had been spending a great deal of money to fund special education, began demanding evidence of its effectiveness. In essence, they employed the old saying, "The proof of the pudding is in the eating"—arguing that it matters little what you do if it does not produce what you want.

In 1994, the Clinton administration specified a set of national education goals. Called "Goals 2000," these were a list of goals that students should achieve by the year 2000. The 1994 reauthorization of the Elementary and Secondary Education Act, known as the Improving American Schools Act, included a requirement that in Title I schools, disadvantaged students should be expected to attain the same challenging standards as all other students. Additional requirements for large-scale assessment and accountability systems designed to measure the performance and progress of all students toward high standards were included in the general and special education legislation that followed (i.e., No Child Left Behind (NCLB) Act of 2001 and the 1997 and 2004 reauthorizations of the Individuals with Disabilities Education Act), and represents a continued emphasis on promoting high achievement across all students. The status of related legislation as we write this chapter is provided in the following section; however, you are encouraged to consult the web using the guidelines listed at the end of the chapter for more recent updates.

1 Legal Requirements

During the 1990s, state educational agencies put forth great efforts in the development of educational standards and large-scale assessment programs to measure student progress toward those standards. However, the extent to which students with disabilities were included in those efforts was questionable. The 1997 reauthorization of the Individuals with Disabilities Education Act (IDEA) included provisions specifying that students with disabilities should participate in states' assessment systems, and that statewide assessment program reports would include information on the extent to which *all* students, including students with disabilities, met state-specified standards. Recognizing that some students with disabilities had unique assessment needs, and that the regular assessment programs might not allow for appropriate measurement of their achievement toward state standards, IDEA 1997 introduced the requirement for IEP teams to determine which accommodations (if any) were needed for individual students to effectively participate in the statewide assessment program. It also required the development of alternate assessments for those students who could not effectively participate in the regular assessment even with accommodations. The 2004 reauthorization of IDEA contains those same requirements.

NCLB included the requirement that states have assessment and accountability systems, and report annually on the performance and progress of all students in reading, math, and science. In 2003, the U.S. Department of Education issued a set of guidelines for alternate assessments that included the concept of alternate achievement standards. The law requires that school systems consider not only how their students are doing as a whole but also how particular groups of students are doing, with a focus on the following groups: economically disadvantaged, students with limited English proficiency, students receiving special education services, students from major racial/ethnic groups. To be considered successful, schools must succeed with all students. States, school districts, and individual schools are required by law to measure the performance and progress of all students. Schools that don't make adequate yearly progress are subjected to certain sanctions (see the Types of Accountability section below for more information on NCLB accountability requirements). School personnel need to know much about how assessment information is used by State Education Agency personnel to make accountability decisions.

Reauthorization of the NCLB is expected to occur in the very near future. Given the impact of federal legislation on statewide assessment and accountability systems, we anticipate that many things that we write about in this chapter will change by the time it goes to print. We certainly do not expect accountability to go away; in fact, most believe that legislative changes will have an even greater emphasis on holding schools accountable for the achievement of all students. You can find more information about recent legislative changes related to accountability systems and related assessment information using the guidance included at the end of this chapter for navigating various websites, so be sure to go there for current information.

2 Types of Accountability

Accountability systems hold schools responsible for helping all students reach high challenging standards, and they provide rewards to schools that reach those standards and sanctions to schools that do not. Today, the consequences of accountability systems are becoming more significant, often referred to as "high stakes." As we write this chapter, NCLB accountability requirements are in effect, which require state educational agencies to have an accountability system that includes certain key components. However, states may choose to add additional features to their accountability system. Although all states include system accountability, some additionally include accountability for students.

System accountability is designed to improve educational programs, and is the focus of federal education reform efforts. NCLB requires that states develop adequate yearly progress (AYP) targets for schools that are based primarily on student progress as measured by statewide assessment programs, assessment participation rates, and student attendance/graduation rates. Schools that do not make AYP in consecutive years experience the following:

- After two years of not making AYP, the school must allow students to attend a higher performing school in the district.
- After three years of not making AYP, the school must provide supplemental supports to low-achieving disadvantaged students.
- After four years of not making AYP, the school must take corrective action that may include replacing school staff or restructuring the organizational structure of the school.
- After six years of not making AYP, the school must develop and implement an alternative governance plan.

All states are expected to publicly report on the performance of their students and school systems. States may additionally decide to incorporate additional

SCENARIO *in* ASSESSMENT

STEVEN | Steven is a third-grade student diagnosed with autism. Steven receives instruction in the general education setting for most of his day, although he needs a teacher assistant to assist with implementation of his comprehensive behavior plan. This plan involves providing him with a variety of cues and reminders about the daily classroom schedule and how he is expected to behave during various activities. He has a very difficult time behaving appropriately when there are changes in the classroom schedule; in such cases, he often becomes very anxious, sometimes throws tantrums, and rarely completes his work.

This is the first year that Steven is expected to complete the statewide assessment used for accountability purposes, and his individualized education program team must determine how he can best participate. At first, Steven's parents are very concerned that he will have an anxious reaction to testing, and they do not want him to participate. His general education teacher is also fearful that he will not be able to focus and complete the test.

Steven's school district has been warned by the state that it needs to increase its rates of participation of students with disabilities in the statewide assessment; in the past, many students with disabilities were excluded from statewide testing. Steven's school is under considerable pressure to show that it is including all students, particularly those with disabilities, in the accountability program. At the meeting, the administrator, special educator, and school psychologist explain how important it is for Steven to participate in order for the education that he and students like him receive to be of concern to those who help in determining how resources will be allocated throughout the district. They also point out how he is working toward all the same grade-level achievement standards as other students, and that his participation may help them determine what he can and cannot do. They explain the variety of ways in which Steven can be accommodated during testing. For instance, they can continue to have the teacher assistant implement his behavior management plan. They can role play in the days prior to the test what the test will be like. Also, they can develop a picture schedule that is similar to the one he uses in the classroom to go along with the testing schedule.

After presenting the underlying rationale for having Steven participate, as well as the ways in which he could be accommodated during testing, the team agrees that it is appropriate to have Steven attempt the statewide assessment toward grade-level achievement standards. His teacher assistant is provided specific training on how she can and cannot assist Steven during testing in order to ensure that his results are as accurate as possible.

The day of the test is considerably draining for Steven and his teacher assistant, but Steven manages to complete the test. Although his total score ends up falling below the proficiency standard, and his teachers question whether it is an optimal measure of his skills and knowledge, his teachers and parents are impressed with the fact that he did not score in the lowest proficiency category. In fact, Steven was able to correctly answer many of the items on the test; he was able to demonstrate some of what he knew when provided appropriate accommodations during testing.

What implications about your own professional role can you draw from this scenario? Go to the Education CourseMate website for this textbook for more reflection questions about this Scenario in Assessment.

school rewards and sanctions for schools based on student performance. Among the sanctions that states commonly use are assigning negative labels to schools, removing staff, and firing principals. Rewards include assigning positive labels to schools and giving extra funding to schools or cash awards to staff. *Student accountability* is designed to motivate students to do their best. Nothing in NCLB requires that states attach rewards or sanctions to individual student performance; however, some states have chosen to do so. The most common high-stakes use of assessment evidence for individual students is to determine whether a student receives a standard high school diploma or some other type of document. Another type of student accountability, that has appeared is the use of test scores to determine whether a student will move from one grade to another.

3 Important Terminology

The standards-based assessment and accountability movement and the federal laws that accompany it have brought a new assessment vocabulary that includes terms such as "alternate achievement standards," "adequate yearly progress," and "schools in need of improvement." Some of these terms are used in many different ways in the professional and popular literature. In fact, the multiple uses of the terms cause confusion. The Council of Chief State School Officers publishes a *Glossary of Assessment Terms and Acronyms Used in Assessing Special Education*, which is a good source of definitions for terms used in assessment and accountability systems. We include an adapted version of this glossary in Table 28.1.

4 It's All About Meeting Standards

Assessments completed for accountability purposes involve measuring the extent to which students are learning what we want them to learn, or the extent to which school systems are accomplishing what we want them to accomplish. To do this, state education agency personnel must specify the standards that schools and students will work toward. They typically do so by specifying a set of *content standards*, which are statements of the subject-specific knowledge and skills that schools are expected to teach students, indicating what students should know and be able to do. States are required by law to specify academic content standards in reading, math, and science. Many states specify academic content standards in other areas. States must also specify *achievement standards* (sometimes called *performance standards*), which are statements of the levels at which or the proficiency with which students will show that they have mastered the academic content standards. Academic achievement standards use language drawn directly from the NCLB law, and they have the force of law. States are required to define at least three levels of proficiency (usually called basic, proficient, and advanced). Some states specify more than three levels of proficiency (for example, they may choose to indicate that a student's level of performance is below basic). The law requires that all students be assessed related to the state content and achievement standards. The state must provide for students with disabilities reasonable adaptations and accommodations necessary to measure their academic achievement relative to state academic content and state student academic achievement standards. It is important to know that all students, including students with disabilities, must have access to the same content standards. However, it is possible for students with disabilities to be instructed and assessed according to different achievement standards.

The two other kinds of standards that apply specifically to students with disabilities are alternate achievement standards and modified achievement standards. Although most students with disabilities are expected to be instructed and assessed according to the grade-level achievement standards, it can be determined that some will work

TABLE 28.1 Glossary of Assessment Terms Used Within Accountability Systems

Academic standards. There are two types of standards: content and performance.

- *Content standards.* Statements of the subject-specific knowledge and skills that schools are expected to teach students, indicating what students should know and be able to do in reading/language arts, math, and science. Many states have content standards in other academic areas as well. These standards must be the same for all schools and all students within a state.
- *Achievement (performance) standards.* Specifications of how well students need to know the academic content standards. They must have the following components:
  1. Specific levels of achievement: States are required to have at least three levels of achievement—basic, proficient, and advanced. Many states have more than three levels and may use different names for the levels.
  2. Descriptions of what students at each particular level must demonstrate relative to the task.
  3. Examples of student work at each level illustrating the range of performance within each level.
  4. Cut scores clearly separating each performance level.

Accommodations. Changes in the administration of an assessment, such as setting, scheduling, timing, presentation format, response mode, or others, including any combination of these that does not change the construct intended to be measured by the assessment or the meaning of the resulting scores. Accommodations are used for equity, not advantage, and serve to level the playing field. To be appropriate, assessment accommodations must be identified in the student's individualized education plan (IEP), limited education proficiency document, or Section 504 plan and used regularly during instruction and classroom assessment.

Accountability. The use of assessment results and other data to ensure that schools are moving in desired directions. Common elements include standards, indicators of progress toward meeting those standards, analysis of data, reporting procedures, and rewards or sanctions.

Accountability system. A plan that uses assessment results and other data outlining the goals and expectations for students, teachers, schools, districts, and states to demonstrate the established components or requirements of accountability. An accountability system typically includes rewards for those who exceed the goals and sanctions for those who fail to meet the goals.

Adaptations. A generalized term that describes a change made in the presentation, setting, response, or timing or scheduling of an assessment that may or may not change the construct of the assessment.

Adequate yearly progress (AYP). The annual improvement that school districts and schools must make each year in order to reach the NCLB goal of having every student proficient by the year 2014. In order to meet AYP requirements, schools must test at least 95 percent of their students in each of the subgroups, and schools must demonstrate sufficient progress for students in each of eight subgroups (for example, students with disabilities, students with limited English proficiency, and students who are members of specific racial/ethnic groups). Nontest indicators, such as attendance or high school graduation rate, are also used as indicators of AYP.

Alignment. The similarity or match between or among content standards, performance standards, curriculum, instruction, and assessments in terms of knowledge and skill expectations.

Alternate achievement standards. Expectations for performance that differ in complexity from a grade-level achievement standard but are linked to the content standards.

Alternate assessment based on alternate achievement standards (AA-AAS). An alternate assessment for which the expectation of performance differs in complexity from grade-level achievement standards and that is designed for use with students whose significant cognitive disabilities preclude their participation in the regular grade-level assessment.

Alternate assessment based on grade-level academic achievement standards (AA-GLAS). An instrument in a different format than the regular test, but it defines for students with disabilities a level of "proficient" performance as equivalent to grade-level achievement and same difficulty as on the state's regular grade-level assessment.

Benchmark. A specific statement of knowledge and skills within a content area's continuum that a student must possess to demonstrate a level of progress toward mastery of a standard.

Body of evidence. Information or data that establish that a student can perform a particular skill or has mastered a specific content standard and that was either produced by the student or collected by someone who is knowledgeable about the student.

Cut score. A specified point on a score scale. Scores at or above that point are interpreted differently from scores below that point.

continued on the next page

TABLE 28.1 Glossary of Assessment Terms Used Within Accountability Systems *(continued)*

Disaggregation. The collection and reporting of student achievement results by particular subgroups (e.g., students with disabilities and limited English-proficient students) to ascertain a subgroup's academic progress. Disaggregation makes it possible to compare subgroups or cohorts.

Norm-referenced test. A standardized test designed, validated, and implemented to rank a students' performance by comparing that performance to the performance of that student's peers.

Opportunity to learn. The provision of learning conditions, including suitable adjustments, to maximize a student's chances of attaining the desired learning outcomes, such as the mastery of content standards.

Out-of-level testing (off-grade or off-level). Administration of a test at a level above or below a student's present grade level to enable the student to be assessed at the level of instruction rather than the level of enrollment. According to federal education law, this practice is not allowed for accountability purposes.

Standards-referenced test (sometimes called a criterion-referenced test). A standardized test designed, validated, and implemented to rank a students' performance by comparing that performance to the specific standards for the state in which the student resides. Students are said to have met or not met the state standards.

Student accountability. Consequences exist for individual students and are based on their individual assessment performance. For example, students might not be promoted to the next grade or graduate if their assessment results do not meet a prespecified level.

System or school accountability. Consequences exist for school systems and are based on the assessment performance of a group of individuals (for example, the school building, district, or state education agency). For example, a school might receive a financial award or special recognition for having a large percentage of students meeting a particular assessment performance level.

SOURCE: Adapted from the Council of Chief State School Officers (CCSSO) (2006). "Assessing Students with Disabilities: A Glossary of Assessment Terms in Everyday Language." Washington, DC: Author; and Cortiella, C. (2006). *NCLB and IDEA: What Parents of Students with Disabilities Need to Know and Do.* Minneapolis, MN: University of Minnesota, National Center on Educational Outcomes.

toward these other two types. *Alternate achievement standards* are expectations for performance that differ in complexity from grade-level achievement standards, but they are linked to those general education standards. States are permitted to define alternate achievement standards to evaluate the achievement of students with the most significant cognitive disabilities. *Modified achievement standards* are intended to provide reliable and valid information about the academic achievement and progress of a unique group of students. These students are pursuing grade-level academic content standards, but they have "persistent academic disabilities"—that is, their performance may be hampered by significant learning disabilities and other cognitive limitations. These students' IEP teams are reasonably certain they are not likely to achieve grade-level proficiency within the school year covered by the IEP. It is important to know that the usefulness of modified achievement standards has been a topic of debate among assessment and accountability experts. Determining which students should be instructed in modified achievement standards has proved to be quite challenging, and many question whether such a "third" type of achievement standards is truly necessary. These standards may no longer exist in the near future (even as this book goes to print).

For quite some time, each state educational agency was expected to develop its own academic content and achievement standards. As a result, standards, and the focus of grade-level instruction, varied across states. Alicia might be taught multiplication in third grade in Michigan, while her cousin Dennis, who lives in Missouri, might not be taught multiplication until fourth grade. This could cause substantial problems for students who move from state to state and consequently miss out on important instruction. Furthermore, statewide assessments designed to hold schools and students accountable for achieving state standards also varied, making comparisons across states inappropriate. Arizona might report having 76 percent of students proficient on the statewide assessment, and Alaska might report 90 percent of students proficient. Does this mean Alaskans have higher achievement? Not necessarily—the differences in content and achievement standards (and consequent difference in statewide assessments) might be such that one test is much more difficult than another.

See the suggestions for navigating web at the end of this chapter for more information on the Common Core State Standards Initiative.

Given these and related concerns, the Council of Chief State School Officers (CCSSO) and the National Governors Association Center for Best Practices (NGA Center) are leading efforts in the development and implementation of common core standards through the Common Core State Standards Initiative. Forty-eight states were involved in the development of these standards in math and English/language arts, and forty states have adopted the final standards that were released in June of 2010. In addition, two consortia have been formed and are currently developing assessments to measure progress toward the common core standards: the PARCC RttT Assessment Consortium and the SMARTER Balanced Consortium.

Standards-based assessment is characterized by specifying what all students can be expected to learn and then expecting that time will vary but that all will achieve the standards. States are required to have in place assessments of student proficiency relative to academic content standards. The following are reasons why school personnel would want to assess student performance and progress relative to standards in addition to the state tests:

- To ascertain the extent to which individual students are meeting state standards—that is, accomplishing what it is that society wants them to accomplish
- To identify student strengths and weaknesses for instructional planning
- To allocate supports and resources
- To ascertain the extent to which specific schools within states are providing the kinds of educational opportunities and experiences that enable their students to achieve state-specified standards
- To provide data on student or school performance that can be helpful in making instructional policy decisions (curricula or instructional methodologies to use)
- To decide who should receive a diploma as indicated by performance on tests that measure whether standards are met
- To inform the public on the performance of schools or school districts
- To know the extent to which specific subgroups of students are meeting specified standards

ALTERNATE ASSESSMENT

Regardless of where students receive instruction, all students with disabilities should have access to, participate in, and make progress in the general curriculum. Thus, all students with disabilities must be included in state assessment systems and in state reporting of AYP toward meeting the state's standards. We have noted that states must specify academic content standards and academic achievement standards, and they must have assessments aligned to those standards. To address the needs of students with substantial concerns, states may choose to develop alternate achievement standards and modified achievement standards that are based on the expectations for all students.

States must include all students in their assessment and accountability systems. However, not all students can participate in the general state assessments, even with assessment accommodations designed to compensate for their specific needs. IDEA 1997 included a provision that by the year 2000 states would have in place alternate assessments intended for use with those students who evidenced severe cognitive impairments. In August 2002, the U.S. secretary of education proposed a regulation to allow states to develop and use alternate achievement standards for students with the most significant cognitive disabilities for the purpose of determining the AYP of states, local education agencies, and schools. In August 2003, the secretary specified that the number of students considered proficient using alternate assessments toward alternate achievement standards could not exceed 1 percent of all students, and on April 7, 2005, the secretary of education issued a rule that states could have an alternate assessment for an additional group of students who evidence persistent academic difficulties and thus are working toward "modified achievement standards." However, states could not count as proficient more than 2 percent of students based on the AA-MAS. As noted earlier in the chapter, however, the usefulness of modified achievement standards and the associated alternate assessments has been questioned, and may not be around much longer.

An *alternate assessment* is defined in the NCLB federal regulations as "an assessment designed for the small number of students with disabilities who are unable to participate in the regular state assessment, even with appropriate accommodations." It is further indicated that "an alternate assessment may include materials collected under several circumstances, including (1) teacher observation of the student, (2) samples of student work produced during regular classroom instruction that demonstrate mastery of specific instructional strategies ..., or (3) standardized performance tasks produced in an 'on demand' setting, such as completion of an assigned task on test day" (p. 68699). The assessments must yield results separately in both reading/language arts and mathematics, and they must be designed and implemented in a manner that supports use of the results as an indicator of AYP.

Alternate assessments are not simply compilations of student work, sometimes referred to as box or folder stuffing. Rather, they must have a clearly defined structure, specific participation guidelines, and clearly defined scoring criteria and procedures; must meet requirements for technical adequacy; and must have a reporting format that clearly communicates student performance in terms of the academic achievement standards specified by the state. They must meet the same standards for technical adequacy as does the general assessment. It has been a struggle for some states to satisfy this requirement. Alternate assessments may be needed for students with a broad array of disabling conditions, so a state may use more than one alternate assessment.

Alternate assessments can be designed to measure student performance toward grade-level standards, alternate achievement standards, or modified achievement standards. Recall that an alternate achievement standard is an expectation of performance that differs in complexity from a grade-level standard. For example, the Massachusetts Curriculum Frameworks include the following content standard: "Students will identify, analyze, and apply knowledge of the purpose, structure, and elements of nonfiction or informational materials and provide evidence from the text to support their understanding." A less complex demonstration of this standard is "to gain information from signs, symbols, and pictures in the environment"; a more complex demonstration is to "gain information from captions, titles, and table of contents in an informational text" (Massachusetts Department of Education, 2001). As previously mentioned, modified achievement standards are a controversial topic, and at the current time it is not clear whether they will continue to be a part of standards-based reform efforts.

You can learn about the current status of related efforts by visiting the websites provided at the end of this chapter.

As the *Common Core State Standards* project and related work of the two assessment consortia discussed earlier gain momentum, and legislative updates occur, we anticipate that there may be similar combined efforts to develop alternate assessments in a collaborative manner across states.

5 Important Considerations in Assessment for the Purpose of Making Accountability Decisions

As a result of accountability system implementation, student assessment data have become much more readily available to the public. Although this public reporting is intended to promote better student instruction and learning, it is important that those who have access to the data know how to appropriately interpret the information. Without these skills, poor judgments and decisions may be made that are harmful to students. For instance, it is important for consumers of accountability information to understand that most tests used for accountability purposes are intended to measure performance of an entire group of students, and that the tests do not necessarily provide reliable data on the skills of individual students. Without this knowledge, consumers may make unwarranted judgments and decisions about individual students based on their test scores.

In addition, it is important for people to recognize that not all students need to be tested in the same way; it is often important for students to be tested using different formats. Some students have special characteristics that make it difficult for them to demonstrate their knowledge on content standards in a traditional paper-and-pencil format. These students may need accommodations to demonstrate their true knowledge. What is most important is that students' knowledge and skill toward the identified achievement standards are measured. Those with assessment expertise can help determine what accommodations or alternate assessments might be necessary for students to best demonstrate their skills and knowledge.

6 Best Practices in High-Stakes Assessment and Accountability

It is critical that accountability systems include and report on the performance of all students, including those with disabilities and limited English proficiency. Personnel at the NCEO (Thurlow, Quenemoen, Thompson, & Lehr, 2001) specified a set of principles of inclusive assessment and accountability systems. These are listed in Table 28.2. The principles address who should participate, the kinds of guidelines states should have, how scores should be reported, the use of scores in accountability systems, and the fundamental belief system that should guide practice.

TABLE 28.2 NCEO Best Practices in Inclusive Assessment and Accountability

Principle 1: All students with disabilities are included in the assessment and accountability system.
Principle 2: Decisions about how students with disabilities participate in the assessment and accountability system are the result of clearly articulated participation, accommodations, and alternate assessment decision-making processes.
Principle 3: All students with disabilities are included when student scores are publicly reported, in the same frequency and format as all other students, whether they participate with or without accommodations, or in an alternate assessment.
Principle 4: The assessment performance of students with disabilities has the same impact on the final accountability index as the performance of other students, regardless of how the students participate in the assessment system (that is, with or without accommodations, or in an alternate assessment).
Principle 5: There is improvement of both the assessment system and the accountability system over time, through the processes of formal monitoring, ongoing evaluation, and systematic training in the context of emerging research and best practice.
Principle 6: Every policy and practice reflects the belief that *all students* must be included in state and district assessment and accountability systems.

SOURCE: Thurlow, M., Quenemoen, R., Thompson, S., & Lehr, C., *"Principles and characteristics of inclusive assessment and accountability systems"* (Synthesis Report 4, Table 1). Copyright © 2001 University of Minnesota, National Center on Educational Outcomes. Reprinted by permission.

Chapter Comprehension Questions

Write your answers to each of the following questions and then compare your responses to the text.

1. What legal requirements for state and school district assessment and accountability systems are specified in NCLB and IDEA 2004?
2. What is the difference between content and achievement standards? Why is there a current movement toward the development of common core state standards?
3. What is an alternate assessment and why is it important?
4. State two important considerations in assessment for purposes of making accountability decisions.

Web Activities 

1. Search the Internet for the common core state standards. Review and describe the process used to develop the standards. What mention of students with disabilities and English language learners is made in these efforts?
2. Go to the websites of the two assessment consortia that are development assessment programs for the states (i.e., search the Internet for Achieve PARCC and SMARTER Balanced Consortium). To which consortia does your state belong (if any)? What is the current status of work among the two consortia?
3. Go to the website for the United States Department of Education and search for the most recent information on the Elementary and Secondary Education Act. What changes are being proposed and/or have been made?

Web Resources

National Center on Educational Outcomes
www.education.umn.edu/NCEO
The website for this organization provides summaries of what is currently going on across the nation to include students with disabilities in large-scale assessment and accountability programs, as well as resources to help in promoting related best practices.

National Center for Research on Evaluation, Standards, and Student Testing (CRESST)
http://www.cse.ucla.edu/
This website includes many great resources that include summaries of research and innovative practices associated with large-scale assessment and accountability programs.

Additional resources for this chapter can be found on the Education CourseMate website. Go to CengageBrain.com to access the site.

Collaborative Team Decision Making

CHAPTER GOALS

1 Understand several characteristics of effective school teams.

2 Be familiar with various teams that are commonly formed in school settings.

3 Know strategies for effectively communicating assessment information to parents.

4 Know a variety of ways in which assessment information is communicated and maintained in written formats, and various related rules about data collection and record keeping.

KEY TERMS

schoolwide assistance teams

intervention assistance teams

multi-disciplinary teams

problem-solving teams

groupthink

Family Educational Rights and Privacy Act (FERPA)

Many important decisions are not made individually but by groups of people. In schools, important decisions are made by teams of individuals. Some team members may be well versed in assessment concepts; however, research conducted through the Center for Research on Evaluation, Standards, and Student Testing suggests that many educational professionals do not know how to carefully examine and use assessment data (Baker, Bewley, Herman, Lee, & Mitchell, 2001; Baker & Linn, 2002). Parents may need considerable support to understand and make appropriate use of assessment information that are collected. Some professional associations (for example, the American Psychological Association, the Council for Exceptional Children, and the National Association of School Psychologists) specify in their ethical standards or principles that their members are responsible for accurate and sensitive communication of assessment information.

In this chapter, we provide information on the many different teams that may be formed to examine assessment data and suggestions for making appropriate team decisions. We offer guidelines for communicating assessment information in both oral and written formats, as well as regulations governing record keeping and the dissemination of information collected in school settings.

1 Characteristics of Effective School Teams

Many individuals play important roles in promoting student learning; each brings unique expertise that can be useful in the process of decision making. In using assessment data to make decisions, you will work with special and general educators, administrators, speech/language pathologists, school psychologists, social workers, nurses, physicians, physical therapists, occupational therapists, audiologists, counselors, curriculum directors, attorneys, child advocates, and probably many others. Effective communication and collaboration is essential to promoting positive student outcomes. Although the expertise each individual offers can be an asset to decision making, it is important to recognize that group decision making does not necessarily result in better decisions than individual decision making. Unfortunately, there are many ways in which group dynamics can hinder appropriate decision making. Gutkin and Nemeth (1997) summarize ways in which group decision making can go awry, including (1) the tendency for groups to concede to the majority opinion regardless of its accuracy, and (2) group polarization, in which groups tend to become more extreme in their decision making than what any individual originally intended (which could either hinder or promote best practice). In order to avoid making poor decisions, it is important to adhere to several principles when working as a team. Although the goals and purposes of school teams may vary, certain principles of effective teaming appear to be universal.

Have shared goals and purpose. Unnecessary conflict and inefficiencies in decision making occur when team members do not understand the team's purpose and when their activities do not reflect that purpose. For example, some members of prereferral intervention teams may view the team's purpose as "just one more hoop to jump through" before a referral for evaluation to determine special education eligibility is made, whereas others may view it as an opportunity to identify the conditions under which a student learns best. Those holding the former perspective may be less inclined to put forth substantial effort in associated team activities, which may reduce team effectiveness. It is important for the team's purpose and function to be clearly articulated when the team is formed and for all team members to be committed to working toward that goal.

Clearly articulate the roles and functions of team members. Team composition needs to be determined carefully, balancing the need for unique expertise and the need for a team to efficiently complete commissioned tasks. Those team members who are selected for participation need to be fully aware of the unique expertise that they bring as well as their knowledge limitations. More team members is not always better; managing large teams can be overwhelming and may intimidate important members of the team (for example, some parents may be intimidated when they walk into a team meeting that includes many school professionals). In addition, large teams may lead to decisions that are informed by just one or two particularly dominant team members (Moore, Fifield, Spira, & Scarlato, 1989). The appointment of a team meeting facilitator can be helpful in assisting the team in following appropriate organizational procedures and ensure that all team members are fully able to share their expertise and knowledge in ways that facilitate progress toward the team's goal.

Listen to and respect each team member's contributions. Teams sometimes gravitate toward "groupthink" (that is, agreeing with the majority opinion), despite the fact that group decisions can be inaccurate (Gutkin & Nemeth, 1997). It is important for those with minority opinions to be given the opportunity to express their positions and for their ideas to be respected and considered within the group's functioning. Effective problem solving can occur when all individuals are encouraged to contribute.

Balance structure and flexibility within team meetings. It can often be helpful for teams to develop and implement systematic procedures for operation. In many cases, teams may have forms that facilitators use to guide team meetings (see Figure 29.1 for an example of such a form). The facilitator might create a written agenda for team meetings, in which there is time for those who have collected information to present their findings, time for additional input from team members, and time for group decision making. Such procedures and structures can help teams maintain attention to task and promote efficiency toward addressing the team's goals. When team members want to discuss important issues that are not associated with the specific decisions to be made, it is important to know how to tactfully address those concerns. We have found the following statement to be helpful in such circumstances: "That's an important issue, but it will take us away from the decision that we are trying to make now. Can we discuss it later or at another meeting?" Some decisions that school teams make are associated with a substantial amount of conflicting opinion and emotionality. For example, discussing certain disability labels such as "student with mental retardation" and "student with an emotional disturbance" can be very troubling to parents. It is important that team meeting facilitators be willing to shuffle the agenda or even stop and reschedule meetings when the emotional nature of the meeting is such that progress toward the team's goals cannot be made.

Use objective data to guide decision making. Often, educational decisions are made without appropriate attention to relevant student data (Ysseldyke, 1987). Without the appropriate collection of and adherence to using data to guide team decision making, the subjective preferences of team members may take precedence over what is truly in the best interest of the student being served. The appropriate use of data to inform decision making can (1) ensure that appropriate practices are put into place and (2) help eliminate conflicting viewpoints on how to proceed.

Ensure confidentiality—it's the law! Those who study team decision making find that confidentiality can break down. Ultimately, it is against the law to break confidentiality rules, and such breaches can be grounds for termination. When confidentiality rules are not followed and a member learns that someone betrayed confidentiality, the team ceases to function well. It is suggested that regular reminders are provided by an administrator, school psychologist, or other team leader that meeting discussions are confidential. We suggest that the leader tell members at the very first meeting that confidentiality is critical and that he or she will be reminding members of this regularly. Then the reminders do not raise questions of "I wonder who talked inappropriately about what we are discussing."

Regularly evaluate team outcomes and processes to promote continuous improvement in team functioning. Team processes and procedures can always be improved. It is important for the team to engage in periodic self-evaluation

FIGURE 29.1
Completed Example Form to Guide Initial Problem-Solving Team Meeting

Date of meeting: 01/30/11
Student name: Jesse Johansen
Student's grade: 3
Teacher's name: Darcy Dunlap
School: Eastern Elementary
Name and title of those attending the meeting (note facilitator and recorder):
Carrie Court (3rd grade lead teacher), Darcy Dunlap *(recorder)*, Greg Gorter *(guidance* counselor), Jackie Johansen (mother), Eric Enright (principal, facilitator)

A. Student Strengths (Provide brief summary of student strengths; 2–3 minutes)
Jesse has many friends and gets along really well with all the other students. He likes to play *soccer, and* is very good at math.

B. Nature of Difficulties (In 2 minutes, circle all that apply)

Academic

(Reading) Writing Spelling Math Social Studies History Other:____

Behavioral

Aggression Attention Task Completion Homework Attendance Tardiness Other:____

Social/Emotional

Depression (Anxiety) Peer Relationships Social Skills Other:____

Physical

Body Odor Headaches Nausea Fatigue/Sleeping in Class Other:____

C. Summary of Data Collected to Support Difficulties Circled Above (2–3 minutes per area)
Jesse performed in the at-risk range on the Fall and Winter DIBELS benchmarking tasks during third grade. When asked to read in class, his voice becomes shaky, and he shuts down, and he refuses to read. His mother reports that he is beginning to not like going to school, and doesn't eat his breakfast (most likely due to his nervousness about having to go to school).

D. Prioritization of Difficulties (2–3 minutes)
#1 Most Problematic of the Above Listed Difficulties: Reading (the team believes that his poor skills in reading are what are contributing to his anxiety).

#2 Most Problematic of the Above Listed Difficulties: Anxiety

#3 Most Problematic of the Above Listed Difficulties: ____

E. Problem Definition in Observable and Measurable Terms (2 minutes)
Currently when presented with a third grade DIBELS benchmark passage, Jesse reads a median of 60 words correctly in one minute.

F. Goal (2 minutes)
Eight weeks from now when presented with a third grade DIBELS benchmark passage, Jesse will read a median of 75 words correctly in one minute.

FIGURE 29.1
(Continued)

G. Suggested Intervention Ideas for Addressing #1 of Prioritized Difficulties (15 minutes)
Intervention Idea #1: After school tutoring with an eighth-grade student.

Intervention Idea #2: Flashcards of phonics patterns that Jesse's teacher would administer after school two days per week, and Jesse's mom would administer at home the other three days each week

Intervention Idea #3: Read Naturally® program that would be administered after school.

H. Description of Final Intervention Selected (10 minutes)
i. What will the student do? Jesse will be taught how to use the Read Naturally® program, and will practice listening to and reading aloud with the tapes.

ii. How often and when will this occur? Two times a week for 45 minutes after school (Tues./Thurs.).

iii. Who is responsible for implementing the intervention? Jesse's mom and teacher

iv. How will progress be measured? DIBELS progress monitoring probes will be administered once a week.

v. Who is responsible for measuring progress? Jesse's teacher

vi. How, when, and to whom will progress be reported? Progress will be reported at the follow-up meeting, unless four consecutive data points fall below the aim line, in which case an earlier meeting will be convened.

I. Date and Time of Follow-Up Meeting (2 minutes): April 9, 2011

in order to ensure that it is meeting identified goals and objectives and that it is respectful of all team members' contributions. In some cases, it may be helpful to ask someone uninvolved in the team functioning to do an anonymous evaluation of a team's functioning. This can help to ensure that all team members are able to contribute their skills and knowledge in a way that is most beneficial to students.

2 Types of School Teams

There are many different teams created to examine assessment data and inform decision making in schools. These teams may have very different names and be composed of professionals with varying expertise. Although all the teams described here are typically involved in examination of data for the purpose of decision making, the teams vary considerably in the types of decisions made and, therefore, the nature of data collected, analyzed, and interpreted. Although we provide titles for these teams, it is important to recognize that there may be a variety of different terms used to describe similarly functioning teams in the schools and districts you encounter.

SCHOOLWIDE ASSISTANCE TEAMS

With the development of technology for managing large amounts of student data, as well as increased attention to accountability for student outcomes, teams of educational professionals are more frequently being formed to collect, analyze, and interpret data on students across the entire school or district. The ultimate purpose of these teams is to inform instructional planning and resource allocation at school and district levels such that student achievement is optimized. They can be thought of as teams intended to ensure that the fundamental level of support within MTSS (core instruction) is effective. Sometimes these teams are referred to as "resource teams." Team members may consist of those with special expertise in data analysis, curriculum, and instruction. These individuals come together to examine statewide assessment data, results from schoolwide screening efforts, and information on existing educational programming, with the purpose of identifying strategies for improving student achievement. In some cases, such teams may be created by grade level, such that all teachers from a particular grade meet on a regular basis with the administrator and someone with expertise in assessment in order to identify areas for instructional improvement. Following a systematic analysis of data, the team may make recommendations for professional development and changes in school programming.

Participants on these teams who have specialized expertise in assessment can contribute to the team by (1) helping the school identify methods for collecting relevant data on all students effectively and efficiently, (2) creating and interpreting visual displays of assessment data for the purpose of decision making, (3) recognizing areas in which additional assessment is needed prior to making substantial changes in school programming, and (4) identifying methods for monitoring the effectiveness of any associated changes in school programming.

INTERVENTION ASSISTANCE TEAMS

Intervention assistance teams are formed to address difficulties that small groups of students or individual students experience within general education classrooms. The purpose of the team is to define the specific problem, analyze the problem in order to develop a targeted intervention plan, implement the intervention plan, monitor the plan implementation and student progress, and evaluate the effectiveness of the plan. Initially, the team may simply consist of a general education teacher and parents of the child involved. However, if the problem is not solved, additional school professionals may be added to the team in order to more systematically define and analyze the problem and to inform the development of interventions that are of increasing intensity. The parent–teacher team might be expanded to include other teachers or the school guidance counselor; these individuals could help conduct a more in-depth problem analysis and brainstorm additional ideas for intervention. If that plan does not lead to progress, other personnel, such as the school psychologist, social worker, or special education teacher, might be added to the intervention assistance team to provide additional support for assessment and intervention. In other words, as a student is determined to need a higher level of support through the MTSS, additional expertise is sought to assist with development of a more intensive intervention. Names for teams with a function similar to that of an intervention assistance team described previously include "teacher assistance teams," "student assistance teams," "building assistance teams," "problem-solving teams," "child study teams," and "instructional consultation teams."

Those with expertise in assessment can assist these teams by helping to select and administer assessment tools that help with defining and analyzing the problem, as well as select tools for monitoring intervention integrity and student progress.

MULTIDISCIPLINARY TEAMS

These teams are convened when a child has not made appropriate progress following support provided through multiple levels of MTSS and is being considered for special education evaluation; the function and activities of these teams are more fully discussed in Chapter 27. They are charged with the responsibility of determining whether a student has a disability and is in need of special education services according to the Individuals with Disabilities Education Act (IDEA).

INDIVIDUAL EDUCATION PLAN TEAMS

After a student is found eligible for special education services under IDEA, the individualized education program is developed by a team of individuals who have specialized knowledge in the specific areas of the child's disability, as well as those who will be responsible for carrying out the plan and the child's parents. These teams typically meet on an annual basis to review the progress and programming for each student receiving special education services individually.

3 Communicating Assessment Information to Parents

Parents and guardians usually have more information about certain aspects of their child's life than any other person involved in the assessment process. However, many parents have limited knowledge and skill in understanding assessment and can find it challenging to take in all of the information presented by different individuals and understand what it means in terms of what is best for their child. Given the influential role that they play in the lives of their children, it is crucial that they understand the assessment results to participate fully in the decision-making process. Many parents (as well as other team members) may lack the knowledge to understand assessment results without additional explanations. Some parents may themselves have disabilities. However, not all parents will lack knowledge or technical expertise; some parents are themselves professionals—psychologists, special educators, attorneys, therapists, and so forth. Other parents will have educated themselves about their child's needs. Regardless of their backgrounds, all parents may need to be empowered to be active and helpful members of school decision-making teams.

A variety of things can limit parent understanding of assessment information and participation in team decision making. Language barriers can clearly hinder effective communication. Many parents may not have a schedule that permits participation in meetings as scheduled by school professionals. They may feel intimidated by various school professionals. They may not recognize the important knowledge that they can bring to the team or not understand how to effectively communicate that knowledge to the team. They may have strong emotional reactions to data that are presented about their child's academic successes and failures, which may hinder rational decision making. They may have strong feelings and opinions about the quality of educational services provided to their child and about how their child's needs might best be met by educational professionals. Unfortunately, parents' unique knowledge about their child is often disregarded or ignored by school professionals, who often make decisions prior to team meetings.

Schools can take several steps to make communication with parents more effective. Better communication should result in more effective parental participation in associated team decision making.

- *Communicate with parents frequently.* In the past, it was often the case that parents were not made aware of difficulties that their child was having until the child was being considered for special education evaluation. When this happens, it can lead to strong emotional reactions and frustration among parents. It can also lead to unnecessary conflict if parents do not think that special education services would be in the best interest of their child. It is important that parents are provided frequent and accurate information on the progress of their child from the very beginning of their child's enrollment in school. By providing this information, parents of those students who are consistently low performing may become more involved in helping to develop intervention plans that may reduce their child's difficulties. Furthermore, when parents receive frequent communication about their child's progress (or lack thereof), they may more readily understand why a referral for special education eligibility evaluation is made. Communication with parents can occur more frequently within MTSS as teachers communicate more frequently with parents about the level of support their child needs.

- *Communicate both the child's strengths and the child's weaknesses.* Parents of students with special needs are often reminded of their child's weaknesses and difficulties in school and may rarely be alerted to their child's successes and strengths. Other parents may overvalue their child's relative strengths and ignore or minimize their child's weaknesses. In order to work effectively with parents, and to facilitate creative problem solving as a part of a team, it is important to recognize and communicate about a child's specific strengths as well as weaknesses.
- *Translate assessment information and team communications as needed.* Assessment data that are reported to all parents (for example, statewide assessment results and screening results) should be made available in the parent's primary language or mode of communication. To facilitate participation in team meetings, interpreters should be provided. In order to interpret well, they may need special training in how to communicate the pertinent information to parents, as well as how to ensure that parents' questions, concerns, and contributions have a voice within team meanings. For all parents, even those who have English as their primary language, it is important to avoid jargon and acronyms, and to use figures and graphs to show assessment results as much as possible to facilitate their understanding.
- *Be aware of how cultural differences may impact the understanding of assessment information.* It is also suggested that when cultural differences exist, a person who understands both the student's culture and educational matters be present. This may be necessary even when language differences are nonexistent (for example, the student is Amish and the culture of the school is not Amish). This can help a team identify issues that may be cultural in nature. Sometimes communication modes that are a normal part of school functioning (e.g., email) are not part of the home environment, and it is important to be aware of these differences.
- *Schedule meetings to facilitate parent attendance.* Efforts should be made to schedule meetings at a time when parents can be present. Challenges associated with transportation should be addressed. In certain circumstances, it may be necessary for school professionals to meet at a location that is more convenient for parents than the school setting. It may also be necessary for school personnel to communicate directly with an employer, encouraging the employer to allow the parent to be excused from work. This is especially true in communities in which one company (for example, a paper mill, an automobile factory, or a meat packing plant) is the employer of many parents. In this case, a blanket arrangement could be made in which the company agrees to release the parent for school meetings if a request is made by the school.
- *Clearly explain the purpose of any assessment activities, as well as the potential outcomes.* Whereas school professionals may be very familiar with assessment-related processes and procedures, and associated decisions that are made, parents often are new to the process. It is important to prepare them for what to expect as it relates to administration of assessment instruments, and using the results of assessment data that are collected. It is important to let the parents know up front what will be involved in assessing the child (e.g., when it will occur, what assessment materials are used, etc.), and how the assessment process will be explained to the child. Sometimes, it can be helpful for school professionals to contact parents before a meeting to explain the purpose of the meeting and what they can expect to happen at the meeting. Parents should be informed of all potential outcomes of a particular meeting (for example, development of an intervention plan, decision to collect more data, and decision that the student is eligible to receive special education services) so that they are not caught off guard.

SCENARIO *in* ASSESSMENT

AMELIA

Ineffective Communication of Assessment Information with Parents

In early November, Mr. and Mrs. Martinez were notified that a meeting was being scheduled to discuss their third-grade daughter Amelia's failure to make progress in reading. The meeting was scheduled as part of a series of intervention assistance team meetings, in which a total of seven children from her elementary school would be discussed by a team of individuals who included the principal, guidance counselor, and the students' general education teachers. General educators were rotated into the meeting at 10-minute intervals, as each child was being discussed. Although Mr. and Mrs. Martinez were notified by Amelia's teacher that the meeting would be held, they were told that it was not important for them to attend, and that it would probably be better for them to plan to attend the meeting that would likely be held in mid-December to discuss Amelia's need for special education services. A few days later, Amelia's parents received a letter and consent form in the mail asking them to sign for permission to conduct an evaluation to determine whether Amelia was eligible to receive special education services. Amelia's parents, although discouraged and confused about what this meant, promptly signed and returned the form, assuming that the school knew what was in Amelia's best academic interests.

On December 15, a multidisciplinary team meeting was held. Mr. Martinez could not make it to the early afternoon meeting, given his work schedule. Mrs. Martinez was able to catch a bus and arrive at the school with her two young children 30 minutes prior to the meeting. At the meeting, several different professionals shuffled into the room at different times, with each presenting results from speech/language testing, intelligence testing, achievement testing, and classroom observations of Amelia. Toward the end of the meeting, a special education teacher asked Mrs. Martinez to sign some forms, which she was told would allow Amelia to get the services she needed, given that Amelia was in the words of her teacher "clearly a student with a learning disability."

Effective Communication of Assessment Information with Parents

In January of Amelia Martinez's first-grade year, Mr. and Mrs. Martinez received a phone call from her teacher. The teacher indicated that although Amelia was making many friends in first grade and seemed to get along very well with her classmates, she was performing below expectations in her development of early literacy skills as measured by the early literacy screening measures administered to all students in the fall and winter. The teacher invited Amelia's parents to attend a meeting in which they would discuss strategies for targeting instruction to Amelia's needs and discuss the possibility of implementing strategies at home for helping her develop early literacy skills.

At the meeting, Mr. and Mrs. Martinez, along with the classroom teacher and a more experienced first-grade teacher, discussed the fact that Amelia did not demonstrate adequate letter–sound correspondence. They developed a plan that allowed her to receive additional instruction and practice in this area at both home and school (with the teacher assistant) each day for 6 weeks, after which they would reconvene as a team to examine the progress that she had made. After 6 weeks, the two teachers and Amelia's parents met, and an additional person (that is, an intervention specialist) was added to the team to help identify any additional assessment and intervention that might be applied, given that Amelia had not made the progress needed to put her on track for learning how to read by the end of third grade. After reviewing Amelia's progress together, and recognizing that she had made small gains as a result of the intervention, they decided to intensify the support she was receiving by providing her more intervention time during the school day, and they continued to monitor her progress. Her mother was provided simple phonemic awareness development activities to practice with Amelia at home in the evening.

Soon after spring break of her first-grade year, the team reconvened to examine Amelia's progress, which continued to be below expectations. Together, the team decided that an evaluation for special education services was warranted. Mr. and Mrs. Martinez were provided information on their rights as parents of a child undergoing evaluation to determine special education eligibility. They were briefly told about the types of testing that would occur and how this would help determine whether Amelia might be in need of and benefit from special education services. At the end of her first-grade year, the team was brought together to examine the assessment results. Based on the information collected, it was clear that Amelia met the state criteria for having a specific learning disability in reading, and the team identified instructional strategies that were beneficial to include as part of an individualized education program for Amelia.

What implications about your own professional role can you draw from this scenario? Go to the Education CourseMate website for this textbook for more reflection questions about this Scenario in Assessment.

- *Communicate using nontechnical language as much as possible.* By now, you have most certainly recognized that language used in educational circles is full of acronyms. It is important for these, as well as all of the other technical terms that may be used, to be fully explained to parents so that they can be in dialog with team members. Whereas some parents may understand technical terms associated with assessment data, others may not. It is more appropriate to err on the side of using language that is easier to understand than to assume that parents understand terminology that is used by school professionals. Figures and graphs can often help to convey student progress in an understandable way.

- *Maintain a solution-focused orientation and avoid pointing blame.* Just about every school team meeting is intended to promote student achievement, whether directly or indirectly. Making this goal happen requires that individual team members focus on alterable rather than unalterable variables and on what can be changed in the future to promote student learning rather than dwelling on what has happened in the past. Unfortunately, there can be a tendency to focus on what people may have done or failed to do in the past rather than making plans for the future. Although it is important to learn from past mistakes, team members should focus on what can be done in the future to improve student learning. Focusing on past failure can decrease morale and contribute to unnecessary conflict and blame among team members.

4 Communicating Assessment Information Through Written and Electronic Records

Although presentation of assessment information and related decision making is frequently done verbally and in team meetings, assessment data are also collected, summarized, and interpreted in written form. Policies and standards for the collection, maintenance, and dissemination of information in written formats must balance two sometimes conflicting needs. Parents and children have a basic right to privacy; schools need to collect and use information about children (and sometimes parents) in order to plan appropriate educational programs. Schools and parents have a common goal: to promote the welfare of children. In theory, schools and parents should agree on what constitutes and promotes a child's welfare, and in practice, schools and parents generally do work cooperatively.

In 1974, many of these recommended guidelines became federal law when the Family Educational Rights and Privacy Act (Public Law 93-380, commonly called FERPA) was enacted. Now these are incorporated with IDEA (IDEA §300.560–300.577). The basic provisions of the act are quite simple. All educational agencies that accept federal money (preschools, elementary and secondary schools, community colleges, and colleges and universities) must grant parents the opportunity to inspect and challenge student records; however, parents typically lose this right when their child turns 18. Regardless of whether the school decides to change the records according to parent input, parents have the right to supplement the records with what they understand to be true or an explanation as to why they believe the file to be inaccurate. The only records to which parental access may be denied are the personal notes of teachers, supervisors, administrators, and other educational personnel that are kept in the sole possession of the maker of the records. Also, educational agencies must not release identifiable data without the parents' written consent. However, at age 18 years, the student becomes the individual who has the authority to provide consent for his or her data to be released to others. Violators of the provisions of FERPA are subject to sanctions; federal funds may be withheld from agencies found to be in violation of the law.

The following section discusses specific issues and principles in the collection, maintenance, and dissemination of pupil information through written records and electronic reports.

COLLECTION OF PUPIL INFORMATION

Schools routinely collect massive amounts of information about individual pupils and their parents, and not all of this information requires parental permission to collect or maintain. As discussed in Chapter 2, information can be used for a number of legitimate educational decisions: screening, progress monitoring, instructional planning and modification, resource allocation, special education eligibility determination, program evaluation, and accountability. Considerable data must be collected if a school system is to function effectively, both in delivering educational services to children and in reporting the results of its educational programs to the various community, state, and federal agencies to which it may be responsible.

Schoolwide Screening

Many schools systematically collect and keep written records of hearing, vision, and basic skill development across all students. The associated screening measures are intended to identify all students who have the potential for additional difficulties very early in time, and they are purposely developed to overidentify students. This can help to ensure that true difficulties are not missed, and that difficulties can be addressed earlier rather than later in time. When students fail to meet minimum thresholds of performance on screening measures, they may be referred for additional assessment to determine whether true difficulties exist. Vision and hearing screening records are typically maintained at the school for a substantial amount of time; review of this information can help determine that basic abilities such as hearing and vision are not contributing to difficulties that a student may experience. For more information on assessment of hearing and vision, refer to Chapter 20.

In addition to hearing and vision information, individual student academic records may also contain results from group-administered district- and statewide assessment programs. With the increasing application of MTSS, schools are implementing additional screening and monitoring programs in order to ensure early identification of academic problems. Programs such as DIBELS, AIMSweb, and others described in Chapter 8 may be used to screen for academic problems and monitor student progress. Some screening is done schoolwide; however, other screening may occur for individual students who are initially identified as having difficulties. Students who do not meet benchmark levels on screening measures and fail to make expected levels of progress toward meeting proficiency may be identified for additional assessment and referred to an intervention assistance team. Although it is best practice to remain in frequent communication with parents about data that are collected about their children, it is not always necessary to get their explicit permission for data collection. For example, prior to holding an intervention assistance team meeting, a school professional may collect data to inform the selection of an intervention that would target a student's individual academic deficits. Such assessment would not necessarily require explicit parent permission.

Consent for Additional Data Collection

Although it is best practice to communicate with parents frequently about student progress, and to alert them to any academic difficulties that the student is having as soon as possible, schools are not required to have parent consent for additional data collection unless a change in educational placement or the provision of a free and appropriate public education according to the Individuals with Disabilities Education Act (IDEA) is being considered.[1] In the section on procedural safeguards, IDEA mandates that prior written notice be given to the parents or guardians of a child whenever an educational agency proposes to initiate or change (or refuses to initiate or change) either the identification, evaluation, or educational placement of the child or the provision of a free and appropriate education to the child. It further requires that the notice fully inform the parent, in the parent's native language, regarding all appeal procedures available. Thus, schools must inform parents of their right to present any and all complaints regarding the identification, evaluation, or placement of their child; their right to an impartial due process hearing; and their right to appeal decisions reached at a due process hearing, if necessary, by bringing civil action against a school district.

[1] This is also the case if data are to be collected for the purpose of research. The collection of research data requires the individual informed consent of parents. Various professional groups, such as the American Psychological Association and the National Association of School Psychologists, consider the collection of data without informed consent to be unethical; according to the Buckley amendment, it is illegal to experiment with children without prior informed consent. Typically, informed consent for research-related data collection requires that the pupil or parents understand (1) the purpose of and procedures involved in the investigations, (2) any risks inherent in participation in the research, (3) the fact that all participants will remain anonymous, and (4) the participants' option to withdraw from the research at any time.

Verification

Verifying information means ascertaining or confirming the information's truth, accuracy, or correctness. Depending on the type of information, verification may take several forms. For observations or ratings, verification means confirmation by another individual. For standardized test data, verification means conducting a reliable and valid assessment. (The concepts of reliability and validity are defined and discussed in detail in Chapter 5.)

Unverified information can be collected, but every attempt should be made to verify such information before it is retained in a student's records. For example, serious misconduct or extremely withdrawn behavior is of direct concern to the schools. Initial reports of such behavior by a teacher or counselor are typically based on observations that can be corroborated by other witnesses. Behavior that cannot be verified can still provide useful hints, hypotheses, and starting points for diagnosis. Ultimately, when the data are not confirmable, they should not be collected and must not be retained. We believe that this requirement should also apply to unreliable or invalid test data that cannot otherwise be substantiated.

Summarization and Interpretation

When additional assessment data are collected as a part of an evaluation to determine whether a student is eligible to receive special education services under IDEA, a written report is typically developed prior to the multidisciplinary team meeting that is held to determine whether a student is eligible for services. The purpose of the report is to summarize the assessment data collected. Written reports communicate information to both existing team members and those who may review the child's file in the future. Although the content of these reports will vary depending on the nature of data needed to determine eligibility, certain principles should be used to promote effective written communication about the data that are collected. These are discussed here.

Organize the report. In general, an eligibility evaluation report will include the following information: a reason for referral, identifying and background information about the student, a description of the assessment methods and instruments used, documentation of interventions used and the associated results, information on observations conducted while assessment data were being collected (that is, to substantiate that test results represent accurate measures of typical student behavior), assessment results, recommendations, and a summary of the assessment procedures and results. In order for readers to easily access the information presented, it can be helpful to present assessment results in tables and figures.

Use language that is easily understood by team members. As when communicating assessment information orally, it is important that your language is accessible to parents and other school professionals. Avoid jargon, and carefully explain all terminology that may be unfamiliar to any members of your audience. When reporting scores, it is important to use scores (like percentiles) that are easily interpreted by those who will read your report. When you are not sure whether readers will understand reported scores, explain them clearly. It is always best to err on the side of "overexplaining" than "underexplaining."

Focus on the reporting of observed behaviors. In report writing, it is important to be transparent in how you describe assessment tasks and results. In your writing, clearly communicate that scores represent performance on particular tasks rather than innate student qualities or characteristics. In doing so, you will more accurately reflect the nature of the data collected and help to avoid misinterpretations and high-level inferences based on collected data.

> *Poor example of a report statement*: John is average in his short-term memory capabilities.
>
> *Better example of a report statement*: On tasks that required John to listen to and recall numbers in the order that were verbally communicated to him by the examiner, John performed in the average range in comparison to his same-grade peers.

However, it is important to ensure that the specific content of test items remains secure. When offering example items in written reports, avoid providing the exact content of test items and/or paraphrasing or revising an item in such a way that the item is essentially the same as the original.

Focus on relevant information. You will likely sift through and collect a large amount of information in the process of conducting a special education eligibility evaluation. Instead of reporting on all information examined and collected, it is important to report only the most relevant information. In order to determine whether the information is relevant, ask yourself the following: (1) To what extent is the given information needed to answer the specific referral question? and (2) To what extent will the given information promote the provision of better educational services to the student? Include only those data that address these questions.

Clearly convey your level of certainty. The potential for error is always present. When reporting the results of tests, it is important to convey this potential. In the presentation of test scores, we suggest explaining and providing confidence intervals for reported scores in order to appropriately communicate the existence of error in testing.

Make data-based recommendations. The assessment summary and recommendations sections are by far the most frequently read sections of assessment reports. Recommendations are perhaps the most important aspect of reports; it is important that they are made very carefully and are clearly supported by the data collected. Although it is expected that the recommendation section will document what students need in order to ensure that they receive a free and appropriate public education, recommendations that are made carelessly and without adequate support can result in inefficient use of educational resources.

MAINTENANCE OF PUPIL INFORMATION

The decision to keep test results and other information should be governed by three principles: (1) retention of pupil information for limited periods of time, (2) parental rights of inspection and amendment, and (3) assurance of protection against inappropriate snooping. First, the information should be retained only as long as there is a continuing need for it. Only verified data of clear educational value should be retained. A pupil's school records should be periodically examined, and information that is no longer educationally relevant or no longer accurate should be removed. Natural transition points (for example, promotion from elementary school to junior high) should always be used to remove material from students' files.

The second major principle in the maintenance of pupil information is that parents have the right to inspect, challenge, and supplement student records. Parents of children with disabilities or with special gifts and talents have had the right to inspect, challenge, and supplement their children's school records for some time. Parents or guardians must be given the opportunity to examine all relevant records with respect to the identification, evaluation, and educational placement of the child and the free and appropriate public education of the child, and they must be given the opportunity to obtain an independent evaluation of the child. Again, if parents have complaints, they may request an impartial due process hearing to challenge either the records or the school's decision regarding their child.

The third major principle in the maintenance of pupil records is that the records should be protected from snoopers, both inside and outside the school system. In the past, secretaries, custodians, and even other students have had access, at least potentially, to pupil records. Curious teachers and administrators who had no legitimate educational interest had access. Individuals outside the schools, such as credit bureaus, have often found it easy to obtain information about former or current students. To ensure that only individuals with a legitimate need have access to the information contained in a pupil's records, it is recommended that pupil records be kept under lock and key. Adequate security mechanisms are necessary to ensure that the information in a pupil's records is not available to unauthorized personnel.

DISSEMINATION OF PUPIL INFORMATION

Educators need to consider both access to information by officials and dissemination of information to individuals and agencies outside the school. In both cases, the guiding principles are (1) the protection of pupils' and parents' rights to privacy and (2) the legitimate need to know particular information, as demonstrated by the person or agency to whom the information is disseminated.

Access Within the Schools

Those school professionals desiring access to pupil records must sign a form stating why they need to inspect the records. A list of people who have had access to their child's files and the reasons that access was sought should be available to parents. The provisions of FERPA as well as IDEA state that all persons, agencies, or organizations desiring access to the records of a student shall be required to sign a written form that shall be kept permanently with the file of the student, but only for inspection by the parents or student, indicating specifically the legitimate educational or other interest that each person, agency, or organization has in seeking this information (§438, 4A; §300.563).

When a pupil transfers from one school district to another, that pupil's records are also transferred. FERPA is very specific with regard to the conditions of transfer. When a pupil's file is transferred to another school or school system in which the pupil plans to enroll, the school must (1) notify the pupil's parents that the records have been transferred, (2) send the parents a copy of the transferred records if the parents so desire, and (3) provide the parents with an opportunity to challenge the content of the transferred data.

Access for Individuals and Agencies Outside the Schools

School personnel collect information about pupils enrolled in the school system for educationally relevant purposes. There is an implicit agreement between the schools and the parents that the only justification for collecting and keeping any pupil data is educational relevance. However, because the schools have so much information about pupils, they are often asked for pupil data by potential employers, credit agencies, insurance companies, police, the armed services, the courts, and various social agencies. To divulge information to any of these sources is a violation of this implicit trust unless the pupil (if older than 18 years) or the parents request that the information be released. However, many schools create forms that parents can sign to indicate their willingness for information to be exchanged about their child between the school and certain outside agencies. Note that the courts and various administrative agencies have the power to subpoena pupil records from schools. In such cases, FERPA requires that the parents be notified that the records will be turned over in compliance with the subpoena.

Except in the case of the subpoena of records or the transfer of records to another school district, no school personnel should release any pupil information without the written consent of the parents. FERPA states that no educational agency may release pupil information unless "there is written consent from the student's parents specifying records to be released, the reasons for such release, and to whom, and with a copy of the records to be released to the student's parents and the student if desired by the parents" (§438, b2A).

Electronic Communication

The increasing use of technology in schools has strong potential to promote student learning, as noted in Chapter 23. Large files containing student performance data can be maintained on computers and allow for more efficient analysis of student data. The use of e-mail can also greatly enhance the speed with which information is disseminated. However, with these advances also comes a need for guidelines to prevent misuse and mishandling of this information, given that such information can be more easily transmitted to those who do not have a right or a need to have the given information. Password protection systems should be developed and used to ensure that only those who have a legitimate need can access specific student information electronically (this includes password protecting flash drives or CDs). Separate identification codes should be developed and used rather than actual student names and identification numbers within large datasets that include sensitive information. Also, e-mail messages should be encrypted or worded in a way that avoids use of actual student names in order to prevent accidental transmission or forwarding to those who do not need the given information.

Chapter Comprehension Questions

Write your answers to each of the following questions and then compare your responses to the text.

1. Describe four characteristics of effective school teams.
2. Name and describe the functions of three types of teams commonly formed in school settings.
3. What are some potential barriers to communicating effectively about assessment with parents? What are some ways to overcome these barriers?
4. What are some ways in which assessment information is communicated in written form in schools? What are the rules governing who has access to this information?

Web Activities

1. Go to the Education CourseMate website for this textbook and examine the evaluation report examples provided there. To what extent do these reports represent the best practices for communication of assessment information? How could they be improved?
2. Search the Internet for materials that are available to parents about RTI/MTSS and evaluation of students for special education services. To what extent are these available in multiple languages?

Web Resources

Syracuse City School District School-Based Intervention Team Resources
http://www.lefthandlogic.com/htmdocs/interventions/sbit.php
This website provides materials used to facilitate the teaming process within the Syracuse, NY, City School District.

OSEP Toolkit on Teaching and Assessing Students with Disabilities, Parent Materials
www.osepideasthatwork.org/parentkit/index.asp
This website provides information about a variety of assessment issues in parent-friendly language.

TeachSource Video Case

Go to the Education CourseMate website to watch the video entitled, *Collaborating with School Specialists: An Elementary Literacy Lesson.*

1. What does the featured teacher find beneficial about his collaboration with the specialist?
2. Describe the approach the specialist uses in working with the featured teacher. What is it about her approach that encourages teachers to work with her?

Additional resources for this chapter can be found on the Education CourseMate website. Go to CengageBrain.com to access the site.

GLOSSARY

504 plan An accommodation plan that is developed to ensure a student with an educationally related disability who does not require special education services has appropriate access to participation during instruction and testing

abscissa The horizontal axis of a graph, representing the continuum on which individuals are measured

access Availability of an assessment to consumers

accommodation A change in testing materials or procedures that enables students to participate in assessments in ways that reflect their skills and abilities rather than their disabilities

accommodative ability The automatic adjustment of the eyes for seeing at different distances

accountability, accountability system The use of assessment results and other data to ensure that schools are moving in desired directions; common elements include standards, indicators of progress toward meeting those standards, analysis of data, reporting procedures, and rewards or sanctions

acculturation A child's particular set of background experiences and opportunities to learn in both formal and informal educational settings

acculturation pattern Used to describe how an individual adapts to a new culture, including the extent to which the individual maintains a connection with their native culture

accuracy Usually the percentage of a student's attempted responses that are correct; accuracy is most important during a student's acquisition of new information

accountability decision A decision about whether students are making the annual progress that is required by state and federal law

achievement What has been learned as a result of instruction

achievement standards Statements of the degree of mastery (such as "with 80 percent accuracy") that students are expected to demonstrate (same as performance standard)

achievement-standards referenced A type of test that involves ascertaining the degree to which students are meeting state and national standards, which specify the qualities and skills that competent learners need to demonstrate

achievement test A measure of what students have been taught and learned

acquisition deficit Failure to learn a particular skill

ADAA Americans with Disabilities Act Amendments of 2008

adaptations A generalized term that describes a change made in the presentation, setting, response, or timing or scheduling of an assessment that may or may not change the construct of the assessment

adaptive behavior Behavior that allows individuals to adapt themselves to the expectations of nature and society

adequate yearly progress (AYP) A provision of the federal No Child Left Behind (NCLB, 2001) legislation requiring schools, districts, and states to demonstrate that students are making academic progress based on test scores; each state was required by NCLB to submit by January 31, 2003, a specific plan for monitoring AYP

affective comprehension A reader's personal and emotional responses to the reading material

age equivalent A derived score that expresses a person's performance as the average (the median or mean) performance for that age group; age equivalents are expressed in years and months, with a hyphen used in age scores (e.g., 7-1 is 7 years, 1 month); an age-equivalent score is interpreted to mean that the test taker's performance is equal to the average performance of an X-year-old

aid An error in oral reading, recorded when a student hesitates for more than 10 seconds and the word or words are supplied by the teacher

aided observation Use of recording devices to allow for review of observations

aimline On a graph, a line connecting the point representing the level of performance and date when instruction begins to the point representing the desired or criterion level of performance and date when instruction is to end

algorithm The steps, processes, or procedures used for solving a problem or reaching a goal

alignment The similarity or match between or among content standards, performance standards, curriculum, instruction, and assessments in terms of knowledge and skill expectations

alternate achievement standards Expectations for performance that differ in complexity from a grade-level achievement standard but are linked to the content standards

alternate assessment Substitute way of gathering data, often by means of portfolio or performance measures; alternate assessments are intended for students with significant disabilities that keep them from participating in the regular assessment

alternate form reliability The correlation of student performance on multiple equivalent forms of the test

alternate forms Two tests that measure the same trait or skill to the same extent and that are standardized on the same population; alternate forms offer essentially equivalent tests and are sometimes called "equivalent forms"

Americans with Disabilities Act (ADA) A 1990 federal law which expands the definition of handicap and requires that people with disabilities have access and necessary accommodations so they can participate in a variety of services and events

amplitude The intensity of a behavior

assessment The process of collecting data for the purpose of (1) specifying and verifying problems, and (2) making decisions about students

assessment portfolio A portfolio in which the contents are rated to make an assessment of student progress

attainment What an individual has learned, regardless of where it has been learned

audiogram A graph of the results of the pure-tone threshold test

audiologist A professional trained and licensed to conduct hearing evaluations

audiometer An electronic device use to test a person's threshold for hearing sound

basal That item in a test below which it is assumed the student will get all items correct

basic interpersonal communication skills Language skills described by Cummins as those necessary for engaging in social conversations

behavioral contexts The array of setting events and discriminative stimuli that may be associated with demonstration of a particular behavior

behavioral observation Observation of spontaneous behavior, which has not been elicited by a predetermined and standardized set of stimuli (that is, not test behavior)

behavioral topography The way in which a behavior is performed

benchmark A specific statement of knowledge and skills within a content area's continuum that a student must possess to demonstrate a level of progress toward mastery of a standard

beneficence Responsible caring; educational professionals do things that are likely to maximize benefit to students, or at least do no harm

bimodal distribution A distribution that has two modes

biserial correlation coefficient An index of association between two variables, one of which has been forced into an arbitrary dichotomy (e.g., smart/dull) and one of which is equal interval (e.g., grade point average)

body of evidence Information or data that establish that a student can perform a particular skill or has mastered a specific content standard and that was either produced by the student or collected by someone who is knowledgeable about the student

capacity building Working with systems (community agencies, schools, families, churches, businesses, related services personnel) to help enhance student competence

cash validity The notion that frequently used tests are valid tests

Category A data The basic, minimum information schools need in order to operate an educational program, including identifying information, as well as information about a student's educational progress

Category B data Test results and other verified information useful to the schools in planning a student's educational program or maintaining a student safely in school

Category C data Information that may be potentially useful to schools, including any unverified information, scores on personality tests, etc.

Cattell-Horn-Carroll (CHC) theory A theory of intelligence that articulates intelligence as being composed of several factors

ceiling That item in a test above which it is assumed the student will fail all items

celeration Celeration is the slope of a trend line; the extent to which the trend of behavior is increasing or decreasing

celeration charts Charts based on the principle that changes (increases or decreases) in the frequency of behavior within a specified time (e.g., number of correct responses per minute) are multiplicative not additive; also called standard behavior charts, semilogarithmic charts, or seven cycle charts

central auditory hearing loss An inability to process or understand sounds in difficult hearing environments. Individuals with this type of loss may have normal air conduction hearing and middle ear functioning

child find The federal requirement that school entities conduct public awareness and screening activities to locate and serve all students with disabilities within their jurisdiction

classification A type of decision that concerns a pupil's eligibility for special services, special education services, remedial education services, speech services, etc.

classroom response systems Handheld devices, often called "clickers," that are used in class to simultaneously assess all students: students are presented with a multiple choice question, and click the responder to indicate their answer; teachers get an immediate graph or table showing all students' responses

clinical low vision An uncorrectable impairment resulting in poor acuity, reduction in visual field, distortion, and heightened light sensitivity

coefficient alpha The average split-half correlation based on all possible divisions of a test into two parts; coefficient alpha can be computed directly from the variances of individual test items and the variance of the total test score

cognitive academic language proficiency Language skills described by Cummins as those necessary to interact with most academic content.

common core standards The educational outcomes expected of all students by the U.S. government.

competence enhancement Helping students build those skills and behaviors that enable them to meet standards or achieve desired outcomes; basically, this involves helping students get better at what they do

comprehensive core standards Curricular goals established by federal and/or state regulations in any content area, but always in reading and mathematics

computer adaptive testing An assessment method whereby items are selected for administration based on the student's performance on earlier items within the test

computer-generated reports A feature of many standardized tests in which a report is generated based on data about the student that the examiner enters into the computer; when used to inform special education eligibility, these decisions may not allow for appropriate tailoring based on individual characteristics and needs

computerized scoring A feature of many standardized tests that has the potential to increase efficiency and accuracy in scoring; an examiner enters student responses and the computer calculates scores

concurrent criterion-related validity A measure of how accurately a person's current test score can be used to estimate a score on a criterion measure

conductive hearing loss Abnormal hearing associated with poor air-conduction sensitivity but normal bone-conduction sensitivity

confidence interval The range of scores within which a person's true score will fall with a given probability

construct validity A measure of the extent to which a test measures a theoretical trait or characteristic

consultation A meeting between a resource teacher or other specialist and a classroom teacher to verify the existence of a problem, specify the nature of the problem, and develop strategies that might relieve the problem

content specificity The degree to which the items or facts with a curriculum are assessed; instead of identifying mathematics content as "addition," it is delineated as 4 + 3, 2 + 7, etc.

content standard Statement of the specific content or skills that students are expected to have mastered at a specific point in time

content validity A measure of the extent to which a test is an adequate measure of the content it is designed to cover; content validity is established by examining three factors: the appropriateness of the types of items included, the comprehensiveness of the item sample, and the way in which the items assess the content

continuous recording A way to record behavior in which the observer counts each occurrence of a behavior in the observation session; the duration or latency of each occurrence within the observation session can be timed

continuous technology-enhanced measures Computer-administered tests that are used in continuous (ongoing or daily) progress monitoring

contrived observations An observation in which a situation is set up before a student is introduced into it

correlation A measure of the degree of relationship between two or more variables; a correlation indicates the extent to which any two variables go together—that is, the extent to which changes in one variable are reflected by changes in the second variable

correlation coefficient A numerical index of the relationship between two or more variables

criterion-referenced test Test that measures a person's skills in terms of absolute levels of mastery

criterion-related validity A measure of the extent to which a person's score on a criterion measure can be estimated from that person's score on a test of unknown validity

critical comprehension Analyzing, evaluating, and making judgments about material read

crystallized intelligence (*gc*) General knowledge and skill that an individual acquires over time (compare with **fluid intelligence**)

curriculum-based assessment Use of assessment materials and procedures that mirror instruction in order to ascertain whether specific instructional objectives have been accomplished, and monitor progress directly in the curriculum being taught

curriculum-based evaluation (CBE) A decision-making framework to guide data collection and analysis that can inform instruction

curriculum-based measurement (CBM) A standardized set of procedures that are brief and intended to ascertain student progress in the development of basic academic skills

curriculum match The degree to which curricular content is assessed by a test and vice versa

cut score A specified point on a score scale; scores at or above that point are interpreted differently from scores below that point (also called a cutoff score)

daily living skills A domain measured within the Vineland Adaptive Behavior Scales, 2nd edition that consists of personal, domestic, and community living skills

data-driven decision making Decisions which are decided by objectively measured student performances

decile A band of percentiles that is 10 percentile ranks in width; each decile contains 10 percent of the norm group

decision-making rules Rules commonly applied to progress monitoring results to inform the need for instructional change

derived score A general term for a raw score that is transformed to a developmental score or to a score of relative standing

descriptive statistics Numerical values, such as mean, standard deviation, or correlation, that describe a data set

developmental age A test score expressed as an age equivalent; the score represents the average score earned by individuals of a specific age

developmental equivalent A type of derived score in which raw scores are converted to the mean or median for a particular age or grade (e.g., a grade equivalent expresses a test taker's raw score as the mean of a school grade; a grade equivalent of 7.0 means that the raw score was the mean of students in the beginning of seventh grade. An age equivalent of 7-0 means that the raw score was the mean of seven-year-old test takers. Age equivalents are also sometimes divided by chronological age to create a developmental quotient.)

developmental milestones Significant developmental accomplishments (such as using words and walking) commonly used to determine whether infants and toddlers are developing as expected

developmental score A raw score that has been transformed into age equivalent (AE) (e.g., mental age), grade equivalent, or developmental quotient

deviation IQ A standard score with a mean of 100 and a standard deviation of 15 or 16 (depending on the test)

deviation score The distance between an individual's score and the average score for the group, such as *z*-scores and *T*-scores

diagnostic achievement test A test designed to identify a student's specific skill development strengths and weaknesses

diagnostic report A report commonly generated by technology-enhanced assessment programs that can provide data on individual students, classrooms, schools, and districts

disaggregation The collection and reporting of student achievement results by particular subgroups (e.g., students with disabilities, limited-English-proficient students) to ascertain the subgroup's academic progress; disaggregation makes it possible to compare subgroups or cohorts

discrepancy A difference between two scores or a score and a standard or criterion

discriminative stimulus A stimulus that is consistently present when a behavior is reinforced and that elicits the behavior even in the absence of the original reinforcer

disregard of punctuation An error in oral reading in which a student fails to give appropriate inflection in response to punctuation; e.g., a student may not pause for a comma, stop for a period, or indicate voice inflection at a question mark or exclamation point

distractor An incorrect option contained in a response set

distribution The way in which scores in a set array themselves; a distribution may be graphed to demonstrate visually the relations among the scores in the group or set

due process A constitutional guarantee that the various procedures specified in federal and state regulations will be followed in legal and quasi legal proceedings

due process provisions A set of legal provisions specifying that schools and the personnel who work in schools must respect all the rights that students are entitled to as persons; specifically, IDEA includes specification of steps school personnel must go through before assessing or changing the placement of students, or resolving conflicting opinion between school personnel and parents

duration The length of time a behavior lasts

ecobehaviorial assessment Observations of functional relationships between student behavior and ecological or environmental factors (What environmental factors are related to specific student behaviors?); enables educators to identify natural instructional conditions that are associated with academic success, behavioral competence, or problem behaviors

ecobehavioral observation Observation targeting the interaction among student behavior, teacher behavior, time allocated to instruction, physical grouping structures, the types of tasks being used, and instructional content

ecology Mutual relationships between organisms and their environments

Education for all Handicapped Children Act Public Law 94-142, passed in 1975, was the first national comprehensive federal law governing how special education must be provided to every student with a disability

Elementary and Secondary Education Act of 2001 See No Child Left Behind

efficiency The speed and economy with which data are collected

eligibility decision The decision that determines if a person has met the criteria to receive certain services or benefits

English language accommodation A change in a test for an English language learner that involves providing support using the English language

English language learner (ELL) An individual who is acquiring the English language and has a non-English primary language

entitlement In special education, the right to a free and appropriate education, related services, and due process

equal-interval scale A scale in which the differences between adjacent values are equal, but in which there is no absolute or logical zero

error Misrepresentation of a person's score as a result of failure to obtain a representative sample of times, items, or scorers

estimated true scores The best estimate of the score a person would receive on a test if there were no error of measurement

ethnographic observation Observation in which the observer does not participate in what is occurring

etiology The cause of a disorder

evidence-based An assessment or instructional approach that has been shown through research to be effective

expectancy The tendency of an observer to see behaviors consistent with her or his beliefs about what should happen

expressive language The production of language

extended responses A testing format in which student response is in the form of an essay; typically it is most useful for testing comprehension, application, analysis, synthesis, and evaluation objectives

externalizing problems Problems in social–emotional functioning that are characterized by aggressive and acting-out behavior

evidence-based instructional practice See "evidence-based" practice

Family Educational Rights and Privacy Act (FERPA) Federal legislation that describes parental rights to inspect and challenge student records, as well as the rights associated with maintaining privacy of the student's records

fluency The rate and automaticity with which an individual can complete a given task

fluid intelligence (*gc*) The efficiency with which an individual learns and completes various tasks (compare with **crystallized intelligence**)

focal points A small number of mathematical topics that should be focused on at each grade level and serve as areas teachers should focus on; the National Council of Teachers of Mathematics published a document detailing these topics

formative assessment Administration of a continuous or periodic tests and use of the test results to adjust teaching or learning while they are happening

formative evaluation Ongoing frequent evaluation as the thing being evaluated is occurring; in instructional evaluation, collection of data as instruction is occurring

free operant A test situation that presents more problems than a student can answer in the given time period

frequency The tabulation of the number of behaviors with discrete beginnings and endings that occur in a predetermined time frame; when the time periods in which the behavior is counted vary, frequencies are usually converted to rates

frustration level Usually accuracy that is less than 85 percent correct; when a student is performing at frustration level, the material is too difficult

functional behavioral assessment Collecting data in order to identify the function of a student's problematic behavior, which is then used to inform the development of an intervention

function of behavior The reason a person behaves as he or she does, or the purpose the behavior serves

functional vision The use of vision spontaneously that depends on the interactions among visual disabilities (poor acuity), individual differences (e.g., stamina), and environmental factors (e.g., lighting)

general outcome measure (GOM) A measure that can be administered on a frequent basis and used to measure student progress toward long-term goals

goal line On a progress monitoring chart, a line that connects a student's baseline performance level with a goal performance level to show an expected rate of growth over time

grade equivalent A derived score that expresses a student's performance as the average (the median or mean) performance for a particular grade; grade equivalents are expressed in grades and tenths of grades, with a decimal point used in grade scores (e.g., 7.1 is grade 7 and one-tenth)

graphomotor skills In education, the skills associated with printing or writing such as letter writing and spacing

gross mispronunciation An error in oral reading in which a student's pronunciation of a word is in no way similar to the word in the text

groupthink When decisions are made by a team of individuals, the tendency to agree with the majority opinion and fail to bring up important alternate ideas

halo effect The tendency of an observer to make subjective judgments on the basis of general attributes, such as race or social class

handheld observation system Observational systems available for personal digital assistants (PDA) that can facilitate observation of classroom behavior

harassment Behavior that is intended to disturb, offend, or upset another.

Head Start/Early Head Start Established in 1995, early Head Start is a federal program for low-income families intended to promote healthy pregnancies, child development, and family functioning

hesitation An error in oral reading in which a student pauses for two or more seconds before pronouncing a word

histogram A representation of frequency distribution by means of rectangles whose widths are class intervals and whose areas are proportional to corresponding frequencies

historical information Information that describes how a person has functioned in the past

holistic evaluation An appraisal made of a product as whole without separate evaluations made of component parts

honing-in phase A preliminary review to see if a test meets general criteria, such as the right age student, the necessary examiner qualifications

inclusive education Education of people with and without disabilities in the same classes or school environments

independent level Usually accuracy that is 95 percent or higher

indicator The symbolic representation of one or more outcomes that can be used to make comparisons among students or schools

Individuals with Disabilities Education Improvement Act (IDEA) The 2004 revisions to the Individuals with Disabilities Education Act

Individuals with Disabilities Education Act The primary federal legislation governing special and related services education in the United States

individual consent Consent by parent (or pupil) required for the collection of family information (religion, income, occupation, and so on), personality data, and other noneducational information

individualized education program (IEP) A document that specifies the long- and short-term goals of an instructional program, where the program will be delivered, who will deliver the program, and how progress will be evaluated

Individual Growth and Developmental Indicators (IGDIs) Individual Growth and Developmental Indicators consist of a few important items that repeatedly assessed during an early intervention to assess a youngster's progress

inferential comprehension Interpreting, synthesizing, or extending the information that is explicit in the reading material

informal assessment Any assessment that involves collection of data by anything other than a norm-referenced (standardized) test

informal reading inventory (IRI) Usually a test without a normative sample, consisting of graded reading passages and vocabulary words that span a wide range of skill levels; IRIs are used to assess decoding and comprehension in order to locate the level at which a student reads at an instructional level (with about 90 percent accuracy)

informed consent Consent that a parent or a student gives for the collection or dissemination of information not directly relevant and essential to the child's education; the assumption underlying the notion of informed consent is that the parent (or pupil) is "reasonably competent to understand the nature and consequences of his [or her] decision" (Goslin, 1969, p. 17)

insertion An error in oral reading in which a student inappropriately adds one or more words to the sentence being read

instructional ecology Relationships between students and their instructional environments

instructional environment Those contexts in which learning takes place (schools, classrooms, homes), as well as the interface of essential contexts for children's learning (home–school relationships)

Instructional Groupings Report Part of STAR Math, this report suggests which students should be grouped together for instruction

instructional level Usually accuracy that is between 85 and 95 percent correct

instructional match Instruction that is matched to a student's specific level of skill development

instructional planning decisions There are three instructional planning decisions: what should the student be taught, how should the student be taught, and what levels of attainment should be expected

intelligence An inferred ability; a term or construct used to explain differences in present behavior and to predict differences in future behavior

intelligence factors Components that are considered to be part of intelligence

interinterviewer reliability The extent to which multiple interviewers who rate behavior of an individual based on interviews with a respondent at different times rate the individual's behavior similarly

internal consistency A measure of the extent to which items in a test correlate with one another

internalizing problems Problems in social–emotional functioning that are characterized by withdrawn, anxious, or depressed behaviors

interobserver agreement The extent to which results can be generalized to different observers, which is determined by having two observers provide scores/ratings, and then determining either percent agreement or the correlation between scores/ratings

interrespondent reliability The extent to which multiple respondents who indirectly rate behavior of an individual based on cumulative exposure to the individual rate the behavior similarly

interscorer reliability An estimate of the degree of agreement between two or more scores on the same test

intervention assistance team (IAT) A group of teachers (and sometimes other professionals, such as school psychologists or speech–language pathologists) who meet to review student difficulties, try to ascertain the kinds of interventions to implement to try to alleviate difficulties in the regular classroom, and monitor the extent to which the interventions work; sometimes called "mainstream assistance team" or "prereferral team"

intervention integrity The fidelity with which an intervention is applied. Was the intervention conducted as intended?

inversion An error in oral reading in which a student says the words in an order different from the order in which they are written

Iowa problem-solving model A systematic process used to assess and intervene on behalf of students with academic and behavioral problems

IQs Intelligence quotients

item reliability The extent to which one can assume that performance on a set of items can generalize to performance on other items within the domain

keyed response The correct answer in a response set

KR-20 An estimate of the internal consistency of a test when test items are scored dichotomously

kurtosis The peakedness of a curve, or the rate at which a curve rises

language A code for conveying ideas; although there is some variation, language theorists propose five basic components to describe the code: phonology, semantics, morphology, syntax, and pragmatics

language mechanics Punctuation and capitalization

latency The amount of time between a signal to initiate the behavior and the actual beginning of the behavior

LEARN Literacy Education for All, Results for the Nation Act, part of the Elementary and Secondary Education Act of 2010

least restrictive environment The specification in IDEA that to the maximum extent appropriate students with disabilities are to be educated with children who are not disabled, and that they should be removed to separate classes, schools, or elsewhere only when the nature or severity of their disability is such that education in regular classes with the use of supplementary aids and services cannot be achieved satisfactorily

leptokurtic curve A fast-rising curve; tests that do not spread out (or discriminate among) those taking the test are typically leptokurtic

lexical comprehension Knowing the meaning of key vocabulary words

Likert scale A technique in which a set of attitude statements is presented and respondents are asked to express degree of agreement or disagreement, usually on a five- or seven-point scale ranging from *strongly agree* to *strongly disagree*; each degree of agreement is given a numerical value, and a total numerical value can be calculated from all the responses

limited English proficiency (LEP) Used to describe an individual who has a native language other than English, such that it affects the individual's ability to learn in an English-speaking classroom

literal comprehension Understanding information that is explicit in the reading material

maladaption Behavior that does not promote surviving and thriving as an individual; often, it is determined based on context, age, and social/cultural expectations; an absence of this is sometimes used in definitions of adaptive behavior

mandated tests Tests that are administered as a result of legislation

mastery Usually accuracy that equals or exceeds 90 to 95 percent correct

mean The arithmetic average of scores in a distribution

measurement error The difference between observed score and true score; the distribution of measurement error can be determined using the test's standard deviation and reliability

median A score that divides the top 50 percent of test takers from the bottom 50 percent; the point on a scale above which 50 percent of the cases (not the scores) occur and below which 50 percent of the cases occur

metalinguistic Relating to the direct examination of the structural aspects of language
mixed hearing loss Abnormal hearing attributed to abnormal bone conduction and even more abnormal air conduction
mode The most frequently obtained score in a distribution
modified achievement standards Expectations for performance that are lower than the grade-level achievement standards, but linked to or aligned with the content standards; this term will be further defined by policy makers in the near future
momentary time sampling A procedure used in systematic observation to determine when observations will occur; a behavior is scored as an occurrence if it is present at the last moment of an observation interval; if the behavior is not occurring at the last moment of the interval, a nonoccurrence is recorded
morphology The use of affixes (prefixes and suffixes) to change the meaning of words used in sentences
multidisciplinary team A general description for a group of educators from a variety of backgrounds and a student's parent or parents who make various educational decisions on behalf of the student. The composition of some multidisciplinary teams (e.g., IEP teams) are specified by law; the membership on other teams (e.g., student assistance teams) are determined locally
multi-tiered system of supports (MTSS) (Chapter 1) A service delivery model in which increasing intensive interventions (supports) are provided to students who exhibit greater and greater needs
multiple gating A method for conducting assessment that involves screening, followed by increasingly comprehensive assessment for students who are identified to be at-risk
multiple-skill battery A test that measures skill development in several achievement areas

native language accommodation A change in a test for an English language learner that involves providing support using a student's native language
naturalistic observations Observations that occur in settings that are not contrived
NCTM Standards Math standards and results specified by the National Council of Teachers of Mathematics
need for special education One of two criteria for special education eligibility. Need is established by a student's failure to respond to validated interventions or when a successful intervention is too intensive or extensive to be implemented in a regular education classroom
procedural safeguards Federal requirements for guaranteeing that the parental and student rights are not violated during all special education processes
negatively skewed distribution An asymmetric distribution in which scores tail off to the low end of the continuum; a distribution in which there are more scores above the mean than below it
No Child Left Behind Act (NCLB) The primary federal legislation governing elementary and secondary education in the United States
nominal scale A scale of measurement in which there is no inherent relationship among adjacent values
nondiscriminatory assessment As provided in special education law, nondiscriminatory assessments are those that do not penalize students for their disabilities unless the assessment is specifically intended to measure performance in the area of disability. For example, students who are blind should not fail a math test because they cannot read the test (e.g., it can be given orally), but it is not discriminatory if the test assesses the ability to read billboards
nonsystematic observation Observation in which the observer notes behaviors, characteristics, and personal interactions that seem of significance
nonverbal tests Tests, such as some intelligence tests, where students can understand and respond to items without verbal language
normal-curve equivalent Standard score with a mean equal to 100 and a standard deviation equal to 21.06
normative sample (norm group) A group of subjects of known demographic characteristics (age, gender, grade in school, and so on) to whom a person's performance may be compared
normative update The restandardization of a test by giving it to a new norm sample without changing the test items
norm group See **standardization sample**
norms In assessment, the group of students to whom a person's tested performance is compared and from which various descriptive statistics are calculated
norm-referenced device Test that compares an individual's performance to the performance of his or her peers

objective-referenced assessment Tests referenced to specific instructional objectives rather than to the performance of a peer group or norm group
objective scoring Scoring that is based on observable qualities and not influenced by emotion, guess, or personal bias
observation The process of gaining information through one's senses—visual, auditory, etc.; observation can be used to assess behavior, states, physical characteristics, and permanent products of behavior (such as a child's poem)
obtrusive observations Observations in which it is obvious to the person being observed that they are being observed
omission An error in oral reading in which a student skips a word or a group of words
operationalize To define a behavior or event in terms of the operations used to measure it; e.g., an operational definition of intelligence would be a score on a specific intelligence test
ophthalmologist A medical doctor who specializes in diseases and conditions of the eye
oral reading A skill often measured in diagnostic reading tests; students are asked to read a series of passages and the examiner takes note of fluency, accuracy, errors, and other characteristics of reading quality
oral reading errors Instances in which a student misreads a printed word

ordinal scale A scale on which values of measurement are ordered from best to worst or from worst to best; on ordinal scales, the differences between adjacent values are unknown

ordinate The vertical axis of a graph of a distribution, showing the frequency (or the number) of individuals earning any given score

outcome The result of interactions between individuals and schooling experiences

out-of-level test A lower- or higher-level test that is judged appropriate for the student's developmental level rather than the student's age/grade level

partial-interval recording A procedure used in systematic observation in which an occurrence is scored if the behavior occurs during any part of the interval

partial-interval sampling A time sampling procedure in which a behavior is scored as present if it occurs at any part in the time interval

partial mispronunciation One of several kinds of errors in oral reading, including partial pronunciation, phonetic mispronunciation of part of the word, omission of part of the word, or insertion of elements of words

participant–observer observation Observation in which the observer joins the target social group and participates in its activities

Pearson product-moment correlation coefficient (*r*) An index of the straight-line (linear) relationship between two or more variables measured on an equal-interval scale

peer acceptance nomination scales Scales that provide an indication of an individual's social status and may help describe the attitude of a particular group (such as the class) toward a target student

penmanship The formation of individual letters and letter sequences that make up words

percent correct The number correct divided by either the number attempted or the total number

percentile rank (percentile) Derived score that indicates the percentage of people whose scores are at or below a given raw score; percentiles are useful for both ordinal and equal-interval scales

perception Any ability or skill involving the interaction of perception and voluntary movement (e.g., typing)

perceptual–motor skills Motor behavior (usually fine motor) that is regulated by perception (usually visual) such as drawing

performance deficit A particular skill that has been learned, but is not used appropriately

performance standard A statement of the degree of mastery (such as "with 80 percent accuracy") that students are expected to demonstrate

periodic technology-enhanced measures Computer-administered tests that are used in periodic (biweekly, monthly, quarterly) progress monitoring

phi coefficient An index of linear correlation between two sets of naturally dichotomous variables (e.g., male/female, dead/alive)

phonology The hearing and production of speech sounds

platykurtic curve A curve that is flat and slow rising

point biserial correlation coefficient An index of linear correlation between one naturally occurring dichotomous variable (such as gender) and a continuous, equal-interval variable (such as height measured in inches)

point-to-point agreement A method of determining inter-observer agreement, calculated by dividing the number of observations where both observers agree (occurrence and nonoccurrence) by the total number of observations and multiplying the quotient by 100

portfolio A collection of products that provide a basis for judging student accomplishment; in school settings, portfolios typically contain extended projects and may also contain drafts, teacher comments and evaluations, and self-evaluations

positively skewed distribution An asymmetrical distribution in which scores tail off to the higher end of the continuum; a distribution in which there are more scores below the mean than above it

power test An untimed test in which the interest is in how many items a student can complete correctly

pragmatics The social context in which language occurs

predictive criterion-related validity A measure of the extent to which a person's current test scores can be used to estimate accurately what that person's criterion scores will be at a later time

prereferral Activities that occur prior to formal referral, assessment, and consideration for placement; the goal of prereferral and intervention is twofold: (1) verification and specification of the nature of a student's difficulties and (2) provision of services in the least restrictive environment

prereferral assessment An evaluation made prior to referral to a multidisciplinary team to determine eligibility for special education and related services

prereferral intervention Instruction or intervention made prior to referral to a multidisciplinary team to determine eligibility for special education and related services

prereview A preliminary survey of what is available prior to conducting a more extensive review

presentation accommodation A change in how a test is presented that facilitates appropriate testing of an individual student

probe A special testing format that is well suited to the assessment of direct performances; probes are brief (usually three minutes or less), timed, frequently administered assessments that can be used for any purpose

procedural safeguards Federal requirements for guaranteeing that the parental and student rights are not violated during all special education processes

process (or processing) deficits Low, absent, or aberrant ability to act mentally on sensory information. Deficits in cognitive functioning that are sometimes used in definitions of learning disabilities

process standards Statements of the specific processes students should go through in solving problems

professional judgment The conclusions or judgments made by another professional (e.g., an MD or physical therapist) about a student

prognosis A prediction of future performance

program evaluation decision A decision about the degree to which a student's curriculum, methods, and materials have resulted in the desired level (generally improvement) of performance

progress monitoring The collection of data that is used to determine the impact of instruction and intervention over a short period of time

progress monitoring decision A decision about the extent to which a student is attaining individual goals or other standards

protection in evaluation procedures provisions The specification in IDEA that assessment procedures and activities must be fair, equitable, and nondiscriminatory

"prove it" mind-set A skeptical attitude whereby one requires clear evidence for assertions made in test materials

Public Law, 94-142 See Education for All Handicapped Children Act of 1975

qualitative data Information consisting of nonsystematic and unquantified observations

qualitative observation A description of behavior, its function, and its context; the observer begins without preconceived ideas about what will be observed and describes behavior that seems important

quantitative data Observations that have been tabulated or otherwise given numerical values

quantitative observation A type of observation that is focused on quantification of a specific behavior, with procedures for recording that behavior at selected times and in selected places

quartile A band of percentiles that is 25 percentile ranks in width; each quartile contains 25 percent of the norm group

random error In measurement, sources of variation in scores that make it impossible to generalize from an observation of a specific behavior observed at a specific time by a specific person to observations conducted on similar behavior, at different times, or by different observers

range The distance between the extremes in a set of scores, including those extremes; the highest score less the lowest score, plus one

rate The number of responses per minute; rate measures are thought to indicate a student's fluency or automaticity of response

rate of reading Often used to measure reading skill; tells how quickly and automatically a student can decode words

rating scale A standardized assessment procedure whereby behavior, states, or feelings are quantified; most rating scales rely on ordinal measurement of recalled observations

ratio IQ A derived score based on mental age (MA), in relation to chronological age (CA), in which IQ equals

$$\frac{\text{MA (in months)}}{\text{CA (in months)}} \times 100$$

ratio scale A scale of measurement in which the difference between adjacent values is equal and in which there is a logical and absolute zero

raw score The quantified evaluation of a test item or group of test items such as right or wrong on a specific item, or the number of right or wrong items on a student's test; in standardized testing, raw scores are usually transformed to derived scores

readiness The extent of preparation to participate in an activity; most often refers to readiness to enter school, but applies to all levels

receptive language The comprehension of language

recollections In assessment, memories of a person's behavior, skills, and conditions that are elicited through rating scales or interviews and incorporated into an evaluation

referral A request for help from a specialist; e.g., a teacher or parent may refer a student to a specialist who can provide the student with an appropriate educational program

reliability In measurement, the extent to which it is possible to generalize from an observation of a specific behavior observed at a specific time by a specific person to observations conducted on similar behavior, at different times, or by different observers

reliability coefficient An index of the extent to which observations can be generalized; the square of the correlation between obtained scores and true scores on a measure r^2_{xt}

repetition An error in oral reading in which a student repeats words or groups of words

representational consent Consent to collect data, given by appropriately elected officials such as members of a state legislature

resource allocation decision A decision about whether a student requires more supports than are found in general education classrooms These supports may be people (e.g., teachers or aides) or materials (i.e., curricula, technology, or aids)

respondent A person who is relied on to provide judgment about behavior based on cumulative observations

RTI (response to instruction) How students respond to core instruction or universal programming (the everyday instruction that occurs for students)

response accommodation A change in how a student may respond to a test that facilitates appropriate testing of that student

response to intervention Students' responses when substantial changes are made in regular classroom instruction

retention The percentage of correct responses recalled following learning; also called "maintenance," "recall," or "memory"

sample A representative subset of a population

scheduling accommodation A change in the scheduling of a test that facilitates appropriate testing of an individual student

schoolwide assistance teams A team of school professionals developed to work together in order to promote better outcomes for all students at the school

scoring rubric An ordinal scale used to rate a product; rubrics typically use verbal descriptions to anchor the end intermediate points of the scale

scotoma A visionless spot in the eye

screening An initial stage of assessment in which those who may exhibit a particular problem, disorder, disability, or disease are discriminated from the general population

screening decision The decision, based on the results of some form of evaluation (usually a test), that a student does or does not require a follow up evaluation by a specialist to determine if a student has the problem for which he or she was screened; for example, a student who does not pass a vision screen is referred to an eye doctor

Section 504 of the Rehabilitation Act of 1973 This federal laws requires that individuals with handicaps have equal access to services and programs funded by the federal government

selection format A method of presenting test questions in which students indicate their choice from an array of the possible test answers (usually called "response options"); true-false, multiple-choice, and matching are the three most common selection formats

semantics The study of word meanings; although the scope of the term can extend beyond individual words to include sentence meaning, the term generally applies to words

sensitivity An assessment procedure's capacity to detect small differences among or within students

sensorineural hearing loss Abnormal hearing associated with both poor bone-conduction sensitivity and poor air-conduction sensitivity

setting accommodation A change in the testing environment that facilitates appropriate testing of an individual student

setting event An environmental event that sets the occasion for the performance of an action

showcase portfolio A collection of work intended to show a person's best or most representative work (however defined)

simple agreement A method of determining interobserver agreement, calculated by dividing the smaller number of occurrences by the larger number of occurrences and multiplying the quotient by 100

single-skill test A test designed to measure skill development in one specific content area (e.g., reading)

skew Asymmetry in a distribution; the distribution of scores below the mean is not a mirror image of the distribution above the mean

skill-based measure (SBM) A measure that can be administered on a frequent basis and used to measure progress toward skill mastery

Snellen chart A wall chart that is used to assess visual acuity; a person stands 20 feet away from the chart and attempts to read lines of random letters

social comparison Observing a peer whose behavior is considered to be appropriate and using the peer's rate of behavior as the standard against which to evaluate the target student's rate of behavior

social skills and relationships A domain measured within the Vineland Adaptive Behavior Scales, second edition that consists of Relating to Others, Playing and Using Leisure Time, and Adapting

social tolerance The threshold above which behaviors are viewed as undesirable by others

social validity A consumer's access to and satisfaction with an intervention or assessment

sociometric ranking Provides an indication of an individual's social status and may help describe the attitude of a particular group (such as the class) toward a target student

Spearman rho An index of correlation between two variables measured on an ordinal scale

specificity see content specificity

speed test A timed test

spelling The formation of words from letters according to accepted usage

split-half reliability estimate An estimate of internal-consistency reliability derived by correlating people's scores on two halves of a test

stability The degree to test scores remain the same or fluctuate over time

stability coefficient Another name for test-retest reliability coefficient; quantifies the consistency of scores over time

standard deviation A measure of the degree of dispersion in a distribution; the square root of the variance

standard error of measurement (SEM) The standard deviation of error around a person's true score

standardization sample The group of individuals on whom a test is standardized; also called "the norm group"

standards Statements of desired goals or outcomes

standard score The general name for a derived score that has been transformed to produce a distribution with a predetermined mean and standard deviation

standards referenced Standards referenced achievement test items are associated with specific educational outcomes (standards) that comprise a state's curriculum standards for elementary and secondary education.

stanine Short for *standard nines*; a standard-score band that divides a distribution into nine parts; the middle seven stanines are each 0.50 standard deviation wide, and the fifth stanine is centered on the mean

status of the class report Part of STAR Math, this report provides the status of students in a class, a list of students who need assignments or help with two or more practice objectives, and the objectives that are causing difficulty for two or more students

stem In selection formats, the part of a problem that contains the question

student accountability The idea that consequences exist for individual students, and are based on their individual assessment performance; for example, students might not be promoted to the next grade or graduate if their assessment results do not meet a prespecified level

subjective evaluation An appraisal not made on the basis of objective, verifiable evidence and/or criteria

subjective scoring Scoring that is not based on observable qualities but relies on personal impressions and private criteria

subskill mastery measure (SMM) A measure that can be administered on a frequent basis and used to measure whether a student has mastered a particular subskill

substitution An error in oral reading in which a student replaces one or more words in the passage with one or more meaningful words (synonyms)

supply format A method of presenting test questions in which a student is required to produce a written or oral response; this response can be as restricted as a number or a word and can be as extensive as a sentence, a paragraph, or several pages of written response

supralinguistics A second order of analysis required to understand the meaning of words or sentences

syntax Word order of sentences; includes a description of the rules for arranging the words into a sentence

system accountability The idea that consequences exist for school systems, and are based on the assessment performance of a group of individuals (e.g., school building, district, or state education agency); for example, a school might receive a financial award or special recognition for having a large percent of students meeting a particular assessment performance level

systematic bias A type of error that can threaten validity; it can consist of the method of measurement, enabling behaviors, differential item effectiveness, systematic administration errors, and unrepresentative norms

systematic error A consistent error that can be predicted; bias

systematic observation Observation in which an observer specifies or defines the behaviors to be observed and then counts or otherwise measures the frequency, duration, magnitude, or latency of the behaviors

targeted supports help provided to students beyond what is typically provided to students in general

test A predetermined set of questions or tasks to which predetermined types of behavioral responses are sought

test purposes The types of decisions and activities for which a test is claimed to be useful

testing Administering a particular set of questions to an individual or group of individuals in order to obtain a score

testing formats The methods by which test items are presented and responded to

test-retest reliability An index of stability over time

test translation A test that was developed in one language and converted into another language

tetrachoric correlation coefficient An index of correlation between two arbitrarily dichotomized variables (e.g., tall/short, smart/dull)

topography of behavior The way a behavior is performed

TOPS report Part of STAR Math, *The Opportunity to Praise Sheet* is the computer generated feedback for student worksheets

transformed score A special form of z-score that allows the transformation of a z-score to a distribution defined by the user:

$$\text{Transformed score} = \text{Mean} + (z^{*}\text{Standard deviation})$$

where the z-score is computed from existing data and the mean and standard deviation are defined according to the needs of the user

trendline On a progress monitoring chart, a line that represents the student's actual growth

true score The score that a student would earn if the entire domain of items was assessed

T-score A standard score with a mean of 50 and a standard deviation of 10

tunnel vision Normal central visual acuity with a restricted peripheral field

tympanometry An assessment energy transmission through the tympanum (eardrum) and the ability of the bones of the middle ear to conduct sound

universal design for assessment The design of assessment programs that involves consideration of the needs of all participants

universal screening Assessments performed on all students to locate those who may have a problem; examples of universal screening include checking all students for head lice and performing a visual screen on all students

unobtrusive observations An observation in which the people being observed do not realize they are being watched

validity The extent to which a test measures what its authors or users claim it measures; specifically, test validity concerns the appropriateness of the inferences that can be made on the basis of test results

validity coefficient A coefficient that measures the correlation between a test of unknown validity and an established criterion measure

variance A numerical index describing the dispersion of a set of scores around the mean of the distribution; specifically, the average squared distance of the scores from the mean

visual acuity The clarity or sharpness with which a person sees

visual discrimination The ability to see the difference between two or more objects

visual–motor integration See perceptual–motor skills

whole-interval recording A procedure used in systematic observation in which an occurrence is scored if the behavior is present throughout the entire observation interval

whole-interval sampling A time sampling procedure in which a behavior is scored as present only when it occurs throughout the entire time interval

word-attack skills Skills used to derive the pronunciation or meaning of a word through phonic analysis, structural analysis, or context cues

word recognition skills Used to refer to skills in recognizing words by sight rather than through use of word attack skills

writing style Rule-governed writing, which includes grammar (e.g., verb tense and use) and mechanics (e.g., punctuation and capitalization)

***z*-score** Standard score with a mean of 0 and a standard deviation of 1

REFERENCES

Achenbach, T. M. (1986). *The Direct Observation Form (DOF)*. Burlington: University of Vermont, Department of Psychiatry.

Achenbach, T. M., & Rescorla, L. A. (2000). *Manual for the ASEBA Preschool Forms and Profiles*. Burlington: University of Vermont, Department of Psychiatry.

Achenbach, T. M., & Rescorla, L. A. (2001). *Manual for the ASEBA School-Age Forms and Profiles*. Burlington: University of Vermont, Department of Psychiatry.

Adams, M. (1990). *Beginning to read: Thinking and learning about print.* Cambridge, MA: MIT Press.

AIMSweb (2010). *Research*. [Retrieved at http://www.aimsweb.com/research/articles/]

Alberto, P. A., & Troutman, A. C. (2005). *Applied behavior analysis for teachers* (7th ed.). Upper Saddle River, NJ: Prentice-Hall.

American Association for the Advancement of Science. (1987). *Science for all Americans*. New York: Oxford University Press.

American Association for the Advancement of Science. (1993). *Benchmarks for science literacy*. New York: Oxford University Press.

American Educational Research Association (AERA), American Psychological Association, & National Council on Measurement in Education. (1999). *Standards for educational and psychological testing.* Washington, DC: American Educational Research Association.

American Psychological Association. (1992). *Ethical principles of psychologists and code of conduct.* Washington, DC: Author.

Ames, W. (1965). A comparison of spelling textbooks. *Elementary English, 42,* 146–150, 214.

Ardoin, S. P., & Christ, T. J. (2009). Curriculum based measurement of oral reading: Estimates of standard error when monitoring progress using alternate passage sets, *School Psychology Review, 38,* 266–283.

Armbruster, B., & Osborn, J. (2001). *Put reading first: The research building blocks for teaching children to read.* Jessup, MD: Partnership for Reading. Available from the National Institute for Literacy website: www.nifl gov.

Assisting Students Struggling with Mathematics: Response to Intervention (RtI) for Elementary and Middle Schools. National Center for Educational Evaluation and Regional Assistance 2009. What Works Clearinghouse: http://www.whatworks.ed.gov.

Ayers, A. (1981). *Sensory integration and the child.* Los Angeles, CA: Western Psychological Services.

Bachor, D. (1990). The importance of shifts in language level and extraneous information in determining word-problem difficulty: Steps toward individual assessment. *Diagnostique, 14,* 94–111.

Bachor, D., Stacy, N., & Freeze, D. (1986). *A conceptual framework for word problems: Some preliminary results.* Paper presented at the conference of the Canadian Society for Studies in Education, Winnipeg, Manitoba.

Bailey, D. B., & Rouse, T. L. (1989). Procedural considerations in assessing infants and preschoolers with handicaps. In D. B. Bailey & M. Wolery (Eds.), *Assessing infants and preschoolers with handicaps.* Columbus, OH: Merrill.

Baker, E. L., Bewley, W. L., Herman, J. L., Lee, J. J., & Mitchell, D. S. (2001). *Upgrading America's use of information to improve student performance* (Proposal to the U.S. Secretary of Education). Los Angeles: University of California, National Center for Research on Evaluation, Standards, and Student Testing.

Baker, E. L., & Linn, R. L. (2002). *Validity issues for accountability systems.* Los Angeles, CA: University of California, National Center for Research on Evaluation, Standards, and Student Testing.

Bandura, A. (1969). *Principles of behavior modification.* Oxford: Holt, Rinehart, & Winston.

Barsch, R. (1966). Teacher needs—motor training. In W. Cruickshank (Ed.), *The teacher of brain-injured children.* Syracuse, NY: Syracuse University Press.

Baumgardner, J. C. (1993). *An empirical analysis of school psychological assessments: Practice with students who are deaf and bilingual.* Unpublished doctoral dissertation, University of Minnesota, Minneapolis.

Bayley, N. (2006). *Bayley Scales of Infant and Toddler Development.* San Antonio, TX: Psychological Corporation.

Beck. R. (1979). *Great Falls Precision Teaching Project: Report for Joint Dissemination and Review Panel.* Great Falls, MT: Great Falls Public Schools.

Beery, K. E. (1982). *Revised administration, scoring, and teaching manual for the Developmental Test of Visual-Motor Integration.* Cleveland, OH: Modern Curriculum Press.

Beery, K. E. (1989). *The Developmental Test of Visual-Motor Integration.* Cleveland, OH: Modern Curriculum Press.

Beery, K. E., & Beery, N. (2004). *Beery VMI.* Minneapolis, MN: NCS Pearson.

Bell, P. (1992). Effects of curriculum-test overlap on standardized achievement test scores: identifying systematic confounds in educational decision-making. *School Psychology Review, 21*(4), 644–655.

Bender, L. (1938). *Bender Visual-Motor Gestalt Test.* New York: Grune & Stratton.

Bergen, J. R. & Kratochwill, T. R. (1990). *Behavioral consultation.* Columbus, OH: Merrill.

Bess, F. H., & Hall, J. W. (1992). *Screening children for auditory function.* Nashville, TN: Bill Wilkerson Center Press.

Betebenner, D. (2008). Towards a normative understanding of student growth. In K. E. Ryan & L. A. Shepard (Eds.), *The future of test-based educational accountability* (pp. 155–170). New York: Taylor & Francis.

Betebenner, D. (2009). Norm- and criterion-referenced student growth. *Educational Measurement: Issues and Practice, 28,* 42–51.

Betebenner, D. & Linn, R. L. (2010). *Growth in student achievement: Issues of measurement, longitudinal data analysis and accountability.* Princeton, NJ: Educational Testing Service.

Betts, J. (2005). *Evaluating different methods for making value-added decisions across classrooms.* Minneapolis, MN: Minnesota Public Schools: Research, Evaluation and Assessment.

Betts, J. (April, 2010). *Measuring academic growth with growth norms: A method for RTI models.* Paper presented at the annual meeting of the National Council on Measurement in Education conference. Denver, CO.

Blake, J., Austin, W., Cannon, M., Lisius, A. & Vaughn, A. (1994). The relationship between memory span and measures of imitative and spontaneous language complexity in preschool children. *International Journal of Behavioral Development, 17*(1), 91–107.

Boehm, A. E. (2001). *Boehm Test of Basic Concepts—Third Edition.* Bloomington, MN: Pearson.

Bolt, D. M, Ysseldyke, J. E. & Patterson, M. J. (2010). Students, teachers, and schools as sources of variability, integrity, and sustainability in implementing progress monitoring. *School Psychology Review, 39*(4), 612–631.

Bond, G., & Dykstra, R. (1967). The cooperative research program in first-grade reading instruction (1967). *Reading Research Quarterly, 2,* 5–142.

Bracken, B., & McCallum, R. S. (1998). *Universal Nonverbal Intelligence Test.* Itasca, IL: Riverside Publishing Company.

Brannigan, G., & Decker, S. (2003). *Bender Visual-Motor Gestalt Test* (2nd ed.). Itasca, IL: Riverside Publishing.

Breland, H. (1983). *The direct assessment of writing skill: A measurement review* (College Board Report No. 83-6). New York: College Entrance Examination Board.

Breland, H., Camp, R., Jones, R., Morris, M. M., & Rock, D. (1987). *Assessing writing skill.* New York: The College Board.

Briggs, A., & Underwood, G. (1984). Phonological coding in good and poor readers. *Reading Research Quarterly, 20,* 54–66.

Broderick, C. B. (1993). *Understanding family process: Basics of family systems theory.* Newbury Park, CA: Sage.

Brown, L., & Hammill, D. (1990). *Behavior Rating Profile* (2nd ed.). Austin, TX: Pro-Ed.

Brown, L., Hammill, D., & Wiederholt, J. L. (1995). *Test of Reading Comprehension–3.* Austin, TX: Pro-Ed.

Brown, L., Sherbenou, R., & Johnsen, S. (1997). *Test of Nonverbal Intelligence–3.* Austin, TX: Pro-Ed.

Brown, V., Wiederholt, J. L., & Hammill, D. D. (2009). *Test of reading comprehension* (4th ed.). Austin, TX: PRO-ED.

Bruininks, R., Woodcock, R., Weatherman, R., & Hill, B. (1996). *Scales of Independent Behavior, Revised, comprehensive manual.* Chicago: Riverside Publishing Company.

Butcher, N. N., Graham, J. R., Ben-Porath, Y. S., Tellegen, Y. S., Dahlstrom, W. G., & Kaemmer, B. (2001). *Minnesota Multiphasic Personality Inventory–2.* Minneapolis, MN: University of Minnesota Press.

Caldwell, J., & Goldin, J. (1979). Variables affecting word problem difficulty in elementary school mathematics. *Journal of Research in Mathematics Education, 10,* 323–335.

Camarata, S.M. & Nelson, K.E. (1994). Comparison of conversational recasting and imitative procedures for training grammatical structures in children with specific language impairment. *Journal of Speech, Language and hearing Research, 37,* 1414–1423.

Campbell, D., & Fiske, D. (1959). Convergent and discriminate validation by the multi-trait–multi-method matrix. *Psychological Bulletin, 56,* 81–105.

Caplan, G. (1964).*The principles of preventive psychiatry.* New York, NY: Basic Books.

Carrow-Woolfolk, E. (1995). *Manual for the Listening Comprehension and Oral Language Subtests of the Oral and Written Language Scales.* Circle Pines, MN: American Guidance Service.

Carrow-Woolfolk, E. (1999a). *Comprehensive Assessment of Spoken Language.* Circle Pines, MN: American Guidance Service.

Carrow-Woolfolk, E. (1999b). *Test for Auditory Comprehension of Language* (3rd ed.). San Antonio, TX: Harcourt.

Center for Universal Design. (1997). *The principles of universal design, version 2.0.* Raleigh: North Carolina State University.

Chafouleas, S.M., Riley-Tillman, T.C. & Christ, T.J. (2009). Direct Behavior Rating (DBR): An emerging method for assessing social behavior within a tiered intervention system. *Assessment for Effective Intervention, 34,* 195–200.

Chafouleus, S., Briesch, A., Riley-Tillman, T.C., Christ, T.J., Black, A.C., & Kilgus, S. P. (2010). An investigation of the generalizability and dependability of Direct Behavior Rating Single Item Scales (DBR-SIS) to measure academic engagement and disruptive behavior of middle school students. *Journal of School Psychology, 48,* 219–246.

Chall, J. (1967). *Learning to read: The great debate.* New York: McGraw-Hill.

Chase, J. B. (1985). Assessment of the visually impaired. *Diagnostique,* 10, 144–160.

Christ, T. J., & Ardoin, S. P. (2009). Curriculum-based measurement of oral reading: Passage equivalence and probe-set development. *Journal of School Psychology, 47,* 55–75.

Conners, C. K. (1997). *Conners Parent Rating Scale–Revised.* New York: Psychological Corporation.

Connolly, J. (2007). *KeyMath 3 Diagnostic Assessment (KeyMath 3 DA).* Minneapolis, MN: Pearson.

Cooper, C. (1977). Holistic evaluation of writing. In C. Cooper & L. Odell (Eds.), *Evaluating writing: Describing, measuring, judging.* Buffalo, NY: National Council of Teachers of English.

Crocker, L. M., Miller, M. D., & Franks, E. A. (1989). Quantitative methods for assessing the fit between test and curriculum. *Applied Measurement in Education,* 2(2), 179–194.

Cronbach, L. (1951). Coefficient alpha and the internal structure of tests. *Psychometrika, 16,* 297–334.

CTB McGraw-Hill (undated). *Yearly Progress Pro.* Monterey, CA: author.

CTB/McGraw-Hill. (2004). *Guidelines for inclusive test administration 2005.* Monterey, CA: Author.

CTB/McGraw-Hill. (2008). *TerraNova—Third Edition.* Monterey, CA: Author.

Cummins, J. (1984). *Bilingual special education: Issues in assessment and pedagogy.* San Diego, CA: College Hill.

Das, J., & Naglieri, J. (1997). *Cognitive Assessment System.* Itasca, IL: Riverside Publishing.

Deming, W. E. (1994). *The new economics for industry, government and education.* Cambridge, MA: MIT, Center for Advanced Educational Services.

Deming, W. E. (2000). *The new economics for industry, government and education* (2nd ed.). Cambridge, MA: MIT Press.

Deno, S. L. (1985). Curriculum-based assessment: The emerging alternative. *Exceptional Children, 52,* 219–232.

Deno, S. L., & Fuchs, L. S. (1987). Developing curriculum-based measurement systems for data-based special education problem solving. *Focus on Exceptional Children, 19,* 1–16.

Deno, S. L., & Mirkin, P. (1977). *Data-based program modification: A manual.* Reston, VA: Council for Exceptional Children.

Derogatis, L. R. (1993). *Brief Symptom Inventory.* Minneapolis, MN: National Computer Systems.

Diana v. State Board of Education, 1970 (*Diana v. State Board of Education*, C-70: 37RFT) (N.D. Cal., 1970).

Doman, R., Spitz, E., Zuckerman, E., Delacato, C., & Doman, G. (1967). Children with severe brain injuries: Neurological organization in terms of mobility. In E. C. Frierson & W. B. Barbe (Eds.), *Educating children with learning disabilities.* New York: Appleton-Century-Crofts.

Dunn, L. M., & Dunn, M. (2007). *Peabody Picture Vocabulary Test* (4th ed.). San Antonio, TX: Pearson Assessment.

Dunn, L. M., & Markwardt, F. C. (1970). *Peabody Individual Achievement Test.* Circle Pines: MN: American Guidance Service.

Dunn, L. M., & Markwardt, F. C. (1998). *Peabody Individual Achievement Test—Revised/Normative Update.* Circle Pines, MN: American Guidance Service.

Edformation (2006). *AIMSweb.* Available at www.edformation.com.

Educational Testing Service. (1990). *Exploring new methods for collecting students' school-based writing: NAEP's 1990 portfolio study* (ED 343154). Washington, DC: U.S. Department of Education.

Elmore, R. (2002). *Bridging the gap between standards and achievement.* Washington, DC: The Albert Shanker Institute.

Englemann, S., Granzin, A., & Severson, H. (1979). Diagnosing instruction. *Journal of Special Education, 13,* 355–365.

Englert, C., Cullata, B., & Horn, D. (1987). Influence of irrelevant information in addition word problems on problem solving. *Learning Disabilities Quarterly, 10,* 29–36.

Epstein, M. H. (2004). *Examiner's manual for the Behavioral and Emotional Rating Scale* (2nd ed.). Austin, TX: Pro-Ed.

Fernsten, L., & Fernsten, J. (2005). Portfolio assessment and reflection: Enhancing learning through effective practice. *Reflective Practice* 6, 303–309.

Figueroa, R. (1990). Assessment of linguistic minority group children. In C. R. Reynolds & R. W. Kamphaus (Eds.), *Handbook of psychological assessment of children.* New York: Guilford Press.

Flesch, R. (1955). *Why Johnny can't read.* New York: Harper & Row.

Foorman, B., Francis, D., Fletcher, J., Schatschneider, C., & Mehta, P. (1998). The role of instruction in learning to read: Preventing reading failure in at-risk children. *Journal of Educational Psychology, 90,* 1–13.

Freeland, J., Skinner, C., Jackson, B., McDaniel, C., & Smith, S. (2000). Measuring and increasing silent reading comprehension rates: Empirically validating a related reading intervention. *Psychology in the Schools, 37*(5), 415–429.

Frostig, M. (1968). Education for children with learning disabilities. In H. Myklebust (Ed.), *Progress in learning disabilities.* New York: Grune & Stratton.

Frostig, M., Maslow, P., Lefever, D. W., & Whittlesey, J. R. (1964). *The Marianne Frostig Developmental Test of Visual Perception: 1963 standardization.* Palo Alto, CA: Consulting Psychologists Press.

Fuchs, D., & Fuchs, L. S. (1989). Effects of examiner familiarity on black, Caucasian, and Hispanic children: A meta-analysis. *Exceptional Children, 55*(4), 303–308.

Fuchs, L. S., Deno, S. L., & Mirkin, P. (1984). The effects of frequent curriculum based measurement and evaluation on pedagogy, student achievement and student awareness of learning. *American Educational Research Journal, 21,* 449–460.

Fuchs, L. S., & Fuchs, D. (1986). Effects of systematic formative evaluation: A meta-analysis. *Exceptional Children, 53,* 199–208.

Fuchs, L. S., & Fuchs, D. (1987). The relation between methods of graphing student performance data and achievement: A meta-analysis. *Journal of Special Education Technology, 8*(3), 5–13.

Fuchs, L. S., Fuchs, D., Hamlett, C. L., Walz, L., & Germann, G. (1993). Formative evaluation of academic progress: How much growth can we expect? *School Psychology Review, 22*, 27–48.

Fuchs, L. S., Fuchs, D., & Maxwell, L. (1988). The validity of informal reading comprehension measures. *Remedial and Special Education,* 20–28.

Gilliam, J. E. (2001). *Manual for the Gilliam Asperger Disorder Scale*. Circle Pines, MN: American Guidance Service.

Ginsburg, H., & Baroody, A. (2003). *Test of Early Mathematics Ability* (3rd ed.). Austin, TX: Pro-Ed.

Gioia, G. A., Isquith, P. K., Guy, S. C., & Kenworthy, L. (2000). *Behavior Rating Inventory of Executive Functioning (BRIEF)*. Lutz, FL: Psychological Assessment Resources.

Goldman, R., & Fristoe, M. (2000). *Goldman-Fristoe Test of Articulation* (2nd ed.). Circle Pines, MN: American Guidance Service.

Good, R. H., & Kaminski, R. A. (Eds.). (2002). *Dynamic Indicators of Basic Early Literacy Skills* (6th ed.). Eugene, OR: Institute for the Development of Educational Achievement. Available at dibels.uoregon.edu. Also available in print form from Sopris West Educational Publishers (sopriswest.com).

Good, R. H., & Salvia, J. A. (1988). Curriculum bias in published norm-referenced reading tests: Demonstrable effects. *School Psychology Review, 17*(1), 51–60.

Gottesman, I. (1968). Biogenics of race and class. In M. Deutsch, I. Katz, & A. Jensen (Eds.), *Social class, race, and psychological development.* New York: Holt, Rinehart, & Winston.

Graden, J., Casey, A., & Bonstrom, O. (1983). *Prereferral interventions: Effects on referral rates and teacher attitudes* (Research Report No. 140). Minneapolis: Minnesota Institute for Research on Learning Disabilities.

Greenspan, S. I. (2004). *Greenspan Social Emotional Growth Chart: A Screening Questionnaire for Infants and Young Children.* San Antonio, TX: Harcourt Educational Measurement.

Greenspan, S. I. (2006). *Bayley Scales of Infant and Toddler Development: Socio-Emotional Subtest.* San Antonio, TX: Harcourt Educational Measurement.

Gresham, F., & Elliott, S. N. (1990). *Social Skills Rating System.* Circle Pines, MN: American Guidance Service.

Grimes, J., & Kurns, S. (2003, December). Response to intervention: Heartland's model of prevention and intervention. National Research Center on Learning Disabilities Responsiveness to Intervention Symposium, Kansas City.

Gronlund, N. E. & Waugh, C. K. (2008). *Assessment of student achievement* (9th ed.). New York: Allyn & Bacon.

Guilford, J. P. (1967). *The nature of human intelligence.* New York: McGraw-Hill.

Gutkin, T. B., & Nemeth, C. (1997). Selected factors impacting decision making in prereferral intervention and other school-based teams: Exploring the intersection between school and social psychology. *Journal of School Psychology, 35,* 195–216.

Hammill, D. (1998). *Examiner's manual: Detroit Tests of Learning Aptitude.* Austin, TX: Pro-Ed.

Hammill, D., & Larsen, S. (2008). *Examiner's manual for the Test of Written Language, Fourth Edition.* Austin, TX: Pro-Ed.

Hammill, D. D., & Larsen, S. C. (2009). *Written language observation scale.* Austin, TX: Hammill Institute on Disabilities.

Hammill, D., Mather, H., & Roberts, R. (2001). *Illinois Test of Psycholinguistic Abilities* (3rd ed.). Austin, TX: Pro-Ed.

Hammill, D., & Newcomer, P. (2008). *Test of Language Development–Intermediate* (4th ed.). Austin, TX: PRO-ED.

Hammill, D., Pearson, N., & Voress, J. (1993). *Examiner's manual: Developmental Test of Visual Perception* (2nd ed.). Austin, TX: Pro-Ed.

Hammill, D., Pearson, N., & Voress, J. (1996). *Test of Visual-Motor Integration.* Austin, TX: Pro-Ed.

Hammill, D., Pearson, N., & Wiederholt, L. (1997). *Comprehensive Test of Nonverbal Intelligence.* Austin, TX: Pro-Ed.

Hanna, P., Hanna, J., Hodges, R., & Rudoff, E. (1966). *Phoneme-grapheme correspondence as cues to spelling improvement.* Washington, DC: U.S. Department of Health, Education, and Welfare.

Harcourt Assessment, Inc. (2004). *Stanford Achievement Test series, Tenth Edition technical data report.* San Antonio, TX: Author.

Harcourt Brace Educational Measurement. (1996). *Stanford Diagnostic Mathematics Test 4.* San Antonio, TX: Psychological Corporation.

Harcourt Educational Measurement. (2002). *Metropolitan Achievement Test* (8th ed.). San Antonio, TX: Author.

Harcourt Educational Measurement. (2003). *Otis Lennon School Ability Test* (8th ed.). San Antonio, TX: Author.

Harrison, P. (2006). *Bayley Scales of Infant and Toddler Development: Adaptive Behavior Subtest.* San Antonio, TX: Harcourt Educational Measurement.

Harrison, P., & Oakland, T. (2003). *Adaptive Behavior System, Second Edition.* San Antonio, TX: Harcourt Educational Measurement.

Hasbrouck, J. & Tindal, G. (2006). Oral reading fluency norms: A valuable assessment tool for reading teachers. *The Reading Teacher, 59*(7), 636–644.

Herrnstein, R., & Murray, C. (1994). *The bell curve: Intelligence and class structure in American life.* New York: The Free Press.

Hintze, J., Christ, T., & Methe, S. (2005). Curriculum-based assessment. *Psychology in the Schools, 43*(1), 45–56.

Horn, E. (1967). *What research says to the teacher: Teaching spelling.* Washington, DC: National Education Association.

Hosp, M. K., & Hosp, J. L. (2003). Curriculum-based measurement for reading, spelling, and math: How to do it and why. *Preventing School Failure, 48*(1), 10–17.

Hosp, M., Hosp, J., & Howell, K. (2007). *The ABCs of CBM: A practical guide to curriculum-based measurement.* New York: Guilford.

Howell, K. W., & Nolet, V. (2000). *Curriculum-based evaluation* (3rd ed.). Atlanta, GA: Wadsworth.

Hresko, W., Peak, P., Herron, S., & Bridges, D. L. (2000). *Young Children's Achievement Test.* Austin, TX: Pro-Ed.

Hresko, W. P., Schlieve, P. L., Herron, S. R., Swain, C., & Sherbenou, R. J. (2003). *Comprehensive Mathematical Abilities Test.* Austin, TX: Pro-Ed.

Isaacson, S. (1988). Assessing the writing product: Qualitative and quantitative measures. *Exceptional Children, 54,* 528–534.

Jacob, S., Decker, D.M. & Hartshorne, T.S. (2011). *Ethics and law for school psychologists.* New York: Wiley.

Jenkins, J., & Pany, D. (1978). Standardized achievement tests: How useful for special education? *Exceptional Children, 44,* 448–453.

Jensen, A. R. (1980). *Bias in mental testing.* New York: The Free Press.

Jimerson, S. R., Burns, M.K. & VanDerHeyden, A. M. (Eds.) (2007). *Handbook of response to intervention: The science and practice of assessment and intervention.* New York, NY: Springer.

Johnson, D., & Myklebust, H. (1967). *Learning disabilities: Educational principles and practices.* New York: Grune & Stratton.

Johnson, J. S., Newport, E. L. (1989). Critical period effects in second language learning: The influence of maturational state on the acquisition of English as a second language. *Cognitive Psychology, 21,* 60–99.

Kaplan, E., Fein, D., Kramer, J., Morris, R., Delis, D., & Maerlender, A. (2004). *Wechsler Intelligence Scale for Children* (4th ed., Integrated). San Antonio, TX: Psychological Corporation.

Kaufman, A.S. (2009). *IQ testing 101.* New York, NY: Springer.

Kaufman, A. S. & Kaufman, N. L. (1998). *Kaufman Test of Educational Achievement—Second Edition.* Circle Pines, MN: American Guidance Service.

Kaufman, A., & Kaufman, N. (2004). *Kaufman Assessment Battery for Children, Second Edition.* Bloomington, MN: Pearson.

Kephart, N. (1971). *The slow learner in the classroom.* Columbus, OH: Merrill.

Kirk, S., & Kirk, W. (1971). *Psycholinguistic disabilities.* Urbana: University of Illinois Press.

Kirk, S., McCarthy, J., & Kirk, W. (1968). *Illinois Test of Psycholinguistic Abilities.* Urbana: University of Illinois Press.

Kline, M. (1973). *Why Johnny can't add: The failure of the new math.* New York: St. Martin's Press.

Koppitz, E. M. (1963). *The Bender Gestalt Test for Young Children.* New York: Grune & Stratton.

Kovacs, M. (1992). *Children's Depression Inventory: Manual.* North Tonawanda, NY: Multi-Health Systems.

Kovaleski, J., & Glew, M. (2006). Bringing instructional support teams to scale: Implications of the Pennsylvania experience. *Remedial and Special Education, 27,* 16–25.

LaBerge, D., & Samuels, S. (1974). Toward a theory of automatic information processing in reading. *Cognitive Psychology, 6,* 293–323.

Larsen, S., Hammill, D. D., & Moats, L. (1999). *Test of Written Spelling–4.* Austin, TX: Pro-Ed.

Lindsley, O. R. (1964). Direct measurement and prosthesis of retarded Behavior. *Journal of Education, 147,* 68-81.

Linn, R., Graue, E., & Sanders, N. (1990). Comparing state and district test results to national norms: The validity of claims that "everyone is above average." *Educational Measurement: Issues and Practice, 9*(3), 5–14.

Loeding, B. L., & Crittenden, J. B. (1993). Inclusion of children and youth who are hearing impaired and deaf in outcomes assessment. In J. E. Ysseldyke & M. L. Thurlow (Eds.), *Views on inclusion and testing accommodations for students with disabilities.* Minneapolis: University of Minnesota, National Center on Educational Outcomes.

Lohman, D., & Hagan, E. (2001). *Cognitive Abilities Test.* Chicago: Riverside Publishing.

Maddox, T. (Ed.). (2008). *Tests, sixth edition—A comprehensive reference for assessments in psychology, education, and business.* Austin, TX: PRO-ED.

Mardell-Czudnowski, C., & Goldenberg, D. (1998). *Manual: Developmental indicators for the assessment of learning* (3rd ed.). Circle Pines, MN: American Guidance Service.

Markwardt, F. (1998). *Peabody Individual Achievement Test–Revised–Normative update.* Circle Pines, MN: American Guidance Service.

Marston, D., & Magnusson, D. (1985). Implementing curriculum-based measurement in special and regular education settings. *Exceptional Children, 52,* 266–276.

Marston, D., Muyskens, P., Lau, M., & Canter, A. (2003). Problem-solving model for decision making with high-incidence disabilities: The Minneapolis experience. *Learning Disabilities Research and Practice, 18*(3), 187–200.

Martin, R. P. (1988). *Assessment of personality and behavior problems: Infancy through adolescence.* New York: Guilford Press.

Massachusetts Department of Education. (2001). *Resource Guide to the Massachusetts Curriculum Frameworks for Students with Significant Disabilities–English Language Arts Section.* [Retrieved April 5, 2005, at www.doe.mass.edu/mcas/alt/rg/ela.pdf]

Mather, N., Roberts, R., Hammill, D. D. & Allen, E. A. (2009). *Test of orthographic competence.* Austin, TX: Pro-Ed.

Mather, N., Hammill, D., Allen, E., & Roberts, R. (2004). *Test of Silent Word Reading Fluency.* Austin, TX: Pro-Ed.

Maynard, F., & Strickland, J. (1969). *A comparison of three methods of teaching selected mathematical content in eighth and ninth grade general mathematics courses* (ED 041763). Athens, GA: University of Georgia.

McBride, J. & Martin, J.T. (1983). Reliability and validity of adaptive ability tests. In D.J. Weiss (Ed.), *New horizons in testing: Latent trait test theory and computerized adaptive testing* (Chapter 11, pp. 224–225), New York: Academic Press.

McCarney, S. B. (1992a). *Early Childhood Behavior Scale: Technical manual.* Columbia, MO: Hawthorne Educational Services.

McCarney, S. B. (1992b). *Preschool Evaluation Scale.* Columbia, MO: Hawthorne Educational Services.

McGraw-Hill Digital Learning. (2004). *Yearly Progress Pro.* Columbus, OH: Author.

McGrew, K., Thurlow, M. L., Shriner, J., & Spiegel, A. N. (1992). *Inclusion of students with disabilities in national and state data collection programs* (Technical Report 2). Minneapolis: University of Minnesota, National Center on Educational Outcomes.

McGrew, K. S., & Woodcock, R. W. (2001). *Woodcock-Johnson III: Technical manual.* Itasca, IL: Riverside Publishing Company.

McNamara, K. (1998). Adoption of intervention-based assessment for special education: Trends in case management variables. *School Psychology International, 19,* 251–266.

Meller, P. J., Ohr, P. S., & Marcus, R. A. (2001). Family-oriented, culturally sensitive (FOCUS) assessment of young children. In L. A. Suzuki, J. G. Ponterotto, & P. J. Meller (Eds.), *Handbook of multicultural assessment: Clinical, psychological, and educational applications* (2nd ed., pp. 461–496). San Francisco: Jossey-Bass.

Mercer, C., & Mercer, A. (1985). *Teaching students with learning problems* (2nd ed.). Columbus, OH: Merrill.

Merrell, K. W. (1994). *Assessment of behavioral, social, and emotional problems.* New York: Longman.

Miller, J. (1981). *Assessing language production in children.* Austin, TX: Pro-Ed.

Moore, K. J., Fifield, M. B., Spira, D. A., & Scarlato, M. (1989). Child study team decision making in special education: Improving the process. *Remedial and Special Education, 10,* 50–58.

Mullen, E. (1995). *Mullen Scales of Early Learning: AGS Edition.* Circle Pines, MN: American Guidance Service.

Myles, B., Bock, S., & Simpson, R. (2001). *Examiner's manual for the Asperger Syndrome Diagnostic Scale.* Circle Pines, MN: American Guidance Service.

Naglieri, J. (2008). *Naglieri Nonverbal Ability Test* (2nd ed.). San Antonio, TX: Pearson Assessment.

National Association for the Education of Young Children. (2003). *Position statement on early childhood curriculum, assessment, and program evaluation.* Washington, DC: Author. [Retrieved June 14, 2008, at www.naeyc.org/about/positions/pdf/pscape.pdf]

National Association of School Psychologists. (2002). *Principles for professional ethics.* Bethesda, MD: Author.

National Association of State Directors of Special Education (2005). *Response to intervention: Policy considerations and implementation.* Alexandria, VA: National Association of State Directors of Special Education.

National Center for Educational Statistics. (1995). *Trends in International Mathematics and Science Study.* Washington, D.C.: Institute for Educational Sciences.

National Center for Educational Statistics (2002). *Fourth grade students reading aloud: NAEP 2002 special study on oral reading.* Washington, DC: U.S. Department of Education, Institute of Education Sciences.

National Center on Response to Intervention Technical Review Committee. (2010, April 19). *Progress monitoring tool chart: Reading and math.* [Retrieved at http://www.rti4success.org/tools_charts/supplementalContent/progress/ProgressMonitoring.pdf]

National Commission of Excellence in Education. (1983). *A nation at risk: The imperative for educational reform.* Washington, DC: U.S. Government Printing Office.

National Council of Teachers of Mathematics. (2000). *Principles and standards for school mathematics.* Reston, VA: Author.

National Institute of Child Health and Human Development. (2000). Report of the National Reading Panel. *Teaching children to read: An evidence-based assessment of the scientific research literature on reading and its implication for reading instruction* (NIH Publication 00-4). Washington, DC: U.S. Government Printing Office.

National Institute of Child Health and Human Development. (2008). Report of the National Mathematics Advisory Panel. (2008). *Foundations for success: The final report of the National Mathematics Advisory Panel.* Washington, DC: U.S. Department of Education.

National Reading Panel. *Teaching children to read: An evidence-based assessment of the scientific research literature on reading and its implication for reading instruction: Reports of the Subgroups* (Chapter 2, Part II). Available at www.nichd.hih.gov/publications/nrp/ ch2-II.pdf.

Neisworth, J., Bagnato, S., Salvia, J. A., & Hunt, F. (1999). *Temperament and Atypical Behavior Scale.* Baltimore, MD: Paul H. Brookes.

Newcomer, P. (2001). *Diagnostic Achievement Battery* (3rd ed.). Austin, TX: Pro-Ed.

Newcomer, P., & Hammill, D. (2008). *Test of Language Development–Primary* (4th ed.). Austin, TX: Pro-Ed.

Nihira, K., Leland, H., & Lambert, N. (1993a). *AAMR Adaptive Behavior Scale–School* (2nd ed.). Austin, TX: Pro-Ed.

Nihira, K., Leland, H., & Lambert, N. (1993b). *Examiner's manual, AAMR Adaptive Behavior Scale–Residential and Community* (2nd ed.). Austin, TX: Pro-Ed.

Northern, J. L., & Downs, M. P. (1991). *Hearing in children* (4th ed). Baltimore, MD: Williams & Wilkens.

Nunnally, J. (1967). *Psychometric theory.* New York: McGraw-Hill.

Nurss, J., & McGauvran, M. (1995). *The Metropolitan Readiness Tests: Norms book* (6th ed.). San Antonio, TX: Harcourt Brace.

Olson, D. (1964). *Management by objectives.* Auckland, NZ: Pacific Book Publishers.

Otis, A. S., & Lennon, R. T. (2003). *Otis-Lennon School Ability Test* (8th ed.). San Antonio, TX: Harcourt Educational Measurement.

Paul, D., Nibbelink, W., & Hoover, H. (1986). The effects of adjusting readability on the difficulty of mathematics story problems. *Journal of Research in Mathematics Education, 17,* 163–171.

Pearson. (2001). *AIMSweb*. San Antonio, TX: Author.

Pflaum, S., Walberg, H., Karegianes, M., & Rasher, S. (1980). Reading instruction: A quantitative analysis. *Educational Researcher, 9*, 12–18.

Phillips, K. (1990). *Factors that affect the feasibility of interventions*. Workshop presented at Mounds View Schools, unpublished.

Prutting, C., & Kirshner, D. (1987). A clinical appraisal of the pragmatic aspects of language. *Journal of Speech and Hearing Disorders, 52*, 105–119.

Psychological Corporation. (2009). *Wechsler Individual Achievement Test* (3rd ed.). San Antonio, TX: Author.

Rayner, K., Foorman, B., Perfetti, C., Pesetsky, D., & Seidenberg, M. (2001). How psychological science informs the teacher of reading. *Psychological Science in the Public Interest*, 2, 31–73.

Reid, D., Hresko, W., & Hammill, D. (2001). *Test of Early Reading Ability* (3rd ed.). Austin, TX: Pro-Ed.

Renaissance Learning. (1997). *Standardized test for the assessment of reading*. Wisconsin Rapids, WI: Author.

Renaissance Learning. (1998). *STAR Math*. Wisconsin Rapids, WI: Author.

Renaissance Learning. (2006). NEO-2. Wisconsin Rapids, WI: Author.

Renaissance Learning. (2007). DANA. Wisconsin Rapids, WI: Author.

Renaissance Learning (2009). *STAR Math technical manual*. Wisconsin Rapids, WI: Author.

Renaissance Learning (2009). *STAR Reading technical manual*. Wisconsin Rapids, WI: Author.

Resnick, L. (1987). *Education and learning to think*. Washington, DC: National Academy Press.

Reynolds, C. R. (2007). *Koppitz Developmental Scoring System for the Bender Gestalt Test–Second Edition (Koppitz-2)*. Austin, TX: Pro-Ed.

Reynolds, C. R., & Kamphaus, R. W. (2004). *Behavior Assessment System for Children–Second Edition–Manual*. Circle Pines, MN: American Guidance Service.

Reynolds, C. R., & Richmond, B. O. (2000). *Revised Children's Manifest Anxiety Scale*. Los Angeles: Wester Psychological Services.

Roach, E. F., & Kephart, N. C. (1966). *The Purdue Perceptual-Motor Survey*. Columbus, OH: Merrill.

Roid, G. (2003). *Stanford-Binet Intelligence Scale* (5th ed.). Chicago, IL: Riverside Publishing.

Roid, G., & Miller, N. (1997). *Leiter International Performance Scale–Revised*. Chicago: Stoelting.

Salvia, J. A., Neisworth, J., & Schmidt, M. (1990). *Examiner's manual: Responsibility and Independence Scale for Adolescents*. Allen, TX: DLM.

Santangelo, T. (2009). Collaborative problem solving effectively implemented, but not sustained: A case for aligning the sun, the moon, and the stars. *Exceptional Children, 75*, 185–209.

Schmidt, M., & Salvia, J. A. (1984). Adaptive behavior: A conceptual analysis. *Diagnostique, 9*(2), 117–125.

Shapiro, E. S. (2003). *BOSS—Behavioral Observation of Students in Schools*. San Antonio, TX: Psychological Corporation. [Software for PDA platform]

Shapiro, E. S. (2004). *Academic skills problems workbook*. New York: Guilford Press.

Shapiro, E. S., & Derr, T. (1987). An examination of overlap between reading curricula and standardized reading tests. *Journal of Special Education, 21*(2), 59–67.

Shapiro, E. S., & Kratochwill, T. (Eds.). (2000). *Behavioral assessment in schools: Theory, research, and clinical foundations* (2nd ed.). New York: Guilford Press.

Share, D., & Stanovich, K. (1995). Cognitive processes in early reading development: A model of acquisition and individual differences. *Issues in Education: Contributions from Educational Psychology, 1*, 1–57.

Sharpe, M., McNear, D., & McGrew, K. (1996). *Braille assessment inventory*. Columbia, MO: Hawthorne Educational Services.

Shinn, M. (1998). *Advanced applications of curriculum-based measurement*. New York: Guilford Press.

Shinn, M. R. (Ed.). (1989). *Curriculum-based measurement: Assessing special children*. New York: Guilford.

Shinn, M., Tindall, G., & Stein, S. (1988). Curriculum-based measurement and the identification of mildly handicapped students: A review of research. *Professional School Psychology, 3*(1), 69–85.

Shriner, J., & Salvia, J. A. (1988). Content validity of two tests with two math curricula over three years: Another instance of chronic noncorrespondence. *Exceptional Children, 55*, 240–248.

Sindelar, P., Monda., L., & O'Shea, L. (1990). Effects of repeated readings on instructional- and mastery-level readers. *Journal of Educational Research, 83*(4), 220–226.

Snow, C., Burns, M., & Griffin, P. (1998). *Preventing reading difficulties in young children*. Washington, DC: National Academy Press.

Sparrow, S., Cicchetti, D., & Balla, D. (2005). *Vineland Adaptive Behavior Scales* (2nd ed.). Circle Pines, MN: American Guidance Service.

Stanovich, K. (1986). Matthew effects in reading: Some consequences of individual differences in the acquisition of literacy. *Reading Research Quarterly, 21*, 360–406.

Stanovich, K. (2000). *Progress in understanding reading: Scientific foundations and new frontiers*. New York: Guilford Press.

Stevens, R., & Rosenshine, B. (1981). Advances in research on teaching. *Exceptional Education Quarterly, 2*(1), 1–9.

Stevens, S. S. (1951). Mathematics, measurement, and psychophysics. In S. S. Stevens (Ed.), *Handbook of experimental psychology* (p. 23). New York: Wiley.

Suen, H., & Ary, D. (1989). *Analyzing quantitative behavioral observation data*. Hillsdale, NJ: Lawrence Erlbaum Associates.

Sugai, G. & Horner, R. (2009). Responsiveness-to-intervention and school-wide positive behavior supports: Integration of multi-tiered systems approaches. *Exceptionality, 17*, 223–237.

Sulzer-Azaroff, B., & Mayer, G. Roy (1986). *Achieving educational excellence: Using behavior strategies*. New York: Holt, Rinehart, and Winston.

Taylor, B., Harris, L., Pearson, P. D., & Garcia, G. (1995). *Reading difficulties: Instruction and assessment* (2nd ed.). New York: McGraw-Hill.

Tharp, R. G., & Wetzel, R. J. (1969). *Behavior modification in the natural environment.* New York: Academic Press.

Therrien, W. (2004). Fluency and comprehension gains as a result of repeated reading: A meta-analysis. *Remedial and Special Education, 25*(4), 252–261.

Thompson, S., & Thurlow, M. (2001). *State special education outcomes: A report on state activities at the beginning of the new decade.* Minneapolis: University of Minnesota, National Center on Educational Outcomes.

Thompson, S. J., Johnstone, C. J., & Thurlow, M. L. (2002). *Universal design applied to large scale assessments* (Synthesis Report 44). Minneapolis: University of Minnesota, National Center on Educational Outcomes. [Retrieved April 9, 2008, at http://cehd.umn.edu/NCEO/OnlinePubs/Synthesis44.html]

Thorndike, R. L., & Hagen, E. (1978). *Measurement and evaluation in psychology and education.* New York: Wiley.

Thurlow, M. L., Elliott, J. L., & Ysseldyke, J. E. (2003). *Testing students with disabilities: Practical strategies for complying with district and state requirements* (2nd ed.). Thousand Oaks, CA: Corwin Press.

Thurlow, M. L., Elliott, J. L., & Ysseldyke, J. E. (2003). *Testing students with disabilities: Procedures for complying with district and state requirements.* Thousand Oaks, CA: Corwin Press.

Thurlow, M. L., Quenemoen, R., Thompson, S., & Lehr, C. (2001). *Principles and characteristics of inclusive assessment and accountability systems* (Synthesis Report 40). Minneapolis, MN: National Center on Educational Outcomes, University of Minnesota.

Thurlow, M. L., & Thompson, S. (2004). *2003 state special education outcomes.* Minneapolis: University of Minnesota, National Center on Educational Outcomes.

Thurstone, T. G. (1941). Primary mental abilities in children. *Educational and Psychological Measurement, 1,* 105–116.

Tindal, G., & Hasbrouck, J. (1991). Analyzing student writing to develop instructional strategies. *Learning Disabilities: Research and Practice, 6,* 237–245.

Torgesen, J., & Bryant, B. (2004). *The Test of Phonological Awareness, Second Edition: Plus, Examiner's Manual.* Austin, TX: Pro-Ed.

U.S. Census Bureau. (1998). *Current population survey.* Washington, DC: Author.

U.S. Census Bureau (2006). *American Community Survey.* Washington, DC: Author.

U.S. Census Bureau (2010). *Language Use in the United States 2007: American Community Survey Reports.* Washington, DC: Author.

VanDerHeyden, A. M., & Burns, M. K. (2005). Using curriculum-based assessment and curriculum-based measurement to guide elementary mathematics instruction: Effect on individual and group accountability scores. *Assessment for Effective Intervention, 30,* 15–31.

VanDerHeyden, A. M., Witt, J. C., & Gilbertson, D. A (2007). Multi-year evaluation of the effects of a response to intervention (RTI) model on identification of children for special education. *Journal of School Psychology, 45,* 225–256.

Venn, J. J. (2000). *Assessing students with special needs* (2nd ed.). Upper Saddle River, NJ: Merrill.

Voress, J., & Maddox, T. (1998). *Developmental assessment of young children.* Austin, TX: Pro-Ed.

Wagner, R., Torgesen, J., & Rashotte, C. (1999). *Comprehensive Test of Phonological Processing.* Austin, TX: Pro-Ed.

Walker, D. K. (1973). *Socioemotional measures for preschool and kindergarten children.* San Francisco: Jossey-Bass.

Walker, H. M., & McConnell, S. R. (1988). *Walker-McConnell Scale of Social Competence.* Austin, TX: Pro-Ed.

Walker, H. M., & Severson, H. H. (1992). *Systematic screening for behavior disorders* (2nd ed.). Longmont, CO: Sopris West.

Wallace, G., & Hammill, D. (2002). *Comprehensive Receptive and Expressive Vocabulary Test* (2nd ed.). Austin, TX: Pro-Ed.

Warren, C. (2005). Creating portfolios of schools. *Education Week, 24*(41), 47, 56.

Wechsler, D. (1939). *Wechsler-Bellevue Intelligence Scale.* New York: Psychological Corporation.

Wechsler, D. (1974). *Manual for the Wechsler Intelligence Scale for Children–Revised.* Cleveland, OH: Psychological Corporation.

Wechsler, D. (2001). *Wechsler Individual Achievement Test—Second Edition.* San Antonio, TX: Psychological Corporation.

Wechsler, D. (2002). *Wechsler Preschool and Primary Scale of Intelligence* (3rd ed.). San Antonio, TX: Pearson Assessment.

Wechsler, D. (2003). *Wechsler Intelligence Scale for Children* (4th ed.). San Antonio, TX: Psychological Corporation.

Wechsler, D. (2004). *Wechsler Intelligence Scale for Children, Fourth Edition–Integrated: Technical and interpretive manual.* San Antonio, TX: Psychological Corporation.

Wechsler, D. (2008). *Wechsler Adult Intelligence Scale* (4th ed.). San Antonio, TX: Pearson Assessment.

White, O., & Haring, N. (1980). *Exceptional teaching* (2nd ed.). Columbus, OH: Merrill.

Wiederholt, L., & Bryant, B. (2001). *Gray Oral Reading Tests–4.* Austin, TX: Pro-Ed.

Wiederholt, L., & Bryant, B. (2001). *Examiner's manual: Gray Oral Reading Tests–3.* Austin, TX: Pro-Ed.

Wilkinson, G. S., & Robertson, G. J. (2007). *Wide Range Achievement Test 4 (WRAT 4).* Lutz, FL: Psychological Assessment Resources.

Williams, K. (2001). *Group reading assessment and diagnostic evaluation.* Circle Pines, MN: American Guidance Service.

Williams, K. T. (2004). *Group Mathematics Assessment and Diagnostic Evaluation*. Circle Pines, MN: AGS Publishing.

Woodcock, R. W. (1998). *Woodcock Reading Mastery Tests–Revised: Normative update*. Circle Pines, MN: American Guidance Service.

Woodcock, R. W., Mather, N., & Schrank, F. A. (2004). *Woodcock-Johnson III Diagonistic Reading Battery.* Itasca, IL: Riverside Publishing.

Woodcock, R. W., McGrew, K. S., & Mather, N. (2001). *WJ-III Tests of Cognitive Abilities and Tests of Achievement*. Itasca, IL: Riverside Publishing.

Woodcock, R. W., McGrew, K. S., & Mather, N. (2003). *Woodcock-Johnson III Tests of Cognitive Abilities*. Itasca, IL: Riverside Publishing.

Woodcock, R. W., Schrank, F. A., McGrew, K. S., & Mather, N. (2007). *Woodcock–Johnson III Normative Update*. Itasca, IL: Riverside.

Ysseldyke, J. E. (1987). Classification of handicapped students. In M. C. Wang, M. Reynolds, & H. J. Walberg (Eds.), *Handbook of special education: Research & practice* (vol. 1, pp. 253–271). New York: Pergamon.

Ysseldyke, J. E., & Christenson, S. L. (1987). *The Instructional Environment Scale*. Austin, TX: Pro-Ed.

Ysseldyke, J. E., & Christenson, S. L. (2002). *Functional assessment of academic behavior: Creating successful learning environments*. Longmont, CO: Sopris West.

Ysseldyke, J. E., Christenson, S. L., & Kovaleski, J. F. (1994). Identifying students' instructional needs in the context of classroom and home environments. *Teaching Exceptional Children, 26*(3), 37–41.

Ysseldyke, J. E., & McLeod, S. (2007). Using technology tools to monitor response to intervention. In S. R. Jimerson, M. K. Burns, and A. M. VanDerHeyden (Eds.), *Handbook of response to intervention*. New York: Springer.

Ysseldyke, J. E., & Salvia, J. A. (1974). Diagnostic-prescriptive teaching: Two models. *Exceptional Children, 41,* 181–186.

Ysseldyke, J. E., & Thurlow, M. L. (1993). *Self-study guide to the development of educational outcomes and indicators*. Minneapolis: University of Minnesota, National Center on Educational Outcomes.

INDEX

Note: Page numbers followed by *n* indicate footnotes.

Melott Cemetery
Brown Co. (408-01)

Guardians of the Soul

Angels and innocents, mourners and saints— Indiana's remarkable cemetery sculpture

John Bower

Foreword by Claude Cookman

STUDIO INDIANA

Published by:

Studio Indiana
430 N. Sewell Road Bloomington, IN 47408
(812) 332-5073 www.studioindiana.com

Publisher's Cataloging-in-Publication Data
Bowver, John.
Guardians of the Soul: Angels and innocents, mourners and saints—Indiana's remarkable cemetery sculpture / by John Bower; foreword by Claude Cookman.

p. cm.
ISBN 0-9745186-1-1
1. Sepulchral monuments—Indiana. 2. Sculpture, Victorian—Indiana.
3. Photography, Artistic. 4. Indiana—Pictorial works.
I. Bower, John, 1949-. II. Title.
NB 1841.B69 2004
779.9'7365—dc22
Library of Congress Control Number: 2004096555

Maple Hill Cemetery
Posey Co. (345-10)

Green Hill Cemetery
Lawrence Co. (284-11)

Foreword

A vivid image from a story read in my youth hovers in my memory. Although I can no longer recall the title or author, one passage persists: In the afterlife, a man gazes down upon a field of stars. Little by little, they twinkle and burn out. Over time they grow scarce and, eventually, the last one disappears. The narrator explains that the stars were people who had known the deceased during his life. As each of them dies, his or her star is extinguished until finally the man's sky is impenetrably black—all memories of him have been erased from the world of the living.

The story evokes two intertwined threads of humanity's response to death: our desire for eternal life in another sphere and our desire to leave a lasting trace of our existence in this world. We can only imagine at what point in the human trajectory the second longing surfaced, but eventually, rude markers began to be erected as locators of burial sites and as memorials for the people interred there. By the era of the pharaohs, both desires were accommodated: elaborate embalming to preserve the individual for eternity and massive pyramids to proclaim his majesty to future generations.

What the richest and most powerful enjoyed was, naturally, coveted by those further down the social ladder. For those who could not command a pyramid in their honor—nobles, court officials and chief scribes—there was little choice but to settle for smaller, flat-roofed mastabas. Centuries later, in western cultures, the same hierarchical approach to memorials persisted. In England, kings, queens, great knights, and ladies were interred above ground in cathedrals with life-sized marble sculptures atop their stone vaults. Women and men of the humble classes were buried in the church cemetery with little more than a cross to testify to their days on earth.

In the mid 1700s, the British poet Thomas Gray meditated on this state of affairs in his "Elegy Written in a Country Churchyard." In it, he celebrated the lives and talents of anonymous country folk. For him, the modest inscriptions and humble sculptures served to memorialize their lives. They were reminders that, in Gray's most famous line, "The paths of glory lead but to the grave." Whether a passerby knew the deceased or not, the wellsprings of feeling were enough to prompt "the passing tribute of a sigh" for a fellow human being.

As a latter-day Thomas Gray, John Bower has wandered the country graveyards of Southern Indiana and offers us, in this book, a photographic meditation on the human response to death. Dorothea Lange, the great documentarian, once said, "The camera is an instrument that teaches people how to see without a camera." Surely, Bower's work proves her point. Perhaps because of our modern culture's discomfort with the idea of death, perhaps because of a preoccupation with the graves of our own loved ones, few of us have invested the time to look intently at this cemetery art.

John Bower has done that for us. With a clear eye and pure technique, he has studied hundreds of cemetery statues. With angle, framing, depth of field, and camera distance, he isolates each one, showing us what makes it unique. Here, an angel framed against a cloudy sky inscribes a name in the Book of Life. Over there, a Saint Christopher-like fire fighter carries a cherubic infant. In another corner, lies a prostrate lion, his massive head weighted down with grief. Towering on his pedestal, Saint Michael—curiously missing his sword—bestrides the vanquished dragon. And what shall we say of the girl who died on the cusp of womanhood? Her fine features, long braided hair, ankle-top shoes, and bouquet of flowers reveal her character. But the most telling detail is her left knee, slightly bent as if ready to take the next step forward.

These statues tell us much about the people who erected them. Some, no doubt, were commissioned by the subjects themselves before their deaths. Most were probably erected by loved ones to memorialize a parent or child. All of them testify to the human struggle against oblivion. Against that pitch-black, starless sky they shout, "I was here. I did live a life. I knew joy and struggle, heartache and accomplishment. I deserve to be remembered."

Beyond the deceased and their loved ones, a third group of people is present in this book. These photographs witness the proud and loving craft of the stone cutters and bronze fabricators who fashioned the sculptures. Bower's photographic craft is a fitting tribute to the work of these artisans.

For me the most poignant of these images shows a seated boy, gazing slightly upward. The real child suffered an early death; his stone effigy suffers a prolonged demise. The left hand is missing. The jacket and trousers are dotted with clumps of moss. A leprous weathering has eroded the stone until the eyes and lips recede into the face. Notwithstanding this deterioration, the statue conveys a strong sense of life. I can feel the boy it represents. Despite his fancy bow tie, ruffled shirt and serious demeanor, I know he was a real boy, who, like Booth Tarkington's Penrod, ran and joked and played throughout his few short years. With Thomas Gray, I look at this statue and sigh for a life lost too soon. With John Bower, I look at all these obituaries in stone and bronze and celebrate the human spirit that produced them.

I will never see cemeteries the same way again.

Claude Cookman
Indiana University
September, 2004

Greenwood Cemetery
Perry Co. (448-11)

Introduction

There was a time in America when people decorated the graves of loved ones with beautiful statues. This Age roughly coincided with the period between two major milestones in our country's history—the Civil War and the Great Depression. During these half-dozen decades, a stone-carving industry flourished, both in this country and abroad. And the quality of the statuary created was exceptional. There were angels, in all sizes, as well as statues of adults and children which were sometimes stylized, sometimes perfect likenesses. These monuments could be pricey, with the larger ones costing as much as a modest house. But, if you could afford it, statues were fashionable.

Until recently, I had no idea just how much of this sculpture existed in cemeteries. Then, as I was photographing Southern Indiana for my book, *Lingering Spirit*, I began visiting more and more Hoosier graveyards—and I started discovering so much extraordinary statuary, and I was so impressed, that I knew it needed to be seen and appreciated by more than the occasional cemetery visitor. I'd already come across books filled with photos of sculpture from the world's most famous cemeteries, but I was finding scores of equally enchanting stone carvings here in the Midwest—as well as unexpected castings, superbly crafted in bronze and zinc.

The more I looked at these statues, the more I began to sense that they had a significance beyond being elaborate decorations. They were something very special a survivor could do, something more than a marker, a remembrance, or a memorial. In fact, I got the impression that they existed to watch over, or accompany, the departed souls, as attendants, as protectors—as guardians.

At first, I planned to photograph in cemeteries throughout the entire State of Indiana but, once I got started, I realized how many memorable statues there were. While they only resided in a minority of cemeteries, there seemed to be far too many for a single book. So I decided to concentrate on half the state, and U.S Highway 40 (the old National Road) seemed like a perfect dividing line. So, *Guardians of the Soul* covers all of Indiana south of that historic highway, an area that includes all, or part, of 48 out of Indiana's 92 counties. Because I live in Bloomington, this is my own backyard.

As I've been working on this project, I've had people tell me that cemeteries make them uncomfortable. To which I reply that cemeteries certainly evoke thoughts of death—but they are also places we can go to quietly remember all the pleasant memories of the friends and relatives who have gone before. And, even though we don't like to dwell on our own mortality, death is our most basic fact of life—a passage of such magnitude and mystery, of such finality and inevitability, that cultures feel compelled to mark it with some type of ritual. Cemeteries are an important part of that ritual

Although many of today's cemeteries have a serene and calming, park-like atmosphere, the concept of a spacious, attractive, landscaped burial ground is only 200 years old, with the first—Père Lachaise—being established in Paris, France in 1804. Previously, Christian cemeteries (particularly in Europe) tended to be morbid, gothic places of loathsomeness and fear, with terrifying images of death and Hell. But the concept behind Père Lachaise was completely different. Instead of being run by the Church, it was a secular, municipal concern, designed with rolling hills, winding lanes, and plenty of trees. Because the plots could be purchased by individual families, permanent monuments, dedicated to the memory of fathers, mothers, and children, were soon being erected. There was no longer the likelihood that others would be buried on top of your deceased relatives, or that a church official would disallow a particular monument's design. With this new freedom, people with sufficient financial resources began contracting for large and elaborate monuments, memorials, and tombs. The skills of sculptors and journeymen stone carvers were employed in the creation of majestic angels, mourning women, fallen doves, innocent children, and much more.

Understandably, the general public, particularly the middle classes, quickly embraced these new garden cemeteries, and they were soon established all over Europe. In an era when public parks were still few and far between, cemeteries became popular open-air places to congregate. People began picnicking, having secret meetings—even making love—in them. By the 1860s, there were 70,000 people a week visiting Paris' major garden cemeteries.

In the United States, by the mid-1850s, garden cemeteries began to be established across the continent. At first, they were popular recreational destinations—just like those in Europe—but, by the turn of the 20th Century, Americans began finding other places to draw their attention. Still, today, you can occasionally spot a few people on a sunny afternoon meandering among the tombstones of an American garden cemetery, or playing catch with their dog, or pushing a baby carriage, or jogging, or simply driving down the quiet, winding, asphalted drives.

Personally, I rather enjoy visiting cemeteries—but not the ones filled with simple, flat, ground-level stones, nor the ones with the subdivision-like regularity of standard granite monuments. I prefer cemeteries that contain older, distinctive, elaborate grave markers and statuary. I don't find them particularly sad places. Instead, I sense in them the deep love the still-living have for those who've passed on. So, when I see a magnificent winged angel, hand-carved in white marble, I consider how much a father, mother, or child cared for their lost loved one. After all, you don't erect a beautiful statue for a lecherous uncle, a mean-spirited parent, or an adulterous husband. You only commission an expensive sculpture for someone who was very special to you—an innocent daughter, a caring relative, a soul mate. And these relationships have a timeless quality—an abiding love that transcends death.

As I walk through these cemeteries, stopping, looking, and touching the weathered monuments, I find them perfect places for relaxation and contemplation. Because of all the artwork, statues, bas-reliefs, etc, I see cemeteries as nothing less than outdoor museums. In fact, I will go so far as to say they constitute a national treasure. Although the individual sculptors are rarely known by name, their work is often spectacular. Some of the statuary was created overseas, but much of America's cemetery sculpture was carved by talented local craftsmen.

Unfortunately, outside of cemeteries, the United States simply doesn't have a significant tradition of public sculpture. Yes, many municipal buildings have classically-inspired figures on their pediments, the lawns of courthouses often have "Lest we forget" monuments to those who served in various wars, and there is the occasional statue of an important local historical figure, but it is in older cemeteries where you regularly find the most captivating sculpture—often in abundance. And while some of these monuments are dedicated to wealthy, influential citizens, they are also erected in the memory of people who were important only to a handful of friends and relatives.

The beauty of the statuary found in graveyards routinely draws photographers and tourists to the larger, better-known cemeteries—Père Lachaise, Montparnasse, and Montmartre, all in Paris; or Metairie in New Orleans; or Mount Auburn in Cambridge, Massachusetts. Because of this, there are guidebooks to these, and most other, major "cities of the dead." But there is much, much, more outstanding cemetery sculpture to be found—often in your own neighborhood. For example, it isn't unusual to find nearly 100 statues in a single large Midwestern city cemetery—if it was established in the 19th century. But I've also been delighted to discover a single charming statue in a tiny, small-town or country cemetery. Anyone can admire these works of art—all you need do is locate an older cemetery and walk or drive thorough the front gate.

Having visited dozens and dozens of cemeteries, I've discovered countless angels, cherubs, young children, and grieving women carved in stone or cast in metal. Some of the statues are very similar, although particular features may differ slightly. And there are certain predictable motifs—the outstretched hand, the beatific look skyward, the innocent expression of a child. But there are also many one-of-a-kind statues. Most are meticulously crafted, with fine details, correct proportions, and balanced design. But, sadly, for many, the beauty is slowly vanishing.

The fact is, the delicate quality of our cemetery statues is fading—for a variety of reasons. Vandalism can certainly be a problem in some areas—monuments being damaged and toppled for the thrill of it, statues being stolen, bases chipped by lawnmowers. But, as bad as wanton or accidental desecration can be, the real damage to these irreplaceable works of art is time. Those of marble and limestone, are slowly eroding away due to natural weathering—and this is dramatically speeding up due to the effects of acid rain. Then, too, lichens and mosses damage surfaces, and vines and roots strangle bases causing them to lean precariously. Only those monuments that were carved in much-harder granite will last for centuries—but those statues are in the minority because granite is more difficult and, therefore, more costly, to chisel.

Because of the expense, the scarcity of skilled stone sculptors, modern cemetery regulations, as well as current tastes and practices, newly created cemetery statues are very rare indeed. Sadly, the carving of sculpture to honor the dead has almost become passé. But, as with much of our history, it is an art that needs to be recognized and documented. And that has been my goal in creating *Guardians of the Soul*.

John Bower

St. Joseph's Cemetery
Dubois Co. (378-05)

Cloverdale Cemetery
Putnam Co. (343-05)

Angels

As with most people, when cemetery statues come to mind, I automatically think angels. While these heavenly visitors occasionally reside in secular burial grounds, they are more often located in those affiliated with churches. For, in our predominantly Christian culture, an angel is an obvious choice to stand—eternally—above a loved one's grave. I suspect that the majority were erected either as symbolic protectors—guardian angels—or as guides to lead the departed into the afterlife. In size, they range from awe-inspiring larger-than-life adult versions, to more diminutive childlike angels, to plump infantile cherubs. Most have been carved by highly skilled, professionally trained artisans of fine white marble or high-quality limestone. A few are more simply chiseled by local craftsmen. Although less sophisticated, these project a most appealing folk-art quality. Not surprisingly, most of these winged beings possess angelic expressions, which is both beatific and reassuring. They succeed in filling us with hope, grace, and comfort.

St. Michael's Cemetery
Franklin Co. (453-04)

Carlsile IOOF Cemetery
Sullivan Co. (311-09)

Greenwood Cemetery
Perry Co. (448-15)

St. Joseph/Holy Cross Cemetery
Marion Co. (292-12)

Fairfield Friend's Cemetery
Hendricks Co. (353-05)

St. Joseph/Holy Cross Cemetery
Marion Co. (320-06)

Old City Cemetery
Fayette Co. (452-04)

St. Joseph's Cemetery
Vanderburgh Co. (357-06)

St. Joseph's Cemetery
Dubois Co. (444-02)

South Park Cemetery
Decatur Co. (432-08)

South Park Cemetery
Decatur Co. (431-13)

Bicknell Memorial Cemetery
Knox Co. (384-12)

Greenwood Cemetery
Johnson Co. (294-14)

Vevay Cemetery
Switzerland Co. (336-09)

Charlestown Cemetery
Clark Co. (332-15)

Wickliffe Cemetery
Crawford Co. (338-01)

Calvary Cemetery
Marion Co. (256-01)

Springdale Cemetery
Jefferson Co. (333-07)

St. Joseph 's Cemetery
Vanderburgh Co. (349-05)

Owensville IOOF Cemetery
Gibson Co. (382-08)

St. Joseph/Holy Cross Cemetery
Marion Co. (290-04)

Fairmount Cemetery
Dubois Co. (427-15)

St. Joseph/Holy Cross Cemetery
Marion Co. (292-06)

Kraft Graceland Cemetery
Floyd Co. (325-01)

Sunset Hill Cemetery
Spencer Co. (445-10)

Greenwood Cemetery
Perry Co. (449-07)

Calvary Cemetery
Perry Co. (446-11)

Maple Hill Cemetery
Posey Co. (345-02)

St. Martin of Tours Cemetery
Perry Co. (308-07)

32

St. Vincent de Paul Cemetery
Shelby Co. (435-13)

South Park Cemetery
Decatur Co. (433-04)

Garland Brook Cemetery
Bartholomew Co. (265-04)

Greenwood Cemetery
Johnson Co. (294-03)

36

Scotland Cemetery
Greene Co. (278-06)

South Liberty Cemetery
Orange Co. (337-12)

Concordia Cemetery
Marion Co. (268-05)

St. Joseph/Holy Cross Cemetery
Marion Co. (293-02)

St. Anthony's Cemetery
Clark Co. (332-07)

Green Hill Cemetery
Lawrence Co. (283-11)

Maple Grove Cemetery
Warrick Co. (362-10)

St. Joseph's Cemetery
Dubois Co. (378-07)

Children

Without a doubt, the statues of children are the most poignant I've come across in cemeteries. These innocents, who were supposed to outlive their parents, but didn't—having passed on, barely tasting life—leave a deep, enduring ache in the hearts of those left behind. In fact, seeing them can make me feel a little less trusting of Life. However, while I can't help but share a profound sadness, I sense, much more strongly, the extraordinary love that the family—especially the parents—had for their offspring. I can feel how a particular child, whether an adolescent or an hours-old infant, made an unalterable difference in their lives. For me, it's quite a moving experience, and I'm not alone in being affected—across the years—by this love, because other cemetery visitors seem to be similarly touched. For, as I drive the winding lanes, I regularly see flowers placed on the statues of youngsters—even 100 years after the boy or girl has passed.

St. Peter's Cemetery
Daviess Co. (366-10)

Oak Hill Cemetery
Vanderburgh Co. (361-02)

Scotland Cemetery
Greene Co. (278-10)

St. Joseph's Cemetery
Dubois Co. (338-12)

Lexington Cemetery
Scott Co. (371-05)

Van Pelt Cemetery
Shelby Co. (436-09)

Riverview Cemetery
Jackson Co. (330-05)

Presbyterian Cemetery
Monroe Co. (317-02)

Park Cemetery
Hancock Co. (300-12)

Hope Moravian Cemetery
Bartholomew Co. (455-05)

Green Hill Cemetery
Lawrence Co. (296-01)

Westport Cemetery
Decatur Co. (374-03)

Rest Haven Cemetery
Johnson Co. (263-06)

Locust Hill Cemetery
Vanderburgh Co. (354-11)

Crown Hill Cemetery
Washington Co. (297-08)

Caddy Naugle

Whenever master stonecarver John Naugle came home from work, his young daughter Caddy would meet him at the gate to their yard. So, when John neared home one day and she wasn't there, he knew something was amiss. As he entered the house, he learned that Caddy was sick. Sadly, she died a few days later. According to local legend, John was so distraught that he lost interest in his work, and many of his duties were taken over by an itinerant stone mason who just happened to be passing through town. This fellow worked diligently to complete John's regular projects, and also took the time to carve this life-size monument of Caddy, standing at the gate waiting for her daddy. Then he disappeared, as mysteriously as he had arrived and, to this day, no one knows his name.

Forest Hill Cemetery
Shelby Co. (369-07)

Rest Haven Cemetery
Johnson Co. (375-06)

Guardian Angel Cemetery
Franklin Co. (456-13)

Maple Hill Cemetery
Posey Co. (344-10)

Locust Hill Cemetery
Vanderburgh Co. (352-08)

Fairview Cemetery
Floyd Co. (328-06)

Orleans IOOF Cemetery
Orange Co. (323-03)

Union Cemetery
Ohio Co. (388-01)

Green Hill Cemetery
Lawrence Co. (283-08)

South Park Cemetery
Decatur Co. (455-11)

Simpson Chapel Cemetery
Greene Co. (279-03)

Greenlawn Cemetery
Johnson Co. (321-12)

St. Francis Cemetery
Franklin Co. (443-05)

Owensville IOOF Cemetery
Gibson Co. (382-09)

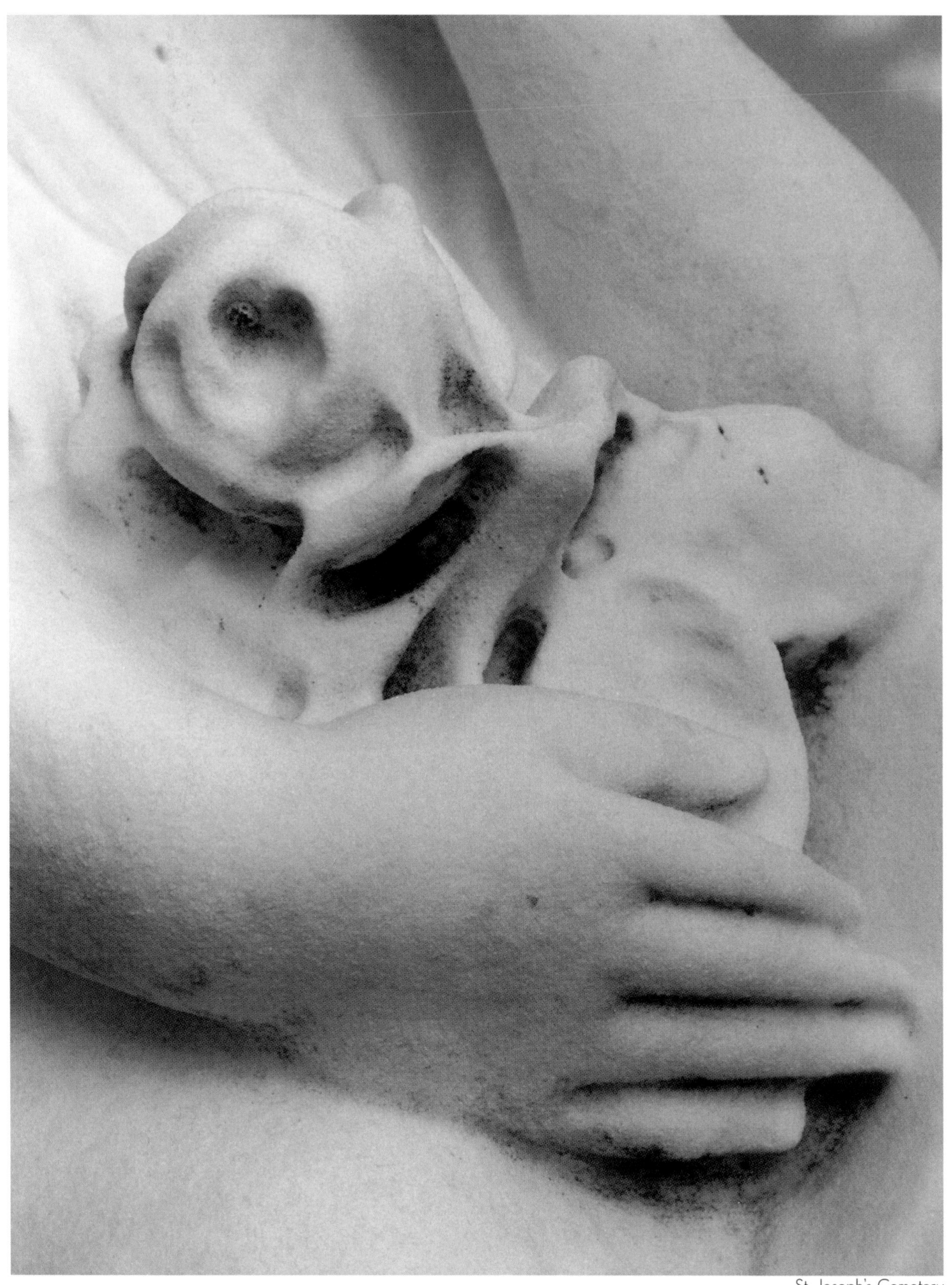

St. Joseph's Cemetery
Gibson Co. (383-10)

Oak Grove Cemetery
Daviess Co. (365-08)

Hays Cemetery
Lawrence Co. (281-06)

Hillcrest Cemetery
Jennings Co. (372-08)

Green Hill Cemetery
Lawrence Co. (284-05)

Adults

The statues decorating courthouse lawns and city parks are almost exclusively male. But, in cemeteries, the vast majority of the adult statues are idealized young women—and they are often mourners. They weep, they lament, they look skyward with sorrowful expressions. Yet, others have upturned faces filled with radiance, jubilation, and joy. In their rapture, they look toward the glory of the celestial kingdom to come. To have one of these beautiful females eternally guarding the grave of a man must have had great appeal. But these statues were also erected over the resting places of women, having, no doubt, been commissioned by grieving husbands. It's touching to me that, in an age when women were often undervalued, these men chose to show a special honor to their departed wives. Of the statues depicting men, many are soldiers—in the traditional male role of protector and defender. These uniformed warriors, as well as all the other men, tend to have a stoic, serious appearance, lacking in any emotion, such as sorrow or rejoicing.

St. Joseph's Cemetery
Dubois Co. (339-11)

Sunset Hill Cemetery
Spencer Co. (444-11)

St. Mary's Cemetery
Perry Co. (448-02)

72

Lexington Cemetery
Scott Co. (371-13)

Walnut Hill Cemetery
Gibson Co. (381-06)

Robert and Anna Anderson

When Robert "The Major" Anderson died in 1895, he left a small fortune in cash, and 900 acres of farmland, to his beloved wife, Anna. To celebrate their life together, Anna commissioned an Italian sculptor to create, from a single block of marble, an imposing monument to them both. The double statue reportedly cost her $8,000, and there was another $5,000 spent on the 16-foot-high granite base. Decades later, the monument remains straight and plumb, thanks to an underground subbase containing enough rock and gravel to fill a railroad-car. Anna was a wealthy woman at the time of The Major's passing, and she donated much of her money to charity. However, this, and her lack of business skills, left her penniless, and she lived as a pauper in her final years. When she died in 1921, there wasn't even enough money to carve her date of death on the monument, but, when this fact was reported in a newspaper article in 1976, an anonymous donor paid to have the date inscribed.

Cliff Hill Cemetery
Ripley Co. (385-15)

Calvary Cemetery
Rush Co. (370-03)

East Hill Cemetery
Rush Co. (434-11)

Lutheran Cemetery
Vanderburgh Co. (356-02)

Crothersville Cemetery
Jackson Co. (307-05)

Forest Lawn Cemetery
Johnson Co. (375-09)

Hope Moravian Cemetery
Bartholomew Co. (451-10)

Maple Hill Cemetery
Posey Co. (344-13)

St. Matthew's Cemetery
Posey Co. (346-14)

St. Joseph/Holy Cross Cemetery
Marion Co. (289-03)

East Hill Cemetery
Rush Co. (435-07)

St. Joseph/Holy Cross Cemetery
Marion Co. (273-10)

St. Joseph/Holy Cross Cemetery
Marion Co. (289-09)

84

Greenwood Cemetery
Perry Co. (451-02)

St. Joseph/Holy Cross Cemetery
Marion Co. (271-05)

Oak Hill Cemetery
Vanderburgh Co. (361-11)

Greenwood Cemetery
Perry Co. (449-03)

Belle Fontaine Cemetery
Posey Co. (346-01)

Governor Alvin P. Hovey

Sometimes a large, heavy marker turned out to be difficult to transport. According to the June 8, 1893 *Western Star*, "The monument to be erected over the grave of our late Governor, Alvin P. Hovey, is now being transferred from the L&N depot to the Bellefontaine cemetery. One of the pieces, weighing seventeen tons, loaded on a wagon imported expressly for this purpose, and pulled by two traction engines, mired on Main Street about one square from the depot, Tuesday. The wagon went down to the hubs and it will take several days work to extricate it."

The youngest of eight children, and an orphan at the age of 15, Hovey was a man with a remarkably varied career. After working as a bricklayer, teacher, and lawyer, he joined the military. During the Civil war, he served under Uylsses S. Grant, Lew Wallace, and William T. Sherman in Missouri, Kentucky, Tennessee, Arkansas, Mississippi, Indiana, and Georgia. During his 70 years of life, he was also an Indiana Supreme Court judge, a U.S. district attorney, a U.S minister to Peru, as well as a U.S. Congressman. He died in 1891, in his 3rd year as Indiana governor.

St. Joseph's Cemetery
Vanderburgh Co. (348-14)

Cliff Cemetery
Perry Co. (421-01)

Springdale Cemetery
Jefferson Co. (335-03)

St. Mary's Cemetery
Floyd Co. (327-07)

St. Joseph/Holy Cross Cemetery
Marion Co. (289-05)

Southpark Cemetery
Morgan Co. (277-13)

Old City Cemetery
Bartholomew Co. (264-05)

Greenwood Cemetery
Perry Co. (448-05)

Oak Hill Cemetery
Vanderburgh Co. (361-06)

Fairmont Cemetery
Jefferson Co. (335-14)

Riverview Cemetery
Jackson Co. (305-06)

Walnut Hill Cemetery
Gibson Co. (381-09)

Fairview Cemetery
Floyd Co. (327-14)

Firefighters' memorial

"The splendid monument to commemorate the memory of the Volunteer Fire Department of New Albany, has been completed, and was set up on Friday afternoon in Fairview Cemetery. It will perpetuate the memory of 800 men who served the Volunteer Fire Department in the years 1825 to 1865. The monument is 15 feet 9 inches in height from the base to the top of the surmounting figure. It is of Bedford light colored stone, and all the work upon it was done in New Albany. It is a work of genuine art in sculpture, being especially elegant in its bas reliefs and in the distinctness of touch and finish in every elaboration. The material is indestructible. This handsome monument is surmounted by the figure of a Volunteer Fireman, in the uniform of the old Volunteer days, holding in his arms a child rescued from a burning building, and rushing to safety with it. The figure is a work of genuine art, and rises above the cap of the shaft, which is also a splendid specimen of art. On the West side of the shaft, just under the cap, is an old-time hand engine resting on a base cut out of the stone and the base bearing the legend—1825-1865—which dates cover the years of the Volunteer Fire Department. "

Excerpted from the *Daily Ledger*, Saturday Evening, August 30, 1902

Riverview Cemetery
Dearborn Co. (439-03)

Greenwood Cemetery
Perry Co. (416-11)

St. Joseph's Cemetery
Vanderburgh Co. (350-05)

St. Joseph/Holy Cross Cemetery
Marion Co. (270-04)

College Corner Cemetery
Union Co. (304-08)

College Corner Cemetery
Union Co. (304-04)

Fairview Cemetery
Greene Co. (309-07)

Rose Hill Cemetery
Monroe Co. (266-06)

Forest Hill Cemetery
Shelby Co. (368-12)

Hymera Cemetery
Sullivan Co. (280-03)

Oak Hill Cemetery
Vanderburgh Co. (362-02)

Fairview Cemetery
Greene Co. (279-07)

Stephen's Memorial Cemetery
Vigo Co. (313-01)

Park Cemetery
Hancock Co. (300-07)

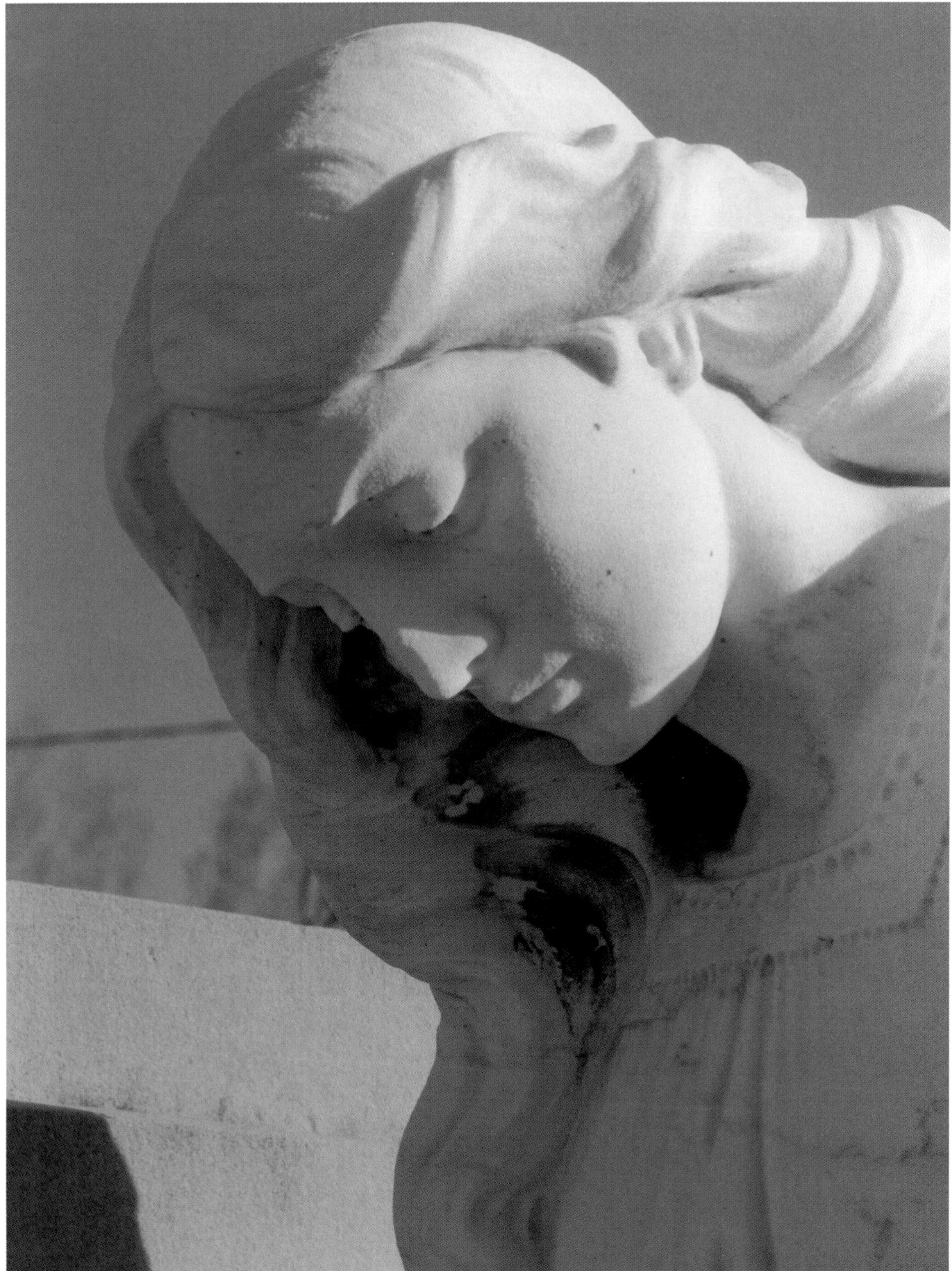

Calvary Cemetery
Rush Co. (370-04)

Lutheran Cemetery
Wayne Co. (303-06)

Fairview Cemetery
Floyd Co. (328-01)

Greenwood Cemetery
Perry Co. (450-02)

Oak Hill Cemetery
Vanderburgh Co. (360-01)

Riverview Cemetery
Dearborn Co. (440-15)

Riverview Cemetery
Owen Co. (314-04)

Fairview Cemetery
Greene Co. (279-09)

St. Joseph's Cemetery
Vanderburgh Co. (349-03)

Oak Hill Cemetery
Vanderburgh Co. (357-15)

Hilldale Cemetery
Morgan Co. (317-14)

Calvary Cemetery
Marion Co. (256-04)

St. Joseph's Cemetery
Vanderburgh Co. (349-11)

Religious

For the purposes of this book, I've distinguished between angels and other religious figures, such as Jesus, Mary, and Joseph (either singly or as a family) and various apostles, saints, and clergy. Crucifixions are common, with larger, life-sized versions often in the centers of Roman Catholic cemeteries. Most are carefully crafted of marble or limestone, but others are cast of metal, or even molded of fiberglass. Sometimes, small weather-worn stone crucifixes mark individual graves. There are also depictions of Jesus kneeling in prayer or standing with a hand raised in blessing. Mary is also a popular figure, usually with welcoming, outstretched arms, or holding the baby Jesus. All these statues vary in style, with some being traditional, familiar representations, while others are wonderfully unique interpretations by artisans interested in showing honor in their own special way. These are the ones I'm most drawn to because they are so unexpected.

St. Joseph's Cemetery
Vanderburgh Co. (356-14)

St. Michael's Cemetery
Franklin Co. (454-04)

St. Martin's Cemetery
Martin Co. (376-12)

St. Joseph/Holy Cross Cemetery
Marion Co. (320-15)

St. Joseph/Holy Cross Cemetery
Marion Co. (320-04)

Eastern Cemetery
Clark Co. (332-12)

Holy Family Cemetery
Franklin Co. (443-10)

St. Mary's Cemetery
Floyd Co. (326-06)

118

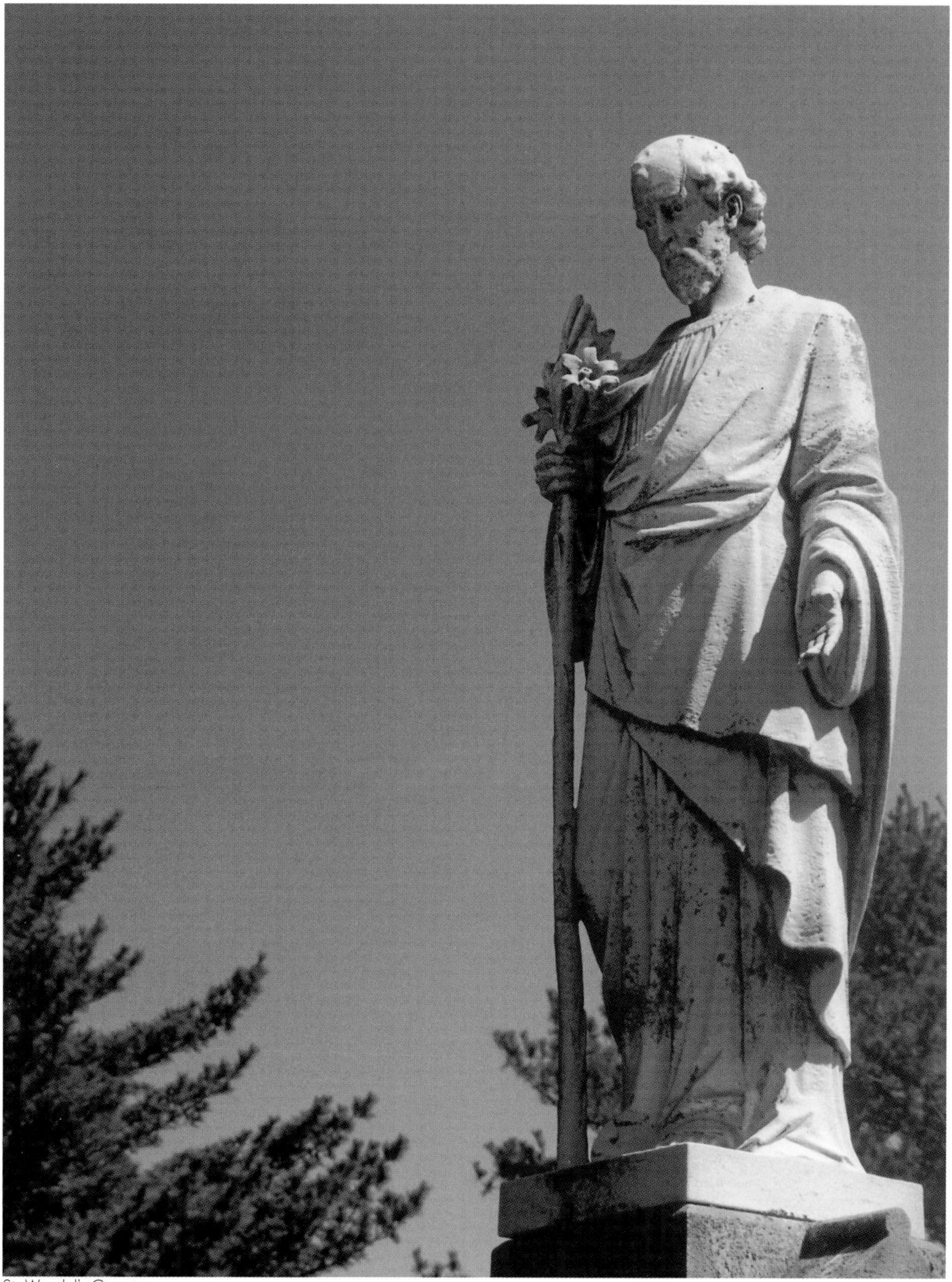

St. Wendel's Cemetery
Vanderburgh Co. (344-03)

St. Phillip's Cemetery
Posey Co. (347-10)

St. Maurice's Cemetery
Ripley Co. (392-08)

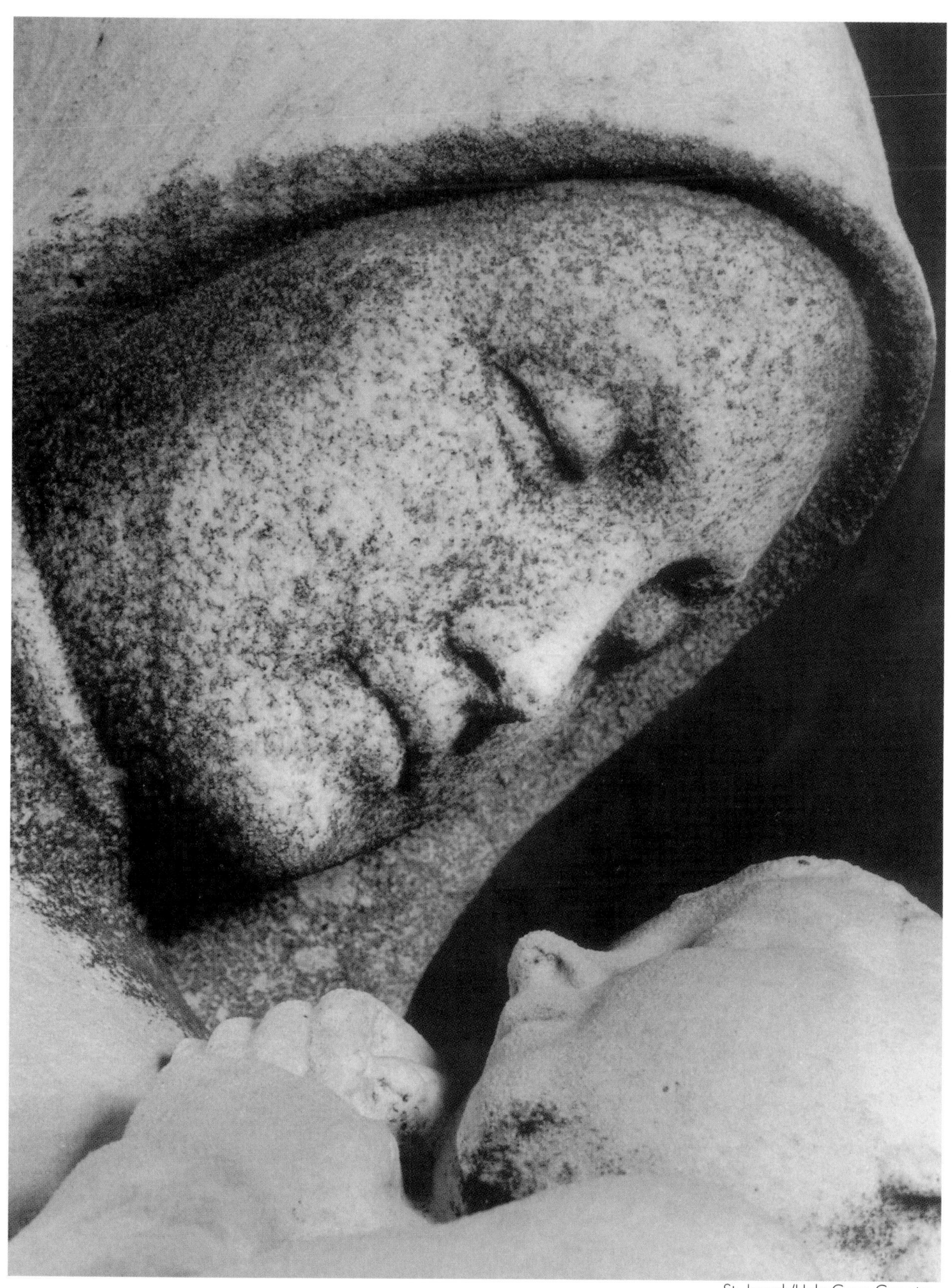

St. Joseph/Holy Cross Cemetery
Marion Co. (291-09)

St. Michael's Cemetery
Franklin Co. (453-08)

Calvary Cemetery
Perry Co. (447-06)

Hilldale Cemetery
Morgan Co. (318-13)

St. Phillip's Cemetery
Posey Co. (347-15)

Fairview Cemetery
Greene Co. (310-14)

Walnut Hill Cemetery
Pike Co. (378-12)

Animals

I didn't originally plan to include animals in this book. However, after I started seeing them, in such wonderful interpretations, and in a variety of settings, I decided to photograph them as well. It was as though, through their uniqueness, they told me they wanted to be included on these pages. Obviously important, they were erected either as symbols or as reminders of lifetime companions. By far, the most common cemetery animals are lambs and doves—representing innocence—which often sit atop the gravestones of children. Sadly, time and acid rain have eroded, into unrecognizability, the smaller of these marble or limestone beasts. But I've also found a variety of other larger, handsome animals, and many are in much better condition—among them are several dogs, lions, and eagles, two horses, two swans, and a cat. Of those that were faithful pets, I sense a deep and abiding love that the survivors who erected them must have known quite well. All patiently sit, perch, stand, and kneel for eternity.

St. Mary's Cemetery
Floyd Co. (327-10)

Oak Grove Cemetery
Daviess Co. (366-04)

Riverview Cemetery
Dearborn Co. (440-06)

Rose Hill Cemetery
Monroe Co. (275-15)

Mt. Zion Cemetery
Spencer Co. (445-13)

Ina Axton

"One of the most beautiful as well as unique works of art in the county was erected in Mt. Zion cemetery, at the grave of Mrs. Ina Axton, this week. The monument is cut from Green River lime stone, and is the figure of a horse about seven-eighths size. The model from which the work was made was a beautiful Kentucky animal, as nearly perfect as could be found and the stone since completion is almost a perfect likeness of the model. Every line, muscle and vein are carved perfectly delineated and marks the skill of the artist Mr. Ira Correll. The model from which the figure was cut was kept standing in the yard of the marble works of Reavis and Beloat at Princeton for forty days while the cutters were engaged up in the work. The figure is placed in the cemetery with the head to the west and stands about twelve feet high. Upon the die underneath the figure is cut the emblems of the IOOF and the K of P and the inscriptions Ina L. Palmer, wife of W. H. Axton, born Jan. 21, 1871, died Feb. 4, 1898. Mr. Axton was led to adopt this novel design of monument by reason of love Mrs. Axton had for that most faithful of man's servants, the horse, and the design, although different from the ordinary, is very beautiful indeed."

Excerpted from the *Rockport Democrat*, July 15, 1898

Oak Hill Cemetery
Vanderburgh Co. (359-07)

Locust Hill Cemetery
Vanderburgh Co. (352-04)

Old City Cemetery
Bartholomew Co. (264-08)

Kraft Graceland Cemetery
Floyd Co. (324-14)

Fairview Cemetery
Greene Co. (310-11)

Pollie Barnett

When Pollie Barnett's daughter, Sylvanie, went mysteriously missing, it was rumored that she had been murdered by her sweetheart, but her body was never found. Pollie couldn't allow herself to believe that her daughter was dead, and she spent her remaining 25 years roaming Greene and the surrounding counties, looking for her. Believed by many to be insane, Pollie was known as "The Lost Wanderer," "the well known and eccentric old wanderer," or, sometimes, "The Catwoman" because of the feline companion she had in her last years.

For a time, Pollie's younger daughter, Olive, accompanied her on the search for Sylvanie. After Olive died and was buried, a newspaper reported that Pollie was dissatisfied with Olive's burial plot, and "with her own hands dug up the remains and carried them in her apron to some unknown spot."

Pollie's love for Sylvanie was so deep, and her determination to locate her was so strong, that, according to a local newspaper article "She trampled over the country through sunshine and storm, undergoing hardships that would destroy the strongest constitution."

Minutes before her death, Pollie asked friends to let her large black cat go, so it could continue looking for Sylvanie. When she died, on February 27, 1900, Pollie was given a church funeral and the burial expenses were paid for by donations from the citizens of Linton.

The inscription on Pollie's monument reads: "Here Pollie Barnett is at rest from deepest grief and toilsome quest. Her cat, her only friend, remained with her until life's end."

Greenwood Cemetery
Perry Co. (450-14)

Green Hill Cemetery
Lawrence Co. (284-11)

Green Hill Cemetery
Lawrence Co. (286-10)

Green Hill Cemetery
Lawrence Co. (282-09)

Carvers

While an accurate history of Indiana's skilled limestone carvers doesn't exist, a number of them are buried near the monument (left), which was erected in memory of all Bedford, Indiana stonecutters. Standing on the top is the likeness of master carver **Johnny Caspar** who emigrated to America from Germany. According to local legend, Caspar planned to work hard, and save his money diligently, until he had enough to pay for a house. Then he would send to Germany for his bride-to-be. As his nest egg began to grow, two local women convinced him that he could save on his expenses if he moved into their boardinghouse—which he did. Unfortunately, Caspar soon died of arsenic poisoning, under mysterious circumstances, and his savings disappeared.

Bedford Indiana's Master Stone Carver **Frank Arena** was 101 years old when he was buried beneath a simple carving of his hat (above), which was crafted by someone else. Frank's work can be seen all across the U.S., but he was proudest of a massive sculpture (completed in his seventies) of Washington crossing the Delaware River, which was commissioned for the Nation's Bicentennial.

Springdale Cemetery
Jefferson Co. (334-08)

Carver **George Grey Barnard** honored his parents' grave with the limestone statue (previous page, lower right), which is titled "Immortality." It was described in an early newspaper account as "an incomparably beautiful figure of a woman in the matching loveliness of mature perfection and form...(and) the lovely hands are uplifted, parting the veil that encircles the voiceless silence of dreamless dust." Barnard was a prolific and talented carver. Examples of his work can be found in Cairo. IL (Abraham Lincoln), the Langesand Cemetery in Norway, and the Metropolitan Museum of Art in New York.

Master stone carver **Harold "Dugan" Elgar** began his career in 1927 but it was interrupted by World War II and a return to school. While at the John Herron Art Institute in Indianapolis he created the model of a Pietà which was accepted for a national competition, and won him fame as a sculptor. However, it wasn't until years later, in 1968, after suffering a heart attack, that he began working on the full-size version (below left). Today, it sits atop his grave and that of his wife.

Of the many statues **Ernest M. Viquesney**—a nationally recognized sculptor—created, he is best known locally for his World War I doughboys, which decorate Midwestern courthouse lawns and cemeteries. A native of Spencer, Indiana, he crafted "The Unveiling" (below right) for the grave of his wife Cora, who died in 1933. At a church service, in which Viquesney was being honored, and a model of the statue was presented to the public, Viquesney read a poem he wrote. Here are the first few lines:

What is it in lifeless clay, the sculptor finds,
From which to mould his living thought?
The clay, insensate, cannot think, nor act,
Just lifeless cold—it stands for naught.
But spark of life, and form and beauty rise,
When sculptor's hands the vision realize.

Clear Creek Cemetery
Monroe Co. (267-04)

Riverview Cemetery
Owen Co. (317-05)

Catalogs

While there were talented stone carvers working in many Hoosier communities who could create one-of-a-kind cemetery monuments, there were also mail-order catalogs available that offered standard designs. These catalogs mostly contained conventional markers, but some had a few statues as well. The partial page shown above depicts one of several statues available through an early edition of *Vermont Marble Company's Designs,* whose headquarters was in Proctor, Vermont. Note how an early monument dealer has penciled in the sizes that were available with an M or L designation for Marble or Limestone.

During the early decades of the 20th century, Sears Roebuck & Company sold a limited selection of grave markers in its large general-merchandise catalog. But Sears also offered its customers several specialty catalogs. The advertisement on the following page is reproduced from its special 1907-1908 *Tombstones and Monuments* catalog. A similar marker can be seen on page 55 of this book.

142

WONDROUS ART, AND MORE WONDERFUL VALUES

The Designer's Art and the sculptor's genius bring to your door this beautiful specimen of their inspiring handicraft, executed in all the beautiful soft lines possible in this, the world famous White Acme Rutland Italian Marble. In the execution of statuary work, bringing out the rounded contour of the human figure, or the soft lines of drapery shown in this beautiful design, we always recommend our White Acme Rutland Italian Marble, but the great beauty of our Acme Blue Dark Vein Marble is not to be ignored in work of this kind, so we quote this high art design in both colors

Send Us Your Order for one of these beautiful tombstones, and we will cut, shape and carve it out of a solid block of beautiful marble, finish it in the highest manner known to the statuary art, place upon it any lettering you may desire, and ship it to you with the distinct understanding and agreement that if it does not prove to be nicer and better than our most extravagant description, if it does not reach you in perfect condition, free from the slightest injury in transportation, is not lettered exactly as you have instructed us, we will take the risk of a total loss and dispose of it at our own expense, refunding your money, together with any freight charges you have paid See page 3, where we tell you all about the cost of freight.

$38.40 in Acme Blue Dark Vein Marble, and $40.20 in White Acme Rutland Italian Marble, delivered on the cars at the quarry and marble works in Vermont. These wonderfully low prices place within your reach this most beautiful, delicate work of memorial art at about half the price you could possibly obtain it for elsewhere, and the quality of the workmanship is the finest the world can produce.

Seldom, if ever, has such an opportunity been offered to own a child's memorial of this character at even double the price we ask. The space allowed for lettering is the straight narrow polished surface directly below the drapery and the polished surface of the upper base These spaces allow ample room for a reasonable amount of lettering See page 77 for prices of inscriptions on marble.

MADE IN ONE SIZE ONLY

DIMENSIONS: Nos 61B730 and 61B731. Total height, 2 feet 2 inches. Bottom base 1 foot 8 inches long by 1 foot wide and 8 inches high. Upper base, 1 foot 4 inches long, 8 inches wide and 4 inches high. Shell cove die 1 foot 2 inches high 1 foot 2 inches wide at base and 6 inches thick at base. Shipping weight, 384 pounds.

No 61B730 Price, Acme Blue Dark Vein Marble $38.40
No 61B731 Price, White Acme Rutland Italian Marble 40.20

GIVE US FOUR TO SIX WEEKS TO FINISH, LETTER AND SHIP THIS BEAUTIFUL DESIGN.

A small sample piece of polished marble will be mailed on receipt of 15 cents.

SAVED MONEY AND IT IS ADMIRED BY EVERYONE

Sears, Roebuck & Co., Chicago, Ill. Webster, Iowa.

Dear Sirs:—The tombstone has been received and is very satisfactory. Everyone admires it and I saved money on it. My neighbors and friends ask where I got it and how much it cost.

Yours truly, C. F. SIEVERT.

In the closing pages of this book we show illustrations of this beautiful marble, indicating the popular styles of lettering, and some desirable verse inscriptions.

Union Cemetery
Ohio Co. (437-15)

photo by Lynn Bower

Afterword

When the idea for this book first started to gel, my wife, Lynn, and I knew of a number Indiana cemeteries that contained statues. In fact, we photographed some for my last book, *Lingering Spirit*. Although we didn't know for sure, we assumed there would be many more statues besides those we'd already seen. And our assumption proved correct.

According to the Division of Historic Preservation and Archaeology, which is a part of Indiana's Department of Natural Resources, there are an estimated 125,000 graveyards and cemeteries in Indiana. Some are very large, particularly those in cities and towns, but the ones out in the country tend to be quite a bit smaller. In fact, many are family plots containing as few as one or two graves.

Even by limiting the scope of this project to the southern half of Indiana, we knew we couldn't possibly visit every single cemetery. That would be too daunting a task. So, I started contacting people in each county who I thought might be familiar with the area's cemeteries. Over several weeks, I spoke to, or emailed, dozens of county historians, funeral-home directors, monument dealers, groundskeepers, and grave diggers, as well as librarians and genealogical-society personnel. Most were quite helpful, and I'd like to thank them all for their time and enthusiastic tips. I'd also like to sincerely thank Claude Cookman for his wonderful Foreword. He truly understood my mission.

After getting leads for the entire area, Lynn and I prepared to start out, on a series of day trips, looking for cemetery statues. Lynn is a exceptional partner, and she's a tremendous help when I'm shooting—scouting for good shots, locating smaller interesting statues, holding a reflector to balance the lighting, and offering helpful suggestions.

With an accordion folder full of county maps, we plotted routes that would connect all the cemeteries on our list. A few leads turned out to be duds, but most led us to some lovely statues. Of course, we checked out all the cemeteries we passed, even though they weren't on our list—and were pleased to locate a number of additional statues. Sometimes we paid 2 or 3 visits to a cemetery to get better light, or more interesting clouds.

I have no idea how many cemeteries we actually visited, but we found something to photograph in nearly 200 of them. All in all, we discovered over 600 statues (and that doesn't include the many small eroded lambs and doves, or newer concrete statues), and I took about 3,000 photographs of them. I ended up with so many images that it was difficult to choose which ones to include on these pages. Most of what I photographed are three-dimensional statues, but I also captured some outstanding two-dimensional bas-reliefs. Based on what we saw, I'd say that there are probably cemetery statues in every single one of Indiana's 92 counties.

My camera is a Mamiya 645 medium-format model and I almost always use a tripod. For many of the shots herein, I used a filter (red, orange, or yellow) to darken the blue sky. For film, I tend to use Ilford's FP-4+, which I process in my own darkroom. Because a number of the statues we encountered were up in the air, on top of a pedestal, I rigged a special mount for my camera so I could clamp it to the top of an 8' step ladder, which I used as an extra-tall tripod. Overall, this project took approximately a year to complete, and we put over 10,000 miles on our Toyota RAV4 (which is equipped with a roof rack for the ladder).

When all the photography and darkroom work was completed, Lynn took over the project to do the design and layout for this book. This is one of her specialties, and it amazes me how fast she can transform a stack of images into pages as coherent and beautiful as these. So, in closing, I'd like to say "Thanks, Honey."

Belle Fontaine Cemetery
Posey Co. (346-09)

For information about John Bower and his work, please visit www.studioindiana.com